Milton Criticism: A Subject Index

Milton Criticism
A Subject Index

WILLIAM C. JOHNSON

DAWSON

First published in 1978

British Library Cataloguing in Publication Data

Johnson, William C.
Milton Criticism.
1. Milton, John — Bibliography
I. Title
016.821'4 Z8578

ISBN 0-7129-0787-4

Printed litho in Great Britain by W & J Mackay Limited, Chatham

Contents

Introduction vii
Acknowledgements ix
How to Use the Index x
List of Books Indexed xi
Abbreviations xviii
The Subject Index 1–450

Introduction

This work presents a detailed and relatively complete index to subjects referred to, or covered in, a carefully selected group of 150 books of criticism pertaining to the life and writings of John Milton. No other subject index of its particular nature and scope exists: as such it is a new type of reference tool, and one whose usefulness might perhaps encourage the compilation of similar works pertinent to other authors.

The increasing number of articles, monographs, and books on Milton testifies to a continuously growing and very considerable interest in his life and works. Some out-of-print books are now being republished, and Milton is the topic of papers and discussions at most large literary conferences. Yet the increase in popularity and publication has increased proportionately the difficulty in gaining access to what already has been published. Libraries have partial collections which most often duplicate the standard critical works found in other libraries. Some out-of-print books are almost completely inaccessible; some of those still in print are almost as difficult to acquire as the out-of-print ones.

Although a researcher might have difficulty in locating books of criticism, he does have access to a variety of indexes, concordances, and lexicons in which he may locate where Milton wrote on a particular subject. Available too are several bibliographies which direct him to hundreds of articles and books in which he may locate where Milton wrote on a particular subject. There are, for example, several concordances, among them those by Charles Dexter Cleveland (*A Complete Concordance to the Poetical Works of John Milton, 1867*), John Bradshaw (*A Concordance to the Poetical Works of John Milton.* Hamden, Conn: rpt., 1965), a computerized work by Gladys W. Hudson (*Paradise Lost: A Concordance,* Detroit: 1970), and Lane Cooper (*Concordance of the Latin, Greek and Italian Poems of John Milton.* Halle: 1923).

Other aids to assist the researcher with Milton's writings by defining terms, or identifying names, appear in a number of forms. Frank A. Patterson's 'Glossary' at the end of *The Student's Milton* (New York: 1933) is very helpful in this respect, as is Walter Skeat's 'A Reader's Guide' at the end of the Oxford World's Classics edition of *The English Poems of John Milton* (Oxford: 1940). The monumental Index to the Columbia Edition of the *Works of John Milton,* compiled by Frank A. Patterson and French Fogle (Columbia: 1940), is indispensible for locating what Milton himself said about any particular subject, or where he used a particular name or phrase. Various dictionaries offer aid in understanding many of Milton's references and allusions. Among these are Edward S. Le Comte's *A Milton Dictionary* (New York: 1961), and Allan Gilbert's *A Geographical Dictionary of Milton* (New Haven: 1919).

Still other works treat critical interpretation of Milton. Among such tools is *The Complete Prose Works of John Milton,* edited by Don M. Wolfe, Ernest Sirluck, *et. al.* (New Haven: 1953–). In addition, the *Variorum Commentary on the Poems of John Milton,* edited by Douglas Bush, J. E. Shaw, *et. al.* (1970–), contains invaluable commentary on Milton's poetry.

Finally, of great importance to the student and scholar are the various Milton bibliographies: David H. Stevens' *A Reference Guide to Milton from 1800 to the Present Day* (Chicago: 1930), Harris F. Fletcher's *Contributions to a Milton Bibliography* (Urbana: 1931), James Holly Hanford's Goldentree Bibliography of *Milton* (1966), and Calvin Huckabay's *John Milton: An Annotated Bibliography* (Dusquesne 1969).

Yet even with the availability of these reference tools, at the initial stages of research at least three serious problems can impede the progress of investigation: (1) even the best of the annotated bibliographies lacks the specificity and detail often required by investigators examining particular subjects, (2) only perusal of a book's table of contents and index, short of reading the entire text, can provide a good indication of an author's approach to, and treatment of, any given topic, and (3) no single library contains all the books one would hope to have for a thorough investigation of critical writings on a research subject.

This work aims to prevent some of these troublesome and time-consuming problems. With the aid of *Milton Criticism: A Subject Index,* a reader can know at a glance which of the indexed books contain information relevant to his pursuit, and which do not. He may then pursue acquisition of the necessary works, and eliminate from his general search those books from the list which do not touch on his own study. The *Subject Index* will not eliminate, nor is it designed to discourage, 'book searching,' but it can reduce significantly the amount of time spent in the initial stages of research when a topic's coverage by previous critics is of concern. It is a guide to, not a substitute for, the critical works themselves.

The books indexed here provide a wide and varied list of research subjects. While Milton is the primary focus, much of the criticism written on his works and his life lends itself to scrutiny by students of non-literary disciplines. As such, extensive entries appear on such matters as the political, social, and economic backgrounds of Milton's England, the Civil Wars, music, geography, rhetorical theory, philosophy, and theology. Furthermore, the *Subject Index* can be used, with equal dexterity, by students as well as advanced scholars – from the undergraduate preparing a term paper to the specialist pursuing in-depth research.

As used here, 'Milton Criticism' refers to published critical works which, if not entirely, then in large part, treat John Milton the man, the artist, and his works. Each of the works selected for inclusion contains some type of index; materials in these indexes, combined with further materials gleaned from each of the books, form the *Subject Index.* I recognize that criteria for inclusion in indexes vary from author to author, with some writers attempting to include every name and subject and other writers selecting only the most important topics. For this reason I have frequently supplemented a particular book's index with topics and names I have extracted from the book, but which the author has not included in his index. Short of re-indexing all the books, this method seemed likely to provide the most consistency in approach.

Ultimately, the user of a reference work such as this one is subject to the editorial discretion of all the authors involved. For this reason I have included almost *all* the information included in all the indexes used, and in my own indexing of texts have attempted to be as full and complete as possible. Because of the nature of this *Index,* completeness was deemed more valuable than selectivity, providing, as it does, more latitude for large numbers of researchers with various investigative demands. While perusing an author's index, or referring to this one, is no substitute for reading a critical text itself, the fact remains that in the early stages of research it is the book's index which a researcher first examines. This *Index* provides a guide to those books.

In all, *Milton Criticism: A Subject Index* catalogues the material in 150 books of Milton criticism. While most of the books were published in this century, some nineteenth-century critical material has been included as well. The neophyte should bear in mind that most earlier works have been supplanted by modern studies; the experienced researcher can use the older books for the value of earlier critical views.

Most of the books included focus on Milton's works; some, however, have a biographical aim. In subject matter the works range from broad analysis of Milton and his times, to specific examination of such detailed topics as Milton and Lactantius, and Milton's knowledge of music. No particular subject has been given more emphasis than any other.

Unpublished dissertations, theses, and monographs are not included in the list. Unindexed material is likewise absent, as well as editions of Milton's works. Books in languages other than English have been omitted, although foreign words appearing in the indexes of the books included have been translated to their literal meanings, and put in their appropriate places in this Index.

Occasionally, I have included books which only partly focus on Milton, such as Curran and Wittreich's *Blake's Sublime Allegory* and Mohl's *Studies in Spenser, Milton, and the Theory of Monarchy.* In such cases only the material pertinent to Milton has been indexed. Each book selected was chosen on the basis of its subject matter, its availability, and the quality of its material. Hard-to-find books, particularly out-of-print books, have been given some preference over those likely to be found in college libraries on both sides of the Atlantic (and where the investigator could easily peruse the book himself). The 'final list' changed several times. Many more books were indexed than are here represented; many were eventually eliminated because a more thorough book on the same subject was found to replace the previously-indexed one. Ultimately, the parameters of time and space necessitated limitation to 150 books, and the 'final final' list was arrived at after careful consideration by a number of individuals.

As each book was indexed, the material was verified to ascertain that the book did indeed contain the subjects listed. Any inaccurate pagination in the original critical books did not affect this work, since this *Index* does not include page references to the indexed books. What was of concern was that the material included would correspond to the respective book(s), and that it would do so with approximately the frequency suggested by the asterisked and unasterisked numerals (explained below).

A number of significant Milton studies have been omitted; had I world enough and time many other works would have found themselves among the list of books included. William Riley Parker's monumental *Milton: a Biography* certainly contains something valuable on almost every topic, and is likewise one of the most readable and up-to-date sources in almost all cases. It is not included solely because its own index is so complete, and because it is by now readily available. And so it is with the Yale *Complete Prose of John Milton,* the very size of which prohibits inclusion. The difficulty has never been in finding worthy books to include, but in limiting the number to a workable figure.

The computer:

Enough has been written in the last few years about computer-assisted reference works to make extensive elaboration unnecessary. Suffice it to say that five years of hand-indexing 150 books produced some 35,000–40,000 note cards, all of which were eventually fed into an IBM 360/367 computer during five less-than-exciting months. The computer sorted the enormous bulk of this material, altered, alphabetized, adjusted, aligned, and provided printouts in a comparatively few hours of actual programmed time.

Unlike many earlier computer-printed works, this one does contain both uppercase and lowercase letters. However, while the computer can now print underlines as well as a variety of accent marks, the programming for such processes would have taken more time than inserting such figures by hand (which is what was done in this case). The only operation we were unable to program involved the sequence of numbers in each entry. Because the final list of books changed several times, the books' corresponding numbers changed as well. Thus a book which at one time might have been indicated by a 4, might in the final version be listed as 17. While the computer could quickly change the 4 to 17, it could not rearrange the sequence of numbers without upsetting the order of other numbers in any given line. This accounts for some entries containing numerical references out of sequential order.

Acknowledgements

During the five-year gestation of this *Index,* I had the benefit of advice and assistance from many persons. My large debt to them, like the *Index* itself, has grown and grown, and acknowledgement can never be more than a partial repayment for the many hours of counsel and help.

First of all, to the librarians and staff at the libraries I used, my gratitude is extended for their assistance and – especially – their patience. The libraries of the University of Chicago, the University of Iowa, the University of Illinois, Cambridge University, and Oxford University provided many of the materials. The British Library, the Bodleian Library, the Library of Congress, and the Newberry Library, provided the rest.

Monies for clerical and computer assistance were generously provided by a Northern Illinois University Deans' Fund grant, and some of the earlier research was completed through the assistance of an American Philosophical Society grant.

This work would have taken twice the time to complete were it not for the cooperation and assistance of the Northern Illinois University Computer Services Department. To Steven Weiland, Judy Knutson, and Michael Sestric, and the various operators who assisted in programming and printing, I proffer this acknowledgement and my gratitude.

John D. Robinson, moving agilely between the technical world of computers and the aesthetic realms of literature, got me through the final stages of the work with helpful words – and good programs.

Many years ago, Rosalie Colie, Rhodes Dunlap, and John F. Huntley stimulated my appetite for Milton; in more recent years William J. Roscelli, respected colleague, has done the same.

Grant Voth, congenitor of the project, provided much assistance in the earlier stages of organization and indexing; his direction and help are deeply appreciated and warmly acknowledged.

Jenefer Giannasi, perceptive reader and dear friend, aided in proofreading portions of this work – as she has assisted by proofreading almost everything I have written for the last ten years.

J. Max Patrick has been more generous with his time and counsel than I could ever have hoped. His advice in matters practical, especially in compiling the final list of books to be indexed, has been invaluable. With few exceptions, his 'nay' has been 'nay,' his 'yea,' 'yea.'

For any discrepancies or errors in the text I am fully responsible. For the vast accumulation of material, however, I am indebted to Bobbie L. Russell and Evelyn Zimmer, whose assistance was of much value. Janet M. Youga, careful critic and gentle counselor, not only helped with extensive indexing, but advised and directed more than I can adequately acknowledge. She saved me from many serious mistakes, and provided suggestions for many valuable additions. And of Jill Catherine Garzone, who diligently and carefully typed the entire corpus of materials onto the computer, and who saw the work through one stage after another until its final computer generation, it truthfully can be said, and without exaggeration, that the *Index* would not have taken shape without her. Her diligence has been amazing; her assistance invaluable.

Finally, of my wife, Nancy Malos-Johnson, I can only add that her understanding and patience throughout this long project are appreciated more than I could ever show or she could ever know. It is to her that I dedicate this long labour.

William C. Johnson
De Kalb, Illinois

How to Use the Index

Immediately preceding the *Index* proper, is the numbered List of Books Indexed. The 150 books have been numbered consecutively in the order in which they have been alphabetically listed. The numbers represent the books wherever reference is made to them in the body of the *Index*.

Each subject entry has a number or a series of numbers immediately following it. These numbers indicate that information on that subject may be found in the book corresponding to the number. If a number is followed by an asterisk, it signifies that ten or more references are made to the subject in that particular book, thus distinguishing works in which more than passing reference is made to the topic.

Because of the enormous quantity of subjects treated here, and in order to conserve space, it has been necessary to create some groupings which, under other circumstances, might not appear. In particular, the reader will find that most indexed individuals with the same surname, whether or not related to one another, are listed under the single surname. Thus two figures such as Nathaniel Brooke and Tucker Brooke, separated by three hundred years and not at all related, appear alphabetically under the major classification of Brooke. The arrangement should pose no problems though, if one remembers that the reference numbers refer specifically to the item immediately preceding them. In the following example, 'Arbuthnot: Alexander: 40. Dr. John: 91, 161,' book number 40 refers only to Alexander, while books 91 and 161 refer only to Dr. John.

Subtopics are listed as they appear in the respective indexed books. Thus in 'Ego: 96. Egotism: Milton's: 113, 146,' the ego in general is discussed in the first reference, and Milton's ego in particular in the second two.

When peripheral information, such as birth or death dates, occupations, relationships, appears, it does so because such information also appears in one or more of the respective books to help identify the subject or to distinguish it from another similar one.

In the larger entries, such as God, Milton, *Paradise Lost,* and Satan, while all the information from the books is included here, it was impossible to organize it all systematically into workable units. Representative sub-topics are extensively indicated, but readers should peruse the rest of the Index for particular and associated topics. Information on Satan not found under 'Satan,' for example, will be found under the specific sub-topic.

Inconsistencies in spelling, especially of proper names, are the bane of anyone engaged in this type of compilation. For the sake of consistency, I relied upon Chambers' *Biographical Dictionary,* New Edition (New York: St. Martin's Press, 1962), to provide a standard format. For the many names of Milton's contemporaries not listed in that work, I went to William Riley Parker's *Milton: a Biography,* for standardization. In most cases cross-references in the text of the *Index* direct readers to the alternate spellings.

As each book was indexed, misspelled words or incorrectly indicated references were occasionally noted in the book's index. When the error was obviously typographical, the information was included in its corrected form in the appropriate place. Other kinds of 'inaccuracies' have been included in the *Index* as they appear in the particular critical book, but have been 'corrected' by a 'see also' reference to the correct subject or title.

The computer affected the alphabetization of material. If upon occasion it seems odd, for example, that Charles Anthony should appear before St. Anthony, it is because the computer is a very literal reader, paying respect only to properly consistent alphabetical order, and not to rank or, at times, human logic. The computer 'reads' everything, and assigns a value to each letter, punctuation mark, and space. Uppercase letters have different values than their lowercase parallels, a space carries a value unique from a comma, and so on. One peculiarity in particular should be noted: the computer attributes to colons less value than it does to other punctuation marks. This results in an alphabetization somewhat different from that which one is likely to find in some other works. For example, the topic 'Life:' appears here after Knight's book *Life of Colet,* because of the higher value of the space after 'Life' in the book title. When there appeared the possibility of confusion because of this arrangement, I moved the entries, by hand, to where one might usually find them. In most cases, however, the listings appear in their computer-assigned places. One should also be aware, and watchful, of the computer's distinguishing between uppercase and lowercase letters, the former of which are valued more highly than the latter. Thus, 'English writers' appears before 'English Company.' Again, when I felt there might be any confusion, I rearranged the entries. I have generally acted on the premise that anyone dealing with the corpus of Milton's works is familiar with printed eccentricities – those of the computer should pose little, if any, problems.

While many 'See also' references have been included, one can never cross-reference as completely as one would wish. The usefulness of this index, as with that of any other work of reference, depends largely upon the reader. He would be well advised to check *all* the subjects which pertain to a topic, and to scan the pages for associated topics and names that occur to him as he pursues his research.

List of Books Indexed

1 Adams, Robert Martin.
Ikon: John Milton and the Modern Critics
Ithaca: Cornell University Press, 1955.

2 Addison, Joseph.
Criticisms on Paradise Lost
Ed. Albert S. Cook. Boston: Ginn and Co, 1892.

3 Ainsworth, Oliver M.
Milton on Education
New Haven, Conn.: Yale University Press, 1928.

4 Allen, Don Cameron.
The Harmonious Vision: Studies in Milton's Poetry
Baltimore: The Johns Hopkins Press, 1954.

5 Arthos, John.
Dante, Michelangelo and Milton
London: Routledge and Kegan Paul, 1963.

6 Arthos, John.
Milton and the Italian Cities
London: Bowes and Bowes, 1968.

7 Bailey, Margaret Lewis.
Milton and Jakob Boehme: a Study of German Mysticism in Seventeenth-Century England
1914; rpt. New York: Haskell House, 1964.

8 Banks, Theodore Howard.
Milton's Imagery
1950; rpt. New York: AMS Press, Inc, 1969.

9 Barker, Arthur E.
Milton and the Puritan Dilemma: 1641–1660.
1942; rpt. Toronto: University of Toronto Press, 1964.

10 Barnett, Pamela R.
Theodore Haak, F.R.S. (1605–1690): The First German Translator of Paradise Lost
The Hague: Mouton, 1962.

11 Bouchard, Donald F.
Milton: a Structural Reading
London: Edward Arnold, 1974.

12 Brett, R. L.
Reason and Imagination: a study of form and meaning in four poems
London: Oxford University Press, 1960.

13 Brinkley, Roberta Florence, ed.
Coleridge on the Seventeenth Century
1955; rpt. New York: Greenwood Press, Publishers, 1968.

14 Brisman, Leslie.
Milton's Poetry of Choice and Its Romantic Heirs
New York: Cornell University Press, 1973.

15 Broadbent, J. B.
Some Graver Subject: An Essay on Paradise Lost
1960; rpt. New York: Schocken Books, 1967.

16 Brown, Eleanor Gertrude.
Milton's Blindness
1934: rpt. New York: Octagon Books, 1968.

17 Burden, Dennis H.
The Logical Epic: A Study of the Argument of Paradise Lost
Cambridge, Mass.: Harvard University Press, 1967.

18 Bush, Douglas.
The Renaissance and English Humanism
1939; rpt. Toronto: University of Toronto Press, 1965.

19 Cawley, Robert Ralston.
Milton and the Literature of Travel
Princeton: Princeton University Press, 1951.

20 Clark, Donald Lemen.
John Milton at St. Paul's School: a Study of Ancient Rhetoric in English Renaissance Education
1948; rpt. Hamden, Conn.: Archon Books, 1964.

21 Condee, Ralph Waterbury.
Structure in Milton's Poetry
University Park, Penn.: Pennsylvania State University Press, 1974.

22 Conklin, George Newton.
Biblical Criticism and Heresy in Milton
New York: King's Crown Press, 1949

23 Cope, Jackson I.
The Metaphoric Structure of Paradise Lost
Baltimore: The Johns Hopkins Press, 1962.

24 Corcoran, Mary Irma.
Milton's Paradise with Reference to the Hexameral Background
Washington, D.C.: The Catholic University of America Press, 1945.

25 Curran, Stuart and Wittreich, Joseph Anthony, Jr., eds.
Blake's Sublime Allegory
Madison: University of Wisconsin Press, 1973.

26 Daiches, David.
Milton
London: Hutchinson's University Library, 1957.

27 Daniells, Roy.
Milton, Mannerism and Baroque
Toronto: University of Toronto Press, 1963.

28 Darbishire, Helen, ed.
The Early Lives of Milton
London: Constable and Co, Ltd, 1932.

29 Demaray, John G.
Milton and the Masque Tradition: The Early Poems, 'Arcades', and Comus
Cambridge, Mass.: Harvard University Press, 1968.

30 Diekhoff, John S., ed.
Milton on Himself
2nd Ed., 1939; rpt. London: Cohen and West Ltd, 1966.

31 Diekhoff, John S.
Milton's Paradise Lost: A Commentary on the Argument
1946; rpt. New York: Humanities Press, 1963.

32 Duncan, Joseph E.
Milton's Earthly Paradise
Minneapolis: University of Minnesota Press, 1972.

33 Elledge, Scott.
Milton's 'Lycidas': An Introduction to Criticism
New York: Harper and Row, 1966.

34 Empson, William.
Milton's God Revised ed.
1961; rpt. London: Chatto and Windus, 1965.

35 Empson, William.
Some Versions of Pastoral
1935; rpt. New York: New Directions, 1960.

36 Evans, J. M.
Paradise Lost and the Genesis Tradition
Oxford: Clarendon Press, 1968.

37 Fish, Stanley E.
Surprised By Sin
New York: St. Martin's Press, 1967.

38 Fixler, Michael.
Milton and the Kingdoms of God
London: Faber and Faber, 1964.

39 Fletcher, Angus.
The Transcendental Masque: An Essay on Milton's Comus
Ithaca, New York: Cornell University Press, 1971.

40 Fletcher, Harris Francis.
The Intellectual Development of John Milton
2 vols. Urbana: University of Illinois Press, 1956 and 1961.

41 Fletcher, Harris Francis.
Milton's Rabbinical Readings
1930; rpt. New York: Gordian Press, 1967.

42 Fletcher, Harris Francis.
Milton's Semitic Studies and Some Manifestations of them in His Poetry
1926; rpt. New York: Gordian Press, 1966.

43 Fletcher, Harris Francis.
The Use of the Bible in Milton's Prose
University of Illinois Studies in Language and Literature, XIV, No. 3. Urbana, University of Illinois Press, 1929.

44 French, Joseph Milton, ed.
The Life Records of John Milton
5 vols. New Brunswick, New Jersey: Rutgers University Press, 1949–58.

45 French, Joseph Milton.
Milton in Chancery: New Chapters in the Lives of the Poet and His Father
New York: Modern Language Association of America; London: Milford, Oxford University Press, 1939.

46 Frye, Northrop.
Five Essays on Milton's Epics
London: Routledge and Kegan Paul, 1966.

47 Frye, Roland Mushat.
God, Man, and Satan: Patterns of Christian Thought and Life in Paradise Lost, Pilgrim's Progress, and the Great Theologians
Princeton, New Jersey: Princeton University Press, 1960.

48 George, A. G.
Milton and the Nature of Man
London: Asia Publishing House, 1974.

49 Gilbert, Allan H.
A Geographical Dictionary of Milton
New Haven, Conn.: Yale University Press, 1919.

50 Gilbert, Allan H.
On the Composition of Paradise Lost: A Study of the Ordering and Insertion of Material
1947; rpt. New York: Octagon Books, 1966.

51 Gilman, Wilbur Elwyn.
Milton's Rhetoric: Studies in His Defense of Liberty
Columbia: University of Missouri Press, 1939.

52 Grace, William Joseph.
Ideas in Milton
Notre Dame, Indiana: University of Notre Dame Press, 1968.

53 Grose, Christopher.
Milton's Epic Process
New Haven, Conn.: Yale University Press, 1973.

54 Halkett, John.
Milton and the Idea of Matrimony: A Study of the Divorce Tracts and Paradise Lost
New Haven, Conn.: Yale University Press, 1970.

55 Hanford, James Holly and Taaffe, James G.
A Milton Handbook
5th ed. New York: Appleton-Century-Crofts, 1970.

56 Harding, Davis P.
The Club of Hercules: Studies in the Classical Background of Paradise Lost
Urbana: University of Illinois Press, 1962.

57 Hartwell, Kathleen Ellen.
Lactantius and Milton
Cambridge, Mass.: Harvard University Press, 1929.

58 Havens, Raymond Dexter.
The Influence of Milton on English Poetry.
1922; rpt. New York: Russell and Russell, Inc, 1961.

59 Honigmann, E. A. J., ed.
Milton's Sonnets
New York: St. Martin's Press, 1966.

60 Hughes, Merritt Y.
Ten Perspectives on Milton
New Haven, Conn.: Yale University Press, 1965.

61 Hyman, Lawrence W.
The Quarrel Within
Port Washington, New York: Kennikat Press, 1972.

62 Jenkins, R. B.
Milton and the Theme of Fame
The Hague: Mouton, 1973.

63 Kelley, Maurice.
This Great Argument: a Study of Milton's De doctrina christiana as a Gloss upon Paradise Lost
Princeton, New Jersey: Princeton University Press, 1941.

64 Kirkconnell, Watson.
Awake the Courteous Echo
Toronto: University of Toronto Press, 1973.

65 Kirkconnell, Watson.
The Celestial Cycle: The Theme of Paradise Lost in World Literature, with Translations of the Major Analogues
Toronto: University of Toronto Press, 1952.

66 Kranidas, Thomas.
The Fierce Equation: A Study of Milton's Decorum
The Hague: Mouton and Co, 1965.

67 Kranidas, Thomas, ed.
New Essays on Paradise Lost
Berkeley: University of California Press, 1969.

68 Krouse, F. Michael.
Milton's Sampson and the Christian Tradition
Princeton: Princeton University Press, 1949.

69 Laguardia, Eric.
Nature Redeemed: The Imitation of Order in Three Renaissance Poems
The Hague: Mouton and Co, 1966.

70 Langdon, Ida.
Milton's Theory of Poetry and Fine Art
1924; rpt. New York: Russell and Russell, 1965.

71 Larson, Martin.
The Modernity of Milton
Chicago: University of Chicago Press, 1927.

72 Lawry, Jon S.
The Shadow of Heaven
New York: Cornell University Press, 1968.

73 Le Comte, Edward S.
A Milton Dictionary
New York: Philosophical Library, Inc, 1961.

74 Lewalski, Barbara Kiefer.
Milton's Brief Epic: The Genre, Meaning, and Art of Paradise Regained
Providence: Brown University Press, 1966.

75 Lieb, Michael.
The Dialectics of Creation: Patterns of Birth and Regeneration in Paradise Lost
Boston: University of Massachusetts Press, 1970.

76 MacCaffrey, Isabel Gamble.
Paradise Lost as 'Myth'
Cambridge, Mass.: Harvard University Press, 1959.

77 McColley, Grant.
Paradise Lost: An Account of Its Growth and Major Origins, with a Discussion of Milton's Use of Sources and Literary Patterns
1940; rpt. New York: Russell and Russell, 1963.

78 McLachlan, Herbert.
The Religious Opinions of Milton, Locke, and Newton
Manchester: Manchester University Press, 1941.

79 Madsen, William G.
From Shadowy Types to Truth: Studies in Milton's Symbolism
New Haven, Conn.: Yale University Press, 1968.

80 Marilla, E. L.
Milton and Modern Man
University of Alabama: University of Alabama Press, 1968.

81 Martz, Louis L.
The Paradise Within: Studies in Vaughan, Traherne, and Milton
New Haven, Conn.: Yale University Press, 1964.

82 Mohl, Ruth.
John Milton and his Commonplace Book
New York: Frederick Ungar Publishing Co, 1969.

83 Mohl, Ruth.
Studies in Spenser, Milton, and the Theory of Monarchy
New York: Columbia University Press, 1949.

84 Muir, Kenneth.
John Milton
London: Longmans, Green, 1955.

85 Muldrow, George M.
Milton and the Drama of the Soul
The Hague: Mouton, 1970.

86 Murray, Patrick.
Milton: The Modern Phase; A Study of Twentieth-century Criticism
London: Longman, Green, and Co, Ltd, 1967.

87 Nelson, James G.
The Sublime Puritan: Milton and the Victorians
Madison: University of Wisconsin Press, 1963.

88 Oras, Ants.
Milton's Editors and Commentators from Patrick Hume to Henry John Todd (1965–1801)
London: Oxford University Press, 1931.

89 Orchard, Thomas Nathaniel.
Milton's Astronomy: The Astronomy of Paradise Lost
1896; rpt. London: Longmans, Green, and Co, 1913.

90 Osgood, Charles G.
The Classical Mythology of Milton's English Poems
New York: H. Holt and Co, 1900.

91 Parker, William Riley.
Milton's Contemporary Reputation
Columbus: The Ohio State University Press, 1940.

92 Parker, William Riley.
Milton's Debt to Greek Tragedy in Samson Agonistes
Baltimore: The Johns Hopkins Press, 1937.

93 Patrides, C. A.
Milton and the Christian Tradition
Oxford: Clarendon Press, 1966.

94 Pattison, Mark.
Milton
1879; rpt. London: Macmillan and Co, 1932.

95 Peter, John Desmond.
A Critique of Paradise Lost
New York: Columbia University Press, 1960.

96 Plotkin, Frederick.
Milton's Inward Jerusalem
The Hague: Mouton, 1971.

97 Pointon, Marcia R.
Milton and English Art
Manchester: Manchester University Press, 1970.

98 Pommer, Henry Francis.
Milton and Melville
Pittsburgh: University of Pittsburg Press, 1950.

99 Pope, Elizabeth M.
Paradise Regained: The Tradition and the Poem
Baltimore: The Johns Hopkins Press, 1947.

100 Qvarnström, Gunnar.
The Enchanted Palace: Some Structural Aspects of Paradise Lost
Stockholm: Almqvist and Wiksell, 1967.

101 Rajan, Balachandra.
The Lofty Rhyme
London: Routledge and Kegan Paul, 1970.

102 Rajan, Balachandra.
Paradise Lost and the Seventeenth Century Reader
1947; rpt. London: Chatto and Windus, 1962.

103 Raymond, Dora B.
Oliver's Secretary: John Milton in an Era of Revolt
New York: Minton, Balch and Co, 1932.

104 Reesing, John.
Milton's Poetic Art: A Mask, Lycidas, and Paradise Lost
Cambridge, Mass.: Harvard University Press, 1968.

105 Ricks, Christopher.
Milton's Grand Style
Oxford: Clarendon Press, 1963.

106 Riggs, W. G.
The Christian Poet in Paradise Lost
Berkeley: University of California Press, 1972.

107 Robins, Harry F.
If This Be Heresy: A Study of Milton and Origen
Urbana: University of Illinois Press, 1963.

108 Ross, Malcolm Mackenzie.
Milton's Royalism: A Study of the Conflict of Symbol and Idea in the Poems
Ithaca, New York: Cornell University Press, 1943.

109 Rudrum, Alan.
Milton
London: Macmillan and Co, 1968.

110 Ryken, Leland.
The Apocalyptic Vision in Paradise Lost
Ithaca: Cornell University Press, 1970.

111 Samuel, Irene.
Dante and Milton: The Commedia and Paradise Lost
Ithaca, New York: Cornell University Press, 1966.

112 Samuel, Irene.
Plato and Milton
Ithaca, New York: Cornell University Press, 1947.

113 Saurat, Denis.
Milton: Man and Thinker
1925; rpt. London: Dent, 1944.

114 Schultz, Howard.
Milton and Forbidden Knowledge
New York: Modern Language Association of America, 1955.

115 Sensabaugh, George F.
Milton in Early America
Princeton, New Jersey: Princeton University Press, 1964.

116 Sensabaugh, George F.
That Grand Whig, Milton
1952; rpt. New York: Benjamin Blom, 1967.

117 Shawcross, John T., ed.
Milton 1732–1801
London: Routledge and Kegan Paul, 1972.

118 Shumaker, Wayne.
Unpremeditated Verse: Feeling and Perception in Paradise Lost
Princeton, New Jersey: Princeton University Press, 1967.

119 Sims, James H.
The Bible in Milton's Epics
Gainesville: University of Florida Press, 1962.

120 Smart, J. S.
The Sonnets of Milton
1921; rpt. Oxford: Clarendon Press, 1966.

121 Spaeth, Sigmund Gottfried.
Milton's Knowledge of Music: Its Sources and Its Significance in His Works
Princeton, New Jersey: The University Library, 1913.

122 Steadman, John M.
Milton and the Renaissance Hero
Oxford: Clarendon Press, 1967.

123 Steadman, John M.
Milton's Epic Characters: Image and Idol
1959; rpt. Chapel Hill: University of North Carolina Press, 1963.

124 Stein, Arnold.
Answerable Style: Essays on Paradise Lost
Minneapolis: University of Minnesota Press, 1953.

125 Stein, Arnold.
Heroic Knowledge: An Interpretation of Paradise Regained and Samson Agonistes
Minneapolis: University of Minnesota Press, 1957.

126 Stroup, Thomas B.
Religious Rite and Ceremony in Milton's Poetry
Lexington: University of Kentucky Press, 1968.

127 Summers, Joseph H.
The Muse's Method: An Introduction to Paradise Lost
1962; rpt. New York: W. W. Norton and Co, 1968.

128 Svendsen, Kester.
Milton and Science
Cambridge, Mass.: Harvard University Press, 1956.

129 Thompson, Elbert N. S.
Essays on Milton
New Haven, Conn.: Yale University Press, 1914.

130 Thorpe, James E., Jr.
Milton Criticism: Selections from Four Centuries
London: Rinehart and Co, 1950.

131 Tillyard, E. M. W.
The Metaphysicals and Milton
London: Chatto and Windus, 1956.

132 Tillyard, E. M. W.
Milton
London: Chatto and Windus, 1930.

133 Tillyard, E. M. W.
The Miltonic Setting: Past and Present
1938; rpt. London: Chatto and Windus, 1947.

134 Tillyard, E. M. W.
Studies in Milton
London: Chatto and Windus, 1951.

135 Treip, Mindele.
Milton's Punctuation and Changing English Usage, 1582–1676
London: Methuen and Co, Ltd, 1970.

136 Visiak, E. H.
The Portent of Milton: Some Aspects of His Genius
London: Werner Laurie, 1958.

137 Wagenknecht, Edward.
The Personality of Milton
Norman, Oklahoma: University of Oklahoma Press, 1970.

138 Waldock, A. J. A.
Paradise Lost And Its Critics
1947; rpt. Cambridge: Cambridge University Press, 1966.

139 Watkins, W. B. C.
An Anatomy of Milton's Verse
1955; rpt. Hamden, Conn.: Archon Books, 1965.

140 Weber, Burton Jasper.
The Construction of Paradise Lost
Carbondale, Illinois: Southern Illinois University Press, 1971.

141 Werblowsky, Raphael Jehudah Zwi.
Lucifer and Prometheus: A Study of Milton's Satan
Introduction by C. G. Jung. London: Routledge and Kegan Paul, 1952.

142 West, Robert Hunter.
Milton and the Angels
Athens: University of Georgia Press, 1955.

143 Whiting, George Wesley.
Milton and This Pendant World
Austin: University of Texas Press, 1958.

144 Whiting, George Wesley.
Milton's Literary Milieu
1939; rpt. New York: Russell and Russell, Inc, 1964.

145 Williamson, George.
Milton and Others
2nd ed., 1965; rpt. Chicago: University of Chicago Press, 1970.

146 Wittreich, Joseph Anthony, Jr., ed.
The Romantics on Milton
Cleveland: The Press of Case Western Reserve University, 1970.

147 Wolfe, Don M.
Milton in the Puritan Revolution
1941; rpt. New York: Humanities Press, 1963.

148 Woodhouse, A. S. P.
The Heavenly Muse
Toronto: University of Toronto Press, 1972.

149 Woodhull, Mariana.
The Epic of Paradise Lost: Twelve Essays
New York: G. P. Putnam's Sons, 1907.

150 Wright, B. A.
Milton's Paradise Lost: A Reassessment of the Poem
London: Methuen and Co, Ltd, 1962.

Milton Criticism
A Subject Index

Abbreviations

In yet another effort to conserve space, various abbreviations are employed throughout the *Index*. Milton appears both as 'M' and as 'Milton', and the substitution appears at times even in titles (as in *M, Man and Thinker*). The abbreviations should pose no difficulties. The same has been done with many numerals ('1st' for 'First'), and with the following:

Abp.	Archbishop	lit.	literature
Attr.	Attributed to	PL	Paradise Lost
Bp.	Bishop	pr.	printer
bks.	bookseller	PR	Paradise Regained
c.	Century	SA	Samson Agonistes
Eng.	England	univ.	University

-A-

A., J. (John Aiken?): 117

A., R. (Robert Austin, pr. 1642-56?): 91, 117

Aarhus (Denmark): 44

Aaron, Jacob Hason: 41

Aaron: 4, 73, 32. Aaron's breastplate: 128

Abaddon: 73

Abaelardus, Petrus. See Abelard, Peter

Abailard, Peter. See Abelard, Peter

Abarim: 49, 73. The mountains: 144

Abassin: 73

Abbana: 19, 49, 73, 144

Abbati, Bocca degli: 111

Abbetmeyer, C.: 36

Abbondanti, Antonius: 64'

Abbot: George, 1562-1633 (Abp. of Canterbury): 19, 40, 44, 145, 91. Robert: 40, 64, 54

Abbott: Edwin, A.: 144. C. C.: 86. John: 114. Lyman: 137. Wilbur C.: 44*, 45

<u>ABC</u> (hornbook): 40

Abcie: 40, 73

Abdiel: 1, 2, 4, 17, 31*, 41, 50*, 56, 57, 60, 63, 73, 76, 98, 102, 103, 104, 112, 111, 123, 124, 127*, 141*, 142, 144, 3, 32, 36, 46, 62, 72, 109, 130, 55, 140*.

Abdy: Anthony: 44. Humphrey: 44

Abel: 68, 73, 102, 123, 127, 32, 36, 72. Diabolic parentage of: 36. Murder of: 109

Abelard, Peter: 40, 65, 68, 114, 32, 36, 137, 77, 71, 93. <u>Commentary on Genesis</u>: 36. <u>Exposition of the Epistle to the Romans</u>: 36. <u>Sic et Non</u>: 77 <u>Hex</u>: 77

Abele, tramelogedia: 65

Abelson, Joshua: 100

Abercrombie: James: 115. Lascelles: 1, 86, 98, 132, 133, 134, 138, 141, 130, 21; works: <u>The Epic</u>: 60; <u>The Idea of Great Poetry</u>: 60

Abergavenny: House: 40. Lord: 44

Abernethy, John: 114

Abert, Hermann: 93

Abiathar: 73

Abilities, M's: 40

Abimelech the Usurper: 73

Abinglon, co. Berks.: 44, 45. Abingdon Grammar School: 40

<u>Abington Bible Commentary</u>: 99

Abiram: 73

Abishai: 44

Ablative absolute: 98

Abney Hall, Cheshire: 44

Abnormal, the Richardsons' dealings with: 88

Abolition: of Catholicism: 58. Of cathedral establishments: 51

Abortion: 128

Abra: 73, 3. River: see Humber

Abraham (Abram): 1, 2, 40, 60, 68, 73, 123, 127, 141, 142, 143, 144, 3, 11, 32, 72, 91. Departure from Ur and third age: 3. Covenant with: 126

Abraham de Balmes: 40

Abraham ibn Ezra: 40

Abraham Farrisol: 41

Abrahams, Israel: 22

Abram, Nicolas: 32

Abramites: 73

Abrams, Meyer H.: 52, 69, 79, 53, 61, 101, 146, 25. On <u>Lycidas</u>: 104

Abravanel: 32

<u>Abridgement of Christian Divinity, The</u>: 142. See also: Wolleb

Absalom: 73, 32, 72

<u>Absalom and Achitophel</u> (Parts I and II): 51, 116, 142, 71

Abskonet, co. Surrey: 44

Absolute, the: 7, 27*. Predestination: 71. M's conception

of: 113

Absolutism: 27. Relation of M's views to 19th c.: 113. M condemns: 147

Abstinence: 93, 9

Abstract, the: 51. Subjects: 51

Abul Wefa: 89

Abyssines: 144

Abyssinia: 19*. Abyssinians. See Ethiopians; Negus, Empire of

Academe: 30, 49, 73, 3

Academic exercises: 30. See also: Prolusions: 132, 112, 147*; Milton, John, Works

Academic life (M's), decided against by 1628: 40

Académie de poésie et de musique: 29

Académie des Sciences (Paris): 44

Academies of Italy (M's views of): 30 44. Italian: 103. See also Della Crusia, and Svogliati

Academy, Gaddian: 30

Academy: 7*, 44*, 45, 51

Acanthus (plant): 73

Accaron (Ecron): 19, 49, 73, 144

Accent: Bentley on, and emphasis: 88. Equals intonation in Lofft's terminology: 88

Accents, old: Pearce, Newton, Todd on: 88

Acceptance: 47

Accia: 128

Accidence (grammatical): 40, 44, 73

Accidence (Colet): 20

Accidence commenced Grammar: 112, 116, 3. See also: Milton, John, Works

Accidence of Armorie: 40

Accidence, Latin: 40

Accommodation: 60, 66, 79, 118, 47*, 110, 122. Theory of: 93, 25. Doctrine of medieval and Renaissance versions: 107, 110, 122. Examples of, passim, incarnation, demonic, Holy Spirit: 47*. M's formulation of: 110. In PL: 110, 79. Theory of in Bible: 79. In Biblical truth: 118. See also Scripture

Accompaniment: 121

Accomplishments (M's) by 1625: 40

Account of the English Dramatick Poets: 116

Account of Persecutions and Oppressions: 116

Account of Private League: 116

Accounts, casting of: 40

Accuracy of M's references: 121

Acevedo, Alonso de: 65 77

Acha, Rabbi: 88

Achaemeniae(n): 73

Achan: 73

Achates: 123, 2

Acheloian, Achelous: 73

Achelous: 49, 90

Achemenides: 56

Acheron: 49, 73, 90, 111

Acherontaeo(n): 73

Achilleid: 111

Achilles Tatius: 90, 122

Achilles: 2, 17, 44, 56*, 60, 70, 73, 90, 123*, 3, 72, 130

Achish: 73

Achitophel: 44, 60, 73, 91

Ackermann, Rudolph: 40, 97

Acontius, Jacobus (Acontio, Jacopo): 40, 114, 93

Acosta, Joseph de: 128

Acrasia: 60, 123, 32

Act of Oblivion: 116, 94. Act of Pardon: 103. Act for Suppressing Blasphemy: 78

Acta Archelai: 36

Actaea(n): 44, 73

Actaeon: 90, 123

Actio or pronuntiato (part four of

rhetoric): 20

Action: vs. contemplation: 114*. As theme in PR: 125. In SA: 125. As withdrawal: 125. And pure intelligence: 125. Virtuous: 31. Demonic parody of: 46. Dunster examines connection between characters and development of: 88

Action: 8, 31, 114*, 125, 118, 46*

Actions: in PL: 118. Punishment of evil: 118. Giving reward and comfort: 118

Actisanes: 73

Active: life: 70, 123*. Good: 60, Hero: 122.

Activity: 141

Acton: Henry: 63. J. E. E. D.: 148. Samuel: 44

Actors, silent: 92

Acts and Ordinences: 9

Acts of Parliament: Act of uniformity: 116, 94

Acts: 3, 88. In SA: 92. Peck divides M's dramatic works into: 88. Of Apostles: 51

Actual meaning of words: Pearce's keen analysis of: 88

Acworth, George: 73

Ad Demonicum (Isocrates): 20

Ad Herennium: 20, 40, 66, 21

Ad Joannem Rousium: 9, 133. See also: Milton, John, Works

Ad Leonorum: 112, 14. See also: Milton, John, Works

"Ad Messallam": 21

Ad Patrem: 112, 121, 129, 4, 6, 8, 9, 20, 27, 30, 40, 42, 44, 45, 59, 70*, 73, 74, 128, 132, 133. See also: Milton, John, Works

"Ad Pisonem": See "Laus Pisonis"

Ad Pyrrham: 72

Adagia (Erasmus): 20

Adair, Douglass: 115

Adalhard: 64

Adam: 1*, 4*, 17*, 19, 24, 31*. 40, 41, 42, 44, 51, 52, 54*, 57, 37*, 50*, 60*, 63*, 67*, 68, 70, 73, 76, 89, 98*, 102*, 103*, 104*, 112*, 111*, 113*, 114*, 122, 123*, 124*, 125, 127*, 128*, 129*, 142*, 143*, 144*, 3*, 11, 32*, 36*, 71*, 72*, 96*, 109*, 130*, 140*, 25, 55*. Associated with: Abraham: 119; with Cain: 119; with Joshua: 119; with Moses: 119. Attains sum of wisdom: 119. Compared to reaper: 119. Dissociated from Abraham after the Fall: 119. Escorted into Paradise: 119. Expulsion of associated with Lot's from Sodom: 119. Fall of foreshadowed: 119. Fallen character of: 119. Reassociated with Abraham: 119. Repentence of: 119, 101. Sum of wisdom learned by: 119. Fall of: 54, 25. State of: 25. Completion of, in Eve: 101. Divine image, in: 101. Education of: 54, 101, 36. Hierarchical function of: 101. Paradise, departure of, from: 101. As contraction: 146. As a character, development: 55. In account of his origin: 72. In colloquy with Raphael: 37, 50, 60, 72*. In his Fall: 17, 72. In judgment upon history: 72. In pre-Satanic Eden: 72. In recognition of Death: 72. In reconciliation: 72. In repentence: 72. In tutelage of Eve: 72. In "wedded love": 72. As a Christian: 93. Equated with Christ: 99*. Sources: 55*. Adam's sin is mankind's: 107. In the image of God: 36. In the image of the angels: 36. Name of: 36. Tasks of: 36*, 32. As "mind": 36. Solitude of: 36. Sleep of: 36*. Type of Christ: 36. Attitude to Eve: 36*. Warning to Eve: 36. Return of: 36. Motive for Fall: 36*. Revelation to: 36. Philosophic discussion with Raphael: 89. Moral consciousness of: 104. Relationships with Michael: 17, 50, 60, 104. Awareness of death: 104. Spiritual regeneration of: 104. Tonal patterns of: 104. As a type: 129. His sin: 67, 129. His future: 129*, 76. As hero: 129. And dark future: 143. The prophecy: 143. Instructed: 50, 143. And Eve in Garden: 143. His original crime: 143. Michael reveals future to: 143. Adam to Noah, first age: 143. As Christian soldier: 76. Vision of future: 67, 76. Knowledge: 76. As ideal man: 76. Attitude toward Eve: 37, 76. Fall: 76. Ruler of Eden: 76. As Everyman: 76. Meaning in Hebrew: 47. His discrimination between Good and Evil: 41. Nature of his knowledge before Fall: 41. His language: 37, 67. And heroism: 37*. Symbolism of 81*. Temptation of: 37*, 54*. Relationship of Eve and: 52, 54*. Samson as another: 52. And Reason: 37*. And Raphael: 37*, 89. And Faith: 37*. And Eve's Dream: 37*. As character: 11. His use of language: 11. Christ parallel: 122, 123. Angelic messengers to: 123. As prophet: 123. Foreknowledge of his posterity: 123. His responsibility for his Fall: 123. Associated with Saturn: 32. As first man: 32. Symbolic meaning of: 32. As Cynic: 32. As Stoic: 32. Original perfection of: 32*. In Jewish tradition: 32. Not first man: 32. Lack of original perfection: 32. Dominion of over animals: 32. And origin of natural rights: 32. Dwelling place of: 32. Creation of: 32, 36*. Relation to Christ: 32. As mankind: 32. Temptation and Fall of: 32, 36*. Adam (literary character): 32*. Original perfection of: 32. In legend: 32. As first man: 32. Work of: 32. And origin of monarchy: 32. Immortality of: 32. Relation to Christ: 32. Symbolic meaning of: 32. Contrasted with historical man: 32. Adam, "the second": 72*. See also: Son, Man, PL; Man; Fall; Atonement; Triple Equation; Christ

<u>Adam</u> (Lipiner): 65. <u>Adam</u> (Lorca): 65. <u>Adam</u> (Roll): 65. <u>Adam</u> (Old French): 77.

Adam and Eve: 50, 54*, 75*, 83, 136, 32*, 36*, 46*, 106*, 25*. Loss of freedom: 46. Corruption after Fall: 46, 32, 36. Innocence of: 106, 46. And knowledge: 106*. And the Fall: 106*. And poetry: 106. And inspiration: 106*. Fall manifold in sin: 107. Adam and Eve (literary characters): Life of in paradise: 32. Compared with Indians: 32. And nature: 32. Inner paradise of: 32. Adam and Eve: Historical importance of: 32. Of Hebrew writers: 32. Tasks of: 32. Marital relations of: 32. Original perfection of: 32*, 83, 36. Temptation and Fall of: 32, 46. Symbolic meaning of: 32*. As first parents: 32. And problem of chronology: 32. Expulsion of: 32, 36*, 75. And natural law: 32. Salvation of: 32. And beginning of Church: 32. Dwelling place of: 32. Description of: 32. Like primitives: 32. Creation of: 36*. As mankind: 50. Bower of: 54. In the image of God: 36. As an hermaphrodite: 36. Marriage of: 36. Type of Christ and Church: 36. Sexual innocence of: 36. Nakedness of: 36. Original imperfection of: 36*. Separation of: 17, 36. Opening of the eyes: 36*. Hiding of: 36. Quarrel of: 36. Interrogation of: 36. Condemnation of: 36*. Clothing of: 36. Repentance of: 36. 1st experience of night: 36. And unfallen creativity: 75*. The uncreation of: 75*. Character: 46. The re-creation of: 75*. Relationship: 46. Joint hero of PL: 83. Worship of: 32. And natural rights: 32. See also: Warning

<u>Adam et Eve</u>: 65

<u>Adam i Ewa</u>: 65

<u>Adam in Ballingschap</u>: 17, 65*

<u>Adam in Banishment</u>: 50

Adam of Bremen: 93 <u>Adam und Eva</u>: (texts by Baggesen, Hartmann, Lutwin, Nocken): 65

<u>Adam und Eva</u> (Baggesen): 65. <u>Adam und Eva</u> (Hartmann): 65. <u>Adam und Eva</u> (Lutwin): 65. <u>Adam und Eva</u> (Nocken): 65. <u>Adam und Heva</u> (Ruff): 65

<u>Adam Cast Forth</u>: 65

Adam Kadmon: 40

<u>Adam Unparadised</u>: 126, 145, 85, 101, 55, 50*, 102, 122

<u>Adam, en ander gedigte</u>: 65

<u>Adam, ou La création</u>: 65

Adam, Book of: 42

<u>Adam, Ein dramatisches Gedicht</u>: 65

<u>Adam, Fragmente</u>: 65

<u>Adam, Life of</u>: 113

Adam, Mr.: 44

<u>Adam's Complaint</u>: 65

<u>Adam's Garden</u>: 65

Adamant: 128

Adamites: 73

<u>Adamo</u> (Andreini): 65*, 70, 94. <u>Adamo</u> (Campailla): 65. <u>Adamo</u> (Loredano): 65. <u>Adamo</u> (Pona): 65

<u>Adamo cacciato del Paradiso</u>: 65

<u>Adamo ed Eva</u>: 65. <u>Adam og Eva</u>: 65

<u>Adamo Caduto</u>: 17, 65*

Adams: Mr.: 44. Abijan: 115. Charles Francis: 58, 115. Clement: 19, 73. Daniel: 115; works: <u>The Thorough Scholar</u>: 115; <u>The Understanding Reader</u>: 115. E. K.: 44. Elizabeth (wife of Thomas Milton): 45. Frank O'Br.: 44. George: 44. H. M.: 44. Hannah: 115; <u>The Truth and Excellence of the Christian Religion Exhibited</u>: 115. Henry: 108. Henry Hitch: 29. J. Q.: 40. James L.: 93. John: 117.

John (the poet): 115; works: Poems on Several Occasions, Original and Translated: 115; To a Gentleman at the Sight of Some of his Poems: 115; The Revelation of St. John the Divine: 115. John (the 2nd president of the U.S.): 115*; works: A Defense of the Constitution of Government of the United States of America: 115; Thoughts on Government: 115. John (gunner): 44. John Quincy: 115; Lectures on Rhetoric and Oratory: 115. Joseph Quincy, Memorial Studies: 44. McKay: 115. Philip: 44. R. M.: 86*, 39. Richard P. 1, 4, 21. Robert Martin: 74, 107, 64, 101, 137, 146, 15, 23, 27, 29, 34, 52*, 60, 105, 122, 128, 143, 14; comment on Comus: 143; on Allen: 143; demise of M's ideas: 143. Robert P.: 93. Samuel: 60, 115. T., Trafalgar: 58. Thomas: 40, 44, 79, 114, 143, 36, 93; State of church: 143; and glassy sea: 143; Meditations on the Creed: 36

Adams and Evens Erschaffung: 65

Adams erstes Erwachen: 65

Adams Klage: 65

Adamson: J. H.: 23, 60, 74, 75, 79, 110, 93. J. W.: 20. Patrick ("Jobus"): 74, 64

Adamus peccans: 65

Adamus Exul (Grotius): 17, 65*, 70, 94. (Barham tr.): 65

Adamus, fabula: 65

Adamus, Melchior: 73

Adao e Eva no Paraiso: 65

Adapa: 32

Adaptation: 51

Adderbury: 45

Addison, Galston: 44

Addison, Joseph: 1, 7, 12, 15, 17, 24, 31, 37, 41, 44, 3, 56, 58*, 60, 70*, 73, 81, 86, 87, 93, 100, 102, 105, 104, 118, 138, 109, 116, 127*, 128, 144, 53, 71, 85, 91, 97, 115, 130*, 146*, 150, 117*, 140, 141, 3, 74, 120, 132, 133, 134, 142, 88*, 94, 149. On the "Pleasures of the Imagination" in The Spectator papers: 87. The Spectator: 115. On Italy: 55, Poem on M: 55. On M: 55. And M compared: 146. Addison on PL, edited by Cook: 70. His objection to learning in PL: 83. On the theme of PL: 83

Additional Discovery of Mr. Roger L'Estrange: 116

Addlegate: 49, 73. See also: Algate

Address to Melancholy: 115

Address, Office of: 44

Adeimantus: 112

Adelard of Bath: 128

Adelkind, Cornelius: 41

Adelung: 100

Ademollo, A.: 6

Ades: 73, 90. See also: Pluto

Adiabene: 19, 49, 73, 144

Adimari, Allesandra: 6, 44

Adjectives, compound: 98. Post positional: 98

Adler: Alfred: 27. E. N.: 123. Jacob H.: 115

Adlerblum, Nima H., A Study of Gersonides: 41

Adlington, William: 117

Admetus: 73, 90

Admiral's Theatre: 68

Admirality judges: 44

Admiralty Committee: 44

Admiralty, Commissioners of: 44

Admiralty: 44

Admiration: 51, 73. See also: Wonder

Admission records (M's to Christ College): 40

Admissions, The Book of: 45

Admonition of John Knox to the Commonality of Scotland (Knox): 147

Admonition to Parliament, a Puritan appeal for civil protection: 147

Adney, T.: 58

Ado of Vienne, St.: 93

Adolphus: 73. See Christina

Adonais: 27, 130.

Adonia: 90

Adonibezec: 73

Adonis, Garden of: 49, 32. See also: Alcinous; Hesperian; Solomon

Adonis: 1, 2, 19, 49, 57, 69, 73, 90, 104, 144, 3, 72, 25

Adoption: 63

Adoram: 73

Adoration (latria) of God: 40

Adrammelech: 73, 142

Adria (Adriatic): 49, 73

Adrian: V, Pope: 111. VI, Pope: 73. Friar: 73

Adrian's Well: 73

Adriani, Messrs.: 44

Adriatic: 3

Adrichomius: 19. Christianus: 144

Adult Baptism: 78

Adultery: 54*, 71

Advancement of Learning (Bacon): 51, 20, 112, 134, 3, 26

Adventurer, The: 88, 117

Adventurous Muse, The (Watts): 70

Adversaries (of M): 30*. Descriptions of, names of: 30*

Adversity: 123*. Argument from: 123*. Tempest as symbol of: 123*

Advertisement for Moore and Company: 25

Advertisement of religion, Dunster on artistic aspect of poetry as mere: 88. See also: Didacticism

Advice to the Commons Within All His Majesties Realms and Dominions: 116

Advice: 51

"Advices to a Painter" (attr. to M): 44

Advocate: 45 51

Ady, Thomas: 142

Aeacus: 44, 73

Aeaea: 144

AEditio (Colet): 20

AEgean (AEgaeus): 49, 73, 90, 123, 3

AEgelands: 49

Aegeria: See Numa

Aegeus: 92

Aegialus: 73

Aegidius of Colonna: 40

Aegisthus: 92

Aegle: 44, 73

Aegon: 44, 73

Aegus: 44

Aelfric, MS. and Fall of Angels: 143. Exameron: 36. On the Beginning of the Creation: 36

AElfric: 40, 68, 36, 99

Aelian: 19, 40, 44, 57, 128, 64

AEmilian Road: 49, 73, 144

Aemilius Probus: 40

AEneas (Silvius): 2*, 17, 56*, 60, 70, 73, 90, 123, 3, 114, 32, 72, 130, 148. See also: Virgil

AEneid: 2*, 20, 27, 70, 111, 118, 11, 46, 92, 94, 130*, 37, 50. See also: Virgil

AEnesidemus: 114

AEnon: 49, 73

Aeolian: charms: 73, 3. Mood (music): 40, 121

Aeolides: 73. See Cephalus

Aeolus: 73, 90, 123, 3. As epic machinery: 123. See also: Virgil

Aerians: 73

Aeschines: 73, 112

Aeschylus: 1, 2, 6, 12, 15, 20, 30, 34, 40, 52, 56, 57, 58, 60, 68, 18, 64, 70, 73, 90*, 113, 114, 127, 128, 132, 133, 141*, 3, 26, 32, 39, 53, 71, 72, 82, 88, 92*, 101, 130, 146, 149, 148, 117, 25, 21, 13, 92*, 94, 82. Persae: 92*. Agamemnon: 92*, 94. Cheophorai: 92*. Eumenides: 92*. Prometheus Bound: 1, 91*. The Suppliants: 82. Septem: 92*. Supplices: 92. Debts to: 92*. Text of: 92. Influence on M: 141

Aesculapius: 16, 73, 90, 144. See also: More, A.

Aeson: 90

Aesonian (Aesonios): 73. Spindles: 3

Aesop: 20, 40, 44, 73, 95, 128, 53, 72, 25. Fables: 3

Aesop's Fables in True Orthography (Bullokar): 20

Aesthetic(s): 25. Aesthetic values: 51. Aesthetic universe as self-sufficient: 118. Aesthetic theory, M's: 70*. Attitude in Pearce's notes, relative rareness of: 88. Aims of Warton's commentary: 88. And psychological examination of M's sentence structure by Pearce: 88. In Patterson's commentary: 88. Discrimination in Warton's illustrations: 88. And in his criticism (due to his literary practice): 88. As distinct from personal experience, Warton on: 88. Considerations in Lofft's phonetic investigations: 88. Method combined by Dunster with biographical considerations: 88. And psychological considerations applied by Dunster to chronological problems: 88. Criticism, Dunster's, far superior to Todd's: 88. Tendencies and didacticism in PL discussed by Dunster: 88. Touch in Thyer's criticism: 88. Effects, Thyer regards PR as principally aiming at: 88. Interpretation, lack of, in Callander's commentary: 88. Character of M's poetry, careful study of facts in Callender's notes helping to elucidate: 88. Sensibility, Massey's: 88. Aspect of M's poetry, Warton's erudition necessary for eludicating: 88. Warton's tendency towards: 88

Aetatis suae: 40

Aether: 73

"Aethiop". See More, A.

Aethon: 44, 73, 3

Aethra: 44

AEtna: 3, 72. Mt.: 19, 44, 49, 73, 3

Afer, Leo: 73, 90, 144

Affectation: Warton dislikes pompous Italianate: 88

Affective Fallacy, The: 12

Affidavit: 45

Affinity, in courtesy books: 54. In M: 54*. In preachers: 54

Affirmation: 47

Affirmative theology: 93

Afranius: 73

Africa, he surnamed of: 73

Africa: 19, 44, 49, 73, 150. Africanism: 70, 73. Africa: 62

Aga Bashas of Algiers: 44

Agag: 44, 73, 91

Agamemnon: 56, 60, 73, 90, 123, 71, 92. See also: Homer

Agape: 141

Agar: 73. Family: 44. Ann (M's niece): see Moore. Anne (M's sister): see Phillips, Anne. Herbert: 9, 60, 102, 112*, 93. John: 44, 45. Mary (M's niece): 45. Mary Rugeley: 44. Thomas: 44, 45, 94. Thomas (M's brother-in-law): 44*, 45. Thomas (M's nephew): 44. Agas, Ralph: 20

Agatha, Council of: 44, 73, 113. Town: 49

Agathias (the historian): 44, 73

Agathon: 112

Age of gold: 72

Age of students on admission: 40

"Age of the antonimes," the: 98

Age of Reason, The: 71

Age: 54. Infirmities of: 144. Old age: 144

Ages of history. See Six Ages

Ages of World: 143*. Classical division of: 143. Scriptual division of: 143*. Aid structure in PL: 143

Agesilaus: 73, 123, 3

Agis: 73

Aglaophamus: 112

Agnelli: 111

Agnew, T., and sons: 44

Agnifilo, Amico: 65, 77

Agnosticism: 47

Agnus Dei: 73

Agon, concept of life as: 68*

Agonistes: 92. Significance of, as epithet: 68*

Agostino, Niccolo d': 122

Agra: 19, 49, 73

Agramante: 1. See also: Jove

Agrarian laws: 60

Agreement: 103. Agreement of the People: 9*, 116, 147*

Agrican: 73

Agricola: Georg: 150, 3. John: 114. Julius: 51, 73. Rudolph: 20, 40

Agricola: 3

Agriculture, M on: 51. Agricultural images: 8

Agrippa: (Henry) Cornelius von Nettesheim: 7, 40, 54, 60, 113, 114*, 123, 128*, 142*, 32, 39, 93; works: Female Preeminence: 142; Occult Philosophy: 142. II, Herod: 73. Marcus: 73. Menenius: 73

Agylla: 73

Ahab (Achabus, Old Testament figure): 44, 73, 98*, 128, 3

Ahab, Capt. (in Melville's Moby Dick): 136

Ahania: 25. Ahania, Book of: 25

Ahaz: 73, 144

Ahaziah: 73

Ahmed IV (Hamet Basha), Dey of Algiers: 44

Aholah and Aholibah: 73

Ahriman: 71

Aialon (Ajalon): 49, 73

Aidoneus: 2. See also: Pluto

Aidos: 90. See also: Justice

Aiken, Conrad: 14

Aikin, John: 44, 58, 97, 115. The Calendar of Nature: 115

Ailsbury: 49

Ailsford: 49

Aims of Creation: 113

Ainger, A.: 23

Ainsworth: Edward G., Jr.: 51, 64, 101. Oliver M.: 51, 102, 112. Robert: 44, 117

Ainsworth: Henry: 7, 9, 60, 77, 79, 102, 114, 142, 32, 36, 93. Ann: 77. Works: Annotations upon...Exodus: 74; Annotations upon...Genesis: 74; Annotations upon...Numbers: 74; Annotations upon...1st book of Moses: 36

Air: 121, 128*. Form of composition: 121. Empyreal air: 128. Three regions of: 128*

Aird, Thomas: 58, 65

Airs (H. Lawes): 121

Airy, H.: 58. Osmund: 116

Aistulphus the Lombard: 73

Aithiopis: 74

Aitken, G. A.: see Marvell, whose Works Aitken edited

Aix (Aquisgrani): 44

Aizema (Atzema), Leo(n) van (M's friend/visitor): 30, 44*, 59, 73, 91, 64

Ajax: by Augustus Caesar: 70. By Sophocles: 70. See also: Homer

Ajax: 60, 73, 123, 92

Ak-lea: 49

Akalon: 49

Akbar: 19

Akenside, Mark: 44 58*, 86, 105, 146. Influenced by L'Allegro and Il Penseroso: 58.

Akiba ben Joseph: 93. Rabbi: 123, 38. See also: Zohar

Akkadians: 89, 32

Akrigg, G. P. V., "The Curious Marginalia of...Stanhope": 44

Al-Batani: 89

Alab(l)aster: 73

Alabama Indians: 118

Alabaster, William: 10, 44, 81

Aladeule, King: 19. Realm of: 49,

73

Alaham: 60

Alain de Lille: 40, 69, 79, 32

Alamanni, Luigi: 56, 122, 123, 64

Alanus: 40

Alanus ab Insulis: 68

A Lapide: see Steen, C.: 93

Alaric: 73, 71, 93. Alaricus II: 73

Alarm to the Armies (attr. to M): 44, 91

Alarum to the House of Lords (Richard Overton): 147

Alasco, Albertus: 40

Alastor, i.e., Salmasius: 44

Alaun: 3

Alaunus (Alan) River: 44, 49, 73

Alba Aula. See Whitehall

Alba, Duke of: 103. Julia: 49

Albany academy: 98

Alberigo: 111

Albermarle, George Monck, Duke of: 44*

Albert Hall, the: 97

Alberti, Leon Battista: 6, 40, 100, 120, 39, 93

Albertus: 142. Albertus Magnus, St.: 6, 7, 15, 40, 41, 114, 128, 32, 137; In Job: 74

Albiac, Aquace d', Livre de Job: 74

Albigensians: 38

Albinism, alleged cause of M's blindness: 16, 113. Albino: 44

Albion(um): 73, 25. Death of: 25. As Eternal Man: 25. Garments of: 25. Rejects Divine Vision: 25. Daughters of: 25. Sons of: 25

Albion's Triumph (Townshend): 29*

Albireo, double star: 89

Albracca: 49, 73. See also: Agrican

Albricus, De Deorum Imaginibus: 74

Albright, William F.: 68, 32

Album Amicorum: 103

Albumasar: 128

Alcaeus: 40, 73

Alcairo: 73

Alceati, Andrea: 29. See also: Alciati

Alcestis (Euripides): 70, 73, 3, 130

Alcestis: 90, 92

Alchemist (Jonson): 34, 131

Alchemist, the: as creator: 75*. And the return to the underworld: 75

Alchemy: 7*, 114, 128. Metal: 128. And Mic scholarship: 75. And the dialectical approach: 75. And the 17th c.: 75. M's knowledge of: 75. Presence of in PL: 75. And unnatural creativity: 75. And the "lapis": 75. And the quaternity: 75 And the production of gunpowder: 75. And natural creativity: 75

Alchindo: 123. See also: Gratiani

Alchymy: 121

Alciati, Andreas: 40, 44, 60, 73

Alcibiades (Plato): 112,

Alcibiades: 6, 44, 3, 112. See also: Cliniades: 73

Alcides: 60, 90. See also: "Hercules"

Alcimedon: 70

Alcina: 123. See also: Ariosto

Alcinous: 44, 73, 90, 128, 3, 72. Garden of: 49, 144, 32*

Alcmaeon: 3

Alcman: 40

Alcock (Allecock), John: 44

Alcohol, M and: 137

Alcoran: 73

Alcuin: 40, 73, 103, 143, 3, 36*, 64. In Apocalypsin: 74. Questions and Answers on Genesis: 36*

Alcyone (Halcyone): 73

Alden: Abner: 115; The Reader: 115. R.: 135

Aldenham, Lord: 44

Aldermanbury, London: 103

Aldermen of London: 44

Aldersgate Street (M's home in): 30, 40, 42, 44*, 45, 103, 136, 94. M's academy in: 89. M lives in: 94

Aldgate, London: 44

Aldhelm: 74, 3, 36. Opera: 74

Aldis Wright: 132

Aldovrandus, Ulisse: 60

Aldrich: George: 44. Henry: 44. Thomas: 40

Aldrovandi: 120, 128

Aldus Manutius: 74, 64. See also: Collection of Ancient Christian Poets

Aldwinkle, co. Northants.: 44

Aleian Field: 49, 73, 3

Aleman, Mat(h)eo: 60, 88

Alès, Adhémar d': 93

Alethia: 90

Alexander: of Hales: 24*, 41, 128. Of Alexandria: 128, 88. The Phrygian: 73. Sir Anthony: 64. Jannaeus: 73, 38. Jerome: 44. Peter: 86. R. G.: 97. W. J.: 18. Sir William: 64. Sir William, Earl of Stirling: 15, 44, 60, 65, 36, 93. William: works: Anacrisis: 74; Doomsday: 74, 36; Jonathan: 74

Alexander the Great: 40, 44, 59, 73, 103, 120, 122, 123, 128, 32, 38, 62, 72. Messianic honors: 38

Alexander Book: 74

Alexander: 90, 71, 3, 35; I: 73. II: 73. III: 73. VI, VII: 27

Alexander's Feast (John Dryden): 70

Alexandra: 73

Alexandria: 40, 44, 49, 51, 107, 3, 32. Description of in Origen's day: 107. Alexandrian school: 89

Alexandrines: 40

Alexandrinus, Codex: 40

Alexandro, Alexander de: see Alexander of Alexandria

Alexipharmaca (Nicander): 3

Alexis I (Mikhailovich): 44

Alfani, Antonio: 15, 65, 77

Alfaric, P.: 113

Alfieri, Vittorio: 65, 120

Alfonso: V, King of Portugal: 44. X el Sabio: 93. X of Castile: 114

Alford: Daniel: 44. H.: 58. John: 44

Alfraganus: 128

Alfred the Great: 73, 103, 123, 46, 3, 93. Alfred, King: 17, 50, 108, 122. Alfred: 133. As subject for Epic: 133. Alfred, epics on: 58. "Alfred" (attr. to M): 44. Son of Oswi: 3

Alfrey: (Alphry), Mr.: 44. Richard: 44. Thomas: 44

Algarsife: 73, 3. See also: Cambuscan

Algate: 49. See also: Addlegate

Algazel: 128

Algebra: 40

Alger, Ellice: 16

Algiers (Argiers): 19, 44, 49. See also: Almansor

Algol, "the demon" (star): 89

Alienation: 47. Of land: 45

Alighieri, Dante: 65. See also: Dante

Alimental nourishment of the Heavenly bodies (ancient theory of): 89

Alimoni, Peloni: 144

Alison, A.: 97

"All" (associated with God): 93

"All in all" (God in Origen and M): 107

All Hallows, Bread St., (Church) London: 40, 44*, 45, 103

All Saints Church, Cambridge: 40

All Saints Church, Maldon, co. Essex: 44

All Saints Church, Oxford: 44

All Saints: 45

All Souls College, Oxford: 44, 45*

All Souls, London: 103

Allacci, Lione: 68

Allam: Andrew: 40, 44, 63, 91. Edward: 44

Allatius, Mr.: 44

Allbutt: 3

Allecock (see Alcock)

Allecto: 56

<u>Allegations for Marriage Licenses: Issued by the Bishop of London</u>: 45. <u>Issued from the Faculty Office</u>: 44

<u>Allegiance Vindicated</u>: 116

Allegory: 8, 15*, 27*, 29, 50*, 70, 79, 122, 123*, 146, 25, 139, 93. In PL: 113. In PR: 113. As related to animism: 118. Of Sin and Death: 118. In epic and tragedy: 149. Sublime: 25. Veils of: 25. Systematic: 25. M as allegorical artist: 146. As form of Biblical interpreation: 68*. Distinguished from "type": 79. And Scripture: 93. Beings: 124. Interpretations: 24; 69. See also: Faith; Sin; Typology; titles of individual works

Allen (river): 49. See also: Maes German

Allen, Don Cameron: 1, 4, 20, 23, 29, 37, 60, 66, 68, 74, 75, 79, 81, 110, 125, 128*, 134, 139, 142, 143, 145, 14, 36, 39, 53, 72, 85, 93, 64, 101. 106, 148, 21. "M and the Descent to Light": 60. "Francis Mere's Treatise 'Poetrie.' A Critical Edition": 82. <u>The Harmonious Vision</u>: 60, 74, 48. <u>Comus</u>, a patchwork: 143. Critic of <u>Comus</u>: 143. On Samson's use of strength: 61

Allen: Alice (wife of Thomas Milton): 45. D. C.: 27. Edward E.: 16. Elizabeth: 44. Francis: 44. Fred: 40. J. W.: 9, 18. John (bricklayer): 44, 79. Jonathan: 115; "A Poem, On the Existence of God": 115. P. S.: 40, 144. Paul: 115; <u>Original Poems, Serious and Entertaining</u>: 115. Robert (J.): 44, 93, 99. Thomas: 10. William (pseud.): 44, 38; <u>Killing No Murder</u>: 91

Allers, Rudolf: 93

Allestree, Richard: 40, 44, 54. See also: Packington, Lady Dorothy

Allestry (Allestree), James, pr. and bks.: 44, 135, 91, 55

Alley: J., <u>Judge</u>: 58. William: 93

Alleyn, E.: 59

Allibone, Samuel A.: 44

Alline, Henry: 115. Two Mites, Cast into the Offering to God: 115

Allison, William T.: 51, 60, 144, 91

Alliteration: 98. Newton on: 88

Allnut, W. H.: 44

Allodoli, E.: 6, 111

Allot, Robert (bks., 1626-36): 40, 128, 91

Allston, W., sonnets of: 58

Allusion(s): 51, 117. And Simile: 106. Literary, explained by first English commentators: 88

Almack, Edward: 44

<u>Almanac for Students of Eng. History, An</u>: 45

<u>Almanack for the Year of Christian Account, An</u>: 115

<u>Almanack of Poor Richard the Second</u>: 115

<u>Almanack For the Year of Our Lord Christ, 1761, An</u>: 115

Almanacs: 40, 44, 128

Almansor (Almanzor), Kingdoms of: 19, 49, 73, 123. See also: Algiers; Bocchus; Fez; Marocco; Sus; Tremisen; Gratiani

"Almes Houses," Cambridge: 40

Almireno: 123. See also: Gratiani

Almon, John: 117

Almoni, Peloni: 9, 44. (Pseud.), Compendious Discourse: 91

Alney (Olanege): 49

Alpenden: 45

Alpers, Paul: 14

Alpha Arietis: 89

Alphabetical: 73

Alphesiboeus: 44, 73

Alpheus: 1, 49, 73, 90, 72. See also: Arethusa

Alphonsine system: 89

Alps: 19, 44*, 49, 3, 103, 8, 73

Alsop: B. (pr.): 44. John: 40. Richard: 115. Aristocracy: An Epic Poems: 115. The Political Green-House, for the Year 1798: 115

Alspach, Russell, K.: 115

Alsted: 10. Henry: 32. Johnann Heinrich: 40, 93

Altdeutsche Genesis, Die: 65

Altdorfer, A.: 97

Alteen (Alty): 49. See also: Tooma

Altercator: 40

Alternatives: atmosphere of: 119. Nature of: 119

Altham, R.: 6

Althamer, Andreas: 32

Althaus: 7

Althusius, Johannes: 32

Altitude circle: 89

Altmann, A.: 93

Altruism: 51

Alumni Cantabrigienses: 45

Alumni Oxonienses: 45*

Alva, Duke of: 103

Alvarez: Emmanuel: 40. Francisco: 32

Alves, R.: 58

Alvetheli: 49

Alvey, Henry: 40

Alvie, Richard: 44

Alvord, John: 40

Alylias (see Mylius, H.)

Amadis de Gaul: 40, 73

Amadis de Grecia: 88

Amadis: 123

Amale(c)k(ites): 73

Amalia Elisabeth (Landgräfin von Hessen-Kassel): 10

Amalthea: 19, 73, 90, 144, 64

Amama, Sixtinus: 40. Amama's Hebrew Grammar: 42

Amanuenses: 19, 28*, 44*, 43, 94. Latin Illiteracy of M's Amanuenses: 43

Amara, Mt.: 19, 49, 73, 32*

Amaranth: 44

Amaryllis in the shade: 73

Amaryllis: 90

Amasis II: 73

Amata: 56

Amateurs in music: 121

Amathus: 49

Amathusia: 73. See also: Venus

Amatus Lusitanus: 32

Amaurosis. See Gutta serena

Amaziah: 73

Amazonian targe (see targe): 19

Amazons: 90, 128

Ambiorix (see Ariovistus)

Ambition: 122*, 123*, 144. See also: Eve; woman

Ambiguous effects, Warton's study of: 88

Ambivalence: 139

Ambler, Humphrey: 44

Amboyna: 19, 44, 103, 150. See also: Moluccae

Ambrogio, Teseo: 40

Ambrose, St.: 4, 15, 18, 24*, 27, 44, 54, 57, 60, 73, 74, 77, 102, 100, 113, 118, 123, 143, 32, 38, 93*, 99*, 68*, 128, 36, 71, 82, 121. Rebuke of Emperor Theodosius: 38. Beyond creation: 143. And man's Fall: 143. De Incarn. Dom. Sacr.: 77. Hexaemeron: 77, 36. On Paradise: 77, 36. Letters: 36. De Interpellatione Job et David: 74

Ambrose, Isaac: 142*, 93. The Compleat Works: 142. War with Devils, and Ministration of and

Communion with the Angel: 142. The Works: 142

Ambrosia: 90, 144, 73

"Ambrosiaster": 36, 93. Questions on the Old Testament: 36

Ambulones: 144

Amelin, Jean de: 40

Amenemhat III! 35

Amenophis! 64

America (American, Americanus): 19, 49, 73, 32, 150, 25. As prophecy: 25. See also: India (West); Peruana

American Almanac, The: 115. American Art Association: 44. American Book Prices Current: 44. American Lady's Preceptor, The: 115. American Magazine, The: 115. American Magazine and Historical Chronicle: 115. American Magazine and Monthly Chronicle, The: 115. American Monthly Review, The: 115. American Museum Or Repository of Ancient and Modern Fugitive Pieces, Prose and Poetical: 115. American Museum Or Universal Magazine, The: 115. American Review and Literary Journal: 115. American Magazine or a Monthly View of the Political State of the British Colonies: 117

American Revolution: 25

Ames: 115. Fisher: 115, 55. Joseph: 135. Nathaniel: 98, 115; An Astronomical Diary: 115. Russell: 52. William: 9*, 17, 41, 44, 54, 63, 69, 73, 102, 113, 114, 123, 142, 32, 74, 38, 93, 101, 148; works: The Marrow of Sacred Divinity: 74, 142; Conscientia: 44

Aminta (see Tasso)

Ammanati, Bartolomeo: 27

Ammian: 90

Ammianus Marcellinus: 19

Ammon (see More, A.)

Ammon (Hammon): 57, 73, 90, 144

Ammon, Jupiter (Jove): 1, 73

Ammonite(s): 49, 73, 144. See also: Basan

Ammonius Saccas (teacher of Origen and Plotinus): 44, 57, 65, 107, 114

Ammosis: 73. See also: Actisanes, and Amasis

Amnon: 73

Amodei, Mgr.: 6

Amor (see Cupid)

Amor ferinus: 72

Amores (Ovid): 139

Amoretti (Spenser): 58*, 70. See also: Spenser

Amorites: 144

Amorrean: 73. See also: Seon's Realm

Amory, T.: 58

Amos complains: 73

Amphiaraus: 44, 73

Amphion: 73

Amphitrite: 1, 73, 90

Amphitryon: 92

Amphitryoniaden: 73

Amphytrio, Plautus': 70

Amplification: 123

Ampthill, co. Bedford: 44

Amram: 73

Amsterdam (Amstelodamensis, Amsterodamensis, Amsterodamus): 44*, 49, 103, 94, 150

Amusements, M's views on: 30

Amvrosii, Serebrennikov: 117

Amymone: 90

Amyntas: 44, 73

Amyntor: 116, 3

Amyntorides: 73. See also: Phoenix

Amyot, Jacques: 40

Amyraut, Moses: 114

An Account of the Late Terrible Earthquake in Sicily (1693): 128

An Answer to Sundry Matters, An: 116

Anabaptists, History of the: 60

Anabaptists: 7*, 9, 44, 51, 73, 113, 114*, 22, 38, 92, 3, 94. 1st congregation: 147. Persecution of:

93. See also: Baptists

Anac: 1

Anachronisms: Thyer on: 88. Condemned by Newton: 88

Anacreon: 40, 44, 70, 132, 82, 64, 13. Anacreontics: 90

Anael: 142

Anagoge, as form of Biblical interpretation: 68

Anagram, astronomical discoveries announced in: 89. Anagrams, phonemic: 118

Anak: 73, 3

Anakim: 123. See also: Giants, Biblical

Analectic Magazine, The: 115

Analogy: 51

Analysis: 51*. Of authors: 20. Precepts and examples: 20. Little, in Paterson's commentary and *The State of Innocence*: 88. Lack of, in Todd's notes: 88

Analytical Art (algebra): 40

Anamnesis: 81. See also: Augustine; Memory

Anania, Giovanni Lorenzo d': 142

Ananias: 73

Anapologesiates Antapologias (John Goodwin): 147

Anarch, the Old: 71

Anarchia Anglicana: 103

Anarchy of a Limited Monarchy (Robert Filmer): 147

Anastasius the Sinaite: 65, 77

Anastasius Bibliothecarius: 44, 73

Anathemas of the Second Council of Constantinople: 74

Anatolius, St.: 73

Anatomy of Abuses, The: 45

Anatomy of Melancholy (Burton): 52*, 70, 88. M's indebtedness: 80. See also: Burton, Robert

Anaxagoras: 89, 128

Anaximander: 89, 128, 92, 93, 77. See also: Hippolytus

Anaximenes: 89, 114

Ancestry, Phillips' account: 55

Anchises: 2, 27, 56, 73, 90, 123. See also: Virgil

Anchor (sign): 44

Ancient: Christians: 51. Classics: 51. Law (Maine): 134. Literature (compared with modern): 87

Ancient Bounds (Liberty of Conscience): 9*, 27, 148

Ancient Britons, The: 25

Ancient Cornish Drama: 65

"Ancient Mariner, The" (S. T. Coleridge): 136, 88, 131

"Ancients" and "moderns,": 70, 87, 146. In opposition: 145. Dispute between: 109

Ancren Riwle: 128

Andalusia: 44, 112

Andaman Islanders: 118

Anderdon, Jr.: 44

Anderson Galleries, New York: 44

Anderson: Jr. (Eng. sculptor): 44. Alice: see Cotton, Alice (Constable). Andrew Runni, "Heracles and His Successors": 74. Dorothy: see Cotton, Dorothy. Edmund: 45. John: 7, 115; *A Mirror Representing Some Religious Characters of the Present Time*: 115. Maxwell: 108. Olivia Cushing: 65. Paul B.: 44. R.: 58. Sir Robert: 40, 117. Ruth L.: 128

Anderton: James: 93. Lawrence: 93

Andes: 19

Andover (town in Hampshire): 49

André, Père, de Rouen: 58

Andrea (Terence): 20

Andreae, Johann Valentin: 7*, 10, 54

Andreas Lundensis: 65

Andred (Andred's League, Andred's Wood): 49

Andredchester (Newenden): 49. See also: Pevensey

Andreini, Giovanni Battista: 6*, 15,

44, 50, 65, 70, 77, 84, 123, 129, 64, 142, 32, 88, 94, 130, 137, 149, 117, 13. L'Adamo: 42, 77, 36, 109, 44, 149. Summary: 149*. Temptation: 149. Eve: 149*. Translated: 58. Necessity of epic treatment of theme: 149. Influence: 55

Andreini, Guido: 6

Andrelini, Publio Fausto: 64

Andrew: 73, 72. Of St. Victor: 32. Of Wyntoun: 93. Andrew, St.: 4, 44.

Andrewes, Bp. Lancelot: 60, 68, 73, 74, 84, 86, 102, 114, 126, 145, 32*, 64, 72, 93, 101, 148, 21*, 4, 15, 20, 23, 40, 44, 99*. M and: 32. Liturgies: 126. And church consecration: 126. Wonderfull Combate: 74. XCVI Sermons: 74. Moral Law Expounded, Private Devotions: 91

Andrewes, John: 93

Andrews, John: 93

Andrews, R. (Eilyllia, Virgil): 58

Andrews, St. (Univ.): 40

Andria: 73. See also: Charinus

Androdeism: 71

Andromache: 73. See also: Euripides

Andromeda: 73, 89, 90

Andronicus Comnenus: 70, 3

Androutsos, Christos: 93

Anecdotes of Painting (Vertue): 70

Anenge: 65

Angel: 7, 15*, 17*, 24*, 31*, 41*, 44, 50*, 57, 60*, 63*, 67, 73, 118, 121*, 143, 128, 129, 110, 113, 114, 102, 107*, 142*, 144, 36*, 46*, 106*, 130, 117. Belief in: 142. Apparition of: 142. Corporeity of: 142, 46. Fall of: 17, 50, 113, 142*, 46, 102. Function of: 142*. As guardians: 142. Creation: 93, 102, 144, 107, 142, 36. Nature: 93, 119. Hierarchy: 93, 36, 107, 41, 129, 114, 142*, 46. Number: 93. Leader: 93. Response to music: 93. Guardian: 93. Ministry of: 99. And poetry: 106*. And light: 106*. Substance of: 142*, 128. Tests for: 142. Worship of: 142. Reproduction of: 36. Chorus of: 36. Food of: 102, 36, 107, 128, 142. Good and evil: 144. Debate of: 36. Envy of: 36. Apostolic Age dependent on Jewish speculation regarding: 41. In Apostolic Age: 41. Concern of early fathers with: 41. Doctrine of Spirituality of: 41. In Old Testament: 41. Not subject to Quantity: 41. Scholastic discussion of: 41. Archangels: 41. Cherubim: 41. Dominations: 41. Orders: 41. Powers: 41. Principalities: 41. Seraphim: 41. Seven angels of the Presence: 41. Seven eyes of God: 41. Seven ministering angels: 41. Thrones: 41. Have bodies and take nourishment according to Justin Martyr: 107. Hierarchically ranked by pseudo-Dionysius Areopagiticus: 107. Concerned Origen's: achieve rank through merit: 107*. Concerned with affairs of men: 107*. Created before the world: 107*. Feast with men: 107*. Not ranked hierarchically: 107*. In PL: achieve rank through merit: 107*. Victorinus of Petlau says one-third fell: 107*. Effects of on nature: 142. Names of: 142. Location of: 142. Powers of: 142. Minds or souls of: 142. Sources and Development of M's ideas of Theory of Angels at close of Middle Ages: 41. World of Angels in Bible: 41. Four Angels of the Presence: 41. Virtues: 41. Armor of: 119, 142*. Angel, materialism of: 110. Theory of Angels at close of Middle Ages: 41. Knowledge and power of: 114. Unfallen as defined by synecdoche and metonymy: 118. As musical: 121. Sex: 128. Sexual love: 128. Worship of Christ: 143. And Saints in Aquinas: 143. Labors of: 143. In Holkham Bible: 143. Angels: Abdiel: 106. Michael: 106*. As poet: 106. Raphael: 106*. As poet: 106*. Uriel: 106. See also: Satan and Uriel; Angelology and Angelology of M, The; Fallen angels; War in Heaven

Angelology: 15, 93. M's: 137. Angelic eating: 142. Angelic love: 142. Borrowings from the Bible: 142. Direct borrowings: 142. Casual borrowings: of names: 142. Of orders: 142. On missions: 142. Christian, in Graeco-Roman world: 41. Development of Christian: 41. Development of Jewish: 41. Development of Scholastic: 41. Last works: 41. Of the New Testament: 41. In De Doctrina: 142*. Dramatic use of: 142. Significance of: 142*. Worship of angels: 142. Guardians: 142. Unorthodoxies in: 142*. History of: 142. Attitude towards: 142. Of M's time: 142.

Angel (sign): 44

Angel of marriage: 50

Angel Court, Westminster: 44

Angel-trumpets: 121

Angeleida, L': 65*

Angelica (see Agrican)

Angelio, Pietro: 64

Anger: 51*, 123. Moderation of, a heroic virtue: 123. Divine: 47

Anglen: 49

Angles, East: 44

Anglesey (Mona, Island): 45, 144, 49. See also: Man

Anglesey Memorandum: 116*

Anglesey: Arthur Annesley, 1st Earl of: 44, 103, 28, 116. Arthur Annesley: 55. Earl of (another): 44

Anglia: 44

Anglican Church: 9*, 103, 114*, 70, 40, 143. Reformation of: 143. Strengths of: 143. And Puritanism: 143. And fallibility: 143. And loyalty to crown: 143. On divorce and marriage: 54. Psalter: 40. Anglican ordinals, use of staff: 104. Anglican priesthood aim of M's education: 40. Reaction to Puritans: 87. Anglicisms: 3. See also: High Church; Episcopacy

Anglo-Italians: 40

Anglo-Saxon: 40. Law: 54. Genesis: 24. Gill's enthusiasm for: 20. Forms in Spight's glossary: 88. Hume's knowledge of: 88. Spellings, Bentley's: 88. Richardson's inadequate acquaintance with, the: 88. Literature, Todd's references to: 88

Angola: 19, 49, 73, 144. See also: Congo

Angronia: 49

Anguilla: 73

Angustiae aurium: 72

Anicetus: 73

Anidmadversions on Lillies Grammar ...(Wise): 20

Anima, prima and secunda: 72

Animaduersions vppon the Annotacions...of Chaucers workes...by Francis Thynne: 88

Animadversions on the Last Speech and Confession: 116

Animadversions on the Remonstrant's defence against Smectymnuus: 8*, 30*, 113, 83, 103, 112, 88, 116. M's use of the term "Perfection" in: 83. Occasion for: 47. See also: Milton, John, Works

Animals: 24*, 50, 128*, 118, 36*. Effect of the Fall on: 128, 36. Language: 128. Images: 8*. Power to reason: 128. Spirits: 118. Naming of: 50, 36*. Treatment of in M's Paradise: 118, 137. Creation of: 36. Equals passions: 36. Adder (stops ears): 128. Amphisbaena: 128. Ape (lecherous): 128. Asp (chaste): 128. Ass: 128. Basilisk: 128. Behemoth: 128. Boar (lecherous): 128. Camel (accustomed to thirst): 128. Cerastes: 128. Chimera: 128. Cockatrice: 128. Cock's egg: 128. Crocodile: 128. Cynocephali: 128. Dipsas: 128. Dog: 128. Reason in: 128. Dragon: 128. Elephant (chaste): 128. Frogs (speechless): 128. Goat (lecherous): 128. Gorgon: 128. Gryphon: 128. Gulon: 128. Hedgehog (foreknowledge of): 128. Hippogrif: 128. Hippopotamus (lets blood): 128. Horse: 128. Hyena (guileful): 128. Lion: 128. Mantichora: 128. Mare (impregnated by wind): 128. Mice: 128. Morse (climbs rocks with teeth): 128. Ox: 128. Python: 128. Rossomakka: 128. Scorpion: 128. Scytall: 128. Serpent, as carnality: 128. As Satan: 128. Egg of: 128. Stag: 128. Sheep: 128. Tiger: 128. Toad: 128. Unicorn: 128. Viper: 128. Wolf: 128. Wolverine: 128

Animism: 118*, 141. In childish thought: 118. In primitive and childish minds: 118. In common speech forms: 118. In inert objects: 118. Source of in PL: 118. In Book VII of PL: 118

Anisio, Giano: 64

Anisotrophy, temperal and visual: 96

Anjou, France: 44. Margaret of: 64

Anna Comnena: 44

Anna: 73

Annales Veteris Testamenti (Ussher): 118

Annan, Noel: 87

Anne of Austria, Queen of France: 103

Anne of Cleves: 73. Promised to Henry VIII: 83. Marriage of to Henry VIII: 83. Rejected by Henry VIII:

83. Stigel's epigrams to: 83. Praised in Stigel's Epithalamium: 83. Pomp of her departure for England: 83

Anne of Denmark: 40

Anne, Queen (Gt. Brit.): 16, 29, 45, 116, 21

Annesley, Arthur (1614-86): 91

Anniversaries (John Donne): 131

Anno aetatis: 40*

Annotation: value of M's: 88. Rise of, of Eng. poets: 88

Annual Catalogue...of the Company of Scriveners: 44

Annunciation: 126, 139, 32, 72*

Anonymous Biographer of M, The (John Phillips?, Dr. Paget?, Cyriak Skinner?): 59, 63, 86, 77, 136, 91, 150, 55. Quoted: 55. M's first marriage: 55. M's library: 55

Anonymous Life of M: 73.

Anonymous: portrait of M: 44. Attack on M: 44. Publication: 51. Contributors to Newton's commentary: 88

Anselm of Laon: 40

Anselm, St.: 60, 73, 143, 93, 77, 142, 36, 71. Why God Became Man: 36, 77

Anstey, New Bath Guide: 58

Anstey: C.: 58. J.: 58

Answer to a Book Entitled the Doctrine and Discipline of Divorce: 103, 91

Answer to a Late Pamphlet: 116

Answer to an Infamous Libel, An: 116

Answer to the London Ministers Letter (Samuel Richardson): 147

Answer to Doctrine and Discipline of Divorce: 9, 30, 44, 3

Answer to Dutch Agents: 44

Answer to Eikon Basilike: 78

Answer to Pauw: 44

Answer to...Humble Remonstrance: 136, 26. See also: Smectymnuus

Answerable Style (Arnold Stein): 139

Antaeus: 60, 68, 73, 90, 111, 123, 46. Prototype of Satan: 46

Antagonism: 51

Antal, Frederick, on Henry Fuseli: 87, 97

Ante-Nicene Fathers: 107. Accept Philo's teachings: 107. Character of: 107. Climate of opinion among: 107. How educated: 107. As judges of orthodoxy: 107. Shapers of the church: 107

Antenor: 56

Anteros: 73, 136. M's myth of: 136

Antesignani, Commentary to Clenard's Grammar: 20

Anthelme (monk): 89

Anthem: 121

Anthemius, Emperor: 44, 21

Anthologia (Greek): 40

Anthology: Latin: 90. Palatine: 90

Anthony: Charles: 93. Francis: 40

Anthony's, St. (school): 40

Anthony's, St.: church: 40. School: 40

Anthropomorphism: 47, 107, 110*, 146. M warns against: 107. Origen warns against: 107. Of angels: 110. Of God: 110*. See also: Accommodation

Anti-classic: 27

Anti-clericalism: 9

Anti-epic: 21

Anti-episcopal pamphlets: 60*. M's account: 55. Discussed: 55*. See also individual titles

Anti-intellectualism: 114, 128

Anti-novel: 21

Anti-Arminianisme: 71

Anti-Catholicism: 63

Anti-Cavalierisme (John Goodwin): 147

Anti-Christ: 7, 47, 51, 73, 114*, 32, 25. Meaning of, compared with Christ, and papal pretension: 47. As Pope: 93. See also: Demonic; Self-deification

Anti-Jacobin: 58

Anti-Miltonists. See Milton controversy

Anti-Remonstrance: 91

Anti-Royalist: 51. Antiroyalism, M's: 40

Anti-Toleration (anonymous): 147

Anti-Trinitarianism: 63*, 107*

Antica Velierymе: 44

Antichristians: 51. Antichristian Tyranny, the: 51

Anticyra: 73

Antidosis (Isocrates): 20

Antidote Against Poison, An: 116

Antigenes: 64

Antigone: 60, 92. Antigone (Sophocles): 70

Antigonus (son of Aristobulus, claimed throne of Judea): 73, 38

Antijacobin Review: 25

Antilia-Macaria: 7

Antilians: 7

Antimachus: 40

Antimaco, Giulio: 122

Antimask (antimasque): 72, 70

Antinomian(ism): 73, 114*, 141, 38, 78. Antinomians: 7, 9

Antioch (Theopolis): 49, 19, 27, 44, 73. See also: Daphne

Antioch (another city): 49

Antiochus Epiphane(s): 73, 38. Desecration of Jewish Temple: 38

Antiopa: 73, 90

Antipapist, the: 51

Antipater the Edomite: 73

Antipater Sidonius: 70

Antipathy: 51

Antiquarian Magazine and Bibliographer: 44

Antiquarian: bent, Hume's and Peck's: 88. Knowledge, Peck's: 88. Warton's: 88*. Of Warton's predecessors: 88. Temper, Newton's lack of the: 88. Interests, Todd's: 88

Antiquaries, Society of: 44

Antique, The: 97

Antiquitarians: 51, 57

Antiquity: 51

Antona: 49

Antoninus Pius: 73

Antoninus, St.: 93

Antonio da Ferrara: 120

Antony and Cleopatra: 40

Antony, Marc: 73

Ants: 144

Antwerp (Belgium): 3, 44, 103. Polyglot: 22

Anubis: 19, 73, 144

Anwykyll, John: 40

Anxiety: 47

Anytus: 112

Aodis: 44

Aonian stream: 44

Aonian Mount (Helicon): 49, 19, 73, 3, 72. See also: Aracynthus; Cirrha; Circe

Apaches, Jicarilla: 118

Aparticas: 144

Apasti: 103

"Apathy and Enthusiasm": 98

Apelles: 73

Apeltre: 49

Apennine Mountains (Apenninus, Appenninus): 44, 49, 73, 3

Aphrodisea, Alexander: 128

Aphrodisia: 49, 73

Aphrodite: 2, 44, 60, 90, 112. See also: Venus

Aphthonius: 20*, 40, 59, 82. Progymnasmata: 82

Apian: 128

Apician(am): 73

Apion: 73

Apis: 57, 144. Aegyptian: 73

Apocalypse (St. John): 30, 67*, 62, 78. Structual relation to PL: 67*. As tragedy: 30. See also: Revelation

Apocalypse of Adam: 65

Apocalypse of Moses: 24, 55

Apocalypse, the: 70, 73, 142, 72*, 3, 25. Sermons on: 87

Apocalyptic: 110, 87*. View of history: 93. Defined: 110. Difficulty of portrayal: 110. Portrayed through analogy: 110; through contrast: 110; through distance: 110; through negation: 110. Imagery: 110. Painters and paintings: 87. "Apocalyptic" poetry: poets: 87*; response to sublime in M's epics: 87*.

Apocrypha: 15*, 74. Views on: 93. Wisdom of Solomon: 15, 60, 36. Wisdom of Moses: 60, 36. Enoch: 15. Esdras: 15. Jewish Angelological: 41. Judith: 15. Secrets of Enoch: 15, 36*. Three Holy Children: 15. Tobet: 15. Apocrypha and Pseudepigrapha of the Old Testament: 36*. Baruch, Syriac Apocalypse of: 36. Enoch, Ethiopic Book of: 36. Ezra, Fourth Book of: 36. Jubilees, Book of: 36*. Sirach, Book of: 36.

Apocryphon of John: 36

Apographum Literarum...Cromwelli: 44

Apollinarius (Apollinarii, Claudius): 44, 51, 63, 74, 93, 113. Apollinarii, the two (father and son): 73. Elder, the: 32

Apollo, Or Weekly Literary Magazine, The: 115

Apollo: 1, 2, 44*, 60, 73, 103, 90*, 111, 121*, 125, 128, 71, 72*, 92, 3, 97. Worshipped in Britain: 121. As a musician: 121*. See also: Phoebus

Apollodorus: 4, 40, 44, 70, 90*, 123

Apollonian: 125

Apollonius: Of Perga: 73. Of Rhodes (Rhodius): 40, 73, 90*, 44, 56, 60, 64. Thyanaeus (of Tyana): 73. The grammarian: 90. The Sophist: 39

Apollos: 73

Apollyon: 60

Apollyonists: 65

Apologetical(l) Narration: 9, 103, 147, 148

Apologeticall Account: 9

Apologeticall Declaration, Of...Presbyterians: 147

Apologia (Ficino): 29

Apologia pro Confessione: 44

Apologie of the Power and Providence of God: 26

Apologist Condemned (John Goodwin): 147

Apologus de Rustico et Hero (Fable of the Peasant and his Landlord): 73

Apology (Justin Martyr): 3

Apology (Plato): 112*

Apology (Xenophon): 112

Apology for the Liberty of the Press, An: 116. Compared with Areopagetica: 116

Apology for Poetry, An: 12. Sidney's: 70

Apology for Smectymnuus: 8*, 30*, 112*, 111, 114, 55. M's account: 55. Biographical significance, necessity for self vindication, occasion of, misleading suppression of information in: 30. Presentation copy: 44. M's use of the term "Perfection" in: 83

Apology of Raymond de Sebonde (Montaigne, trans. Florio): 134

Apophthegmatum (Lycosthenes): 20

Apophthegmatum: by Erasmus: 20. By Lycosthenes: 20

Apostasy: 47. See also: Psuedo-pilgrims

Apostates and the faithful: 47. See also: Psuedo-pilgrims

"Apostles," the (Cambridge Univ. Society), attitude toward M: 87

Apostles: 143, 3, 72. And reformers: 143. Authority to preach: 143. Duty of: 143

Apostles' Creed: 126, 78

Apostolic times: 51

Apothecaries, chartered by James I:

16

Apothecary: 123

Apothegms: 40

Apparent (truth): 51. (Goods) argument from: 123

Apparition. See Superstition

Appeal from the Country to the City, An: 116

Appeal to all Englishmen, a Diggers' manifesto (Gerrard Winstanley): 147

Appeal to the House of Commons (Diggers): 147

Appeal: 51*. Based on sense of justice: 51. Religious: 51*

Appeals: 51*

Appearance and reality (of sin, love, Eve): 54

Appearance, personal (M's): 28*, 30*, 44, 137. Anonymous biographer's account: 55. Richardsons' account: 55. M's as a boy: 40. Appearances: 96

Appendix to the Cleargie of the Four Great Parties (Roger Williams): 147

Appenzell. See Swiss Evangelical Cantons

Appetites: 17*

Appian Claudius: 73

Appian Road: 49, 73, 144

Applausi poetici alle glorie delle signora Leonara Baroni: 44

Apple of ashes: 98

Appleton, Henry (Captain): 44. R. B.: 92

Applewhite, Matthew: 103

Appollinarii: 3

Apposing (at St. Paul's School): 40

Apposition, defined: 20

Approach: 51

Approval in moral life: 17*

Apries: 73

Apriorism, anthropological and empirical: 96*

Apulia: 49, 73

Apuleius: 1, 40, 44, 70, 73, 90, 114, 142, 64, 117. Golden Ass: 91

Aquaeductus: 40

Aquaria: 49

Aquaviva, Claudio: 40

Aquila (the apostate): 73, 142, 93

Aquilo (Greek Boreas): 73, 90

Aquinas, St. Thomas: 4, 5, 74, 79*, 7, 15, 18, 24*, 27, 31, 34*, 40, 44, 47, 51, 52, 63, 67, 68, 69, 70, 73, 76, 102, 108, 112, 111, 113, 114*, 116, 120, 123, 124, 128, 142*, 143, 11, 32*, 36, 71, 99*, 137, 150, 3, 48. Summa Theologica: 74, 142, 48. De Regimine Principum: 83. De...Prin., his definition of the term "Perfection": 83. De Malo: 142. Summa Contra Gentiles: 142. Basic Writings: 48. On the image of God in man: 48. On the active intelligence: 52. Meaning of grace in: 52. Meaning of nature in: 52. Spenser better teacher than: 52. Thought compared with M's: 52. M and Aquinas: 32. Aquinas and supreme good: 143. Degrees of angelic order: 143. And glassy sea: 143. Human intelligence: 143

Aquitain (Aquitania): 49

Arab: 72. Conceptions of music: 72. Philosophy: 42. Medical debt to, and treatment of blind by: 16. Astronomy: 89

Arabia (Araby): 19*, 44, 49, 73, 144. See also: Sabean; Thebes; Egypt

Arabia Felix: 40

Arabian Nights: 94

Arabic text of Aristotle: 40

Arabic: 40, 42. Numbers: 40

Arachosia: 19, 49, 73, 144

Aracynthus: 49, 73

Araignment of Mr. Persecution (Richard Overton): 147

Aram: 144. P.: 58

Aramaic: 40, 42*, 3

Ararat, Mt.: 32

Arator: 74, 64. De Actibus Apostolorum: 74. "Epistola ad Vigilium": 74

Aratus: 73, 90, 32, 3, 94, 64. Phenomena: 40, 44

Arausi: 73

Araxes River (Aras): 19, 49, 73, 144

Arbaces: 73

Arber, Edward (ed. Stationer's Register to 1640): 40, 44*. Term Catalogues: 91. See also: Stationer's Register

Arbesmann: 23

Arbiter, Petronius: 103

Arbuthnot: Alexander: 40. Dr. John: 91

Arcades: 87, 103, 113, 121, 3, 14, 72*. Ascent in: 72. Music in: 72. Myth in: 72. Stances in: 72. Pageantry of the Heavens: 8

"Arcady, Star of" (masque): 104

Arcadia (place): 1, 49, 32, 72. In pastoral poetry: 118

Arcadia (Sanazzaro): 29

Arcadia (Sidney): 29, 30, 70, 103, 118, 116, 26, 88, 3, 94. The Pamela Prayer in: 30

Arcadian Rhetoric (Fraunce): 20

Arcadius, Emperor: 73

Arcangelo (Archangelus): 40

Arcesilaus: 114

Arcetri: 44. d'Arcetri, villa: 103

Archaemenius: 32

Archaeological Institute: 44

Archaeological Journal: 44

Archaic: language, Hume on: 88; his method of dealing with: 88. Expressions, Thynne, E. K. and Hume on: 88. Words now archaic, but used at Hume's time: 88. Usage neglected by Hume: 88. Dealt with superficially by Bentley: 88. Bentley's attempts at restoring: 88. Pearce on: 88. Inadequate treatment of, by the Richardsons, Peck and Paterson: 88. Language, studied by Hawkey: 88. Newton on: 88. Insufficient knowledge of, Massey's: 88. Warton's treatment of: 88. Dunster on: 88. Todd on: 88. Errors regarding, checked by Todd: 88. Accents and phraseology, Todd on: 88

Archaism: 15

Archangel (Arkania): 49

Archangel: 19, 41, 142. Or Bene Elohim: 142

Archangelus of Borgo Nuovo: 142

Archangelus Mercenarius: 40

Archbishop of Canterbury: 51

Archdale: family: 44, Mr.: 45. Miss: 44; see also: Moulton, Mrs. Abraham: 45. Alice: see Ayloffe, Alice. Bernard: 44. Elizabeth: 44; see also: Fleetwood. Martin: 45. Matthew: 45. Richard: 44, 45. Thomas: 44

Archelaus: 73

Archer: F. S.: 97. Henry: 9, 38. J. W.: 44

Archery: 40

Archetectonic power: in Comus: 143. M's mastery of structure: 143. Three movements in PL: 143

Archetypal Patterns in Poetry: 12

Archetype: 123*. See also: Example; Pattern; Hero

Archilochus: 5, 40, 73

Archimago: 87

Archimedes: 6, 44, 59, 73, 3

Architect: 70. God as: 128. Satan as: 128

Architecture: 70*. Painting and sculpture, M and: 137. Ancient, Warton on: 88

Archivist: 44

Archpoet: 64

Archytas: 4, 121, 123

Arco, Niccolo d': 64

Arctic (Hyperborean): 44, 150

Arctos: 73

Arcturus: 89

Arcucci, Giovanni Battista: 64

Arden, Forest of: 118

Arden, John: 44

Arderne, James: 145, 91

Ardor imbued under a Commonwealth: 51

Arecca betula: 19

Arendt, H.: 34. Hannah: 39

Arenne: 49

Areopagite. See Dionysius the Areopagite

Areopagitica: 8*, 37, 30*, 51*, 83, 98, 102, 103, 112*, 111, 113, 116*, 121, 80, 3*, 55. On Christian liberty: 83. On the need of learning: 83. Defense of sects in: 83. M's use of the term "Perfection" in: 83. Compared with A Just Vindication: 116. Compared with Apology: 116. Compared with Reasons Humbly Offered: 116. Thesis of: 51. M's conception of man in: 80. Cited to illustrate M's disapproval of utopian schemes: 80. Aims of: 30. Presentation copy of: 44. Purpose in: 51

Areopagus: 44, 51, 3, 91

Ares: 2, 90. See also: Mars

Arethusa (Arethuse): 1, 49, 90, 144, 72. See also: Alpheus

Aretia: 123. See also: Gratiani

Aretine, the. See Pietro, Aretino

Aretino, Leonardo. See Bruni

Aretino, Pietro: 6, 44, 132, 91, 18

Aretius, Benedictus (Problems): 44, 73, 99, 64

Arezzo: 49, 73

Argantes: 1. See also: Tasso

Argelander: 89

Argent, Abel d': 74. Sepmaine: 74

Argestes: 90, 144

Argo: 44, 73, 90

Argob: 49, 73, 144. See also: Basan

Argonautica: 44

Argonautics: 30, 44

Argonauts: 90, 123

Argos: 49, 92

Argument or Debate in Law (J. M. C. L.): 44

Argument Proving, That the Abrogation of King James, An: 116

Argument: 92. A fortiori: 51, 123*. Consentany: 123. Dissentany: 123. From the greater: 123. From the lesser: 123. From name: 123. Inartificial: 123. From adjuncts: 123. From adverses: 123. Derived: 123. And appeal, alternative: 51. Ad hominim: 123. From conjugates: 123. Subject of poem: 123*. Of Homeric and Virgilian epic: 123. Relation to history: 123. Divine: 123. See also: Cause; Demonstrative rhetoric; Delibertive rhetoric; Controversy

Argumentative force: 51

Arguments, invention of: 20

Argus: 73, 90

Argyll, Archibald Campbell, Marquis and Earl of: 44, 54

Aria parlante: 121

Ariadne: 44

Arian(ism): 15, 27, 34, 40, 47, 60*, 73, 113, 78*, 117*, 3, 71, 72. As heresy: 139, 71. M's: 132; in DDC: 93; in PL: 93; alleged: 137. See also: Trinity

Ariana: 121

Ariel: 41, 73, 142. Ariel's flight: 89

Aries: 89, 90

Arietis: 40

Arimaspi: 144. Arimaspian: 49, 73, 90. See also: Cronian Sea

Arimathea: 49

Ariminum: 49, 73

Arioc: 142

Arioch: 4, 41, 73

Arion: 44, 70, 121, 144, 3

Ariosto: Gabriello: 40. Ludovico: 1, 2, 4, 6, 10, 15, 19, 30, 40, 44, 50, 18, 51, 52, 54, 56, 64, 60, 68, 70, 73, 77, 84, 90, 102, 108, 111, 114, 120, 122*, 123, 126, 127, 128, 3, 132, 133, 135, 26, 32, 38, 46, 53, 82, 88, 93, 94, 101, 106, 115, 130, 137, 146*, 117*, 55, 21. Orlando Furioso: 74, 77, 129, 46, 82. Comus: 129

Ariovistus, Ambiorix (Henry Erastius):

44

Aristarchus: 44, 73, 89, 64

Aristide quintilianus: 100

Aristides: 90, 121

Aristippus: 32, 62. "Aristippus with all his Cyrenaic route": 73

Aristobulus: I: 73. II: 73. III: 73

Aristophanes: 23, 40, 51, 66, 70, 73, 90, 112, 123, 128, 82, 92, 3, 13, 18, 64

Aristorides: 73

Aristotle: 1, 2*, 4, 5, 6*, 7, 9, 12, 15, 17, 18*, 19, 20*, 23, 24, 27, 30, 31, 35, 37, 40*, 41, 44*, 45, 50, 51*, 52, 56, 60*, 63, 70*, 73, 74, 76, 79, 90, 95, 103, 100, 105, 108, 112*, 111, 89, 121, 116, 122*, 123*, 124, 125, 127, 128*, 3*, 132, 133, 134, 142, 145, 11, 26, 32, 39, 46, 53, 71, 72*, 82*, 85, 88, 91, 92*, 93, 94, 101, 109, 130*, 131, 137, 146, 149, 148, 150, 117*, 64, 25, 21, 13. Idea of Perfection in Metaphysics: 83. Galileo's examination of: 89. Canons of rhetoric: 51, On decorum: 66. Golden Mean of: 71. Virtues, according to: 71. M and: 32. M's use of Aristotelian rhetorical techniques: 51. Works: Organon: 82; Posterior Analytics: 82; Topica: 82; Politics: 51, 60, 83, 82; Metaphysics: 60; De Generatione et Corruptione: 60; Nicomachean Ethics: 44, 60, 74, 51, 82; Poetics: 2*, 74, 92*, 48; on the plot: 48; Prior Analytics: 44, 82; Rhetoric: 44, 51, 82. Works (ed. W. D. Ross): 82. Aristotle On the Art of Poetry (Cooper): 70. Aristotle's Theory of Poetry and Fine Art (Butcher): 70

Aristotelian(ism): 114*, 125, 32*, 71, 13. Aristotelian: essentials of ethical proof: 51; modes of persuasion: 51; topic of degree: 51. See also: Degree

Aristoxenus: 121

Aristrocracy: of Grace 9*; of Nature: 9*

Aristyllus: 89

Arithmetic: 40. See also: Mathematics

Arithmetica Universalis: 78

Arius: 57, 74. "Confession of the Arians": 74

Ark: 128, 144. Origin of: 41. See also: Symbolism

Arkwright, G. E. P.: 44

Arles: 49. Synod of: 36

Arlington, Henry Bennet (1st Earl of): 44

Armageddon: 113

Armagh, Ireland: 44, 45, 49

Armagh, James, Abp. of: 51, 103. See also: Ussher

Armenia: 19, 42, 144, 32

Armenian Life of Adam: 65

Armida, Garden of: 70

Armida: 103, 123. See also: Tasso

"Armies of the Wilderness, The": 98

Armies Vindication: 9

Armin, Philip. See Glisson, Francis

Armin, R.: 105

Arminian(s): 51, 73, 145, 22, 3, 146. Teachings: 147. Magazine, The: 115

Arminianism: 7, 9, 44, 60, 103, 63*, 113, 114*, 22, 32, 38, 71, 93, 13

Arminius, Jacobus: 40, 52, 73, 113, 122, 123, 32, 71, 93, 101, 142. Works of: 142. Challenges Calvin's damnation by predestination: 147

Armitage, G. J.: 45

Armorica (Britain in France): 44, 49, 73, 3

Arms: 122

Armstrong: Arthur H.: 93. Edward A.: 128. Dr. J.: 58*. J. Tarbotton: 44. John (Albert): 58, 32, 117

Army: 51, 60, 44, 103*, 9*. Control of: 51. Regime, collapse of: 51. Dissension caused by: 22. Parliamentary: 9*. Scottish: 51. M and: 44. And radical propaganda: 147

Army's Plea (by the officers): 147

Arnald, S. W.: 97

Arnalt and Lucenda: 40

Arnauld D'Andilly, Robert (Poème sur la Vie de Jésus-Christ): 74, 64

Arndt, Johann: 7, 10

Arne, Thomas: 39, 146, 117

Arnisaeus, Heningus (of Halberstadt): 44, 73

Arno River: 40, 44, 49. See also: Valdarno

Arno: 73, 3

Arnobius: 57, 70, 73, 82

Arnold: Andrew: 10. Christopher: 10, 30, 44, 91, 94. C.: works: Commerce: Distress: 58. E. V.: 79. Gottfried: 7. James: 29. Matthew: see separate entry. Samuel: 117. Thomas: 146

Arnold, Matthew: 15, 17, 18, 27, 31, 50, 58*, 60, 73, 83, 84, 86, 64, 87*, 95, 3, 98, 105, 125, 132, 133, 134, 136, 138, 26, 71, 91, 92, 130*, 150, 55. His definition of culture: 83. Politcal sonnets of: 87. Criticized demand for "engage" literature: 87. Merope: 87. Essays in Criticism: 82. Pertaining to M: Preface to 1853 ed. of Poems: 37; "To a Friend": 87; "To the Hungarian Nation": 87; M's influence on "Sohrab and Rustum": 87; opinion of M as artist: 37; attitude toward M: 87; on M's puritanism: 87; M's puritanism as a limitation: 87; on Renaissance-Puritan elements in M: 87; admired M's artistry: 87; on classical qualities in M's poetry: 87; On PL as a commentary on Genesis: 87; attitude towards PL: 87; on the theme of PL: 83.

Arnoldus Villanovanus: 7

Arnon, river: 144

Arnon: 49, 73. See also: Seon's Realm; Moab

Aroar (Aroer): 73

Aroer: 49, 144. See also: Arnon

Arraignment of the Present Schism (John Brinsley): 147

Arraignment, Tryal and Condemnation of Algernon Sidney, Esq., The: 116

Arrangement of composition: 121

Arras: 49

Arrest, M's: 44, 136

Arrow Against All Tyrants (Richard Overton): 147

Arrowhead: 98

Ars dictandi: 20

Ars poetica: 40

Ars Grammatica (Donatus): 40

Ars Poetica (Horace): 20, 70, 88

Arsaces, King: 19

Arsaces: 73

Arseniev, Nicholas: 93

Arsochis, Francesco de: 64

Art: 70*, 11. M's: 129*. Ancient, studied by Warton: 88. Art (ars), meaning of term: 20, 30. Art for art's sake: 70. Art, inspired by M: cartoons for Houses of Parliament: 87. See also: Blake; Doré; Fuseli; Martin

Art (of M): 129*. Dependent on knowledge and on character: 129. Subjective element in: 129. Versification: 129. Pictorial power: 129*

Art of music (as opposed to theory): 121

Art of rhetoric: 51

Art of Candle-Making: 58

Art of Government: 103

Art of Logic, arranged after the method of Peter Ramus: 37

Art Union, The: 97

Artabanus: 73

Artaxerxes I: 73, 3. Artaxerxes Mnemon (Artaxerxes II): 73. Artaxerxes Ochus (Artaxerxes III): 73

Artaxta (Artaxata): 19, 49, 73, 144

Arte of English Poesie, The (Puttenham): 20, 70, 135

Arte of Rhetorique (Wilson): 20, 3

Arteldi, Paulo: 64

Artemis: 68, 90, 72. See also: Diana

Artes (Celsus): 3

Artes of Logike and Rhetorike, The (Fenner): 20

Artes praedicandi: 40

Arthos, John: 29, 60, 105, 111, 32,

39, 93, 101, 64

Arthur, King: 17, 19, 30, 44, 50, 70, 73, 103, 108*, 122, 123, 38, 46, 60, 3, 137. Quasi-messianic legend of: 38. As subject for M: 137. "Arthur" (epic attr. to M): 44. Arthuriad, M's projected: 132*, 133*. Arthurian epic: 21. Arthurian legend(s): 8, 92, 94, 55

Arthur, Prince of Wales; 40, 73, 103

Articles of Oxford: 44*

"Articles of Peace": 103. Images derived from mythology, occupation: 8. See also: Milton, John, Works

Articles of Religion (Anglican): 40

Articles, Commissioners for: 44

Artificial music: 121. M as artificial poet: 146

Artificiality: Hume's dislike of: 88; Peck on M's: 88; Pope on same: 88; Ovid's contrasted by Newton with M's simplicity: 88

Artillery Company, Honourable: 44

Artillery Row: 94

Artillery Walk (M's last house): 103. See also: Bunhill

Artillery, Use of by Rebel Angels: 41

Artis Logicae: 103

Artist: and material reward: 70; and the public: 70 Artistic proof: 51. Modes of persuasion: 51. Aims and learning: 40. Tendency of the Richardsons: 88. See also: Aesthetic

Artist: 70. M as consumate artist: 87

Artistry: 50

Arts of Empire, The: 116

Arts, seven liberal: 40. Images derived from: 8

Arts, trivial: 40

Artz, Frederique B.: 100

Arundel (earldom): 49

Arundel, Duke of: 10. Earl of: 103

Arundell, Thomas Howard (Earl of): 44

Arur(r)u: 32, 36

Arviragus (Arvirach): 44, 73, 3

Arwaker, Edmund: 37

Arzina: 19, 49

As You Like It: 34, 45

Asa: 73

Asam brothers: 27

A Satana: 65

Asbury, Francis: 115

Ascalon (Askalon): 19, 49, 73, 144

Ascalonite: 73

Ascan, Mr.: 73

Ascanius: 2

Ascensius: 123. See also: Badius, Jodocus

Ascent of Soul: 79

Asceticism: 143, 71. And fear of moral contagion: 143. Rejected by Protestants: 143

Ascham, Anthony: 44, 103, 38, 91. "Eutactus Philodemus": 38

Ascham, Roger: 1, 18, 20*, 40*, 44, 52, 56, 60, 66, 114, 120, 122, 145, 3, 93, 64, 148, 112. The Schoolmaster: 51, 82. Toxophilus: 82

Asclepiades: 128, 64

Asclepius: 57, 72

Ascot under Wychwood: 45

Asgrimsson, Eysteinn: 65, 64

Ashburnham, Earl of, Catalogue...of Books: 44

Ashburnham, W.: 58

Ashby de la Zouch, school: 20

Ashdod (Azotus): 49, 73

Ashdown (Ashdune, Escedunc, Eskesdun): 49

Ashdown (Assandune, Assehill, Assendune): 49

Ashe: John: 44. Simeon: 40

Ashenhurst, Dr.: 88

Ashfield, Edmund (artist of M portrait): 44

Ashkelon: 92

Ashmole, Elias: 7, 10, 77, 114, 142. Way to Bliss, 1658: 77

Ashmolean Museum, Oxford: 44, 45

Ashridge (Egerton home): 29

Ashridge Library: 88

Ashtaroth (Ashtoreth): 68, 73, 128, 142, 144, 57

Ashton: Abdias: 40. John: 91. Leigh: 44. Partridge: 45. Trevor: 39

Ashurst, Sir William: 44

"Ash-Wednesday" (T. S. Eliot): 131

Ashworth case: 45

Ashworth family: 45. Ashworth, Mr.: 44. Ashworth, Mrs. (Downing): 45. Ashworth, Anne: 45. Ashworth, Dorothy: 45. Ashworth, Edwards: 44*, 45*. Ashworth, Elizabeth: 45. Ashworth, Elizabeth (Duffield): 45. Ashworth, Elizabeth (Mrs. Edward): 44*. Ashworth, Elizabeth (Weaman): 45*. Ashworth, Gervase: 45. Ashworth, Henry: 44*, 45*. Ashworth, Jane: 45. Ashworth, Jervace: 45. Ashworth, John: 45. Ashworth, Thomas: 44, 45. Ashworth, Ursula: 45. Ashworth, Ursula (Edwards): 45

Asia (Asis): 44, 49, 51, 3, 150. Asia Minor: 150. Asiatics: 51

Asianism: 70

Asilas: 56

Askew, Egeon: 114

Asmadai, Asmodai, Asmodeus: 4, 73, 71, 142, 1, 124, 142, 130

Asopus (river): 49, 73

Asperges: in Comus: 126; in Fletcher's The Faithful Shepherdess: 126

Asphalt: 144

Asphaltic Pool (Asphaltis, Bituminous Lake, Dead Sea): 49, 73, 144. See also: Sodom

Aspinwal, William: 9

Aspramont (Aspromonte): 19, 49, 73

Assassination, M's fear of: 44

Assemblies, defects and distrust of popular: 51

Assembly of the Synod: 44

Assembly of Divines: 44, 45

Assembly, Glasgow: 51

Assembly's Annotations: 99*

Assent: 47

Asser, Bishop: 44

Assertion without proof: 51

Assimilation of the style of the originals in M's imitations: 88

Assington, co. Sussex: 44

Associations: literary, influencing the value of common words, Hume on: 88; of ideas, complexity of M's, Warton on: 88

Assumption(s): 51*. See also: Premises

"Assurance" (ship): 44

Assurance of Salvation: 63

Assurbanipal: 64

Assyria (Asshur): 19, 44, 49, 32

Assyrians: 32. Assyrian Garden: 144; blasphemer: 73; Mount: 144; Queen: 73, 90. See also: Venus

Ast: 112

Asta (Asti): 49

Astacides: 64

Astarte: 144, 32, 72

Astell, Mary: 54

Asteyn: (Astyn, Astin, Aston), Edward: 44, 45. Grace (Chesterman): 45. James: 45

Asthall: 45

Astle, D.: 58

Astolat Press: 97

Astolpho: 111

Aston, Middle: 45

Aston: Mr.: 44. Sir Thomas: 9

Astoreth: 42, 127, 144

Astracan: 19*, 49, 73

Astraea: 52, 73, 90, 32, 72

Astrolabe: 40

Astrology: 7, 3, 89, 114*, 128*, 93. Images: 8. M's knowledge of: 89. Judicial: 123. See also: Magic

Astronomica (Manilus): 3

Astronomical observations first made by the Chaldeans: 89

Astronomical: dialogue: 100; refractions: 89. Diary, Or, An Almanack for the Year of Our Lord Christ, 1746, An: 115

Astronomy: 8, 17*, 40*, 47, 50, 67, 89, 114*, 121, 128*. Urania, goddess of: 89. M's learning and knowledge of: 89, 102. M and the New Astronomy: 128. M and astronomers: 128. M's knowledge of astronomy: 129, 61. Images derived from: 8. Brief history of: 89. Associated with astrology: 89. Introduction to Western Europe: 89. Study of, in England: 21. Period of transition in: 89. Invention of telescope: 89. Phraseology of, in M's time, indefinite and vague; 89. See also: Poetic Universe; Stars; Planets; Sun; Moon

Astrophel, Spenser's expression of admiration for Rosalinde in: 83

Astyn, Edmond: 44

Asymmetry, patterns of: 96*

Atabalipa: 19, 73

"At a Solemn Music" (M): 8, 89, 134, 121, 72*. Text: 55. Artist in: 72. Christianity in: 72. Music in: 72. Stance in, as prayer: 72. Moral approval of music: 8. See also: Milton, John, Works

"At a Vacation Exercise": 134. See Milton, John, Works

Atchley, Cuthbert: 40

Athaliah: 73

Athamantaeos: 73

Athanasian creed: 71, 78

Athanasius: 5, 15, 27, 20, 47, 57, 68, 73, 74, 123, 142, 36, 71, 78, 88, 113, 93, 65, 77, 32. "Against the Arians": 74. Against the Heathen: 36. "Fragmenta in Job": 74

Atheism: 47, 51, 114*. And superstition, theological via media between: 114

Atheists: 51. M as: 146

Athelney (Edelingsey): 49

Athelstan, King: 44, 73, 3

Athena (Pallas): 60, 90, 72, 92, 1, 2. See also: Minerva

Athena. See Athene

Athenae Oxonienses: 45, 116. See also: Fasti Oxonienses

Athenaeum: 40, 44*, 45, 87

Athenaeus: 70, 90, 123, 82, 112, 73, 64

Athenagoras of Athens: 107

Athenagoras: 57, 73, 93

Atheneus: 120

Athenian Mercury: 116. On M: 58

Athenian, Commonwealth: 51, 3. Democracy, experience of: 51. Ideas on education: 40. Schools: 40

Athens: 9, 19, 30, 44*, 49, 51, 70, 112, 3*, 72*. Erechtheum: 27

Atheomastix: 40

Atherstone, Edwin: preferred M to Homer: 87. Collaborated with John Martin: 87. The Fall of Nineveh: 87

Atherton, John: 44

Athletics, M and: 137

Athos: 49, 73

Atkins: Edward: 44. J. W. H.: 66, 122. Samuel D.: 44. Thomas (alderman): 44. William: 44

Atkinson: Brooks: 79. Elizabeth: see Willoughby, Eliz. Ernest G.: 45. John: 45, 58. Thomas Dinham: 40. Troilus: 44

Atkyns, Sir Edward, Baron: 44

Atlantean: 73

Atlantic: 49, 103. Sisters: 73. Stone: 73. And Utopian politics: 3. See also: Azores

Atlas, Mt.: 19, 44, 49, 32

Atlas: 60, 73, 90, 121, 3

Atlases, M's interest in: 144. See also: Maps

Atom bomb: 136. And international

belligerency: 136

Atomism: 32, 36

Atomy, Mrs. See Attaway

Atonement: 17, 36. Meaning of: 83. Vicarious, doctrine of: 71. Mary's role in: 93. Theories of: 60, 123, 25. Traditional theories: 93. Protestant theory: 93. See also: Christ; Son of God; Redemption

Atreus: 56, 90, 123

Atrides(ae): 73

Atropatia: 19, 49, 73, 144. See also: Media

Atropos ("inflexible"): 73, 90, 72

Attachment: 45

Attack, on the bishops: 51. Upon the established order: 51

Attacking an opponent's argument/ statement: 51

Attalic: 73

Attaway (Atomy), Mrs.: 44, 91, 94

Attendant Spirit: 1*, 29*, 73, 143, 72*. As divine symbol: 143. Advocate of marriage: 143

Attention: 51*

Atterbury: Bp. Francis: 44, 58, 68, 117, 97. Lewis: 45. Stephen: 44, 45

Atterbury: 88

Attic Tragedies: 51

Attic(a) (Actaeus): 44, 49. Bird: 73. Boy: 73. Atticism: 70, 3. See also: Athens

Attica Bellaria: 40

Atticus, Titus Pomponius: 73

Attis: 44

Attitude: 51

Atto of Vercelli: 68

Attorney: 45

Attorney's Academy, The: 45, 73

Attributed writings (M's): 44*. See also: Milton, John, Works

Attributes: 107. Of God: 93

Attrition: 47

Atzberger, Leonhard: 93

Au désert: 65

Aubert, Jean-Marie: 93

Aubigné, Théodore Agrippa d', Creation: 74

Aubrey, John, diarist (1626-97): 1, 7, 9, 10, 16, 20*, 28*, 30, 40*, 44*, 45, 103, 3, 59, 63, 70, 73, 77, 86, 102, 105, 121, 116, 120, 128, 134, 136, 142, 144, 26, 39, 62, 88, 91, 94*, 137, 150, 117, 132, 149, 55.

Auden and Isherwood: 133

Auden, W. H.: 15, 33, 105, 108, 128, 14, 101, 150

Audience: 146, 143, 25, 30*, 31*, 51*. Fit: 143. Learning of: 143. And the Muse: 143. Vulgar: 70. Poet's relation to: 25. Prophet's relation to: 25. Orator's relation to: 25. M's sense of attitude toward: 30*, 31*, 51*, 146. M's fit audience: 25 M's contemporary: 146. M's 18th c.: 146. M's lack of: 146. M's reception by: 146. Romantic: 146. Romantic conception of: 146. Romantics' idea of: 25. See also: Blake; Jerusalem; Milton; Poet; Poetry; Prophecy

Auditory imagery: 118*. Definition of: 118. Acoustic metaphor in: 118. As including all of PL: 118. Difficulties in analyzing: 118. Confusion of spellings with sounds: 118. Apparent strain in analysis of: 118. Necessity of slow and repeated reading for analysis of: 118. Sample analysis: 118. Subtlety in: 118

Audland, John: 7

Audley End, co. Essex: 44

Audley, William: 44

Audlin Hill: 44, 45

Aue, Hartmann Von: 100

Auerbach, Erich: 69, 76, 79, 111, 36, 39. "Figura": 74. Mimesis: 74

Augeas: 3

Auger, Lord: 3

Augier, René (Augerium): 30, 44, 73

Augsburg Confession: 27, 83, 99

Augusta: 49

Augustan. See Augustus

Augustan(s): 53*. The, attitude of, towards M: 58*

Augustine, St.: 1*, 4, 5, 6, 7, 15*, 17, 19, 20, 23, 24*, 27, 34, 37, 40, 44, 18, 69, 47*, 51, 52*, 54, 57*, 60*, 63, 67*, 68*, 73, 74, 77, 79, 81*, 84, 3, 86, 90, 102, 112*, 110, 127, 111, 113*, 118, 122, 123*, 124, 125, 126, 128, 141*, 142*, 143, 144*, 32*, 36*, 38, 39, 62, 72, 82, 88, 93*, 99, 101, 109, 130, 137, 148*, 150, 48. His theory of knowledge: 96. City of God, influence: 55. On reason and rationality: 48. Beata vita, concept of: 81. Beatitudo, , concept of: 81, 38. Chaos, concept of: 81. Concupiscence, doctrine of: 81. Depravity, doctrine of: 81. Illumination, concept of, defined: 81. Meditative method, defined: 81. Love: 47. Fear; Degeneration: 47. On Good and Evil; on wisdom: 47. Memory, theory of: 81*. Mystical principles: 81. Platonism: 81. Desire, concept of: 81. Powers of the soul, action of: 81. Repetition, technique of: 81*. Search for truth, method of: 81. Time, concept of: 81. On Esthetics: 100*. Influence on M: 113. Unique importance of: 144. Vive's commentary: 144*. M interested in: 144. On soul's progress: 143. And glassy sea: 3. And ages of world: 143. On the Nature of sin: 83. On the Nature of perfection: 83. Read by Thomas Ellwood: 83. Cited on divorce: 83. Views on millennium: 38. Works: De Beata Vita: 81; De Haeres: 77; De Magistro: 81; De Musica: 81; De Quantitate Animae: 81; Faith, Hope, and Charity: 36; Genesis according to the Letter: 36; Genesis against the Manichees: 36; On Marriage and Concupiscence: 36; On Nature and Grace: 36; On the Grace of Christ: 36; On the Merits and Forgiveness of Sins: 36; City of God (De Civitate Dei): 52*, 60, 74*, 81, 77, 142, 144*, 36, 57, 46, 82; Enchiridian: 77, 142; De Urbis Excido: 74; Enarrationes in Psalmos: 74; Harmony of the Evangelists: 74; De Doctrina Christiana: 11, 36; Contra Faustum: 74; On the Trinity: 74, 48; De genesi ad litteram imperfectus liber: 60, 77; as paraphrased by Peter Lombard: 77; Retractions: 81; Soliloquies: 81, De Trinitate: 81*; De Vera Religione: 81; "Catechising of the Uninstructed": 74; Confessions: 52, 81*; style of: 81; decorum: 66, on meaning of nature: 52; title, meaning of: 81; on original sin: 52. Anti-Pelagian writings: 81. Basic writings: 48. See also: Austin; Migne

Augustine of Chisamensis: 32

Augustine of Hippo: 114*

Augustine Reprint Society: 44

Augustine, St. (another): 73

Augustine, St. (church): 40

Augustinianism: 71*.

Augustinians, late: and illumination: 52. And primacy of will: 52

Augustus, Caesar: 52, 56, 70, 73

Augustus: 35, 3, 72. Augustan empire: 3

Auld, J. B.: 98

Aulén, Gustaf E. H.: 15, 68

"Aulico, De" (Clerke, Castiglione): 40

Aulos: 121

Aulre (Aldra): 49

Aulus Gelius: 82

Auran: 49, 73, 144. See also: Eden

Auranitis: 144

Aurelio et Isabelle (Jean de Flores): 40

Aurelius: Abraham, Jobus: 74. Marcus: 35, 60. Victor: 40, 73

Aureolus: 142

Aurora: 44, 73, 90*, 72

Aurum potabile. See Minerals and metals

Auslander, Joseph: 16

Ausonius: 40, 90, 64. Ausonian: 73

Austen: E. M.: 44. Jane: 1, 58, 133, 39. William: 93

"Austen St." See Augustine

Auster: 73, 3

Austerity: and SA: 143. Of M's later work, Warton on: 88. Of M's sonnets praised by Warton: 88. Of religious poetry, Dunster on: 88

Austin. See Augustine, St.

Austin: Alfred: 111. John: 147; seeks leniency for the Papists: 147; wrote The Christian Moderator: 147.

Samuel: 65, 93. W.: 58. W. W.: 39

Austins Urania: 65

Austria, Archduke of: 6

Austria: 44, 49, 103, 3

Authentic: texts, *M Restor'd* demanding study of: 88. Meaning, M's, the Richardsons' insistence on its being restored: 88. Text, Hawkey's aim of restoring the: 88. Material, Newton anxious to base his edition on: 88. Text of M, Marchant's demand of in: 88. Facts, Lofft's endeavour to ascertain: 88. Texts, studied by Todd: 88. Documentation, wealth of, in Todd: 88. Fenton's doubts as to: 88

Author of our church history: 73

Author's: point of view, understanding of, demanded by the Richardsons: 88. Spirit, need of insight into, emphasized by Marchant: 88

Authoritarianism: 27, 30

Authorities: 27, 30*. M's contempt for: 113. M's use of, names of, works of: 30*

Authority: 50*

Authorized Edition of the English Bible (1611), *The* (Scrivener): 135

Authorship: of *M Restor'd and Bentley Depos'd*: 88. Of *The State of Innocence*: 88

Auto da Vida de Adam: 65

Auto de fés: 71

Auto de los los primeros hermanos: 65

Auto de Sanson: 68

Autobiography in M's works: 44, 20, 30*. In PL I, III, VII, IX: 50. Various passages: 55*. In SA: 92

Autobiography of John Milton (James J. G. Graham): 136

Autogeny: 47

Autograph Prices Current: 44

Autographic Mirror: 44

Autographs, M's: 16, 44

Autolycus: 89

Autonomy: 47

Auvergne, William of: 32

Auxerre: 49

Auzout: 10, 88

Avalos, Hernando d': 64

Ave Maria: 40

Aven: 49. See also: Kerdicsford

Avena: 121

Avenarius (Habermann): 40

Avenging Spirit: 92

Aventine (Aventinus): 49, 73

Averay, R.: 58

Avernarius, Johann: 41

Avernus: 49, 73

Averroes: 18, 123, 128, 32

Avery, Joseph: 10

Aves: 126

Avianus' *Hebrew Grammar*: 42

Avicenna: 122, 123, 128

Avis, Symon: 44

Avison, Charles: 117

Avitas, Alcimius Ecdicius, St.: 65*, 74, 77, 102, 141, 32, 36*, 64, 55; *Ad Apollinarem Episcopum*: 74. *De Spiritalis Historiae Gestis*: 74. *De Virginitate*: 74. "Epistle XLV": 74. *Poematum de Mosaicae Historiae Gestis Libri Quinque*: 36*, 55. Marcus Maecillius: 73. Quintus Octavius: 34, 56

Avon (Afene): 49. Rocky: 73. See also: Bradford

Awareness, total, as outrunning discursive thought: 118

Awbrey, J.: 58

Awdley, William: 44

à Wood, Anthony. See Wood, Anthony à

Axelrad, Arthur M.: 54. "One Gentle Stroking: M on Divorce": 82

Axon, W. E.: 64

Aylesbury, co. Bucks.: 44

Aylesbury, Sir Thomas: 40

Aylesford, co. Kent: 44

Aylett, Robert: 44, 45, 74, 114, 93, 64. Works of: David's Troubles Remembered: 74; Joseph: 74; Susanna: 74; Urania: 74

Aylmer, Brabazon (pr., publisher, bks., 1670-1707): 91, 6, 44*, 116, 134, 94, 117

Ayloffe: 45*. Agnes (Archdale): 45. Agnes (Byrch): 45. Agnes (West): 45. Anne: 45. Anne (Barnardiston): 45. Barbara (Sexton): 45. Sir Benjamin: 45. Catharine: 45. Catharine (Sterne): 45. Elizabeth: 45. Elizabeth (Penyston): 45. Elizabeth (Walsingham): 45. George: 45. Gyles: 45. James: 44*, 45*. Jane (Harris): 45. Jane (Suliard): 45. John: 45. Margaret: 45. Margaret (Fanshawe): 45. Margaret (Foster): 45. Mary: 45. Maud (Shad): 45. Raffe: 45. Thomas: 45. William: 40, 45

Aynho: 45

Ayres, Henry M.: 44, 58

Ayres, P.: 58

Ayscue (Ayscough, Ascue), Sir George: 44

Az ember tragediaja: 65

Azael: 142

Azariah: 73

Azazel: 1, 2, 4, 41, 57, 73, 89, 102, 107, 113, 142, 144, 55. In Origen: 107. A Cherub: 41, Herbraic Origin of name: 41. Name of Evil Spirit in Spenser: 41. As name of great Demon: 41. Origin of idea of, for M: 41. Rabbinical treatment of name: 41. 17 ideas of: 41. Spirit of Evil dwelling in Wilderness: 41. Standard bearer of Rebel Angels: 41, 55

Azevedo: 15

Azimuth circle: 89

Azores: 49. See also: Atlantic

Azotus (Ashdod): 19, 73, 143, 144

Aztecs: 34

Azza: 73, 72

-B-

B., A.: 117

B., C. W.: 44

B., C.: 117

B., J. (commissioner): 44

B., J. (pr.): 44

B., M. See Braithwaite, Michael

B., Q. N.: 44

B., R. W.: 44

B., S. See Barrow

B., S. (pr.): 44

B., T.: 44

B., W.: 117

Baader, Franz von: 7

Baal and Baalim: 143

Baal-peor: 73

Baal-zebub. See Beelzebub

Baal-Bosheth: 41

Baal: 42, 68, 73, 141*, 142, 144, 72

Baalim: 73, 128, 144

Baas, Paul de Castelmore, Baron de: 44

Babb, Lawrence: 128, 148

Babbitt, Irving: 70, 130

Babel: 1, 2, 19, 51, 73, 3, 143, 144, 72, 109, 141, 96*. Meaning of: 143. Ruled by Nimrod: 143. Built in 2nd age: 143

Babergh, co. Suffolk: 44

Babington: 23. Gervase: 77, 102, 142, 36. Notes upon every Chapter of Genesis: 36. The Works: 142

Babrius: 114

Babylon: 19*, 27, 49, 73, 3, 103, 122, 143, 144, 72, 25. Harlot of: 54. Meaning of: 143. Modern: 143. Symbol of tyranny: 46

Babylonia: 89, 32, 92, 118. Records of astronomy in: 89

Babylonian woe, the: 73

Babylonian Epic of Creation: 65

Baca: 49, 73

Bacchae: 5, 11

Bacchanalia: 44. Bacchanalians: 144. Bacchanalian Stream: 3

Bacchantes: 44

Bacchus: 1, 40, 44, 51, 70, 73, 3, 103, 90*, 121, 123, 143, 144, 72. And revelers: 143. As epic machinery: 123

Bacchylides: 40

Bach, J. S.: 15, 70, 100, 124, 39, 46

Bachelors of arts: 40. Number of in 1629: 40

Bachiler, John: 9, 44, 147, 91. Licenses the Sectaries books: 147

Bachmann, Conrad: 40

Back to Methusaleh: 65

Back, Shepherds: 121

Backer, Augustin de: 40

Backgammon: 40

Background: 51

Backus, Azel: 115. An Inaugural Discourse, Delivered in the Village of Clinton: 115

Bacon: Anthony: 145. Francis: See separate entry. Justice: 59. Nathaniel (?): 44. Bacon, Roger: 7, 16, 44, 114, 128, 32, 71

Bacon, Sir Francis: 1, 4, 7, 9*, 10, 12, 40*, 41, 44, 15, 35, 91, 64, 16, 17, 18, 20*, 23, 29, 37*, 45, 51, 52, 54, 82, 88, 93, 57, 59, 60, 67, 69, 70, 73, 3, 76, 79, 86, 90, 114*, 120, 123, 124, 125, 128*, 134, 135, 136, 109, 100, 142, 144*, 145*, 26, 32, 38, 39, 53, 71, 115, 130, 137, 146*, 148, 117, 55, 13, 112, 89, 132, 133, 94, 113. Works: Advancement of Learning: 60, 83, 142, 80, 82; Advertisement touching Controversies in the Church: 144; Certaine Considerations: 144; Essays: 82; The New Atlantis: 80; De Augmentis Scientianum: 60; Magna Instauratio: 80; Sermones Fideles Ethici, Politici, Oeronomici: 82; A Wise and Moderate Discourse, Concerning Church-Affaires: 82. Creation a natural process: 144. M's knowledge of Bacon's church tracts: 144. His and M's interest in reform: 144. His attitude: 144; on ceremony: 144; on church government: 144; against dissention: 144; for change: 144. Program of church reform: 144. Contrast with M: 144, 80. As a Christian: 80. Knowledge, purpose of: 80. On "schools": 80. And M compared: 146. Baconians, or educational reformers: 132. Baconian philosophy: 71.

Bactra: 73, 144, 49

Bactria: 19. See also: Boghar

Bactrian: 49, 73. See also: Bactra; Casbeen; Tauris

Baculus: 40

Badburie: 49. See also: Winburne

Badcock, Mr.: 58

Baddeley, Richard (publisher and bks.): 44

Baddily: Joan: 44. John: 44

Badiley: 10. Capt.: 44

Badius, Jodocus Ascensius: 123, 40

Badon: 49

Bag-pipe: 121

Bagehot, Walter: 4, 27, 29, 70, 86*, 87*, 105, 138, 144, 109, 130, 137. On M's Satan: 87. Analysis of M's character: 87. On changes in theology since PL: 87. On realism of Satanic council scene in PL: 87. On "Begat" passage in PL: 87. Effect of PL on 17th-c. mind: 87. On theology of PL: 87.On theme of PL: 83. Works: Literary Studies: 60; "Wordsworth, Tennyson, and Browning": 60

Baggesen, Jens: 65

Baggott, Robert: 44

Bagnall, co. Staffs.: 44

Bagnall: Elizabeth: 40. Robert: 93

Bagot, L.: 58

Bagshaw, Edward: 9, 116, 91, 148

Bagwell, John: 114

Baharim (Bahreim): 150

Baiana fabula: 73

Baif, Ian Antoine de: 64

Baildon: John: 40. W. P.: 45

Baiie: 28. See also: Bayle, Pierre

Bailey: Benjamin: 44. Derrick S.: 93. Isaac: 115; A Poem Delivered Before the Philermenian Society of

Brown Univ.: 115. John: 16, 86, 102, 110, 142, 113, 132, 133, 92; M: 142. John Eglington: 40, 44. Margaret L.: 9, 60, 63, 75, 77, 142; M and Jakob Boehme: 142. Philip James: Miltonic elements in poetry of: 87, 58; works: Festus: 87; A Spiritual Legend: 87; The Angel World: 87; The Mystic: 37. Thomas: 45

Baill(i)e: 7. Donald: 47. John: 47. Robert (Bayle, 1599-1662): 9, 16, 40, 44*, 51, 59, 103, 114, 120, 143, 38, 93; Dissuasive: 91

Baily, E. H.: 97

Bainbridge: 128. Thomas: 40, 44, 103, 116

Baines, A. H. J.: 44

Bainger. See Bangor

Bainton: 45. Roland H.: 93

Bajona: 49

Bakeless, John: 142. The Tragicall History of Christopher Marlowe: 142

Baker: family: 44. Mr.: 44. Augustine (the Venerable): 7. Sir Brian: 44. C. D.: 23, 63. Carlos: 14. Col.: 44, 116; Blazing Star: 91. Herschel: 17, 69, 128, 85, 93; tradition in Renaissance: 143; influence of Protestants: 143; works: Invocation of Health: 58; The Dignity of Man: 48. J. N. L.: 144. J. T.: 23. Sir Richard: 40, 44, 93. Thomas: 40, 45. W. P.: 128. William: 44. Winifred: 44

Baker's Biographia Dramatica: 88

Balaam: 73

Balak: 73

Balbie, Ceward: 44

Balbuena, Bernardo de: 123

Bald, Robert Cecil: 44, 93

Baldac: 49

Baldacci, Luigi: 5

Baldini, Baccio: 143

Baldinucchi, F.: 6

Baldwin Britwell, co. Oxon.: 44, 45

Baldwin, Alice M.: 115

Baldwin: Charles S.: 20, 123. Edward Chauncey: 1, 41, 42, 74, 60, 86, 102, 112, 113, 123, 32, 93; Types of Lit. in the Old Testament: 74. Katherine: 120. Thomas Whitfield: 20, 40*, 41, 56, 43, 21; William Shakespere's Small Latine and Lesse Greeke: 82. Thomas: 40. Sir Timothy: 45

Bale, John: 15, 65, 114, 143, 38, 93, 64, 99*. The Word: 143. The glassy sea: 143. Temptacyon of Our Lorde: 74

Bale: 132

Balearic: 73

Balearicus: 49

Balesham: 49

Balet Comique de la Royne (Beaujoyeulx): 29*

Balfour, Andrew: 16

Ball: Ann: 40. George: 44, 45. John: 114, 22, 93. Lewis: 108, 133. Thomas: 45

Ball: 10

Ballad (tune, writer): 121

Ballard, J. F.: 44

Ballatry: 121

Ballet de cour: 29

Balliol College, Oxford: 40, 45

Ballou, Hosea: 115

Bally, G.: 58

Balsamon, Theodore: 44, 73

Balsara: 19, 49, 144. See also: Teredon

Balsara: 73

Balsham: 40

Balston, Thomas, on John Martin: 87

Baltasar, Juan de: 32

Baltic Sea (Balticum Mare): 44, 103, 49

Balticum Fretum: 49

Baltimore, Maryland: 44

Balus, Alexander: 117

Balzac, Honoré de: 60, 136

Bamburger, Bernard J.: 142. Fallen

Angels: 142

Bamfield, Mr.: 44

Bampfylde: C. W.: 58. J., sonnets of: 58

Bampton: 45

Banbury, co. Oxon.: 44, 45*

Banbury, The History of: 45

Bancroft: John (Bp. of Oxford): 45, 64. Richard (Abp. of Canterbury): 40, 44, 45. Thomas: 114, 32

Band: 121

Banda: 19, 49. See also: Amboyna; Pularonis Insula; Ternate

Bandello, Matteo: 40

Bandini, A. M.: 6

Bañez, Domingo: 93

Banger: Mrs.: 45. Bernard: 45. George: 44, 45

Bangor: 49

Bangs, Carl: 93

Banister. See Bannister

Banister: John: 128. (Bannister), Richard: 16

Bankes, Thomas: 44

Banks: Sir John: 44, 117, 64. Sir Joseph: 44. T.: 135. Theodore Howard: 60, 63, 75, 102, 110, 125, 128, 143, 85, 99. On M's imagery: 143. "Spenser's Rosalinde: a Conjecture": 83. See also: Denham

Bankside, the: 70

Bannatyne Club: 40

Bannerman: A.: 58. W. Bruce: 40, 44

Bannister (Bannester, Banister) family: 45. Bannister, Mr.: 44, 45. Bannister, William: 45

Bannister-Ducket voyage: 19

Banquet (Xenophon): 112

Banquet of Jests: 44, 91

Banquet, celestial, in PR: 123

Banqueting scene: 99*

Banqueting House (Whitehall): 29, 103

Bantam: 150

Bantamus: 49

Banyan: 128. See also: Trees and Plants

Baptism of Christ: 139

Baptism: 47, 63, 126, 143, 93. M's conception of: 80. Infant: 7. M's: 40, 44. 1st sacrament: 143. Roman Catholic interpretation of: 143

Baptist(s): 7, 9, 103, 114*, 147, 38, 71, 78. Congregation, founding of: 147. Origin of Quakerism in: 83. Arminian nature of: 83. M's tenets like those of: 83. Early history of: 83. M's idea of perfection unlike that of: 83. 1st to ask for toleration: 147. Issued Persecution for Religion Judg'd and Condemned: 147. Issued Propositions and conclusions: 147. Prominent army men: 147. Wrote A Most Humble Supplication; a plea for liberty of conscience: 147

Baptist, John the. See John the Baptist

Baptista Mantuanus: 40, 57

Baptistes: 136, 94. By George Buchanan: 88

Bar Kokhba: 36

Bara: 49

Barabbas: 45

Barac: 68

Barak: 92

Baram Down: 49

Barba, Alonso: 128

Barbados: 49

Barbandt, Carl: 117

Barbaro, Francesco: 54

Barbary: 19

Barbauld, Mrs. Anna Letitia: 12, 58*, 115

Barber: family: 45. Rev. A. D.: 63*, 102, 71. C. L.: 15, 29, 39*. Joseph: 45. Robert: 44

Barberini family: 6*. Barberini, Anna: 6. Barberini, F.: 6*, 121, 94. Barberini, Cardinal Francesco: 30, 44*, 73, 103, 64, 26, 6, 137, 55; entertained M at Rome: 87.

Barberini, Maffeo: 6*, 55, 64. See also: Urban VIII

Barberini: Palace: 27, 103. Theater: 55

Barbers (as connected with music): 121

Barbican, London (M's house in): 44*, 45, 103, 121, 94

Barbitos: 121

Barbo, Paolo: 40

Barbour: 133

Barca: 49, 73. See also: Cyrene

Barcephas, Moses: 88

Barcham: 49

Barchard, Mrs.: 44

Barchly, John: 40. See also Barclay

Barckley, Sir Richard: 15, 19, 123, 93, 74. Discourse of the Felicitie of Man: 74

Barclay: 3. Alexander: 44, 64. David: 40. John: 6, 40, 73, 64. Robert: 7, 9, 83. William: 64

Bard: 25, 144, 121. See also: Poet

Bardi, Cannon Vincenzio: 44

Bardi, G. dei: 6, 29

Bards, Welsh: 25

Bardsey Ferry, co. Suffolk (?): 44

Bardsey: 144

Barebones Parliament: 51, 103, 147. M and: 147. Wanted to abolish national ministry: 147. Criticized by M: 147

Barebones, Praisegod: 1, 44, 91

Barents, William: 19

Baret, John: 40

Baretti, Giuseppi: 117

Barfield, Owen: 76

Barford St. Johns: 45

Barford, R.: 58

Bargaeus, Petrus Angelius: 122

Bargrave: Isaac: 44, 93. Portrait of M: 44. R.: 6

Barham, Francis Foster: 65, 123

Barhebraeus: 24*

Barignano: 120

Baring-Gould, Sabine: 110

Barish, Jonas A.: 29, 37, 39

Barker Street, Nantwich: 44

Barker, Arthur E.: 1, 4, 23, 27, 37, 40, 44, 52, 54, 66, 68, 79, 86, 100, 102, 108, 112, 104, 116, 126, 128, 11, 36, 39, 53, 72, 85, 93, 101, 106, 109, 148, 21, 61. On PL: 104. Works: "M and the Puritan Dilemma": 60, 83, 82, 48; "Structural Patterns in PL: 60. "M's Schoolmasters": 82

Barker: C. J.: 7. Christopher (pr.): 40, 44. Sir Ernest: 144, 93. John: 44, 45; sonnets of: 58. L. F.: 16. Robert (pr.): 40, 44. William: 10

Barking: 45, 49

Barklay, Alexander: 40

Barksdale, Clement: 45

Barkshire (Berkshire): 49

Barlaeus, Caspar: 65, 117. Paradisus: 74

Barlement, Noel: 40

Barley, William: 44

Barlow: Joel: 115; works: Columbiad: 58, 115; An Elegy on the Late Honourable Titus Hosmer, Esq.: 115; The Prospect of Peace: 115; The Vision of Columbus: 115. John: 58. Bp. Thomas: 93, 44. William: 77

Barnabus: 73, 107, 38

Barnachmoni: 73

Barnard: E.: 58. James: 44. John: 44. M., Odyssey: 58. R.: see Bernard, R.

Barnard's Inn: 45

Barnarde, Ralph: 44

Barnardiston: Anne: see Ayloffe, Anne. Sir Thomas: 45

Barnes: 45, 120. B.: 58. Emmanuel: 40. J. (plagiarist): 94. Jean H.: 79. Joseph (pr.): 40, 44. Robert: 40. W. E.: 40

Barnett, H. A.: 143

Barney, Thomas: 20

Barnfield, Richard: 59, 129, 39

Barnwell(ianos), argos: 73

Barnwell: 40

Barocci, Federico: 27

Baroco: 27

Baron: (Barrowe), Christopher: 44. George: 44. Hans: 13. John: 44. Richard: 44, 116, 117; ed. Works: 44*; praises M: 58. Robert: 44, 88; Cyprian Academy, Pocula Castalia: 91; plagiarizes M: 58. Sarah: 44. William: 115

Baronetcies of England, Genealogical ...History of the Extinct and Dormant: 45

Baroni, Leonora: 6, 44, 103, 59, 87, 121, 142, 26, 39, 94, 137

Baronius: 42. Caesar (Cardinal): 73, 93

Baroque in poetry, M's use of: 52, 101

Baroway, Israel M.: 40, 93. "Hebrew Hexameter": 74

Barozzi, Francesco: 40

Barrell, Robert: 93

Barrera y Leirado, A. de la: 68

Barret: C. K.: 79. Robert: 44. Roger W.: 44. William: 44

Barret's Alvearie: 88

Barrimore, Richard Barry, Earl of: 28, 44, 103, 120

Barrington: Mr.: 44. S.: 58

Barrow: Mr.: 44. Henry: 114. Dr. Isaac: 40, 150, 94, 58; on M: 58; master of Trinity: 94. R. H.: 81. Dr. Samuel (1525?-82): 10, 44, 60, 73, 128, 46, 91; physician to Charles II: 94

Barrowe, Christoper. See Baron

Barry: James: 97*, 146, 117. Richard. See Barrimore

Barrymore, Earl of. See Barrimore

Barstable: 45

Bart(h)olommei, G.: 6*, 44

Bartas, Guillaume de Salluste du. See Du Bartas

Barth, Karl: 47*, 48. Church Dogmatics: 48. On creation: 48. On accommodation, God's righteousness, chaos, Hell, the sexes, image of God, incarnation, sin, faith, misuse of the Scripture: 47

Barthélemy, Dominique: 93

Barthes, Roland: 11

Barthlet, John: 93

Bartholemew: 142. John: 40, 45

Bartholinus: Caspar: 40, 44. Thomas: 44

Bartholomaeus Anglicus: 1, 65, 123, 128*; Beastiary: 83

Bartholomew Close, London: 44, 103, 94. Bartholomew Fair: 103

Bartholomew, St., massacre: 44

Bartisch, George: 16

Bartlet, James V. (Acts of the Apostles): 51

Bartlett, J. R. See Williams, R.

Bartlett, John: 21

Bartolini, Thomas: 44

Bartolinus, Erasmus: 89

Bartolozzi, F.: 97

Barton: R.: 58. William: 42, 44

Barwellianus: 49. See also: Sturbridge

Barwick: G. F.: 44. John: 44

Barwicke, Peter: 44

Barzizza: 20

Barzun, Jaques: 1

Basan: 49, 73, 144

Basel (Bale, Basle), Switzerland: 44, 73, 3, 49

Basemore, Edward: 44

Basha of Memphis: 44

Basil, St.: 1, 15, 18, 24, 44, 57, 73, 3, 102, 122, 32*, 88, 77, 40, 60, 36, 93. His commentary: 51. His 1st Homily on the Psalms: 20. Works: Hexaemeron: 36, 77; That God is not the Author of Evil: 36; De Spiritu Sancto: 74; Homily VIII on Genesis: 82; Homily on Psalm 1: 82; Opera: 82; Homilia in Illud, in Prinicipio erat Verbum: 57; Psalm 33: 77; De Par: 77; De Hom. Struct.: 77. See also: Pseudo-Basil

Basil, Switzerland. See Basel

Basil: 68, 128*, 142, 71. Of Ancyra: 74. Martin (examiner in Chancery): 44, 45

Basili, Adriana: 103

Basilikon, Doron: 116

Basilius: 44

Basing (town): 49

Basing House, Hampshire: 40

Basingstoke, co. Hants.: 40, 44, 45

Baskerville, John: 117

Basle: 44

Basore, John W.: 33

Bass viol: 121

"Bassa," Capt.: 44

Bassano, Cesare: 123

Bassel (Bussel), Thomas: 44

Bassett, Thomas (bks.): 44

Bastard, Thomas: 40

Bastian, Ralph J.: 81

Bastide, Charles: 44

Bastwick(e), Dr. John: 9, 33*, 59, 116, 55. His Letany reflects his hatred of prelates: 147. Imprisoned for attacking Episcopacy: 147. Opposes toleration in The Utter Routing of the Whole Army of all the Independents and Sectaries: 147. Works: A Just Defense of John Bastwick: 147; Letany: 147

Batard, Yvonne: 60

Bate: George: 60, 116. George (author): 44. George (bks.): 44. W. Jackson: 86, 14

Bateman: Richard: 44, 45. Stephen: 123, 128*, 142; Batman Vppon Bartholome: 65. William: 44

Bates: Dr.: 97. Isaac: 115; An Oration, Pronounced Before the Washington Benevolent Society of the County of Hampshire: 115. Mary Dexter: 115. W. N.: 92. William: 93

Bateson: F. W.: 12, 40, 86*, 133, 76. Frederick: 21. Thomas: 44

Bath (Badencester, Caerbadus), co. Somerset.: 44, 45, 49

Bath: Earl of: see Bourchier, Henry. Sir Henry Frederick Thynne, 6th Marquess of: 44. Thomas Henry Thynne, Marquis of: 44

Bathe, William: 40

Batheaston, literary coterie at: 58

Bathing in the Cam River: 40

Batho, Edith C.: 44; Later Wordsworth

Bathurst: Allen, Earl Bathurst: 12. Ralph: 10, 44

Batley, Mr.: 44

Batrachomyomachia: 73, 3

Battagia, M.: 6

Battaglia celeste: 65

Batten: John: 44. Milton: 93

Battenhouse, Roy W.: 100, 36

Batteux, Charles: 117

Battie (an Anabaptist): 113

Battisford: 45

Battle in Heaven: 72*. See also: War in Heaven

Battle of Maldon: 15, 36

Battle-pieces: 98

Battleswade: 45

Batto: 49

Batty, Robert: 44

Baucis: 44, 73

Baudelaire, Charles: 86, 88, 97, 35

Baudele: 123. See also: Gratiani

Baudius: 149

Baudoin, Jean, Iconologie: 74

Baudry, Paul: 44

Baugh, A. C.: 135

Baughan, B. E.: 58

Baum, Paull F.: 68, 113, 85, 92*

Baumer, Franklin Le V., Early Tudor Theory of Kingship: 83

Baumgartner, Paul R.: 59, 122, 14, 93

Bava, Joannes Baptista: 64

Bavaria (Noricum): 44, 49

Bavius: 73, 3

Bawdry: 128

"Baxius": 40

Baxter: 130. C.: 97. Richard: 7, 9*, 15, 37, 40, 44, 54, 59, 79, 108, 114*, 116, 142*, 144, 32, 38, 46, 93, 99, 115, 148, 117; works: Life of Faith: 74; Paraphrase of the New Testament: 74; Be Domes Daege: 74; The Certainty of the World of Spirits: 142; Forty Popish Frauds Detected and Disclosed: 142; A Key for Catholics: 142; Of the Immortality of Man's Soul: 142; On the Nature of Spirits: 142; The Reasons of the Christian Religion: 142; The Saint's Everlasting Rest: 142. 109. Wynne E.: 23, 44, 43

Bay Psalm Book: 126, 71

Bayer, star altas of: 89

Bayer, Raymond: 5

Bayes (town): 44

Bayfordbury (M, portraits): 44

Bayfordbury, co. Herts.: 44

Bayle, Pierre: 7, 18, 44, 150, 117

Bayley: C.: 58. Harold: 93. Joan: 44. (Bailey), John: 44. Peter: 58, 115; Poems: 115. Robert: see Baillie, R. William: 7

Baylie, Robert: 103

Bayly: Anselm: 25. John: 93. Bp. Lewis: 93, 40. Thomas: 44

Baynard's Castle, London: 44

Bayne, Peter: 37. On M and Dorothea Brooke: 87. M's political activities defended: 87. M humorless: 87. On M's treatment of women: 87

Baynes: Paul: 114, 93. Ralph: 22

Baynton, Mr.: 44

Bayona's hold (Bayona): 19, 49, 73. See also: Guarded Mount; Namancos

Be Domes Daege: 74

Be Merry And Wise, Or a Seasonable Word (L'Estrange): 147, 103, 91. See also: L'Estrange, R.

Beacon, M.: 79

Beacons Quenched (pamphlets on censorship): 147

Beaconsfield: 44, 45

Beadle of univ. See Ridding

Beal, John: 142

Beale: 7. John: 40, 44. Mary (painter of M portraits): 44

Bealozera: 49

Beamflet (Benflet, Essex): 49

Beamont, Mr.: 44

Beandune (Bindon): 49

Beane, Joseph: 44

Bear Inn, Oxford: 44, 45

Bear Tavern: 45

Bear-baiting: 40

Bear, the Great (Ursa major): 89, 3

Beardsley: A.: 97. M. C.: 12, 123, 128

Beasts: 17*. In Paradise: 17. Jesus among during wilderness temptation: 119

Beatitude: 122, 123, 139. See also: Felicity

Beatrice (Dante's): 44, 103, 60, 70, 73, 3, 111*, 64

Beatrice-Joanna: 60

Beatson, J.: 58

Beattie: James: 115, 146, 117; on blank verse, diction: 58; on the Utility of Classical Learning: 115. W.: 58

Beatty: A.: 58. J. M.: 70

Beaty, Frederick L.: 44

Beau Chesne, John de: 40

Beauchatel, Christophle de: 40

Beauforest: Anne: see Lyde alias

Joyner, Anne. Richard: 45

Beaufort: John: 40. Lady Margaret: 40

Beaufrons: 116

Beaujoyeulx, Baltasar de: 29, 64

Beaulieu, M.: 29, 40

Beaumont and Fletcher: 37, 133, 88, 137, 13

Beaumont: Francis: 27, 35, 95, 108, 128, 39, 82, 83, 146, 117, 55. Herst. Van: 44. Joan: 142; A Treatise of Spirits: 142. Joseph: 1, 4, 15, 17, 19, 23, 60, 65*, 64, 74, 84, 102, 77*, 142, 26, 32, 36*, 93, 101, 149; Psyche: 74, 77*, 142, 36*; quoted, speech of Satan: 149. Robert: 40. Stephen: 44

Beautiful simplicity valued by Todd: 88

Beautiful, M's love of the: 129

Beauty: 8, 69, 70. As epic motif: 122*. Eve's and Woman's: 54. In landscapes, melancholy as an integral element of, Warton on: 88. Emotional: 88. Of discords, Dunster on: 88. Of creation: 93

Beaux' Stratagem, The: 71

Beavan, E.: 58

Beaver, Joseph: 128

Bebbanburg (Bamborrow): 49

Becanus, Gropius: 123, 128. See also: Gropius, Johannes

Becanus, Martin: 60

Beccafumi, Domenico: 27

Beccaria, Cesare: 146

Beck, Cave: 37, 44

Becker, G.: 36

Beckersteth, E. H.: 58

Becket, A.: 58

Becket, St. Thomas a: 13, 35, 73

Beckett, Samuel: 23, 51, 72

Beckford, William: 58, 97, 150

Beckley Coppice: 45

Beckman, W.: 58

Becmanus: 10

Becon, Thomas: 18, 20, 79, 143. The Word: 143. On preaching: 143. And wolves in the church: 143

Beconshaw, Elizabeth. See Tipping, Elizabeth

Bedanhafde: 49

Bede (Beda), Venerable: 24, 40, 67, 68, 73, 3, 128, 32, 36, 133, 99*, 64, 149. St. Bede: 123, 93. Works: De Arte Metrica: 74; De Schematis et Tropis: 74; Quaestiones super Regum Libros: 74; Super Exodum: 74; Super Librum Judicum: 74; Ecclesiastical History: 36, 46, 82

Bedecanwillan: 49. See also: Pictland

Bedell: Gabriel (bks., 1646-68): 91. William: 40, 42

Bedford (Bedanford, city or co.): 44, 45, 49

Bedford: Countess of: 10. Duke of: 45, 97. Jasper Tudor, Duke of: 44. William Russell, 1st Duke of: 44

Bedhampton: 45

Bedingfield: Sir Henry, Chief Justice: 44. Thomas: 44

Bedmakers: 40

Bedwell, William: 40

Bee, Book of: 42

Beech, William: 144

Beecher, Henry Ward: 137

Beeching: 70. H. C.: 1, 105, 113. H. D.: 122

Beelzebub: 2, 4, 17, 19, 31, 40, 50, 56, 60*, 67, 70, 73, 76, 98, 102, 103, 111, 113, 123*, 124, 126, 128, 72, 142, 144, 36, 46, 71, 109, 130, 55, 140*, . On ruin of man: 104. See also: Demonic

Beer: E. S. de: symbolism in Lycidas: 104; see also: Evelyn. John: 97, 146

Beerbohm, Max: 68, 85, 92

Beers, H. A.: 58

Beers's Almanac for the Year of Our Lord 1799: 115

Beersaba: 49, 144. Town: 73

Bees: 144. Government of: 83. Simile: 8

Beeseley, Rev. Claude A.: 44

Beesly, Alfred: 45

Beethoven, Ludwig van: 60, 124, 125, 135, 39, 46, 64, 149

Begemann: 7

Begley, Walter: 44, 91

Behemoth: 142, 73

Behn, Mrs. Aphra: 32

Beianus: 49

Beiblatt zur Anglia: 44

Being, God's plan of: 113. Diagram of: 113

Being: 96*

Bekker, Balthasar: 142. The World Bewitched: 142

Bel(l)ua: 73

Bel: 73, 144

Belasyse, Baron John: 44

Belcari, Feo: 93

Belden, H. M.: 51

Belerium: 144

Belfast, Ireland: 44, 103, 49

Belgia: 3

Belgiojoso, Baltazarini de: 29

Belgium: 44. See also: Low Countries

Belial: 1, 2, 4, 40, 50, 56, 60, 68, 73, 76, 98, 102, 103, 112, 111, 113, 123, 124, 125, 128, 136, 141, 142, 143, 144*, 46, 71, 72*, 109, 130, 55, 140*. The advocate of expediency: 136. Character in PL: 144. Contemporary significance: 144. Sons of Belial: 144. And Christ: 144

Belief: 47, 50, 128. Nature of: 132

Belin, Mr.: 44

Belinus: 44, 3

Belinus: 73

Belisarius: 3, 44, 70, 73, 122

Bell: 121

Bell (sign): 44

Bell Inn: 40

Bell: Dorothy: 40. E. Ingress: 44. G. (publisher): 97. J. (publisher): 97. Millicent: 15, 17, 37, 95, 110, 118, 128, 36, 93, 101, 106, 137, 140*, 48; "The Fallacy of the Fall in PL": 48. R. Anning: 97. Sir Robert: 40, 44. Walter G.: 93. Walter William Rouse: 40

Bella-Insula: 49

Bellamy: D., trans. Muscipula: 58. John: 91. Joseph: 115; works: The Great Evil of Sin as it is Committed Against God: 115; The Wisdom of God in the Permission of Sin: 115; Sermons Upon the Following Subjects: 115. T.: 58

Bellaria Attica: 40

Bellarmine, Robert(o), Cardinal: 40, 44, 60, 73, 79, 114, 116, 128, 142, 32, 93. De Scriptoribus Ecclesiasticis: 74. Bellarmine's Hebrew Grammar: 42

Bellassis, Thomas. See Falconbridge

Bellay, Joachim du. See Du Bellay, Joachim

Belle Isle, France: 44

Belleau: 40, 64. Remy (Amours de David): 74

Belleforest, Francesco: 40

Belleperche, Gautier de (Maccabees): 74, 64

Beller, Elmer A.: 44, 116

Bellerophon: 73, 90, 141, 144, 3, 106

Bellers, Fulk: 93

Bellerus, Fable of: 49, 73. See also: Langoëmagog

Belli, F.: 6

Bellingham, S.: 44

"Bellipotens Virgo" (to Queen Christina, attr. to M): 44

Belloc, Hilaire: 9, 15, 18, 44, 52, 60, 68, 86, 108, 130, 133, 136, 148

Bellona: 2, 73, 90

Belloni, Antonio: 6, 122

Bellot, Hugh H. L.: 44. Jacques: 40

Bellow, Saul: 14

Bellowings of a Wild-Bull, The: 116

Bellum angelicum: 65

Bellum Episcopale: 44. See also: Bishop's War

"Bellum Jugurtha": 40

Belly: 143. Fable of belly and members: 8, 128. And false clergy: 143

Beloe, W.: 58

Belon: 73

Belsham, W., Essays: 58

Belshazzar: 56, 60, 73, 77

Belsirena: 123. See also: Gratiani

Belstead, co. Suffolk: 44

Belus: 19, 73

Belvoir Castle: 44

Bely, Maldon, Essex: 44

Bembe, John Vande: 10

Bembo, Pietro, Cardinal: 5, 20, 30, 44, 59, 70, 73, 3, 26, 55, 112, 114, 120, 132. See also: Benbow

Ben Gerson: 63

Ben Naphtali: 41

Benacense. See Lancetta

Benbow, John: 44. See also: Bembo

Benbrigge, John: 144

Bence: Alexander: 44. Elizabeth: see Upton, Eliz. Rachel: see Fane, Rachel

Bendish: Bridget: 44; see also: Ireton. Henry: 44. Thomas: 44. Sir Thomas: 44, 45

Bene dicere: 40

Bene Elohim: 142. See also: Archangels

Benedicite, omnia opera Domini: 126

Benedicite: 72

Benedict XIV (Pope): 60, 122, 123

Benedict, John: 40

Benedict, St.: 143. Twelve steps of humility: 143. And Jacob's dream: 143. And life on earth: 143

Benedictus es, Domine: 126

Benedictus: 126, From Luke: 126

Benefactor: 122. Hero as: 123

Benefield, Sebastian: 64

Benet College, Cambridgeshire: 40. Benet Street, Cambridge: 40

Benevolence: 54

Bengal: 150

Bengala: 19, 49, 73

Benger, E., Poems on Slave Trade: 58

Benhadad: 73

Benham, Allen R.: 44, 63, 128, 91

Beni: 70. Paolo: 122*

Benin: 1, 34

Benivieni, Girolamo: 93

Benjamin, Metropolitan: 31

Benjamin, Walter: 39

Benjamin: 144

Benjamites: 73

Benlowes, Edward: 44, 100, 93

Benndorff: 3

Bennet: Henry: see Arlington. Thomas (publisher): 44

Bennett: Arnold: 92. C. E.: 56. H. S.: 40. John: 115; Letters to a Young Lady: 115. J.: 23. Josephine Waters: 60, 77, 128, 69, 59, 14, 80; Plato's "Myth of Er", M's use of: 80; The Evolution of the Faerie Queen: 83. Roger E.: 131. (Bennet), Sir Thomas: 45

Benoît, Pierre: 64

Benson (Bensington): 45, 49. W.: 105, 97; admires M, and on blank verse: 58. William (auditor): 44, 88. William (critic): 117

Bentham: 94. Jeremy: 34, 44, 87

Benthem, H. L.: 10

Bentley: E.: 58. G. E., Jr.: 39, 25. Richard: 1*, 15, 16, 17, 18, 28, 34, 35*, 37, 40, 44, 57, 58, 133 88*,

60, 73, 76, 86, 102, 127, 128, 134, 135, 142, 14, 32, 97, 54, 101, 115, 137, 130, 146, 150, 117*, 55, 105*; works: edition of M's Poems: 43; edits PL: 58; Dissertation upon the Epistles of Phalaris: 57; Letter to Mill: 57; Proposals for Printing a New Edition of the Greek Testament: 57; M's PL: 142. Thomas: 117. Bentley's M (J. W. Mackail): 88; see also: Mackail

Bentzen, Aage: 93

Benvenuti, E.: 6

Benvenuto: 40

Benziger, James: 1

Beorford: 49

Beowulf: 1, 45, 76, 128, 36, 46, 137

Bequests, from Bradshaw, from Cousin John Jeffrey: 44

Beranvirig (Banbury): 49

Berchet, Toussaint: 40

Berdan, John: 44

Berecynthia: 44

Berengarius (poem on Emperor): 133

Berens: 7

Berenson, B.: 15

Berenson, Bernard: 123

Beresford, B.: 58. J. (Aeneid): 58. Richard: 115; Nugae Canorae: 115

Bereshith Rabbah: 24*

Beresithias, sive Mundi Creatio: 65

Berg Visiting Professorship, New York Univ.: 44

Berg. See Frederick William

Berga: 49

Berge, Ernst Gottlieb von: 7, 10*, 91

Berger: Harry, Jr.: 39. P., on Blake: 58

Bergomum: 49

Bergonzi, Bernard: 37, 52, 66, 86*, 105, 48. "Criticism and the M Controversy": 48

Bergouignan, Paul and Andre: 93

Bergson, Henri: 1, 23, 125, 141, 14*, 53

Berkeley: 7. Mr.: 44. David S.: 14; on Lycidas: 104. Bp. George: 12, 44, 115

Berkhof, L.: 63

Berkin Manor: 44

Berkshire County: 44, 3, 45. Visitation of: 45. Record Office: 44.

Berlaymont: 40

Berlin, Isaiah: 125

Bermudas: 32

Bern: 44. City: 49. See also: Swiss Evangelical Cantons

Bernard: 73, 128. Mr.: 44. Francis: 44, 116. John Peter: 117. Of Chartres: 20. Of Clairvaux, St: 7, 52, 54, 60, 70, 79, 123, 114*, 142, 143, 32, 36, 93; on worldly clergy: 143; and Jacob's ladder: 143; on humility: 143; Opera Omnia: 142. Of Morlais: 64. Of Silvester: 79. (Barnard), R., his Terence in English: 20. Richard: 44, 54, 60, 93. Robert: 45

Bernards of Abingdon, The: 45

Bernardus: 130

Bernau, Charles V.: 44*

Bernays, J.: 92

Berne, Switzerland: 44

Bernegger: 7

Bernhard de Trevigo: 7

Bernhold of Constance: 40

Berni, Francesco: 6, 120, 122, 82, 64. Orlando Innamorato: 82, 64

Bernicia: 49

Bernini: Giovanni Lorenzo: 1, 6*, 27*, 39, 64. P.: 6

Beroalde, Mathieu: 32

Beroaldus: 74. Philippus: 40, 123

Beroeans: 51

Berri: 44

Berry: James: 44. Lloyd E.: 104, 64

Berthelet, Thomas (pr.): 40

Bertie, Montaque, Earl of Lindsey: 45

Bertinus: 40

Bertoni, Giulio: 5, 40

Berwick-in-Elmet: 40

Berwick-upon-Tweed: 44

Berwick, E.: 44

Besantinos: 64

Besaucèle, Berthé de: 122

Bessanyei, Sándor: 117

Bessarion, Cardinal: 32. Johannes: 6, 40

Bessel, stellar parallax of: 89

Best: John (pr., 1660-65): 91. Paul (author of <u>Mysteries Discovered</u>): 44

Besterman, Theodore: 93

Bestiaries: 128

Bethabara (Ford of Jordan): 49, 73, 72

Betham, M.: 58

Bethany: 49, 73, 72

Bethel (Luz): 49, 73, 144

Bethell, S. L.: 23

Bethesda: 49, 73

Bethlehem (Bethleem): 49, 3, 72, 21

Bethnal Green (Bednollgreene), London: 44. Academy: 78

Bethpeor: 41

Bethshemesh: 49, 73

Bethune-Baker, J. F.: 93

Betkius (Beets): 7

Betrothal: 54

Betson, A.: 58

Bett, H.: 35

Betterton: 94. Thomas: 44, 86, 136. Sir William: 44

Bettesworth, John: 44

Betuleius, Xystus: 65

Beulah: 25. Contraries of: 25. Description of: 25. Lament of: 25. Daughters of: 25. State of: 25. Song of: 25

Beum, Robert: 39

Beumer, Johannes: 93

Bevan, Edwyn: 110

Bevenot, Maurice: 93

Beverege: 49

Beverning, Mr. (Dutch agent): 44

Bevershal: Elizabeth: 91. Sir William: 91

Beverstan: 49

Bevill, Mr.: 45

<u>Bevis of Southampton</u>: 15

Beye, Charles R.: 25

Beyerlinck, Laurentio: 142. <u>Magnum Theatrum Vitae Humanae</u>: 142

Bèza, Théodor(us)e de: 40, 44, 73, 103, 74, 22, 72, 99, 115, 117, 135, 123, 93. <u>Job Expounded</u>: 74; <u>Poëmata Varia</u>: 74

<u>Bhagavad-Gita, The</u>: 146

Bi-form man: 69

Biaea: 44

Bianchi, Giacinto: 64

<u>Biathanatos</u> (Donne): 135, 131

<u>Bible Moralisee</u>: 143

<u>Bible</u>: 1, 7*, 15, 17*, 19*, 20, 24, 27*, 28, 34*, 40, 41*, 42*, 44*, 50, 51*, 54*, 57, 59*, 60*, 63, 68*, 70, 73, 74*, 87*, 98, 103*, 100*, 104*, 112, 111, 118, 123, 127*, 128*, 129*, 83, 113*, 132*, 133, 135*, 136, 144*, 145*, 147, 3, 32*, 36*, 46, 43*, 53, 71, 72*, 88*, 94, 97*, 149, 117*, 21, 25*

Bible, and scholars: Bentley's principle of adherence to, infraction of: 88. Blake's debt to, and illustrations: 25. Derivations from, condemned by Callander: 88. Erasmus on reading of: 147. Fuller's <u>Pisgah -Sight</u>: 144. Authority ascribed by Hume to: 88; classical lit. supposed by Hume to be based on: 88. Classics as derived from, Paterson and The State of Innocence on: 88. Pearce's knowledge of Eng. language: 88. Newton expect poetry to conform: 88

Bible, editions, versions, various: Bomberg Rabbinical: 42, 44. Buxtorf: 24, 42. Calvinistic: 40. Cambridge, Chapman and Bible, study of Greek and Hebrew: 20, 40. Clerks: 40. Bookshop: 44. Hebrews: 101. M's knowledge of Greek and Hebrew: 22* Streane Leviticus: 41. Century, W. H. Bennett, Genesis: 41. Complutensian: 40. Coverdale: 42. Diodati's Italian translation: 42. Douai: 24, 40. Erasmus' edition of Greek N.T.: 147. French: 40. Geneva: 123, 68, 24, 40, 42, 43, 32, 101, 143*; the word: 143; the ladder, Christ: 143; the Protestant Bible: 143; published: 143; and PL: 143*; commentary of: 143; examples from: 143; and SA: 143*. Great: 123, 40, 42. Greek: 40; Greek text of N.T.: 43*; Beza's Greek: 43. Hebrew: 3; Kettell's: 41; Massoretic text: 41; Rabbinical: 41; text of O.T.:

Bible, individual books: Acts: 15, 44, 32, 36. Amos: 32. I Chronicles: 41. Chronicles: 74. Collossians: 15, 73, 74, 148. I Corinithians: 15, 17, 27, 148, 44, 128, 36. II Corinthians: 17, 51, 60, 127, 32, 36. Daniel: 15, 17, 27, 41, 60, 101, 25. Deuteronomy: 41, 44, 74*, 36, 46, 101, 148, 25. Ecclesiastes: 15, 41, 74, 36, 46. Ephesians: 15, 32, 36, 148. Esther: 68. Exodus: 15, 41, 60, 74, 46, 148, 25. Ezekiel: 15, 60, 127, 32, 36, 46, 148, 25; structure of: 25. Ezra: 41. Ezdras: 148. Galatians: 51, 74, 101, 148. Genesis: 15*, 17*, 27, 34*, 41*, 44, 60*, 74, 127, 128, 32*, 36*, 46, 53, 101, 148, 25; as epic: 25, as tragely: 25; commentators on: 32; defense of: 32. Gospels: 53. Gospel of Nicodemus: 74. Hebrews: 15, 17, 60, 68, 74, 127, 32, 148.

Bible, individual books, cont.: Isaiah: 15, 41, 60, 127, 32, 36, 46, 53, 148. James: 15, 74, 127, 148. Jeremiah: 15. Job: 15, 17, 41, 60, 68, 128, 36, 46, 53, 148, 25; as tragedy: 25; as epic: 25. Joel: 36. John: 15, 27, 60, 127, 32, 36, 148*. Jonah: 17, 19, 46. I John: 15, 74, 36, 148. Joshua: 17, 74. Jude: 15, 17. Judges: 17, 27, 41, 68*, 74, 46, 148, 25. Kings: 15, 74. I Kings: 53. Lamentations: 15, 74. Leviticus: 41. Luke: 15, 27, 51, 60, 32, 101, 148. II Maccabees: 148. Mark: 74, 36, 148. Matthew: 15, 17, 27, 40, 60, 74, 127, 36, 101, 148. Numbers: 41, 51, 60, 74, 148, 25. Paul, Epistles of: 74, 53. Peter: 15, 127, 36. II Peter: 17, 60, 127, 101. Phillipians: 74. Proverbs: 15, 41, 51, 60, 70, 74, 128, 36, 148. Psalms: 15*, 17, 60*, 70, 74*, 127, 128, 32, 36, 46, 101, 148.

Bible, individual books, cont.: Revelation: 15*, 17, 51, 60, 74, 127, 32 36, 46, 101, 148, 25; Blake's knowledge of: 25; commentary on: 25; obscurity of: 25; clarity in: 25; relation to earlier prophecy: 25; genre of: 25; structure of: 25; influence on M: 25; as tragedy: 25; chorus in: 25; as dramatic structure: 25; as epic: 25; imagery in: 25; influence on Blake: 25; inspiration in: 25; and oratory: 25; time in: 25; seven visions of: 25; perspectives in: 25; characters in: 25; songs in: 25; continuity in: 25; repetition in: 25; Last Judgment in: 25; climax in: 25. Romans: 15, 17, 51, 60, 74, 32, 36, 148. I Samuel: 27, 60, 74, 53. II Samuel: 41, 74, 36. Song of Solomon: 15, 60, 36, 32, 25. Thessalonians: 51. I Timothy: 17, 68, 74, 36. II Timothy: 148. Titus: 51. Wisdom: 148. Zechariah: 41, 25. See also: Newton; Pareus; Prophecy

Bible, Priestly Code: 32. Symbolic interpretation of: 32. Exegesis: 32. Mosaic law: 32. Apocrapha: 32, 43. And Yahwist writers: 32. Typological interpretations of: 32*. As unified structure: 25. Allegory in: 25, 93. Mythology: 25. As epic poem: 25. Theme of wandering: 25. Theme of return: 25. Primacy: 93. Interpretation of: 148. View of nature in: 93. Burning of: 147. Interpretation of, individualistic: 147. Language of, in speeches and pamphlets: 147. Reading, the, effect of: 147. Apocalypse: 97. Citations of: 101. Joseph's Dream in: 136. An infallible guide: 144

Bible, M and: 144, 113*, 132*. Attitude toward: 137. Interpretation of: 32. M's knowledge of: 40. As the source of PL: 83, 129*, 118; read with PL by the Victorians: 136. Main source of SA: 144. On women, marriage, divorce: 54*. Not understood by indolent reader: 107. Use of the term "Perfection" in: 83. Foundation of his thought: 143. Use of: 63. Variants Reflecting Direct Use of Hebrew Text: 43. Chief source: 83. Illustration: 97*. M's attitude toward text of scripture: 43. M's family Bible: 63. M's acceptance of: 129*. Maps in: 144. More-Speed map: 144. Use of Biblical critical apparatus: 43. Material fitted to context: 43; citation without quotation: 43; clipping: 43; M's own version of Scripture: 43; Latin quotation differing from Junius Tremellius; quotations in pro populo: 43; Eng. quotations agreeing with definite text: 43; quotations differing from any recognized text:

43; peculiarities of M's quotation from New Testament: 43; shortened quotations changed in phrasing: 43; table of M's Biblical quotations before and after blindness: 43; true paraphrastic variants: 43; use of marginal readings of Authorized Version: 43; use of scriptural material with no indication of origin: 43; variants from Junius Tremellius: use of Adonai, Dominus, Elohim, and change of "qu" to "c": 43*. M's Bible(s): 28, 40, 44*; usual Eng. version: 43; usual Hebrew text: 43; usual Latin O.T. version: 43; usual Latin Apocrypha: 43; usual Latin N.T.: 43

Bible, The Baskett: 97

Bible, The Kitto: 97

Bibles, editions and versions: American: 41. Arabic: 24. Aramaic Targums: 43. Authorized Version: 123, 135*, 43*; 143; M's: 143; infallibility of: 143; influence of: 143. Bishops: 123, 40 42, 32. 43*; Buxtorf's Hebrew Bible: 43. Interlinear Greek-Latin: 40. Italian: 40. King James: 1, 24, 40, 41, 42, 32. Latin: 40, 41; Junius-Tremellius: 43*, 123, 1, 24, 40, 32; Tremellius's notes and commentary: 43; Tremellius's Latin trans. of Syriac N. T.: 43. Moralized: 74. New Testament: 60*, 74, 46. Old Testament: 60*, 74, 97. Pauline Epistles: 43. Polyglot: 123, 40. Septuagint: 123, 24, 32, 43. 1683 ed. of 1611 Version: 135. Sixtine-Clementine: 40. Solomon: 43. Spanish: 40. Syriac: 24. Trans. of the Bible in Middle Ages and Renaissance: 43. Vulgate: 123, 1, 15, 19, 24, 40, 32, 43. See also: Word of God

Biblia Pauperum: 74

Biblia Sacra (ed. Franciscus Junius and Immanuel Tremellius: 74

Bibliander (Buchmann), Theodore: 82, 93

Bibliander: 40

Biblical allusions: 51. Authorities: 51. Authors: 51. Command: 51. Lore: 51. Source, expansion of in PL: 118. Biblical images: 8*

Biblical: sources of PL studied by Hume: 88. Erudition, Hume's: 88. Learning, Bentley's, weak points in: 88. Expressions, Peck's ignorance of: 88. Knowledge, Newton's classical and, his chief assets: 88. Parallels, Gellies's: 88. Learning, Dustern's copious application of his: 88. Style, Dunster's respect for: 88. References in Todd: 88

Bibliographer: 44

Bibliographical Society of America, Papers of: 44

Bibliographical Society Transactions: 44

Bibliography of Eng. History, Stuart Period 1603-1714: 45

Bibliotheca Bigotiana: 44

Bibliotheca Fratrum Polonorum: 22

Bibliotheca Heberiana. See Heber

Bibliotheca Scholastica (Drax): 20

Bibliothecarii: 40

Bibliothek des Litterarischen Vereins in Stuttgart: 44

Bibliothèque Nationale, Paris: 40, 44

Bibliothèque Universelle: 78

Bicester: 45

Bicknell, Edward J.: 93

Bicton, co. Devon: 44

Biddle, John: 114, 74, 93. Works: Apostolical...Opinion concerning the Holy Trinity: 74; Testimonies of Irenaeus, etc.: 74

Bidenbachius, Felix: 44, 73

Bidlake, J., The Sea: 58

Bidle, John: 148

Biebel, Franklin M.: 44

Bienne: 44. See also: Swiss Evangelical Cantons

Biese, Alfred: 118

Bifield, Nicholas: 114

Bigamy: 78

Bigelow, Andrew: 115. An Oration Delivered Before the Washington Benevolent Society at Cambridge: 115

"Bigge Bulles of Basan": 83

Bigg-Wither, L., Odyssey: 58

Biggs, Miss. See Freeman, Mrs. Biggs, John: 45

Bignon, Philip: 40, 42

Bigongiari, Dino: 39

Bigot, Emeric: 16, 28, 30, 44*, 70, 73, 3, 137. John: 44. Nicholas: 44

Bigotiana Bibliotheca: 44

Bigres, P., Jesus Mourant: 74, 64

Bilborough: 45

Bilderbeck, Heinrich: 10

Bilderdijk, Willem: 65

Bill, John (pr.): 44

Bill: 45. Of Indemnity: 103

Billesley (Bilsley), co. Warwick: 44, 45

Billing, Samuel (engraver): 44

Billinge, C., influence by PL: 58

Billingsgate, London: 44

Billingsley: Catherine: see Chilcott, Catherine. Henry: 40. Nicholas: 93. Thomas: 45

Bills of Exclusion: 116*

Billson, C. J., Aeneid: 58

Billy Budd (Melville): 98*, 136. Billy Budd: 98

Bilson, Bp. Thomas: 73, 116, 3, 93, 99

Binary star systems: 89

Binckes, William, Dean of Lichfield: 44, 116

Bindemann: 100

Binderton, co. Sussex: 44

Bindley, James: 44, 88

Bingham, John: 40

Binney, Barnabas: 115. An Oration Delivered on the Late Public Commencement at Rhode-Island College in Providence: 115

Binns, Henry Bryan: 136

Binsfield, Peter: 142

Binyon, Laurence: 52, 58, 65, 87, 110, 97. And M's imagery: 143

Biographer(s): 132. M's contemporary: 55. Early: 55. 18th c.: 55, 87*. Masson: 55. Stern: 55. 20th c.: 55. M's: anonymous: 132; early: 30, 86. See also: Aubrey; Phillips; Richardson; Toland; Wood

Biographia Literaria (Coleridge): 70

Biographical: documentation in Peck's notes: 88. Facts, Thyer sees connection between, and M's poetry: 88. Method applied by: Newton: 88; Warton: 88; Dunster: 88. Method combined by Dunster with artistic and psychological considerations: 88

Biographies of M: 20*. In 19th c.: 87. Reaction to 18th-c. biographies: 87. Biased and unbalanced: 87. Over elaborate and expensive: 87. Treatment of M's prose in: 87. "Three periods" approach to M's life: 87

Biography: 20*, 117*. Materials for: 55*. Chronology, with historical events: 55

Bion: 4, 33, 40, 73, 90, 72, 93, 64

Biondello, Francesco: 5

Birch: 7. A pr.: 94. A. H.: 93. Col. John: 44. Peter: 116. Thomas: 28, 40, 44*, 58, 73, 116, 43, 91, 146, 150, 117. Ed Works: 44*

Birchen Rod for Dr. Birch, A: 116

Bird-song: 121

Bird: Mr.: 44. Agnes: 44. Samuel: 40 Bird Cage Walk: 103

Birds (fellows?): 40

Birds: 128*, 144. Foreknowledge of: 128. Solar: 128. M's descriptions of: 150. Cormorant: 128. Cranes: 128*. Imagery: 8*. Cuckoo: 128. Daw: 128. Dove, chaste: 128. Eagle: 128; regeneration of: 128; solar: 128. Geese, confused with cranes: 128; flight: 128; silence: 128. Halcyon: 128. Hoopoe: 128. Ibis, purging: 128. Nightengale: 128. Ostrich: 128. Owl: 128; foreknowledge of: 128. Phoenix: 128*. Raven, foreknowledge of: 128. Swallow, builder: 128. Swans, chaste: 128; flight: 128. Vulture: 128; foreknoweldge of: 128

Birdwood, Sir George: 150

Birken, Sigmund von: 10

Birkenhead: Earl of: 59. Sir John (1616-79): 44, 91

Birkhead, Mr.: 44

Birks, pacification of: 44

<u>Birmingham Halpenny, Upon a</u>: 58

Birmingham: 40

Birnwud: 49

Birrell: A.: 130. Augustine: 16, 44, 58, 86, 87. F.: 133

Birt, Mr.: 44

Birth: 128, 141. Image of: 141. M's: 28*, 44, 84

Birthplace, M's: 44

Birthric: 3

Birthright, as criterion for nobility: 123*

Bisbie, Nathaniel: 116

Biscay, Bay of: 49

Bischoff, E.: 100, 142. Die Elemente der Kabbalah: 142

Bischop, Simon: 40

Biserta: 49, 73

Bishop of London: 40, 51

Bishop of Winchester: 112. See also: Elegy III

<u>Bishop Burnet's History of His Own Time</u>: 116

<u>Bishop Parker's History of His Own Time</u>: 116

Bishop, George: 40. S.: 58. W. W.: 40

Bishop's foot (proverbial expression): 8

Bishop's Head (sign): 44

Bishop's Reigstry of Oxford: 44

Bishop's Palace, St. Paul's: 103

Bishop's War: 44

Bishops Land: 45

Bishops, contempt for: 30, 51

Bishops, restriction upon authority of: 51

Bishops: 51*, 103*, 113*. M's pamphlets against: 113. M attacks their worldliness: 147. M's hatred of: 147

Bishopsgate, London: 44, 45.
Bishopsgate Street, London: 44

Bismarck: 130

Bisset: 120. J.: 58

Bissill, George: 35

Bister. See Bicester

Bisterfeld: 10

Bistichius: 16

Bitumen: 144

Bix (Dent-du-Midi): 44

Bixby, William K.: 44

Bizance (Byzantinus, Constantinople): 49, 73

Bizari, Pietro: 40

Black Bear, St. Paul's Churchyard: 40

Black Spread Eagle Court; 40, 44

Black: J.: 58. John: 21. M. (M. Treip): 135. Matthew W.: 44; <u>Shakespeare's 17th. C. Editors</u>: 44

Blackall, Offspring: 116

Blackamores Head Inn: 40

Blackborough: 28. Mr.: 44

Blackborow: Abraham: 44. Hester Jeffrey: 44; Hester (daughter of Hester): 44. Hester (another): 44. Jane: 44. Joan: 44. Sarah: 44. William: 44; William (son of William): 44

Blackburn Grammar School: 20

Blackburn, S.: 97

Blackburne: F.: 58. Francis: 44*, 116, 146, 117; <u>Memoirs of Thomas Hollis</u>

Blacker, Mr.: 44, 45

Blackett: J.: 58. M. D.: 58

Blackfriars, London: 44, 45

Blackie, J. S.: 58

Blacklock, Thomas: 16, 58

Blackmoor Sea: 49, 73

Blackmore, Sir Richard: 1, 6, 15, 56, 58*, 65, 95, 142, 32, 46, 88, 91, 115, 146, 13. <u>Paraphrase on the Book of Job</u>: 74

Blackmore: 133, 130

Blackmur, R. P.: 60, 76

Blackstone: Mr.: 45. Bernard: 81, 25. Sir William: 45; Lawyer's Farewel: 58

Blackwall, Anthony, author of Introduction to the Classics: 88

Blackwater Bay (Essex): 44. See also: Chelmer River

Blackwell, B. H., Ltd.: 44

Blackwood: Christopher: 99*; Expositions and Sermons upon... Matthew: 74. Henry: 101

Blackwood's Edinburgh Magazine: 87, 146

Blackwood's Magazine on Callander: 88

Blaeu, Le Grand Atlas: 144

Blaeu: (Blaviana), Jan (Dutch publisher): 24, 44, 73, 3. Willem: 114

Blagrave: Mr.: 45. Daniel, regicide: 44. John: 40. Mary: see Fleet, Mary. Thomas: 44, 45

Blair: Hugh: 12, 58, 117. Lectures on Rhetoric and Belles Letres: 82. On M: 58. Robert (1593-1666): 51, 91, 97, 115. Grave: 58

Blake: Catherine: 25. Charles: 117. Francis: 45. Mary (Cope): 45. Admiral Robert: 44, 59, 103, 94

Blake, William: 1, 5, 7, 15*, 27, 34, 52, 58*, 60, 73, 76, 44, 112, 120, 123, 79, 81, 98, 111, 84, 86, 87, 113*, 118, 123, 126, 128, 132, 134, 136*, 143, 138, 139, 141*, 25*, 14*, 38, 39, 46, 93, 97*, 106, 109, 115, 130*, 131, 137, 146*, 148, 150, 117, 55, 21. The artist: full page designs: 25; his visual art: 25; 1809 Exhibition: 25. The poet: as prophet: 25; system of: 25; and tradition: 25; mythology of: 25; personae: 25; aesthetics of: 25; obscurity of: 25; narrative art: 25; contexts for poems: 25; topical concerns: 25; use of grammar: 25; imagery: 25; career of: 25; irony of: 25; humor of: 25; early prophecies: 25; language of: 25. And philosophy: 25. As iconoclast: 25. Isolation of: 25. As Biblical exegete: 25. Humanism of: 25. Genius of: 25. As cosmologist: 25. Knowledge of weaving: 25. Biography of: 25. Others' reminiscences of: 146. Portrait heads: 97. And Burney: 97. And Hayley: 97. Illustrations to: Comus: 97; L'Allegro and Il Penseroso: 97; Ode: 97; PL: 97*; PR: 97; M: 146. Annotations to: Reynolds's Discourses: 97, 146; Boyd's Inferno: 146; Lavater's Aphorisms: 146; Swedenborg's Heaven and Hell: 146; Watson's Apology: 146. Letters: 146. Notebook: 146. Works: Description of Illustrations to L'Allegro and Il Penseroso: 146; Descriptive Catalogue: 146; Four Zoas: 146; Island in the Moon: 146; Jerusalem: 146; Marriage of Heaven and Hell: 146; Prospectus: 146; Public Address: 146; "Milton": 97, 146*; Songs of Experience: 46

Blake, William, and M: 58*. On M's Satan: 87. His interpretation of PL: 83. Relationship with Fuseli: 87. Art work inspired by M: 87. Blake's idea of, criticism of M: 25. As poetic influence: 25. Blake's debt to: 25. And poetic tradition: 25. And orthodoxy: 25. As revolutionary artist: 25. Poetical form: 25. Myth-maker: 25. Blake's knoweldge of: 25. Illustrations for M: Comus: #1 through #8: 25; Il Penseroso: 25; L'Allegro: 25; PL: 25, 143; PR: 25. See also: Individual titles

Blake and M (Saurat): 113

Blakeney, E. H.: 92, 99

Blakiston, Noel: 40, 44

Blakmorè, Thomas: 44

Blakston, Ralph: 40

Blamire, S.: 58

Bland: 98

Blandford Forum: 45

Blane, W.: 58

Blank verse: 44, 58*, 146, 25. Milton on: 58. As a development of rhymed epic verse: 118. The Richardsons on flexibility and intricacy of: 88. Discussed: 87, 55*. Blank verse too "solid" for some readers: 136

Blankenham-upon-the-hill, co. Suffolk: 44

Blasphemy: 9, 51

Blastfield, Master: 45

Blau, Joseph L.: 93

Blauvelt, Samuel: 115. Fashion's Analysis: 115

Blavatsky, Madame: 1, 142

Blazing Star, or Nolls Nose, The: 103, 116

Bleau, Edouard: 65

Blebelius, Thomas: 40

Blechinion, co. Berks.: 44

Bledington: 45

Blegabredus: 70

Blemishes of PL: 88

Blenheim: 70, 27

Blenner-Hasset, R.: 1, 54

Blessed Isles: 90

Blest, Islands of the: 32. See also: Fortunate Islands

Bliemetzrieder, Franz Pl.: 40

"Blind mouths": 113

Blindness and light: 105*. See also: Angels and light; Son of God and light

Blindness, M's: 16*, 20*, 28*, 30*, 40, 44*, 51, 60, 98, 113, 121, 132*, 137, 84, 89, 90, 114, 136, 94, 128. See also: Sonnets: XVIII; XIX; XXII

Blindness: probable causes of: 113. Anonymous biographer's account: 55. Phillips' account: 55. M's statements in Second Defense, discussed: 55. Prayer to Light in PL: 55. And SA: 55. In poetry about M: 55. Effect on M: 55. Images derived from or influenced by: 8*

Bliss, Philip B.: 20, 44, 45*, 116. See also: Wood, Anthony

Blissett, William: 60

Block, Edward: 44

Blockley: 45

Blois: 49

Blome, Richard: 44, 45

Blomefield, Francis: 40

Blomfield, Robert: 44

Blondel, Jacques: 60, 81, 39

Blondell, David: 44

Blood: 128

"Bloody Assizes": 44

Bloody Tenant of Persecution, The (Roger Williams): 51, 147, 103, 26, 91

Bloody Tenant Yet More Bloody (Roger Williams): 147

Bloom, Harold: 110, 14, 146, 25*

Bloomfield, Morton: 25. N., Essay on War: 58

Blore, W. P.: 44

Blos, Peter: 14

Blosse, Darcy: 44

Blossom, The (John Donne): 131

Blount: Charles: 114, 116*, 128, 32, 115. (Blunt), Edward (bks., 1594-1632): 40, 91, 64. Sir Henry: 40. Thomas: 19, 44, 45, 116, 128, 145, 92; Glossographia: 91

Blow, John: 39

Blower, Peter: 44. Thomas: 44. See also: Bower, Thomas

Bloxham: 45

Bloys, William: 93

Blue Anchor (sign): 44

Blue Ball (sign): 44

Blume, Friedrich: 39

Blunden: 7. Mr.: 44. E.: 133. Edmund: 44, 145. Elizabeth: see Moore. Humphrey (bks., 1637-54): 91

Blundeville, Thomas: 40*

Blunt: Anthony: 93. Sir Anthony: 97. Rev. J. J.: 16, 87; on De Doctrina Christiana: 87; on M's puritanism: 87. W.: 6

Blunte, Oswald: 44

Bluntness of style, Manboddo opposed to: 88

Boaden, J.: 58

Boadicea, Queen: 103

Boaistuau, Pierre. See Boaystuau

Boanerges: 59

Boarding School: On Lessons of a Preceptress to her Pupils, The: 115

Boars (seniors): 40

Boas: Franz: 118. Frederick S.: 40. George: 79, 36. See also: Boase

Boase: (Boas), George C.: 44, 69, 81. T. S. R.: 97

Boasts, heroic: 123

Boaystuau, Peter: 128

Boaz: 73

Boccaccio, Giovanni: 1, 4, 6, 18, 37, 40, 41, 44, 57, 68, 69, 79, 90, 33, 120, 122, 123, 133, 36, 39, 62, 88, 64, 146. Works: Genealogiae De orum: 57, 74; Filocolo: 74; Life of Dante (Vita di Dante): 74, 82; Genealogy of the Pagan Gods: 36

Boccage, Mme. Marie Ann du: 117

Boccalini, Trajano: 2, 40, 145, 82, 130. Ragguagli di Parnasso: 82

Bocchus: 73, 49, 144. See also: Almansor

Bochart, Samuel: 1, 19, 41, 44, 90, 142, 22, 32, 128. Hierozoicon sive Bipertitum Opus de Animalibus Sacrae Scripturae: 142

Bochenski, Innocentius: 40

Bode, Anne. See Jeffrey

Bodenheimer, F. S.: 128

Bodin, Jean: 9, 15, 18, 40, 44, 51, 60, 73, 102, 116, 123, 132, 142*, 32*, 82, 93, 55. Works: Refutation des Opinions de Jean Wier: 142; De la Demonamanie: 142; Heptaplomeres: 132, 142

Bodington, Over (Upper): 45

Bodkin, Maud: 1, 12, 60, 75, 76, 86, 118, 123, 128, 133, 138, 141, 32, 130

Bodleian Library: 40, 44*, 45, 103, 92, 94. MS. Aubr. 8, f. 63: 40. MSS. Rawlinson: 45, 103. MSS. Wood: 45. Library Record: 44. Quarterly Record: 44

Bodley, Sir Thomas: 40

Bodmer, Johann Jacob: 10, 65, 97, 149, 117, 94

Bodotria: 49. See also: Dunbritton

Body and soul: 107. Unity of in M's thought: 113

Body politic, the: 83. And human: 125. And life of the spirit: 125

Boecler, John Henry: 44

Boehme, A. W.: 7

Boehme, Jakob: 7*, 10, 54, 60, 77, 114, 123, 142, 32, 38, 71, 93, 97, 146, 148, 55. Academies, alchemy, Antilians, authority, critics, democracy, Jews, life, literary influence, politics, Quakers, science, social reform, spread of interest in, students of, style, teachings: 7*. Works: The Three-fold Life of Man: 60; A Description of the Works: The Three Principles of the Divine Essence: 60, 77

Boehmenists: 7*

Boehner, Philotheus: 40

Boemer, A.: 40

Boemus, Joannes Aubanus: 40, 32

Boeotia: 49. See also: Aonian

Boeschenstein, Johannes: 40

Boethius: 15, 17, 40, 47, 52, 63, 69, 79, 100, 102, 114, 121, 122, 128, 134, 3, 32, 46, 62, 71, 72, 82, 93, 64. Works: Consolation of Philosophy: 60; De Musica: 60

Boghar: 19, 49. See also: Bactra

Bogholm, N.: 142. M and PL: 142

Boguet, Henry: 142. An Examen of Witches: 142

Bohemia: 44, 49. Rose de: 40. Bohemian History: 73

Bohn, H. G. See Lowndes

Bohn's Standard Library: 44. Bohn edition: 73, 87. See also: Milton, Prose Works

Bohun, Edmund: 116

Boiardo, Matteo Maria: 19, 40, 44, 120, 133, 46, 88, 117 73, 90, 111, 122*, 123, 82, 93, 64, 55, 21. Orlando Innamorato: 74, 82

Boileau-Despreaux, Nicolas: 2, 15, 58, 70, 87, 105, 122, 115, 149, 117, 146, 150, 21. Works: "Lettre...a l'Autheur du Jonas et du David": 74; Lutrin: 2; Translation of Peri Hupsous: 87; Art Poetique: 74

Boineburg, Christian von: 40. Johannes Christanus de, Baron: 44

Bois, John: 40

Boismorand, C. J. Chéron de: 117

Boissard (Boissardus), Jacob: 142. De Divinatione et Magicis Praestigiis: 142

Boisset, Jean: 93

Boissonade, J. F.: 6

Boius, Cornelius: 117

Boke called the Governour (1531). See Book of the Governour

Bold: Mr.: 44, 45. (Bould), Edward: 44. Matthew: 117. Norton: 45. William, father's servant: 44

Bolde, Thomas: 40

Boldness of M's style, Peck unaware of: 88

Boldu, L.: 6

Bolgar, R. R.: 123

Bolingbroke, Henry St. John, Viscount: 12*, 142, 32, 82, 115. The Works: 142

Bolington. See Bullingdon

Bolland, W.: 58

Bollingdon. See Bullingdon

Bologna: 44, 103, 3, 94. Medical school of: 16

Boloigne (Bononiensis Portus, Gessoriacum): 49

Bolsover Castle: 29

Bolte, J.: 68

Bolton: Edmund: 39. John: 44. Joseph: 40. Robert: 40, 60, 142, 93, 148; Of the Foure Last Things: 142. Samuel: 40, 79. William: 116

Bolzano, Bernard: 110

Bombast von Hohenheim: 93. See also: Paracelsus

Bomberg Rabbinical Bible: 22

Bomberg: Cornelius: 41. Daniel: 40, 41

Bona fides, Bentley's, and Mackail: 88

Bonamattei, Benedetto: 26

Bonamicus, Lazarus: 21

Bonaparte, Lucien: 146. And M compared: 146

Bonaparte, Napoleon: 146

Bonavento. See Welcome

Bonaventura(us), St.: 7, 24*, 41, 60, 79, 77, 81, 102, 111, 32, 36, 93. Works: In...Evangelius Secundam Lucam: 74; Itinerarium: 81*; Sent.: 77; Centiloquium: 77

Bonciani, Francesco: 6. Difesa di Dante: 74

Bond: Mr.: 44. Dennis: 44*. Elizabeth: 44. John: 20, 40, 38, 93; Sermon by: 38. John J.: 44. Richmond P.: 122

Bond: 45

Bondage. See Slavery

Bonde, Christiern (Swedish agent): 44

Bonfigli, Luigi: 122

Bonfrerius, Jacobus: 68

Bongianni, F. M.: 5

Bongo, Pietro. See Bungus

Bonham, William: 40

Bonhoeffer, D.: 36

Boniface: 36. VIII: 64

Boniform faculty: 123

Bonmattei (Bonmatthei, Baonmatteoi), Benedetto: 28, 30, 40, 44*, 73, 114, 137. See also: Buonmattei, Bonmattei

Bonnard, G. A.: 44

Bonnard, J.: 36

Bonnell, J. K.: 36

Bonner of Rotherham School: 20

Bonner, Edmund: 64

"Bonner's broth, Bonner-like censure to burn": 73

Bonney, Henry Kaye (?), Archdeacon of Lincoln: 44

Bononia: 44, 49, 73

Bontia: 73, 103. See also: Pontia

Bonus, Jacobus; 68, 74, 64. Works: De Raptu Cerberi: 74; De Vita Gestis Christi: 74; Sub Figura Herculis: 74

<u>Book of the Governour</u> (Elyot): 29, 40

<u>Book of the Secrets of Enoch</u>: 65

<u>Book of Adam and Eve</u>: 65, 123

<u>Book of Adam's Daughters</u>: 65

<u>Book of Common Prayer</u>: 27, 40, 54, 59, 103, 126*, 143, 25. Elizabeth's: 126. Gospel for Christmas Day: 126. Evening Prayer: 126. Morning Prayer: 126. Collect for Visitation of the Sick: 126. Commination against sinners: 126

<u>Book of Enoch</u>: 57, 65, 142

<u>Book of John the Evangelist</u>: 123

<u>Book of Jubilees</u>: 65

<u>Book of Judgment</u>: 111

<u>Book of Nature</u>: 60. Book of nature: 79, 93. See also: Natural theology

<u>Book of Tobit</u> (Apocrypha): 139

<u>Book of Wisdom</u>: 88

<u>Book Auction Records</u>: 44*

<u>Book Prices Current</u>: 44*

"Book was Writ of Late call'd Tetrachordon, A": 26

Book-licensing: 51

<u>Book-Lore</u>: 44

Bookbinders: 40

Booker, Francis: 44. John: 114. L.: 58*

Books: 8*, 51*, 70, 44, 30, 40, 113. Confiscated and burned: 44. M's acquisition of: 30, 40. M's access to as a boy: 40. Bought in Italy: 44. M's promiscuous reading: 51. Manufacture: 40. M's praise of: 113. M on good and evil books: 51. And learning: 8*

Booksellers, London and Cambridge: 40

Bookshops (in London, Cambridge): 40

Booktrade: 40

<u>Bookworm</u>: 44

Boone, Thomas: 44

Boote, Anne: 44

Boötes: 73, 89, 3

Booth faction, the: 51

Booth: Anne: see Cope, Anne. Sir George: 38. Philip: 45. Wayne: 37, 110

Boothby, Sir B.: 58

Borck, Oluf: 44

Bordeaux-Neufville, Antoine de (French ambassador): 44

Bordeaux: 21. School at: 40. Gloss: 73

Border Ballads: 35

Boreas: 73, 90, 144

Boreel, Adam: 7. See also: Borellius

Borelius (Boreel), W. (Dutch envoy): 44

Borellius, Adam: 44

Boreman, Robert: 114

Boreplace: 45

Borges, Jorge Luis: 11, 39

Borghese Gallery: 27

Borgia: Alexander: 120. Caesar: 52, 122

Borinski, Karl: 5, 100

Boristhenes: 49

Borlase, Col. Nicholas: 44

Born, L. K.: 40

Borowe Hill Coppice: 45. See also: Borrowhill

Borrichius, Olaus: 44

Borromeo, St. Charles: 27

Borromini, Francesco: 6, 27*, 39

Borrowhill Copse: 44

Borrowing, literary: 20

Bors, Sir: 60

Borso of Ferrara: 39

Borzelli, A.: 6

Bos, Jean de: 44

Bosbury, co. Herefordshire: 44, 45

Boscan Almogaver, Juan: 56, 64

Boscawen, W.: 58

Bosch: 15

Boscham: 49

Boscobel: 59

Bosheth: 73

Bosporus: 49, 73. See also: Justling Rocks

Bosseville, William: 44

Bossu: 149, 117. Charles: 2, 15, 130

Bossuet: 15. J. B.: 32

Bostock: J. K.: 36. Robert (pr.): 44

Boston, publications: Boston Evening Post, The: 115; Boston Gazette and Country Journal, The: 115; Boston Magazine, The: 115; Boston Repertory: 115; Boston Spectator, The: 115

Boston, Lincolnshire: 49

Boston, Mass.: 44

Bostwick, Dr.: 103

Boswell: Jackson C.: 101. James: 9, 12, 35, 44, 58, 86. James (son of biographer): 44, 58, 136, 137, 146. Sir William: 10, 40

Bosworth, Henry: 44. Jacob: 44

Botany: 128*. See also: Trees and Plants

Boteler, Noel: 40, 44. See also: Butler

Botero, Giovanni: 40

Botsford, Mr.: 44

Bottari, S.: 6

Botticelli, Sandro: 5, 15, 27, 70, 74, 90

Bottkol, J. McG.: 6, 44

Bottral, Margaret: 141

Bottsford (Botsford), William: 44

Bouchard, J.-J.: 6*

Bouche, P. P.: 97

Boucher, F.: 97

Boughen, Edward: 114

Boughner, Daniel C.: 4, 68, 122, 123, 101, 85

Bouhereau: Elie: 44. Richard: 44

Bould, Edward. See Bold

Boullée, E. L.: 97

Boulliau, Ismael: 10

Boultbee, J.: 97

Boulter, Robert (pr.-bks., 1666-83): 44, 91

Boulting, William: 71

Boulton, John: 44

Bounden, J.: 58

Bouques, Charles de, Merveilles de Jésus-Christ: 74, 64

Bouquet, J. (pr.): 44

Bourbon, Mlle. de: 44

Bourchier, Henry, 6th Earl of Bath: 45. John: 40

Bourchier, Rachel. See Cranfield, Rachel

Bourdeaux-Neufville, Antoine. See Bordeaux-Neufville

Bourdelotius, Petrus: 44

Bourgeois, Emile: 44

Bourges (Avaricum): 123. See also: Alamanni

Bourke, Vernon J.: 81

Bourne: Mr.: 44. Benjamin: 79. E. C. E.: 66. Immanuel: 93. Nicholas (bks., 1609-57): 44, 91. Richard: 44. William: 44, 128

Bourse. See Exchange

Bouschart: 44. See also: Bochart

Bousset, W.: 113

Boustrophedon: 118

Boutflower, John: 40

Bouton, A. L.: 58

Bouwsma, William J.: 69

Bouyer, Louis: 93

Bovet, Richard: 142. Pandaemonium: 142

Bovie, Smith Palmer: 81

Bovillus, Carolus: 39

Bowden: John: 115; works: The Apostolic Origin of Episcopacy Asserted: 115; A Full-Length Portrait of Calvinism: 115. S.: 58

Bowdler, J.: 58

Bowdoin, James: 115. The Younger: 115

Bowe, William: 120

Bowen, Catherine Drinker: 115

Bower: Geoffrey: 44, 45. Thomas (scrivener): 40, 44*, 45*. William (scrivener): 44, 45

Bowers: Fredson: 1. R. H.: 29

Bowes, Jerome: 19

Bowghton: 45

Bowick, J.: 58

Bowle: 88. Oxford tutor: 94

Bowles, William L.: 58*, 37, 53, 146, 117. Influenced by PL: 58. Borrows from Comus: 58

Bowling: 40

Bowmen of the Arches: 73

Bowra: 17, 52, 56, 60, 76, 79, 86, 102, 110, 123, 125, 138, 142, 62, 122; From Virgil to M: 142; on PR: 143; on SA: 143; and Samson's sin: 143. Sir Maurice: 39, 93

Bowtell, Stephen: 38

Bowyer, William (pr.): 44

Box, G. H.: (and Oesterley): 40, 142. A Short Survey of the Lit. of Rabbinical and Medieval Judaism: 142

Boxall, Sir W.: 97

Boyce, Benjamin: 4, 44. S. P.: 63

Boyd: Eleanor: 44. Ernest: 60. Henry (critic): 88, 117*. Julian P.: 115. M. C.: 40. Zachary (Psalm paraphrases): 126

Boydell, John: 97, 146

Boydell's Shakespeare Gallery: 87

Boyette, Purvis: 75

Boyhood, M's: 51; images dealing with: 8

Boyle, Hon. Robert: 7, 10*, 16, 44, 93, 113, 114, 128, 142*, 115, 55. Works: The Christian Virtuoso: 142; A Disquisition about the Final Causes: 142; The Usefulness of Natural Philosophy: 142; Considerations touching the Style of the H. Scriptures: 74; The Works: 142

Boyle's Critical Dictionary: 88

Boyle's Head (sign): 44

Boyne, D. (publisher): 97

Boyneburg, Johann Christian von: 10

Boynton, Percy: 16

Boys, John: 44, 114, 93

Boyse, S.: 58

Bracciolini, F.: 6

Brach, Pierre de, Monomachie: 74, 64

Brachin, P.: 6

Brackenridge, Hugh Henry: 115. Works: Gazette Publications: 115; A Poem on Divine Revelation: 115; The Rising Glory of Americana: 115; Modern Chivalry: 115

Brackley: Elizabeth, Cranfield, Lady: 44. Lord (John Egerton): 121, 94, 64. Viscount: 40

Braclavia: 49

Bracton: 45. Henry of (de): 73, 116

Bradamante: 123. See also: Ariosto

Bradbrook, M. C.: 35, 39

Bradburn, E. W., PL for Children: 58

Bradbury: clergyman: 94. S.: 58. Rev. Thomas: 44

Braden Heath, Hampton, co. Salop: 44

Bradenham: 45

Bradford (Bradanford): 49

Bradford: A. M.: 58. Alden: 115; Memoir of the Life and Writings of Rev. Jonathan Mayhew, D. D.: 115. William: 147, 115; Reaveals Pilgrims' distrust of Roger Williams: 147; writes of life in Holland: 147; Of Plimoth Plantation: 115

Bradley: A. C.: 23, 59, 25; on Shakespeare's sonnets: 87. F. H.: 86, 125. Henry: 44. Thomas: 45. W.: 58

Bradnemore: 45

Bradner, Leicester: 44, 68, 64. Influence of Fletcher on M: 104. "Neo-Latin Dramas": 74

Bradshaigh, Lady: 117

Bradshaw Press Act: 103

Bradshaw-Isherwood, Mr.: 44

Bradshaw: 51, 112, 94. Family: 44. Henry: 40, 44, 64. John (Joannes Bradscianus, 1601-59, regicide): 28, 30, 33, 40, 44*, 45, 59, 73, 113, 144, 3, 38, 91, 103, 137, 55. John (another): 44. John A.: 100. Richard (agent to Russia): 44. Sarah: 40. William: 9

Bradshawe, John: 116

Bradstreet, Anne: 71

Bradwardine, Abp. Thomas: 93

Brady, N., <u>Aeneid</u>: 58. Robert: 116

Bragadino, A.: 6

Bragaglia, A. G.: 6

Braggadocchio: 123, 92. See also: Spenser

Bragge, Richard: 44

Brahe, Tycho: 3, 34, 40, 60, 73, 77, 100, 128, 144, 137, 149. <u>Opera</u>, ed. Dreyer: 77

Brahma: 47, 25. Brahamanas, Sanskrit: 118. Brahmanism: 47. See also: Indian religion

Brain: 128

Braine, T.: 97

Brainford. See Brentford

Braithwaite: 7. William C., works: <u>The Second Period of Quakerism</u>: 83; <u>The Beginnings of Quakerism</u>: 83

Bramante, D. D.: 6

Bramhall: a detractor: 94. John (Abp. of Armagh): 44*, 60, 114, 32, 91, 93; <u>Serpent Salve</u>: 91. Mr. (son of Abp.): 44. Dr. (Bp. of Londonderry): 103

Bramshill, facing: 45

Bramston, George: 44. J.: 58

Bran(d)t, Sebastian: 73, 44, 57. Ship of Fools: 44

Branagan, Thomas: 115. <u>The Flowers of Lit.</u>: 115

Brand, Mr.: 44. C. P.: 6. Hennig: 10

Brandeis, Irma: 53

Brandenburg: 103. Brandenburg, Frederick William, the Great Elector of (Brandenburgicus Ducatas): 49, 103, 91

Brandolinus, Lippus: 20

Brandon, S. G. F.: 36, 39

Brannell (Branwell): 44

Branston, Sir John: 40

Branthwaite, Michael: 6, 44, 103. William: 40

Brasenose College: 45

Brasidas: 123

Brasil: 49

Brass, Henry de: 44*, 103, 134

Brathwait(e), Richard: 54, 79, 114, 93

Bray: Dr.: 44. E. A.: 58. René: 100. William: see Evelyn

Braybrooke, Henry Seymour Neville, 9th Baron: 44

Braybrooke, Richard Griffin Neville, 3rd Baron: 44

Brazen George Inn, Cambridge: 40

Brazil: 150

Breacon. See Brecknock(shire)

"Bread." See PR Bread Street, London: 40, 44*, 45*, 103, 94

Breadstreet Hill: 40

Breath: 128

Breckly Copse: 44

Brecknock(shire): 45, 49. See also: Bricnam-Mere

Breda: France: 44. Declaration of: 51

Bredvold, Louis I: 1, 40, 44, 69, 86, 102, 113, 123, 128, 132, 142

Breerewood (Brerewood, Breerwood), Edward: 40, 73

Brehaut, Ernest: 128

Brehier, Emile: 5, 79

Brehmer's, Aug., (British) Successor, Ltd.: 44

Breife Memento, A. (William Prynne): 147

Breitinger, Johann Jacob: 149, 117

Bremen: 44*, 103; see also: Charles X. Prince Aop. of: 10. Senate of: 3

Bremensis Civitas (Brema): 49

Brendan, St.: 32

Brenius, Joannes, Hiob: 74

Brennecke, Ernest: 20, 40, 44*; John Milton the Elder and His Music

Brennus: 44, 73, 3

Brent: John: 45. Sir Nathaniel: 44; tr. Paolo Sarpi's Historia del Concilio Trilentino: 82. Susan: see Freeman, Susan

Brentford (Brainford, Branford): 40, 44, 49, 73, 103, 94

Brenz, Johann: 68

Brereley, John. See Anderton, James

Breres, Edmund: 45

Brereton: Peter: 44*. William: 10

Brerewood, Edward: 10, 44

Brest, France: 44

Brestensis Portus (Brivatis): 49

Bretaynes: 45

Breton, Nicholas: 108, 129, 133, 145, 93, 55

Brett: R. L.: 79. S. Reed: 60

Bretton, Spencer: 44

Breval, J. D. de: 58

Breve Sumario: 65

Breviarum Lingua Graeca: 40

Brevint, Daniel: 44

Brevissima Institutio seu Ratio Grammatices...(Lily): 20

Brewen. See Bruern

Brewengrange, co. Oxon.: 44, 45

Brewer, Wilmon: 68, 92

Brewerne: 44

Brewster, Sir David: 7. Edward (publisher): 44. Thomas (bks.): 44, 116

Brewster's "Martyrs of Science": 89

Breydenbach: 19

Brian: Sir Francis: 131. Rev. Robert: 44

Briant, Lemuel: 115

Briareo(u)s: 1, 56, 60, 73, 90, 123

Brias (Bryas, Dryas, son of Lycurgas): 44

Bribery: 82

Bribes, M accused of taking from Mylius: 44

Brice, Edmund: 7

Brick Lane, London: 44

Brickner, Richard M.: 60

Brickston, Peter: 44

Bricnam-Mere: 49. See also: Brecknock

Bridegroom, the: 72

Bridenbaugh, Carl: 115

Brideoke, Dr.: 45

Bridewell, London: 44, 45, 103

Bridge Street, Cambridge: 40, 49, 73

Bridge Ward: 45

Bridge, William: 59, 114, 120, 38, 93. Sermons by: 38

Bridge: 143. By Death and Sin: 143. Contrasted with ladder: 143. Like a saw: 143. Through Chaos, Biblical basis for: 119. See also: Sin and Death

Bridgeman: Sir John: 29. Sir Orland, Lord Keeper: 44. Richard: 44

Bridger: Lowther: 44. William Milton: 44

Bridges series: 45

Bridges, Dr. Robert: 40, 64, 86, 87*, 133, 88, 130, 150. Interest in M's artistry: 87. Attitude toward M: 87. Attitude toward PL: 87. Interest in prosody of SA: 87. Sonnets in M tradition: 87. Works: The Growth of Love: 87; Keats: 58; M's Prosody: 87, 109; Prometheus the Firegiver: 87

Bridges: Henry: 45. Bp. John: 93. Thomas: 44, 53. William: 44

Bridgewater (town), co. Somerset: 40, 44

Bridgewater: circle: 44. House: 44. MS.: 104, 27, 29*, 44, 136. Papers: 40

Bridgewater: family: 27, 40, 44. Frances Stanley, Countess of: 44. John Egerton: Viscount Brackley, 1st Earl of: 27, 64, 121, 120, 38, 94, 25, 1, 103, 29*, 113, 44, 91; see also: Egerton, Sir John; 2nd Earl of: 29, 44. Elizabeth Cavendish, Countess of: 44

Bridgman, P. W.: 37

Brief notes upon a late sermon: 103, 116, 147

Brief Anatomie of Women, A: 54

Brief Chronicle Of the Late Intestine Warr, A: 45, 116

Brief Description of Fanatics: 91

Brief Description of Genoa: 44

Brief History of the Unitarians: 78

Brief Lives: 45

Brief Relation of certain... passages, and speeches in the Starre-Chamber: 33*

Brief Relation of Some Affairs: 44

Brigg(s): Charles Augustus: 22. Henry: 10, 40. K. M.: 39. M. S.: 27. William: 16, 40

Bright polar sea in M's cosmology: 89

Bright: George: 40, 44. James W., "Relation of the Caedmonian Exodus to the Liturgy": 74. Timothy: 16, 41, 128. William: 44

Brightman: Edgar Sheffield: 137. Thomas: 38, 93

Brightwell: 45

Brinckl*é*, J. G., Electra: 58

Brindley, co. Chesire: 44

Brinkley: Florence: 108. Roberta Florence: 23, 60, 122, 133, 145, 93

Brinnin, John Malcolm: 60

Brinon, Jean: 64

Brinsley, John: 20*, 40*, 44, 54, 56, 114. Alarmed by the sectaries in Arraignment of the Present Schism: 147. The elder: 114. The younger: 114

Brinton: Anna C., Maphaeus Vegius: 74. Crane: 60

Briseis: 56

Bristol: 44, 45. Gazette: 146

Bristow (Eristow): 49, 73

Britain (Albion, Britannia, Samothea): 49, 3, 103, 51, 72, 25. See also: Utmost Isles

Britain's Remembrancer (Wither): 135

Britain's Triumph: 103, 116

Britannia (Blome): 45

Britannia (Camden): 45. See also: Camden, William

Britannia's Pastorals: 29, 88

Britenburgh: 49

British Chronicle: 44

British Museum: 44*, 45, 103. Brit. Museum, Additional Charters: 45. Additional MSS.: 45. Catalogue of Additions to the MSS. in: 44. Cottonian Charters: 45*. Harleian Charters: 45. Harleian MSS.: 45. Lansdowne MSS.: 45. Library: 40. Add. MS. 5584: 40. Royal (Reg) MSS.: 45. Add. MS.: 5843: 40. Add. MS.: 10,338: 40 British, Journal (publications): Archeological Assn.: 44. Of Ophthalmology: 44

British Record Society, Publications of the: 45

British Themis: 3

British: Academy: 40, 143, 92; proceedings of Academy: 44, 144. Apollo: 58. Chronologist: 44. Council of Fine Arts Committee: 44. Critic: Empire: 45. History: 40. British islands: 3. Isles: 3. Name: 3. Nation: 3 War: 3

Britons: 3, 32

Britons: 44, 3

Brittain's Ida: 15

Britten, Richard: 40

Brittington: 45

Britton: John: see Aubrey. Lionel, Hunger and Love: 35

Britwell, co. Bucks.: 44

Broad Church Party: 51

Broad Street. See Bread Street

Broadbent, J. B.: 17, 23*, 29, 37, 66, 75, 81, 86, 105, 110, 111, 123, 127, 128, 14, 32, 36, 53, 93, 101, 106, 140. Works: "M's Rhetoric": 74; "Links between Poetry and Prose in M": 60; "M's Hell": 60; Some Graver Subject: An Essay on PL: 60*, 48

Broaddus, Andrew: 115. The Age of Reason and Revelation: 115

Broadgates Hall, Oxford: 40

Broadhead, H. T.: 58

Broadhurst, Jean: 16

Broadley, A. M.: 44

Brobdingnag: 139, 72

Brocardus, Jacob: 40

Brocas, Elizabeth. See Cotton, Elizabeth

Brochard, James: 143. Glassy sea and the gospel: 143

Brockbank: J. P.: 93. Philip, on cyclical rhythm of light and darkness in M: 61

Brocke, James: 44

Brocklesby, Richard: 117

Brockunier, Samuel Hugh: 115

Brockway, Thomas: 115. The Gospel Tragedy: An Epic Poem: 115

Broken style, Bentley on: 88

Brokesby family: 45. Brokesby, Jane: 44, 45. Brokesby, Jane (Powell): 45

Brokesley. See Brokesby

Brome: family: 45. Mr.: 45. Mrs. (Hampden): 45. Audrey (Man): 45. Sir Christopher: 45*. Edmund (Browne): 44, 45*. Eleanor (Windsor): 45. Elizabeth: 44, 45. Elizabeth (Weynman): 45. Frigwith: 45. George (Broome): 45. Henry (bks.): 44, 45, 91. Jane: 45. John: 45*. Sir John: 45. Margaret (Rous): 45. Mary: 45. Nicholas: 45. Richard: 108. Robert: 45. Thomas: 45. Ursula: see Whorwood. William: 45

Bromehead, Joseph: 44

Bromeley: 7

Bromfield, Col. Lawrence: 44

Bromhall, Thomas: 142. Works: Learned Treatise Confuting the Opinions of the Sadduces: 142; Treatise of Specters: 142

Bromion: 25

Bromius: 73

Bromley, W.: 97

Bronchorst, Johann: 32

Bronson, W. C.: 58

Bronte: Charlotte: 136. Emily: 133

Bronze Age: 36

Bronzino, Allesandro: 27

Brook, Fulke Greville, Lord: 103. See Brooke

Brooke: 130. Family: 45. Dorothea (George Eliot's character), on M: 87. H., Constantia: 58. Henry: 147; wrote The Charity of Church-Men: 147. Lord: 44, 45, 144*, 134; his Discourse and M's Of Prelatical Episcopacy: 144; M's debt to: 144; his tolerance: 144; A Discourse Opening the Nature of...Episcopacie: 147; see also: Greville, Sir Fulke; Willoughby, Robert. Nathaniel (bks., 1646-77): 91. Ralph: 44. Sir Robert Greville, 2nd Baron: 44, 73, 51. Rupert: 35, 86. S.: 99. S. A.: 68. Thomas: 40. Tucker: 60. William T.: 122

Brooklyn, N.Y.: 44

Brooks Wharf: 44

Brooks: Anthony: 44. Cleanth: 1, 4, 12, 23, 29, 60, 79, 81, 86, 100, 102, 105, 110, 125, 128*, 14, 61, 93, 101, 109, 131, 146, 148, 21, 25; ambivalence in M's religous feelings: 61; dramatic irony and tension in Comus: 61; on M's pagan vs. Christian poetic tensions: 61; on the vision of promise and hope in Lycidas: 61; and Hardy, John E.: 1*, 29, 59, 139; Poems of Mr. John Milton: 74. E.

L.: 64. Nathan: 116

Brooks: 130

Broome: (Brome), George (scrivener): 44, 45. William: 58; influenced by Lycidas, Il Penseroso: 58

Brosted: 45

Brother(s) (Younger and Elder in Comus): 29*, 40, 73, 72*

Brothers Karamazov, The: 52

Brougham, Lord Henry, on M: 87

Broughton: B., Views: 58. Dorothy: 128. Hugh: 40, 42, 74

Broukhusius, Janus: 64

Brouncker, Lord William: 10

Brown: A. R.: 118. Charles Raymond: 115. Clarence Arthur: 115. Driver and Briggs Hebrew Lexicon of O.T.: 41, 43. (Browne), Edmond: see Brome. Eleanor G.: 8, 9, 20, 44, 59, 110, 128, 144, 92, 21. Hawkins: 44; De Animi Immortalitate: 44. J. Wood: 128. James, D. D., Britain Preserved: 58, 128. James (freemason): 58. John: 44, 116, 143. John, D.D., poem on moonlight: 58; a profane use of churches: 143. John Edwin: 16. Lancelot: 70. Louise Fargo: 9, 83; The Political Activities of the Baptists and 5th Monarchy Men in England during the Interregnum: 83. N., "North-Country Wedding": 58. Norman O.: 75, 118, 32. R. C.: 70. Robert: 44, 58, 32. Ruth Wentworth: 115. Samuel (pr.): 44. Sir Thomas: 44, 58, 69, 84, 132, 64. W.: 45. W. H.: 97. William: 64

Brownbaker's Hall: 44

Browne: Edward: 123. Emma: 143; worships God in window: 143. Hablot K.: 97. Isaac Hawkins: 44, 58. John: 40. M., imitates Lycidas: 58*. Martin: 45. Moses: 117. R. C.: 1, 19, 33. Sir Richard: 44. Robert, 1550-1633: 7, 9, 45, 114, 147; leader of the 1st separatists: 147; wrote A Treatise of Reformation without Tarrying for Anie: 147. Samuel (bks. at Hague, 1543-60): 91. Thomas: see separate entry. William of Tavistock: 16, 40, 29, 44, 73, 84, 108, 128, 129, 133, 26, 32, 39, 132, 91, 117; influence: 55; Britannia's Pastorals: 82

Browne, Sir Thomas: 1, 7, 15*, 16, 17, 18, 19, 24, 35, 40, 44, 45, 59, 76, 79, 86, 102, 108, 114*, 124, 128*, 129, 135*, 136, 133, 32, 142, 145*, 36, 38, 39, 71, 91, 93*, 109, 115, 130, 131, 146, 150, 101. Works: Religio Medici: 60, 142, 83; on dangers of knowledge: 83; Pseudodoxia Epidemica: 144, 36; Christian Morals: 60. Browne, Sir Thomas, The Works of: 45

Browning: 149. Elizabeth Barrett: 16, 65, 98, 142; reaction to PL: 87; sonnets of: 37; Sonnets from the Portuguese: 87. John: 44. Robert: 1, 40, 44, 45, 86, 95, 105, 139, 3, 26, 39, 46, 71, 92, 64, 109, 137; version of the Agamemnon quoted: 95; on the sonnet: 87

Brownists (Brownism): 7, 44, 73, 103, 147, 38, 92. Antagonism to kingship: 147. Imprisonment: 147. Influence of: 147. Radical implications of their reforming zeal: 147. Brownists Humble Petition (author unknown): 147

Broxolme, Charles: 54

Bruce, Robert (the): 40, 45, 93

Bruegal: 27

Bruern (Brewen): 45

Bruges (city): 49, 3

Bruges: Agnes (Ayloffe): 45; John: 45

Brunacci, G.: 6

Brunanburg (Bruneford, Wendune): 49, 3. See also: Glendale

Brunel, Sir M.: 97

Brunelleschi, F.: 6

Brunetto Latini. See Latini, B.

Brunetto: 40

Bruni: 40, 3. Leonardo (Aretino): 18, 93

Brunne (town): 49

Brunner, E.: 15. Emil: 47, 93, 48; Man in Revolt: A Christian Anthropology: 48. H.: 9

Brunnquell, Ludwig: 7

Bruno Astensis, St.: 36, 99. Expositions on the Pentateuch: 36

Bruno, Giordano: 5, 7, 27, 34, 40, 77, 112, 113, 114, 122, 123, 39, 71, 93, 55, 13. Works: De gli Eroici Furori: 60, 74; Lo Spaccio de la Bestia Trionfante: 60; Infinito Universo: 77

Brunschvicg, Léon: 81

Bruser, Fredelle: 69, 101

Brushfield, T. N.: 44

Brussels, Belgium: 44, 49, 97

Brut, legend of: 93

Brute: 73

Brutishness: 122, 123. Feritas, contrary of heroic virtue: 123*, 122

Bruto, Giovanni: 40, 64

Brutus (legendary founder of Britain and grandson of AEneas): 40, 90

Brutus (pen-name): 44. Lucius Junius: 44, 73. Marcus Junius: 60, 73, 103. The Trojan: 123, 72

Brutus (Cicero): 20

Bruxelleae. See Brussels

Bruyne, Edgar de: 5, 79, 93

Bryan: Dr. (of Coventry): 40, 97. Daniel: 115; Oration on Female Education: 115. Michael: 44. Robert A.: 37, 101

Bryanston: 45

Bryant: 149. Joseph A., Jr.: 19, 44, 58, 93. William Cullen (Homer): 58, 115

Bryce, James, Studies in History and Jurisprudence: 83

Brydges: Egerton: 63, 97, 146; considered political controversy harmful to M: 87; Life of M: 87. Robert: 56. Sir S. E.: 45, 57, 58; on M's sonnets: 58

Bryskett, Lodowick: 27, 33, 64

Bryson, W. A.: 58

BTR News: 44

Buber, Martin: 23, 125

Buc (Buck), Sir George: 40

Bucanus, Gulielmus: 93

Buccina: 121

Buccleuch and Queensberry, Dukes: Walter Francis Scott, 5th: 44; William Henry Walter Montagu-Douglas-Scott, 6th: 44; Walter John Montagu-Douglas-Scott, 8th: 44

Bucer, Martin: 20, 30*, 31, 40, 41, 42, 44, 3, 103, 54, 59, 60, 68, 74, 112, 113, 3, 32, 38, 82, 93, 99, 55. Works: De Regno Christi: 60; Sacra Quattuor Evangelia: 60.

Bucerian conception of Christian Kingdom: 38

Buchan, J.: 9, 144

Buchanan: 132. Edith: 101. George: 6, 9, 20, 40, 42, 44, 60, 73, 90, 116, 26, 32, 82, 88, 64, 148, 117, 55, 21; works: Franciscanus: 88; Rerum Scoticarum Historia: 82. James: 88, 117. J., 6 Books of PL: 58

Buchanan's Head (sign): 44

Bücher Mosis, Die: 65

Buchlein Adam, Das: 65

Buchler, Joannes: 20, 40, 44. Buchler, John, Thesaurus: 91. Phrasium Poeticarum Thesaurus, ed. Phillips: 44

Buck, Collections: 44

Buck: Albert: 16. John: 40. P.: 9

Buckenham, Richard: 40

Buckeridge, John, Bp. of Ely, sermon: 126

Buckhurst, Lord: Spenser's letter to: 88

Buckingham Palace, decoration of the garden pavilion: 97*

Buckingham, co.: 49

Buckingham: Countess of: 57. Duke of: 144. George Villiers, Duke of: 20, 33, 40, 44, 57, 73, 103, 103, 116, 64; Essay on Poetry: 58; see also: Villiers, George. Thomas: 115

Buckingham: 49, 130

Buckinghamshire: 45*, 103, 62

Buckle, H. T.: 34

Buckler, John (artist): 44, 73

Bucklesham, co. Suffolk: 44

Buckley: George T.: 128. William: 40

Bucknell, co. Oxon.: 44

Bucks county: 44

Budden, John: 64

Buddha: 34, 86. Buddhism: 47, 71.

See also: Indian religion

Budé: Eugène: 40. Guillaume: 18, 40, 123

Budeus: 10

Budge, Sir Frederick: 40

Budgen, F.: 23

Budworth, J., "Windermere": 58

Buelth: 49

Buff, F.: 122

Buffeid, John: 44

Buffler, Peter: 42

Buffon: Comte de: 32. Georges Louis de: 87

Buffum, Imbrie: 27

Bugge, Richard: 45

Buhl, F. P. W.: 40

Bukofzer, M(anfred) F.: 27, 39

Bulendun: 49

Bulgarini, Bellisario: 111

Bulkeley, J.: 58

Bull Head Tavern: 44, 103

Bull Inn, London: 40

Bull-baiting: 40

Bull: Bp. George: 142; Sermons and Other Discourses: 142. John (composer): 44

Bullen, A. H.: 45

Bulletin of the History of Medicine: 44

Bulletin of Medical Library Association: 44

Bullingdon (Bolington) hundred, co. Oxon.: 44

Bullingdon (Bullington): 45

Bullinger, Henry (Henrich): 41, 54, 68, 79, 123, 142, 143, 32, 38, 93, 101. The keys: 143. And glassy sea: 143. Works: The Christian State of Matrimony: 109; Fiftie Godlie and Learned Sermons, trans. H.I.: 74; The Decades: 142

Bullokar: John: 40. William: 20, 40, 44, 97

Bullough: G.: 86. Geoffrey: 128, 144

Bullyn (Bulleyn), Alicia: 44

Bulow, Hans von: 39

Bulstrode family: 29, 44

Bulteel: Mr.: 44, 45. Jean: 10. Peter: 45

Bulwer-Lytton, Edward George: 16. "M": 87

Bunce, James: 44

Bundt, Count Christian: 16, 103

Bundy, Murray W.: 5, 41, 3, 142, 137. "M's View of Education in PL": 83, 113

Bungus, Petrus: 100*

Bunhill Fields or Row (Artillery Walk), London: 44*, 103, 94

Bunny, Edmund (1540-1618): 44, 91, 93

Bunting Preacher: 40

Bunyan, John: 1, 7, 9, 15, 17, 23, 27*, 33, 35, 37, 47, 60, 76, 79, 108, 110, 114, 121, 122, 133, 32, 71, 92, 93, 94, 130, 149, 117. Prose of: 87. Works: Pilgrim's Progress: 79, 46, 109; Grace Abounding: 109

Buonamici, F.: 6

Buonarotti, Michelangelo. See Michelangelo

Buonconte: 111. Guido de: 111

Buonmattei, Benedetto: 6, 44, 70, 111*, 3, 38, 120. M to: 112. See also: Bonmattei

Buontalenti, B.: 6

Burbage, Richard: 39, 21

Burckhardt: 130. Jakob: 18, 23, 27, 60, 39, 62. Sigurd: 23, 53

Burdach, Konrad: 18

Bürde: 10

Burdeaux (Bordeaux, Burdegala): 49

Burden, Dennis: 110, 123, 101, 106

Burdett-Coutts family: 44

Bureau Or Repository of Lit., Politics, and Intelligence, The: 115

Buresch, C.: 4

Burford Records, The: 45

Burford, co. Oxon.: 44, 45

Burg, Burgesse, Burghers: 97

Burgersdijck, Franco Peter: 40*

Burges: Cornelius: 38; sermons by: 38. G., "Ajax": 58. J. B.: 58. Tristam: 115; Liberty, Glory and Union, or American Independence: 115. "Burges, To Master John": 45

Burgess: 58. Anthony: 40, 93. Cornelius: 9. Theodore: 21. Thomas: 63. W. H.: 9

Burgh: Dr.: 70. James: 115; The Art of Speaking: 115. William: 44

Burghclere, Lord: 58

Burghley, Lord: 33, 54

Burgidolensis, Herveus: 60

Burgoyne, General: 58

Burgum, Edwin Berry: 108

Burgundie (Burgondy): 49

Burgundy, Mary of: 73

Burial, M's: 44

Buridan: 128

Burke: 133. Arthur M.: 44. Edmund: 5, 58, 60, 87, 105, 136, 46, 71, 97, 115, 146, 148, 150, 117; praises M: 58. John: 45. Kenneth: 15, 67, 69, 110, 125, 39

Burkitt, F. C.: 36

Burlamachi, Philip: 120

Burleigh, John, H. S.: 81

Burlesque blank-verse poetry: 58*

Burlington Magazine: 44

Burlington, Lord: 97

Burman, Peter: 44*

Burmann, Franz: 47; on faith and works: 47. Pieter: 64

Burnaby, John: 81, 93

Burnell, Thomas: 44

Burnet, Bp.: 103

Burnet: 130. Bp.: 28. Bp. Gilbert: 44, 58, 116, 93, 115. J.: 132. James: 115; An Oration Delivered on the 4th of July, 1799: 115. Professor: 40. Thomas: 44, 128, 32, 93; The Sacred Theory of the Earth an influential theodicy: 87. Burnet's History of My Own Time: 116

Burnett: Frances Hodgson: 118. George: 6, 44; ed. Prose Works: 44. John: 48; "The Socratic Doctrine of the Human Soul": 48

Burney: 121. Charles: 40, 58, 88; Charles Jr.: 117; Charles Sr.: 117. E. F.: 97*. F.: 58

Burnley, James: 88

Burns, Robert: 1, 58, 98, 120, 71, 82, 130, 146

Burr, George L.: 142. The Lit. of Witchcraft: 142

Burrell Rhetoric lecture at Cambridge: 40 Burrough: Charles: 44. John: 44. Stephen: 19. William: 44

Burrell, Lady S.: 58

Burroughs: 7. F.: 97. Jeremiah: 114, 120, 93

Burrow Bridge: 73

Burrow, Hugo: 44

Burrows, John: 44

Bursebell: 45

Burt, T(homas) S.: 58, 93

Burthogge, Richard: 142. An Essay upon Reason and the Nature of Spirits: 142

Burton Constable, co. York: 44

Burton-on-Trent: 45

Burton, co. Sussex: 44

Burton: Mr.: 44. Dr. Henry: 9*, 66, 103, 116, 147, 38, 55. Toleration for Independent worship: 147. Conformitie's Deformity is against a state church: 147. Persecuted and imprisoned by the bishops: 147. For God and King, pamphlet against the prelates: 147. Narration relates his persecution: 147. Protestation Protested: 147. Vindiciae veritatis, portrays Jesus as a heretic: 147. Writes A Vindication of Churches Commonly Called Independent: 147

Burton: Hezekiah: 44. John: 45. Richard: 102. Robert: see separate entry. Samuel: 44*, 45*. Thomas: 44, 120. William: 20, 144

Burton, Robert: 1, 4, 8, 15, 16, 33*, 40, 44, 52, 68, 73, 84, 108, 114, 122, 128, 129, 133, 144*, 142*, 145, 53, 88, 91, 93, 54, 109, 148, 117, 55. Intensive study: 144. Marriage: 144. And L'Allegro: 144. And Il Penseroso: 144. And Comus: 144. The Anatomy and PL: 144*. The Fall: 144. Devils: 144. The well: 144. Cosmography: 144. Divine mysteries: 144. Temperance: 144. War condemned: 144. And M compared: 146. Works: Anatomy of Melancholy: 142, 144*, 80; "Digression of the Nature of Spirits": 142. "Abstract": 144. See also: Anatomy of Melancholy

Burtt, E. A.: 23, 79, 142. Works: The Eng. Philosophers from Bacon to Mill: 142; The Metaphysical Foundations of Modern Physical Science: 142

Bury, Suffolk: 49. Bury St. Edmunds, co. Suffolk: 44

Bury: J.: 44. Jacob: 116. J. B.: 132. R. G.: 50. Richard: 40

Busby, T.: 58

Busenello, G. F.: 6

Bush, Douglas: 1, 4, 9, 12, 19, 20, 29, 37, 40, 52*, 66, 68, 77, 76, 86*, 95, 98, 102, 105, 112, 110, 111, 122, 123, 125, 127, 128, 135, 139, 142, 143, 144, 39, 53, 141, 62, 85, 91, 101*, 64, 106, 130*, 137, 146, 148, 140*, 21, 48. On misunderstanding of the theme of PL: 83. Christ's divinity and humanity contrasted: 61. His interpretation of its theme: 83. On Samson's request for guidance: 61. On M's humanism: 83. On Mask: 104. On Lycidas: 104. On M's puritanism: 104. On Satan's tragic potentialities: 61. On M: 80. Jonson's influence on M: 143. Comus unromantic: 143. On M's asceticism: 143. Spiritual struggle in Lycidas: 143. M's humanism: 143. On M's religion: 143. And M's merit: 143. Works: "PL" in Our Time: 60, 95, 142, 48; Eng. Lit. in the Earlier 17th Century: 74; Mythology and the Renaissance Tradition in Eng. Poetry: 60; Renaissance and English Humanism: 74, 77

Bush, Geoffrey: 69

Bushe, A.: 58

Bushell: Thomas: 45. William: 44

Busher, Leonard: 60. Baptist tolerationist, wrote Religious Peace: 147

Bushnell, Horace: 137

Business practice and theory: 8

Busino, Orazio: 29

Busiris: 73, 90, 123, 144

Busnelli, G.: 5

Bussell, Thomas. See Bassel

Bust of M (Simon or Pierce): 44

Bust, Henry: 64

Butcher: Francis: 44. S. H.: 27, 70, 123, 92, 64, 101

Butler: Anne (Truelove), cousin: 44. Bp.: 94. Charles: 20, 40*, 44, 56, 128, 135*, 144; The Feminine Monarchie: 88. Cuthbert: 81. E. M.: 142; Ritual Magic: 142. H. E.: 128, 64. Bp. John: 32. (Boteler), Noel: 44, 45. Samuel (1612-80): 15, 35, 40, 44, 59, 100, 105, 114, 116, 142, 145, 32, 71, 64, 115, 131, 146, 148, 117; works: Geniune Remains: 82; Remains: 53; Hudibras: 15, 87, 115; Satires and Miscellaneous Poetry and Prose: 142. Thomas: 44

Butler: 35, 130

Butlin, M.: 97

Butt: G.: 58. T.: 58

Butter: Nathaniel (pr., bks., 1604-64): 44, 91. Peter: 110

Butterfield: H.: 142; The Origins of Modern Science: 142. L. H.: 115

Butterworth, C. C.: 40

Buttingtun: 49

Butts: Henry: 40. Thomas: 39, 146

Buxtorf Rabbinical Bible: 22*

Buxtorf, Johann(es): 1, 40, 41*, 42, 44, 68, 22, 142. Lexicon Chaldaicum, Talmudicum et Rabbinicum: 41, 142. Buxtorf II (Johannes, the Younger): 41, 44, 73, 22

Byfield: Adoniram (?): 44. Nicholas: 54, 93

Byles, Mather: 115*. Works: The Comet: 115; Eternity: 115; Goliah's Defeat: 115; Poems on Several Occasions: 115; The Glorious Rest of Heaven: 115; For the Memory of a Young Commande: 115

Byng, Alexander: 42

Bynneman, Henry (pr.): 40

Byrch, Agnes. See Ayloffe, Agnes

Byrch: William: 45

Byrd: 121. William: 40, 44, 115; The Secret Diary of William Byrd of Westover: 1709-11: 115

Byrom, John: 7, 58, 65, 32

Byron, George Gordon, Lord, 6th Baron: 1, 27, 31, 35, 44, 52, 58*, 65, 70, 86, 87, 107, 113, 118, 120, 136, 141, 46, 71, 97, 109, 130, 131, 146*, 149, 148, 150, 55. Influenced by PL: 58. On PL: 87. Glorification of Satan by: 83. Cain reviewed: 107. And M compared: 146. Others' reminiscences of: 146. The Byronic hero: 150. Works: Vision of Judgment: 146; Hints from Horace: 87, 146; Manfred: 87; Cain: 87, 146; Diary: 146; Letters: 146; Childe Harold's Pilgrimage: 146; Don Juan: 146; Eng. Bards: 146; Reply: 146

Byse, Fanny: 44. M on the Continent: 44

Byshop (Bishop), John: 93

Bysshe, E.: 58

Bythner, Victor: 40, 123

Bywater, Ingram: 70, 92, 101

Byzantine authors: 40. Greeks: 40. Histories: 44; in M's library: 113. Type: 40

Byzantium: 19, 144

-C-

C., A.: 91. See Coe, Andrew, Jr. (pr., 1644-67)

C., C.: 44

C., E. (pr.): 44. Ellen Cotes or Edw. Crouch (pr.): 91

C., E.: 44, 117. See also: Carey, E.

C., J.: 117

C., R.: 44

C., S.: 44. See also: M portraits (Cooper)

C., T. (pr.): 44, 91. Glass for the Times: 91

Cabala, Mysteries of State (1654): 40

Cabanis, Charles: 44

Cabannes, Camille: 16, 113

Cabbala: 39, 88, 7, 15, 40, 41, 42, 54, 68, 132, 139, 44, 112, 116, 123, 22, 142*, 144, 32, 55. Cabalists(ism): 73, 60, 114. Cabalistic ideas: 93; theories: 139; writings: 40, 7. Allusion to M: 44. See also: Kabbalah

Cabell, James Branch: 137

Cabinet of Characters, A.: 45

Cabinet Council, The: 116, 103. See also: Sir Walter Raleigh

Cabot, Sebastian: 19

Cacciaguida: 111

Caccini, Guilio: 6, 39

Cacus: 44, 73, 90

Cadbury, John: 44

Cadbury: North: 45; South: 45

Cade: Ann: see Comyn alias Chilcott. Anthony: 93. Waller: 45

Cadence: 121. Equals rhythm in Lofft's terminology: 88

Cadiou, René: 107. Says Rufinus does not do violence to Origen's works: 107

Cadiz. See Gades

Cadmus: 1, 90, 92. Founder of Thebes: 73, 111. Public executioner: 73

Cadwell, J. (pr., 1659-1662): 91

Cady, Edwin, H.: 115

Caecias: 73, 90, 144

Caecilius Metullus, Lucius: 73

Caedmon: 4, 15, 77*, 102, 129, 36, 46, 94, 99, 64, 55. Works: Caedmonian Genesis: 65*, 149; poems: Caedmon Poems, tr. Charles W. Kennedy: 74; Christ and Satan, ed. Merrel D. Clubb: 74; Exodus, fragment: 74; Genesis A, fragment: 74; Genesis B, fragment: 74. See also: Junius, Franciscus

"Caelius Rediginus": 40

Caen Book (ex libro Cadomensi): 73

Caeneus: 73

Caer-Caradoc: 49

Caerleon (Caerlegion, Caerose): 49

Caermarthenshire (Carmarthen): 45

Caernavon: 44

Caersws, co. Montgomery: 40, 44

Caesar (Lucan): 1

Caesar: Augustus: 122, 123, 128; see also: Ajax. Gaius Julius: 73. Julius: 20, 40, 44, 51, 56, 60, 120, 122, 123, 128, 64, 3, 82, 21; Commentaries: 82. Octavius: 3. Pagan: 3

Caesar: Sir Charles: 44

Caesarea: 49

Caesarius, Johann: 40

Caesura in Greek poetry: 40

Caetani family: 6

Caffey, George: 44

Caffi, F.: 6

Caiaphas: 73

Cailleux, Ludovic de: 65

Cain and Abel, sacrifices of: 126

Cain the Wanderer: 65

Cain, A Mystery: 65

Cain: 2, 4, 73, 102, 127, 141, 143, 32, 72*, 25. And insincere sacrifice: 143

Cain's Lamentations over Abel: 65

Caine, T. Hall: 87, 146

Cairns: David: 93; The Image of God in Man: 48. Earle E.: 93. Huntington: 93; comments of, on, PL: 83. Wm. B.: 115

Cairo: 19

Caius: 77. John: 40

Cajetan (Cajetanus): 24, 88, 99. Cardinal, Jacob de Vio: 142. Cardinal Thomas: 32, 93. Tomasso de Vio Gaetano: 68. Thomas, In Librum Job: 74

Cal To All The Souldiers Of The Armie (Wildman): 147

Calaber, Quintus: 44

Calabrese, G.: 6

Calabria: 19, 49, 73

Calais, France: 44, 45, 103

Calamato, Allesandro: 60

Calamy: Edmund (1600-66): 44, 51, 114, 38, 91; sermon by: 38. Edward: 93

Calandrini, Jean Louis: 30, 44

Calandrino: 73, 3

Calandrinus: 73

Calater (Calaterium): 49

Calboli, Rinieri da: 111

Calchas: 73, 3

Calcott, A. W.: 97. Samuel: 45

Caldcleugh, W. G.: 58

Calderón: 92 Calderón de la Barca, Don Pedro: 39, 145

Caledonia(n): 73. Caledonian Market, London: 44

Calendae (Statius): 88

Calendar, Christian: 44. Calendar of Clarendon Papers: 44. Calendar of the Committee for (on) Compounding: 44*. Calendars of State Papers, Domestic: 44*, 103, 116. Calendars of State Papers, Venetian: 44. Calendars of Treasury Books: 44

Calendrium Carolinum: 44

Calepino, Ambros(g)io: 40, 22, 123

Cales: 49, 73. See also: Gades

Calfhill, James: 68

Caliban: 2, 128

California and Oregon Trail, The: 98

Caligula, Gaius Caesar: 73

Calisthenes: 128

Calisto (Callisto): 73, 90

Callander, John (of Craigforth): 40, 41, 57*, 58, 88

Callicles (the rhetorician): 60, 73, 112

Calliepeia (Drax): 20

Callimachus: 15, 30, 40, 44, 58, 60, 70, 73, 74, 90, 120, 64, 133, 3, 62, 88, 94, 101. Works: Hymn to Jupiter: 88; Hecale: 74

Calling: 9, 63

Callinus of Ephesus: 40

Calliope: 73, 90, 111, 72

Cailot, J.: 97

Calmet, Augustine: 142. The Phantom World: 142

Calne: 45. Caln.: 49

Calovius, Abraham: 22, 99

Calpurnius, Siculius: 64

Calston: 45

Calthorp: 45

Calton: 99, 88. Mr.: 45, 57. Sir Francis: 44. Thomas: 44

Calvary: 32, 72, 103

Calvert: Oliver: 40. Sarah: 44, 91

Calves' heads (sophomores): 40. Calves-Head Club: 44

Calvin, John: 1, 9*, 15*, 17*, 18, 23, 24*, 27, 40, 41, 42, 44, 47*, 50, 51, 54, 60, 63, 67, 68, 73, 74, 77, 79*, 83, 102*, 103, 108, 110, 113, 114*, 122, 123*, 128, 134, 137, 142*, 143, 146, 147, 22, 32*, 36*, 38*, 39, 43, 71*, 82, 93*, 99*, 64, 3, 143, 101, 109, 115, 148*, 48, 25. Differs from the Independents: 147. Prepared the way for democratic philosophy: 147. Repudiates the doctrines of Knox: 147. Shadow on family life: 147. On: accommodation, Antichrist, Hell, the Fall, God's anger, Holy Spirit, formalism, sacrament and scripture, faith: 47. Theology of: 147. On decorum: 66. On the dignity of man: 48. "Perfection" defined by: 83. Influence of, on Robert Barclay: 83. Cited on divorce: 83. Views on preaching: 143. Place among Protestants: 143. And Geneva Bible: 143. Calvin Theology: 48. Works: "Commentary on Daniel": 60; Commentary on Genesis: 77*, 142, 36; Institutes: 33, 147, 94; The Institutes of the Christian Religion: 60, 142, 48, 77; Commentarie upon ...Josue (tr. William Fulke): 74; Commentaries upon Daniell (tr. Arthur Golding): 74; Four Last Books of Moses: 74*; Harmonie upon... Matthewe, Marke, and Luke (tr. Eusebius Pagit): 74; Institutes (tr. Thomas Norton): 74*; Sermons...upon ...Job (tr. Arthur Golding): 74; A Commentary upon the Prophecie of Isaiah: 142; The Holy Gospel... Christ...John...of M. John Calvin: 142

Calvinsism: 7, 60, 63, 81, 113, 114*, 38*, 71, 78. M's break with: 83. And grace: 52. Opposed by Arminius and the Cambridge Platonists: 83. Opposed by Baptists, Mennonites, and Quakers: 83. Imputed righteousness: 52. M's agreement with: 83. And the outsider: 52

Calvinists: 9*, 34, 40, 44, 73, 136, 71. The Calvinist: 71

Calypso: 90

Cam (river): 40, 44, 3, 21, 103

Cama: 49. See also: Nagay

Camalodunum (Colchester, Colnchester): 49. See also: Maldon

Camball: 3

Cambalu (Cathaia, Paquin), alternative name for Peking: 49, 73, 144. See also: Cathay

Cambaluc: 19

Cambden family: 20

Camberwell, London: 44

Cambridge: 121, 135, 3, 32, 72, 94, 150. Visitation of: 45. See also: Cambridge University. Cambridge (Cantabrigia, Grantbrig), town: 40, 42, 44*, 49, 51, 57, 70, 112

Cambridge University: 19, 29, 40, 44*, 45*, 49, 51, 113, 62, 137, 21, 103*. Library: 44

Cambridge (Milton): M at: 16, 20, 30*, 40*, 136. His opinions of: 87, 94. English poems: 55. Popular at: 58*. Views on: 20, 30*. Account of: 55. Prose writings: 55. Latin poems: 55

Cambridge Bibliography of Eng. Lit.: 44

Cambridge History of Eng. Lit.: 3

Cambridge Manuscript: 15, 16, 44, 50*, 70*, 73, 76, 112, 63, 129. Described: 55. Comus date: 55. Lycidas date: 55. Sonnet, dates: 55. See also: Manuscripts; Letter to a Friend (M's)

Cambridge Modern History, The: 59

Cambridge Platonists: 1, 15, 63, 81,

112, 83, 132, 78, 92, 109. "Perfection" defined by : 83. Perfection achieved by man through reason and experience, taught by: 83. M's indebtedness to: 83. Influence of, on the sectaries: 83. M's idea of perfection like (and unlike) that of: 83

Cambridge Portfolio: 44

Cambridge Review: 44

Cambridge, Mass.: 44

Cambridge, The Book of Matriculations ...in the Univ. of: 45

Cambridgeshire: 45, 49

Cambuscan: 73, 3

Cambyses: 73

Camden Society Publications: 44*, 45

Camden, Car(r)oll: 128, 93

Camden, William: 20, 40*, 42, 45, 51, 73, 82, 88, 93. Works: Greek Grammar: 20; Britannia: 144; Annales: 83, 82*

Camel: 42

Camelford (Gasulford): 49

Camenick: 49

Camerarius, Joachim: 10, 40, 66, 123, 99, 64. Phillip: 40, 128, 93

Camerini: 40, 120

Cameron: A.: 68. John: 73, 148

Camfield, Benjamin: 142, 93. A Discourse of Angels: 142

Camilla: 2

Camillus, our (i.e. Cromwell): 73, 123

Camm, John: 7

Camõe(n)s, Luis(z) de (Vaz): 15, 84, 133, 19, 65, 122, 123, 93, 115, 137, 64, 146, 150, 117. Lusiads: 115

Campagnac, E. T.: 23, 112, 135

Campailla, Tommaso: 65

Campanella, Thomas (Tommaso): 6, 7, 44, 79, 77, 128, 142. Works: Poetica: 74; The Defense of Galileo: 77, 142; An Apology for Galileo: 109

Campania: 44, 49. Campanian: 73

Campanus: 40

Campaspe (Lyly): 131

Campbell: Archibald: see Argyle, Marquis of. Colin: 27. John, 1st Baron: 44, 139. Joseph: 75, 76, 118. L.: 59. Lewis: 120, 148. Lily Bess: 23, 29, 58, 60, 68, 102, 122, 128, 133, 144, 64, 39, 93, 106; Divine Poetry and Drama in 16th-c. Eng.: 74. Roy, The Albatross: 35. Thomas: 58, 87, 146

Campeggi, Ridolfo, Lagrime di Maria Vergine: 74, 64

Campensem: 73

Campion: 121, 132, 133. Edmund: 82, 93. Edward: 44. Thomas: 20, 29*, 40, 56, 58, 59, 108, 39, 46, 55. William: 44

Campsey, John: 44

Camus: Albert: 14. Bp. Jean Pierre: 93

Camus: 1, 49, 104, 111, 21; in "Lycidas": 72. Rev. sire: 73

Can: 73. Cathaian: 1

Cana: 44

Canaan (Holy Land, Palestinus, Promis'd Land): 44, 49, 73, 3, 72. Spy of: 73. Canaanite(s), Canaanitish: 73, 68. See also: Israel; Palestine

Canace: 3

Canada: 19, 49, 3

Canariae Insulae (Canary Islands): 49, 32. See also: Azores; Hesperides; Palma; Teneriffe

Canaries: 19

Canby, Henry Seidel: 115

Cancellations, Bentley's: 88. Motives for: 88. Apparent metrical plausibility of: 88

Candace: 32

Candaor (Candahar): 49, 73, 19, 144. See also: Arachosia

Candelabrum: 20

Candidus, Pantaleon: 65. Candidus: 77

Candinos: 49

Candish, Hugh: 44, 45

Candlemas Day (Feb. 2): 40

Candy, Hugh C. H.: 16, 20, 44. "M's Early Reading of Sylvester": 74

Canidia: 73

Canker: 73

Canne, John: 9, 44, 113, 114, 144*, 147, 38. And M's Tenure: 144. Seneca quoted: 144. Tyrants to be resisted: 144. King's power limited: 144. Political power rests in people: 144. Kings subject to punishment: 144. And M: 144. Justification of regicide: 147. Works: The Golden Rule: 147; date of: 144; Time of Finding: 74

Canneh: 144

Cannibalism: 139

Canning: G.: 58, 87. Richard: 44

Cannon, Charles K.: 79

Canon law: 54

Canon Frome: 45. Canon-ffrome Court: 45

Canon: 121

Canonical hours: 24

Canons (summarized from Horace's Ars Poetica by Fabricius): 70

Canons Ashby: 45

Cantacuzene, John, Historia: 82

Cantbrig: 49

Canterbury (Caerkeynt, Cantuariensis, Doroverne): 44, 49, 3, 103

Canterbury Report, use of staff: 104

Canterbury Tales (Chaucer): 131

Canterbury, Abp. of: 103, 94. See also: Laud, Cranmer

Canterbury, Cathedral Register: 40

Canterbury, Prerogative Court of. See Prerogative Court of Canterbury

Canterbury's Dream (attr. to M): 44

"Canticle A": 98

Canticles: 2

Canticum de Creatione (Auchinleck MS): 65, 36. Canticum de Creatione (Trin. Coll. MS): 65

Canto fermo: 40

Canto, Charles: 44

Canton, G.: 58

Canute: 73

Canzone: 40, 132. Italian: 132

Caos, Il: 65

Cap(p)ellus, Ludovicus: 73. See also: Capel(l)

Capaccio, G. C.: 6

Capaneus: 111, 123

Cape of Good Hope: 19, 49, 150. Cape Verde: 144. See also: Ethiopian

Cape, the: 73

Capel(l): E.: 58. Edward: 88. Louis: 68, 22, 73. R.: 99. See also: Cappel

Capella, Martinus: 40

Capello, B.: 6

Capernaitans: 73

Capgrave, John: 93

Caphtor: 49. Sons of: 73

Capitals, used by the Richardsons to indicate emphasis: 88

Capito: 44, 73. Wolfgang F.: 40, 42

Capitol (Tarpeian Rock): 49

Capitol or capital: 50

Capitoline: 73

Capitolinus, Julius: 73

Caplan, Harry: 40

Cappadocian(s): 73, 32

Cappadocus: 49

Cappel, Louis. See Capel(l)

Capponi, Vincenzio, Marchese: 44

Caprara, Antonio: 120

Capras, tripudiantes: 73

Capreae: 19, 49

Capriano, G. P., Della Vera Poetica: 74

"Capt. or Col., or Knight in Arms": 26

Captain (as epic person): 122*

Captivity of Jews: 142

Capua, Francesco di: 5

Caracalla, Antoninus: 73

Caracci, Annibal: 128

Carapetyan, A.: 6

Caravaggio, M. Da: 6

Carbery: Richard Vaughan, 2nd Earl of: 30, 44; John Vaughan, 3rd Earl of: 44

Carbo, Caius: 73

Card-playing (only at Christmas): 40

Cardan, Jerome: 60, 73, 114, 128, 142*. Works: De Rerum Varietate: 142; De Subtilitate: 142; Hyperchen: 142; Opera Omnia: 142

Cardano, Geronimo (Gerolamo): 16, 40

Cardenas, (Lord) Don Alonzo (Alphonso): 44*

Cardew-Rendle, H. C.: 44

Cardi, Capt.: 44

Cardigan, co. Caridganshire: 44. Cardiganshire: 45

Cardinal, the French (Richelieu): 73

Cardouin (Cardoyn), Camillus (Camillo): 30, 44, 6

Carducci, G(iosue): 6, 40, 65, 120, 133, 64

Care, Henry: 128

Carelia (Karelia). See Charles X

Carensdale, Robert: 44

Caresano, Pier Antonio: 120

Carew: 120, 35, 133, 130. Matthew: 44. Richard: 1, 40. Sir Thomas: 15, 29*, 40, 59, 86, 38, 69, 39, 131, 146, 150, 64, 55; Caelum Britannicum: 94. Carew's Survey of Cornwall: 88

Carey: Edward: 44, 83. Elizabeth, suggested as Rosalinde: 83. G. S.: 58. H.: 58. Henry, Lord Hunsdon: 128. J.: 59. John: 39, 64, 148. Mathew: 115; The Olive Branch, Or Faults on Both Sides; Federal and Democratic: 115. N.: 94. Patrick: 131. Lady Philadelphia: 40. Sir Robert: 40

Carfax: 45

Cargill, Oscar: 44

Caribiae Insulae: 49

Carill. See Caryl

Carion: 128. Johann: 40, 93

Carisbrooke Castle: 45, 103

Carissimi, G.: 6

Carle, Lancelot de: 64

Carleton: Sir Dudley: 45; see also: Dorchester, Viscount. George (Bp. of Chichester): 10, 40

Carlile (Cairleil): 49

Carlisle: Earl of: 40, 58. Nicholas: 20

Carlo Emanuele II: 59

Carlson, C. Lennart: 115

Carlstadt, Andreas: 114

Carlyle, A. J.: Political Liberty, A History of the Conception in the Middle Ages and Modern Times. Carylye, A. J. and R. W.: 116. A History of Medieval Political Theory in the West: 83. J. A.: 5

Carlyle, Thomas: 7, 87*, 98, 111, 133, 136, 146, 25. M compared with Shakespeare: 87. On Shakespeare's sonnets: 87. Read M's prose: 87. Admired M's character: 87. Life of Schiller: 87

Carlyon, Dr.: 136

Carmarrthen. See Caermarthenshire

Carmel: "hilly promentory": 49, 73. Town: 49

Carmelites: 142

Carmen: 121. Carmen de Deo: 65. Carmen de Figures (Mancinelli): 20. Carmen de Moribus (Lily): 20, 40. Carmen de providentia divina: 65. Carmen heroicum: 65. Carmen Paschale: 65

Carmerthen. See Caermarthenshire

Carmichael, James: 40

Carmina (Horace): 70

Carmina Elegiaca (M): 40, 73

Carnal reliance: 123

Carnall, Geoffrey: 128

Carnap, Rudolf: 37

Carnarvon, Earl of: 58

Carnarvonshire: 45

Carne, Mr.: 45

Carneades: 4, 73, 3

Carnivals: 29

Carnokehill: 45

Carnovia. See Frederick William

Caro: 120. Annibale: 123, 130. Hannibal: 56, 145

Caroline, Queen: wife of George II: 1, 44, 88

Caroline: poetry: 129. Poets (Saintsbury): 131

Carolus: 115. Prince of Saxony: 64. Carolus I Britanniarum Rex: 91

Caron, Antoine: 39

Carpathian: 49. Wizard: 73

Carpathos: 90

Carpe diem: 69

Carpenter: Edward: 44, 71. H.: 71. John: 93. Nan Cooke: 100, 126, 21. Nathaniel: 114, 128, 32. Richard: 40, 93. Thomas: 45. William: 87, 146; on Tory biographers of M: 87; The Life and Times of John Milton: 87

Carpentier, J., de Marigny: 44, 91

Carr (River Char, Dorsetshire): 49

Carr: J., Filial Piety: 58. (Carre), Nicholas: 40, 73. R.: 40. Ralph: 93. Robert: 64, 39. W. W.: 58. William: 31

Carrafa, Vincenzo: 21

Carrara, Enrico: 64

Carrell: Mr.: 44. Alexis: 60

Carrent, Mr.: 44, 45

Carriere: 7

Carrington, N. T.: 58

Carrithers, Jr., Gale H.: 39. On Mask 104

Carroll, Lewis: 1, 35, 39

Carron: 49

Carruthers, Robert: 44

Carswell, Mr.: 44

Cartaeret, Sir George: 44

Cartagena: 44. See also: Carthage

Cartari, Vincenzo: 39. Fountaine of Ancient Fiction, tr. Richard Linche: 74

Carter: E.: 58. G.: 58. H., ed.: 135. John: 44; see also: Caster. Peter: 40. Timothy: 45

Carteret, Philip: 91

Cartesianism: 32

Carthage: 56, 25. Carthaginian: 19; Council: 73; phrase: 73. Carthago: 49

Cartright, Thomas, Puritan intellectual: 147. A 2nd Admonition: 147. See also: Cartwright

Cartwright: 19, 41, 51, 120. Mr.: 45. Christopher: 1, 22. E.: 58. John: 45. Thomas: 9, 60, 73, 87, 114, 123, 32, 38, 93, 99; Confutation of the Rhemists Translation: 74. William: 59; Cartwright's Ordinary: 88. See also: Cartright

Carus, P.: 92

Carver: Marmaduke: 32. P. L.: 138, 142, 93

Carvilius: 73

Cary: Barbara: see Powell, Barbara. Sir Henry: 58*; see also: Falkland, Viscount. John: 45. John Patrick: 6, 40. Lucius, Viscount Falkland: 9, 40, 114, 55. N.: 44. Patrick: 44. Valentine: 40

Caryl, Joseph (1602-73): 30, 40, 44, 74, 114, 135, 38, 91, 55, 103. Sermon by: 38. Exposition...upon... Job: 74*

Carysfort, Earl of, Revenge of Guendolen: 58

Casa, Giovanni della: 40, 44, 58, 103, 64

Casady, Edwin: 93

Casaubon (George Eliot's character), M identified with: 87

Casaubon, Isaac: 40, 42, 44, 114

Casaubon, Meric (Mark): 7, 40, 142*, 39. Works: The Origin and Cause of Temporall Evils: 142; The True and Faithful Relition of What Passed Between Dr. John Dee and Some Spirits: 142

Casaubon: 94, 64, 149. Exercitations on Baronius: 94

Casbeen: 49, 73. See also: Bactrian; Hispahan

Case of the Armie truly Stated: 147

Case of Resistance of the Supreme Powers, The: 115

Case of Succession to the Crown of Eng., the: 115

Case Stated Touching the Soveraign's Prerogative: 147

Case: Arthur E.: 44. John: 40. Thomas: 9. W.: 58

Casella: 59, 121, 128, 120

Casimir, translated: 58

"Casimiri Poemata": 40

Casimire, John: 114

Casius, Mt.: 49, 73. See also: Serbonian Bog

Casman, Otho: 142. Angelographia: 142

Caso di Lucifero, Il: 65

Cason, John: 44

Casparson, W. J. C. S.: 117

Caspian Sea: 19*, 49, 73. Lake: 144. See also: Hyrcanian

Cassandra: 92

Casse, Capt. John: 44

Casselden, William: 40

Casserly, J. V. Langmead: 143. On ideal of secular life: 143. And progress: 143

Cassia: 73, 144

Cassian: John: 71. St.: 143. Cassianus: 68, 73, 36; works: Consolations: 74; Conferences: 36. Cassianus: 68

Cassibelan(us): 40, 44, 73, 3. Cassibelauni: 40. Jugera: 49. See also: Colnus

Cassini: Giovanni Domenico: 89. J. D.: 10. Jacques: 89

Cassiodorus, St.: 143

Cassiodorus: 40, 93, 99. Works: De Schematibus et Tropis: 74; Expositio in Psalterium: 74

Cassiopeia: 90

Cassirer, Ernst: 5, 15, 23, 60, 69, 75, 76, 79, 81, 112, 118, 122, 125, 39, 93, 48. Works: An Essay on Man: 48; The Logic of Humanities: 48

Cassius, Mt.: 19

Casson, Richard: 44

Cassubia (Kassubia). See Charles X

Cassuto, U.: 36

Casta, Giovanni della: 55

Castalia: 44, 90

Castalian Spring: 49, 73, 144, 3. Wine: 3

Castalione, Sebastiano: works: Biblia...cum...Annotationes: 74; Sibyllina Oracula: 74

Castalis: 49

Castel Hill, Cambridge: 40

Castelgandolfo: 103

Castell, Edmund: 22. Lexicon Heptaglotton: 41, 42

Castelli: B.: 6. O.: 6

Castellinus, Lucas: 123

Castellio(n), Sebastian: 123, 93

Castelnau: 40

Castelvetro, Lodovico (Ludovico): 17, 44, 66, 70*, 73, 100, 112, 111, 122, 123, 3, 53, 92. Castelvetro's Theory of Poetry (Charlton): 70

Castenaei Distinctiones: 40

Caster: Harbert: 44. (Carter), John: 44. Sylvester: 44

Castiglione, Baldassare, Conte: 1, 4, 5, 18, 27, 33, 40, 5, 18, 51, 5, 18, 60, 76, 112, 114, 125, 39, 93, 101, 55, 21, 64. The Courtier: 51; tr. Thomas Hoby: 74

Castile (Casteel): 49, 3

Casting Down of the Last and Strongest Hold of Satan, The: 26

Castle of Perseverence, The (morality play): 60, 122, 132

Castle Baynard Ward: 40

Castle Cary: 45

Castle Howard: 27

Castle, John: 45

Castlemaine, Roger Palmer, Earl of: 44

Castleton: 45. Castleton, Baldwin (scrivener): 44

Caston: family: 44. James: 44. Sarah: see Jeffrey

Castor: 89, 90, 122

Castration: 141

Castri-Brienii, Ludovici Henrici, Comitis: 44

Casuists: 44

Caswall, Elizabeth: 44

Caswell, Wynema: 128

Cataia: 144, 3

Cataio: 73. See also: Cathay

Cataline War: 44

Catalog of devils: 144*. Source of in PL: 144*. Conventional interpretation: 144. Relation to Ross's Pansebeia: 144. Other sources: 144*. Conclusions: 144

Catalogi Codicum Manuscriptorum Bibliothecae Bodleianae: 44

Catalogue of the General Sects. etc.: 103

Catalogue of the M Collection of Wynne E. Baxter: 44

Catalogue of the Severall Sects and Opinions in England: 44, 91

Catalogue of the Stowe Manuscripts in the B. M.: 44

Catalogue of Additions to the Manuscripts in the B. M.: 44

Catalogue of Books (between 1670 and 1674): 44

Catalogue of New and Old Books in Arts, Sciences, and Entertainment, A: 115

Catalogue of Prints and Drawings in the B. M.: 44

Catalogues of stars: 89

Catalogues, M's Epic: Miltonic, appreciated by the Richardsons: 88; Newton and Virgil's and M's: 88

Catalogus...Collegii...Trinitatis ...Dublin: 44

Catalogus Bibliothecae Conringianae: 44

Catalogus Universalis...Collegii Sionis: 44

Catana: 3

Cataneo, Johannes Maria: 20

Cataphryges: 73

Cataract (of the eyes), possible accompanying cause of M's blindess: 16

Cataracta: 49

Catarino, Ambrogio: 123

Catastrophe of epic or drama: 123

Cataudella, Quintino: 5

Catch: 121

Catechesis Ecclesiarum in regno Poloniae et ductu Lithuaniae: 44

Catechism(s): 40, 44

"Catena d'Adone": 29, 72

Catesby: Margaret: 40. Robert: 73

Cathaian: 73

Catharan: 40

Catharine Hall, Cambridge: 40

Catharinus: 77

Catharist: 73

Catharsis-Clause in German Criticism (Gillet): 70

Catharsis: 17, 70*

Cathay (Cathaian, Cataio, China, Sinaean): 19*, 44, 49, 3, 103. See also: Cambalu; Sericana; Vaiguts

Cathedral(s): 121. An expression of Renaissance: 71. Establishments: 51

Catherine of Aragon: 103

Catherine: Marie de Castelnau: 40. Catherine of Alexandria: 32. Catherine of Braganza, Queen of Charles II: 44. Catherine of Sienna: 27

Cathness: 49

Catholic(s): 147. Pleas for toleration of by: John Austin: 147; Overton: 147; Roger Williams: 147. M on toleration of: 147. Regime: 51. Rule, Roman: 51. Apostolic Church: 78. Encyclopedia: 63, 57; quoted: 95. Roman: 143; interpretation of ladder: 143; ritual: 143, 71. Religious imagery: 8. See also: Wolf

Catholicism: 7, 27, 44, 51*, 52, 113, 114*, 53, 72, 103. 16th c., in conflict with Protestantism: 83. Roman. Warton attracted by aesthetic aspect of: 88. Protestant attitude toward: 93. M's (alleged): 44; intolerance of: 147; attitude toward: 114; aversion to: 51; antagonism to: 147; hatred of: 113. See also: Pope

Catholicity of Warton's taste: 88. Enables him to appreciate the austere manner of M's later work: 88

Catilinarian War (Sallust): 3

Catiline: 123. Lucius Sergius: 73

Cato: 2, 20, 23, 40, 44, 51, 56, 70, 123, 130, 117, 3, 103. Dionysius: 115. Marcus Porcius: the Elder, the Censor: 73; the Younger, Uticensis: 73. Of Utica: 111

Cats, Jacob (Dutch agent): 44, 65, 117

Catsfield, co. Sussex: 44

Cattieuchlani: 40

Catullus, Gaius Valerius: 1, 4, 6, 20, 40, 44, 59, 70, 73, 90, 36, 146, 117, 64. Works: Peleus and Thetis: 74; Epithalamion: 36

Caucasus: 19, 44, 49, 73, 144, 92, 3. See also: Hyrcanian

Caudwell, Christopher: 25

Causality: confusion of with intention in childish thought: 118. The principle of: 48

Causation, claims and principles of: 96*

Cause(s): 123*. Relation to effect: 123. God not cause of Adam's Fall: 123*. Satan as persuading: 123. 1st of all arguments: 123. Types of final: 123*. Instrumental: 123*. Efficient: 123*. Per se: 123. Per accidens: 123. First: 123. Principal: 123*. Procatarctic (external): 123*. Proegumenic (internal): 123*. Direct: 123. Indirect: 123. Compelling: 123. Impulsive: 123. Mediate: 123. Immediate: 123. Remote: 123. Counselling: 123. Assisting: 123. Sufficient: 123. Persuading: 123. Moral: 123. Procreant: 123. Second: 123. Proximate: 123

Causeway from Hell, the, in PL: 89

Causham. See Cosham

Caussin(us), Nicola(u)s: 40, 32, 93, 117

Cauvin, Jean. See Calvin

Cavalcanti: Mr.: 44. Guido: 120

Cavalier(s), the: 121, 150, 51, 54, 71, 103*

Cavalieri, E. Del: 6

Cavalli, (P.) F.: 6

Cavallieri, Tommaso de': 5

Cavanaugh, Jean Carmel: 40

Cave of Treasures, The: 65

Cave: Edward (pr.): 44. Sidney: 93

Cavendish: Charles: 10. Margaret, Duchess of Newcastle: 128. Richard: 69. Thomas: 19. Cavendish's Memoirs of Wolsey: 88

Cawdry: Robert: 123. Thomas: 38; sermon by: 38

Cawley, Robert R.: 15, 19*, 40, 110, 128, 32

Cawood, John: 40

Cawsome-House: 29

Caxes, Juan: 65

Caxton: 105, 133. William: 40, 65, 68, 128*, 32, 36, 93. Works: Recuyell of the Historyes of Troye: 57; Golden Legend: 36, 88; Mirrour of the World: 36, 53

Cayré, Fulbert: 81

Cazan (Casan): 49

Ceba, Ansaldo, Reina Esther: 74, 64

Cebes: 8, 40, 51, 73, 112, 3

Cecil: family: 40. Lord Burghley: 40. Lord David: 1, 4, 81, 86, 141. Elizabeth (Cope): 45. Sir Robert: 45, 39. Sir Thomas: 91. William, Lord Burghley: 18, 40, 39

Cecita: 143

Cecropios...sales: 73

Cedren(us), Georges (Georgius): 41, 68, 73, 65, 77. Compendium Historiarum: 32

Ceillier, Rémi, Histoire Generale des Auteurs Sacrées: 74

Celano, C.: 6

Celestial: music: 121*. Motions: 128; retrogradation: 128. Cycle: 118, 32; writers of: 32*

Celestina: 40

Celibacy: 54

Celine, Voyage au Bout de la Nuit: 35

Cellarius, Christopher: 44

Cellini, Benvenuto: 5, 27

Cello: 40

Celsus, Aulus Cornelius: 18, 44, 73, 4, 44, 107, 114, 36, 88, 3. Attacks on Christianity: 107

Celtes, Conrad: 20

Celtic: 73

Cenci, Giacomo: 120

Censorship: 51*, 113. M complains of the indignity of: 147. M's opposition to: 113. See also: Freedom of the press: 147

Censura Literaria: 44

Censure of the Rota upon Mr. M's Book, The: 9, 44, 51, 116, 147, 91*, 117, 103. Outburst against M: 147

Centaur: 73, 128

Centaurus: 89

Centones Virgiliani: 65

Cephalus: 73, 90

Ceporinus, Jacobus: 40

Ceraste horn'd: 73

Ceraunia: 49, 73

Cerberean mouths: 73

Cerberus: 1, 73, 90, 111

Cerdagni, Camillo: 103

Ceremonies: 47, 51. Ceremony: 144

Ceres: 1, 44, 73, 90, 102, 112, 144, 72, 3

Certain Brief Treatises: 44, 91

Certain Considerations: 9. Touching The Present Factions In the Kings Dominions, tract listing the factions of 1648: 147

Certain Observations, etc: 103

Certain Passages Which Happened at Newport: 116

Certain Quares: 9

Certaine Additionall Reasons, tract against toleration: 147

Certainty, of salvation: 114*. Perceptual and impirical conditions of: 96

Certificate: 45. See also: Reports and certificates

Cervantes, Miguel de: 1, 27, 40, 58, 87, 122, 136, 39, 149, 64, 117

Cesare(o), Alfredo: 5. Mario di: 64

Cessiéres, G. de: 58

Cestine V (Pope): 111

Ceylon: 19, 144

Chabod, Federico: 123

Chadband, Mr. (Dickens' character): 87

Chadwick: John: 118. N. K.: 36. O.: 36.

Chaeronea: 49

Chain of Being: 8, 8, 60, 63, 76, 123, 128*, 46, 101. See also: Scale of Nature

Chain(s): 34, 51*. Of reasoning: 51*. Lack of: 51. Homeric chain: 17, 93. Chain of devils: 93. Chain of history: 93 Chaine, J.: 123

Chair of State: 29

Chalcedon: 44, 49. The English Bp. of: 73. Chalcedonian Council: 73;

Decree: 74

Chalcides: 40

Chalcidia: 44. Chalcidian: 73

Chalcidica Ripa: 49

Chalcidius: 40, 93

Chalcondyles: Demetrius: 40. Leonicus: 40

Chaldaea (Chaldee): 19, 44, 49, 73, 3, 103. Chaldean(s): 73, 51, 32, 3; and astronomy: 89

Chaldey: 51

Chaldon: 143

Chalfont St. Giles: 103, 40, 94, 55. Co. Bucks.: 44*

"Challenge-and-Response" theme: 48*

Challenor, Mr.: 44

Challoner, Richard: 40

Chalmers, A.: 58. George: 40, 44

Chaloner: Edward: 93. (Chalonerus), Sir Thomas: 20, 44*, 73

Chalybean: 49, 73, 90

Cham: 1, 73, 90, 144

Chamberlain, Basil Hall: 118

Chamberlain, Thomas: 44

"Chamberlain of England": 44

Chamberlaine (Chamberleyne): Mr.: 45. Alice: 45. Anne: see Raleigh, Anne. John: 45. Joseph: 45. Sir Thomas: 45. Sir William: 45

Chamberlayne: 133. J.: 58. William: Pharonnida: 88

Chamberlin: Hugh: 16. M.: 53

Chambers: Mr.: 44. A. B.: 60, 122, 75, 79, 85, 93, 101, 106. E. F.: 40. E. K.: 29, 92. Ephraim: 128. L. H.: 44. R. W.: 13, 52, 83, 86, 108; "Poets and Their Critics: Langland and M": 83. Robert: 45. Chambers' Cyclopaedia: 86, 150. Chambers' Handbook of Astronomy (cited): 89

Chamier, Daniel: 44, 73

Champants: 44

Champion, Larry S.: 101

Champion: Christ as: 123. Satan as: 123. Samson as: 123*

Chance: 17*, 90, 132, 93, 48. Element of, in epic: 132

Chancellor of Cambridge Univ.: 40

Chancellor, Richard: 19, 103

Chancellor's Court (of the Univ. of Oxford): 45

Chancellors, A Catalogue of the Lords: 45

Chancery Lane, London: 44, 45

Chancery: 45. Court of: 45*. (The) History...of the High Court of: 45. Proceedings: 45. Select Cases in: 45. Suits: 44

Chancy. See Chauncy

Chandler: John: 44. Joseph: 115; The Young Gentleman and Lady's Museum: 115. M.: 58. Thomas: 44. See also: Chaundler

Chandlers, Company of: 44

Channing, William Ellery: 98, 115, 130, 117

Chanson de Roland: 26

Chansonnette, Hilaire: 64

Chant: 121

Chantal, Jean Frances de, St.: 81

Chanting of epic: 118

Chaos: 1, 41, 44, 47, 50*, 56, 73, 75, 76*, 89*, 90*, 98, 107, 111*, 113, 118, 128*, 143, 144*, 3, 46, 71, 93. Importance of: 75. As center of opposition: 75. And Night: 75. Diabolic attitude toward: 75. And loss of identity: 75. And earth: 75. As prototype: 76. M's description of: 76. M on the origin of: 113. After the Fall: 76. In world mythology: 118. And Deluge: 76. As character and setting: 72, 89. And Satan's voyage: 76. In M's cosmology: 89. "The womb of Nature and perhaps her grave": 89. Ancient conceptions of, and modern science: 89. Origin of idea of, unknown: 89. Evolution of the cosmos out of: 89. Storms of, allusions to: 89. Wild waste: 89. Anarchy of: 89. Of Hesiod: 89; in Hesiod's Theogony: 144. "Inner": 93. King of, associated with demons: 119. In boundless space: 143. Without law and order: 143. A time of: 143. And Cupid: 144. In PL: 144. In

Raleigh's *History*: 144. In Mercator's *Atlas*: 144. See also: Night; Satan and Chaos

Chaonian mothers: 3

Chaonis: 44, 73

Chapel books: 40

Chapel Perilous: 72

Chapel Royal: 40, 121, 136

Chapelain, Jean: 6, 44, 123, 122. Works: "Lettre...sur le Poeme d'Adonis": 74; Dialogue de la Gloire: 60; La Pucelle: 74, 60

Chapman: George: 15, 29, 44, 60, 69, 86, 98, 108, 128, 18, 35, 64, 145, 39, 53, 93, 131, 146; and M compared: 146. George (another): 44. Livewell (publisher, bks., 1651-55): 44, 51, 91, 103. M. J.: 64. Raymond: 93. Robert: 44

Chapone, Hester Muslo: 58, 98

Chappel (Chappell), William (1581-1649), M's tutor: 15, 20, 28, 30, 103, 40*, 42, 44*, 84, 113, 132, 26, 91, 137, 55

Chappell: 94

Character of the Rump: 44, 116, 147, 91. Singled M out as the goose-quill champion of the Rumpers: 147

Character of Mercurius Politicus: 103

Character-writing in 17th c.: 132

Character: 51*, 121. Analysis: 34. Developed by a commonwealth: 51. In musical instruments: 121. In epic and tragedy: 123. Hume on Satan's: 88. And rapidity of speech, the Richardsons on: 88. The Richaradsons on Satan: 88. M's: 28*, 51; and personality: 60, 84

Characteristics of Men, Manners, Opinions: 12

Characterization, Newton's insight into relativity: 88

Characters: M's, dealt with by Hume: 88. Of PL, for the first time examined in detail by the Richardsons: 88. Of fallen angels, the same on: 88. Development of, in PL, the Richardsons on: 88. The same on graphic details in, of PL: 88. Infernal, of PL preferred by Paterson to celestial: 88. Meadowcourt's superficial treatment of M's: 88. Callander on Spenser's proper names as chosen to suit his: 88. M's, Gillies on: 88. Dunster examines connection between, and development of action: 88. M's Stillingfleet on: 88. Todd on: 88. Number of: 92

Chardin, Teilhard de: 52, 111

Charenton, France: 44, 73, 103

Charge for "waggon to London": 40

Charing Cross: 44, 49, 73, 94, 103

Charinus in Andria: 73

Chariot of paternal deity: as throne: 100*. As thunder: 100*

Charis: 73

Charitology. See Grace

Charitopulus, Manuel: 82. *Solutiones, in Leunclavius' Iuris Graeci-Romani...Tomi Duo*: 82

Charity of Church-Men (Henry Brooke): 147

Charity: 51, 54, 73, 136, 143. In court masque: 143. And ladder: 143. In Donne's sermon: 143. As heroic virtue: 123*. As heroic norm: 122. Modern alienation of sympathy from: 118. As bait: 125

Charland, Thomas M.: 40

Charlbury: 45

Charlemagne: 18, 19, 44, 60, 70, 73, 122, 123, 93, 103, 3, 64

Charles I, of Eng. (1600-49): 6, 8, 8, 9*, 10*, 16, 17, 27, 29*, 30*, 33, 34, 40*, 44*, 45*, 51*, 52, 59*, 60*, 70*, 73, 81, 84, 87, 100, 108*, 113, 114, 3*, 103*, 116*, 120, 122, 123, 128*, 132, 135, 145, 147*, 26, 32, 38*, 39, 71, 62, 64, 93, 94, 137, 150, 55, 21, 13. M's loyalty to: 60. And the Army's *Heads of Proposals*: 147. And the Dethroning Bills: 147. Defends his own cause at his trial: 147. His apology, *Eikon Basilike*: 147. Reliance on his word impossible: 147. Relies on Church of Eng.: 147. War against inevitable: 147. Compared to Turkish Tyrant in *Eikonoklastes*: 60. Execution: 147. Accused of parricide: 103. Negotiations with Presbyterians: 103. Influence of his look: 103. Attacked in Eikonoklastes: 103. Defended by Salmasius: 103. Restrictions on press: 103. Goods sold: 103. Attacked in *Defensio*: 103. Portrait of: 103. Posthumous reputation: 103. Treats with Scotch: 103. Deposition proposed: 103. Negotiations of: 103. Execution proposed: 103. Portrait of: 103. His trial: 103. Execution: 103, 147. Publication of Eikon Basilike: 103. Posthumous strength: 103. Treaty with Ireland: 103. Need of money: 103. Addressed by M: 103. Compared to Samson: 103. At York: 103. At Nottingham: 103. Orders retreat: 103. At Oxford: 103. Ballads to: 103. At Hampton Court: 103. Flees to Isle of Wight: 103. Religion of: 103. At Cambridge: 103. Illegal taxation of: 103. At Ludlow Castle: 103. Despotism of: 103. Contrasted with Cardinal: 103. Personal rule: 103. Summons Wentworth: 103. Difficulties of: 103. Policy towards Scotland: 103. Relations with Dutch: 103. Opposes religious freedom: 103. Harrington's friendship for: 103. Opponents attacked: 103. Criticized in Tenure of Kings: 103. Dedication to: 103. Anniversary of execution: 103. Overthrown: 103. M's appeal to in Reason of Church Government: 60. Works: Book of Sports (1633): 53

Charles II, of Eng.: 9, 10, 16, 18, 20, 34, 40, 44*, 45, 51, 54, 3, 103*, 59, 60, 73, 84, 87, 108, 114, 116*, 128, 136, 141, 145, 26, 32, 38, 71, 72, 94, 62, 64, 137, 150, 55. Anticipating the return of, M strikes back at royalist pamphleteers: 147. At Hague: 103. Attitude of powers toward: 103. Publishes Defensio Regia: 103. Accredits ambassadors: 103. Coronation: 103. Awards Salmasius: 103. Directed by M: 103. Acknowledged as King: 103. Fear of accession: 103. Defended by Leviathan: 103. Restoration considered: 103. Restoration: 103. Declaration of Breda: 103. Proclaimed King: 103. Enters London: 103. Spares M: 103. Hears du Moulin: 103. Licensing system of: 103. Praised by poets: 103. Tomkyn's fear of: 103. Sells Dunkirk: 103. Welcome recalled: 103. Rumor of divorce: 103. Religious policy: 103

Charles IV: 73. Charles V (Holy Roman Emperor), of Spain: 6, 41, 51, 60, 73, 38, 21. Charles VIII, of France: 64. Charles IX, of France: 73, 91, 64. Charles XI (son of Charles Gustavus): 44. Charles, Earl of Halifax: 40. Charles, Prince (M's verses on): 44. Charles, Prince Edward ("Bonnie Prince Charlie"): 116. Charles Emmanuel I, Duke of Savoy: 70. II: 44*. Charles (X) Gustavus, King of Sweden: 44*, 59, 73, 120, 103. Charles Louis, Count Palatine: 44

Charles Martel: 73

Charles: John, M. D.: 44. R. H.: 41, 57, 100. R. M.: 15, 113

Charleton, Walter: 40, 142, 145, 93. The Immortality of the Human Soul Demonstrated by the Light of Nature: 142

Charlewood, J. (pr.): 40

Charlotte, Electress Palatine: 10

Charlton: H. B.: 70. Sir Job: 44

Charm: 121

Charman, Derek: 44

Charmides (Plato): 5, 112

Charnock: Mr.: 44, 45. John, Jr.: 44

Charon: 44, 73, 111

Charondas: 73, 3

Charran: 144

Charron, Peter (Pierre): 102, 114, 123, 142, 93, 128. Of Wisedom: 142

Charterhouse, London: 44, 45

Chartist(s): movement: 87. Interest in M's prose: 87. Attitude toward M: 87. Chartist Circular: 87. See also: Cooper, Thomas

Charwomen: 40

Charybdis: 19, 44, 49, 56, 70, 73, 90, 144, 71

Chasles: Monsieur: 44. V. P.: 44

Chasteigner de la Roche-Pozai, Henri Louis: 40

Chastel: André: 5, 60. Jean: 44

Chastity: 9, 27, 30, 69*, 113*, 122, 132, 136, 143, 144, 46, 82, 93, 25. Doctrine of: 132. The discipline of: 136. And virginity: 143. Not repudiated: 143. M and, on: 113*, 137; theme of Comus: 143; as title for Comus: 143. See also: Purity; Virginity

Chastleton: 45

Chateaubriand: 136, 94, 149, 117. François René, Vicomte de: 44, 60, 111

Châteauneuf, M. de: 40, 103

Châteillon, Sebastien. See Castellio

Chatham, co. Kent: 44

Chatsworth: 143

Chatterton: 15, 133, 130. Thomas: 44, 98, 146; Poems on: 53

Chaubon, Abbé de: 10

Chaucer Society Publications: 44

Chaucer: 4, 6, 15, 18, 19, 20, 27, 30, 35, 37, 40, 44, 51, 57, 58, 59, 3, 60, 63, 68, 73, 79, 84, 86, 87, 89, 90, 105, 108, 121, 120, 122, 123, 127, 128, 132, 134, 133*, 134, 139, 145, 14, 71, 72, 82, 88*, 93, 64, 109, 115, 130, 131, 137, 146*, 149, 150, 117, 13. Blake's design for: 25. On decorum: 66. Works: Second Nun's Prologue: 57; Wife of Bath's Prologue: 82; Wife of Bath's Tale: 82; Doctor of Physic's Tale: 82; Merchant's Tale: 82; Romance of the Rose: 82

Chauncy: Charles: 115; works: A Discourse Occasioned by the Death of the Rev. Jonathan Mayhew: 115; Divine Glory Brought to View in the Final Salvation of All Men: 115; The Mystery Hid from Ages and Generations, Made Manifest by the Gospel-Revelation: 115. Lady Eleanor: 45. Sir Toby: 45. (Chancy), Sir William: 45

Chaundler (Chandler, Chandeler), George: 45. Thomas: 45

Chauvet, Paul: 63

Chauvin, Victor: 40

Chavance, Philibert (French pr.): 44, 91

Chaworth: Anne. See Cope, Anne. Elizabeth. See Cope, Elizabeth. Sir G.: 45

Cheam, co. Surrey: 44

Cheapside: 40, 44*, 45, 103

Chebar: 49. Flood: 73

Chedworth: 45

Cheek (Cheke), Sir John: 70, 120, 27, 40, 59, 112, 135. Philip Macon: 122

Cheetham, James: 115. The Life of Thomas Paine: 115. R. F.: 58

Cheever, Henry T.: 98

Cheila: 49

Cheke: 3. Sir John: 13

Chelmer River: 44

Chelmsford (Chensford), co. Essex: 44

Chelsea: 45

Chelys: 121

Chemistry in M's time unknown as a science: 89

Chemmis: 73

Chemnitius, Christianus: 64

Chemnitz, M(artin): 99*, 93

Chemos: 73, 127, 142, 143, 144

Chenu, M. D.: 79, 39

Chephren or Khafre: 73

Chepping Wycombe, co. Bucks.: 44

Cherbonnier, E. la B.: 93

Cherefeddin Ali: 88

Cherfield: 44. See also: Sherfield

Cherith: 49. Brook of: 73

Cheron, L.: 97*

Cheroness: 144

Chersonese (the golden): 19, 49, 73

Chertsey, co. Surrey: 44

Cherubim: 41, 142*. Ophanim: 142. Origin of: 41

Cherubini, Alexander (Allesandro): 6, 30, 44, 73

Cheselden, William: 16

Chesewright, John: 44

Cheshire: co.: 40, 44, 45, 49; see also: Lancashire. History of: 45. Rebels: 73

Chess: 40

Chest of viols: 121

Chester Plays: 65, 36*, 99

Chester: Allen G.: 144. Col. Joseph Lemuel: 40, 44*, 45. Robert: 128. Bp. of: 44

Chester: 45, 49, 73, 21. Town: 40, 44*. Architectural Society of, Journal of: 44. See also: Cheshire

Chesterfield, Lord: 86, 97. Philip Dormer Stanhope, 4th Earl of: 44

Chesterman: Grace: 45. Grace: see Asteyn, Grace. James: 44, 45. John: 45.

Chesterton, G. K.: 18, 15, 40, 52, 86, 136, 130, 137

Chetham Society, Publications of: 45, 44

Chetwode, Mr.: 44, 45

Chevalier, Antoine: 40, 42

Chew: Beverly: 44. Samuel C.: 36, 93

Cheyne: 7

Cheynell: Francis: works: Chillingworthi Novissima: 114, 71, 93; sermons by: 38. John: 45

Chi Soffra Speri: 103

Chiabrera, Gabriello: 6, 40, 44

Chicago: Illinois: 44. Univ. of: 44

Chichele, Abp.: 45

Chichester (Cichester) (town): 44, 49

Chichester, Francis Leigh, Baron Dunsmore, Earl of: 44

Chichirin, Georgi Vasilyevich: 60

Chidley, Katherine: 9

Chief Promises of God, The: 65

Chifos, Eugenia: 40, 44

Chilcott: Ann: 45. Catherine (Billingsley): 45. Mary (Newman): 45. Sarah: 45. Robert: 45. (Chilton), William: 45. See also: Comyn alias Chilcott

Child-baptism: 71

Child: Mr.: 44. F. J.: 64. Sir Francis: 45. Harold: 16. J.: 45. Richard: 44, 45. (Childe), William (scrivener): 44*, 45*

Childe, Vere Gordon: 64

Childerditch, co. Essex: 44

Childeric: 116

Childhood, symbolism of: 81*. See also: Traherne; Vaughan, Henry

Children, G.: 58

Children's Canticle: 126

Childrey: 45

Childs: B. S.: 36. George W.: 134

Chiliasm: 107*, 38*, 93. In ante-Nicene times, orthodox: 107*. In Commodianus: 107*. In "Epistle of Barnabus": 107*. In Justin Martyr: 107*. In Lactantius: 107*. In Methodius: 107*. In Papias of Hierapolis: 107*. In Tertullian: 107*. In Victorinus of Pettau: 107*. Not in Origen: 107*. Chiliast, M: 107

Chillingworth: Roger: 148. William: 9, 20, 113, 114, 143, 22, 38, 71, 94; and Mosaic Law: 143 143

Chilpericus: 73

Chiltern Hills: 44, 49, 103

Chilton, William. See Chilcott, William

Chimaera: 90. See also: Chimera(s)

Chime: 121. Church: 121

Chimentelli, Valerio: 6, 44. The Younger: 44

Chimera(s): 73, 144

Chimney: 45

China (Cathay): 19*, 44, 144, 32, 150. Astronomy in: 89

Chinard, Gilbert: 115

Chinese(s): 19, 44, 73, 3

Chinnock and Galsworthy (bks.s): 44

Chios: 49, 73

Chippenham, co. Wilts.: 44, 49

Chipping Norton: 45

Chipping Wycombe, co. Bucks.: 44

Chiron: 44, 73

Chiselhampton: 45

Chissell: 45

Chiswell, Richard (pr.): 44

Chivalry: 92. And the Christian ideal: 136

Chloe: 73, 3

Chloridia (Jonson): 29*, 143

Chloris: 44, 73, 90, 3. See also: Flora

Chmielnicki, Bogdan, Massacres of Jews: 38

Choaspes River: 19, 49, 73, 144

Choheleth: 58

Choice of Emblems (Whitney): 29

Choice Drollery. See Phillips, John

Choice Psalms (Lawes): 121

Choice, moral: 122

Choir: 121. Books: 121. Choirboys: 40; At St. Paul's Cathedral: 40

Cholder, Jane: 45

Choral: 121

Chord: 121

Choristers: 40

Chorus Vatum: 44

Chorus: 92*. Chief characteristics of: 92*. Leaving stage: 92. Sex of: 92. In Tragedies: 50*, 70. As audience function: 72. In SA: 70, 72*. In consideration of Fortune: 72. In despair: 72. In offer of catharsis: 72. In reconciliation: 72. See also: Semi-chorus

Chote, Thomas: 40

Chreia (exercise in dilation of a theme): 20

Chrestien, Florent: 40

Chrétien de Troyes: 70

Christ: 1*, 4*, 7*, 15, 17, 19*, 41, 44*, 47*, 51*, 56, 57*, 60*, 70*, 73, 87*, 98, 102*, 103*, 107*, 112, 111, 113*, 83*, 121, 123*, 125*, 128*, 141*, 132, 139, 141*, 143*, 144*, 32*, 36*, 46*, 71, 96*, 101, 109*, 130*, 149*. As Adam/2nd Adam: 99, 101, 107, 32, 46. Exemplar, "perfect man," prototype: 80, 46. As hero: 93, 46, 101*. As Oedipus, Orpheus, Samson: 93. As Hercules: 101, 123*, 144. As the Greater Man: 113, 83. As power figure: 141. As judge: 107*. As priest: 125. As king: 125*. As Prophet (symbolic illumination of mind): 125. As Creator: 144, 143, 101. As creative principle of God: 46. As 2nd Isreal: 46. As Word of God: 46. As Pure Intelligence: 125. As God's agent: 143. As Ideal of harmonious life: 121. As Manifested God: 113. As Divine Reason: 113. As symbol of paradise: 32. As Son of God: 57*. As truth: 47

Christ (continued): divine and human: 93. Embodiment of the Church: 46. And saints: 32. And celestial light: 101. Two meanings for name: 107. As harmonizing Greek and Biblical anthropologies: 125. And Platonic tripartite soul: 125. And Platonic integrity of style and man: 125. And ministers, preachers: 143. Royalist symbolism applied to: 8

Christ, and life: divine and human: 93. Motivation: 99*. Fasting (quadraginta dies): 99. Acknowledged divine at end of temptation: 99. Dies body and soul: 107. Passion of: 32. Temptation of: 46*, 144, 36. Crucifixion of: 36. Descent into Hell: 36. Four epiphanies: 46. Incorporate: 107. Millennial reign of: 107. Prophecies: 123*. Power over death and Hell: 143. Exalted: 143. And salvation: 143. Blood of: 143. His victory and kingdom: 143, 149*. Non-human sexual qualities increase distance from us: 61. On inner paradise, and as door to paradise: 32. Incarnation of: 36. Life of: 36. Military spirit: 61. Image of: 52 Nature of Perfection in: 83*

Christ (and Satan): 101*, 65, 144, 141, 36; as brother of Satan: 125.
Christ and Satan (Middle English): 77

Christ (M's conception/delineation of): 141, 137, 61, 125. In PL: 55*, 132; word "Christ" not used in PL: 107. In PR: 55*, 87, 60*, 113, 132*. Not mentioned in SA: 113. Dramatic problems of the dual nature of: 125

Christ (others' views): Augustine's conception of: 113. In "Epistle of Barnabus": 107. Sermons of Edward Irving on 2nd Coming of: 87. In Montgomery's Messiah: 87

Christ: See also: Atonement; Jesus; Messiah; Nativity; Redemption; Son of God; Temptation; Trinity; Word of God

Christ Church: 45. London: 44. Canterbury: 40. Oxford: 40, 44

Christ's College, Biographical Register of: 45

Christ's College, Cambridge: 40*, 44*, 45, 112, 121, 94, 103. M at: 44

Christ's Hospital, London: 40

Christ's Lane, Cambridge: 40

Christ's Piece, Cambridge: 40

Christ's Suffering (formerly ascribed to Gregory Nazianzen): 70

Christ's Thorn: 1

Christ's Victory and Triumph (Fletcher): 25, 94

Christ's Victory in Heaven: 65

Christabel: 136, 88, 103

Christendome: 51

Christensen, Merton A.: 115

Christiad, authored: by Clarke: 65. By Vita: 70

Christiade, La: 65

Christiados libri VI: 65

Christian (of Pilgrim's Progress): 31

Christian Advocate: 44

Christian Doctrine, Treatise of: 8, 100, 95, 107*, 129, 111, 118, 85*, 143, 148*. On Christian liberty: 83. The greater man in: 83. On the fall of Adam and Eve: 83. M's definition of "Perfection" in: 83*. Tenets of sects in: 83. Additional and revisions: 85*. M's attitude towards: 85. Book One: adoption: 85; Christ's mediatorial office: 85; Christ's nature: 85; Christian liberty: 85; compulsory necessity: 85; creation of man: 85; evil will: 85; exaltation of Christ: 85; faith: 85; 4 degrees of death: 85; free will: 85; function of Christ's ministry: 85; good works: 85; imperfect glorification: 85; justification by faith: 85; Mosaic law: 85; natural renovation: 85; new law: 85; perfect glorification: 85; perseverance of believers: 85; predestination: 85; prelapsarian Adam: 85; punishment of sin: 85; redemption: 85; regenerate reason: 85; regeneration: 85, 143; repentance: 85; results of Fall: 85; sanctification: 85; supernatural renovation: 85; supplication: 85; tree of knowledge: 85. Book Two: bodily gratification: 85; Christian liberty: 85; evil conscience: 85; external worship: 85; fortitude: 85; good conscience: 85; internal worship: 85; love of God: 85; lowliness of mind: 85; magnanimity: 85; man's duty to himself: 85; patience: 85; prudence: 85; self-discipline: 85; trust: 85; virtues: 85; wisdom: 85; zeal: 85. Angelic creation, date of in: 102. Arianism in: 102. Battle in Heaven described in: 102. Composition date of: 102. Hell, location of in: 102. Materialism of: 102. Mortalism in: 102. Mosaic law, relation to Gospels in: 102. Its growth and nature characterized: 148. Outline of Book I: 148*. Assurance of salvation: 143. Revelation by stages: 143. Free grace: 143. General depravity: 143. Individual conscience: 143. Discovery of: 87. Latitudinarian tone of: 87. Effect of: 87. Macaulay on: 87. Various responses to: 87. Conception of God in: 87. Use of Scripture: 148. On creation: 148*, 143. On the Trinity: 148*. Corrupt: 107. To be derived from Scripture alone, under guidance of Spirit: 107. Stated by Ussher: 143. Farming and travel images: 8; Nature and philosophy of nature: 8. See also: De Doctrina Christiana

Christian Examiner and Theological Review: 117

Christian Liberty: 103

Christian Magazine, The: 117

Christian Moderator (John Austin): 147

Christian, of Denmark: "Christiern" II: 73. III: 73. IV: 10*

Christian: Charles: 44. Diane: 39. Duke of Brunswick-Wolfenbuttel: 40, 21. Terence: 40. Thomas: 117

Christian(s): 103, 71. Before Christ: 93. Authors in schools: 20. Brotherhood: 51. City: 73. Discipline: 51. Doctrine, definition of: 63. Form of church organization: 51. Humanism: 47, 110, 148. Idea of education: 40. Knowledge: 51. Basic ethical aim of: 143. Liberty as birthright of: 143. Truth and faith of: 143. The ideal of: 143. Every individual sacred to: 143. Principles and politics of: 143. Era: 143. Poetry: 106*. Rationalism: 20, 40. Ministry: 51. Morality: 51. Study of Oriental languages in Middle Ages and Renaissance: 41. Study of Semetic and Rabbinical lit. in 16th and 17th c.: 41. Anthropology: 48. Talmudical learning of M's time: 41. Tolerance: 51. Tradition, meaning of: 51. Virtues, not tenable under kingship: 51. Writers: 51. Myth, use of by M rather than Christian theology: 61. Myth and Christian theology compared: 61. Renaissance: 71. Culture and PL: 143. Infrequently in Comus: 143. Dignity: see Dignity of Man. Humanist, M as: 80. Liberty: 27, 51*, 63, 102, 103, 148*. See also: Word of God; Son as creative agent; Adam and Eve and poetry; Angels and poetry

Christian's, Scholar's and Farmer's

Magazine, The: 115

Christiani hominis institutum: 40

Christianity: 7, 31, 147, 51*, 141*, 36*, 71, 72*, 146, 25. And Biblical thought: 141*. And Greek thought: 141. And "higher castration": 141. And the "world": 141. Historical: 71. Medieval: 71. Principles of: 71*. Virtues according to: 71. Of, and M: 121, 137. See also: Powers; Christ; Civilization

Christie-Miller, S. R. Catalogue of Books: 44

Christie, Agatha: 118

Christie's auction rooms: 44

Christine(a), Queen of Sweden: 6, 30, 40, 44*, 59, 73, 120, 132, 136, 82, 91, 3, 103, 137

Christmas: 72. Day: 40. Date of: 44. Term: 40. Vacation: 40

Christocentric view of history: 93*

Christology, M's: 15, 40

Christopher, William: 45

Christus Patiens (a projected work): 136, 94

Chromatic: 121

Chromosphere: 39

Chronica Hungaorum: 143

Chroniche: 111

Chronicle form of PL XI valued by Hume: 88

Chronicles, British: 40

Chronicon Paschale: 68

Chronographia: 15

Chronology of Ancient Kingdoms: 78

Chronology: chronological order: 50*. Chronological structure. See Temporal structure. Chronologies: 93

Chronos: 71. See Time

Chroust, Anton-Hermann: 93

Chrysaor: 90

Chryses: 56, 71

Chrysippus: 73, 112, 3

Chrysogenee: 72

Chrysologus, Peter: 68

Chrysoloras, Michael: 40

Chrysostom: 77, 128, 142, 3. St: 18, 3. John: 23, 24, 27, 40, 47, 51, 57, 68, 70, 73, 74, 102, 123, 36, 88, 99*, 101. John: works: "Fragmenta in...Job": 74; "Homily VIII, Philippians ii:12-16": 74; Opera: 82*; Homilies on John: 36; Homilies on Timothy: 36. Homilies on Genesis: 36

Chub, William: 93

Church: 7*, 17, 27, 30*, 47, 51*, 63*, 113, 143, 32*, 36*, 103. And secular power: 122*. Lutheran: 7. Roman Catholic: 27. State: 7. And State: 7, 9*, 51, 136; separation of: 71. Censure: 9*. Discipline: 9*, 51. Fathers: 51, 57*. History: 51. Incomes decrease of: 51. Music: 40. Organization: 51. Militant: 143. Edifice a symbol: 143. Purpose of: 143. Of the Spirit: 143. Medieval abuses in: 71. Modern, development and evolution in: 71. Levellers: 9. Powers of: 9*. Symbolized by paradise: 32. And classical tradition: 32. Symbolic representation of: 32. Biblical interpretation of: 32. And covenants: 32. Beginnings of in paradise: 32. Of Christ: 32. In relation to state: 32. Represented by Adam and Eve: 32. Symbolized by Eve: 32. Attendance mandatory: 40. Censure: 9*. Symbol of New Jerusalem: 32. The Christian: 46. And M: endowment of, condemned by M: 147; career: 44; as reformer: 144; on the: 113; government pamphlets on: 51. 16th c.: conditions: 83; in Eng.: 83; in Wales: 83; on the Continent: 83

Church of England: 7, 8, 8, 27, 44, 51; as centralized authority: 147. Church establishment. See also: Established church; Episcopal establishments

Church Floor, The (George Herbert): 131

Church: Mr.: 45. Misses: 44. A. J.: 16, 68. Benjamin: 115; The Choice: 115. Henry: 93. Richard: 45. R. W.: 70. Thomas: 45, 44

Churchill, co. Oxon.: 44

Churchill: 45. Awnsham (bks.): 44. Charles: 58, 115; parodies imitations of L'Allegro and Il Penseroso: 58. John: 44, 45

Churchman, Theophilus. See Heylyn,

Peter

Churchyard, Thomas, identified as Diggon Davie: 83

Chute d'un Ange, La: 65

Chypri: 44

Cianfa: 111

Ciardi, John, on imaginative unity: 104

Cibber, Theophilus: 44, 58, 117

Cicerchia, Nicolo (Passione): 74, 64

Cicero, Marcus Tullius: 1, 2, 4, 5, 6, 8, 8, 9, 15, 18*, 20*, 23, 31, 37, 40*, 44, 51, 52, 56, 57, 59, 60, 66, 70, 73, 79, 89, 90, 100, 112, 114*, 121, 116, 120, 122, 123, 125, 127, 128, 132, 133, 136, 141, 145*, 26, 38, 53, 71, 62, 54, 82*, 3*, 88, 91, 93, 94, 109, 115, 130, 146, 148, 117, 25. Works: Tusculan Disputations: 60; De Finibus: 60, 74; De Officiis: 60, 74; De Natura Deorum: 74; De Re Publica: 74; De Inventione: 82; Dream of Scipio: 149; "Epistulae ad Atticum": 74; Phillippics, a source for M's conception of the law of nature: 147; Opera: 82; Topica: 82; Twelfth Philippic: 82. "Cicero." See Ad Herennium. Ciceronianism: 40, 66

Ciceroianus, authored: by Erasmus: 20. By Harvey: 20. By Ramus: 20

Cicogna, Strozzio: 142. Magiae Omnifariae: 142

Cicuta: 40, 121

Cicutis: 40

Cid: 149

Cif(r)a, Antonio: 6, 44, 121

Cilicia: 49, 3. Cilician: 73

Cimbrica: 73

Cimbricus: 49

Cimmerian: 90, 72. Desert: 19, 49, 73

Cimon: 123

Cinematographic technique: 118

Cinnamus, Joannes: 44

Cino da Pistoia: 120

Cinque Ports: 44, 103

Cinthio (Cintio), Giraldi: 6, 60, 66. Discorsi...intorno al Comporre de i Romanzi: 74, 111, 129

Cionacci, Francesco: 111

Cipriani, Giovanni Battista (engraver, M portrait): 20, 44

Circassia: 49

Circe: 1, 2, 8, 8, 29*, 44, 70, 73, 90*, 121, 123, 144, 32, 72*, 25, 3
Circe's Island: 49

Circle: 8, 8, 41. Significance of: 75. Domination of cosmos by: 128. Associated with God: 93. Associated with creation: 93. See also: Square

Circuitus spiritualis: 72

Circumcision: 126, 141, 93. And Eucharist: 126. Collect for: 126. As transformed into baptism: 126. As considered by St. Paul: 126

Circumnavigation of Britain: 40

Cirencester: 45, 49

Cirillo, Albert R.: 60, 93

Cirrha: 49, 73

Cirrillo, Albert L.: 101

Cithaeron, Mount: 2, 49, 73

Cithara: 121

Cities, Two: 93

Citizenship, M and the concept of: 52

Cittern: 121

City of God: 118. See also: De Civitate Dei; Augustine, St.

City Council, London: 103

City-Ministers unmasked: 147. Berates persecuting prelates: 147

City: in Heaven: 51. City Mercury, the: 116. Of God: 72. Of Men: 72. Of the World (civitas Terrena): 123. Party, the: 51. Petition: 73. City life: 8; images derived from: 8

Ciudad Real: 64

Civil Power in Ecclesiastical Causes: 9*, 132

Civil War: 7, 8, 30, 113, 103; M's role in the: 113

Civil: law, regius professorship of: 40. Government: 9*, 51. Authorities, function of in religious matters: 51. Law, study of: 40. Liberty: 51, 60. Magistrate, relation of to religious matters: 51. Power, Treatise of, in relation to religious matters: 51*. See also: Magistrates; Government; Social contract

Civilization: 50, 51, 141*. The causes of genesis: 43. Hybridic: 141. Condemned: 141*. Affirmed: 141. And Satan: 141. In Christianity: 141. In Judaism: 141. Regarded as corrupt by the Richardsons: 88. See also: Prometheus

Claggart: 93

Clamor Regii Sanguinis (P. du Moulin): 28, 44, 150

Clandeboy: 49, 73

Clannesse: 65

Clanvowe, Sir Thomas: 59, 120

Clapham, Henoch: 68, 114

Clapmarius, Mr.: 44

Clapton, Anthony, M. D.: 44, 45*

Clare College, Cambridge: 40

Clare, J.: 58

Clarel: 98*

Clarence, George, Duke of: 111

Clarendon Press: 112

Clarendon, Edward Hyde, Earl of: 40, 44*, 59, 91, 97, 137, 117, 13. See also: Hyde, Edward. Clarendon Code: 116

Claretta: 120

Clarges, Sir Thomas: 44, 91, 94, 103

Clarinet: 121

Clarion: 121

Clark(e)son, George: 45

Clark, William Andrews, Memorial Library: 44

Clark: A. M.: 55. Andrew: 40, 44, 45, 116, 120. Catherine: 44. Donald Lemen: 31, 40*, 44, 56, 66, 122, 123, 82, 21; works: John M at St. Paul's School: 82; "The Rise and Fall of Progymnasmata in 16th and 17th Century Grammar Schools": 82. Sir Edward: 45, 58. Elizabeth: 120. Evert M.: 9, 15, 19, 51*, 68, 79, 110, 128, 144; on M: 80; see also: M, Readie and Easie Way. F. Le Gros: 16. G. N.: 86, 144. Harry Hayden: 115. Ira: 106. J.: 58. John Willis: 40. K.: 36. Sir Kenneth: 27. Kitson: 87. Marguerite: 137. Mary: 120. Richard: 45. Samuel: 10. W. K. Lowther: 139. And Gray: 40. See also: Clarke; Clorke

Clarke-Papers: 147

Clarke: 130. family: 44. Mr.: 28, 44. Abraham (M's son-in-law): 44*. Abraham (M's grand-son): 28, 44. Alured: 44. Anna (w. of Abraham): 44. Caleb (M's grandson): 29, 44*. Deborah (M's daughter): 44*; see also: Milton. E. (M's granddaughter): 59. Elizabeth: 28, 44; see also: Foster. Frederick Seymour: 44. G. R.: 44. Hyde, discoveries concerning M's ancestry: 44*. Isaac (M's great-grandson): 44. Jathniel: 44. John: 40, 112, 117. Joseph (bks., 1670-3): 91. Mary (w. of Caleb): 44; their daughter, Mary: 44; their grandaughter, Mary: 44. Richard: 44; see also: Clorke. Robert: 65, 64; Christiados: 74. Samuel: 40, 32; works: Life and Death of Alexander the Great: 74; Life and Death of Julius Caesar: 74. T. E. S.: 116. Urban (M's grandson): 44

Clarkenwell: 44. See also: Clerkenwell

Clarkson: Laurence: 45

Claros: 3

Classes of society: origin of: 83. Duties of: 83. Faults of: 83

Classic(s): 8*, 19*, 27*. M regarded as a: 88

Classical code: 97*

Classical tradition: 70. In Eng. poetry: 87. See also: Greeks, the

Classical Journal: 63

Classical Mythology of M's Eng. Poems (Osgood): 3

Classical: writers, authority of, overrated by Hume: 88. Lit., charged by Hume of lacking decorum: 88. Supposed by him to be based on Bible: 88. And regarded as inferior to PL: 88. Criticism, methods of Bentley's misapplied in his M: 88. Authorities confirming Bentley's appreciation of virgorous ruggedness of metre: 88. Annotation influencing Eng. scholarship: 88. Sources of PL examined by Hume: 88. Scholarship influencing Bentley: 88; and Newton: 88. Tenets, Bentley's: 88. Parallelisms borrowed by later commentators from Hume: 88. Idioms studied by Hume: 88. M's use of classical authority: 51. Theory of verse misapplied by Bentley: 88. Scholarship, weak points in Bentley's: 88. Lit., Pearce's solid knowledge of: 88. Allusions in M, Pearce on: 88. Writers, authority attr. by Pearce to: 88. Idioms examined by Hume and Pearce: 88. Pronunciation of proper names, Pearce on: 88. Dramatic chorus, Pearce examining influence of style of, on M: 88. Scholarship, the elder Richardson's lack of: 88; and his son's competence in: 88. Idioms studied by the Richardsons: 88. Style, the Richardsons on M's wise utilization of the advantages of a: 88. Grace, majesty and simplicity, and preferableness of classical languages for poetry, the Richardsons on: 88. Flavour of M's language, the Richardsons on: 88. Style and Christianity combining to make M incomparable, according to the Richardsons: 88. Lit., superiority of, the Richardsons on: 88. Syntax in M, the Richardsons on: 88. Models of M's verse examined by the Richardsons: 88. Idioms and shades of meaning studied by Peck: 88. Models, Peck on M's: 88. Writers, Peck does not overrate the authority of: 88. Lit., regarded by Paterson as based on Bible: 88; and as inferior to M: 88

Classical, editors: Paterson's commentary to rival the work of: 88; and Newtom's edition imitating them: 88. Scholarship, Jortin's: 88; and Biblical reading Newton's main assets: 88. Authority, Newton's excessive respect for: 88. Tradition, Newton's explanation of the value of: 88. Drama and SA, Newton on: 88. Preferred by Newton to modern languages: 88. Allusions, uncommonness objected to by Newton except in: 88. Writers, Callander's overvaluation of authority of: 88. Traits in M, Callander on: 88. Lit., Thomas Warton's familiarity with: 88. Features mixed with elements of medieval Romance, Warton on: 88. Training reflected in Lofft's method: 88. Learning, Dunster's: 88. Allusions and metre regarded by Dunster as mere decorations of poetry: 88. Idioms, Dunster on: 88. Prosody, Dunster on Newton's misapplication of principles of: 88. References in Todd: 88. Parallelisms in Stillingfleet's notes: 88. Traits in M, Monboddo on: 88. Idioms in M, Monboddo on: 88

Classical, education system: 20. Authors, veneration of in schools: 20*. Critics: 31. Dialectic in support of Christian ethics: 40. Dramatic form: 70. Ideals, M's: 51. Rhetoric: 51. Texts: 40

Classicism: in 18th c.: 58. As opposed to Romanticism: 87

Classicist: tendencies in Newton: 88. Standards: Bentley's rigorous: 88; their definition: 88; their positive features: 88. Prejudices, Pearce's: 88. Tendencies, Peck's, superimposed on Dryden's views regarding poetry: 88. Meadowcourt as a: 88. Regularity of metre, Sympson's dissatisfaction with: 88. Tendencies in Callander: 88. Spirited opposed by Massey: 88. Superficiality disliked by Warton: 88. Moderation, Warton's occasional taste for: 88. Perfection, Warton on lack of stimulus in cold: 88. Tendencies, Dunster's: 88. Style, romance, Todd on: 88

Classification: rigorous, opposed by the Richardsons: 88. Peck takes into account M's literal views with regard to literary: 88. Newton's interest in: 88

Claude Lorraine: 133, 97

Claude, Jean: 116

Claudia: 128

Claudian: 19, 40, 44, 57, 58, 70, 90, 128, 133, 32, 64, 3, 88, 94, 130, 117, 55; works: <u>De Consulatu Stilichonis</u>: 57; <u>Epigram de Phoenice</u>: 57; <u>De Raptu Proserpine</u>: 74; <u>In Rufinum</u>: 74. In Addison: 2. Nickname of friend of Heinsius: 44

Claudianus, Claudius: 73, 21

Claudius, Emperor: 73. Appius: 16. Ptolemaeus: 121

<u>Claustris Musarum</u>: 40

Clavell, Robert (bks.): 44

Clavering, co. Essex: 44

Clavis: <u>Apocalyptica</u> (Mede): 94. <u>Graecae Linguae</u>: 40. <u>Lingua Hebraeae</u>: 40

Clavius: 128. Christopher: 40, 77

Claxton, M.: 97

Claypitts, co. Suffolk: 44

Clayton: H. J., use of staff: 104. Sir Robert: 40. Sir Thomas: 45

Cleanthes: 128. The Stoic: 39

Cleave: 44

Cleaver: Robert: 45; see also: Dod, John and Robert Cleaver. Simon: 45. W.: 58

Cleland: James: 40*. John: 114. Thomas: 115; The Socini-Arian Detected: 115

Clemen, Wolfgang: 128

Clemens Alexandrinus: 4, 24, 40, 54, 144, 71. See also: Clement of Alexandria

Clément, Jacques: 44

Clement: of Alexandria, St.: 57, 68, 73, 74, 90, 107, 113, 114, 125, 142, 26, 32, 3, 36, 82, 93; "Perfection" defined by: 83; father of speculative theology: 107, the Logos: 107; subordinationist: 107; teacher of Origen: 107; works: "Instructor": 74; Protreptikos: 74; Stromata: 74; Miscellanies: 36; Paedogogus: 82. Of Rome, St.: 68, 73, 71; "Perfection" defined by: 83. F. (not Fillippo): 40. John: 45. Theologian: 44. V, Pope: 64. VI, Pope: 33, 64; IX, Pope: 103, 64

Clement: 112

Clementi, Fillippo: 6

Clementillo (Chimentelli), Valerio: 28, 30, 44, 73

Clementine Homilies: 36

Clementis ad Corinthios: 40

Clementius, Antonius: 44, 91. See also: Salmasius, Claude

Clements: Mr. (lawyer): 44. R. J.: 5. Rex: 142, 93

Clenard, Nicholas: 20

Clench: Frances: 44. Meriell: 44. Sir Robert: 44. Thomazine: 44

Cleombrotus: 73, 111, 114, 144

Cleomenes: 123

Cleopatra: 73

Clepsydra: 39

Cleremontanians: 44

Clergy: corrupt practices of: 83. Duties of: 83. Episcopal: 143. Unfaithful: 143. Worthy: 143. Subject to Word: 143. M's attitude toward: 30*, 51, 113

Clerico-Classicum (John Price): 147

Clericus, J.: 99

Clerke: 45. Agnes: 89. Mr. (butler): 44. Bartholomew: 40. John (Col.): 40, 44, 120. See also: Clarke

Clerkenwell, London: 44, 45

Cleve: 45

Cleveland: 94. E., "Identity Motive in PR": 74. John: 33, 44, 84, 145, 103, 64

Cleves: 44, 49. Marie de: 64. See also: Charles X; Frederick William

Cleynaerts, Nicolas: 40

Clifford: Lord: 44. C. C.: 58

Cligés, Chrétien de Troyes: 70

Climate: effects on M: 30. M's complaint of the English: 113. Change of: 50

Cline, James M.: 145

Cliniades: 73, 44. See also: Alcibiades

Clink: 49, 73

Clinton-Baker, Lady Rosa A.: 44

Clinton, DeWitt: 115. An Introductory Discourse: 115

Clio: 73, 121, 44, 3, 103

Clitomachus: 4

Cloanthus: 2

Clock(s): 40. Astronomical, construction of: 89

Clode, C. M.: 44. Memorials of the Guild of Merchant Taylors: 44

Clodius: 120. Publius: 73

Clonto, John: 44

Clopton, co. Suffolk: 44

Clopton, Mr.: 44, 45

Clorinda, pastoral name of Mary Sidney: 83

Clorke, Richard. See Clarke

Close: 121. Rolls: 45

Clothes, attitude toward: 8

Clotho: 90. See also: Fates

Cloud of Unknowing: 7

Cloud(s): 128. Causes and kinds: 128. Of fire and nitre: 128. Machines (in masques): 29*

Clough: Arthur Hugh: 53, 64. B. C.: 58

Clumber: 44

Clutterbuck, Robert: 45

Cluver, Hans: 40

Cluverus, Detlevus: 10

Clyde: Richard: 44. W. M.: 44

Clymene: 73, 90

Clytaemnestra: 54, 111, 72, 92

Clytie: 56, 73

Cnidos: 49, 73

Cnidus River: 44

Coal Sack, the: 89

Coat of arms, M's: 40, 44

Cobb, Elizabeth: 44

Cobbet: Ralph: 91. William: 94. 115; The Bloody Buoy, Thrown out as a Warning to the Political Pilots of America: 115. See also: Corbet

Cobbett's: Complete Colection of State Trials: 143. Parliamentary History of England: 44

Cobham, Thomas: 40

Coblenz, Pr. of: 6

Cobler's Prophecie, The: 88

Coburn, Miss Kathleen: 12

Cocceius, Johannes: 47, 114, 22, 99. In Job: 74

Coccio, Marcantonio. See Sabellicus

Cochet, Mr.: 44

Cochlaeus, Johannes: 60

Cochran, Mr. (Scotch agent): 44

Cochrane: Charles N.: 93. John: 44

Cock Lane, London: 44

Cockayne, Land of: 32

Cockayne, Thomas O.: 128

Cockburn, W.: 58

Cocke, George: 40

Cockes, Samuel: 45

Cockfield, co. Suffolk: 44

Cockings, George: 58. 115. Epics by: 58. War: An Heroic Poem: 115

Cocklehill, co. Oxon.: 44

Cocleus, or Cochleus, Johannes (originally Dobeneck): 73

Cocteau, Jean: 46

Cocytus: 49, 73, 90

Codex: Alexandrinus: 40. Vaticanus: 40

Codinus, Georgius: 44, 73. De Officiis in Byzantinae Historiae Scriptores: 82

Codomannus, Laurentius: 93

Codrus: 123

Cody, Richard: 64

Coe, A(ndrew) C. (pr.): 44

Coeffeteau, Bp. Nicolas: 93

Coelmannus, Petrus: 40

Coelum Stellatum: 121

Coelum: Britannicum (Carew): 29*. Crystallinum: 143

Coelus: 1

Coercion: 143. Rejected by church: 143

Coffin For The Good Old Cause: 147

Coffin, Charles Monroe: 110, 128, 93

Coffman, George R.: 64

Cogan, Henry: 144

Coghlan, Brian: 39

Cognition: 96

Cohen, Ralph: 146

Cohens, Sir George: 44

Cohn, Norman: 39, 101

Cohon, S. H.: 15

Coictus. See Coyet

Coignard, Gabrielle de: 64

Coimbra, Univ. of: 40

Cokayne, G. E.: 45

Coke: Mr.: 45. Bridget: 120. Sir Edward: 16, 33, 40, 45, 59, 73, 103, 120. Sir Francis: 40. Roger: 91. Thomas: 115

Colagrosso, F.: 6

Colasterion: 45, 112, 113, 132, 103. See also: Milton, John, Works

Colbatch, Dr.: 88

Colberg: 7

Colbert, Jean Baptiste: 27

Colbron: James (scrivener): 40, 44. Thomas: 44

Colchester: 44, 49, 103

Colchis: 49, 73

Cole: Henry: 114. J.: 58. Nathanael: 93. Peter: 44. T.: 58. William: 40

Colebrook (now Colnbrook): 73, 49

Coleman Street, London: 44

Coleman: Dr.: 40. Charles: 39. Edward D., Bible in Eng. Drama: 74. Thomas: 38; sermons by: 38. William: 115; A Collection of the Facts and Documents: 115

Colenso, Bp.: 17. Critical study of the Bible: 87

Coleraine, Lord Henry Hare: 32

Coleridge: Hartley: 94. Sara: 58

Coleridge, S. T.: 1, 5, 7, 12*, 15*, 16, 23, 27, 35, 44, 50, 52, 56, 58*, 60, 65, 68, 70, 75, 76, 79, 84, 86, 87, 95, 98, 104, 112, 110, 111, 114, 118, 124, 126, 128, 136*, 138, 142, 143, 14, 32, 39, 53, 71, 88, 92, 94, 64, 97, 101, 109, 131, 137, 146*, 148, 150, 13, 25, 132, 133, 130*. Annotations to: Anderson's British Poets: 146; Barclay's Argensis: 146; Baxter's Life: 146; Birch's M: 146; Chapman's Homer: 146; Cornwall's Dramatic Scenes: 146; Defoe's Robinson Crusoe: 146; Donne's Poems; Sermons: 146; Field's Church: 146; Flogel's Geschichte: 146; Fuller's Church History; History: 146; Hacket's Scrinia Reserata: 146; Hayley's M: 146; Howie's Biographia: 146; Hutchinson's Memoirs: 146; Jonson's Works: 146; Kant's Schriften: 146; Luther's Table Talk: 146; Noble's Appeal: 146; Quarterly Review: 146; Scott's Novels: 146; Sedgwick's Hints: 146; Stockdale's Shakespeare: 146; Swift's Gulliver's Travels: 146; Taylor's Discourses: 146; Theobald's Shakespeare: 146; Warton's Poems: 146*; Waterland's Doctrine: 146. Conversations of: 146. Lecture: 146*. Letters: 146*. And M compared: 146. Notebooks: 146*. Others' reminiscences of: 146*. Prefaces: 146. Projected works: 146. On Shakespeare as an impersonal poet: 87. Attitude toward M: 87. Shakespeare compared with M: 87. Renaissance-Puritan view of M: 87. Influenced by L'Allegro, Il Penseroso, and Lycidas: 58. Lecture on PL: 60. On theme of PL: 83. On nature of symbols: 143. His tribute to M: 143. Works: Literary Remains: 12; Letters: 12; Lay Sermons: 12, 146; Kubla Khan: 12, 25; Destiny of Nations: 12; Dejection, An Ode: 12; Christabel: 12; Biographia Literaria: 12*, 53, 146; Ancient Mariner: 25, 142; Letter to Sotheby: 53; Table Talk: 12*, 87, 146; Shakespeare and Other Eng. Poets: 74; Statesman's Manual, The: 12, 60, 146; On Poesy as Art: 12; Notes and Lectures: 12; Miscellaneous Criticism (ed. Raysor): 12

Coles: 40

Colet: 112. John: 18, 20*, 40*, 42, 57, 66, 74, 110, 129, 142, 39, 82, 93, 3, 103, 148, 55; Two Treatises on the Hierarchies of Dionysius: 142

Colfield, co. Essex: 44

Colgoieve: 49

Coli, Edoardo: 5

Colie, Rosalie L.: 23, 60, 81, 110, 39, 93, 101, 14

Colin Clout, pastoral name for Spenser: 83

Colin Clout's Come Home Againe (Spenser): 70. Spenser's expression of admiration for Rosaline in: 83

Coliseum: 27

Colkitto: 120

Colkyer, James: 44, 45

Collaborate: collaboration of the Richardsons: 88. Collaborators:

Newton's: 88; Warton's: 88; Todd's: 88

Collard, John: 44

Collas, Georges: 60

Collcitto: 59

Collectanea rerum memorabilium (Solinus): 3

Collection of Ancient Christian Poets, ed. Aldus Manutius: 74

Collection of Epitaphs, A: 59

Collection of Poems, By Several Hands: 115

Collection of Recent and Witty Pieces by Several Eminent Hands: 44

Collection of 18 Rare Tracts: 91

Collections (Aubrey): 3

Collections (Hearne): 45

College(s): meaning of word: 40. Rise of in Eng. universities: 40. Invisible, the: 7. Of Arms, London: 44. Of Physicians, London: 40, 44. At Cambridge, list of foundings: 40. Collegiants: 7, 78

Collegium: de Anima: 40. Physica: 40

Colles, H. C. See Grove, George

Collier: *Poetical Decameron*: 94. Mr.: 44. J. Payne: 44, 53, 68, 108; Ed., *Seven Lectures on Shakespeare and Milton by the Late S. T. Coleridge*: 44. Katherine B.: 4, 110, 144. Thomas: 9, 44, 45, 60, 114, 38, 93; sermon by: 38; millennial views: 38. W. F.: 16, 58. William: 115; *The Gospel Treasury*: 115

Collinge, N. E.: 59

Collingwood, R. G.: 79, 93

Collinne, William: 44, 116. *Spirit of the Fanatics*: 91

Collins-Baker, C. H.: 15, 97*

Collins: Mr.: 44. Antony: 44, 45. Arthur: 45; *Letters and Memorials of State*: 83. Baldwin: 40. Daniel: 44. Elizabeth: 44. J.: 58. J. C.: 92. James (bks., 1664-83): 142, 91; *The Thomistic Philosophy of Angels*: 142. John: 10, 16, 44, 45, 110. Joseph: 16, 79. Samuel: 40, 64. William: 58*, 87, 14, 88, 97, 109, 55; influenced by *L'Allegro* and *Il Penseroso*, praises M, uses *Nativity* meter: 58; Series: 45

Collius: 4

Collobria: 40

Collogue: 73

Colloqui Graecae: 40

Colloquia (Erasmus): 20

Colloquia: 40

Colloquialism in M: 70

Collwell. See Colwell

Colman: Benjamin: 115*; works: *A brief Dissertation on the Three First Chapters of Genesis*: 115; *A Discourse on the Incomprehensibileness of God*: 115. George: 58, 117. Henry: 115; *A Sermon on the Character and Conduct of Zaccheus*: 115. Walter, *La Dance Machabre*: 91

Colmanus: 73

Colmogro: 49

Coln: 49

Colnbrook, co. Berks.: 40, 44

Colne: River: 29, 40, 44, 73, 3, 103. Valley: 40

Colney: 49

Colnus: 49

Cologne, Germany: 44

Colombine, P.: 58

Colomiés, Paul: 40

Colonna: family: 6. Stefano: 120. Vittoria: 5, 6, 120, 64

Colonne, Guide delle: 123

Colonus: 92

Color: M's use of: 16; perception in M: 113; effects in M, the Richardsons examine: 88. The Richardsons on, and symbolism: 88. Epithets, Hume on: 88

Colossi: 49

Colossians, St. Paul to the: 73, 74

Colossus: 73

Colt: (Cowlt) Mrs.: 44. Sir Henry: 44, 45

Coltellini (Cultellinus), Agostino:

6*, 30, 44, 73, 111

Coltellino (Cultellino): 28

Coltman, William: 45

Colton, Thomas: 40

Coluga: 49

Colum, Padraic: 98

Columba, the miraculous: 73

Columban: 40

Columbia Milton: 1, 44, 51

Columbia: Univ.: 44, 45; Press: 112. Univ. edition: 73. MS. (M): 45

Columbian: Centinal: 115. Letter-Writer, or, Young Lady and Gentleman's Guide to Epistolary Correspondence, The: 115. Magazine Or Monthly Miscellany, The: 115. Phenix and Boston Review, The: 115

Columbus, Ohio: 44

Columbus: C.: 6, 73. Christopher: 32, 71, 150

"Columbus, the English": 45

Columella: 128, 3. L. J. M.: 44, 73

Colure(s), (the): 89, 128

Coluthus: 40

Colvin, S., on Keats: 53

Colwell (Collwell), Thomas: 44, 45

Comanini, Gregorio: 123

Comba: 120

Combat images: 99

Comberba(t)ch, Roger: 44, 58. Roger C., his son: 44

Combinative logic of M's technique studied by Dunster: 88

Comedy: 27, 146, 70. In PL: 50

Comenius (Komensky), Johann Amos: 5, 7*, 10*, 20, 40, 44, 51, 102, 114, 128, 3*, 142, 147, 26, 32, 53, 93, 94, 137, 148, 55. And M, light for the benighted: 147. M and: 147. Works: A Reformation of Schooles: 147; The Great Didactic: 147; Porta Linguarum: 40; National Philosophie Reformed by Divine Light: 142

Comenius, John Amos (Laurie): 3

Comes, Natale (Natali Conti): 4, 40, 32, 101. Mytholgiae: 74, 38

Comestor, Peter (Petrus): 24, 65, 68, 32, 36*. Historia Scholastica: 74, 36

Comet(s): 89*, 128*, 144. Description of: 89. Harmless: 89. Nucleus of: 89. Orbits of: 89. Researches of Hevelius on: 89. Superstitions regarding: 89. Tail of: 89. Causes and kinds: 128. Sword: 128. Satan as: 128

Comgoscoi: 49

Comic: notes on PL: 104. Relief: 92

Comines (Commines), Philippe de: 73, 40, 82, 88. Memoires: 82

Cominges, Comte de: 44

Comitatus: 36

Comitialis: 40

Commandments, Ten: 40

Commelinus, Hieronymus: 44

Commencement day: 40

Commentaries (Blackstone): 3

Commentariorum in Genesin libri tres: 65

Commentary on Plato's Timaeus, A: 112

Commentary, by author in propria persona: 123*. See also: Bible, Holy

Commings, Comte de: 103

Commissary Court of London: 44

Commission: 45. Commissioner: 45. Commissioners or Committee, of or for: Scottish: 51; Army: 44; Breach of Articles: 44; Compounding with Delinquents: 44*; Custody of Great Seal: 44; Customs: 44; Excise: 44, 103; Foreign Affairs: 44*; Great Seal: 44; Haberdashers' Hall: 44; Navy: 44; Propagation of Gospel: 103, 44; Racovian Catechism: 44; Relief upon Articles of War: 44; Sequestrations: in Cornwall: 44; in Oxfordshire: 44*; in Suffolk: 44; Whitehall: 44; Advance of Money, Calendar of the Committee for: 45*; Compositions: 45, 103; Compounding Calendar of the: 45; Safety: 103; privileges: 103; Religion: 51; printing, legislative: 51

Commodianus: 107. Chiliast: 107. Lust the motive for the angelic Fall: 107. Materialist: 107

Commodus: 73

Common law: 45, 51

Common sense: according to the Richardsons handicapped by pedantry: 88. Newton wants poetry to conform to, and the Bible as well as to give pleasure: 88

Common Pleas, Court of: 45*

Common Prayer, Book of: 40

Commonplace book (M's): 16, 28, 112, 111*, 113, 121, 132, 133, 147, 26, 94, 103, 3. Described: 55. Commonplace Book Out of the Rehearsal Transpros'd, A: 116, 91

Commonplace: in theme writing: 20; 40. Books in Renaissance: 20*, 40. Commonplaces, theological: 63. Commonplaceness of criticism in Paterson's commentary and The State of Innocence: 88

Commons, House of: 44*, 45, 51*. Debates: 44. Journals: 44, 45

Commonwealth of Oceana: 52. Plato's: 3

Commonwealth, the: 9*, 51*, 60, 70, 113*, 71, 103*. M's views of a free; M takes part with the: 51, 113. Men of the: 51. Commonwealth's Man Unmasqu'd, The: 116. M on: 3

Communion: 126, 139. Sacrament of: 47. Of saints: 47, 60, 113

Communism: 9. Communistic state as proposed by Winstanley: 147. See also: Diggers

Community: destroyed by demonic; man requires; God restores; in Heaven; in church: 47*. As theme in SA: 125*. See also: Heaven; Love; Heroic morality

Commena (Commena), Anna: 73

Comnenus, Andronicus: 73

Companion to Greek Studies (Whibley): 3

Company of Stationers: 103

Comparetti, Dominico, Vergil in the Middle Ages: 74

Comparison, in theme writing: 20, 51

Compass(es): 143. Golden: 128; used in creation: 119. See also: Golden Compass; Circle

Compassion: 136. The gift of: 136

Compassionate Samaratane (William Walwyn): 147

Compendious: Discourse: reply to Of Prelatical Episcopacy: 144. Date of: 144. Defends Irenaeus: 144. Defends bishops: 144. Way of Teaching, A (Philipps): 20

Compendium: Malificarum: 97. Of Theology. See also: Treatise of Christian Doctrine

Compilation: Peck's method of: 88. Newton's edition mainly a: 88

Complacence: 54

Complainant. See Plaintiff

Compleat Angler, The: 17

Compleat Gentleman: 121, 141

Complete: Collection, A: 116. Commentary...on M's PL (James Paterson): 88; see also: Paterson. Peerage, The: 45. Completion, metaphors of in Book XII: 118

Complex: plot: 92. Complexity: of M's syntax misunderstood by Bentley: 88. Of M's impressions and associations of ideas appreciated by Warton: 88

Compliance: 54

"Complutenses" (Coimbra): 40

Complutensian polyglot: 22

Composition: 121. Of imitative exercises: 20*. Latin: 40. Practices and habits of M's: 28*, 30, 50, 102. Peck on M's method of: 88

"Compositum mixtum": 69*

Compound: epithets: 13. Words: 98; Hume, Peck on: 88

Comprehensionism: 114

Comptes Rendus hebdomadaires des sceances de l'academie des sciences: 44

Compton: 45

Comte, Auguste: 87

Comus (Thomas Arne, 1738): 39

Comus sive Phagesiposi Cimmeria (Puteanus): 29

Comus II: 112

Comus: 8*, 27*, 104*, 112*, 111, 87, 95, 100, 113*, 118, 121, 125, 126, 129*, 132*, 143*, 144*, 147, 11*, 72*, 101*, 148*, 13, 25. As allegory: 146, 25, 143. As drama: 146, 25. Performances of: 146. Text: 55. "Haemony" in explained: 13. Synopsis of M's vision: 25. Summary of: 25, 148. Characters in: 25. As pilgrimage: 25. M's alternations of: 25. Sexuality in: 25. As dream: 25. Images in: 8*. As Masque: 148, 129, 146, 72, 101. The argument: 148. The epilogue: 148, 87, 101. Wotton's praise: 55. Editions: 55. Discussed: 55*. In 18th c.: 55. Bridgewater MS. of: 40. Disputations in: 40. And chain of being: 134. And Spenser's garden of Adonis: 134. M's doctrine of chastity: 134, 55. Reconciliation of virtue and pleasure: 134, 143. Moly: 144. Intemperance: 144. Bacchus: 144. And melancholy: 144. Redemption in: 72. Stances in: 72*. Chastity in: 101. Christian-classical synthesis: 101. Light imagery in: 101. Textual changes in: 101. Rites described: 126. Asperges, function in: 126. Prologue to in Cambridge MS.: 87. Influence of in Bridges' Prometheus: 87. Sources of: 129, 146*, 144, 143, 55. Criticism of: 29*, 143*. Related to M's prose: 11. Compared to Lycidas: 11. Compared to PL: 11. Ascent in: 72. Christianity in: 72. Debates in: 72*. Methexis in: 72. Prayers in: 72. And masque of Hymen: 143. And Encomium Moriae: 144. The use of myth in: 11*. Its ideal of community: 11. The "woods" of: 11. And the role of violence: 11

Comus, as a figure, character: 1*, 29*, 52, 90, 128, 143, 71, 72*, 92. Dominates Comus: 143. His wit and rhetoric: 143

Comus, Temple of: 97

Comyn alias Chilcott: Ann (Cade): 45. Robert: 45

Conceit: 69

Concent: 121

Concentration, favored by blindness: 16

Concentu: 40

Conceptual: background: 110. Imagery: 110

Concert: 121

Concinnabam: 40

Concio: 40

Conciones ad clerum: 40

Conciones et Orationes: 40

Concise Bible Commentary (W. K. Lowther Clark): 139

Conclusions(s): rhetorical: 51*. absence of, in Hume's notes: 88

Concord: musical: 40, 121. Of fine: 45

Concordance (Bradshaw): 112

Concordance, Biblical: 44

"Concordia mundi": 69*

Concrete: manner, M's; the Richardsons on; details, Newton's occasional appreciation of: 88. Imagery in M: 70. The concrete: 51

Concupiscence: 81, 36. Doctrine of: 81

Condé. Jean de: 120

Condee, Ralph Waterbury: 21

Condell, Henry (pr.): 44. His widow: 44

Condemnation. See Adam and Eve; Animals; Satan; Serpent

Conders, J.: 58

Condivi, Ascanio: 5

Condorcet, Marquis de: 115

Conduct, right: 31

Conduit Head, Cambridge: 40

Cone of night: 128

Confessio Fidei in Conventu: 44

Confessio Fraternitatis: 7

Confession, meaning of: 81

Confessions (Augustine): 112, 118, 71

Confessor, Edward the: 73

Confidant in epic or drama: 123

Confidence Man, The: 98

Confidence: 51*. In the future of the Commonwealth: 51

Confirmatio a causa: 40

Confirmation and refutation as one exercise: 20

Confiteor: 126

Conflagration, final: 93

Conflict: "of convictions": 98. Of good and evil, reason and passion in PL: 83

Conformitie's Deformity (Henry Burton): 147

Conformity: 47, 92*. To image of Christ: 123

Confucius: 34, 136. Confucianism: 71

Confusion: 2

Conger, George P.: 102, 128

Congo: 19, 49, 73, 144, 103

Congregational: Way: 7. Congregationalism: 9*, 44. Congregationalists: 52, 38. See also: Independents

Congregationalist: 44

Congregazione dell' Oratoria della Madonna della Fava: 68

Congreve, William: 58, 145, 97, 146

Congringianae: 44

Coniah: 51

Conimbricensian commentary on Aristotle: 40

Coningh, Abraham de: 68

Conington, J. (on translation): 58. See also: Connington

Conismarck, Capt., of Sweden: 44

Conjectura Cabbalistica: 144

Conjugates: 123. See also: Argument

Conklin, George N.: 1, 23, 34, 107, 110, 14, 93. Bible and Word of God: 107. Bible as M's primary source: 107. PL occasionally heretical: 107. Wolleb and Ames may have contributed to form but not content of De Doctrina Christiana: 107

Connaught, Ireland: 44

Connecticut: Courant, The: 115. Magazine, and Gentleman's and Lady's Monthly Museum, The: 115

Connecticut: 45

Connelly, Marc: 52

Connington (Conington): 45

Conington-Nettleship, edition of Virgil: 150

Connoisseur, The: 44. By J. Richardson: 88

Conqueror: 122*. See also: Warrior

Conquest, the Norman: 3

Conrad, Joseph: 137

Conradus de Mure: 40

Conring, Hermann: 44*

Conringianae, Catalogus Bibliothecae: 44

Consalvo: 123. See also: Gratiani

Conscience, La: 65

Conscience: 47, 51*, 93, 9*. See also: Liberty, religious

Consciousness, structure and perception of: 96*

Conservatives: 51. Conservativism, M's: 51

Consett, Rev. Mr.: 44

Considerations: and Proposals: 103, 116. On M's Early Reading (Charles Dunster): 88

Considerations: touching the likeliest means, etc: 16, 103, 113, 116, 147, 71. Upon a Printed Sheet: 116

"Consilium Regis": 44

Consistency, in poetic characters: 123*

Consolatio, Messianic prophecy as: 123*

Consolation for Our Grammar Schools, A (Brinsley): 20

Consolation: for earthly ills: 143. Of philosophy: 62

Consort: 121

Constable: Alice. See Cotton, Alice. Cuthbert: 44. Henry: 59, 120. Sir John: 45, 58, 118, 117. W. G.: 97

Constance: 49, 73. Constancy: 122*; as heroic virtue: 123

"Constans Thaumatographis": 40

Constant Method (MS): 40

Constantin, Robert: 40

Constantine: 9, 44, 51, 57, 73, 112, 116, 123, 3, 91, 130. The Great, St.: 114, 93. I, emperor: 111, 82*

Constantinople: 44, 45, 73, 3

Constantinus: Leo III: 73. II: 73, 116. III: 73

Constanzo, Angelo di: 123

Constellations: 89. Delineation of: 89. Description of: 89. Little known in M's time: 89

Consternation: 2

Constitutional Documents: 9

Constitutiones (Jesuits): 40

Constitutions and Canons (1604): 40. Ecclesiastical (1640): 66, 116

Construction: 132. Poetic: 132. Constructive: argument: 51. Reasoning: 51

Construing, Latin: 40

Consubstantiation: 71, 93

Consummation: 47

Contarini: Carlo, Doge of Venice: 44. Cardinal Gaspar: 93

Contarinus: 40

Contemplation: 53, 72. And ladder: 143. And discipline: 143. And sin of curiosity: 53. As opposed to "knowledge": 53. And action, in PR, and in SA: 125. Contemplative: life: 70, 123. Hero: 122*

Contemporary: influence, M's: 60. And personal elements of PL ignored by Hume: 88. Background of M's poetry: Dunster's innsufficient study of: 88. Background of M's poetry: Todd on: 88

Contempt: 45

"Contemptu mundi": 69, 123

Contentment: 58

Context: neglected by Bentley: 88. Carefully traced by Pearce: 88. Disregarded by Sympson: 88

Conti: Antonio: 111. Natale (Natali): 1, 40, 44, 60, 123, 128, 64; Mythologiae: 144

Continence: 139. 137

Continent. See Europe

Continental: books soon known at Cambridge: 40. Journey: 40, 51, 89

Contingency: 47, 124

Continuation of the History of Passive Obedience, A: 116

Continue: continuative epithets, Peck on: 88. Continued creation: 93; see also: Providence

Contio (Acontius), Giacomo: 55

Contra-paganos: 114*

Contra-Remonstrants (Gomerists): 40

Contraction(s): metrical: Pearce and Bentley: 88; the Richardsons: 88; Newton: 88; Todd: 88. In documents: 45

Contracts and convenants: 9. See also: Social contract

Contraries: 146, 25. Logical: 122*, 123*

Contrast: 143. In Comus, in PL: 143. Rhetorical device: 51; as an apocalyptic technique: 110

Contrera, Don Fernando Ruiz de: 44

Contrition: 47

Controversy(ies): Biblical: 51. M's aims, achievements, motives, methods: 30*, 40, 51

Convenient, the: 47

Conventicle Act: 44, 116, 94, 103

Convention: 47. Conventionality, occasional: of Thyer's attitude: 88; of Newton's: 88

Conversation, M's: 44. Corrupted by the Fall: 54

Conversion: 9, 25

Convivio (Dante): 70, 112, 111

Conway: Lady Anne: 7, 142. Moncure: 142; Demonology: 142. Secretary: 45

Cook: Mr.: 45. A. B.: 133. Albert S.: 16, 19, 57, 70, 128, 144, 39, 71, 92; on M: 104. Amos Jones: 115; The Student's Companion: 115. Elizabeth Christine: 115. John: 40, 44, 116, 38, 91. Thomas: 128

Cook's Proemium: 88

Cooke: Mr.: 44. Benjamin: 117. Col.: 44. C. (pr., publisher): 44, 97. Edward: 44, 116, 93. Elizabeth: 120. Francis: 40. H.: 58; praises M: 58. Henry (painter): 44; see also: Cook. Henry (another): 44. Increase: 115; The American Orator: 115. Isaac: 44. John: 58, 120. Sir Miles: 45. Richard: 44. Robert: 64. Shadrach: 44. Sir William: 40, 58

Cooke's Pocket Edition of...Poets: 44

Cookson, Edward: 44

Coolidge: John S.: 62. L. W., on M: 80

Cooper: 3. Anthony Ashley, 3rd Earl of Shaftesbury: 115. Charles Henry: 40*. Elizabeth: 58, 117. James Fenimore: 98. John Gilbert: 58. John: 40. John T.: 115; An Oration, and Poem, Delivered before the Government and Students of Harvard Univ.: 115. Lane: 19, 58, 70, 64, 100, 112, 101, 21; ed. and tr. The Rhetoric of Aristotle: 82. Myles: 115; The Patriots of North America: 115. Samuel (artist): 44. Bp. Thomas: 40, 44, 114, 123, 144, 93; effect of PL on: 87; works: The Life of Thomas Cooper Written by Himself: 87; The Purgatory of Suicides: 87. Thompson: 44. William: 44, 45

Coopers' Free School: 40

Coote: Edmund: 40. R.: 58

Cope: family: 44*, 45*. Mr.: 45. Mrs. (Walter): 45. Agnes (Harcourt): 45. Alice (Monoux): 45. Anne (Ann, Anna): 45; see also: Digby, Anne; Lee, Anne. Anne (Booth): 45. Anne (Fermor): 45. Ann (Gardiner): 45. Anne (Paston): 45. Ann (Sanders): 45. Anne (Spinckes): 45. Sir Anthony: 44*, 45*. Bridget (Raleigh): 45. C. W.: 97. Dorothy (Grenville): 45. Dorothy (Waller): 45. Edward: 40, 45. Elizabeth: 45; see also: Cecil, E.; Estcourt, E.; Goldsmith, E.; Greere, E. Elizabeth (Chaworth): 45. Lady Elizabeth (Farre): 44*, 45*. Elizabeth (Mohun): 45. Elizabeth (Sheffield): 45. Frances (Lytton): 45. Frances: see Lee, Frances. George: 45. Hannah: 45. Harry: 45. Henry: 45. Jackson: 14, 85. Jackson I: 52, 75, 79, 81, 105, 32, 53, 61, 93, 101, 106, 140*; on Satan: 61; rhythmical use of antithetical elements by M: 61; The Metaphoric Structure of PL: 48. Jackson I.: 17, 37, 60*, 110. Jane (Crewys): 45. Jane (Spencer): 45. John: 45. Sir John: 44*, 45*. Sir Jonathan: 44, 45. Katern Cull: 45. Katherine: 45. Margaret: see Hewett, Margaret. Mary: 44, 45; see also: Blake, Mary. Mary (Gerard): 45. Mary (Mallory): 45. Mary (Walter): 45. Rachel: 45. Richard: 45. Stephen: 45. Thomas: 45. Ursula (Ursule): 44, 45; see also: Doyley, Ursula. Sir Walter: 44, 45. Will: 45. William: 45*. Capt. William: 45. Sir William: 44*, 45*

Cope: case: 45. Genealogy: 45

Copenhagen: 44, 103

Copeario, Giovanni: 40, 121

Copernicus, Nicolas: 1, 6, 8, 8, 15, 34, 40, 77, 89*, 103, 113, 114, 122, 128*, 142, 139, 71, 72, 93, 149. And the heliocentric system: 128*. His "De Revotulionibus Orbium Celestium": 89. Propounds the Copernican System: 41, 89. Retains the notions of uniformly circular motion: 89

Copernican: System: 102, 144; and PL: 61; hypothesis: 109. Theory: 40, 89*, 94, 55; promulgation of: 89; progress of, retarded by imperfections and inaccuracies: 89; repudiated by Tyche Brahe: 89; supported by Kepler: 89; and Galileo: 89; attitude of other men of eminence: 89; gradual supersession of Ptolemaic system by: 89; confirmed by the advances made in astronomy: 89; condemned by the Inquisition: 89. M and Copernicanism: 89. Theory: 40, 89*, 94, 55. See also: Galileo

Cophteus, Josephus Baroatus: 64

Copia Verborum (Erasmus): 3

Copia, techniques of achieving: 118

Copinger, Edward: 44

Copiousness of words: 40

Copleston, Frederick: 93

Copley, John: 93

Coppe, Abiezer: 7

Coppens, J.: 36

Coppinger, Mr.: 45

Coppock, G. A.: 45

Coppyn, Sir George: 45

Coprario, John (composer): 44

Copreus: 92

Copson, Elizabeth: 40

Coptic: 40, 42

Copulation, in Eden and in Heaven: 137

Copy of a Letter (attr. to M): 44

Copy of a Letter from Lt. Col. John Lilburne to a friend (John Lilburn): 147

Copyright(s): 51

Cor Caroli: 89

Corah (Korah): 73

Corallaei Agri: 49. Corallian fields: 3

Corallaeis: 73

Corantoes: 40

Coras, Jacques de: works: 74, 64; Jonas: 74; Josué: 74; Samson: 74

Corasius (of Toulouse): 44, 73

Corax of Syracuse: 40

Corbet: Henry: 44. John: 37; Self-Imployment in Secret: 37. Miles (regicide): 44. Richard: 45, 64

Corbould: H.: 97. R.: 97

Corcoran Art Gallery, Washington: 44

Corcoran, Sister Mary Irma: 68, 75, 32, 36, 93, 110, 122, 17, 15

Corcyia, Isle of: 32

Cordelia: 73

Corderius, Bathasar: 40, 56, 74. In Librum Job: 74

Cordier: 99

Cordovero: 113

Cordus, Eurycius: 64

Cordy, Peggy: 64

Core Redivious: 116

Corfe (Corvesgate): 49

Corfield, Wilmot: 44

Corinedian Loxo: 3

Corineus: 73

Corinth(ians): 73, 74, 49. Corinthians I: 92. Epistles to: 3, 44, 51. Erasmus on: 3

Coriolanus (Shakespeare): 103, 88, 97

Cork, Earl of: 45

Cork, Ireland: 44

Corker: Mr.: 44. Robert: 44

Cormican, L. A.: 37, 86, 110

Cornazzano, Antonio: 65, 77, 74, 15, 117, 64. Works: Vita de la Gloriosa Vergine Maria: 74; Vita et Passione de Christo: 74

Corneille, Pierre: 6*, 100, 94, 97, 101

Cornelius a Lapide: 23

Cornelius Gallus: 40

Cornelius: Mr.: 44. John: 44

Cornell Univ.: 44. Library: 44

Cornford, Francis M.: 35, 37, 66, 76, 81, 125, 133, 141, 93, 148

Cornhill, London: 44

Cornhill, S.: 58

Cornish rebels: 73

Cornish: Henry: 45. William: 45

Cornock, Irene: 64

Cornozano, Antonio. See Cornazzano

Cornucopia: 49

Cornwall: 45, 49

Cornwallis (Cornwallys): W.: 23, 29. Sir William: 114

Cornwell, Francis: 114

Coromandel coast: 150

Corona: 89

"Corona" (Donne): 135

Coronides: 73

Corot: 70

Corporal punishment of schoolboys: 20

Corporation Act: 116

Corpus Byzantinae Historiae: 55

Corpus Christi College, Oxford: 45, 40. St. Benet's, Cambridge: 40

Corpus Juris Civilis: 82, 3

Corrections, M's of himself, studied by Peck: 88

Corrector, The: 115

Correggio, Niccolà da: 29

Correspondence, M's: 30. Structural principle: 67. See also: Letters

Corro, Antonio de: 40

Corruption: 51, 40, 143, 71. Before Flood: 143. And man's nature: 143. Doctrine a perversion: 143. During the Middle Ages: 71. Human, doctrine of: 71. Of the clergy: 40

Corsamonte: 122, 123

Corseige, Richard: 44

Corser, Thomas: 44

Corson, Hiram: 16, 136

Corton, co. Suffolk: 44

Cortona, P. da: 6, 27

Corus: 73

Corvinus, Matthias: 40

Cory, Herbert E.: 58, 68. _Spenser, the School of the Fletchers, and M_: 74

Coryat, Thomas: 6, 19, 88

Corydon: 73, 90

Cosham (Causham), co. Hants.: 44, 49

Cosimo: 27

Cosmas of Alexandria: 77

Cosmetics: 54

Cosmic: identities: 128*. Disharmony, named as the theme of PL: 83. Cosmography: 40, 144. Cosmology: 89, 113, 123, 50; not literal: 50; of the ancient Greeks: 89; and of M: 39, 113; the Mosaic: 89; of PL: 46*; Copernican: 46; Ptolemaic: 46

Cosmo, Umberto: 5

Cosmographia: 65

"Cosmopolitanism," the beliefs of the Alexandrian Jews: 107

Cosmos, poèmes: 65

Cosmos: 121, 71. Renaissance charts of: 25

Cosmourgia: 65

Cossack(s): 49, 51

Cossall: 45

Cossic numbers: 40

Costanzo, Angelo di: 120, 82. _Historia del Regno di Napoli_: 82

Costar, Pierre: 44

Coste, Bertrand de la: 10

Coste, Hilarion de: 10

Costello: W. J.: 128. William T.: 40

Coster, John: 44

Costobarus: 73

Costumes: 29*

Cote: 45

Cotes: Richard: 40. Thomas (pr., 1627-41): 40, 91

Cotgrave: J., _Treasury of Wit_: 58. Randle: 40

Cothrope: 45

Cotimia (Chocimum): 49

Cotin, (Abbe) Charles, _Magdeleine_: 74, 64

Cotta, Giovanni: 64

Cottaz, Joseph: 122

Cotter, G. S.: 58

Cotterell, Sir Charles: 44

Cotterill, H. B.: 33*, 64

Cottisford: 45

Cottle, J.: 58*

Cotton, co. Suffolk: 44

Cotton: Alice (Constable): 45. Charles: 15, 40, 58. Dorothy (Anderson): 45. Dorothy (Tamworth): 45. Edmund: 120. Elizabeth (Brocas): 45. Elizabeth (Honywood): 45. Elizabeth (Shirley): 45. Frances: 70. Henry: 45. Jane: 45. Joane (Paris): 45. John: 9, 15, 40, 44*, 45*, 147, 32. Lettice: 120. Lucy: see Woodhouse, Lucy. Lucy (Harvye): 45. Margaret (Howard): 45. Robert: 45, 120. Sir Robert

Bruce: 40, 44, 45. Roger: 120, 93. Seaborn: 82. Sir Thomas: 44*, 45*

Cottonian collections: 40

Cottonian Charters. See British Museum

Cotytto: 73, 90, 72, 143

Coulange, Louis. See Turmel, J.

Coulson, C. A.: 143. On conflict of science and religion: 143

Coulton, George G.: 142, 143, 93. Ancestry of Puritanism: 143. Five Centuries of Religion: 142

Councel, Antichristian: 51

Council in, of: Ireland: 44. Articles: 44. Constantinople, 3rd: 71. Nicea, A. D. 325: 78; as terminal date for "original purity" in religion: 107. Of Nice: 71. Of officers: 103. Sardica: 78. State: 16, 30, 40, 44*, 45, 51, 103, 94; M secretary to: 94. Trent: 27, 51, 83, 116, 71. Privy: 44. Of State of Republic: 103*

Council: powers of, etc.: 51. Epic: 122*. In Heaven: 50, 93. Divine: 123. In Hell: 50*, 77, 123. Supplementary analogues may be had in Andreini, Beaumont, Caedman, Cowley, Masenius, Valmarana, Valvasone: 77

Councils: M's contempt for the decisions of: 113. Of the Church: 93

Counsel: 45. Counselor: 45

Counsellours, cabin: 51

Counter-argument: 51

Counter-syllogisms: 51

Counter-Reformation: 27*, 81

Counter-Renaissance: 69

Counterpoint rhythm: 40, 121

Countess Dowager of Derby: 29

Country life near Cambridge: 40

Country-side: Peck's knowledge of: 88. Warton's familiarity with: 88; and with language of: 88. Todd on language of, in Comus: 88

Couplet(s): the heroic: 58. Octasyllabic: 40. See also: Blank verse; Rime

Courage: 51*

Courcelle, Pierre: 81

Courier, The: 146

Courland: Duchess of: 10. Duke of: 44

"Course by": meaning of: 40. Dispute by: 40

Course of study: 51

Course of Time, The: 65

Court and Times of Charles the 1st: 44

Court of Arches: 44. Of Articles: 44. Of High Commision: 116, 103, 40. Of Common Pleas: 44. Of Chancery and its procedings: 44*. Of Common Council, London: 40. Of King's Bench: 44. Of Whitehall: 44. Of Exchequer: 103. Of Law: 103

Court of Sapience, The: 60

Court Hand Restored: 45

Court: 44, 40, 51, 104. M offered position at: 44. Chancellor's of the Univ. of Oxford: 44. Education for: 40. Life, corruption of: 51. Masque: 104

Courtenay, H.: 58

Courtesy-books (mostly on marriage): 54*

Courtesy: 51, 122

Courthope: Mr.: 44. W. J.: 87, 110; on Renaissance element in M: 144

Courtier, P. L.: 58

Courtiers, greed of: 83

Courtin, Nicolas, Charlesmagne Penitent: 74

Courtly love: 122. See also: Frauendienst; Sovereignty

Courtney, Francis: 44

Courtship, M's: 87

Courville, X. de: 6

Coutances, André de (verse paraphrases of Gospel of Nicodemus): 74, 64

Coutts, T.: 97

Covel, John: 40

Covenant of grace, its manifestation and sealing: 63

Covenant(s): 123, 143, 103, 32*. The new: 143. In M's works: 32. Nature and obligations of: 96*. See also: Christ; Church; Tree of knowledge; Tree of life

Covenant, writ of: 45

Covenanters: 51

Covent Garden, London: 44, 45*

Coventousness, abstinence from, as heroic virtue: 123

<u>Coventry Plays</u>: 65

Coventry, co. Warwick: 44, 45

Coventry: F.: 58. Thomas, Lord Keeper of Great Seal: 44, 45

Coverdale, Myles (Miles): 143, 32, 91, 93, 3. On Josiah, destroyer of idolatry: 143, 3. And pains of Hell: 143

Covering Cherub: 25

Cow, P. B. and Co.: 44

Coward, William M. D.: 44*, 58

Cowel (Cowell), John: 45

Cowes, Isle of Wight: 44

Cowie, Alexander: 115

Cowley (?) (Culdehm), co. Oxon.: 44

Cowley, Abraham: 1, 10, 15*, 23, 33, 44, 50, 56, 58, 59, 60, 65, 77, 84, 86, 87, 95, 102, 108, 111, 114, 118, 122, 123, 127, 128, 129, 145*, 38, 39, 88, 91, 93, 64, 106, 130, 131, 137, 146*, 149, 148, 117*, 55, 13, 120, 132, 133. And M compared: 146. Works: <u>Poetical Blossoms</u>: 91; <u>Davideis</u>: 149, 95, 74, 144; Satan, Heaven, angels; comparison with M: 149; <u>The Wish</u>: 145

Cowley: H.: 58. Malcolm: 108

Cowlt, Mrs.: 44. See also: Colt

Cowper: Mr.: 45, 120. A.: 58. James: 44. W., Dr.: 58. William (clerk of Parliament): 44, 102. William: 6, 35, 40, 44, 58*, 70, 79, 86, 87, 98, 107, 142, 103, 3, 88, 97, 64, 137, 146*, 148, 150, 117*, 55, 25, 132, 130, 149. Admiration for M: 58*; borrowings from M: 58; translates M's Latin poems: 58; thought PL orthodox: 107; poem on desecration of M's grave: 87; <u>Three Heavenly Treatises</u>: 74

Cox: Daniel: 10. Rev. F. A., on moral influence of M's Satan: 87. H. Shute (pr.): 44. Mary: 44. Nicholas: 44. R. G.: 86. Richard: 44; his son, Richard: 44. Thomas: 45

Coxe: Dr.: 44. A. C.: 41. Benjamin: 44. Thomas: 44

Coxeter: Jane (Woodroff): 45. Margery (Fowler): 45. Richard: 44, 45*

Coyet (Coictus), Peter Julius (ambassador from Sweden): 44

Coypel, A.: 97

Crabbe: George: 58, 130, 146. G., influenced by M: 58

Crabtree, William: 89. Observation of transit of Venus by: 89. Death: 89

Cracovia: 49

Cradock: Mr.: 44. Francis: 91. S.: 99*. Walter: 9, 44

Craford (Creganford): 49

Craftsmanship: 70

Cragg, Elizabeth: 44

Cragge: Mr.: 44. John: 40, 44

Craig: Hardin: 23, 128, 39; <u>Eng. Religious Drama of the Middle Ages</u>: 74. John: 73, 103. M.: 97. W.: 97

Craik, T. W.: 110

Crakanthorpe, Richard: 40

Cramocke, Peter: 44

Cramoisy, Sebastian (pr.): 40

Cranch, Christopher Pearse: 58, 65

Crane, bookshop in St. Paul's churchyard: 44

Crane: Mrs. C. D.: 45. Hart: 145. R. S.: 12, 23, 58, 113, 145. Verner Winslow: 115. W. G.: 66

Cranes: 144

Cranfield: Lionel, 3rd Earl of Middlesex: 45. Rachel (Fane), Countess of Bath and Middlesex: 45

Cranford, Mr.: 44

Cranmer, Thomas (Abp.): 15, 40, 42, 44, 47, 51, 73, 87, 38, 82, 91, 93, 3,

103. Prayer book: 126

Cransford, co. Suffolk: 44

Crantor: 73, 114, 3

Crantz (Krantz), Albert: 73

Crantz(ius), George (Georgius): 73, 44

Cranwell, J.: 58

Crapulia: 49, 73

Crashaw, Richard: 1, 4, 6, 15, 23, 27, 40, 44, 59, 55, 35, 73, 77, 79, 81, 84, 86, 102, 105, 123, 132, 145, 39, 71, 88, 91, 93, 101, 109, 115, 130, 131, 149, 150, 55, 60. Works: Steps to the Temple: 74; Hymn as Sung by the Shepherds: 115

Crasso: 23

Crassus: Lucius: 73. Marcus Licinius: 73

Craster, Sir Edmund: 44

Crates: 44

Cratylus (Plato): 112

Craven, Isaac: 93

Crawford: C.: 58. G. P.: 44

Crawley: Francis: 44. F. S.: 141

Creacao, A: 65

Creacion del mundo (Acevedo): 65

Creacion del mundo (Vega Carpio): 65

Creacion, La: 65

Creatyon of Eve: 65

Creation: 9, 17, 31, 41, 42, 47, 50*, 60, 63*, 107, 89, 65, 98, 113, 128*, 143*, 144*, 32*, 36*, 46, 72*, 96*, 22, 119. Account in Genesis: 93, 119. A matter of faith: 93. Year of: 93. Council before: 93. A joint labour of the Godhead: 93. Ex Deo: 93. Ex Nihilo: 93. Ex materia praeexistente: 93. Two-fold: 50, 93. Reasons for: 93. End of: 93. Perfection of: 93. Goodness of: 93. Associated with: circle: 93; music: 93. Creatio continua: 93. M's treatment of: 109, 32, 144. M's views on: 137, 22, 107, 32. Sermon on: 32. Mechanistic view of: 32. Fall, renewal, in M: 72*. The first: 107. Knowledge of: 75*. As a dance: 75. Description of: 89, 32. God's activity before: 114. As heroic exploit: 122. Story as metaphor: 128. Two accounts of: 128. The Heavenly: 107. The aims of: 113. Brought about through the Son: 113. Of man: 50, 113. Of man, in world mythology: 118, 144. By retraction: 63. Orthodox ideas of: 32. Myth of: 32. Plato on: 144. And the Word: 144. And Hesiod: 144. Bacon on: 144. Henry More on: 144. Order: 144. Plan of: 144. Initial act: 144. Natural process: 144. Revelation of God through: 119. Details of: 144. Represents sacraments: 143. Illustration of: 143. In Geneva Bible and PL: 143. M and the Mosaic account: 144. Lambertus Danaeus on: 144. Purchas on: 144. See also: Providence; Adam; Adam and Eve; Angels, Animals; Eden; Eve; Books III, VII of PL; Man; Order; Demonic; Perversion; Generation

"Create": 107

Creatio ex nihilo: 71

Creation and Other Biblical Plays: 65

Creation of World in Spring: 77. See also: Heywood; Swan; Syncellus

Creation-myths: Babylonian: 141. Jewish: 141. Greek: 141

Creation, The: 98

Creationism: 93

Creative genius: 136

Creativity of the artist: 5

Creativity, true and perverted: 128*

Creator: the: 111. Celebration of: 75*. Castigation of: 75

Creature, visible and inferior: 51

Creccelius, Johannes: 44. Collectanae: 44

Crecklad (Creclad): 49

Creditor: 45

Creech, T.: 58

Creed Church near Aldgate, London: 44

Creed, the Nicene: 71

Creed, John (bks., 1670-85): 91

Creed: 40, 143. Universally recited and believed: 143. Commentary of the Richardsons, the expression of a personal: 88

Creeds: as test of M's orthodoxy: 107. Importance of during the Middle

Ages: 71. Protestant: 71

Creel, H.: 34

Creet. See Crete

Creighton: Charles: 16, 40. Mandell: 120. Robert: 40

Crellius: Fortunatus: 40. Nicholas: 22

Cremona: 49. Cremona's trump: 73, 121

Crendon. See Long Crendon

Creon: 44, 70, 73, 92, 3

Crespigny, Lady Champion de: 58

Crespin, Jean: 40

Cressy (village): 49

Cressy: Hugh: 79. Father Serenus: 7

Crest, M's: 28

Crestonus, Joannes: 40

Creswick, T.: 97

Crete: 73, 49, 3

<u>Cretensis, A Briefe Answer to an ulcerous treatise...Gangraena</u> (John Goodwin): 147

Creusa: 44, 73

Crevel, M. van: 100

Crewé-Milne, Robert Uffley Ashburton, Marquis of: 44

Crewe, co. Cheshire: 44

Crewkerne: 44

Crewys, Jane. See Cope, Jane (Crewys)

Creyghton, Robert (1593-1572): 44, 91

Crichton, James: 64

Crighton, Marjorie P.: 44

Crim: 49

Cripplegate: 40, 103

Cripps: Henry (bks., d. 1663): 91. Sir Stafford: 143; on economic and social justice: 143

Cririe, J.: 58

Crisis: 123. Heroic: 122

"Crisófilo Sardanápalo": 65

Crisp: Stephen: 7. Tobias: 79, 114

Crispinus: 73

Crispus, Flavius Julius: 73

Cristina di Lorena: 6

Cristina, Queen of Sweden: 38

<u>Critias</u> (Plato): 73, 32, 112

<u>Critic</u> (New York): 44

Critic: 50, 146. Of fine art: 70

<u>Critical Dictionary</u> (Bayle): 88

<u>Critical Dissertation with Notes on M's PR</u> (Meadowcourt): 88

<u>Critical Observations on Shakespeare</u> (John Upton): 88

<u>Critical Review</u>: 88, 115

<u>Critici Sacri</u>: 32

Criticism: 63*, 143, 11, 146*. Modern: 143. Renaissance: 31, 51. Of PL dictated by party allegiance: 107. of M: 58*. Of Lawes: 121. 19th C. concept of M's work: 80. And creation: 146. Illustration as: 146. Imitation as: 146. Adverse: 117*. Commendatory: 117*. Biographical: 25. Historical: 25. Compared to 18th c., Victorian and modern criticism: 146. Debt to M: 146. And genre: 146. And the M tradition: 146. And the periodical press: 146. Revolutionary character of: 146. Shift in interest during 19th c.: 87. M and criticism: 70, 75. See also: Poetic theory

Critics: 143. Character of: 143. Discredited: 143. And the art of the past: 143

<u>Critique on M's PR</u>: 88

<u>Crito</u> (Plato). See Critias

Critolaus: 60, 73, 3

Croce, Benedetto: 123, 64

Crocetti, Camillo Guierrieri: 122

Croese: 7

Croft, Sir James: 40, 3

Crofts, J. E. V.: 145

Croi, François de: 93

Croke: Burton: 45. Charles: 45.

Elizabeth (Wright): 45. George: 40, 44. Sir Richard (Crooke): 44, 45. Unton: 45. Wright: 45

Croker: John: 45. Mary. See Pye, Mary (Croker)

Croker: 130

Croll(ius), Oswald: 79, 93

Croll, Morris W.: 37, 145

Croly, G.: 58

Crompton, William: 54

Cromwell, Oliver: 1, 7*, 9*, 10*, 15, 16, 18, 27, 28*, 30, 31, 33, 34, 40, 42, 44*, 45, 51, 59*, 60, 81, 84, 86, 87, 111, 108*, 113*, 114*, 116, 120*, 103*, 3, 123, 125, 128, 132*, 136, 144, 145*, 147*, 26*, 32, 38*, 39, 46, 71, 72, 82*, 91*, 93, 94*, 97, 115, 137, 148, 150, 117, 13, 25, 141, 130. M's loyalty: 55, 147, 94. M and: 147. M doubts Cromwell's view on the State Church: 147. M relation to: 51, 94. M member of Cromwell's government: 61. And abolition of tithes: 147. Accepts Goffe's proposal of prayer: 147. Agrees with Ireton on property: 147. And the Instrument of Government: 147. And the New Model Army: 147. Consents to Charles' execution: 147. Conservatism of: 147. Contends for liberty of all: 147. Disappoints M: 147. Dissolves the Rump: 147. Fails to satisfy: 147. Fearful of new theories of government: 147. Ignores Winstanley: 147. Immature wrestler with ideas: 147. Levellers lose faith in him: 147. Negotiations with the King: 147. Master of practical psychology: 147. On toleration of Catholics: 147. On vote of No Addresses: 147. Opposes the Agreement: 147. Rebuffs Harrington: 147. Swings to Leveller position: 147. Timer of action: 147. Upholds the Declaration of the Commons: 147. Views on state church issue: 147. As a musician: 121

Cromwell, Oliver, The Writings and Speeches of: 45

Cromwell: Bridget (Oliver's daughter): 44. Richard: 9, 10, 44*, 45, 51, 103, 120, 26, 38, 91, 94. Robina: 10. Thomas: his suggestion of marriage as a source of strength in alliance: 83; his execution: 83; Melancthon's description of his execution: 83

Cromwell's Army (Firth): 3

Cromwellians: 51

Cronian Sea: 19, 49, 73

Cronus: 60

Cronus: 90, 144. See also: Saturn

Crook: John: 147; published Tythes No Property to, nor lawful maintenance for a Powerful Gospel-preaching Ministry: 147. Major: 45

Crooke: Helkiah: 93. John (bks., 1637-69): 91. Richard: see Croke. Samuel: 40. William (bks.): 44. See also: Croke

Croon, Dr. William: 10, 91

Cropley, Edward: 45

Crosfield, A.: 58

Crosland, J.: 36

Crosna. See Frederick William

Crosnier, Jules: 44

Cross currents in Eng. Lit. of the 17th c.: 112

Cross Keys: 45, 44. As Norfolk: 44. Ludgate: 44

Cross, the: 72. In St. Paul's churchyard: 40

Cross: F. L.: 36. William: 44

Crossbows: 40

Crosse: R.: 58. William: 93, 64

Croston, A. K.: 44

Croton: 3

Crouch, John: 103

Crowe: E.: 97. W.: 58

Crowley: John: 44. Robert: 93

Crown: 45. Sign in Pope's Head Alley: 44. Office, Chancery: 44

Crowther, John: 44

Croyland (Croilana): 49

Crucifixion: 113, 32, 72*. Augustine on the: 113. See also: Passion

Crump: C. G.: 44. M. Marjorie: 74, 64; Epyllion from Theocritus to Ovid: 74

Crundell, H. W.: 128

Cruquius: 44

Crusades: 123, 71

Crusca: Accademia della: 88. Dictionary of the: 83. See also: Della Crusca

Crutched Friars, London: 44

Cruttwell, Patrick: 15, 79

Cry of the Royal Blood, The: 30*, 62

Crynes, Nathaniel: 44

Crypsis (structural principle): 67

Crysostom, St.: 5

Crystalline: ocean: 128, 144. Sphere of the Universe: 41, 89, 128*

Ctesias: 73

Ctesiphon (Tesiphon): 19, 49, 73

Cubus, Joannes: 40

Cuckoldry: 54

Cuckoo and the Nightingale: 88

Cuddesdon (Culsden, Cudlesden), co. Oxon.: 44*, 45*

Cuddie, Spenser's: 70

Cudworth: Ralph: 9, 12, 15, 40, 42, 60, 74, 112, 114, 123, 134, 142, 38, 93, 148; sermon by: 38. Robert: 44. W.: 58

Culcares, Guiddon: 44

Cullen (Colonia, Cologne, Coloniensis): 49, 73

Cullimore, W.: 44

Cullman, Oscar: 11, 93

Cullum, Sir Thomas Gery: 44

Culma: 49

Culpeper: John, 1st Lord: 114. Nicholas: 114

Culpepper, Sir Cheney: 10, 44

Cultellino: 44

Cults: 7

Culture: 51, 143*. Medieval: 51. M's individualistic: 143. Philosophical: 143*. Platonic: 143*. Protestant: 143*. Scriptural: 143*. Christian: 143*. And the State: 70

Cultus Dei: 40

Culuehm. See Cowley

Culverwell: Ezekiel: 93. Rev. Nathaniel: 23, 40, 44, 112, 114, 93; Discourse of the Light of Nature: 74. Preacher: 40

Cumanagota: 49

Cumberbatch, Mr. See Comberbach

Cumberland: 45, 49. Earl of: 45. George: 58, 25. Richard: 27, 58*, 68, 92, 88, 117; influenced by PL: 58

Cummings, E. E.: 105

Cumont, F.: 36

Cumulation, use of: 51

Cumulative style, Todd on: 88

Cundall, J. (publisher): 97

Cunizza: 111

Cunningham: A.: 97. Alexander (author of History of Great Britian): 44. Alexander (another): 44. Dolora: 29. Peter: 44, 58. William: 128

Cupid and Psyche: 143

Cupid: 1, 29, 44, 73, 90, 144, 72, 25

Curan, Stuart: 25

Curcellaeus, Stephanus: 123

Curetes: 73

Cureus, Joachim: 40

Curfew: 121

Curial language: 5

Curio: Coelius Secundus: 41. Leo: 41

Curiosities of Literature: 98. By D'Israeli: 88

Curiosity: 114*. Idle: 144

Curius: Marcus: 44. Manius Curius Dentatus: 73

Curling, Nicholas: 45

Curll, Walter, Bp. of Winchester: 44

Currer, Frances M. R.: 44

Curricula of grammar schools: 20*

Curriculum: 51. At Cambridge (M's dislike of): 8

Currier, Thomas F.: 44

Curry, Walter Clyde: 23, 68, 75, 79, 102, 107, 110, 123, 125, 128, 142, 85, 92, 93, 101. M's ideas from Plato and the later neo-Platonists: 107. M's ideas of creation from Fludd: 107. <u>M's Ontology, Cosmogony, and Physics</u>: 74

Curson, Sir John: 44

<u>Cursor Mundi</u>: 55, 68, 123, 133, 32, 36, 88, 149

<u>Cursory Remarks Upon Some Late Disloyal Proceedings</u>: 116

Curtaine-drawer of the World, The: 45

Curteis, T.: 58

Curtes, William: 44

Curtis: Benjamin, Jr.: 115. Mrs. George Vaughan: 44

Curtiss, Joseph T.: 128

Curtius: Ernst Robert: 69, 100, 110, 122, 32, 39, 106; <u>European Lit. and the Latin Middle Ages</u>: 74. Marcus: 27, 73. Quintus: 40, 44. Sir William: 10

Curtney, Hugh: 44

Curzii: 60

Cusa, Nicholas of: 114. See also: Cusanus

Cusanus, Cardinal Nicholas: 77; <u>De Docta Ignorantia</u>: 77

Cusco: 19, 49. In Peru: 73

Cushman, Robert: 37

Cuspinian, Johannes: 82. Works: <u>Historia Caesarum et Imperatorum Romanorum</u>: 82

Custom House: London: 44, 45*. Quay (Key): 45

Custom: 9*. Estates held by: 45

Customs, Commissioners of: 44

Cuthbert (St.) of Lindisfarne: 40

Cutler, Coleman: 16

Cutpurse, Moll: 44

Cutter, Abram G.: 44

Cutteris, Elizabeth: 44

Cutzenellebogen. See William VI

Cuyler, J. P.: 44

Cybele: 73, 90

Cyclades: 49, 73

<u>Cyclopaedia of Eng. Lit.</u>: 45

Cyclops: 56, 73, 123

Cydonius: 49, 73

Cyllene: 49, 90. Hoar: 73

Cyllenius: 73

Cymbal: 121

<u>Cymbeline</u>: 134, 88

Cymbrians. See Danes

Cymenshore: 49

Cynegetica (Oppian): 3

Cynewulf: 15, 36. <u>Christ</u>: 36. And Cyneheard: 36

Cynic impudence: 3

Cynosure: 90

Cynthia: 1, 73, 90, 25. The moon: 89. See also: Diana

<u>Cynthia's Revels</u> (Jonson): 135

Cynthius: 73, 90. See also: Apollo

Cypria (Venus): 143. See also: Cypris

Cypria: 90

Cyprian: St.: 9, 57, 68, 70, 74, 77, 128, 32, 36, 101, 54, 73, 38, 113, 93. Works: "Testimonies against the Jews": 74; <u>On the Good of Patience</u>: 36; <u>Opera</u>: 82*. Of Carthage: 114. Of Antioch: 114

Cyprianus: 149. Gallus: 65, 36*; <u>Heptateuchos</u>: 36

Cypris (Venus): 73. See also: Cypria

Cyprius: 73. See also: Cupid

Cyprus (Cypros): 44, 49, 73

Cyrenaic(k) route: 73

Cyrene: 3, 49, 51, 73, 112

Cyriak Skinner, upon his Blindess, to Mr. (M): 3

Cyril: St. (Patriarch of Alexandria): 57, 65, 68, 77, 73, 93; 2nd Letter to Nestorius: 74; In Jonam Prophetam: 74. St., of Jerusalem: 65, 77, 114, 36, 71, 93; works: Catecheticae Orationes: 74; Catechetical Lectures: 36

Cyropaedia: 72

Cyrus (the Great): 19, 73, 123, 3

Cytherea: 44, 73, 90, 3. Her son, Aeneas: 73. See also: Venus

Czar: 19*

Czech Temptation-play: 65

Czerniechovia: 49

-D-

D., E. See Dering

D., G. (pr.): 44

D., I. (pr., 1637-48): 44, 91. See also: Dawson, John

Dabridgecourt, Mr.: 44, 45

Dacian (Dacizo): 44, 73

Dacier: 2

Dacor (Dacre): 49

d'Acugna, Christ.: 88

Da creacão e composicão do homem: 65

Dacres, Edward: 93

Daedalus: 29

Daemon: 1, 29, 90, 142*. Substance of: 142. Possession by: 142. M on: 142. See also: Demonolgy; Devils

Daemonomachia: 65

Dagon: 19, 68, 73, 125, 143, 144, 72*, 92*. See also: Temple of Dagon

Dagonalia: 50, 92

Dahlberg, C. R.: 59

Dahomean Negroes of Africa: 118

Daiches, David: 4, 27, 37, 52, 66, 75, 79, 100, 86, 110, 127, 143, 62, 108, 93, 101, 21. Works: The Living M: 60; M: 60

Daillé, Jean: 93

Daily schedule, M's: 44

Daily Gazette(er): 117

Daily News, The: 136

Daily Post: 88

Daines, Simon: 135*

Daintry, M. J.: 58

Dainville, Francois de: 40

Dalby (Great Doulby), co. Leicestershire: 44, 45

Dalby: Joseph: 93. William: 44, 45

Dale, T. C.: 44, 45

Dalilah: 1, 4, 52, 56, 68*, 70, 103, 113, 125*, 126, 128, 132, 144, 71, 72*, 92*, 109, 130, 55, 25. Character of: 132. In defense of nationalism: 72. In definition of love: 72. In offer of catahrsis: 72. In temptation of weakness: 72. See also: Delilah

dall' Anquillara, Andrea: 1

Dallas: E. S.: 87; on poetic sensibility of M: 87; The Gray Science: 87. R. C.: 58

Dallington, Sir Robert: 40, 114

D'Almaine, W. F.: 97

Dalmatius: 44, 73

Dalton, Dr. John: 44, 58, 143, 117, 55, 21

Daly, Augustine: 44

Dalziel Bros.: 97

Dam, B. A. P. van: 16

Dama: 73

Damaetas, old: 73, 90

Damascene, St. John: 77, 24*, 142, 123. Works: Opera: 77; De Duo Vol.: 77; De Fide Orth.: 77

Damasco: 19, 49, 73. See also: Damascus

Damascus, St. John of: 32

Damascus: 73, 144, 49, 73

Damasippus: 73

Damasus: 73

Damer, J.: 58

Damiani, Peter: 68, 111

Damiata: 19, 49, 73, 144

Damned, punishment of: 50

Damoetas: 72, 3

Damon and Pythias, the Tragicall Comedie of: 88

Damon: 144. Charles Diodati: 44, 112, 123. See Diodati. S. Foster: 58, 60, 25*

Dampier, Dr.: 88

Damsel train: 92

Dan (city in Palestine): 49, 73. Territory of tribe of Israel: 49, 73

Dana: Francis: 115. Joseph: 115; A discourse on the Character and Death of General George Washington: 115. Richard H: 115; An Oration Delivered Before the Washington Benevolent Society at Cambridge: 115

Danaeus, Lambertus: 65, 79, 102, 123. The Wonderfull Workmanship of the World: 144

Danaids, chorus of: 92

Danaus: 73, 92

Danaw: 73

Danby: Earl of: see Danvers, Henry. F.: 97. John F.: 69, 93

Dance(s): 121*. Music: 121. Masque: 29*. Music: 121. Dancing: 40, 51; masters: 40; M's attitude toward: 137. Images related to: 8. See also: Music

Dandinus: 142

Dandolo, Enrico: 16, 73

Dane, Nathan: 40, 44

Daneau, Lambert: 77, 142, 32, 93. Works: A Dialogue of Witches: 142; Physica Christ, tr. Thomas Twyne, 1578: 77

Danegelt, four nobles of: 73

Danes (Cymbrians): 44, 3. Danish invasion: 3. See also: Denmark

Danes, John: 40

Daniel: "Clackshugh": 58. Arnaut: 100. Bp. of Winchester: 36. George: 44. Peter: 44. Roger (pr., bks., 1622-66): 40, 91. Samuel: 1, 4, 18, 20, 29, 40, 58, 59, 69, 102, 114, 122, 129, 145, 39, 93, 64, 150, 21; sonnets of: 87

Daniel: 51, 57, 60, 68, 73, 74, 90, 120, 133, 3

Daniello da Lucca, Bernardino: 74, 111. Works: ed. Dante: 82. Poetica: 74

Daniells, Roy: 1, 6, 37, 60, 110, 14, 93, 64, 101*. Satan's exercise of unity, power and will: 61. M, Mannerism and Baroque: 74

Danielou, Jean: 79, 36, 39, 93. Origen: 74

Daniels: A. H.: 41. Earl: 21. Edgar: 14

Danish: ambassadors: 44. Resident: see Gioe; Petkum

Danite(s): 73, 72, 92. See also: Israelites

Dansey, Mr.: 44

Danson, G.: 97

Dante and Other Essays (Church): 70

Dante, Alighieri: 1, 4, 5*, 6, 12, 15*, 16, 17, 18, 23, 27, 30, 31, 35, 40, 41, 42, 44*, 45, 50, 51, 52, 54, 57, 58, 59, 60, 69, 70*, 73, 103, 74, 76, 77, 79, 84, 86, 87, 89, 90, 98, 100*, 102, 105, 112, 110, 113, 114, 121, 120*, 118, 122, 123*, 124, 126, 127, 129*, 132, 133, 135, 3, 136, 139, 141, 143, 145, 14, 26, 32*, 38, 39, 46, 53, 62, 71, 72, 82*, 88, 91, 93*, 94, 97, 64*, 101, 109, 130*, 137, 146*, 149, 148, 150, 117, 55, 21, 13, 25. Cary's translation of: 146. And M compared: 146, 37. Sonnets: 146. Vita Nuova compared to Shakespeare's sonnets: 87. Works: Convivio: 82; De Monarchia: 74, 83, 82; Inferno: 60, 82, 146; Purgatorio: 82; Paradiso: 60, 82, 77; Divine Comedy: 60, 74, 83, 87, 46, 146; "Letter to the Can Grande": 74

Dantine, Ramis: 44

Dantiscus: 49

Dan(t)zig: 44, 103

Danube River (Danubius, Danaw): 19, 44, 49, 73, 144

Danvers: Harrington: 45. Henry, Earl of Danby: 45. Sir John: 44, 45, 114. Samuel: 44

Daphne: 1, 73, 90, 104, 3. Grave of: 144, 32. Place: 49

Daphnis: 73, 90

Darbishire, Helen: 1*, 9, 16, 20, 40, 44*, 45, 56, 59, 60, 63, 68, 86*, 100, 105, 118, 128, 135*, 39, 62, 101, 150, 112, 133, 136. Works: ed. MS. Ed. of PL, 1: 44, 135*; "The Chronology of M's Handwriting": 82

Darby: John, Jr. (stationer): 44. S.: 58

D'Arcy, Martin C.: 52, 75, 93. The Mind and Art of Love: 48

Darcy: Elizabeth: 40. Thomas: 40

Dardanian: 73, 3. See also: Trojan

Dardanius: 49

Dardanus: 123

Darent, co. Kent: 44

Dares, Phrygius: 40

D'Argent, Abel: 64

Darien: 19, 49, 73

Darius: the Great, King of Persia: 60, 73, 3. The Mede: 73, 3

Dark Ages: 51

Darkness at Noon: 34

Darkness: 8, 90, 128. See also: Erebus

Darlington: Abraham: 44. John: 44; his son, John: 44

Darmstadt, Germany: 44

Darnley, Robert: 103

Darrel, John: 142

Darrell: Alice: see Holloway, Alice (Darrell). Walter: 45

Darroll, G. M. H.: 93

Dart, Thurston: 39

Dartford: 45

Dartnoll, Jasper: 45

Darwen: 49

Darwent: River in Kent: 49. (Derwent), River in Yorkshire: 49

Darwin: Charles: 15, 34, 35, 128, 139, 71, 149; PL once favorite reading of: 87; voyage of the Beagle: 87; works: Origin of Species: 35, 87; Autobiography: 87. Erasmus: 15, 58, 97

Dasent, J. R.: 40

Dashwood: family: 44. Sir John, 10th Baronet: 44. Sir Robert John, 9th Baronet: 44. Sarah Moore: 44

da Silva, José Amara: 117

Dati MSS.: 45

Dati: C.: 6*, 17, 30, 44, 59, 103, 3. Carlo Roberto: 28, 44*, 73, 84, 111, 121, 120, 134, 26, 38, 91, 149, 117, 55

Dating, method of: 29

Dato, Carlo: 128

Daube, D.: 79

D'Aubigné, Agrippa: 65, 67

Daubray, M. Dreux, Lord of Offemont, Villiers, etc.: 44

Dauby. See Dalby

Daughters of God: 93

Daughters, M's: 44. M's relation with: 94, 137

Daunian: 73

Daunius: 49

Daunus: 73

Dauphin (later Louis XIV): 6

Davantes, Pierre (Antesignanus): 40

Davanzati, Bernardo: 73

Davenant: family: 44. Charles: 44. John, Bp. of Salisbury: 10, 15, 40, 50, 114. William, son of playwright: 44*

Davenant, Sir William: 1, 28, 29, 40, 44*, 50, 56, 59, 60, 70, 103, 84, 86, 133, 120, 122, 136, 94, 144, 145, 26, 39, 91, 101, 131, 137, 150, 117, 55, 130. Saved by M: 136. Gondibert: 74, 91

Davenport: 49. John: 9. R. A.: 58

Davey, Henry: 40

David: 4, 30, 44, 60, 68, 70, 73, 112, 122, 127, 143, 39, 71, 72*, 91, 123, 32, 92, 119, 103, 3. Psalms of: 103. Compared with Samson as giant slayer and hero of faith: 123. Key of: 143. 3rd age to: 143. David and Orpehus: 106*. See also: Cowley; Du Bellay; Walther

David and the Amalekite Upon the Death of Saul: 116

David, J. I.: 97

Davideis (Cowley): 65, 118, 130

Davidson: John: 40. Philip: 115

Davie, Donald: 12, 15, 75, 86, 105, 110, 14, 39, 101. "Syntax and Music": 74

Davies: Ebenezer T.: 93. Lady Eleanor: 58, 114. Godfrey: 9, 44, 45, 116, 144, 101. Hugh Sykes: 138. J.: 58. John: 29, 60, 69, 128. Sir John: 15, 20, 24, 76, 83, 102, 114, 129, 134, 145, 36, 39, 71, 93, 55; Orchestra: 36. John of Hereford: 15, 40, 102, 114, 93. John of Kidwelly: 40. Matthew: 44. Richard, Bp. of St. David's in Wales (Diggan Davie): 83. Samuel: 58, 115; influenced by L'Allegro and Il Penseroso: 58; works: A Poem Wrote by a Clergyman in Virginia in a Storm of Wind and Rain; Sermons on Important Subjects. Sneyd: 117. Sir Thomas (bks.): 44. W. D.: 79, 36. W. H.: 111. William: 120

Da Vinci: 29, 114. See also: Leonardo

Davis: B. E. C.: 83. Miss: (courted by M) and M: 44. Miss: 58, 94, 137. (Davys), Mr.: 44. Daughter of Dr.: 23, 44. Dr. Thomas: 44, 59. C. T.: 79. F. N.: 45. H. (ed.): 135. Norman: 64. Richard B.: 115; Poems by Richard B. Davies: 115. Robert Gorham: 60. T.: 58. Walter Goodwin: 44. Walter R.: 69

Davison: David (grocer): 44. Dennis: 44. Francis: 40, 39

Davity, Pierre: 19, 44, 113, 144, 94

Davus: 73

Davy Dickar's Dream (Churchyard): 83

Davy, Sir Humphrey: 13

Dawe, Donovan: 44

Dawes, Richard: 117

Dawkins, Polecarp: 44

Dawn: 8, 90. See also: Aurora

Dawson: Mr.: 44; see also: Lawson. Anne: 44. Christopher: 52, 56, 69, 143, 93; and spiritual forces: 143. Giles E.: 44. John (I. D., pr.): 44. Martin: 44. Samuel: 44. Thomas (pr.): 40. Wm.: 115; Poems on Several Occasions: 115

Day: 90

Day: division of: 89. And night, according to Ptolemaic theory: 89. Days, in Heaven: 50. For Day of the Lord: see Last Judgement

Day: Angell, letter-writing formulary: 20. Douglas: 110. George: 40. John: 40, 58, 93. Thomas: 128. William: 40

Day of Judgement: 71

Dayton, Hughes: 16

De la Creatione del Mundo (Cornazzano): 65

De la Mare, Walter: 35, 136, 137

De la Republique: 51

De Agri Cultura (Cato): 3

De Aitzema, Leo: 38

De Amicitia: 26

De Anima: 5

De Animorum Immortalitate: 65

De Argumentis Scientiarum (Bacon): 134

De Arte Poetica (Vida): 70

De Barthoma, Lewis: 128

de Baas. See Baas

De Beer, E. S.: 6. See also: Evelyn

De Beneficiis (Seneca): 70, 3

De Bras: 3

De Brass, Henry: 70, 73, 84, 146

De Bry, Theodore: 144

De Burgh: 3

De Cain et Abel: 65

De Chorographia (Mela): 3

De Civili Dominio (Wycliffe): 83

De Civitate Dei (Augustine): 3, 112, 113. See also: The City of God

De Comus à Satan (Morand): 134

De Conscribendis Epistolis: by Erasmus: 20. By Vives: 20

De Copia Verborum (Erasmus): 20

De Corpore Politico (Thomas Hobbes): 147

De Creatione et Lapsu Angelorum: 65

De Creatione Ale: 65

De Creatione Mundi: by Barlaeus: 65. By Lernutius: 65. By Parifioli: 65. By Wandalbertus: 65

de Crevecoeur, J. H. (St. John): 71

De Daemonibus (Psellus): 112

De Diei Septimi Opere: 65

De Dierum Creatione Hymni VI: 65

De Dieu, Louis. See Dieu, Louis de

De Diligendo Deo: 52

De Diversis Quaestionibus (Augustine): 112

De Doctrina Christiana (M): 20, 52*, 63*, 102*, 112, 113*, 116, 22*, 103*. Accomodation: 107*. Anthropomorphism: 107*. Body and soul indivisible: 107*. Chiliasm: 107*. Christ as judge: 107*. Christ dies body and soul: 107*. Demons tempt and punish men: 107*. Editors have not used as commentary upon PL: 107*. The Fall: 107*. God did not make demons: 107*. Logos inspires men with Spirit: 107*. Moses did not see God: 107*. Mutual hypostatic union: 107*. Prov. viii, interpretations of: 107*. Religion in its original purity: 107*. The rule of judgement: 107*. Satan author of evil: 107*. "Shorter systems of the divine," form drawn from: 107*. Son and Father not of same essence: 107*. Treatment of the soul: 22*. Angelic creation, date of in: 102. Arianism in: 102. Battle in Heaven described: 102. Composition date in: 102. History, description, revisions of manuscripts: 63*. Hell location of in: 34. Mosaic law, relation to gospel in: 102. All sins included in the Fall: 52. On Biblical interpretation: 52. Christ died for all men: 52. Meaning of nature: 52. Twofold will denied in God: 52. Hermeneutics of: 22. Treatment of creation: 22. See also: *Christian Doctrine*; Milton, John, Works

De Duplici Copia Rerum ac Verborum Commentarii Duo (Erasmus): 112

De Duplici Copia Verborum ac Rerum (Erasmus): 20

De Elocutione (Demetrius): 3

De Epistolis Latine Conscribendis (Verepaeus): 20

De Fabrica Mundi: 65

De Factis Dictisque Memorabilibus, Libri ix (Valerius Maximus): 20

De Figures (Despauterius): 20

De Filippis, Michele: 144

De Filippis, Michele: 6, 44, 128, 21

De Finibus (Cicero): 112

De Generatione Animalium (Aristotle): 3

de Haro. See Haro

De Hominis Opificio: 65

De Idea Platonica (M): 112, 132

De Inventione Dialectica (Agricola): 20

De Jordy, Alma: 40

De Jure Belli et Pacis: 103

De La Haye, Jean: 68

De Lacy, Hugh: 128

De Lancre, Pierre: 142

De Legibus: 116

De Lingua Latino (Varro): 3

De Loutherbourg, P. J.: 97

De Lyra, Nicholas: 68

de Magny, Constantin: 117

de Maisieres, M. T.: 36

De Man, Paul: 14

De Medici: Catherine: 29. Lorenzo: 29

De Miseria Hominis: 65

De Montezinos, Antonio: 38

De Mundi Creatione: 65

De Mundi Sphaera: 65

De Musica (Boethius): 121

De Musica (Plutarch): 121

de Nonney de Fontenai, C.: 117

De Nuptiis Philologiae: 121

De Officiis: 111

De Opere Sex Dierum: 65

De Operibus Dei: 65

De Operibus Sex Dierum: 65

De Oratore (Cicero): 20, 3

De Ordine Mundi: 65

De Origine Mali: 12

De Paradiso: 65

De Partibus Animalium (Aristotle): 3

De Partitione Oratoria (Cicero): 20

De Patris, F.: 6

De Pauley, W. C.: 9

de Pauw. See Pauw

De Placitis Philosophorum (Plutarch): 112

de Plinval, G.: 36

De Poeta Libri Sex (Minturno): 70

De Praestigiis Daemonum: 117

De Quincey, Thomas: 16, 44, 87, 105, 135, 136, 112, 142, 14, 71, 94, 130, 146. Opinion of PL and M: 87. On Anne Manning's *Life of Mary Powell*: 87. Bibliography of his M criticism: 146. Preface: 146. Works: "On M": 87; *Collected Writings*: 142; *Autobiography*: 146; *Confessions of an English Opium Eater*: 146; *Diary*: 146; *Dr. Samuel Parr*: 146; *Herder*: 146; *Joan of Arc*: 146; *Letters to a Young Man*: 146; *Life of M*: 146; *M's Versus Southey and Landor*: 146; *Notes on Walter Savage Landor*: 146; *On M*: 146; *Orthographic Mutineers*: 146; *Poetry of Pope*: 146; *Postscript Respecting Johnson's Life of M*: 146; *Questions as to Actual Slips in M*: 146; *Rhetoric*: 146; *Rosicrucians and the Free Masons*: 146; *Schlosser's Literary History*: 146; *Shakespeare*: 146; *Sir William Hamilton*: 146

De Ratione Scribendi (Brandolinus): 20

De Ratione Studii (Erasmus): 20*

De Re Poetica: 116

De Re Rustica (Columella): 3

De Re Rustica (Varro): 3

De Republica (Cicero): 112

De Republica Anglorum Instauranda (Chaloner): 20

De Rerum Natura (Lucretius): 118, 3

De Romani Pontificis: 116

De Rougemont, Denis: 47, 60; on demonic anti-model, demonic disguises, temptation: 47

De Sales, Francis: 47. On presence of God: 47

De Santillana, G.: 6

de Saumaise. See Salmasius

De Selincourt, Ernest: 14. On Keats: 58*

De Serpente Seductore: 88

De Servo Arbitrio: 71

de Shamer, Costello, Marquis: 44

De Somniis: 121

De Sphaerarum Concentu: 121. See also: Prolusion II

De Tolnay, Charles: 5

De Tradendis Disciplinis (Vives): 3

De Trevisa, John: 128

De Tribus Impostoribus (attr. to M): 44

De Triplici Vita (Ficino): 29

De Utraque Verborum ac Rerum Copia (Erasmus): 118

De Vere: Aubrey, Jr. and Sr., sonnets of: 58; on the sonnet: 87. Robert: 73

De Victoria Verbi Dei: 65

De Visione Dei: 32

De Vries, Vredeman: 97

De Vulgari Eloquentia: 111, 26

de Wilde, S.: 97

de Wint, P.: 97

De Wit, Mr. (artist): 44

de Wulf, Maurice: 52

Deacon: D.: 58. John: 93. John (and Walker, John): 142; works: *A Dialogical Discourse of Spitits and Devils*: 142; *A Summary Answer to all the Material Points in any of Master Darel, his Books*: 142

Dead Sea (Asphaltic Pool): 19, 49, 128, 144, 72; apples: 123

Deal: 49

Dean: 143. Of M scholars: 143. Joseph Hall: 143. L.: 23

Deane: Charles: 44. C. V.: 108, 110, 133. Mary: 45. Sir Gen. Richard: 44, 45

Deare, J. R.: 58

Death of Adam, The: 65

Death of Cain: 65

Death of King Charles I, The: 116

Death: 1, 2*, 17*, 31, 41, 44, 47*, 50, 56, 102, 107, 111, 63, 90, 113, 124, 125*, 127*, 143*, 144, 46, 71, 93, 96*, 109, 130, 25. Allegorical figure in PL: 70. As character: 72*, 55, 104. Dance of: 97. Personified in pictures: 97. Sources: 55. 4 degrees in M: 107. Theme of PL: 104. Symbolism in PL: 104. M on: 113. Way of: 125*. Death-Wish: 118. Satanic apocalypse of: 125. As theme in SA: 125*. In Greek tragedy: 92. And debts: 92*. And Sin build causeway: 143. And pride: 143. Limited power of: 143. Invades universe: 143. Shadow of Sin and: 143. Interpreted: 143. And purgatory: 143. And eternal: 143. Ways to: 143. M's: 28*, 44*, 84, 94; Phillips' account: 55; anonymous biographer: 55. See also: Sin and Death; Satan; Urizin

Debach, co. Suffolk: 44

Debate, of Comus and the Lady: 29*

Debate: 51

Deborah: 122

Debtor: 45

Debus, Allen G.: 75

Decalogue: 71

Decan (Deccan): 49, 73, 19

Decay: of civilizations: 19. of nature: 128, 93. See also: Nature

Decebalus: 44

Decemviral Laws: 73

Decency: 70. Anglican: 66

Deception, human: 47. See also Demonic; Fraud

Decia Ligenhain. See William VI

Decii (P. Decius Mus, father and son): 60

Decisions, M's, against law, priesthood, any profession: 40

Decius (Emperor): 73, 3

Declamatio, exercise of in ancient and modern schools: 20, 40. Declamations: 40

Declaration...against the Spanish: 44

Declaration...of the Army of God: 9

Declaration of...the Lord General: 9

Declaration of...the Officers of the Army: 9

Declaration of indulgence: 116

Declaration of the...Congregational Churches: 9

Declaration of the Commons...Against ...the 2nd Part of England's New Chains Discovered: 44

Declaration of the Election of this Present King of Poland: 16, 55

Declaration of the Nobility: 44

Declaration of the Parliament of Eng. upon the Marching of the Army into Scotland: 44, 103 Declaration of Scottish Parliament, 1648: 59

Declaration of Breda (1660): 103, 116

Declaration of Congregational Societies: 147

Declaration of Independence: 103

Declaration of Some Proceedings of Lt. Col. John Lilburn: 147

Declaration on Ecclesiastical Affairs: 116

Declarations (of Parliament): 144

Declinations, earliest use of: 89

Decoration: Meadowcourt on poetry as instruction made attractive by: 88. Dunster on imagination as external, serving to advertise religion: 88. Dunster on metre and classical allusions as mere: 88

Decorum: 66*, 67, 69, 70*, 123*, 92. Epic: 122. In characterization: 118. In M's prose: 66. Definition from M's prose: 66. Application to verse: 66. Classics charged by Hume of lacking: 38. Hume's concept of, and Addison: 88. Hume on, and the characters of PL: 88. Newton on: 88. Newton's insistence on: 88. Todd on: 88. M and traditional: 66. "Decorum Personae" (Satan, God, Raphael, Adam and Eve): 66*

Decree(s): and orders: 45. Of God: 113. Of God unchangeable: 93

Dedekind, Constantin Cristian: 65

Dedimus potestatem: 45

Dedington: 44

Deduction: 96. Deductive reasoning: 31, 51

Dee River: 40, 44, 73. See also: Deva

Dee: Arthur: 114. Dr. John: 1, 19, 40, 114, 142, 39

Deering: Sir Edward: 103. Richard (musician): 44

deFaye, E.: 113

Defeasance: 45

Defects: 50*. See also: Inconsistencies

Defence of a Letter Concerning Education of Dissenters: 44

Defence of the Parliament of Eng., The: 116, 103

Defence of the Parliament of 1640: 116

Defence of the People of Eng., A: 16, 52

Defence of the Vindication: 116

Defence of King Charles I, A: 116

Defence of Poetry (Shelley): 70, 131

Defences (M): 45

Defendant: 45

Defender of the Faith (as title): 123

Defens: 40

Defense and Continuation of Ecclesiastical Politie, A: 116

Defense of knowledge. See Prolusion VII

"Defense of Poetry": 98 Defense of the English People, etc.: 103. Presentation copy of: 44. See also: Defensio Pro Popula Anglicano; Milton, John, Works

Defense of the Humble Remonstrance: 26, 62, 103. See also: Milton, John, Works

Defense of Ryme, A (Daniel): 20

Defensio of M: 112. See also: M's Defense

Defensio pro se: 8*, 103, 113, 44. See also: Milton, John, Works

Defensio Fidei Catholicae Adversus Anglicanae Sectae Errores: 116

Defensio Pro Populo Anglicano: 113*, 147*. See also: Milton, John, Works

Defensio Regia (Salmasius): 116, 136, 94, 3

Defensio Regia pro Carolo I: 51, 113, 62, 103

Defensio Secunda: 45, 50, 102, 112, 113*, 132*, 133, 147*, 103. See Milton, John, Works

Defensor Pacis (Marsilius of Padua): 83

Deferrari, R. J.: 79

Defestro, Susanna: 44

Defiance Against All Arbitrary Usurpations (Richard Overton): 147

Definition of Poetry (Coleridge): 70

Definition(s): 51. Perfect and imperfect: 123. By opposition: 123. In verse: 20

Defoe, Daniel: 1, 27, 35, 41, 44, 86, 87, 102, 113, 116, 136, 142, 97, 146, 13. Influenced by PL: 58. Praises M: 58. History of the Devil: 142

Deformity: 70*

Degeneration, human: 47. See also: Demonic

Degree(s): 143. The topic of: 51. Ranks in church: 143. In religion and morals: 143. Three: 93. Seven: 93. Nine: 93. M's: 44. See also: Scale of Nature

Degsastan: 49

Deguilleville, Guillaume de, Pelerinage Jhesucrist: 74

Deianeira: 92

Deichmann: 10

"Deification": 24

Deiope: 73

Deiphobus: 1, 73

<u>Deipnosophists</u> (Athenaeus): 112

Deira: 49

Deism: 15, 114*, 71, 146. Deists: 78. Influence of: 58

Deity: 89. Abode of the, according to Ptolemaic astronomers: 89. Idolatry to portray: 143. Character of: 143. Samson agent of: 143. As represented by artists: 97

Dekker, Thomas: 45, 114, 88, 15, 40, 108, 93, 130. <u>Dekker, Thomas, The Non-Dramatic Works of</u>: 45

Del Rio, Martin: 44, 142, 32. Les Controverses et Recherches Magiques: 142

Del, Will: 79

Delacourt, Raymond: 44

Delacroix, E.: 97

Delahay, Henry: 44

Delambre (cited): 89

Delamere, Thomas Pitts Hamilton Cholmondeley, 4th Baron of: 44

Delamothe, G.: 40

Delany, Mrs., oratorio from PL: 58

Delatte, Armand: 5

Delattre, F.: 133

d'Elbene, M.: 50

Delbene, Bartolomeo: 123

Delft (Delf): 44, 49, 73

Delia: 73

Deliberateness, of M's poetic method over-emphasized by Dunster: 88

Deliberative oratory (rhetoric): 31, 51, 123*

<u>Delices de la Suisse</u>: 44

Delilah: 44, 54, 103, 143. See also: Dalilah

Delille: Jacques: 58, 44, 70, 115

<u>Delitiae Poetarum Germanorum</u> (Stigel): 83

Delius: 60, 73. See also: Apollo

Deliverance: 122*. As heroic theme: 123*

Delivery: 51

Dell: 49. Floyd: 122. William: 7, 9, 60, 108, 114, 148

<u>Della humanita del Figliuol di Dio</u>: 65

Della lingua Toscana: 111

Della Cassa, Giovanni: 1, 44, 56, 59, 120, 127, 26. M's sonnets modeled after: 87. Freedom of his sonnet form: 87

Della Certa, Lodovico: 44

Della Corte, A.: 6

<u>Della Creatione del Mondo</u> (Murtola): 65

Della Crusca Academy: 44. The Della Cruscans: 58. See also: Academies

<u>Della Difesa della Commedia di Dante</u> (Mazzoni): 70, 3

Della Scala, Can Grande: 111

Dellile, Jacques: 44. See also: Delille

Delmenhorst: 44, 49. See also: Frederick III of Denmark

Delos: 19, 44, 49, 73, 90, 3

Delphi (Delphos, Pythian Vale): 49, 73, 72. Delphian oracle: 5, 44, 73; lines: 3.

Delphinatus: 49

Delphinus: 73, 121, 123

<u>Deluge, The</u> (a projected work): 136

Demaray, John G.: 39, 64, 101. On <u>Mask</u>: 104. Reconciliation of Dogma to pleasure in <u>Comus</u>: 61

Demeter: 90. See also: Ceres

Demetia: 49

Demetrius: 44. Of Phalerum: 112. The Rhetorician: 73, 3

Demigod, hero as: 123

Demille, Cecil B.: 137

Demiurge: 113, 36, 71. The Son as a: 113. In the Zohar: 113

Democracy Rampant: 44

Democracy: 7, 9*, 31, 51. M's love of: 51

Democritus: 4, 5, 44, 73, 114, 128, 142, 32, 71, 146

Demodocus: 44, 73, 90, 3

Demogorgon: 40, 57, 73, 90, 144

Demon of Mascon, The: 142. Perraud, Du Moulin: 142

Demon(s): 41, 107*. Achieve rank through merit: 107*. Change shapes at will: 107*. Lose power at Christ's coming: 107*. Not pardoned: 107. Powerless against good men: 107. Take on animal bodies: 107. Eventually pardoned in Origen: 107*. God did not make: 107*. Gods of nations become: 107*. God uses to tempt and punish man: 107*. Greek gods as: 107*. Lust the motive of their Fall according to Commodianus: 107*. Demonic: 47*; power: 107*; suggestion: 107. Demonology: 142. Characteristics and functions of: power seeking, repudiating love, abandoning freedom; degeneration of, deceptions, disguises and poses; possession by; compared with men; strategies of: 47. See also: Antichrist; Perversion; Satan; Daemon; Devils; Self-deification

Demonstrations: 51

Demonstrative rhetoric: 20, 123

Demophoon: 73

Demos in Council, or 'Bijah in Pandemonium, The: 115, 117

Demosthenes: 5, 6, 8, 18, 20, 30, 40*, 44, 51, 52, 56, 70, 73, 112, 136, 145, 82, 94, 146, 117, 13, 3. And M compared: 146

Demurrer: 45

Denbigh: Basil Fielding, 2nd Earl of: 44, 103. Lord: 94

Denbighshire: 44, 45, 49

Denck, Hans: 7, 60, 114

Denderah, temple of: 89

Dendy, Edward, Sergeant-at-Arms: 44*

Denham, Sir John: 1, 15, 28, 44*, 58, 84, 114, 145, 91, 149, 117, 55. Works: *The Sophy*: 149

Denis, St.: 142

Denison, Stephen: 114

Denkinger, M.: 6

Denmark, Frederick III, King of: 91

Denmark: 44*, 49, 103

Denne, Henry: 79, 114

Dennett, Charles: 44

Denney, James: 93

Dennie, Joseph: 115

Dennis: 94. Mr.: 44. John: 58*, 7, 44, 56, 86, 142, 53, 91, 130, 146, 117; advises M: 58; influenced by M: 58; on the Sublime: 87; on PL as a sublime poem: 87; works: *Remarks on a Book...Arthur*: 142; *Age of Pope*: 58; *The Grounds of Criticism in Poetry*: 87

Denny: Sir Edward: 40. Honora: 40. Thomas: 117

Denomy, Alexander J.: 122

Denonain, J. J.: 79

Denores, Giason, *Discorso...che la Comedia...et il Poema Heroico*: 74

Denouement: 92

Dent: Arthur: 114, 93. Edward: 39

Denton: Alexander: 45. T.: 58. William: 44, 116

Deodati. See Diodati

Deodorus, cited: 89

Deorhist: 49

Deorrham: 49

Deposition: 45

Depravity: 9*, 81, 71. Doctrine of: 81. Human, doctrine of: 71. Of man: see Fall; Free Will

Deputy Keeper of Public Records, Reports of: 44, 45

Der andere Milton (Heinrich Mutschmann): 38

Derby (Darby), city and county: 44, 45, 49

Derby (Darby): House: 103. Duchess of: 103. Earl of: 58, 103. Alice Spencer, Countess Dowager of: 33, 44,

26, 55, 113, 121, 136, 72. George S.: 16

Derbyshire (Darbyshire): 45, 49. Visitation of: 45

Derbyshire Archaeological and Natural History Society, Journal of the: 45

Dereliction, temptation of: 123

Derham, William: 115. Physico-Theology: 115

Dering, Sir Edward D.: 9, 44

Dermody, Thomas: 58, 115.

Derrida, Jacques: 11, 14

Derry (Londonderry): 44

Dertmouth (Dartmouth): 49

Desainliens, Claude: 40*

Desborough, co. Bucks.: 44

Desborough, John: 73, 103

Descant: 121

Descartes, René de: 6, 7, 10, 15, 16, 18, 42, 44, 60, 83, 86, 89, 102, 108, 114, 118, 128, 142, 144, 11, 32, 39, 72, 91, 109, 148. "De Sphaerum Concentu": 89

Descent: 143. Through pride: 143. Images of as implying conclusion: 118

Deschamps, Eustache: 120

Description of the World: 40

Description of England: 45

Description, in theme writing: 20. Descriptive poetry of the 18th c.: 58*. See also: Cowper, W.; Thomson, J.; Wordsworth, W.; Topographical poems

Descriptive Catalogue: 25

Desert Islands (W. Dela Mare): 136

Desertion: 54

Deserts: 144

Design: 50

Desire, legitimacy of: 113

Desmarets de Saint-Sorlin, Jean: 70, 122, 74, 64. Works: Clovis: 74; Deffense du Poëme Heroïque: 74; Esther: 74; Marie-Madeleine: 74; Regulus: 74

D'Espagnet, Jean: 10, 44, 113

Despair: 51, 123, 124, 125*. As theme in SA: 125*. Converting itself: 125. And progressive death in Satan: 125

Despauterius, Joannes: 20, 40

Desportes: 40, 120. Marie: 39. P.: 59

Despot, obedience to: 31. Despotism: 51

Despréaux, J. E.: 29, 58

Dessurne, M.: 97

d'Este family: 6, 29, 44, 123

Destiny: 144. M's conception of: 113

Destroyers as heroes and kings: 123

Destructio, exercise in theme writing: 20

Destruction: 122*. See also: Creation

Destructive argument, case: 51

Desvergonia: 49, 73

Detachment in Samson: 125

Details: 88. Pearce takes notice of important little graphic: 88. Graphic, in characters well observed by the Richardsons: 88. Retardation by emphasizing: 88. Newton's sense of concrete: 88. Warton's ability to see essentials in: 88. Individualizing, appreciated by Warton: 88

Determinations (ed. Leavis): 131

Determinism: 96, 25. Determinist philosophy: 31

Detford: 49, 73

Dethick(e), Sir John, Lord Mayor of London: 44, 120, 103

Detraction which followed upon my writing certain Treatises, On The: 113

Detroit, Michigan: 44

Detzel, H.: 99

Deuc(k)alion: 73, 90, 72

Deus absconditus: 96

Deus et Rex: 40

Deus ex machina: 70, 92

<u>Deuteronomy</u>: 139, 3, 99. See also: Bible

Deutsch, Alfred Henry: 142

<u>Deutsches Adambuch</u>: 65

Deva: 49, 73. River: 144

<u>Develis Perlament</u> (ed. F. J. Furnivall): 65, 74, 36

Deventer, school at: 20

Devereux, Robert: 114, 64

Devices, persuasive: 51

Devil: 1*, 31, 44, 60, 141*, 71, 146*. Cast out: 141. Modern resurgence of: 141. See also: Satan; Lucifer

<u>Devil's Challange of God</u>: 48

<u>Devil's Dream, the</u>: 65

Devils: 44, 50*, 107*, 114, 117*, 119*. Nature of: 142. Rank of: 142. Possession by: 142. Miscegenation with: 142. As locusts: 106. And M's politics: 106. As poets and philosophers: 106. Catalogue of: 106. And negative creativity: 106. Beelzebub: 106. Mammon: 106. Number: 50. Mulciber: 106. Revenge planned by: 119. M and "devil's party": 146. Association with NT demons: 119. Biblical language used ironically by: 119. Creation of man discussed by: 119. Defeat of foreshadowed: 119*. Efforts of to be thwarted by God: 119. Find defeat of alluded to in Satan's speech: 119. Names of blotted out in Heaven: 119. Origin of as angels: 119. Perverted idea of God expressed by: 119. See also: Fallen angels; Daemons; Demons; Demonology; Satan

Devizes: 44

Devonshire: 44, 45, 49. Visitation of: 45

Devotion books: 40

Dew, William: 44

Dew: 128. Causes and kinds: 128

D'Ewes, Sir Simonds: 40*, 45, 114, 116, 120. The Journal of: 45

Dewes, Giles. See Duwes

Dewey: Eldad: 115; <u>The American Instructor</u>: 115. John: 144

Dewick, E. C.: 142. <u>Primitive Christian Eschatology</u>: 142

Dexter: George: 55. Gregory (pr.): 44. Samuel: 115; <u>The Progress of Science</u>: 115

D'Herbelot, M.: 123

Diacceto, Francesco Cataneo da: 5

Dial of the moon. See Poetic universe

<u>Dial, The</u>: 12

Dialect: 51. Syrian: 51. Expressions dealt with by Hume and by Warton: 88

Dialectic: 47, 25, 40. In M's works: 46. Kinship with rhetoric: 20, 31. In PR: 123*. Rhetoric a branch of: 123. Heroes skilled in: 123. Dialectics: in the prose: 75; in PL: 75*

<u>Dialectica</u> (Ramus): 20, 112

Dialogue in Heaven: 67

<u>Dialogue with Trypho</u>: 71

"Dialogue between the Soul and Body" (Marvell): 131

<u>Dialogue Between Dr. Sherlock, the King of France, the Great Turk, and Dr. Oates A</u>: 116

"Dialogue of Self and Soul" (W. B. Yeats): 131

Dialogue(s): 96*, 40

<u>Dialogues</u> (Plato): 112*, 70

<u>Dialogues</u> (Vives): 3

<u>Dialogues of Plato</u> (Jowett): 3

Diana: 44, 56, 69*, 73, 90*, 32, 25. Ref. to <u>Diana Enamorada</u>: 73

Dianoia (thought): 123, 92

Diapason: 121

Diapente: 121

Diaper, William: 58, 128

Diaphragm: 136. Dividing intellect and emotion: 136

"Diary of Events in Ireland": 44

Diaspora of Greek Scholarship: 42

Diatessaron: 121

Diatonic scale: 121

Diatribe, brutishness as topic of: 123

Dibdin: T. F.: 58. T. J.: 58

Dicas, Thomas (pr., bks., 1660-69): 44, 91

Dice: 40

DiCesare, Mario A.: 75. Vida's Christiad: 74 Dick: Hugh G.: 40. O. L.: 40

Dickens, Charles: 5, 31, 86, 105, 137

Dickenson, Abraham: 44

Dickins (Dickons), John: 44

Dickinson: Abraham: 45. E.: 105

Dickson: David W. D.: 60, 79, 110, 93. John: 101

Diconson: Abraham: 45. Leonard: 45

Dictaean: 49. Jove: 73

Dictamen: 40

Dictator: 40; obedience to: 31

Diction: 58*, 70, 124*. Poetic: 146. M's influence on, and 18th c. ideas on: 58. of PL: 15*

Dictionary of Christian Biography: 57

Dictionary of National Biography (DNB): 40*, 44*, 45*

Dictionary of Printers: 40

Dictionary: 40. Johnson's: 3

Dictys Cretensis: 40, 90

Didactica Magna (Comenius): 3

Didacticism: 47. In PL, Dunster on conflict of artistic tendency with: 88. Todd's: 88. Didactic: poetry: 58; function of poetry: 123. Didacticism: Patterson's, in judging of PL: 88; of Thyer's theory of poetry: 88; and intellectualism of PR regarded by Thyer as due to the subject: 88; in Thyer's definition of epic poetry: 88; Meadowcourt's: 88; considerable traces of, in Newton: 88; Marchant's: 88; not obtrusive, in Warton: 88; Dunster's: 88

Didactics: 51, 73

Didbin, Sir Lewis and Sir Charles E. H. C. Healey: 54

Diderot, Denis: 40, 113, 32, 97

Dido: 2, 56*, 72

Didot, François: 60

Didron, A.: 99

Didymus: 123. Alexandrinus, "Fragmenta in Job": 74

Diekhoff, John S.: 1, 17, 34, 44, 59, 86, 102, 112, 110, 123, 128, 135, 14, 36, 39, 106, 109, 137, 146, 148, 140*, 48. Works: "The Function of the Prologues in PL": 60; M's "PL": 60, 83, 48

Diels: 141. H.: 4, 68

Dieppe (Diepa), France: 44, 49

Dies irae. See Last Judgement

Diet of Torda: 78

Diet: 51. M on: 51

Dietrich, J. C.: 44

Dieu: Louis de: 22. Ludovicus: 40

Difesa della comedia di Dante: 111

Difesa di Dante: 111

Difference: 11*. In "War in Heaven": 11. And identity: 11. And communication: 11. Basis of human desire: 11*

Digby: Dr.: 44. Anne (Cope): 45. Lord George, Earl of Chester, 2nd Earl of Bristol: 9, 73, 51. Lord: Speech: 144; summary of: 144; M refutes: 144. Sir John: 40. Sir Kenelm: 44, 45, 60, 102, 114, 128, 142, 93; works: Observations on Spenser's F. Q.: 142; Observations upon Religio Medici: 142; Private Memoirs: 142

Digestion: 128. Of angels: 128

Diggan Davie: 83*

Diggers: 7, 9, 60, 32. Communistic movement led by Winstanley: 147

Digges: Sir Dudley: 93. Leonard: 128. Thomas: 40, 128, 142

Dignity of Kingship Asserted (G. Sheldon): 9, 116, 103, 147. See also: Sheldon, G.

Dignity: 124*. Of man: 114*. The conception of: 48*

Digression, method of: 81.

Digressions: 51, 143; in Lycidas: 143

Dijon, France: 44

Dike: 49, 32, 72

Dilemma, use of: 51. Of modern man: 143

Dilherr, Johann Michael: 93

Dillenberger, John: 93

Dillistone, F. W.: 79, 93

Dillmann, A.: 123, 36

Dillon: Capt. (pirate): 44. Richard H.: 44. Thomas, Viscount: 73

Dilmun: 32

Dilthey, W.: 58

Dilworth, Thomas: 115. A New Guide to the Eng. Tongue: 115

Dim, Mr. (scrivener): 44

Diminution: 123

Dimmery, Mr.: 45

Dimond, W.: 58

Dimsdale: Sir John: 44. Sir Joseph Cockfield: 44

Dingley, Robert: 142. The Deputation of Angels: 142

Dini, P.: 6

Dinsdale, J.: 58

Dio Cassius: 90

Dio Chrysostom: "8th Discourse, on Virtue": 74. "1st Discourse, on Kingship": 74. "4th Discourse, on Kingship": 74

Dio: 3

Diocletian: 73, 3, 38. Persecutions of: 38. Emperor: 111

Diodate, J.: 99

Diodati-Florio circle: 40

Diodati: family: 40, 44*, 45, 55. Abigail: 40. Carolo, of Florence: 132; 3. Charles: see separate entry. Elie (1576-1651): 44, 45, 55. Giovanni (Jean, John, 1576-1649): 6, 10, 28, 30, 40, 42, 45, 68, 73, 74, 77, 26, 32, 94, 55; Annotations upon the Holy Bible: 74*. Isabel, mother of Charles: 44. John: 36, 101. John (brother of Charles): 40, 44, 123, 3. John (father of Charles): 44. Philadelphia (sister of Charles): 40, 44. Richard (brother of Charles): 44. Theodore, Dr. (1573-1651): 40, 45, 44

Diodati, Charles: 1, 4, 15, 17, 18, 20, 28, 29, 30*, 33, 40*, 111, 121, 132, 134, 62, 88, 130, 149, 113, 42, 44*, 59, 70, 73, 77, 84, 120, 124, 128, 129, 136, 144, 26, 112*, 32, 38, 53, 71, 91, 92, 94, 64, 109, 137, 146, 148*, 21*, 3, 103. Letters of: 55. Latin Letter, 23 Sept. 1637: 77. Letters to: 112*, 55. Poem on his death: 72. M's friendship with: 113, 132. See also: Damon; Epitaphium Damonis

Diodorus of Tarsus: 68

Diodorus Siculus (of Sicily): 1, 15, 19*, 77, 24, 40, 44, 68, 73, 74, 90*, 128, 144*, 121, 3, 32, 82. Babylon: 144. Asphalt: 144. Thebes: 144. Meroc: 144. Rivers in India: 144. His History and PL: 144*. Purpose of history: 144. Egyptian worship: 144. Nyseian Isle: 144. Sabean odors: 144. Servonian Fen: 144. Pyramids: 144

Diogenes: 4, 74, 128. The Cynic: 123. Of "the Cynic tub": 73. The Stoic: 73, 3. Laertius: 5, 20, 40, 77, 112*, 123, 148; Lives (tr. Hicks): 77

Diomede, Ars Grammatica: 74

Diomedean: 73

Diomedes Grammaticus: 1

Diomedes: 2, 4, 44, 56, 123, 72

Dion: 73, 3, 32. Cassius Cocceianus: 73. Chrysostom (author of Logoi): 44. Prusaeus (surnamed Chrysostomos): 73, 3

Dionysius of Alexandria, St.: 51, 60, 73, 3, 32. Afer: 3. The Areopagite (Pseudo-Dionysius): 18, 41, 44, 60, 73, 79, 81, 111, 114, 142*, 93, 109, 21. Pseudo-Dionysius: 142. The Celestial Hierarchy: 142. Of Halicarnassus: 2, 20, 44, 66, 73, 90, 120, 3, 130. Surnamed Penegetes: 73. Of Syracus: the elder: 3, 70, 73; the younger: 73. Pope: 73

Dionysius: 7, 40, 44, 51, 74, 112, 128, 82. Dionysiac: 125. Dionysian cult: 92. Bacchus: 90

Dionysus: 11

Dioscorides: 128

Dioscuri: 90

Diosemeia (Aratus): 3

Diotima: 73, 112*

Diotogenes the Pythagorean: 73

Diotrephes: 73

Diphilus: 70

Dippers Dipt or the Anabatists Duck'd and Plung'd Over Head and Eares (Daniel Featley): 147

Dippers: 73

Diptychon utriusque Testamenti: 65

Dircaean: 73

Dircaeus: 49

Dircks: 3

Directions to Preachers (James' warning against dangerous doctrines): 147

Directory for Public Worship: 59

Dis, city of: 111, 73, 90

Discipline: 31, 51*, 70, 124. Presbyterian: 51. The artist's: 124. The Richardsons' lack of critical: 88. Peck Lacking: 88. Warburton deficient in critical: 88

Discord: 2, 47, 90, 121*. Musical: 40. Discords: unrhymed lines likened by Peck to: 88; beauty of, Dunster on: 88

Discorsi del Poema Eroico (Tasso): 70, 3

Discorsi dell' Arte Poetica (Tasso): 70, 3

Discorso in Difesa della Comedia: 111

Discourse in Vindication of Bishop John Bramhall: 116

Discourse of the Soveraign Power: 116

Discourse of Devils: 60, 77

Discourse of Ecclesiastical Politie: 116

Discourse of English Poetrie, A: 70

Discourse of Toleration, A: 116

Discourse on the Light of Nature (Culverwel): 112

Discourse on Government: 116

Discourse Opening the Nature of... Episcopacie: 147. See also: Lord Brooke

Discourse Showing...3 Kingdoms (attr. to M): 44

Discourse(s): 53*, 71. For formal delivery: 40. Public: 40. See also: Rhetoric

Discourses (Reynolds): 70

Discourses Concerning Government: 116

Discoverer, The (a tract to discredit the Levellers): 147

Discoveries (Jonson): 3

Discovery of Dangerous Tenets: 91

Discovery of Witchcraft (Reginald Scot): 88

Discretio: 5

Discussion: 51*

Disease(s) and ill(s): 8, 128*, 144. Atrophy: 128. Balaam's: 128. Catalogue of: 128. Disorder of humours: 128. Dropsy, causes and kinds: 128. False pregnancy: 128. Fever: 128. 4 kinds of frenzy: 128. Gangrene: 128. Gout: 128. Gravedo: 128. Gutta serena: 128. Heart: 128. Impotence: 128. Impostume: 128. Indigestion: 128. Insominia: 128. Leprosy: 128. Lethargy: 128. Madness and mental: 128. Megrim: 128. Melancholia: 128. Miscarriage: 128. Nausea: 128. Palsy: 128. Pearl: 128. Plague: 128. Pleurisy: 128. Polyps: 128. Rupture: 128. Skin and flesh: 128. Sores and ulcers: 128. Spasm: 128. Snake-bite: 128. Tumors: 128. Venereal: 128. Wen: 128. Disease and remedy, a dialectic of disorder: 128*

Disestablishment of the Church: 113

Disestablishment: 78. Appeal for: 51

Disguises: Satan's: 50, 123. Alfred's: 123. Odysseus': 123

Disinterment, M's: 44

Disney: Edgar: 44. John: 44. Walt: 95

Disobedience: 122*, 123, 143. Causes of Adam's: 122. Mankind seduced by: 143. Sin and misery reuit of: 143. Samson's: 143. Fatal: 143. Eve's: 143. See also: Obedience; Satan

Dispensary, The: 2, 130. See also: Garth

Dispensing power: 44

Dispositio (part 2 of rhetoric): 20, 40

Disposition, M's: 44

Dispraise and praise, themes in: 20

Disputatio: 40

Disputations Physica: 40

Disputations: 40*. In M's works: 40. "Dispute by course": 40. Disputing, effects of, on M: 40

Disraeli: B., sonnets of: 58. Isaac: 35, 44, 98, 136, 88; Curiosities of Literature

Dissenter(s): 40, 122. Attitude toward M: 87. Fond of PL: 58. _Dissenter's Sayings, Two Parts in in One_: 116. Dissenters' Chapels Bill: 78

Dissimilarity, argument from: 123

Dissociation: 141. Of sensibilities, lack of in Bks. III, IV of PL: 118, 53. And rhetoric: 53. As function of theme: 53. Simile as indicator: 53. See also: T. S. Eliot

Dissonant: 121

Dissuasive from errors of the time: 103

Distance, aesthetic: "distancing" of epic: 118. In Samson: 125*

Disticha Catonis: 59

Disticha Moralia (Cato): 20

Distinction, between false and true in epistemological method: 123

Distinguished visitors, M's: 44

Diston, William: 45

Distraction (Vaughan): 131

Distraint of Knighthood: 103

Distrust: 123

Dithyramb: 92

Ditis Chorus: 58

Ditmarsh (Ditmarsia): 49. See also: Frederick III

Ditty: 121

Diurnall Occurences: 103

Dives: 73

Divine: power: 51. Precepts: 51. Prescript: 9*. Revelation: 51. Touch: 16. Will, as source of all law and order: 121. Vision: 25. Scales, interpreted: 80. Right of kings: 51, 60, 113. M attacked divine right: 147. M's rejection of divine right: 113

Divine Commedia, The: 65, 70, 113, 118, 139, 52. See also: Dante

Divine Epopée, La: 65

Divine Image: 122*, 123*

Divine Poems (Donne): 65, 123, 131

Divine Right of Kings Asserted in General, The: 116

Divine-Demonic encounter: 48

Divines: Protestant: 51

Divinity Books, Catalogue of the Most Approved: 44

Divinity, regius professor of: 40

"Divinity School Address": 71

Divinum somnum: 40

Division(s): 51, 121

Divorce at Pleasure (William Prynne): 73, 147

Divorce: 8, 9*, 17*, 19, 30*, 51, 63, 54*, 136, 46, 93, 109*. M's tenets: 54, 147, 71*, 136. A male privilege: 54. Allowed by Bible: 54. M pleads for open-minded considerations of his divorce views: 144. Concept of nature in divorce tracts: 104. M's tracts on: 60, 149, 146, 113*, 121. Phillips' account: 55. Anonymous biographer's account discussed: 55. _Colasterion_: 55. _Doctrine and Disciple_: 55. _Judgement of Martin Bucer_: 55. _Tetrachordon_: 55. See also: _Doctrine and Discipline_; Marriage

Divorcers: 44, 103, 113

Dixon: Dorothy: 40. Elizabeth: see Haly. Fennor: 44. Frances (Mrs. Fennor): 44. Henry: 117. James: 44. R. W.: 86, 87, 105; correspondence with G. M. Hopkins: 87. W. M.: 58

Dixwell, Col. John: 44

Doane, Richard: 44

Dobinson: Richard: 45. William: 44, 45*

Doble, E. A. See Hearne, William

Dobrée, Bonamy: 86

Dobson: A.: 58. W. (Prussian Campaign and translations by): 58. William (painter, M portrait): 44, 103, 97, 117

"Docetism" in Encyclopedia of Religion and Ethics (ed. James Hastings): 74

Doctor Faustus (Marlowe): 139, 26

Doctor Walker's True, Modest and Faithful Account: 116

Doctor, unnamed, friend of Salmasius: 44

Doctor's Commons: 45

Doctorate in divinity: 114

Doctrina Christiana, De: 104. See also: Christian Doctrine

Doctrine and Discipline of Divorce: 83, 103*, 102, 112*, 113*, 116, 132*, 147, 3*. Presentation copy of: 44. Images in: 8*. Ends of marriage, fitness and unfitness, marriage above human law, divorce as preserver of love, not intended for women, fornication: 54*. See also: Divorce

Doctrine of Polity of Church of England: 44

Doctrine: 51, 143. Protestant: 143. Reformers: 143. Of Reformers: 143. Eroded by time: 143. See also: Christian Doctrine

Doctrines, Presbyterian: 51

Documents Relating to...Cambridge: 40*

Dod: Mr.: 45. John: 40, 114, 93; and Robert Cleaver: 54. Thomas: 44

Dodd: 141. The Rev.: 38. Charles H.: 5, 36, 93. D.: 97. Dr. W., Explanation of M: 58; influenced by M: 58*. William: 117

Dodds, E. R.: 5

Dodge, R. E. Neil: 56, 110, 113

Dodgson: 35. Works: Alice in Wonderland: 35; Through the Looking Glass: 35

Dodington, Bartholomew: 40

Dodoens, R.: 128

Dodona: 49, 73, 90. Dodonian oak: 73

Dods: Marcus: 122. Robert: 45

Dodsley: R., influenced by M: 58. Robert (pr., publisher): 44, 58*, 97, 117

Dodwell, Robert: 44

Dog (star): 73

Dog days, the: 89

Dog Lane (Shrewsbury): 44

"Dog Latin": 40

Dogma and Compulsion (Reik): 139

Dogma: 113*. M's attitude toward: 113. Few traces of in the De Doctrina: 113. Completely absent from Samson: 113. Satan's criticism of: 113

Dogs barred from college: 40

Doig, D.: 58

Dolan, John P.: 101

Dolce Stil Nuovo: 5, 122

Dolce, Lodovico: Vita di Giuseppe: 74, 64

Doleman. See Parsons, Robert

Dollam, Mr.: 44

Dolle, William (engraver, M portrait): 44

Dolman, Richard: 128

Dolon: 56

Dolphin Inn, Cambridge: 40

Dolphin(s): 144

Domandi, Mario: 122

Domenico, Testa: 117

Domesday Book: 73

Domestic: 125. M's domestic life: 87. Liberty: 51. See also: Evil

Domi et foris (domi forisque): 40

Domina: 40

Dominations: 41, 142

Dominical jigs and may-poles, Statute for: 73

Dominican order: 44, 73, 51

Dominicus, Joannes (Corellanus), <u>Theotocon</u>: 74, 64

Dominion: 24. Theory of, Wycliffe: 83

Dominions: 142

Domitian, Roman emperor: 44, 73, 89

Domitius Afer: 40

Domitius, Gnaeus (Ahenobarbus): 73

<u>Don Juan</u>: 130, 146

Don Juan: 40

<u>Don Quixote</u>: 35, 11, 94, 130

Don Quixote: 93

Don, as typical unbeliever: 143

Don, River , in Durham: 49

Donadeus, Natalis, <u>De Bello Christi</u>: 74, 64

Donaldson: E. F.: 37. James: 79. Walter: 40

Donatello, Donato: 5, 27

Donati, Gemma: 64

Donatists: 57, 38

Donato, Eugenio: 11

Donatus, Aelius: 1, 4, 40, 56, 21

Doncaster, Viscount: 40

Done, Abraham: 44

Doni: Giovanni Battista: 6*, 30, 44, 73, 121, 55. N.: 6

Donnadieu, A.: 44

Donne, Edward: 40

Donne, John: 1, 4, 5, 8, 12, 15*, 18, 20, 23*, 27, 33, 34, 35, 37, 40, 44, 52, 54, 59, 60, 63, 63, 73, 77, 79, 81, 83, 84, 86*, 87, 95, 100, 102, 105, 108*, 110, 103, 114*, 118, 120, 123, 124, 132, 125, 127, 128*, 135*, 145*, 133, 143, 26, 32, 38, 39, 53, 71, 85, 88, 91, 93*, 64, 101, 109, 115, 130, 131*, 137, 146, 148, 150, 55, 13. Before the throne: 143. Ranked above M: 143. And Jacob's vision (ladder): 143. Works: The Calme; The Storme: 109. The Crosse, Exstasie, First Anniversary: 35. Metempsychosis: 145*; Ignatius, his Conclave: 145*; <u>Anniversaries</u>: 83, 145*; Holy Sonnets: 35. Devotions upon Emergent Occasions: 126; <u>Donne, the Divine Poems</u> (Helen Gardner): 131; <u>Donne and Paracelsus</u> (W. A. Murray): 131; Donne, J. (the younger): 59

Donoghue, J.: 58

Doomes-Day: 65

Doors, behavior of in PL: 118

Doran, Madeleine: 128

Dorat, Jean: 64

Dorchester, co. Oxon.: 44, 45, 49

Dorchester: Dudley Carleton, Viscount, Secretary of State: 44. Henry Pierrepont, Marquis of: 44, 103

Doré, Paul Gustave: 5, 87, 136, 97, 115

d'Oresme, Nicholas: 128

Dorian, Donald C.: 40, 44*, 59, 14, 143. Ed., "Of Education": 82

Dorian: lyric odes: 73, 3. Mode: 40, 70, 73, 121

Doric: 73, 44

Dorington: Alexander: 44, 45. Mary (Porter): 44

Doris: 73, 3

Dorislaus, Isaac (1595-1649): 40, 44, 103, 134, 91

Dormer, Sir Robert: 44

Dorner, J. A.: 142

Dorset portrait of M: 44

Dorset, Charles Sackville, Earl of: 44, 91. Condemns images: 143

Dorsetshire: 44, 45, 49. Dorset: 45

Dort, Holland: 44. Synod of: 40

Dory, John: 73

Dosiadas: 64

Dostoevsky, Fyodor M.: 35, 52, 141, 46, 64

Dothan (Dothaim): 49, 73

Dottereale, co. Oxon.: 44

Douay Bible: 74*

Double vision, M's: 113

Double Your Guards. See R. L'Estrange

Doubleday Page (publishers): 97

Doubles: 11*. In SA, Comus, and Lycidas: 11. In M's prose: 11. As idols: 11. In the Labyrinth: 11

Doublet (a game): 40

Doubt: 123

Doughty: Charles M.: 58, 65. John: 93

Douglas: Bp. of Salisbury: 94. J.: 58. James W.: 93. John: 117*

Doulby: Great, co. Leicester: 44. See also: Dalby

Douza, James: 64, 117

Dove. See Symbolism

Dove, John: 44, 38, 93; Life of Andrew Marvell

Dover: Henry Jermyn, 1st baron: 44. Simon: 116

Dover: 44, 45, 49

Dowden: 70. Edward: 79, 87, 114, 132, 85; on M's prose: 87; on M's Puritanism: 87; on M's theology: 87; on Puritan elements in M: 37; on effect of De Doctrina Christiana: 87

Dowersey. See Towersey

Dowey: E. A.: 23. Edward R.: 93

Dowham, George: 112

Dowland: 121. John: 40, 108, 39

Dowling, Margaret: 45

Downame: Bp. George (d. 1634): 40, 73, 102, 91, 93; Commentarii: 53. John: 68, 74, 123, 93, 99, 101; Annotations: 74

Downer: John: 44, 45. Rebecca: see Wainwright, Rebecca: Rose: 44*, 45*. Downer-Milton lawsuit: 40

Downes: Mr.: 44. A. H. C.: 79. Andrew: 40, 64. Brian W.: 44

Downham, John: 44

Downing College (Cambridge): 44

Downing: Miss: see Ashworth. Calibut: 45. George: 44. John: 16

Downman, H.: 58*

Downs, the: 44, 103

Downshire, Arthur Wills...Sandys Hill, Marquis of: 44

Dowse, Sir Francis: 40

Dowsing, John: 44

Doxopater: 21

Doyley: family: 45. Sir Cope: 44, 45. John: 44, 45. Martha (Quarles): 45. Thomas: 40. Ursula (Cope): 45. See also: Doyly

Doylie, Sir William: 44

Doyly, Sir Cope: 44. John: 44. See also: Doyley

Doyne, P.: 58

Dr. Hollingworth's Defence of K. Charles: 116

Drabull, John: 44

Draco volans: 128

Dracontius, Blossius Aemilius: 65, 77, 102, 32, 36*. Works: Carmen de Laudibus Dei: 74; Carmen de Deo: 36*

Dradon. See Dryden

Draft: I, II, and III: see PL; Tragedy

Draiton. See Drayton

Drake: Acton: 45. Sir Francis: 19, 40, 108, 150. Jane: see Lowe, Jane (Wright). N.: 58*; praises L'Allegro and Il Penseroso: 58

Drama of Exile, A: 65

Drama: 27*, 30*, 31, 70*, 125*. Medieval religious: 55. Greek influence: 55. M on: 55. And Italian music-drama: 55. Renaissance religious: 55. M's use of: 104. Various forms of: 70. Rules of: 125. Of knowledge: 125*. Of salvation: 125. And definition: 125*. And motivation: 125. And the "summit": 125. And momentum: 125. Images derived from: 8. Academic: 40. Classical, and SA dealt with by Newton: 88. See also: Acts; Tragedies; Dramatic; Stage

Dramatic, the: 124*. Form: 145. Rhythm in SA: 125*. Analyses of style: 124*. Definition: 124.

Immediacy: 124*. Context: 124. Perspective: 124*. Treatment of subject of PL, Pearce on possible model of M's intended: 88. Schemes, M's used by Peck for reconstructing intended play on subject of PL: 88. Plans, M's possible, Peck's conjectures regarding: 88. Works divided by Peck into acts: 88. Sketches, M's studied by Newton: 88. Dramatic readings of PL: 118. Dramatic agent as mouthpiece: 70. Music, ca. 1600: 40. Plot: 70. Structure: 70. See also: Tragedy; subject matter of

Dramatists, Elizabethan: 50

Dramma per musica: 29*

Drant, Thomas: 40, 114

Drap. See Draper

Draper: Mr.: 45. Anne: 45. C.: 45. John W.: 19, 58, 128. John: 44*, 45*. Somerset (bks.): 44. William H.: 44, 45, 58

Drawing: 40

Drax, Thomas: 20, 40

Draycott: 45

Drayton (Draiton): 45, 120, 133. Michael: 4, 15, 16, 20, 29, 40, 77, 102, 108, 110, 122, 128, 129, 142, 32, 39, 88, 91, 64, 130, 150, 13; works: Moyses: 74; <u>David and Goliath</u>: 74; <u>Noahs Floud</u>: 74; <u>The Owle</u>: 109; <u>Poly-Olbion</u>: 109; <u>Song 18</u> (of <u>Poly-Olbion</u>): 77

<u>Dream of the Rood</u>: 15

<u>Dream of Scipio</u> (Cicero): 112

Dream(s): 90, 93, 96. And dream lore: 128. Eve's: 17, 50, 123, 106. Adam's: 106. The stuff of life: 136

<u>Dreer, Ferdinand Julius Catalogue of the Collection of Autographs</u>: 44

Drepanius Florus, "Exhortatio ad Legenda Sacra Volumina": 74, 64

Drepanum: 49

Dress, M's: 44

Dresser, Matthaus: 93

Drevet, P.: 97

Drew: Elizabeth: 12. J.: 44. P.: 59

Drexel, Jeremias: 40

Drexelius, Hieremias: 74. Jobus: 74

Dreyfus, J.: 123

Dring: 3. E. H.: 44. Thomas, Jr. (bks., 1668-94): 44, 55, 91

Drinking and drunkards: 51

Driscoll, Emily: 44

Driver: Samuel R.: 68, 123, 32, 36, 93; <u>Introduction to the Lit. of the OT</u>: 74; and G. B. Gray, <u>Book of Job</u>: 74. Tom F.: 93

Drogheda: 103

Droitwich, co. Worcs.: 44

Drope, John: 64

Drownings in the Cam River: 40

Druid(s): 121, 144, 3, 25. As bards: 121. British: 3. Druidic sources of Eng. civilization: 113

Drum: 121

Drummond: G. H.: 58. T.: 58. Sir W.: 58. William of Hawthornden: 4, 15, 18, 20, 44, 58, 60, 86, 108, 114, 39, 93, 64, 109, 70, 120

Drummond's Bank: 44

Drury Lane, London: 44. Theatre: 44

Drury: Anne (Truelove), cousin: 44. Elizabeth: 35. G. Thorn: 56. William: 44, 64

Drusius, John (Joannes): 1, 40, 41, 42, 123, 22

<u>Dry Salvages, The</u>: 130

Dryades: 90

Dryas: 44 See also: Brias

Dryden Press: 44

Dryden, John: 1, 2, 6, 15, 16, 17, 20, 23, 27, 28, 33, 35, 40, 44*, 51, 56*, 58*, 60, 63, 65, 67, 70, 73, 74, 76, 77, 81, 84, 86*, 103, 105, 108, 110, 114, 116, 118, 120, 123, 127, 122, 128, 132*, 133, 134, 135, 138, 141, 142, 145*, 26, 32, 38, 39, 53, 71, 88, 91, 64, 92, 93, 94, 97, 101, 109, 115, 130*, 137, 146*, 148, 150, 117*, 140, 21, 13, 55, 149. "On M" 58, 87. On M's Satan: 87. Epigraph on M: 146. And M compared: 146. Operatic version of PL: 55. Works: <u>Absalom and Achitophel</u>: 142; <u>All for Love</u>: 109; <u>Religio Laici</u>: 74; <u>Essays of John Dryden</u>: 142; <u>Hymn</u> (<u>Veni Creator Spiritus</u>): 115; <u>Marriage a la</u>

Mode: 35; *State of Innocence*: 146; *The Spanish Friar*: 2

Dryope: 44

Du Bartas, Guillaume de Salluste: 1, 5, 6, 15, 17, 19, 24*, 40, 42, 44, 50, 60, 63, 68, 69, 70, 73, 74, 76, 77, 102, 105, 107, 114, 113, 121, 122, 123, 127, 128*, 133, 143, 142, 22, 26, 32, 36, 88, 91, 93, 64, 130, 137, 149, 148, 117, 55, 94. Seigneur: 107. M does not borrow central beliefs from: 107. On creation: 143. And ages of the world: 143. Works: *La Sepmaine* (tr. Sylvester): 36, 46; *Decay, Vocation, Eden, Imposture, Furies, Handicrafts, Law, Captains, Babylon*: 77*; *Judit*: 74*; *Divine Weekes and Workes*: 60, 65, 118, 26, 144. *Seconde Sepmaine*: 74, 77*. *Sepmaine*: 74, 36, 109; *Uranie*: 74; *La Muse Chrestiene*: 50; *Works*, ed. U. T. Holmes et al.: 74, *La Semaine*: 55. See also: Hudson, Thomas; James I; Sylvester; Joshua; Saluste

Du Bellay, Joachim: 60, 122, 123, 132, 64. Works: *Deffence et Illustration de la Langue Françoyse*: 74; *Lyre Chrestienne*: 74; *Monomachie de David et de Goliath*: 74

Du Cange, Charles du Fresne: 40, 88

Du Chatel, N.: 97

Du Chesne, André, *Histoire D'Angleterre, D'Escosse, et D'Irlande*: 82

Du Faur: 40

Du Guernier, A.: 97

Du Haillan, Bernard de Girard, Seigneur: 73

Du Jon, Francois: 40, 114, 93. See also: Junius, F.

Du Laurens, Andre: 40

Du Monin, Edouard: 65

Du Moulin: 62. Pierre (the elder and younger): 9, 16, 28, 30, 44, 73, 84, 62, 94, 101, 55, 142; works: *Clamor*: 91; *Parerga*: 91; *The Divell of Mascon*: 142. See also: Moulin

Du Plessis, Scipio: 128, 93

Du Ploiche, Pierre: 40

Du Port, Francois, *De Messiae Pugna*: 74, 64

Du Rouveray, F. J. (publisher): 97

Du Vair, Bp. Guillaume: 60, 93

Du Val, Guillaume: 40

Dualism: 47, 113. M's attitude toward: 113

Duality of man's nature: 113

Dublin: 44, 49, 103. Academcy: 78. Castle Record Tower: 44

Dubocage, Madame: 32

Dubois, Peter: 45

Dubuffe, C. M.: 97

Duca, Guido del: 111

Duchesne-Guillemin, J.: 34

Duchess of Malfi, The (John Webster): 131

Duck Lane, London: 44

Duck: Sir Arthur (lawyer): 44*, 45*. Grace (Walker): 45. Katherine: see Waltham, Katherine. Margaret (Southworth): 45. Nicholas: 45. Philip: 45. Richard: 45. S.: 58

Ducket, Gregory: 40

Duckett, Eleanor S.: 36. *Latin Writers of the 5th c.*: 74

Duckworth, George E.: 56

Dudden, F. Homes: 93

Dudley: family: 40, 83. John, Duke of Northumberland: 73

Due Right of Presbyteries: 26

Duels: 44

Duerer, Albrecht: 40. See also: Dürer

Duff: E. G.: 40. J. D.: 122. J. W.: 145

Duffield: Elizabeth: see Ashworth, Eliz. Francis: 45

Dufour, M.: 16

Dufresnoy, C. A.: 58

Dugard: Mrs.: 44. Richard: 44. William (pr.): 44*, 103, 116, 91, 55

Dugdale, William: 40, 45, 116

Duhamel, P. Albert: 1, 23, 37, 123. "M's Alleged Ramism": 82

Duick, J.: 58

Duin, Tower of: 44

Duina: 49

Dujardin, M.: 97

"Duke and Brother": 73

Duke of Guise, The: 116

Duke Humphrey's Walk: 103

Duke Street: 44

Duke, Grand, of Florence: 44

Duke, William: 115. A Clew to Religious Truth: 115

Duke's Palace, London: 44

Dulac, E.: 97

Dulcedine of philosophy: 40

Dulcimer: 73, 121

Dulia: 47

Dulichium: 49

Dulwich: London: 44. College: 44. College Muniment: 45

Duméry, Henry: 81

Dummelow, J. R.: 68

Dumore, Baron. See Lee, Sir Francis

Dun (Don), River: 49, 73

Dunbar (Dumbarrensis): 49, 103. See also: Sonnet XVI

Dunbar: Mrs. A. M.: 58. H. Flanders: 100.

Dunbritton (Alcluith), now Dumbarton: 49. See also: Wall

Duncan: Andrew: 40. Edgar H.: 60, 75, 128. J. E.: 23, 58

Duncan-Jones, Elsie E.: 44

Dunciad: 88

Duncker, P.: 93

Duncomb, flogged in school: 20

Duncombe: Mr.: 44. John: 117. J., praises M: 58. W., quotes Lycidas: 58

Duncon, Mr.: 44

Dundas: Sir David: 44. Henry, Viscount Melville: 13

Dundee Grammar School: 40

Dunedham (Dymedham): 49

Dunfeoder: 49

Dunghill women: 44

Dunham, Josiah: 115. An Oration Delivered at Hanover: 115

Duni (the Downs): 49

Dunkerley, R.: 34

Dunkin: Robert: 44. W.: 58

Dunkirk, France: 44, 45, 103. Dunkirka: 49

Dunmore, John (bks.): 44

Dunn: E. Catherine: 93. W. H.: 63

Dunning, William A.: 83

Duns Scotus: 18, 24, 31, 52, 83, 82, 93, 137

Dunsmore, Lord. See Chichester, Earl of

Dunstan, St.: 73

Dunster Castle: 44

Dunster: Charles: 42, 58, 68, 105, 128, 88*, 117*, 55. Henry: 40, 41. John: 44. T. (pr.): 44

Dupin, L. E.: 57

Duplessis-Mornay, Philippe: 60, 38. Supposed author of Vendiciae Contra Tyrannos: 38

Duport, James: 10, 40, 117, 74

Duppa: Dr., Bp. of Salisbury: 28. Bryan: 45, 64

Dupré: de St. Maur (tr. PL): 58

Duraer. See Dury

Durand, M.: 117

Durandus: 142, 32. Staff as symbol: 104

Durant, Samuel, Histoire de la Tentation: 74

Durante, C.: 58

Durden, Robert F.: 115

Durel, John: 44

Dürer: Mr.: 44. Albrecht: 40, 27, 88, 146. Woodcut of St. Gregory's

Mass: 126

D'Urfe, Anne: 54

D'Urfey, Thomas: 40, 58

Durham, Francis: 40

Durham: 45, 49. College, Oxford: 40

Durie, John (1596-1680): 30, 44, 73, 91. Duraeus: see Dury

Durlach: 44

Durling, Robert M.: 33, 101, 106

Durr, Robert Allen: 23, 69, 81, 128

Durrell, L.: 23

Dury, John: 7*, 10*, 44*, 79, 114, 38, 93, 55. His wife: 44. See also: Durie

Dustoor, P. E.: 102, 77

Dutch Annotations upon the Whole Bible (tr. Theodore Haak): 74, 32, 99

Dutch: 44, 51, 103, 150. Agents: 44*. Ambassador: 44. Company: 44. M, study of language: 44. 36 Articles: 44. War(s): 44, 94. Quoted out of the: 73. Book illustrations: 97. See also: Low Countries

Duties of life, preparation for: 51

Dutton: E. P. and Company: 112. John: 45. Lawrence: 45. Mary: see Fleetwood, Lady Mary. Warren: 115; The Present State of Lit.: 115. William: 44, 45

Duty and Honour of Church Restorers (Herbert Palmer): 147

Duty: to God: 51. To theology: 51

Duwes, Giles: 40

Duyckinck: Evert A.: 98. George: 98

Dvina, River: 19

Dvorak, M.: 27

Dwight: T.: 58. Timothy: 115*; works: The Conquest of Caanan: 115*. The Nature and Danger, of Infidel Philosophy: 115; A Dissertation on the History, Eloquence, and Poetry of the Bible: 115; The Triumph of Infidelity: 115; Theology; Explained and Defended in a Series of Sermons: 115

Dyce Collection, Victoria and Albert Museum: 44

Dyce: Alexander: 86. W.: 97

Dyer: 15. Ancreta: see Ewens, Ancreta. Edward: 20, 40. G.: 58. John: 58*, 97

Dyke: Daniel: 10*, 37, 102, 93, 99*, 101; Two Treatises...of Repentance ...of Christ's Temptations: 74; The Mystery of Selfe-Deceiving: 37. Jeremiah: 10, 93

Dynamism, psychic: 141

Dysart: Grace, Countess of: 44. Lionel: 44

Dyskrasia: 72

Dyson, Anthony E.: 143, 93. And M's Platonism: 143

-E-

E. K.: 56, 66, 83*, 3, 88

E., G.: 128

E., J.: 44. See also: Ernle

E., W.: 116

E Forms in M's handwriting: 40

Ea: 1

Eachard, John (1636?-97): 44, 102, 128, 145. Contempt of the Clergy: 91

Eadmer: 93

Eagle of Jupiter: 111

Ear of God: 93

Earle: Royal chaplain: 94. John: 40, 44, 145. W. B.: 58

Earles, C.: 97

"Earliest" Life of M: 44

Early rising, M's elegy on: 20, 50

Early Lives of M, The (ed. Darbishire): 20, 112

Early Prolusion by John Milton, An (McCrea's tr.): 20

Early, Thomas: 40

Earth, the: 89*, 90*, 144, 143*, 128. Small size: 128. Axis, inclination of: 89. Density: 89. Dimensions: 89. Distance from the sun: 89. Eccentricity of orbit: 89. Form: 89. Perturbation: 89. Revolution: 89. Rotation: 89. Topographical details as viewed from other planets: 89. Velocity: 89. As center of the universe: 89, 144. M's allusions to: 89. Motion of: 114. Her bounty: 144. Wronged by man: 144. This dim spot called: 143. Power of Satan in: 143. Once near to God: 143. Its future revealed: 143*

Earthly Paradise: 111*

Earthquakes: 128. Causes and kinds: 128. Compared to agues and fevers: 128. In Hell: 128

"Earthy man": 122. See also: "Heavenly Man"; "Old man"; "New man"; Adam-Christ parallel; St. Paul

Ease, argument from: 123

East: the: 45. Angles: 49. Cheap (Street, London): 49, 73. France: 49. Hanningfield, co. Essex: 44. India Company: 19, 44, 150; trade: 8. Indies: 150; see also: India. Near and Far: 150. Prussia: 103. Retford Grammar School: 42. Road, Cambridge: 40. Saxons: 3

Easter: 47, 3, 72*. Term: 40. Vacation: 40

Eastern Fathers: 71

Eastlake, Sir Charles: 97

Easton, James: 44

Easy: 45

Eating: and uncreation: 75*. And creation: 75*

Eaton, co. Chester: 44

Eaton: Arthur Wentworth Hamilton: 115. Horace A.: 44. John: 114. Samuel: 79, 148

Ebrew: 73. See Hebrew

Ebsworth, J. W. See Phillips, John

Eburne, Richard: 93

Eburones: 49

Eca de Queiroz, José Maria de: 65

Ecbatana (Ecbatan): 19*, 49, 73, 144

Ecbert: 73. Son of Ercombert: 3. The Abp.: 3. The West-Saxon: 3. King of West Saxons: 38

Ecbryt Stone: 49. See also: Selwood

Eccentricity: of R. Burton, Warton on: 88. And irregularity approved by the Richardsons if artistic: 88. Of the Richardsons' criticism: 88. Of style seldom, of matter only in exceptional cases approved by Newton: 88. Of events condemned by Newton: 88. Of the metaphysical school, Warton on: 88

Ecchius: 73

Eccles: F.: 7. Mark: 44

Ecclesia: 51

<u>Ecclesiastes</u>: 114*, 126, 144, 71, 92. See also: Bible

Ecclesiastic History of Scotland: 73

<u>Ecclesiasticae Historiae Autores</u>: 82, 44

<u>Ecclesiastical History</u> (Bede): 3

<u>Ecclesiastical Sonnets</u> (Wordsworth): 94

Ecclesiastical: display: 51. Hierarchy: 51. Historian: 51. Issues: 51. Officials (hatred of): 51. Organization: 51. Power (abuse of): 51. Ranks: 51. Reforms: 51. Revenues: 51. Constitutions: 51. Pamphlets: 30, 40. Music: 121. Ecclesiastics, royal: 51. Ecclesiastical Court for the Issue of Marriage Licenses: 44. See also: Faculty Office

Echionian: 73

Echo: 90, 72. Sweetest nymph: 73

Eckhart (Meister): 7, 114, 125

Eckman, Frederick: 128

Eclectic method: Newtons: 88. M's, Newton on: 88

<u>Eclectic Review</u>: 63

Eclipse(s): 89, 128. Of sun and moon: 89. Impression of: 89. As supernatural manifestations: 89. Use of the word in M's poems: 89. Caused by Satan: 128. Lunar: 128. Solar: 128

Ecliptic, the: 89. Obliquity of: 89. Circle: 128

<u>Eclogues</u> (Virgil): 20, 70, 3, 26

Economics: 40. Economic factors,

neglect of: 113. M on economic change: 147. M's philosophy of economic reform: 147

"Economy" of the dramatic fable: 70

Economy in structure, Newton's pedantic application of principle of: 88

Ecphantas: 73

Ecphrasis, Greek term for descriptio: 20

Ecstasy: 5, 7

Edda, Icelandic: 118

Eddowes, Joshua (bks.): 44

Edelstein: Heinz: 100. L.: 68

Eden: C. P.: 23. Richard: 19. Thomas, master in Chancery: 44, 45

Eden: 2, 19, 31, 44, 49, 98, 103, 112, 111*, 125, 143, 54, 73, 144, 3, 32, 36*, 72*, 25. Biblical description of: 119, 32. Biblical setting of: 119. And landscape gardening: 97. Garden of: 36*. Creation of: 36. Location of: 36. Delights of: 36. Overabundance of: 36. Associated with the Golden Age: 36. Symbol of relationship with God: 46. Symbol of liberty: 46. As organism: 75. Composition and knowledge of: 96*. And sexuality: 75*. Restored: 143. Meaning of: 32, 119, 36. Situation and extent of: 32. location of in PL: 32. See also: Alcinous; Amara; Auran; Daphne; Euphrates; India; Nysean Isle; Pontus; Punic Coast; Selevicia; Paradise; Tellessar; Tigris

Edersheim, Alfred: 142, 93. <u>The Life and Times of Jesus the Messiah</u>: 142

Edessa: 3

Edethrudus: 54

Edgar: 3. King of Eng.: 44, 73. Thomas: 44

Edgcote: 45

Edgehill: 103. Battle of: 8

Edgeworth, R. L.: 58

Edginton, G. W.: 58

Edgman, William: 44

Edinburgh (Agned, Alclud, Edinborrow, Castle of Maydens): 44, 49

<u>Edinburgh Review</u>: 44, 63, 87, 146

Edindon (Ethandune): 49

Eding: 10

Edith: 3

Editions: 117*

Editor: Bentley's phantom: 88. Editors and commentators: 17th, 18th, 19th, 20th c.: 55*

Edkins, Joshua: 117

Edlington, Joseph: 45

Edman, Irwin: 143. Past echoes: 143

Edmonds: Charles: 44. Cyrus, on M's Puritanism: 87; <u>John Milton</u>: 87. Mary: 44

Edmondson, Joseph: 45

Edmund Hall. See St. Edmund

Edmund, Sir Anthony: 40

Edmunds: Richard: 44. Thomas: 40

Edmundson: Mr. G., on M and Vondel: 95. George: 68, 144, 32, 36

Edolph, Sir Thomas: 45

Edom (Edomoeus, Edomitish, Edomite): 49, 73

Edridge, R.: 58

<u>Education during the Renaissance</u> (Woodward): 3

<u>Education of Children, The</u> (Kempe): 20

<u>Education of Shakespeare, The</u> (Plimpton): 20

Education, Book of: 51

<u>Education, Tractate on</u>: 132*

Education: 8, 9, 20*, 27, 30*, 40*, 51*, 84, 121, 78, 113. Of boys: 114*. As including music: 121. M's theory of: 137, 51, 124, 55. M's account of his: 55, 137. Phillips' account: 55. Cambridge, M's account: 55. M's doctrine of useful: 114*. M's and Renaissance schools: 20*, 30*, 44*, 51. M's criticism of contemporary: 51. Commission for reform of: 51. Humanistic theory of: 51. Philosophy of: 51. Plan of: 51. Provision for in free commonwealth: 51. Traditional: 51. M and Comenius on: 147. The best and noblest way of: 51. Educational, ideas, practice(s), problems, procedure, reform, routine, treatises: 51. Of Education: see Milton

Educational Charters and Documents (Leach): 3

Edward: the Confessor: 70, 3, 94. I, King of Eng.: 44. II: 122. III: 73. V: 45. VI (King of Eng.): 18, 40, 44, 51, 52, 54, 60, 70, 73, 103, 120, 128, 3, 38, 62, 64; Second Prayer Book: 150. VI fellowship: 40. Prince: 44. The elder: 3

Edwards: Mr. (husband to Anne): 44. Anne: 44. J. Passmore: 23, 44. James: 44, 45. John: 45. Jonathan: 98, 71, 115; humility of: 71. Ralph: 27. Richard: 45, 66. Robert: 45. S.: 58. Thomas (1599-1647): 7, 9*, 44, 58*, 59, 79, 113, 114, 120, 147, 26, 32, 101, 148, 117; Gangraena: 91; anti-tolerationist: 147; condemns Robinson: 147; wrote Gangraena: 147. Ursula: see Ashworth, Ursula. William: 45

Effect: 50. Tragic: 123. Of regeneration: 123. Inferior to cause: 123. Of epic poem: 122. Argues cause: 123

Effel, Jean: 95

Effinger, Carl: 117

Egcourte: Mr.: 45. See also: Estcourt

Eger, Hans: 93

Egerton Manuscript: 132

Egerton: family: 40, 44, 143, 72, 88, 94. Lady Alice: 1, 29*, 44, 121, 136, 64, 55, 21*. Lady Alix: 40, 44; ed. of Comus: 44. Lady Catherine: 29, 64. Rev. F. H.: 88. Sir Francis: 44. Lady Frances, Countess of Bridgewater: 29, 21. John, Lord Brackley, 1st Earl of Bridgewater (1579-1649): 29*, 40, 44, 26, 53, 64, 55, 21. John, Viscount Brackley (1623-86): 55, 21. Mary: see Lee, Mary. Lady Penelope: 29, 64. Stephen: 93. Sir Thomas, Baron Ellesmere, Lord, Lord Keeper and Viscount Brackley, Chancellor (1542-1613): 29, 40, 44, 45, 121, 131, 55, 21. Thomas (1625-48?): 54, 55. See also: Bridgewater

Egger, Emile: 100

Eggers, Hans: 100

Egham, co. Surrey: 44

Eglesburh: 49

Eglesfield, F. (pr.): 44

Eglesthrip (Episford): 49. See also: Ailsford

Eglon: 91

Egmondt, Frederick: 40

Ego: 96. Egotism, M's: 113, 146. Ego-ideal: 47

Egremont, Earl of: 88

Egypt (AEgypt, AEgypticus, AEgyptus, Pharan Fields): 2, 19*, 40, 44, 51, 103, 144*, 3, 32*, 72, 150, 25. Blindness in: 16. Symbol of tyranny: 46. Egyptians: 39, 144*, 3; and astronomy: 89. Gods: 144*. Colony: 3. Hall, The: 97. See also: Memphis; Nile

EHA. See Ecclesiasticae Historiae Autores

Ehrmann, Jacques: 11

Ehud: 91

Eidolon: 123*

Eidolopoeia: 20

Eidophusikan, the: 97

Eidora: 49

Eighteenth century: 58*. Attitude toward M and Shakespeare: 87. Attitude toward the sonnet: 87. See also: Augustans; Blank verse; Diction; Milton, John; Moralizing; Prosody; Sonnet; Spenser, Edmund

Eighth sphere, the, distribution of the stars in: 89

Eighth Age: 93

Eike of Repgow: 93

Eikon Aklastos: 44, 116, 91. See also: Jane, J.

Eikon Alethine: 44, 113, 91, 55. Anonymous answer to Eikon Basilike: 147. See also: Milton, John; Eikonoklastes

Eikon Basilike: 8, 9, 20, 28*, 30, 40, 44, 51, 146, 55, 103*, 113, 116*, 128, 132, 3, 11, 26, 53, 62, 71, 82, 91*. Of Charles I: 70. By Dr. Gauden, Charles I's apology: 147, 94. And M's reply: 147

Eikon Episte : 144, 91

Eikonoklastes: 8*, 16, 103*, 112, 113, 121, 116*, 129, 144*, 147, 3*. Compared with A Letter from General

Ludlow to Dr. Hollingworth: 116. Compared with A Letter from Major General Ludlow: 116. Compared with Ludlow No Lyar: 116. Relation to Eikon Alethine: 144. Debt to May's History: 144. Use of Declarations: 144*. M's integrity: 144. Presentation copy of: 44. M's use of "Perfection": 83. Imagery: 8*

Eileithyia: 90

Ein schön lieblich Spiel: 65

Einhard: 93

Einstein, Albert: 23, 40, 112

Eiselen, Malcolm R.: 115

Eisenstein, Sergei M.: 5, 15, 39

Ejection of 1662: 78

Ekfelt, F. E.: 128

Ekins, J.: 58

Ekloge Chronographias: 65

Ekron: 73

El Dorado: 19, 49, 73. See also: Guiana

El Greco: 27

Elcock, Ephraim: 44

Elder Brother: 1, 29, 40, 104. His wisdom: 143. Vindicated: 143. See also: Brothers

Elderkin, G. W.: 39

Elderston: Copse: 44. Coppice: 45

Elderton, Rev. J.: 44

Eldrige: Mr.: 44. Richard: 45

Eldune: 49

Eleale: 49, 73, 144

Elean: 73. Dust: 3

Eleazar: 73. Cf Worms: 113

Elect: 9*, 143, 71. M's conception of the: 113. In Geneva Bible: 143. In PL: 143. Samson among the: 143. Election: 9*, 63, 122; doctrine of: see Grace. See also: Saints; 3 classes of men

Elections: Electors, care in choice of: 51

Electra (character): 73, 90, 91, 92

Electra: 40, 103, 26

Elegance: false, by Peck preferred to vigour: 88. Todd on: 88

Elegantiae (Valla): 20

Elegies (in general): 15, 20, 113, 27. Elegia de angelis: 65. Elegia levis: 40

Elegy in a Country Churchyard: 88

Elegy in Memory of Lady Penelope Noël (Gill the Younger): 20

Elegy on Gustavus Adolphus, Gill the Younger mentioned having written an: 20

Elegy, M's Latin: 8, 40, 129, 112. Attitude toward myth: 8. Elegy III: 112. IV: 112. V: 112; theme of: 104. VI: 112, 61. VII: 112. See Milton, John, Works

Elementals (elemental spirits): 142. See also: Gnomes; Sylphs

Elementarie (Mulcaster): 135. 1st Part of the: 3

Elements of Punctuation (David Steel, Jr.): 88

Elements: vitalism in: 118. Four: 128, 46. Interchange: 128

Elenchus Motuum: 116

Elephant: 17

Eleus: 49

Eleusinian: 73

Eleusinus: 49

Eleusis: 3, 92

Eleutherius, Bp. of Rome: 73

Elfled: 3

Elfresh, F. M.: 71

Elfric (Aelfric): 73

ELH: 44

Eli: 68, 120. Eli's (Ely's) sons: 73

Eliade, Mircea: 69, 75, 118, 125, 32, 39

Elias: 25. The Levite (Levita): 40, 41, 42, 22

Eliberis: 49. Council of: 44, 73, 113

Elijah (Eliah): 70, 73, 123, 125, 139, 3, 32*, 72, 25. Prototype of Christ: 46. See also: Los

Eliot: 112. Andrew: 115, 117. Charles: 34. George: 1, 15, 23; on Young: 58; references in Middlemarch to M: 87. John: 9, 40, 99. Sir John: 103, 120. N.: 117

Eliot, T. S.: 1*, 4, 12*, 15*, 18, 23, 34*, 35, 37, 56, 60, 63, 66, 73, 75, 76, 77, 79, 81, 83, 84*, 86*, 87, 102, 105*, 104, 108, 110, 111, 118, 123, 124*, 125, 126, 127, 128, 132, 133*, 134, 136, 138, 139, 142, 143, 144, 145, 11, 14, 32, 36, 39, 46, 61, 62, 72, 93, 64, 101, 109, 115, 130*, 131, 146, 150*, 48, 25. Attitude toward M: 87. On rhetorical style: 53. On visualization in Dante: 53. On M's dead English: 53. Vision in PL, Bk. I: 53. Works: 4 Quartets: 109; After Strange Gods: 83. Ash Wednesday: 12. Brief Intro. to the Method of Paul Valery: 12; Family Reunion: 12; Lecon de Valery: 12. Milton: 12, 60, 74; Murder in the Cathedral: 12; Music of Poetry, The: 12; Notes toward the Definition of Culture: 12; Poetry and Drama: 12; Possibility of a Poetic Drama, The: 12; Sacred Wood, The: 12, 60; Serpent, Le: 12; Tradition and the Individual Talent: 12; Use of Poetry and the Use of Criticism: 12; A Study of His Writings by Several Hands: 12. T. S. Eliot, The Design of his Poetry: 12

Elisha: 72

Elision: Bentley on: 88. Problem of, left unsolved by Pearce: 88. Explained by the Richardsons according to acoustic impressions: 88. Identified by Peck: 88. Newton, Lofft on: 88

Elizabeth (Elisabeth): Lady: 44. Princess (1635-50): 91. Princess Palatine: 10, 40. Queen of Bohemia: 40, 44. Stuart: 10, 64

Elizabeth, Queen I: 1, 6, 18, 20, 29, 33, 35, 40, 42, 44, 45, 51, 52, 56, 60, 73, 83, 87, 103, 108*, 128, 147, 3, 143, 38, 39, 82*, 93, 94, 64, 13. And the Puritans: 147. Established the Anglican Church: 147. Voids all preaching licenses of nonconformists: 147. Warns James against the Puritans: 147. Opposed by Grindal: 143. Supressed prophesying: 143. Elizabethan Age: 27

Elizabethan Club (Yale): 44

Elizabethan Critical Essays, Introduction to (Gregory Smith): 70

Elizabethan Criticism of Poetry (Thompson): 3

Elizabethan Psychology (Dowden): 70

Elizabethan Puritan, An: 45

Elizabethans, the: 70, 87, 103, 88*. Relation to the: 129*. Audience: 92. Dramatists: 92. Elizabethan Period: 121. Elizabethan Lit.: lyric and drama: 129; pastoral poetry: 129; the elegy: 129; the sonnet: 129, 87; the masque: 129; other forms: 129. Elizabethan taste: 40

Elkin, Robert: 44

Elledge, Scott: 53

Eller, Meredith F.: 93

Ellesmere, Lord, Earl of: 40, 44

Elliot: Benjamin: 115; An Oration, Delivered in St. Philip's Church: 115. E.: 58. James: 115; The Poetical and Miscellaneous Works of James Elliot, Citizen of Guilford Vermont: 115

Elliott: Major Alexander: 44. George R.: 93

Elliptic: constructions, Bentley on: 88. Manner of M, attr. by Pearce to his vigorous enthusiasm: 88. Expressions, misinterpreted by Pearce: 88. The Richardsons' emotional interpretation of: 88. Peck on: 88. Cotton perplexed by M's: 88. Newton's inadequate treatment of: 88. Todd on: 88. Expressions, Dunster, Masson on: 88. Style, Manbaddo on terseness of M's: 88

Ellis-Fermer, Una: 6, 108, 68, 143, 85, 101, 21

Ellis: Messrs. (bks. s): 44. George: 40, 58. Henry: 64. Havelock: 75. John: 44. Robert: 40. (Ell), William: 44

Ellistone, John: 7

Ellman, Richard: 48

Ellmann, R.: 23

Elloway (Elwes, Elwayes, Ellowayes): Mrs. (Raleigh): 45. Sir John: 45

Ellrodt, Robert: 60, 81, 39

Ellston (Elston, Elstone): Elizabeth: 45. John: 44, 45

Ellul, Jacques: 52, 93

Ellwood: 132, 3. Thomas (1639-1713): 1, 7, 16, 28, 44*, 70, 77, 74, 129, 83, 84, 103, 114, 125, 135, 139, 142, 26, 38, 72, 91, 94, 64, 101, 130, 137, 146, 148, 117, 21; quoted: 77, 55. See also Life (Richardson)

Elmer, the monk: 70

Elocutio (3rd part of rhetoric): 20

Elohim: 25. See also: God; Jehovah

Eloquence: 20, 31

Elpenor: 73

Elphin: 44

Elphinston, J.: 58

Elsaezisches, Adam und Evaspiel: 65

Else, G. F.: 6

Elsinore (Elsenora), Denmark: 44, 49

Elson, James H.: 93

Elsynq(e): 51. Henry: 44

Elton: C. A.: 58. Oliver: 58, 86, 138, 130

Eltonhead, Mr., Master in Chancery: 44, 45

Elve: 49

Elversham: 49. See also: Henault

Elwayes. See Elloway

Elwes. See Elloway

Elwood, Thomas. See Ellwood, Thomas

Ely, Benjamin: 44

Ely: co. Cambridge: 44. (Anguilla, Eely, Elie), city: 49. Isle of: 44

Ely: Cathedral: 44. Bp. of: 103, 72

Elye, Rev. Thomas: 44

Elynittria: 25

Elyot: 133, 3*. Sir Thomas: 18, 20, 29, 40, 51, 74, 102, 114, 123, 93; The Boke Named the Governour: 32

Elys, Edmund: 116

Elysium: 1, 73, 90, 142, 72. Elysian: 73; Fields: 144, 32*; flowers: 3

Elzevi(e)r: 91. Family: 44. Daniel (pr.): 44, 63, 94, 150, 55. Ludovicus (Louis), pr.: 44*, 103

Emanation: 25

Emathian (Aemathia): 73

Embellishments: 121

Emblem(s): 15, 123. Emblem books: 114

Emblematum Liber (Alciati): 29

Emendations: Hume preparing the way for Bentley's best: 88. Crude, in Hume: 88. Bentley's, see chapter on Bentley: 88*. Meant to regularize M's verse: 88. Based on literary parallelisms: 88. Valuable, by Bentley: 88. Bentley's, of M's punctuation: 88. Pearce, careful in his: 88. Peck's: 88. In Hawkey's edition: 88. In Newton's edition: 88. Jortin's: 88. Sympson's: 88

Emerson: E. H.: 60. Ralph Waldo: 79, 86, 98, 39, 62, 71, 115, 130, 137; on the Puritan Mind: 147; The American Scholar: 115

Emett, S.: 58

Emilia: 73, 120, 144, 137. Of the sonnets to: 20, 30, 44

Emily: 40. C.: 58

Emim(s): 73, 123. See also: Giants, Biblical

Emma (Jane Austen): 134

Emma, R. D. (editor): 123, 135

Emmanuel College, Cambridge: 40*, 44, 45

Emmanuel Syrus: 65

Emmaus: 72

Emmerich, Katherine: 141

Emmet: 144

Emmons, Nathanaiel: 115, 117. A Sermon Preached at the Installation of the Rev. David Avery: 115

Emotion(s): 7. Appreciated by Thyer even though irregular: 88. Little understanding of, in Newton's comments: 88. Newton's appreciation of geniuine, in SA: 88. And syntax, Newton on: 88. Experimental and aesthetic: 148. Socialization of in 17th c.: 118. Rhetorical appeals to: 51*. Emotional: interpretation in the Richardsons' commentary excessively: 88. Subtleties observed by Thyer: 88. Beauty, Warton's ideal of profound: 88. M's use of emotional appeal: 51

Empedocles: 60, 73, 111, 114, 123, 128, 71, 48

Emphasis, structural (rhetoric): 51. Bentley on accent and: 88. The Richardsons' consistent use of capitals to indicate: 88. And spelling in M, Lofft on: 88

Empire, the: 51

Empneusta (wind instrument): 40

Empson, William: 1*, 12, 15, 17, 23, 37, 52, 56, 66, 75, 76, 81, 86*, 100, 102, 105, 110, 111, 118, 123, 127, 128, 133, 138, 139, 141, 11, 14, 36, 39, 61, 93, 106, 109, 137, 146, 140*, 25. Works: _The Listener_: 60; _M's God_: 60, 109

Empyrean, the: 73, 89, 71. See also: Heaven

En-Sof, conception of in the Zohar: 113

Enakim: 142

Enarationes in rii Psalmos Davidicos: 121

Enarrationes in opus sex dierum: 65

Enchanter: 122

Enchiridion militis Christiani (Colet): 40

Enchiridion Orationes: 40

Encinas, Francis: 40

Encke's comet: 89

Encomium of Folly (Erasmus): 3

Encomium: 20, 122. Heroic virtue in: 123

Encontadas, the: 98

Encyclopedia: 40. Of M research, Todd's edition a veritable: 88. Encyclopaedic: accumulation of matter in Hume: 88. Tendencies of Paterson's notes, Callander's commentary: 88. Encyclopedists: 142

Encyclopaedia of Religion and Ethics ("Usury"): 82

Encyclopaedia Britannica: 1, 44, 51. 1963 edition: 82

Encyclopedias of science: 128*. Conservative attitude, contents, purpose, sources: 128*. See also: Bartholomew; Caxton

Encyclopédie: 32

End, of poetry: 123. See Causes, final

Endeavor (ship): 44

Enderby: 45

Endowment, creative: 70. See also: Inspiration; Nature; Spontaneity

Endurance: 122. See also: Patience; Suffering

Endymion: 44, 73, 3

Energy, primitive awareness of: 141

Enfer, L': 65

Enfield, co. Middlesex: 44, 45

Engagement of Allegiance: 103

Engine: 143. Conflicting interpretations of: 143

England: 9*, 31, 45, 49, 51*, 103*, 112, 3*, 32*, 72. Church of: 3. M's idea of: 113. Popularity of Golden Age in: 32. Writers on Genesis in: 32. Opposition to eternalism in: 32. Atomism in: 32. Ideas of Adam's salvation in: 32. Covenant doctrine in: 32. M's return to: 89. Ideas of Adam's knowledge in: 32. Ideas of marriage in: 32. Landscape of: 8. Ideas of government in: 32. Ideals of natural rights in: 32. Model of paradise in: 32. Ideas of Heaven in: 32. Garden description in: 32. See also: Britain; Logres; Anglia

England's Helicon: 129, 94

England's Proper and onely way (John Hare): 147

England's Sole Remedy: 59

Englands Birth-Right Justified (John Lilburne): 147

Englands New Chains Discovered (John Lilburne): 147

Englefield: 49

Engleheart, F.: 97

Englische Padagogik im 16 Jaarundert (Benndorff): 3

Englische Studien: 44, 45

English writers before 1625: 40

English Company of Merchants, Hamburg: 40, 44

English Court Hand Illustrated: 45

English Dancing Master (Playford): 29

English Expositor: 40

English Garden (William Mason): 70

English Grammar Schools to 1660, The (Watson): 112, 3

English Grammar, The: by Butler: 135*. By Jonson: 135

English Historical Review: 44, 45

English Lit. in the Earlier 17th C.: 83

"English phrases derived from the Latin tongue": 44

English Poems of M (1940, ed. C. Williams): 134

English Pulpit Oratory: 51

English Review, The: 136

English Secretary, The (Day): 20

English, Peter: 44. Survey of Policy: 91

English: 20*, 40, 44, 51*, 70, 103*, 121, 3. Books: 40. Citizens: 51*. Channel: 103. College (Catholic, at Rome): 44. Comedy: 70. Commonwealth: 51. Critics: 70. Jesuit College, Rome: 103. Authors, language, lit.: 40. Jesuits: 103. Music: 121. Nation: 3. People: 103*, 3. Precendent: 70. Theorists: 70. Prosody: 40. Language: 70, 103, 3*; language in grammar schools: 20*; praise of: 44; Old (Anglo-Saxon): 40. English views of M: 149. Trade, M's knowledge of: 19. Tragedy: 70. Universities Press: 44. Englishman (Englishmen): 3. Poet, the (Spenser): 83. Pope, the: 73. Reader, the: 98

Engrossment: 45

Enharmonic genus: 121

Enimie of Idleness, The (Fulwood): 20

Enion: 25

Enipeus: 2

Enitharmon: 145, 25*

Enjambment in PL: 118

Enjoyment, aesthetic: 50

Enki and Ninhursag: 65, 36

Enkidu: 32, 36

Enlightenment: 67

Enna: 19, 49, 73, 72. Field of: 144, 32

Enneads: 112

Ennemoser: 7

Ennius: 56, 57. Translated: 58

Enoch: 1, 17, 68, 102, 111, 113, 123, 127, 32*, 72, 106. Book of: 41, 63, 141, 144, 32, 109. Book of the Secrets of: 41. Enoch II: 24; I: 77

Enort, Thomas: 117

Enos: 123

Enquiry into the Measures of Submission to the Supream Authority: 116

Enrichment of poetry: 19

Enrollment by colleges: 40

Ens: 40, 73

Enséignement des Lettres Classiques d'Ausone à Alcuin (Roger): 3

Ent, Sir George: 10

Entata (plucked instruments): 40

Entertainment: definition of: 29. At Cambridge: 40

"Entertainment at Highgate" (Jonson): 29. "Entertainment at Althorpe" (Jonson): 29. "Entertainment at the Barriers" (Jonson): 29. "Entertainment at the Blackfriars" (Jonson): 29. "Entertainment given by Lord Knowles" (Campion): 29. "Entertainment of Q. Elizabeth at Harefield" (anonymous): 29

Enthronement of Christ: 100*

Enthusiasm: 5, 7, 51, 114*

Enthymeme, in rhetoric: 31, 51*, 73

Entries on the Deadly Sins: Anger (not included), Avarice, Envy, Gluttony and Drunkenness, Lust, Sloth, Pride (not included): 82.

Entries on Opposites of the Deadly Sins: "Of Courage," "Of Duels," "Of Justice," "Of Keeping Faith": 82

Entries on Ways of Speaking: "Of Evil Speaking," "Of Flattery," "Of Lying," "Of Reproof": 82

Entries with Literary Import: "Of the Knowledge of Lit.," "Of Poetry," "Of Music," "Of Curiosity," "Of Consultation": 82

Entropy: 96

Enuma Elish: 36

Environment and human weakness: 31

Envy, by Satan. See Jealousy

Enyo: 2, 73. See also: Bellona

Enys, D.: 58

Eobanus, Helius: 64

Eos: 73, 90. See also: Aurora

Eothen: 15

Epaminodas: 73, 123, 3

Epaphroditas: 73

Epectetus Mannuall and Theophrastus Characters: 29

Epeisodia: 92*

Ephemerides: 45

Ephesus (Ephesians): 44, 49, 73, 126, 3. Ephesians: 92. See also: Bible

Ephialtes, Neptune's son: 73

Ephraim (Ephraem): 49, 73. St.: 123, 77. Ephraim (Ephraem, Ephrem): 49, 73. St.: 123, 77; Syrus: 32

Epic: 17*, 27*, 30, 31, 50*, 70*, 132*, 145*, 72*, 92, 145*, 117*, 25. And tragedy: 149*. Method: 149*. Background: 149*. Classic and Christian: 149*. Sad ending: 149. Happy ending: 149. Future of: 149. Scenes: 149*. Strains: 149. Epical tendency in Shakespeare: 149. Romantic: 25. Convergence with prophecy: 25. Evolution of: 25. As composite form: 25. Rules for: 25. Theorists: 25. M's conception of: 25. Brief and diffuse: 25. Ironic strategy of: 25. As heterocosm: 25. Renaissance: 46. Encyclopaedic: 46. Classical: 46, 25. Brief: 46. And the novel compared: 48. Myth: 48. Figures in the: 70. Function of the: 70. Hero: 60, 70. Poem, design of: 28*. Subject matter: 70*. Subjects, list of: 40. Tradition: 67, 21*, 25. Voice: 37*. Experimentation: 25. Imitation: 25. Death motif: 25. Visionary drama: 25. Mythical plots of: 76. Comedy: 124. M's innovations: 76. Renaissance concept of: 124. Chronology of events: 76. M's concept of as Drama: 124. Diction: 76. M's ideas on: 132*. Trend: 149. Reiteration: air as realm of Satan's dominion and defeat: 119; disobedience of man theme: 119; serpent as subtlest beast theme: 119. Person: 122*, 123*. Machinery: 123. Causes (formal, final, material): 123. National: 123. Sacred: 123. Laws: 123. Marvellous: 123. Catalogue: 123. Effect: 123. Similes: 76, 98; angels like field of grain, like guardian bands of Jacob and Elisha: 119. devils like locusts of Egyptian plague, like Pharoah's armies: 119; Satan like Asmodeus; like Leviathan, like a wolf: 119; stairs to Heaven like Jacob's ladder: 119. Theory, and natural history: 128. Epics of 18th and 19th c.: 58*. Structure of the: 28, 70, 25; see also: proportional structure; symmetrical structure. Epic blocks: see proportional structure. See also: titles of individual works

Epic Structure of PL (E. N. S. Thompson): 70

Epicedion: 21*

Epicedium Cantabrigiense: 40

Epicharnus: 40

Epictetus: 40, 68, 73, 74, 123, 71, 117. Discourses: 74

Epicurus: 30, 57, 74, 112, 114, 123, 128, 32, 71, 142, 146. Epicurean(s): 60, 3. Epicureanism: 5, 27, 40, 32, 3, 73

Epicycles: 73, 144

Epidaurus: 49, 90. The god in: 73

Epideictic: oratory: 31. Rhetoric: 20

Epigonus: 128

"Epigram occasion'd by seeing some Sheets of Dr. B__t__ly's Edition of M's PL": 117

Epigram on Pope Urban VIII (attr. to M): 44

Epigrammata: 65

Epigrammatum Libri Tres: 65

Epigrams: 146. M's Latin: 94. Epigrammatist: 44

Epilogue: conclusion, rhetorical: 51. Comus: marriage proposed in:

143; purpose of: 143. To Elegy VII: 30. To The Passion: 30

Epimenides: 73

Epimetheus: 1, 17, 90, 32

Epinomis: 5

Epiphanies of Christ: 45

Epiphanius, St.: 41, 44, 57, 73, 113, 3, 36, 93. Panarion: 36

Epirot (Epeirot): 49, 3. See also: Sonnet XVII; Pyrrhus

Episcopacy by Divine Right asserted: 51, 26

Episcopacy: 7, 8, 9*, 51*, 144*, 147. Defended: 144. Origin of: 144. And schism: 144. A tyrannical adjunct to the Crown: 147. M on: 51. Conflict with Puritans: 144. Reform of: 144*. Controversy: 84

Episcopal: establishment: 103. Church: 71. Episcopalians: 78

Episcopius, Simon: 22. "Perfection" defined by: 83

Episode: 50*

Epistemology, method and empirical dilemmas of: 95*

Epistles, various: Latin: 20*, 40. "Epistle from a Gentleman": 58. Epistle of Barnabus: 107; Christ exists before the world: 107; God incomprehensible: 107; subordinationist: 107. Epistolae (Cicero): 20. Epistle to the Pisos (Horace); 20. Epistle of Paul the Apostle to the Romans, The: 51, 70, 3, 48. Epistle of Paul to Titus: 51. Epistles (Plato): III, VIII: 112; VII quoted: 149. Epistles (Horace): 70

Epistola ad Pollionem (attr. to M): 44

Epistulae Et Ponte: 62

Epitaphs: Epitaph on Cardinal Mazarin (attr. to M): 44. Epitaph for Damon: 111; Epitaphium Damonis: 45, 111, 121, 129; presentation copy: 44. Epitaph on Elizabeth Swettenham (attr. to M): 44. Epitaphs on Hobson: 72. Epitaph on Lady Talbot (M's): 44. Epitaph on Moll Cutpurse (attr. to M): 44. Epitaph on Thomas Young (attr. to M): 44

Epithalamion: An: 115. The: 83. By Jonson: 135. By Spenser: 70, 88, 130

Epithets: 70. Hume on: 88. Semicolon and Pearce dealing with: 88. The Richardsons on: 88. Compound and continuative, Peck on: 88. Warton on pompous: 88. Warton on individualizing: 88. Literary sources of M's, Warton on: 88

Epitome of Purchas (attr. to M): 44

Epstein, Isidore: 36, 93

Equal(s), argument from: 123*

Equality: 9*, 11. Of Father and Son in PL: 93

Equator: 19, 150

Equicola, Mario: 40

Equinoxes: the, precession of the: 89. Equinoctial: line (Ethiop Line): 49; circle: 128; winds: 150

Equity: 45

Equivoques, Satan's use of: 123

Er: 121

Erasmus Concerning Education (Woodward): 3

Erasmus, Desiderius: 1, 4, 7, 15, 18, 20*, 30, 40*, 42, 44, 51, 54, 56, 60, 66, 68, 73, 74, 77, 79, 103, 107, 108, 112, 114*, 118, 122, 123, 125, 129, 141, 142, 144*, 3*, 22, 26, 32, 71, 82, 93*, 99, 64, 109, 115, 130, 148, 117, 55. Origen his teacher: 107. Preferred Origen to Augustine: 107. Staff as symbol: 104. And Comus: 144. Youth: 144. Stoics: 144. Wisdom: 144. Works: Encomium Moriae: 144; Annotationes: 142; The Lives of Jehan Vitrier and John Colet: 57; Paraphrase upon the Newe Testament (tr. Nicholas Udall, et al.): 74; De Copia: 44, 82; De Ratione Studii: 82

Erastianism: 9, 63, 114, 38

Erastius. See Ariovistus

Erastus, Thomas Liebler: 40, 51, 73, 142, 115

Erato: 103, 3. Muse: 44, 73

Eratosthenes: 89, 90

Erbury, William: 114

Ercilla y Zúñiga, Alonso de: 122

Ercoco: 19, 49, 73, 144. See also: Negus, Empire of

Erdiswick, Mr.: 44, 45

Erdman, David V.: 25

Erebus: 73, 90. See also: Darkness

Erechtheum (Athens): 27, 44

Erectness: 24. Of Adam and Eve, implication of: 118

Eresby: 45

Erigena, John Scotus: 7, 32, 36. On Division of Nature: 36

Erikson, Erik: 53. On negative identity: 53. On "moratorium": 53

Erin(n)ys: 73, 90. See also: Furies

Eris: 90

Erith, L. E. P.: 68

Erling, Bernard: 93

Erminia: 49

Ernaldus, of Bonneval: 36

Ernest of Mansfield, Count: 21

Ernle, Sir John (J. E.): 44

Ernst: J. E.: 9. James: 115

Erondelle, Pierre: 40

Eros: 103, 112. Modern apotheosis of: 118. Eros-Anteros: 128

Errors (Heresys), M's: 44

Erskine; Audrey M.: 44. John: 16, 98, 113, 71, 130, 137, Jone: 128. Thomas: 115; The Speeches of the Hon. Thomas Erskine: 115

Eruditions, M's: 51. Allusions in Comus: 143. As potential encumbrance: 143

Erymanth: 49, 73

Erymanthus: 90

Erythraean main: 73

Eryximachus: 112

Esau: 73, 74, 111

Escalante: Barnardine: 19. Ferdinand de: 79

Escape: 47

Eschatology: 141, 78, 93*. Prophecy and: 96. Typology and: 96*. See also: Last Judgement

Escorbiac, Jean d': 74, 64. Christiade: 74

Escott. See Estcott

Esdras: 113

Eshtaol: 49, 73, 92. See also: Zora

Esnaval, Robert d': 64

Esquire bedell: 40

Essais de Morale: 78

Essamerone, ovvera l'opera de sei giorni: 65

Essays: 114*. Essay concerning Human Understanding (Locke): 78, 130. Essay on Design in Gardening, An (George Mason): 70. Essay of Dramatic Poesy, An (Dryden): 70. Essay on the Learning of Shakespeare: 88. Essay on Man (Pope): 139, 52. Essay on Marriage; Or The Lawfulness of Divorce, An: 115. Essay upon M's Imitations of the Ancients: 88, 117. Essay on the Writings and Genius of Pope: 12. Essayes (Bacon): 135. Essays and Studies by Members of the Eng. Assn.: 44. Essays on M (E. N. S. Thompson): 70

Essence: 96. Of Godhead: 93

Essenes: 73

Essex: 3. Court: 45. Earl of: 45, 103, 120, 39; marriage to Frances Howard: 143. Robert Devereux, 2nd Earl of: 44. Robert Devereux, 3rd Earl of: 44, 73. William: 44

Essex: 45*, 49. County (East-Saxons): 44, 103

Est: Robert: 44. Willem H. van: 93

Established church: 103*

Estates of the world: 83

Estbury: 45

Estcott (Escott, Estcot): Mr.: 45. Richard: 45. Thomas (lawyer): 44, 45. See also: Estcourt

Estcourt: Mr.: 45. Elizabeth (Cope): 45. Thomas: 45. Thomas, Master in Chancery: 44. See also: Estcott

Este, Hercules d': 64

Este, House of: 29

Estenses: 73

Esthambruges: 49. See also:

Henault; Mercator (map)

Esther, Queen: 73, 123

Esthonia. See Charles X

Estienne: Charles: 114, 123; see also Stephanus, Carolus. Henri: 40*, 108, 114; see also Stephanus, Henricus. Robert: 40; see also: Stephanus, Robertus

Estius: 68

Estoire Joseph (12th c. French verse paraphrase): 74

Estotiland: 19, 49, 73

Estrée, Paul d': 44

Etana-myth: 141

Etching Club: 97

Eteocles: 92

Eternal: the: 47. Death: 25. Life: 47. Present: 93. Eternals: 25*. Eternity: 25. Eternal and Immutable Morality: 12

Etham: 49, 73

Ethel, Garland: 93

Ethelbert: 73

Ethelffridda: 54

Ethelred, King of Eng.: 44

Ethelwolf: 3

Etherington: J.: 79. Lewis: 44

Ethics: 51, 40*, 96; definition of: 71; Miltonic concept: 31*, 40, 113*. Ethical: proof(s), rhetorical: 51*, 123; value of music: 121. Ethical power of Lady in Comus: 40

Ethiopia (Ethiop, AEthiopa): 49, 144, 32. Line: 73, 144. Queen: 73. Ethiopian, the wide: 73; Sea: 150, 19, 49. Ethiopic(ians): 42, 44, 32

Ethnics. See Heathen

Ethopoeia, defined: 20

Ethos: 92. Teaching of the doctrine of: 20

Etienne de Bourbon: 40

Etiological argument: 123

Eton, co. Bucks.: 44, 103

Eton: 3. College: 40, 44

Etruria: 19, 44. Etruria(n): 73

Etruscan: 73

Etten, Christopher van: 64

Etty, W.: 97*

Etudes Anglaises: 44

Etymology: 40. And meaning in M, Hume on: 88. Argument from: 123. Of heroes: 123. Etymological: information in Speght's glossary: 88; analysis in Hume, Pearce: 88; method of Paterson's notes: 88. Etymologiae: 121. Etymologicon (Henri Estienne): 40, 123. See also: Argument; Notation

Euan, Teumesian: 73, 3

Euboic: 73. Sea: 49

Eucharist: 71, 72, 93. Symbolism of: 81

Euclid: 2, 4, 40, 59, 73, 100, 108, 133, 3, 130

Euclion: 73

Eudoxus: 89

Euergetae: 73

Eugenius: 73, 74. Hispanus: 65. Of Toledo: 36

Eugippius Africanus: 68

Eugubinus, Augustinus Steuchus: 32

Euhemerus: 57

Eumenides: 73, 90. See also: Furies

Eunapius: 44

Eunomius: 18, 73

Eunuch (Terence): 20

Euoe: 73

Euphony: 70

Euphorian: 64

Euphrasy: 72

Euphrates (Assyrian Flood): 19, 49, 73, 144, 32*, 150. See also: Assyria; Balsara; Tigris

Euphrosyne: 44, 70, 73, 90. See also: Mirth

Euphues (Lily): 88. Euphues Golden Legacie: 40

Euphuism: 27, 132

Euripides: 1, 4, 5, 6, 15, 18, 20, 30, 35, 40*, 44, 51, 52, 56, 57, 59, 68, 70, 73, 74, 81, 90*, 103, 113, 120, 123, 127, 132, 144, 3, 26, 39, 53, 64, 146, 143, 117, 21, 71, 82*, 88, 91, 92*, 94, 101, 130. Translated: 53. Debts to: 92*. Stephen's edition of: 92. M's translation from: 117. Works: Alcestis: 32, 92*, 149; Andromache: 92*; Bacchae: 92*; Electra: 92; Hecuba: 92*; Helen: 92*, 149; Heraclidae: 82, 92*; Hippolytus: 92*; Iphigenia in Aulis: 92*; Iphigenia in Tauris: 92*; Ion: 92*; Madness of Herakles (Hercules Furens): 149, 82, 92*; Medea: 82, 92*, 149; Orestes: 82, 92*; Phoenissae: 92*; Rhesus: 92*; The Suppliants (Supplices): 82, 92*; Troades: 92*

Euripus: 49, 73

Europe: 49, 51, 103*, 3, 71, 25. Ethics in, during Middle Ages: 71

European Magazine: 117. European Magazine and London Review: 115

Eurotas: 49, 73, 90

Eurus: 73, 90, 144

Euryalus (Eurialus): 2, 73

Eurydice: 73, 90, 3, 72

Eurylochus: 73

Eurynome: 1, 50, 73, 90. See also: Ophion

Eusebio, Abate Don: 44

Eusebius: 25, 38, 82*, 55; works: Historia Eccelesiastica: 82; De Vita Constantini: 82. St.: 7, 27, 44, 57, 73, 100, 123. Of Caesarea: 68, 74, 114, 142, 93*, 148; works: De Demonstratione Evangelica: 74; Evangelicae Praeparationis: 74; Onomasticon Urbium et Locorum Sacrae Scripturae: 142. Of Emesius: 77. Pamphilius: 77; Praep. Evang. (tr. Legge): 77. Eusebian book: 3

Eustachius: 40*

Eustathius: 1, 40, 56, 128, 88, 77. Macrembolite: 90. Of Thessalonica: 90

Eusthates of Antioch: 65

Eustochium: 73

Eustratius: 123

Euthydemus (Plato): 112

Eutychian: 71

Eutychius of Alexandria: 68

Eva, L': 65

Eva, Mythologia: 65

Evagrius Scholasticus: 73. Church History: 82

Evan, Enoch: 114

Evander: 2, 73

Evangelic: religion: 51. Evangels: 3. Evangelicals: attitude toward M: 87; reading of Bible: 87. Evangelical Record and Western Review for the Year 1812, The: 115

Evans: Mr. (publisher): 44. B. Ifor: 86. Charles: 115. Florence M. G.: 44. G. Blackmore: 44, 91. J.: 15. J. M.: 32, 106. Joan: 128. Margaret: 40. Mathew: 44; see also: Ewens. Nathaniel: 115, 117; Poems on Several Occasions, With Some other Compositions: 115. Richard: 44, 45. (Ewans), Thomas: 44. W. M.: 59, 100, 39. W. T.: 44. Willa McClung: 29*, 40, 44

Evanscence of human glory: 19

Evaristus, S. Mary: 4

Eve: 1*, 4*, 17*, 19, 24*, 31*, 37, 42, 44, 50*, 54*, 60*, 63, 67*, 70*, 73, 98*, 102*, 103, 112, 111*, 113*, 114*, 123*, 76, 124*, 125, 127*, 128*, 143, 142*, 144, 3, 32, 36*, 71, 72*, 80, 92, 96, 99, 109*, 130*, 140*, 25. As a character: discussed: 55*; sources: 55. And reason, faith: 37*. As recipient of Messianic prophecy: 123. Fatal error of: 143. And classical goddesses: 17, 32, 76. Original perfection of: 32. In relation to Adam's knowledge: 50, 32. Name of: 36. Equals sense: 36. Type of Mary ("2nd Eve"): 72, 36. Alone when tempted: 36. Seduction of: 36*. Creation of: 50. Temptation and Fall of: 36*, 37, 76, 123, 143. Motives for Fall: 36. Motives for tempting Adam: 36. Vision of: 36. Symbolic interpretation of: 32. Creation of: 32, 36*. Work of: 32. Adam's kingship over: 32. In account of her origin: 72. In dream: 72. In her Fall: 72. In implication of Adam: 50, 72*, 123*. In losing Eden: 72. On the morning of the Fall: 17, 72. In pre-Satanic Eden: 72. In repentence: 72. In "wedded love": 72. And the Lady: 101. As preserver: 101. And Satan: 101.

Self-sufficiency of: 101. And Sin: 101. Dream: 17, 50, 76, 37*. As ideal woman: 75. Placed below Adam: 76. Loss of Eden: 76. Her language: 37. Description of: 37. At the pool: 17, 37. Independence from Adam asserted by: 119. Language of Paul used ironically by: 119. Repentant state associated with Mary Magdalene: 119. Sin of foreshadowed: 119. Subjection of to Adam symbolized by hair: 119. Takes the fruit: 119. Tempted by the Serpent: 119. As uncreator: 75. In PL: moral consciousness of: 104; awareness of death: 104; confession of: 104; spiritual regeneration of: 104; tonal and tempo patterns of: 104. See also: Adam and Eve; Woman; Triple Equation; Adam

<u>Eve</u>: by Hodgson: 65. By Howard: 65. By Peguy: 65. By Rossetti: 65. By Stephens: 65. <u>Eve, A Mystery in 3 Parts</u>: 65

Evelyn-white, H. G.: 23

Evelyn: George: 45. Sir John: 6*, 10, 16, 19, 40, 44*, 58, 70, 116, 128, 145, 38, 39, 109, 55

<u>Evening Fire-Side Or Weekly Intelligence, The</u>: 115

Evening: 89. Star: 50, 89; see also: Venus. Evensong: 125

Everard: John: 7, 23, 79, 114. Robert: 9

Everinden, Humphrey: 93

<u>Everlasting Gospel, The</u>: 25

Eversley: 45

<u>Every Man in his Humor</u> (Jonson): 70

<u>Everyman</u>: 125, 72. Everyman: 1, 27, 122, 134, 149. See also: Man

Everyman's Library: 44

Evidence, rhetorical: 51*

Evil: 7, 8, 31*, 47, 51*, 52, 107, 113*, 141, 143*. Definition: 107. Nonexistent until thought becomes action: 107. Origin: 149, 107. Permitted by God: 107. The result of free choice in Origen: 107. The problem of, in M: 113*. In Hebrew speculation: 113. Cosmic: 125. Domestic: 125. Depth and recalcitrance of: 143. Days of: 143. Theory of: 71. M on: 80. Permissive: 93. Converted into good: 93*. Its ultimate desctruction; active and passiveve resistance to: 47. Origin in Lucifer: 149. Conflict with God: 149*. Repulsiveness of: 141. Attract- iveness of: 141. Reality of: 141. And God: 141. On earth: 143. Ignorance of: 143. Conflict of good with: 143. Universality of: 143. Power of: 50. Not pure: 125. And compulsiveness: 125*. And "spiritual death": 125. And imagination: 125. Office of: 125. Limits of: 125. Dalila's: 125. Problem of: 52. Company: 51. See also: Demonic; Sin

Evolution, theory of, as affecting modern views of Genesis: 118

Evremond, St.: 70

Ewald, Johannes: 65

Ewbank, W. F.: 93

Ewelme (Yewelme): 44

Ewelme, co. Oxon.: 44, 45

Ewen, C. L'Estrange: 142. <u>Withcraft and Demonianism</u>: 142

Ewens: Mr.: 45. Alexander: 44*, 45*. Ancreta (Dyer): 45. Andrew: 45. Anne: 45. Barbara: 44, 45. Katherine (Catherine): 44, 45. Elizabeth (Keymer): 45. Elizabeth (Keynes): 45. Frances (Rogers): 45. Gertrude: 45. Gertrude (Stocker): 45. Hastings: 45. Jane: see Freake, Jane. John: 45. Katherine: see Ewens, Catherine; Freake, Katherine. Katherine (Hales): 45. (Evans), Matthew (the Elder): 44*, 45*. Matthew, Jr.: 44. Thomas: 45

Ewer (Ewre): Edward: 44, 45. Francis: 45

Ewert, Alfred: 100

Ewing, D.: 135

Ewre. See Ewer

<u>Ex opere operato</u>: 93

<u>Exact Accompt of the Receipts</u>: 44

<u>Exact Collection</u>: 144

<u>Exact Narrative Of the Tryal and Condemnation Of John Twyn</u>: 116

Exaggeration: 124. In the Richardsons' manner: 88

Exaltation: 34. In Messianic exemplar: 122. Christ's: 123

<u>Examiner, Leigh Hunt's Literary</u>: 146

<u>Examiner, The</u>: 87, 115

Example, rhetorical: 51*. Poetic and rhetorical function: 123*. Examples and precepts, study of: 20, 31

Excellence source of perfection: 83*

Excess: heroic: 122. Of virtue-heroic: 123. Of vice-brutishness: 123. M and theme of: 65*

Exchange (Bourse): 44

Exchequer, Court of: 45

Excise: bond, M's: 44. Commissioners of: 44. Office: 44

Exclusion of bishops: 51

Exclusive Salvation, doctrine of: 71

Excommunication: 45, 51

Excursion, The (Wordsworth): 70

Exe (river): 49

Exegesis: 107. M's: 107. Origen's: 107

Exemplum: 40

Exercise (physical): 40, 44, 51. M's: 137. M on: 51

Exercises (in schools): 20*

Exeter, co. Devon: 44*, 45, 49. Cathedral: 44. College, Oxford: 44, 45

Exhalations: from the celestial bodies, ancient theory of: 89, 128. Causes and kinds: 128

Exhibition to a univ., prize of: 20

Exhibitions from St. Paul's Schools: 40

Existence: 46, 96*. Levels of: 46. Orders of: 46

Existential reality and dialectics: 96*

"Exit Tyrannus" (sign, attr. to M): 44

Exodos: 92*. Exodus: 44, 72, 146; see also: Bible

Exodus (13th c. French verse paraphrase): 74

Exorcism: 51

Exordium: 40, 51*, 123*

Expansum, stretching out of Heavens: 128

Expediency, in deliberate rhetoric: 123*

Expenses, student: 40

Experience: 51*, 96*. As testimony: 123. Of Adam and Eve: 50

Experimental tendency in Peck's notes: 88

Explanatory Notes and Remarks on M's PL (J. Richardson, Father and Son). See Richardson

Explicator, The: 131

Exploration and discovery ca. 1600: 40

Exposition...upon the Book of Job, An (Caryl): 135

Exposition touching All the Bokes of Holie Scripture, and Their Excellence: 74

Exposition, rhetorical: 51

"Expostulation with Inigo Jones" (Jonson): 29

Expulsion: 96. The, as illustrated by artists: 97*. See also: Adam and Eve

Extasie, The (John Donne): 131

"Extempore upon a Faggot" (attr. to M): 44

External, problems of the: 96

Exton, co. Hants.: 44

Exton: John: 44. Sir Thomas: 44

Extract from M's PL, An: 88

Extracts from classical writers, collections of: 40

Extracts from other critics in Todd's edition: 88

Exuberance: the Richardsons' ideal of, quaint: 88. Of imagination, M's youthful, met with reserve by Newton: 88

Eye of God: 93

Eyes: exemptile: 128. Eye Salve: 116, 91. Eye-Salve for the Army: 44. Eye-Salve for the Eng. Army: 44, 103. Eye-Salve For the City of London (a royalist appeal): 147. Eyesight: 128; M's: 44. Eye strain, possible cause of M's blindness: 16. Equated with understanding: 8

Eyewitness: 50

Eyford, co. Gloucester: 44

Eyre-Todd, G.: 133

Eyre: C.: 105. George E. B.: 44; see also: <u>Stationers' Registers</u>

Eysteinn, Ásgrimsson: 65

Eyton: Elizabeth (Guise): 45. Theophilus: 45

<u>Ezekiel</u>: 2, 4, 34, 73, 132, 141, 3, 90, 126, 139, 64, 25. Book of: 95, 118, 144. See also: Bible

Ezra: 68, 73. Book of: 3

Ezzo von Bamberg: 65

-F-

F., D.: 91

F., M. See Flesher, Miles

F., R.: 44

F., S. See Fox, Stephen

F., T. See Forde, T.

Faber: Jacobus: 16; see also: Fabry, Jacobus. Otto: 142. Stapulensis: see Lefèvre d'Etaples. Tanaquil: 44

Fabius: 44, 3, 88. Maximus: 73. See also: Quintillian

Fables: 8, 144. In theme writing: 20. <u>Fable of the Head and the Wen</u> (M's?): 44. <u>Fable of the Bees</u> (Mandeville): 136

Fabre, John. See Fabry

Fabricius: 70, 73, 89, 123, 64. Andreas: 68. Georgius: 40, 74; see also: <u>Opera Christiana</u>. Germanus: 44, 91. Johann Seobald: 10, 40

Fabroni, Angelo: 44

Fabry, Jacobus: 16, 40

Fabyan, Robert: 93

Facsimile Text Society: 44

<u>Facsimiles of...Autographs in the ...British Museum</u>: 44

Facsimiles of National Manuscripts: 44

Fact: poetry not bound to give accurate accounts of historical, according to Pearce: 88. Poetic inaccuracy in handling facts excused by Paterson: 88. By Newton preferred to fiction: 88. Callander on poetry and: 88. Warton on hints in M referring simultaneously to fiction and: 88. Future, rhetoric: 51. Past, rhetoric: 51

Factionalism: 51, 144. M and faction: 144

Faculae: 89

Faculties (rational, irascible, concupiscible): 122. See also: Thymos

Faculty Office of the Abp. of Canterbury (for marriage licenses): 44

<u>Faerie Queene</u> (Spenser): 8, 12, 20, 29, 31, 50, 51, 52*, 70*, 83, 112, 113, 111, 118, 134*, 136, 139, 3, 71, 130, 88, 131, 26, 46*. The, analogies with: 72. See also: Spenser

Faesule: 44, 3. See also: Fiesole

Fagan, Louis: 44

Fage: 128

Fagg, Robert: 44

Fagius: 54, 3. Paulus (Bücher, Paul): 30, 40, 41, 42, 44, 73, 22, 38

Faguet Auguste Emile: 100

Fair Infant, A (M): 112

<u>Fair Mirror of Foul Times</u> (attr. to M): 44

Fair Orian (music): 40

<u>Fair Oriana in the Morn</u>: 121

Fairbairn, Patrick: 93

Fairclough, H. Rushton: 118

Fairebrother, William: 44

Fairfax: Edward: 44, 65, 122, 123, 88, 117. Baron Ferdinando: 103. <u>Tasso</u>: 88, 94; see also Tasso. Mary: 44. Sir Thomas, 3rd Baron: 28, 30, 40, 51, 44*, 59, 60, 87, 114, 120, 145, 38, 62, 26, 82, 132, 94; see also: M's Sonnet XV

Fairies: 15, 144. Fairyland, M's allusions to: 89

Fairmands, Ezra (Esdras): 44

Faith: 7, 9*, 31, 47*, 51*, 122*,

143*, 96, 93. Derived from Bible: 107. Justification by: 93, 143. Saving: 63. Hero of: 123*. Object of: 123. In court masque: 143. As reality for M and others: 143. In Lycidas: 143. Defined by Perkins: 143. In the ladder: 143. And works: 143, 123, 93. Orthodox: 143. Samson's: 143*. See also: Regeneration; Trust

Faithful yet Imperfect Character of ...Charles I: 44

Faithful Portraiture of a Loyal Subject: 44

Faithful Scout: 59

Faithful Shepherdess, The (Fletcher): 29, 134, 26, 83

Faithorne, William (artist, M portrait, frontispiece): 44*, 94, 55

Falconbridge: Thomas Bellassis, Viscount, son-in-law of Oliver Cromwell: 44. See also: Fauconberg

Falcone, Matteo: 64

Falconer: C.: 105. John: 114. J. P. E.: 44, 58. Thomas: 44. Thomas (another): 44. William: 44, 58

Falconry: 40

Falcourt, Andre: 44

Falerne: 49, 73

Falkland: Lord: 51, 94; see also: Cary, Lucius. Sir Henry Cary, 1st Viscount: 44. Henry Cary, 3rd Viscount: 44. Lucius Cary, Viscount: 145, 38

Fall: 9*, 31*, 41, 42, 44, 47*, 50*, 52*, 54*, 57, 83*, 89, 107, 113*, 128*, 132*, 139, 144, 143*, 32*, 36*, 46*, 71, 72*, 93*, 96, 109, 48*, 25, 107. Of Adam: 141; myth of: 141. Of Angels: 17, 41, 103, 46; cause: 93; God's attitude toward: 93; how repaired: 93. The: according to legend preceded by a perpetual spring: 89; problem of in PL: 137; physical change supervenes after: 89; M's conception of: 113*; as the triumph of passion over reason: 113; as sensuality: 113; in SA: 113; of Satan: 113; in Hebrew speculation: 113; in Paul: 113; in the writings of the Fathers: 113*; of man: 47, 128*; cosmic effects of: 128; felix culpa: 128, 143, 93; sexual component of: 128; doctrine of: 132*; from grace: 139; in Conus: 143; man's nature before and after: 47, 143; man doomed to: 143; by his own choice: 143; obsolete doctrine of: 143; man alienated from God by: 143; of nature: 46; cause(s) of: 123, 93, 48; foreknown: 93; God's attitude toward Eve's: 93, 48; the postlapsarian state: 93; the crisis of: 48; the 1st step of: 48; M's treatment of the theme of: 48; moral of: 48; as Original Sin: 48; "The Paradox of the Fortunate Fall": 48; 61; the paradox of Fall and freedom: 48; the psychological treatment: 48; the psychology of man and his Fall: 48; as a qualitative leap: 48; story: 48; the technique of the treatment of: 48; the separate acts of transgression by Adam and Even in the Fall episode: 48; theories of: 48*, the theme of: 48; renewal: in PL: 72*; in SA: 72; fallen condition of man: 25; according to Clarence Green, C. S. Lewis, M, Denis Saurat, Shelley, E. M. W. Tillyard, Charles Williams: 107; in world mythology: 118; among the Andaman Islanders: 118. See also: War in Heaven; Atonement; Sin, Adam; Eve; Lucifer; Satan

Fall and Passion, The: 65, 36

Fall of Man, or the Corruption of Nature, The: 26

Fall of Man, The (Christopher Goodman): 131

"Fall of Richmond, The": 98

Fallacies: rhetoric: 51. Of ignoratio elenchi: 123. Of secundum quid: 123

Fallen angels: 89. Number: 93. Hierarchy: 93. Excluded from Scale of Nature: 93. Chained: 93. Beyond redemption: 93. Respond to music: 93. See also: Angels

Falling: bodies, law of: 139. Motion: as uncreative symbol: 75*. Stars: 89. See also: Rising motion

Falls, multiple: 107

False: generalization, rhetoric: 51. Evils, goods: 123

Falsehood, M's answer to charges of: 30

Falstaff: 87, 72

Fama Fraternitatis: 7

Fama: 90. See also: Rumor

Fame: 70*, 136, 72. Distinguished from reputations: 119. Biblical giants' lust for: 123*. Personification in PL: 2. M's pursuit and achievement of: 30*, 51. M and: 137

Familiae Minorum Gentium: 45

Familiar Epistles: 103

Familiar Explanation of the Poetrical Works of M: 88

Familiar Letters: 129

Familists: 7, 9, 142. Familism: 73, 114*

Family: concept of: 31. Interest in: 51. Life, in 17th c.: 8

Famous: serpents: 77. Pareus: 77. Pererius: 77

Fanatics: 44. Fanaticism: 47

Fanchurche Street. See Fenchurch

Fancy(ies): 70, 128, 121. See also: Imagination

Fane: family: 45. Charles, 3rd Earl of Westmoreland: 45. Lady Elizabeth: see Cope, Lady Eliz. Sir Francis: 44, 45. Francis, 1st Earl of Westmoreland: 45. J. ("Monody"): 58. Mary: see Gerard, Lady Mary. Mary (Mildmay): 45*; see also: Westmoreland, Countess of. Mildmay, 2nd Earl of Westmoreland: 45. Rachel: see Cranfield, Rachel, Countess of Bath and Middlesex. Sir Thomas: 45. Vere, 4th Earl of Westmoreland: 45

Fanfani, G.: 6

Fano, F.: 6

Fanshaw, J.: 58

Fanshawe: C. M.: 58. J. G.: 44. Margaret: see Aylofte, Margaret. Sir Richard: 55, 122, 39. Thomas: 45. Sir Thomas: 45

Fantastic manner of Italian poetry condemned by Newton: 88

Fantasy: 121

Fantom, Capt. Carlo: 45

Faraday: 35

Faraji collection: 22

Farendon: 49, 3

Farewell: Mr.: 45. James: 45. Thomas: 44, 45

Farges, Jacques: 148

Farinata: 111

Farinelli, Arturo: 5

Farley: F. E.: 58. Francis: 44. John: 44; his son, John: 44. Robert: 40

Farmer, R.: 58

Farmer's Almanack, For the Year of Our Lord 1798: 115

Farmingham (Farningham), co. Kent: 44

Farnaby, Thomas: 20*, 40, 44, 82, 88. Works: _Index Rhetoricus_: 82; _Systema Grammaticum_: 82; _Tropes and Figures_: 82

Farnborough: 45

Farnell, Lewis R.: 143. Day of judgement: 143

Farnese, Ottavio, Duke of Parma: 120, 64

Farnesi family: 6, 44. Farnesios: 73

Farnham: Edward: 44, W.: 68. Willard E.: 93

Farnham: 49. Castle, co. Surrey: 44

Farnsworth, R.: 142

Farquhar, George: 35, 71

Farr: D.: 97. Edward: 79

Farrar: Dean: 102. Frederic William: 79, 110, 22, 93. Geraldine: 137. Mildred: 97. Thomas: 44

Farre, Laurence (Lawrence): 44, 45

Farrell: James T.: 142. S.: 58

Farren, Miss: 58

Farrer: Austin: 57, 143, 93, 25. Lucy: 40

Farrerus: 44, 73

Farringdon-Magna, co. Berks.: 44, 45

Farrington, J.: 97

Fasciculus Temporum: 143

Fashionability of M: 58

Fasti Ecclesiae Anglicanae: 45

Fasti Oxoniensis, supplement to _Athenae Oxonienis_: 28*, 45, 63

Fastiogiositate: 5

Fate(s): 17*, 34, 63, 89, 123, 90,

93, 144, 92*. In SA: 143. M on: 80

Father Abraham's Almanack: 115. Father Abraham's Almanack, for The Year of Our Lord, 1770: 115

"Father Hubburd's Tales": 45

Father: the: 71*. In PL: theme of wrath: 104; tonal and tempo patterns of: 104; the deity, praised by angels: 119; and Son not of same essence: 107. See also: God

Fathers: 9, 3, 71, 78, 113*. Values of: 107. Church: 51, 114*, 93. Early, conception of Hell in the: 89. M's contempt for: 107; evaluation of: 107; readings in: 107; use for: 107. Hume on: 88. Peck on, and M: 88

Fatio, Guillaume: 44

Fauconberg: Henry: 44. (Falconbridge), Thomas Belasyse (Bellasis), Viscount: 44

Faukeland. See Falkland

Faulkner: Thomas: 40. William: 124, 127, 32

Faunus, Fauns: 90, 73

Faust: 52, 114, 142, 72

Faust (Goethe): 87, 141, 94, 130, 48. See also: Goethe

Faust-book: 15, 32

Fausta: 73

Faustus (Marlowe): 141, 34, 52, 60. See also: Marlowe

Faustus of Riez: 36

Favaro, A.: 6

Favola di Cefolo (Correggio): 29

Favonius: 73, 90, 3

Favorinus: 60

Fawcett: John: 58. Joseph: 58

Fawkes (Fauxe): F., Parody on PL: 58. Francis: 117. Guy: 73, 116, 62, 72. Guy Fawkes Day: 40, 103

Fawley: 45

Fawnt, George: 44

Fawsley: 45

Fay, Amy: 39

Fazio degli Uberti: 120

Feake, Christopher: 9

Fealty: 123

Fear of God And the King (sermon, Matthew Griffith): 103, 147

Fear: 2, 31, 47*, 51*, 123. Types of: 47. Sinful: 47

"Fearful symmetry": 11

Fearing, Kenneth: 108

Feasts, origin of: 41

Feathers Tavern Petition: 78

Featley, Dr. Daniel (1582-1645): 9, 40, 44, 59, 114, 93, 101, 55. The Dippers Dipt or the Anabaptists Duck'd and Plung'd Over Head and Eares: 147, 91

Fechner, Gustave: 142

Federalist, The: 51

Fee(s): 45. Simple: 45. Tail: 45

Feeling and Form: 12

Feeling: 51*. Large scale movements of in PL: 118. Of God's presence: 47. Quality in Adam's perceptions: 48. See also: Human feeling; Self

Fehr: 141. B.: 113

Feibleman, James K.: 93

Feidelson, C.: 23

Feigin, S. I.: 142

Feigning, poetic, contrasted with method of history: 123

Feil, John Philip: 44

Feilding, B.: 6

Feiling, Keith: 116

Felgenhauer, Paul: 7, 65

Felicianus, Joannes Bernardus: 123

Felicity: 123*. As topic in deliberative rhetoric: 123. As final cause of ehtics, politics, theology and poetry: 123*. Constituents of: 123. See also: Good, highest

Felix culpa, the: 15, 102, 36, 140. See also: Fortunate Fall; Fall

Felix II: 73

Felixstowe, co. Suffolk: 44

Fell: Dr. John: 40, 44, 91; urges restoration of Charles in Interest of England Stated: 147. Kenneth: 143. Samuel: 64

Fellow: commoner: 40. Students: 30*

Fellowes: 70. Sir Charles: 44. Robert: 44

Fellows of the college (Christ's): 40, 44

Fellows: Alfred: 44. J.: 58

Fellowship, M's: 44. M and question of: 94. M's ineligibility for: 40

Fellowship, Southern: 40

Felpham: 97

Feltham, Owen: 114, 128, 145, 93

Feltmakers' Company: 44

Felton: Sir Adam: 44. Sir Compton: 44. Sir Henry: 44, 145. H.: 58. John: 20, 103. Nicholas (Bp. of Ely): 40, 44

Feltre, Vittorino de: 13, 40

Female will: 25*

Femarn: 49

Feminine Monarchie, The (Charles Butler): 88

Feminism: 25

Fen Drayton: 40

Fenchurch (Fanchurche) Street, London: 44

Fencing: M's: 40, 44, 51. Masters: 40

Fénelon, Francesco de Salignac ("Télémaque," translations of): 58, 123

Fennell, James: 115. An Apology for the Life of: 115

Fenner: Dudley: 20, 37, 40, 51, 60, 73, 79. William: 93

Fenns: 49

Fenton: 88. Edward: 128. Elijah: 40, 44, 58*, 115, 146, 150, 117*, 55. E., influenced by PL, on M's minor poems: 58. E.: Life of M: 28. R.: 58

Fenwick: John: 40, 44. Sir William: 45

Ferdinand: Emperor: 103. King of Aragon and Castile: 123. II, Grand Duke of Tuscany: 6, 44*. III, Emperor of Germany: 44. III, King of Romans: 6

Ferguson: John: 36, 93. R.: 23. Wallace K.: 69, 39, 93

Fergusson: Francis: 23, 76, 101. R., influenced by M: 58

Fermor: Amphyllis: 45. Anne: see Cope, Anne

Fermoy, Ireland: 44

Fern, S. Mary: 4

Ferne, Bp. Henry: 9, 93

Fernel, Jean: 93

Ferneley, William: 44

Ferneyhough, W.: 58

Ferrabosco, Alfonso (composer): 44, 39

Ferrar: John: 81. Nicholas: 7, 81, 114, 101

Ferrar: 120. See also: Ferrara

Ferrara, Italy: 29, 44, 49, 103, 120, 3, 94. Univ. of: 40

Ferrari: Benedetto: 6. Portus: 49

Ferrarius: 44

Ferrell, C. C.: 36

Ferrero, G. G.: 5

Ferry, Anne Davidson: 17, 37, 60, 75, 79, 86, 100, 110, 111, 32, 53, 106. Control of mood in PL: 61. M's Epic Voice: 74. Differences between the fallen and unfallen worlds: 61

Fesole (Faesulani Colles): 49, 73. See also: Florence, Valdarno

Fessenden, Thomas G.: 115. Pills, Poetical, Political, and Philosophical: 115

Festing, Michael Christian: 117

Festus, Pompeius: 128

Fethanleage: 49

Fetherstone: Cuthbert: 120. Henry: 59, 120. Mary: 120. Ralph: 120

Fetter Lane, London: 44

Fettiplace: Anne: see Jones, Anne. Edmund: 45. Thomas: 45

Feudalism, dangers of: 33

Fevardentius: 44, 91

Fever: 2

Feversham: 45

Feyerabend, Sigmund: 93

Fez: 49, 19, 73. See also: Almansor

Fichte, J. G.: 113

Ficino, Marsilio: 4, 5, 6, 7, 23, 27, 29, 40, 42, 60, 68, 18, 64, 69, 74, 76, 79, 100, 112, 114, 118, 121, 122, 123, 142*, 39, 72, 93, 101, 21. Works: Ex Michael Psello De Daemonibus: 142; Ex Secundo Libro Porphyrii: 142; "Commentary on Plato's Symposium": 60; <u>De Religione Christiana</u>: 60; <u>Liber de Sole</u>: 60

Fiction: 53. In <u>Prolusions</u>: 53. As criterion in poetry: 53. In <u>Lycidas</u>: 53. In similitude: 53. And doctrine: 53. Everything except Biblical matter regarded by Hume as: 88. Addison on: 33. Hume's theoretical condemnation of romance as: 88. Newton prefers fact to: 88. Regarded by Newton as not justified in itself: 88. Massey on: 88. Warton on allusions in M referring simultaneously to fact and: 88. Fictional world: 69

Fidao-Justiniani, J. E.: 60

Fiddle: 121. Fiddler: 121

Fidelis, Ludovicus: 32

Fides Publica (Morus): 94. See also: Public Faith

<u>Fides Publica contra calumnias</u>: 103

Fiducia (trust in God), opposites to: 123

Field: B. (parodies <u>L'Allegro</u>): 58. John (pr.): 44, 114. Nicholas: 45. Richard: 93

Fielde, Rev. I.: 44

Fielding, Henry: 35, 34, 44, 58, 60, 136, 97, 146, 117. <u>Tom Jones</u>: 82. Jonathan Wild: 35

Fiennes: Mr.: 45. Lady Elizabeth (Temple), Viscountess Saye and Sele: 45. James: 44. James, 2nd Viscount Saye and Sele: 45. Nathaniel: 9, 44, 45, 38. Richard: 44, 45. See also: Saye and Sele

Fierville, Charles: 40

Fiesole: 19, 44

Fifa (Fife): 49, 73

Fifield: 45

Fifth (interval): 121

Fifth Age: 143

Fifth Monarchy: 9, 52, 113, 114, 3, 73. Men: 1, 9*, 51, 71, 94. Fifth Monarchists: 60. Fifth Monarchism: 38*. See also: Kingdom of Christ; Millenarians

Figgis, John Neville: 60, 83, 116, 144, 39

Figino, Ambrogio: 123

Figtree: 19, 144, 36. Indian: 144

Figurative, the: 47. See also: Accommodation

Figures: of style, Peck's observations on, borrowed from Blackwell: 88. Of speech: 20, 70; see also: Schemes; Tropes. Figuralism: 69*

Filelfo, Francisco: 74. <u>De Morali Disciplina</u>: 74

Filippis, M. de: 44

<u>Fille de Caïn, La</u>: 65

Fillon, Benjamin: 44

Filmer: Edward: 91. Sir Edward: 91. John: 91. Reginald: 91. Sir Robert: 9, 44, 60, 103, 116*, 142, 32, 71, 117, 91; works: Anarchy of Limited Monarchy: 91, 147; Freeholders Grand Inquest: 91; Necessity of Absolute Power: 91; Observations: 91; Reflections: 91; in <u>Observations Concerning the Originall of Government</u>: 147, 91; in <u>Anarchy of a Limited Monarcy</u>: 147

<u>Fin de Satan, La</u>: 65

Final cause(s): 114*. Of heroic poem: 122

Final Perseverance of the Saints, doctrine of: 71

Financial dealings, M's: 44*. See also: Cope; Foxcroft; Skinner; Hamey; Hartop; Kensington; Maundy; Powell; Robinson; Warcupp; Wheatley

Finch: Mr.: 44. A.: 58. Mrs. B.:

58. Sir Heneage: 44. Sir Henry: 93. Sir John S.: 44. Richard: 19. S. W.: 58

Fine arts: 70*. And the State: 70

Fines: 44. Land: 45. Penal: 45. With Rudds, M's: 44*

Finitude: 47. See also: Death

Fink, Zera S.: 60, 102, 116. Works: The Classical Republicans: 82; "The Theory of the Mixed State and the Development of M's Political Thought": 82

Finland. See Charles X

Finley: John H.: 56, 59, 14. M. I.: 64

Finmark: 49

Finmore. See Frinnor

Finn: 36

Finnegans Wake (Joyce): 139, 130

Finney, G. L.: 6, 29, 44, 63. Gretchen L.: 100, 125, 14, 39, 93, 101, 137, 148

Finnor. See Frinnor

Fino, Bartolommeo: 64

Fiore, Amadeus P.: 93

Fiorentino, Rosso: 27

Fiorino, Jacopo: 64

Fippes, John (poet's father's servant): 44

Fire of 1561: 20. Great fire of 1666: 20, 40, 44, 94, 93

Fire: of Hell: 93. Of Last Judgement: 93. Balls: 89. Element or sphere of: 114, 128*; mixed with hail: 128; wandering: 128; without light: 128; see also: Ignis fatuus. Firemaking: 123. Symbol: 141

Firmament: 41, 89, 128*, 144, 143. Various meanings: 128. Waters above: 128

Firmin, Thomas: 114

First gospel: 93

First Age: 143

First Bishops' War: 51, 103

First Cause: 72

First Defence. See Milton, John

First Folio, 1623 (Shakespeare): 135*

Firth: 3. Sir Charles Harding: 9, 44, 60, 113, 128, 3, 144, 93, 137; calls the Puritan Rev. the "evolution of democracy": 147

Fisburg: 49

Fisch, Harold: 79, 14, 25

Fischer: Peter F.: 110. W.: 44, 113

Fish, Stanley E.: 110, 123, 11, 14, 53, 101, 106*. Limitations of his views on M: 61. On reader's sympathy to sinful actions: 61. On suffering: 61. "The Harassed Reader in PL" and Further Thoughts on M's Christian Reader": 109

Fish: 128*. Bishopfish: 128. Dolphin, sociability, foreknowledge of: 128. Eels: 128. Remora: 128. Whale: 128*; as Satan: 128; Whale-pilot: 128. Fishing: 40

Fisher: Cardinal: 52. Edmund: 45. Edward: 45. Elizabeth (M's servant): 44*, 55. Henry: 44, 45. J.: 58. James (M's father's servant): 44, 45. John: 40, 44, 45, 68. St. John Cardinal: 93. Mary (M's servant): 44, 94. Dr. Otto O.: 44. Payne: 44. P. F.: 23, 60. Peter F.: 128. "The Jesuit": 57

Fisherton: 45

Fishtoske, co. Lincoln: 44

Fiske: Mrs. as Becky Sharp: 149. Dr.: 45. Horace: 16. John: 16, 142, 137; Outline of Cosmic Philosophy Based on the Doctrine of Evolution: 142

Fison, Bp. Joseph E.: 93

Fitch: Elijah: 115; The Beauties of Religion: 115. Ralph: 150

Fitchett, J.: 58

Fithy, David: 44

Fitness and unfitness: 54*. In courtesy books, preachers, and M: 54*

Fitzgeoffrey, Charles: 64

Fitzgerald: Edward: 60, 136. William: 79

Fitzherbert, Sir Anthony: 44, 45

Fitzmoore family: 44

Fitzpatrick, R.: 58

Five Mile Act: 116, 94

Five Senses, The (Gill the Younger): 20

Fixler, Michael: 17, 37, 79, 110, 39, 53, 85, 93, 101. Works: Banquet scene in PR; 74; M and the Kingdoms of God: 74

Flaccus: 73. Lucius: 73. Valerius: 44, 64. Verrius: 128

Flaminius Nobilius: 123

Flamsteed, 1st Astronomer-Royal: 89

Flanchford in Reigate, co. Surrey: 44

Flanders (Flandria): 49, 103, 3

Flannagan, Roy: 32

Flatman, Thomas (painter, M portrait): 44, 116

Flatter, Richard: 60

Flattery: 51

Flaubert, Gustave: 46, 1

Flaucius Illyricus (Matthias): 79, 93

Flaxman: Anna (Nancy): 25. John: 39, 97*, 146, 117, 25

Flecknoe, Richard: 145

Fleet: family: 45. Edward: 45. Mary (Blagrave): 45

Fleet: Bridge: 40. A stream: 40. Prison, London: 44, 45. Street, London: 44*, 45

Fleetwood: 51, 120. Family: 44. Mr.: 45. Anne: 44. (Fletuode), Gen. Charles: 44, 73, 38, 94. Elizabeth Archdale: 44. George: 44. Sir Gerard: 45. John: 44. Martha: 44. Lady Mary (Dutton): 45. Miles: 44. Sir Richard: 45. Sir Thomas: 44. Sir William: 44. Sir William, of Aldwinkle: 44; his son, William: 44. Sir William, of Great Missenden: 44

Fleming: Abraham: 40, 93. Sir Oliver: 10, 44*

Flemish: music: 121. Book illustration: 97

Flemming (schoolmaster); 20

Flesher: James (pr., 1652-70): 91. Miles (pr., 1619-64): 44, 91

Fleta: 45, 73

Fletcher: Angus: 25. Antony: 128, 93. G.: 129, 99*. G. B. A.: 21. Giles: see separate entry. H. E., on M: 80. Harris: see separate entry. Ian: 39. J.: 129. Jefferson B.: 60, 83. John: see separate entry. Phineas: see separate entry. Robert: 87; on M's biography: 87; defense of M's prose: 87. R. J.: 45. T.: 58

Fletcher, Giles (Elder and Younger): 1, 4, 6, 8, 15*, 19*, 27, 33, 40, 42, 65, 73, 74, 76, 84, 100, 102, 104, 108, 122, 123, 132, 64, 133, 26, 36, 91, 93, 101, 109, 130, 148, 117, 21. Works: Christs Victorie and Triumph: 74*, 60, 126, 36, 46, 94, 149, 55; Sabrina's story: 104

Fletcher, Harris Francis: 1*, 5, 9, 16, 17, 23, 24, 41, 44*, 51, 57, 73, 68, 77, 59, 63*, 100, 102, 60, 75, 81, 86, 107, 111, 123, 128, 132, 135*, 139, 142, 144, 22*, 32, 80, 36, 43, 93, 101, 106, 137, 148, 21. Identifies M's Muse as the spirit who led the Israelites into Canaan: 107. M's indebtedness to Hebrew writers: 107. M's religious background: 104. Works: facsimile ed. of Complete Works: 44*; M's Semitic Studies: 57; M's Rabbinical Readings: 142; Intellectual Development of John M: 74. See also Milton, John, individual titles of MSS. and poems

Fletcher, John: 1, 15, 27, 29, 84, 90, 95, 103, 108, 64, 128, 132, 133, 134, 39, 72, 82, 88, 109*, 146, 117. Works: The Nice Valour: 55; The Faithful Shepherdess: 126, 55. See also: Comus; L'Allegro

Fletcher, Joseph: 65, 77, 36, 93, 64. Works: Christes Bloodie Sweat: 74; Perfect-Cursed-Blessed Man: 74, 36

Fletcher, Phineas: 1, 6, 15, 19, 40, 56, 59, 60, 65*, 68, 73, 77*, 84, 102, 104, 108, 128, 132, 133, 134, 26, 64, 88, 91, 109, 130, 148, 21. Influence: 55. And Giles: 77. Ps.: 77. Pisc. Eclog: 77. T. O. D.: 77 Works: The Purple Island: 46, 77; Apollyonists: 149, 77; Satan, Locustae: 149, 77

Flew, R. Newton, The Idea of Perfection in Christian Theology: 83*

Flight: 2, 17. And the poet: 106

Flint, co.: 44, 45. Flintshire: 49

Flissinga: 49

Flock, Howard: 39

Flood, John: 44

Flood: 17, 50, 144, 143, 32*, 36, 72*. End of 1st age: 143. A parallel among the Andaman Islanders: 118. Events before: 143. Punishment of immortality: 143.

Flora: 73, 90. Joachim of: 18

Florence (Florentia, Thusca Urbs), Italy: 6*, 19, 29, 40, 44*, 49, 51, 103, 112, 111, 121, 3, 94. M's visit to: 6*, 30. Florentine: 3; Academy: 44, 112; Platonism: see Platonism, Florentine. See also: Arno; Fesole; Tuscan; Valdarno; Vallombrosa

Florence: Duke of: 97. Of Worcester: 3, 93

Florentinus, Antonius: 54

Flores Poetarum: 20, 40

Flores Regii: 40

Flores, et Sententiae Scribendique: 20

Flores, Juan de: 40

Florid music: 121

Florida: 49, 144

Florio: 120. John: 40*, 82; see also: Montaigne. Michelangelo: 40

Florus: L. Annaeus: 40. Of Lyons, In Natale Sanctorum Joannis et Pauli: 74, 64

Flower de Luce (sign): 44

Flower, C. T.: 44

Flowerdew, A.: 58

Flowers, naming of: 50. Images derived from: 8

Floyd, Dr.: 44

Fludd, Robert: 1, 7, 10, 15, 23, 60, 63, 100, 113*, 114, 121, 128, 142*, 22, 71, 72, 148*. Influence on M: 113. On the Mortalists: 113. Works: De Macrocosmi Historia: 60; Mosaical Philosophy: 60, 142; Philosophia Sacra: 60, 142; Utriusque Cosmi Historia: 60, 142; Anatomiae Amphitheatrum: 142; Doctor Fludd's Answer unto M. Foster: 142; Integrum Morborum Mysterium: 142; Medicina Catholica: 142; Responsum ad Hoplocrisma-Spongum: 142

Flugel, J. C.: 15

Flushing, Holland: 44

Flute: 40, 121

Flying Post, The: 35

Focillon, Henri: 18

Fock, Otto: 22

Focus, close and diffused, examples of: 118

Foerster: Donald M.: 115. Norman: 115

Fogel, Ephim: 39

Fogg Art Museum, Harvard Univ.: 44

Fogle: F. R.: 68. French: 44, 68, 116, 146

Fokker, T. H.: 27

Folco: 111

Folengo, Teofilo: 65, 74, 64. Works: Agiomachià: 74; Humanita del Figliuolo: 74

Foley, Henry: 40, 44

Folger Library: 40, 44

Foliot, Gilbert: 40

Folklore: 8, 149. The Richardsons' appreciation of: 88. Peck's interest in: 88. Peck on elements and atmosphere of, in Shakespeare: 88. In M: 137. Folklore Society, Publications of: 44, 45. Folk-song: 121

Folly: 90, 144. Parentage: 144. Prime factor in life: 144. And sobriety: 144. See also: Ridicule

Fonesca: Pierre da: 40. Cristobel de: 93

Fonsbury, co. Salop: 44

Fontainebleau: 3

Fontana, Lucio: 27. Marco Publio: 64

Fontani, F.: 6

Fontanus, Robert: 40

Fontarabbia: 19, 49, 73

Fontenelle, Bernard de Bovier de: 1, 4, 93

Food: 17, 51

Foot of fine: 45

Foot, J.: 58

Football: 40

For the Honour of Wales (Jonson): 29

For the Sexes: 25

For God and King (Dr. Henry Burton): 147

Forbes: Elizabeth L.: 69, 79, 81. John: 114. Patrick: 143. William: 114

Forbidden: fruit: 50, 36*, 93; effect of: 36*; see also: Figtree; Tree of Knowledge. Tree: see Tree of Knowledge

Force: 1, 51, 123*. Subject for deliberate epic: 123

Forcellini: 120

Ford: 70. Mr. (auctioneer): 44. Boris: 86. Sir Henry (1619?-84): 91. Hugh: 44. Jeremiah, D. M.: 122. John: 108, 101. T.: 58

Forde: Thomas: 44; *Letters*: 91. W.: 105

Forebearance: 45

Foreign churches in London: 40

Foreign language: 51

Foreign Office, British: 103

Foreknowledge: 50, 143, 80. M on: 80. God: 50. And foreordination: 46. Of God: 93. See also: Free will

Forell, George W.: 93

Forensic: oratory: 31. Theory of the Atonement: 93

Forerunner of Milton, A: 112

Forese: 111

Forest Hill with Shotover: 44

Forest Hill Book: 45

Forest: Louise C. T.: 128. William, *History of Joseph*: 74, 54

Foresthill (Forsthill, Fosthill) (Forest Hill, co. Oxon.): 28*, 40, 44*, 45*, 103, 94, 150

Forgiveness: 47, 25. See also: Reconciliation

Foris domi et: 40

Form(s): 40, 51, 69, 70*, 96*, 146. M's philosophy of: 25. Poetical: 25. Transformation of: 25. Ideologies of: 25. As emblem of order: 25. Transcendental: 25. The elder Richardson's sense of: 88. As structural principle: 25. Discovery as: 67*. See also: Structure; Structural principles

Formal: discourse: 40. Music: 121. Formalism: 47, 51; Massey opposed to literary: 88

Forman, Simon: 114

Formica, Signor: 6

Formula of Concord: 71

Formulae Orationae: 40

Formularies, letter-writing: 20

Formulas, tedious: 51

Fornax noster: 40

Fornication: 54*. Definition of: 71

Forreigne Invasion: 51

Forrest, Thomas: 20

Fors Clavigera (Ruskin): 111

Forshall, J.: 23

Forster: E. M.: 15, 34, 86, 133; *A Passage to India* quoted: 95. John: 40, 44. N.: 58. Richard: 116

Forsthill. See Forest Hill

Forsyth: James: 93. Joseph: 98. P. T.: 71

Forsythe, Robert S.: 98

Fort St. George. See Madras

Fortescue: G. K.: 44, 120, 64; see also: Thomason, George. Sir John: 45, 58, 73, 102. Sir Nicholas the Younger: 44

Forth: 49

Fortherby, Martin: 114

Fortification: 40

Fortinbras: 92

Fortitude: 51, 122*, 123*, 125. And magnaminity: 125. See also: Virtues

Fortuna: 90. See also: Chance

Fortunate Fall: 17, 34, 47, 60, 72, 93, 96

Fortunate Islands: 19, 32. See also:

Blest, Islands of the

Fortunation, Atilius: 73

Fortunatus: 133. Venantius: 40, 74

Fortune: 123, 144, 72, 93. Goods of: 123. Lures of: 123. Inconstancy of: 123. Symbolized by tempest: 123

Fortunes of Nigel, The: 51

Fosbroke, John: 93

Foscarini, Paolo: 77. Trans. Salusbury: 77

Foscolo: 50, 120

Fosdick: Harry Emerson: 71. Thomas: 44

Foss: E.: 59. H. J.: 44. Martin: 83, 143. Martin, The Idea of Perfection in the Western World: 83

Fosse, Edward: 44

Foster: family: 44. Birket: 97. Elizabeth (M's grand-daughter): 16, 28, 44*, 117, 55. Frances E.: 64. Herbert D.: 93. J., praises M: 58. Rev. James: 44. Joseph: 40, 44, 45. Kenelm: 5. M.: 58. Margaret: see Ayloffe, Margaret. Sir Richard: 44. Samuel: 10. Sir Thomas (lawyer): 44. Thomas (husband of Elizabeth): 44*. Sir William: 19, 93, 150. William T.: 67, 142; A Sponge to Wipe Away the Weapon Salve: 142

Foster's Essay on Accent: 88

Fosthill (Forsthill, Forrest-Hall). See Foresthill

Fotherby, Bp. Martin: 40, 93

Fotheringay: 45

Foucault, Michel: 11

Fouqeron, J. (engraver, M portrait): 44

Foulis, Henry: 44, 116

Foulke, William Dudley, Some love songs of Petrarch: 83

Fountain and Bear (sign in Cheapside): 44

Fountain of Slaunder (William Walwyn): 147

Fountain Bleau (Fontainebleau, Fons Belaqueus): 49, 73

Fountain: (Fountayne), Mr.: 45. Mr. (lawyer): 44. Brigg: 45. Hugh: 45. John: 45. Robert: 40

Fountayne. See Fountain

Fouqué, Michel: 7, 64. Vie, Faictz ...de...Jesus-Christ: 74

Four Angels of the Presence: 41

Four Hymnes (Spenser): 112

Four Letters: Being an Interesting Correspondence between Those Eminently Distinguished Characters, John Adams ...And Samuel Adams: 115

Four Monarchies: 93

Four Questions Debated: 116

Four Zoas, The (Blake): 25*. As epic: 25. Structure of: 25. In relation to PL: 25. And Bible: 25. Subtitles for: 25. Garment imagery in: 25. Additions to: 25. Obscurities: 25. Depiction of the last judgement: 25. Perspectives in: 25. Individual nights, I, II, IV, V, VII (A and B), VIII, IX: 25

Fourfold method of Biblical interpretation: 79

Fourme of consecrating of an Archbishop, The: 104

Fournier, E.: 16

Fournival, Richard de: 100

Fourth interval: 121

Fourth Age: 143

Fourth Paper Presented by Maior Butler (Roger Williams): 147

Fowler: Alastair: 100*, 39, 106, 148, 21. B.: 58. Christopher: 142; Daemonium Meridianum: 142. Edward: 44, 142. Margery: see Coxeter, Margery

Fowlmere: 40

Fowns, Richard: 93

Fox-Marcillo, Sebastian: 32

Fox: 3. C. J.: 58. G.: 94. George: 7, 23, 27, 33, 114*, 115, 130, 137, 83*, 146; on tithes and the ministry: 147; Instructions for Right Spelling: 115; pleads for toleration in To All that Professe Christianity: 147. Ralph: 108. Robert C.: 93, 131. Sir Stephen (S. F.): 44. W., Jr., "La Bagatella": 58. William: 44

Foxcroft Bond: 44

Foxcroft: George: 44. H. C.: 116

Foxe, John: 10, 23, 27, 73, 38, 93

Foxes, in Eng.: 83

Foy: 49

Foythe, Abraham: 44

Fracastoro, Girolamo: 58, 74, 21, 64. Works: Joseph: 74. Syphilis: 74

Fradelle, H. J.: 97

Fraenkel, Peter: 93

Fragmenta ex Genesi: 65

"Fragments from a Writing-Desk": 98

Fragonard, J. H.: 97

Frain, Jacques le: 44

France (Celtica, Celtic Fields, Francia, Gallia, Gaul): 31, 44*, 103, 49, 3, 94, 150. M's visit to: 28

France, Anatole: 65, 136, 142

Francesca da Rimini: 111

Franchini, Francesco: 120

Franchise, M's conception of: 147

Francini, Antonio: 6, 28, 30, 40, 44*, 59, 73, 128, 26, 117, 94, 3

Francis(cus), St.: 7, 18, 27, 73, 141, 32. Franciscan order: 44, 73

Francis: Benjamin: 115; The Conflagration: A Poem on the Last Day: 115. J.: 97

Francius, Petrus: 64

Franck, Sebastian: 7, 79, 114, 128, 32, 93

Francklin: Richard: 40. T., Sophocles: 58

Franco, Pierre: 16

Francofurtum: 49

François de Sales, St.: 81, 94. Traité de l'Amour de Dieu: 109

Franekera: 49, 73

Frank: Grace: 93. J.: 23, 37, 58. Leonard, Carl and Anna: 35. Mark: 93

Frankenberg, Abraham von: 7

Frankfurt: 44

Franklin: 3. Benjamin: 115, 117; The Works of the Late Dr. Benjamin Franklin: 115. Edward: 40. James: 115

Franko, Ivan: 65

Franks, Augustus W. See Hawkins, Edward

Franks: 44, 3

Frantze, Wolfgang: 128

Franz, Marie-Louise: 141

Fraser: Dr.: 44. G. L.: 61; continuity of pagan and Christian mythologies in Lycidas: 61

Fraser's Magazine: 44

Fratres Poloni. See Socinians; Socinianism

Fraud: 47, 123*. Subject for deliberative epic: 123. Whether consistent with heroic virtue: 123. In warfare: 123. See also: Deception

Frauendienst: 122. See also: Courtly Love

Fraunce, Abraham: 15, 20, 23, 64. Countesse of Pembrokes Emanuel: 74

Frays, J.: 44

Frazer, Sir James G.: 12, 35, 68, 76, 86, 118, 35, 123, 144, 32, 36, 64

Frazer's Magazine: 87

Frazier, J. G. See Frazer, James G.

Freake (Freke): Jane (Ewens): 45. Katherine (Ewens): 45. Richard: 45. Robert: 45. William: 93

Freculph of Lisieux: 93

Frederic(k): Barbarossa ("red-beard"): 73. II: 73. III, King of Denmark: 10, 44*. V, Elector Palatine: 3, 64. William, Marquess of Brandenburg, etc.: 44. John: 44

Free: Commonwealth: 51*. Council: 51. Government: 51. Press, M's pleas for liberty of press and free speech: 147. Speaking, M's please for liberty of the press and free speech: 147. State, M on dangers to be avoided in: 80. Will: see separate entry. Writing: 51

Free-Mans Freedome Vindicated (John Lilburne): 147

Free will: 7, 24*, 37*, 51, 113*, 143, 36*, 132*, 147, 46, 80, 71. M's belief in: 147, 80. Problem of: 149. Danger of: 149. And causation: 96. Doctrine of: 132*. Granted at creation: 93. Impaired: 93. Dignity of: 149. In created man: 143. As basis of salvation: 143. As source of sin: 143. Satan's, Reader's, Adam and Eve's: 37. See also: Foreknowledge; Salvation

Free Parliament: 103. Free Parliament Litany: 44, 103, 91

Free, J.: 58

Freedman: Morris: 44, 60. Ralph: 39

Freedom: 7*, 17*, 31*, 47*, 50*, 51*, 60*, 107, 122*, 124*, 125, 141, 143, 147*. M and freedom of language: 66*. M champion of: 143. Of Man: 47. Derived from freedom of matter: 107. Of will: 50, 98, 114*; see also: Free will. Of will in PL: 83. Of will in Pursuit of Perfection: 83. Of the press, M on: 147*, 51. And departure from Paradise: 101. In fallen man: 101, 143, 48. And foreknowledge: 101. As nucleus of man's nature: 101. And perfection: 101. Abdiel on: 50, 52. Earthly and Heavenly: 52*. And the demonic: 47. M's concept of: 52. Political: 52. And responsibility: 101. In repentant man: 101. The concept: 47, 48. And rationality: 48. Of the press: Edwards against: 147; Goodwin on: 147; Lilburne on: 147; Overton on: 147; Walwyn on: 147. See also: Slavery

Freeholder's Grand Inquest: 116

Freeman: Mrs. (Biggs): 45. F. Barron: 98. John: 44, 93. R.: 15, 58, 105. Ralph: 45. Susan (Brent): 45. Thomas: 40, 97. William: 45

Freere, Sir Edward: 44

Freesland (Frisia): 49

Freher: 7

Freige, J. T.: 23

Freigius: John Thomas: 40. Thomas: 20

Freind, Dr. John: 44

Freke. See Freake

French: the: 51. Court: 51. Language: 103, 3, 88. Church in London: 40. Dictionary: 40. Element in British education: 40. Influence on octasyllabic couplet: 40. Language, studied by M: 20, 40, 44. Lit., referred to by early commentators (Todd, Warton, Bowle, Stillingfleet): 88. Book illustration: 97. Academy, The: 150. Revolution: 60, 92, 97, 25. New Testament: 40. Teaching: 40. Tutor: 40. Verse: 40. Law: 3. Manners: 3. Must: 3. People: 3. Symbolism: 88. Classical drama: 92

French: John (Registrary of Oxford Univ.): 44. J. Milton: see separate entry. Richard: 16. Roberts B.: "Verbal Irony in PL": 74; change from natural despair to Christian hope in Lycidas: 61

French, J. Milton: 6, 9, 20, 40*, 44*, 45, 59*, 60, 63, 73, 116, 123, 75, 86, 135, 144, 143, 36, 62, 91*, 101. Digressions in Lycidas: 143. The engine: 143. Works: Life Records of J. M.: 82; M in Chancery: 82; "That Late Villain M": 82

"French Critic on M, A": 98

French Revolution, The (Blake): structure of: 25. As epic: 25. As prophecy: 25

Frendraught, Lady: 64

Freneau, Philip: 71, 115*. Works: The House of Night: 115; The Power of Fancy: 115; The Rising Glory of America: 115; A Voyage to Boston: 115

Frénicle, Nicolas: 74, 64. Jésus Crucifié: 74

Frenzy: 2

Frere, J. H.: 58

Fresals, Maistre de: 44

Frescobaldi: 70, 121. Gerolama: 44. Pietro: 6, 28, 30, 44, 73

Fresh Discovery of some Prodigious New Wandring-Blasing-Stars (William Prynne): 147

Fresh Suit Against Independency: 116

Freshman studies: 40

Freshwater, Edward: 40

Fresnaye, Vauquelin de la: 100, 122

Fret: 121

Freud, Sigmund: 12, 15, 35, 52, 75, 76, 86, 95, 118, 123, 128, 11, 32, 72, 109, 131, 137

Frey, D.: 6

Frezzi, Federico: 55, 32

Frick Collection: 44

Friedeberg-Seeley, F.: 79

Friedländer, Gerald: 41, 123

Friedman, M. J.: 23

Friedmann, Wolfgang D.: 93

Friedrich, C. J.: 27

Friedrich: III, Elector Palatine: 10. IV, Elector Palatine: 10. V, Elector Palatine: 10. Wilhelm, Elector of Brandenburg: 10

Friend's Review: 44

Friends: of God: 7. Of m: 30*, 44; see also: Aizema; Arnold, Christopher; Barberini, Francesco; Bendish; Bigot; Diodati, Charles; Durie, John; Ellwood; Gill, Alexander; Old Margaret; Marvell; Paget; Pennington; Ryley; Winthrop. Quakers: 7, 78. Friendship: 30, 51, 122; M's views on: 30. See also: Quakers

Fries, C. C.: 135

Friesland, West: 44

Friex, E (pr.): 44

Frinnor (Finmore, Finnor, Fynmore): John: 45. Richard: 45. William: 45

Frischlin(us), Nicodemus: 40, 44, 117

Frith: John: 143. Mary: 44. W. P.: 97

Fritsch, Charles: 19

Fritwell: 45

Froebel: 3

Frohberger: 70

Froissart, Jean: 27, 60, 32, 88, 93

Frome: 49

Fromm: 141

Fromond, Thomas: 44

Fronde: 60

Frontinus: 44. Sextus, Strategematicon: 82

Frost: Mrs. Gualter and family: 44. Gualter, the elder (secretary to Council of State): 30, 44*. Frost(ium), Gualter Walter: 73. Gualter, the Younger: 44. Joseph: 44. Robert: 14, 72, 80, 93. Stanley B.: 93. W. E.: 97. Walter: 10, 38

Frost: 128

Frothingham, Nathaniel L.: 115

Froude: Hurrell: 87; hatred of M: 87. James Anthony, Oxford Movement: 87

Fruit: 144, 143. Forbidden: 17*, 19. Divine: 143. By their fruits: 143

Frustration: 47

Fry: Edward A.: 40, 45. Mary Isabel: 128

Frye, Northrop M.: 17, 23, 27, 37, 52*, 69*, 75, 76, 79, 86, 110, 118, 123, 125, 14*, 32, 39*, 53, 85, 97, 101, 106, 64, 137, 146, 48, 25. Analogy between Christ and Moses: 61. Christ's temptation and the fulfilling of the law: 61. Variance of Christ's feelings in PR: 61. On M: 104. Works: Anatomy of Criticism: 60; Fearful Symmetry: 60; "Typology of PR": 74

Frye, Roland Mushat: 23, 37, 44, 54, 59, 66, 79, 110, 93*

Fucci, Vanni: 111

Fuchs, R.: 128

Fugue: 121

Fulbrook: 45

Fulfillment: 47

Fulford: 49

Fulgentius, Fabius: 1, 4, 90, 122, 123, 133, 18

Fulham, co. Middlesex: 40, 44, 45, 49

Fulke, William: 40, 128

Full Answer To the Levellers Petition (a royalist pamphlet): 147

Fuller Worthies Library: 44

Fuller: 132. Andrew: 115; Dialogues, Letters, and Essays, on Various Subjects: 115. Margaret: 115. Timothy: 115; An Oration Pronounced at Lexington: 115. Thomas: see separate entry. William: 93

Fuller, Thomas: 1, 7, 8, 15, 19*, 20,

23, 40*, 44, 45, 54, 59, 60, 66, 68, 114, 116, 120, 128, 144*, 93, 99*, 101, 64, 146. Works: <u>Holy and Profane State</u>: 82, 91; <u>A Pisgah Sight of Palestine</u>: 144*; <u>Davids Hainous Sinne</u>: 74

Fulletby, co. Lincs.: 44

Fulman, William: 40

<u>Fulness of Time, The</u>: 65

Fulton, Dr. John: 44

Fulvius: 73

Fulwood, William: 20

Fumaeus, Antonius: 64

Fumagalli, Giuseppina: 5

Funccius, Christianus: 44

Funck, Johann: 93

Function: 70*. Of poetry, moral and political: 123

<u>Fundamenta Graecae Linguae</u>: 40

Fundamentalism: 47

Funeral Tears for the Earl of Devonshire: 121

Funeral, M's: 44

Fürer, Christoph (the Elder and Younger): 10

Furetière: 88

Furio, Federigo: 40

<u>Furius</u>: 117

Furness, Edward: 40

Furniss, W. Todd: 29, 39

Furnivall, F. J.: 44, 45

Furnivall's Inn, London: 44, 45

Furs(e)man, George: 44, 45

Furseman. See Horseman

<u>Further Discovery of the Plot</u>: 116

<u>Further Papers on Dante</u> (Sayers): 111

Fury: 2, 72. Blind: 73. Furies: 90, 92

Fusili (Fuseli), J. Henry: 58, 87, 97*, 14, 115, 146. Special relationship with M: 97. Youth and training: 97. And Blake: 97*. And Hogarth: 97. And James Barry: 97. And Martin: 97. And Ramney: 97*. And Westall: 97. And W. Hamilton: 97. As painter of Miltonic subjects: 87. Relationship to Apocalyptic poets: 87. The influence and success of the M Gallery: 97*. Works: <u>Sin coming between Satan and Death</u>: 87; Vision of the Madhouse: 87

Future: dark: 143. M's vision of: 143. Survey of: 143. Evil: 143

Fux: 70

Fuzon: 25

Fyall, Christopher: 45

Fyfe, W. H.: 5

Fynmore. See Frinnor

-G-

G., E. (Edward Griffin, Jr., pr., 1637-52): 44, 91

G., H. See Guy, Henry

G., J. G.: 116

G., J.: 44

G., R. See Goodgroom, Richard

G., S.: 103. See also: Godolphin, Sidney

G., W.: 44, 116. See also: Goldesborough, William

Gabalis, Comte de: 142. See also: Villars

Gabriel: 1, 2, 4, 17, 41*, 42, 50*, 56, 57, 60, 70, 73, 89, 98, 102, 103, 111, 123, 124, 127, 128, 141, 142*, 32, 36, 71, 72, 130, 55, 140, 80

Gabriellis, the two: 70

Gabrielli, Cleofe: 39

Gadarene swine: 72

Gadbury: Elmer: 45. (Cadbury), John: 44, 45, 128. Oliver: 45. William: 45

Gadd, Cyril J.: 64

Gaddi, J(ames) (Jacopo): 6*, 28, 30, 44, 73

Gaddian Academy: 44

Gades (Cales, Gadier): 49, 73, 144, 3. See also: Hercules' Pillars; Tarsus; Tartessus

Gadire: 73

Gaditanum Mare: 49

Gadites: 73

Gage, Clara Starrett: 142

Gager, William: 64

Gagliano, M. da: 6

Gagnebin, Bernard: 44

Gahagen, V.: 97

Gaia: 57, 90. See also: Earth

Gainsborough, T.: 97

Gainsburrow: 49

Galahad: 60

Galanis, D. E.: 97

Galasp: 120

Galaspy, Mr.: 120

Galataeus de Moribus: 40

Galatians, the foolish: 73

Galatinus, Petrus (Pietro Galatino): 40, 123, 43

Galaxy, the: 89. Milky Way: 128

Galba: 73

Galbraith, Vivian H.: 93

Gale: Theophilus: 81, 114, 93. Thomas, High Master: 10, 20, 40, 56, 123, 32

Galen, Claudius: 4, 16, 73, 128, 145. Galenists: 114

Galerius Armentarius: 128

Galicia: 144

Galilee: 49, 72. Of the Gentiles: 73. Pilot of the Galilean lake (St. Peter): 73

Galilei: Vincenzo (son of astronomer): 6, 44. Virginia: 6

Galileo, Galilei: 1, 6*, 7, 8, 10, 15, 17, 23, 30, 37, 40, 44*, 51, 60, 70, 73, 77, 79, 84, 86, 87, 103, 89*, 112, 111, 113, 114, 121, 128*, 139, 142, 144, 3, 26, 32, 39, 46, 71, 88, 93, 94, 101, 109, 130, 137, 146, 149. His astronomical clock: 89. Early scientific writings of: 89. Examination of Aristotle: 89. Adherence to the Copernican hypothesis: 89. Summoned before the Inquisition: 89. Received by Urban VIII: 89. Publishes the "Dialogue," breach of faith with the Inquisition: 89. Abjuration: 89. Meeting with M: 89, 55. His incredulous opponents: 89. Caution in disclosing his discoveries: 89. Blindess: 89. Death: 89. Salusbury: 77. Characteristics in controversy: 89. Effect of his discoveries on PL: 61. Discoveries of: observation of the moon: 89; Jupiter's moon: 89; observation of the Sun: 89; phases of Venus: 89; stellar structure of the Milky Way: 89; views as to habitability of the moon: 89; views on the stars: 89; telescope constructed and 1st used by: 89; Sidereal Messenger: 142. And M: 89, 97. See also: Copernican theory

Galimberti, Alice: 111

Gallaecia: 49

Gallandi, P.: 60

Gallaphrone: 73

Gallas, Count Matthias, Imperial General: 10

Gallegos Romulo: 83

Gallet, Louis: 65

Galli(c): 73

Gallia: 73, 144. Gallic School of Trevès: 40. See also: Gaul

Galliard, John Ernest: 117

Gallienus: 73

Gallilee, Thomas: 44

Gallinago: 40

Gallus, Cornelius (Gaius Cornelius): 44, 73, 21, 64

Galluzzi: 70

Galton, Major, of Hadzor: 44

Gama, Vasco de: 122, 123. See also: Camoens

Gamaliel: 73

Gamba, Bartolommeo: 44

Gambara, Lorenzo, Tractatio...de Perfectae Poëseos: 74, 64

Gamber, S.: 36

Gamble, John: 39

Games and sports: 8. Backgammon: 40

Gaming: 51

Gamon, Christofle de: 65. Semaine: 74

Gamut: 121

Gandhi: 35, 141, 25

Gandy, J. M.: 97

Gang, Theodore: 93

Ganges: 32, 150. River (Gangetis): 19, 49, 73, 144

Gangraena (Thomas Edwards): 113, 147, 26, 78. Most widely read antitolerationist pamphlet: 147

Ganong, Harry W.: 64

Ganymede: 90, 73, 111. Sigeius: 44

Garamanti: 49

Garden: 17*. Of Adonis: 139. Of Eden: 70*, 76*, 11, 72*; portrayal of: 67; M's as ideal: 118. Garden, The (Andrew Marvell): 131. Garden of Spiritual Flowers, A: 37. See also: Paradise

"Gardener's Chronicle": 44

Gardens Ancient and Modern (Sieveking): 70

Gardiner: 3. Mr.: 44. Bp.: 59, 120. Ann: see Cope, Ann. Bernard: 45. Dorothy: 40, 44. J.: 58. Joan: 120. John S. J.: 115; works: A preservative Against Unitarianism: 115; A Sermon, delivered at Trinity Church: 115; Remarks on the Jacobiniad: Part 1st: 115; Remarks on the Jacobiniad: Revised and Corrected by the Author: 115. R. B.: 20, 40. Ralph: 142. S. G.: 144. Samuel R.: 9, 40, 44, 51, 120; A Student's History of England: 82. Bp. Stephen: 73. Sir Thomas: 28, 44, 45, 103. Gardiner's estimate of Eikonoklastes: 147

Gardner: Helen C.: 12, 23, 37, 60, 75, 86, 100, 110, 143, 32, 36, 93, 97, 106, 131, 137, 148, 150; ambivalence in M's doctrine of woman's inferiority: 61; on Eve's guilt: 61; on Satan: 61. John: 44. Thomas: 44. W. H.: 87

Gareth of Orkney: 60

Garfield, John (bks., 1656-60): 44, 91

Gargrave, Richard: 40

Garin, Eugenio: 5, 79, 93

Garland, John: 40

Garment. See Symbolism

Garner, Ross: 81

Garnett: David (son of Edward): 44. Edward: 44, 130. Richard: 16, 44, 58, 87, 113, 132, 142, 92, 137; on M as a free thinker: 87; on poetical temperament of M: 87; on M's belief in characters in PL: 87; on M's political position: 87; on loss of belief in supernatural and effect on PL: 87; Life of M: 132, 142; see also: Gosse, Edmund

Garnsey, E. R.: 58

Garopoli, Girolamo: 123

Garret, William: 44

Garrett, Christina A., The Marian Exiles: 83

Garrick, David: 44, 58, 97, 115, 117; borrows from M: 58

Garrigou-Lagrange R., Christian Perfection and Contemplation: 83

Garrison, Fielding H.: 16

Garrod, H. W.: 44, 132

Garsington: 45

Garstacke, Ames: 44

Garter, the prelate of the: 73

Garth: 2. See also: Dispensary, The

Garthwait, Timothy (bks., 1650-69): 91

Garver, Willia K.: 41

Garway, Mr.: 45

Gascoigne: George: 40, 58, 68, 71, 88, 66, 79, 102. William: 89

Gascoine (in France): 49

Gaskell, Elizabeth C.: 137

Gassendi: 89, 113, 142, 88; Opera Omnia: 142. Pierre (Peter): 6, 60, 114, 32, 89, 113, 142, 88

Gaster: Moses: 142; Studies and Texts in Folklore, Magic, etc.: 142. Theodore: 144

Gaston de Foix: 60

Gastrell, Peregrine: 44

Gataker, Thomas: 40*, 44, 79, 22, 93, 94

Gate House: 103. Gatehouse prison: 44, 49, 73

Gath: 19, 49, 73, 103, 144

Gattacre (Gataker), Thomas: 40, 54, 114

Gattaker, Mr.: 40

Gaudel, A: 104

Gauden, Bp. John: 10, 28, 44*, 60, 103, 113, 115, 26, 32, 62, 71, 93, 94, 55. His son: 44

Gaul: 3

Gaule, John: 114, 142, 93. *Selected Cases of Conscience, etc.*: 142

Gaunt, W.: 97. John of: 64

Gautier de Metz: 32

Gautruche, Pierre: 1

Gavin, Frank: 93

Gawain and the Green Knight: 76

"Gawdy Day": 44

Gawen, Thomas: 44, 45

Gawler, Christopher: 45

Gawsworth: 40

Gay collection, Harvard College Library: 44

Gay: Elizabeth: 45. John: 35, 58, 88, 64, 146; *The Beggar's Opera*: 35. William: 45

Gay: 120

Gayley, Charles M., and Benjamin P. Kurtz, *Methods and Materials of Literary Criticism*: 74

Gayton, Edmund: 128

Gaza (Azza): 19, 49, 73, 144, 72, 103, 92. Gates of: 92. Prison in: 92. Harlot at: 92

Gaza, Theodorus: 40, 117

Gazaeus: 77. Angelin Gazet: 65, 40. Alardus: 143

Geber (Jabir): 114

Gebhards, D.: 44

Gedeon: 92

Gedicht von der Weltschöpfung: 65

Gee: Edward: 44. John: 40

Geer, Louis de: 10

Geeres, Thomas (judge): 44

Geffroy, A.: 44

Gehazi: 73

Gehenna: 73, 144

Geist, Stanley: 98

Geistlich Spiel, Ein: 65

Gelasius I: 73

Gelber, Jack: 67

Gell, Robert: 40, 44, 114, 120, 93

Gelli. See Gello

Gellian manner: 3

Gellibrand: Henry: 10. Samuel (bks., 1637-75): 91

Gellius, Aulus: 40, 44, 73, 90, 128, 88, 21. *Attic Nights*: 74

Gello, John Baptista (Gelli, Giovanni Battista): 69, 64

Geloni: 49

Gelonos: 73

Gematria: 41

Gemini: 90. See also: Dioscuri

Geminus, Thomas: 40, 44

Gemm, Thomas: 44, 45

Gemma Animae: 104

Gemma, Reinerus Frisius: 40

Gemmingen, Otto Heinrich von: 117

Genealogia deorum: 62

Genealogia Christi: 68

Genealogist: 44

Genebrardus, Gilbert: 74, 123. *Chronographiae*: 74

General Advertiser: 44

General Collection of Treaties of Peace and Commerce: 44

General Magazine: 44

General Theological Seminary: 44

General: Act of Pardon: 103. Confession: 126. Council: 51. Election: 51. Judgement: see Last Judgement. Spirit: 71. To the specific, rhetorical: 51. Generalization: Bentley's tendency towards: 88; opposed by Pearce: 88; rhetorical: 51. Generalized imagery, appreciated by Newton: 88. Generalizing method of Addison's criticism: 88

Generation: 25. Begins with Wisdom: 107. Creative: 75*. Uncreative: 75*. And intemperance: 75*. And privacy: 75. And self-destruction: 75*. Unfallen: 75*. Fallen: 75*. And sleeping and waking: 75*. And language: 75*. And temperence: 75. And union: 75*. And consecration: 75*. And godhead: 75*. And the right hand: 75. And imitation: 75. And reunion: 75. And disunion: 75*. And unfulfillment: 75*. And the left hand: 75. And the mouth: 75. And wounding: 75. And the Chariot of Ezekiel's vision: 75. And water: 75*. And physical posture: 75. And internalization: 75. And incest: 75*. And narcissism: 75*. And transformation: 75*. And blood: 75. And the ear: 75

Generative vocabulary: "reduce," "return," "waste," "womb," "grave," "pyramid," "feed," "brood," "move," "stores," "pour," "bring forth," "mount," "root, " "head," "fruit," "disburden," "breach," "seat," "engross," "devise," "erect," "possess," "issue," "disappeared," "void," "dislodged," "invent," "shoot forth," "hollow," "contrive," "sit," "pensive," "deliberation," "projecting," "hatching," "devising," "breed," "won," "hands," "surcharged," "redundant," "speculation": 75

Generosity: 51

Genesis: 2, 5, 44, 47, 50, 52, 56, 57, 76, 87, 95, 103, 118*, 123, 124, 126, 132, 139, 3, 71, 72, 96, 99, 146, 48, 36. Old English: 123. As myth: 118, 48. Commentaries on: 102. Ante-Nicene: 77. And creation story: 48. And history: 48*. Cabalistic meaning of the opening words of: 40. Composition of imitative exercises: 20*. Story: 65. 12th c. French verse paraphrase: 74. Genesis-A: 65*, 36. Genesis B: 17, 65*, 36*. Genesis (Olinger): 65. See also: Bible

Genêt, Edmond Charles Edouard: 115

Genethliacum: 40

Geneva: 9, 44*, 49, 73, 103, 3, 92, 94. Discipline of: 71. Academy of: 40, 44. Bible: 74*, 36. M's visit to: 6, 28, 30

Genezaret (Galilean Lake): 49, 73

Genghis Khan: 89

Genii: 142

Génin, F.: 40

Genius: 7, 90, 25. Literary: 51. Of the shore: 72. Of the Wood: 29, 73, 72

Genne: Elizabeth: 10. Kateryne: 10

Gennis, Francis: 44

Genoa, Italy: 44, 45, 49, 3, 94

Genocide: 47

Genre(s): 67. M's obedience to: 104. Distinctions in: 123. Or "Kinds," theories of: 66

Gent, Cardinal of: 10

Gent, T.: 58

Gentiles: 51, 3, 72. Semitic studies in Europe: 40. See also: Heathen

Gentili: Alberico: 93. Scipio: 88

Gentium Mores: 40

Gentleman's Magazine: 44*, 45, 94, 117*. Articles on M in: 58

Gentlemen: 51

Genua. See Genoa

Genuineness, of the Richardsons makes up for their frequent heaviness: 88

Genung, J. F., Epic of the Inner Life: 74

Geo-heliocentric universe: 128

Geocentric universe: 128. See also: Ptolemy

Geodaesia: 40

Geoffrey of Monmouth: 1, 4, 17, 57, 70, 73, 90, 114, 133, 64, 3, 39, 88, 93, 137

Geoffrey the Grammarian: 40.

Geoffroy: A.: 9, 116. E. L.: 58

Geography (Strabo): 70

Geography: as a topic: 40, 144. Books: 40. In M's works: 8, 15*, 19*

Geology: 87

Geometry: 40

Geon River: 32

George (sign), Burford, co. Oxon.: 44

George Inn: 45, 40

George, St.: 73, 122, 123. See also: Spenser

George: Charles H. and Katherine: 54, 93. Daniel: 115; works: An Almanack for the Year of Our Lord 1782: 115; An Almanack for the Year of Our Lord Christ 1784: 115. David: 7, 114. Isaac: 44. J.: 44. Rozaling: 44

George: I, of Eng.: 44. II, of Eng.: 44. III: 120. IV, King: 103

Georgeson, Sir P.: 116

Georgia: 19

Georgics (Virgil): 37, 70, 111, 3

Georgius: Cedrenus: 90. Monachus: 65. Pisides: 65

Gerald, Florence: 44

Geraldini, Antonio: 64

Gerard: Baron: 45. Lord Dutton: 45. John: 1, 19, 44, 128. See also: Gerhard. Mary: see Cope, Mary. Lady Mary (Fane): 45

Gerard's Hall Inn: 40

Gerardus, Andreas. See Hyperius

Gerber, J.: 34

Gerbier, Sir Balthazar (painter, d. 1667): 44, 114, 91

Geree: John, seconds the Presbyterian manifesto in Might Overcoming Right: 147. Stephen: 114

Gergessa: 49, 73

Gerhard, John (Johann): 57, 40, 73, 142, 22, 93. Meditations: 142. See also: Gerard

German(us), St.: 73

Germany (Almany, Germania, Teutonici Agri): 40, 44, 49, 3. German(s): 3; educational textbooks: 40; elements in British education: 40. Germanic epic: 118. Migrations: 123

Germershemius, Johannes Posthius: 44

Gerold, Theodore: 100, 93

Gerrish, Brian A.: 93

Gerson: Ben: 1, 41, 42, 73, 128, 144, 60, 22. John: 114. Jean de: 40, 64; Josephina: 74. Levi Ben Gershon (Gersonides): see Gerson, Ben. Gersonides, Levi: see Gerson, Ben

Gertrude, in Hamlet: 72

Gertsch, Alfred: 44

Gerusalemme Liberata: 65, 118

Geryon: 19, 90, 111. Geryon's sons: 73

Gesamtkatalog (Prussia): 40

Gesamtkatalog der Wiegendrucke: 40

Gesamtkunstwerk: 118

Geschaffne, gefallne und aufgerichtete Mensch, Der: 65

Gesenius, Hebrew Grammar: 41

Gesner, Conrad: 128

Gessner: 10. A poet: 94. Solomon: 58, 65

"Gesta Britannica": 44

Gesta Grayorum: 29

Gestures, oratorical: 51

Gésu: 27

Gethsemane: 72

Getto, G.: 6

Gewin (Gewen), Thomas: 45

Geymonat, L.: 6

Gherard, Francis: 44

Gherardo da Borgo San Donnino: 38

Ghilini, G.: 6

Giamatti, A. Bartlett: 110, 32, 101

Giangolino, Carlo: 32

Giannettasio, Niccolo: 64

Giants: 90, 143, 92. Biblical:

122*, 123. Angels as: 123. Heroes as: 123*. Classical: 123

Giattini, Vincento: 68

Gibbens, Nicholas: 102, 93

Gibbon: Edward: 18, 23, 34, 57, 58, 86, 71, 94, 146, 117; Memoirs and Letters: 82. Nicholas: 45

Gibbons: Dorothy: 45. Ellis: 121. James: 45. Orlando: 40. R.: 23. T.: 58

Gibborim: 123. See also: Giants, Biblical

Gibbs: Henry: 44. V.: 45

Gibeah: 49, 73, 144

Gibeon: 49, 73

Giblet, H.: 6

Gibralter (Gibraltar): 44, 49, 73. See also: Hercules' Pillars

Gibson: Archable: 115; An Almanack, For the Year of our Lord 1812: 115. Edmund: 7. James: 73. Samuel: 93. Wilfred: 148. William: 7, 58

Giddy, Paul (fictitious name for pr.): 44

Gide, Andre: 133, 39, 46

Gideon: 68, 73, 123, 141

Giedion-Welcker, C.: 23

Giedion, Sigfried: 23, 37

Gierke, Otto: 9, 83, 102, 93

Giffard, George: 102

Gifford: 130. George: 93. J.: 40. W.: 58, 87. William: 70

Gifftheyl: 7

Gift of Constantine: 111

Gifts, to, from M: 30*

Gigantomachia: 56

Giggleswick School: 40

Gigli, G.: 6

Gigur, Oxford Univ. beadle of beggars: 44

Gihon River: 32

Gil: Alexander: 93. George: 20. See also: Gill

Gilbank, W.: 58

Gilbert: 89. A. A.: 148. Allan H.: see separate entry. Davies: 44. Sir Geoffrey: 45. John: 116. Katherine Everett: 100. Neal: 39. S.: 23. W. S.: 35. William: 1, 44, 77, 142, 32, 45

Gilbert, Allan H.: 6, 9, 15, 17, 19*, 20, 31, 40, 41, 44, 52, 60, 63, 68, 70, 75, 77, 81, 86, 102, 112, 110, 113, 122, 123, 125, 128*, 132, 142, 144, 36, 71, 92, 93, 64, 99, 101, 106, 130, 21. Works: Dante's Conception of Justice: 60; "Form and Matter in PL": 60; "M on the Position of Women": 60; On the Composition of "PL": 60, 142. "The Theological Basis of Satan's Rebellion and the Function of Abdiel in PL": 60; Literary Criticism, Plato to Dryden: 20; Temptation in PR: 74

Gilboa: 49

Gilby, Anthony: 51, 60, 73

Gilchrist: Alexander: 25. Octavius G.: 91

Gildas, St. (Rerum Britannicarum, De Excidio, et al.): 44, 73, 3, 82, 93

Gilded Lion (bookshop): 44

Gilder: Joseph B.: 44. Thomas: 45

Gildon, Charles: 44, 58, 116, 142, 130, 117; praises M: 58; Misc. Letters and Essays on Several Subjects: 142

Gildredge, Nicholas: 10

Giles, Thomas: 29

Gilfillan, George: 16, 60, 87. On Miltonic Satan as sublime figure: 87. On the Satan of PR: 87. On M's character: 87. On many-sidedness of M: 87

Gilgal: 49, 73

Gilgamesh: 1, 141, 36. Gilgamesh Epic: 65, 32, 36

Gill upon Gill: 20

Gill: 3. Dr.: 44. Alexander (Senior and, or, Junior): 15, 9, 19, 20*, 40*, 82, 29, 28, 30, 40*, 42, 44*, 56, 59, 70, 73, 84, 103, 107, 108, 112, 135, 93, 144, 26, 82. Alexander (the Younger, 1597-1642): 91, 137, 148, 132; admired Origen: 107; usher at St. Paul's: 132; M's letter to, quoted: 55; mentioned: 55. The Elder (1564-1635): 132, 148,

55; Headmaster of St. Paul's: 132, 94. Elizabeth: 40. George: 40. John: 143; the sword and Gospel: 143; glassy sea: 143. Nathaniel: 40, 44. Dr. Robert: 44, 103. Thomas: 44. Thomas H.: 44, 116. William Wyatt: 118

Gilles: 3. Pastor Peter: 103. Pierre (Peter): 73; Histoire Ecclesiastique des Eglises Reformées: 82

Gillespie, George: 51, 59, 120

Gillet, J. E.: 70

Gillette, E. H.: 44

Gillies: John: 105, 88; edits PL: 58. Mrs. Leman: 87; on M's treatment of daughters: 87

Gillingham: 49

Gillman, James: 119 Gillray: J.: 97. James: 146

Gilly: 120

Gilman: S.: 23. Wilbur E.: 40, 54, 60, 116, 123, 91. William: 128

Gilmer, Robert: 44

Gilmore, M. P.: 39, 93

Gilpin: Richard: 142; Daemonologia Sacra, or Treatise of Satan's Temptations: 142. W.: 97

Gilson: Etienne: 52, 79, 81, 100, 114, 123, 142, 32, 93; works: The Philosophy of St. Bonaventure: 142; The Philosophy of St. Thomas Aquinas: 142. J. P.: 44

Giltspur Street, London: 44

Gimmer, Thomas: 45

Gin Hall: 44, 45

Ginchi, Gasparo: 40

Ginsburg, Christian D.: 40, 41

Ginzberg, L.: 68, 142. The Legends of the Jews: 142

Gioe, Marcus (Danish resident): 44

Gionnotti, Donato: 5

Giono, J.: 6

Giordano, Luca: 117

Giorgio, Francesco: 100, 93

Giorgione: 39

Giovio, Paolo: 8, 19. See also: Jovius, Paulus

Giphanius, D.: 1

Gipkin, John: 20

Giraldi, Giambattista (Cinthio, Cynthius): 114, 122, 123, 21, 64. Lilio G.: 44

Girard: 121. Bernard de: 82; Histoire de France: 82*. René: 11, 39

Girardi, E. N.: 5

Girardi, E. N.: 5

Girardin, Saint-Marc, Tableau de la Litterature Française: 74

Giraudoux, Jean: 46

Girdler, Lew: 44

Girls: education of: 40. Golden: 40. Girls' Own Paper: 34

Girolami, Mr.: 44

Gisborne: J.: 58. T.: 58

Gish, Lillian: 137

Giuseppi, M. S.: 45

Giustiniano(i), G.: 6, 3

Givens, Sean: 23, 60

Glamorgan: 49

Glanville: Francis: 45. Sir John the Younger: 64. Joseph: 60, 81, 128, 114, 145, 32, 72, 93, 142*; works: Blow at Modern Sadducism: 142; Lux Orientalis: 142; Sadducismus Triumphatus: 142. Ranulf de: 73

Glarus: 44. See also: Swiss Evangelical Cantons

Glasgow, Scotland: 44, 103. Glasgow Assembly: 51

Glasier, Thomas: 44

Glass for the Times: 103

Glass(e): George: 117. Janet: 40, 58. Solomon: 79, 22, 68

Glass, Venetian: 54

Glasse of Godly Love, The: 54

Glasse of Time: 1st Age: 65. 2nd Age: 65

Glassford, James: 87, 120

Glasson, T. Francis: 93

Glassy Sea: 128, 143*. Explained: 143*. Baptism: 143. Theological background of: 143. Spiritual sense of: 143

Glastbrig: 49

Glaston: 49

Glaucoma: 16*

Glaucon: 112

Glaucus: 56, 44, 73, 90, 104

Gleason, Robert W.: 93

Glee: 121

Gleeking (a game): 40

Glendale: 49. See also: Brunanburg

Glenne (the use of): 83

Glickman, Harry: 115

Glicksman, Harry: 44, 113, 93

Glielmo, P. Antonio: 117

Glisson: Dr.: 142. Francis: 10, 44

Globes: 40, 144

Gloriana: 60

Glory: 51, 52*, 122, 123*, 125*. Glorification: 63. Gloria in excelsis: 126. Gloria Patri: 126. See also: Honour

Glossa Ordinaria: 74*, 36

Glossarial character of 1st literary commentaries in England: 83

Glossary to Parochial Antiquities (Bp. Kennet): 88

Glosses: 83*

Glossographia: 45

Gloster: 49

Gloucester: 44, 45. Hall: 45. Journal: 88

Gloucestershire: 45*, 49. Visitation of: 45

Glover: 133. Andrew: 44. Mary: see Roberts, Mary. Richard: 58*. Sir William: 45

Gluck, C. W. von: 39

Gluckstadium: 49

Gluttony: 51, 93

Glycas, Michael (Glyca, Michaelis): 44, 65, 68, 73

Glycera: 73, 3

Glynn: John, Lord Chief Justice: 44. R.: 58

Gmelin, Hermann: 100

Gnerghi, G.: 6

Gnesna (misprinted "Guesna"): 49

Gnomes: 142

Gnomon, the: 89

Gnosis: 36

Gnostics: 34, 40, 73, 79, 95, 113, 71. Gnosticism: 36*, 25

Goadby (publisher): 97

Goats (freshmen): 40

Goclenius: 10, 128

God: 7*, 31*, 44*, 47*, 50*, 51*, 52, 54*, 60*, 63*, 87*, 98*, 17*, 37, 73, 80, 140*, 103*, 107*, 112*, 111*, 113*, 118, 128*, 127*, 141*, 144*, 143*, 32*, 36*, 71*, 72*, 93*, 109, 146. Qualities and characteristics of: anger: 47, 17, 46; foreknowledge: 17, 31, 50, 46, 107, 93; goodness: 17, 31; justice: 9, 17, 31, 50, 32; nature: 83, 36; perfection: 83; pity: 17, 31; providence of: 63, 17, 31; reason of: 9, 17, 31, 37*; jealousy (towards man): 141; jealousy (toward Jews): 141; father figure: 141; demonic character of: 141; liberality: 143; severity: 143; invisibility: 107; benevolence of: 36*; Grace of: 47. omnipotence of: 36*; omnipresence of: 36; omniscience of: 36*. Ways to Man: 36*. Names of: 36. Throne of: 36. After the Fall: 72. Anthropomorphic accommodation, symmetry, respect for man, created man for community: 47. Rhetoric of: 37, 109. Speeches of: 17, 37*. Style of: 37*. Will of: 9*, 51. Image of: 51, 93. Word of: 51. As source of natural Sublime: 87. Plan of creation: 144. Creation natural: 144. And light: 144. And the universe: 144. And man's creation: 144. As a logician: 37. See also: Christ; Holy Spirit; Son of God; Trinity; Diety; Word of God

God, continued: creative power: 46.

1st cause of "great chain of being": 46. Incomprehensibility: 93, 107*. Immutability: 93. As center of circle: 93. "All": 93, 107*. Musician: 93. Eye: 93. Ear: 93. Conceptions of: 93. Knowledge and character of: 96*. Motivation: 99, 51. And ambition: 144. And fortune: 144. Sons of: 144. And law: 144, 51. And Satan: 144*. And Jacob's dream: 144. And marriage: 144. Unworthy servants: 144. His love: 144. Unity: 93. Glory of: 93. And nature: 93. And history: 93*. "God of order": 93. Imitated by Satan: 93. His gifts: 93. Laughter: 93. Daughters: 93. Man's Fall: 144. His secrets: 144, 17. His worship: 144. Defiance of: 144*. His City: 144. His angels: 144. During the Battle of Heaven: 72. In colloquy upon the Fall: 72*. During Creation: 72. As Absolute: 107*. According to Justin Martyr: 107*. Attributes are absolutes: 107*. External efficiency: 107*. And the Son as agent: 75*. As defined by synecdoche and metonymy: 118

God (actions): as calling man: 141. God-Devil encounter: 48. Uses demons to tempt and punish man: 107. Creates good from evil: 107*. Speaks to serpent: 32. Speaks to Adam: 32. Speaks to Adam and Eve: 32. Foresees Heavenly paradise: 32. Patterns paradise on Heaven: 32. Leads Adam to paradise: 32. Ordains work: 32. How engaged before creation: 93. As "Creator": 75, 32*, 93, 144. As "Uncreator": 75*. As "Recreator": 75*

God (in M): in PL: 40, 132. As unamiable figure: 141. As a character: 55*, 140, 144. Function and nature of in PL: 140*, 137, 46. His benevolence and grace in: 118. Portrayed as King: 118, 46. In SA: 92*. In M's religious epics: 87. M's God contrasted with God of Faust: 87. M's heresies concerning: 140. M's interpreation of God's will: 147. Deprived of attributes by M: 107*. "All in All": God in Origen and M: 107. M's conception of: 113*

God, miscellaneous: with compasses: 143. Unlawful to represent: 143. Attributes: 143, 93. His purpose: 143. Relation to man: 143. Not inexorable: 143. Nearness, in old cosmology: 143. Challenged through His creation: 48. God's image and likeness in man: 48*. The doctrine of His image and likeness: 48. Man's Godlikeness and the relationship between Adam and Eve: 48. Personal relationship as an element in man's Godlikeness: 48. Idea of: 107. Did not make demons: 107. Inaudible: 107. Knows evil: 107. Seven eyes of God: 41 Permits evil: 107. Representation of: 141. His kingdom: 143. In the O.T.: 141. Creation of Eve: 32. Promise of to man: 32. Relations with Adam and Eve: 32. And covenants: 32. Adam's knowledge of: 32. Adam's marriage: 32. In relation to social order: 32*. Relation to man: 32. Reflection in nature: 32. Presence of: 32. As a character: sources of: 55; 20th c. criticism: 55. Royalist symbolism applied to: 8

"God send": 51

"God Glorified in Man's Dependence": 71

God, in <u>La Strage degl'Innocenti</u>: 60

Godbid, William (pr., 1656-77): 91

Goddard: family: 44. Elizabeth Woodcock: 44. Jonathan: 10*. Mary: 128

Goddard's drops: 16

Godden, Arthur (coachman): 44

Godeau, Antoine: 129, 64. <u>St. Paul</u>: 74

Godefridus (Abbas), <u>Homiliae</u>: 74

Godefridus Admontensis: 68

Godemann: 10

Godfrey of Bouillon (Boulogne): 6, 44, 60, 70, 65, 73, 123. See also: Tasso

Godfrey: 3. Of Viterbo: 32. Thomas: 115, 117; works: <u>The Assembly of Birds</u>: 115; <u>Court of Fancy</u>: 115; <u>Juvenile Poems on Various Subjects</u>: 115

Godfridus: 128. See also: Godefridus

Godlesford. See Goodlesford

Godless institution: 51

Godlike: man, as hero: 123*. Godlikeness: 123. See also: Divine image

Godolphin: F. R. B.: 64. Sidney, 1st Earl of (S. G.): 44

<u>Godot, Waiting for</u>: 34

Godran, Abbe Charles: works: <u>Historia Crucis Dominicae</u>: 74, 64; <u>Judith Viduae Historia</u>: 74

"God's Ape," devil as: 122

Gods: of Olympus: 90*. Of nations are demons: 107

Godwin: 3. Francis: 128. Thomas: 40, 68. William: 16, 40, 44, 53, 87, 128, 71, 91, 94, 97, 146, 28, 117; Lives of John and Edward Phillips

Goedeke, K.: 68

Goethe, Johann W. von: 4, 12, 41, 42, 52, 58, 87, 105, 113, 120, 136, 141, 14*, 39, 92, 94, 130, 146, 149, 64. The Prometheus of: 141. Classic spirit of: 87. Compared with Shakespeare: 87. Faust compared with M's Satan: 87. Faust: 87. See also: Faust

Goffe: Joseph: 115; The Flaming Sword: 115. Thomas: 40, 64. Goffe's Amurath: 88

Gog Magog Hills: 40

Gohn, Ernest S.: 68, 122

Golartius (Goulart), Simon: 73

Gold, Michael: 1

Golden Age Restored (Jonson): 29

Golden Book of Marcus Aurelius: 133

Golden Bough, The: 12, 118

Golden Grove: 40

Golden Legend (Caxton): 88

Golden Lyon (vessel): 44

Golden Rule: 147. See also: Canne, John

Golden Thoughts on Mother, Home, and Heaven: 44

Golden Treasury, The: 86, 87

Golden: Age: 59, 11, 36*; as affected by harmony: 121; see also: Age of Gold. Ball (sign): 44. Chain: 144. Compasses: 143*; process described: 143; in St. Edmond's Church: 143. Flower: see Symbolism. Ladder, the (in PL): 89. Lane, London: 44. Lion (sign): 44. Rule: 51. Rule of construing: 40

Goldesbrough: William: 45. William, Deputy Registrar of Court of Chancery: 44

Golding: 133. Arthur: 1, 15, 20, 40, 114, 128*, 32, 33, 93. L. T.: 45. William: 15

Goldsmith (Goldsmythe, Gouldsmith): Mr.: 44, 45. Clement: 45. Dorothy: 44. Elizabeth (Cope): 45. Ellen: 44. Henry: 45. John: 44, 45. Margery: 44. Nicholas: 44. Oliver: 35, 44, 58, 86, 87, 98, 105, 128, 133, 131, 146, 117; praises M: 58. Randle: 44

Goldsmiths" Alley, London: 44. Goldsmiths' Company: 40, 44*. Goldsmiths' Hall: 44*, 103; Committee at: 44

Goldwell, Charles: 93

Goldwin, W.: 58

Golf at St. Andrew's: 40

Golgonooza: 25

Golgotha: 19, 49, 73, 72

Golia: 73

Goliath: 91. i.e., Salmasius: 44. Prototype for Harapha: 123

Golius, Theophilus: 40

Goll, Ivan: 65

Gollancz: Hermann: 128. Sir Israel: 33

Golty, Mr.: 44

Golvoe, Antonio: 93

Golzio, V.: 6

Gomar: 41

Gomarus, Franciscus: 40, 63, 73

Gombrich, E. H.: 79

Gomez de Ciudad Real, Alvarus, Thalichristia: 74

Gomme, Sir L.: 120

Gompertz, I.: 58

Gondibert (Davenant): 144, 131

Goneril (Shakespeare's character): 87

Gonfalons: 142

Gonville and Caius College, Cambridge: 40

Gonzaga: 3. Cardinal: 103. Ippolita: 64. Marquis: 44. Vincenzo, Duke of Mantua: 103

Gooch, G. P.: 7, 9. And H. J. Laski: 60

Good Friday: 47, 72. "Good Friday riding westward" (John Donne): 131

Good Morrow, The (John Donne): 131

Good Old Way, The: 116

Good Words: 44*

Good: divine machinery: 149*. Modern conception of: 149. Force of, origin in God: 149. Highest: 123*. Lesser: 123. External: 123. Of the body: 123. As topic in deliberative rhetoric: 123. Indisputable: 123. "Good Authors": 40. And Evil: 7, 31, 129. Versus Evil: 80. Evil results in: 31*. Administration, factors in: 51. Conduct, books on: 40. "Good old cause": 103, 71. Party: 9*. Sense: 51. Spirits, aid men: 107. "Good temptation": 37*. Will: 51*. Works: 63, 123; doctrine of: 71; faith essential form of: 123; causes of: 123; definition of: 123; works of the Spirit: 123

Good: J. M.: 58. Dr. John Walter: 9, 44, 58*, 70, 116, 88, 97, 130, 117; Studies in the M Tradition: 91. Thomas: 81

Goodall, Charles (?): 44

Goodchild, Jeffrey: 44

Goode, W.: 59

Goodfellow, Christopher: 44

Goodgroom, Richard: 44

Gooding, Henry: 44

Goodlesford Andrews (Godlesford Andrews, Gusford Hall): 44

Goodman: 51. Christopher: 60, 73, 131. Bp. Godfrey: 1, 15, 40, 77, 102, 116, 26, 38, 93, 101, 148. P.: 59, 110. Paul: 14

Goodness of God, freely given: 77. See also: Babington; Damascene; Mersenne; Syncellus; Taylor; Robbins

Goodness: of natural instincts: 113. Of matter: 113. In poetic characters: 123. As true criterion of merit: 123. Of created order: 93. And God's glory: 93

Goodwin sands: 19

Goodwin: 7. Arthur: 64. Gordon: 128. John: 8, 9*, 28, 44*, 59, 60, 147, 103, 114, 116, 144, 22, 32, 38, 91, 93, 148, 55; asserts his extreme views in Thirty Queries: 147; defends himself in The Unrighteous Judge: 147; justifies army's purge in Right And Might well Met: 147; on liberty of the press: 147; quotes M in Obstruction to Justice: 147; replies to Edwards in Cretensis, A Briefe Answer to an ulcerous treatise... Gangraena: 147; on right of self-government in Right and Might Well Met: 147; tracts: Anapologesiates Antapologias, a plea for toleration: 141; anti-Cavalierisme: 141; works: Right and Might Well Met: 60; Theomachia: 147; The Grand Imprudence: 147; The Obstructours of Justice: 60, 91; The Apologist Condemned: 147; Imputatio Fidei: 147; A Reply of two of the Brethren to M. S.: 147; Sion College Visited: 91; Twelve Serious Cautions: 91. Thomas: 9, 23, 44, 51, 59, 102, 120, 93, 114, 38

Googe, Barnaby: 65, 74, 128, 46

Gopp, John (apprentice scrivener): 44

Goppelt, Leonhard: 93

Gorboduc (Sackville): 130, 131

Gordian: 73

Gordon: 35, 120. A.: 58. D. J.: 19, 39. E. V.: 64. George, 2nd Marquis of Huntly: 73. James: 93. James D.: 93. John (Viscount): 64. Lord: 40. R. K.: 36. William: 115; The Doctrine of Final Universal Salvation Examined and Shewn to be Unscriptural: 115

Gore, Charles: 68, 93

Gorgades: 144

Gorges: Arthur: 64. Carew: 40

Gorgias (Plato): 112

Gorgon(s) (Gorgonian): 73, 90, 144, 92. See also: Medusa

Goring: George: 73. Sir Henry: 44

Gorky (Gorki), Nicholas: 35, 44

Gorlois: 44, 73, 3

Goropius, Johannes: 32

Gorra, Egidio: 5

Gorting, Mr.: 44

Gorton, J.: 58

Gortyn, Samuel: 114

Goshen: 49. The sojourners of: 73

Gosling (Gostling), George: 44

Gratiani (Graziani), Girolamo: 123

Gratianopolis: 49

Gratianus, Flavius: 73

Gratitude: 51

Grattan, Henry: 117

Gratton, R. H.: 45

Gratz, Simon: 44

Graunt, I.: 79

Grave: 49. Simple: 121. Ladder from to Heaven: 143. Of M, rifled: 87

Gravelot, H.: 97

Graves: 3. Messrs. (art restorers): 44. Frank Pierrepont: 112. Henry (bks.): 44. John: 45. Robert: 1, 33, 34, 58, 66, 32, 137. Thomas: 42

Gravesend, co. Kent: 44

Graveyard poetry: 58. And _Il Penseroso_: 58

Gravitation, universal, discovery of law of: 89

Gravius, Theodoricus: 7

Gray: 132, 133, 130, 149. Mr.: 44, 120. Arthur: 40. F. C.: 68. G.: 44. G. B.: 35; and S. R. Driver; _Book of Job_: 74. John: 44. Ralph: 40. Thomas: see separate entry. Zachary: 44

Gray, Thomas: 15, 16, 35, 40, 44, 58*, 86, 87, 88, 97, 115, 146*, 117*, 55. Borrows phrases from M, influenced by _L'Allegro_ and _Il Penseroso_, praises M, uses Nativity meter: 58*. Blake's designs for: 25. Works: The Bard: 35; Elegy: 35

Gray's Inn, London: 29, 44, 45*, 103. _Gray's Inn Admission Register_: 45*. Gray's Inn Lane: 44, 45. _Gray's Inn, The Pension Book of_: 45

Graziani. See Gratiani

Great men, as precedents: 30*

Great plague, London: 103

Great Bear, the: 89

Great Britain, Ministry of Works: 44

Great Britain, Parliamentary Papers, Reports of Commissioners: 40

Great Britain's Ruin Plotted: 44

Great Britains Vote (anonymous, against Levellers and sectaries): 147

Great Case of Liberty of Conscience: 116

Great Chain of Being: 52, 96. See also: Chain of Being

Great Civil War and Toleration: 147

Great Dalby. See Dalby

Great Didactic (Comenius): 147

Great Doulby: 44, See also: Dalby

Great Dunmow, co. Essex: 44

Great Exhibition, The: 97

Great Fire of 1666: 44, 103

Great Hall, Ludlow Castle: 29

Great Milton. See Milton

Great Missendon, co. Bucks.: 44

Great Mother: 144

Great Queen Street: 44

Great Remonstrance: 103

Great Scotland Yard: 44

Great Seal, Commissioners: 44

"Great Shepherd": 58

Great Turnstile: 44

Great Waldingfield, Suffolk: 40

Greater Man, Christ as the: 113*

Greatheed, B.: 58

Greatness: defined: 30. As criterion of merit: 123

Greaves: John: 10, 19, 40. Thomas: 10

Greban, D'Arnoul: 65

Grebanier, Bernard D., Samuel Middlebrook, Stith Thompson, and William Watt: 44

Greece (Doric Lane, Graecia): 19, 30, 35, 44*, 49, 51, 70, 103, 112, 145, 3*, 72*, 94, 150. See also: Javan

Greek Anthology, The: 87, 117

Greek Medicine in Rome (Allbutt): 3

Greek: 40*, 42, 44*, 51.

Transliteration of: abyss: 119; amarant: 119; demonic: 119; eremite: 119; hyalive: 119; myraids: 119; panoply: 119; tartarus: 119; Urania: 119. Variant translations based on: anxiety: 119; Evil One: 119; tread: 119. Regius professorship of: 40. Tragedy: 150, 101; and SA: 143. Tragic poets: 40. Music: 121. Theory: 121. Writers: 121. Gods: 144*, 71. Literature censured in PR: 93. Comedy: 70, 51. Culture, (apollonian aspect of): 87. Language: 70, 103, 3*. Anthology: 40. Drama (translation of): 53; see also: Drama, Greek. History: 8. Ode: 40. Poets: 51. Prosody: 40. Proverb: 40. M's studies: 44. M's poetry: 40, 44, 117. M's Book of Greek heroic poets: 40. M's study and use of: 20*, 30, 40, 44. M's Greek poems: 88; see also: Burney. See also: Greece

Greeks, the: 70*, 3, 32, 71, 150. Arts and contributions of: 71. Democracy of: 51; treatment of blind by: 16. And astronomy: 89. See also: Classical tradition

Green Cape: 49

Green Dragon (sign): 44

<u>Green Pastures</u>: 52

Green: Mr.: 45. Clarence: 107, 138, 141, 144, 36; Eve falls deceived: 107; Adam undeceived: 107; "The Paradox of the Fall in PL": 48. George Smith: 88, 117; "New Version of PL": 58; see also: Oxford, "Gentlemen of." H.: 10, 15, 58. John Richard: 70, 18. M.: 53. T. M.: 60. Thomas, on M: 58, 117. W. C.: 58. See also: Greene

Greene: Benjamin, M's servant: 44. Clarence E.: 52. E. B.: 58. Graham: 84. Humphrey: 45. J.: 58. Robert: 15, 128, 129. Thomas M.: 37, 45, 110, 122, 39, 93, 101. W.: 44, 45; <u>Friar Bacon and Friar Bungay</u>: 35. William: 45. See also: Green

Greenham, Richard (as Diggon Davie): 83

Greenidge, C. W. W., <u>Slavery</u>: 82

Greenlaw, Edwin: 1, 5, 60, 63, 69, 77, 83, 86, 102, 107, 108, 64, 112, 113, 122, 138*, 141, 144, 71, 88, 93, 130, 137, 48, 132, 133, 36, 128. Spenser's influence on M: 107. "A Better Teacher than Aquinas": 48, 109

Greenville: Sir John: 51. Sir Richard: 44

Greenway (alias Tilney), Anthony: 44

Greenwich, London: 44, 49, 150

Greenwood: Mr.: 45. Elizabeth (Jones): 45. George: 44, 45. Henry: 60, 114, 93. James: 58, 118, 117. Thomas: 45. W.: 58

Greere: Elizabeth: see Hopton, Eliz. Elizabeth (Cope): 45. Thomas: 45

Greever, G.: 58

Greg, W. W.: 44, 148

Gregoras, Nicephoras, <u>Byzantine Historiae Libri XI</u>: 82

Gregorian: calendar: 73. Decretals: 73

Gregory: I, the Great: 60, 68, 74, 77, 114, 73, 116, 123, 64, 36*, 93, 99, 125, 121, 128, 44, 142; works: <u>XL Homiliarum in Evangelia</u>: 74, 77; <u>In Septem Psalmos</u>: 74; <u>Moralia in Job</u>: 74*, 36, 77; <u>Sermon on the Gospel of Sunday</u>: 36; Decretals: 82. VII, Pope: 87, 116. XII, Pope: 32. Nazianzen, St.: 4, 54, 68, 70, 73, 77, 32, 57, 36, 90, 65, 93; <u>Orations</u>: 36, 77. Of Nyssa, St.: 63, 60, 65, 73, 77, 113, 123, 124, 141, 142, 143, 24*, 44, 57, 63, 32, 36*, 39, 71, 93; <u>The Great Catechism</u>: 36; <u>On the Making of Man</u>: 142, 36; <u>On the Baptism of Christ</u>: 36; <u>Opera</u>: 82. Of Rimini: 93. Thaumaturgos, St.: 60, 107; Origen's most famous pupil: 107; materialism: 107. Of Tours, St.: 73, 93

Gregory: Elizabeth: see Hopton, Eliz. Francis: 116. George: 44. J. F.: 44. John: 44, 32, 115; <u>A Father's Legacy to His Daughters</u>: 115. Ruth W.: 115. William: 45

Gregynog Press: 97

Grenander: M. C.: 123. M. E.: 6

Grendel: 36

Grenegras, Richard: 44

Grenewey, Richard: 145

Grenoble, France: 44

Grensted, Laurence W.: 93

Grenville: Dorothy: see Cope, Dorothy. J.: 58. Sir Richard: 45. Collection, Brit. Museum: 44

Greschischev, Ivan: 117

Gresham College: 16, 40, 44

Gresty (Greasty), co. Cheshire: 44

Gretton, Mary Sturge: 45

Greville: Mrs.: 58. Thomasine: 45

Greville: Sir Fulke, Lord Brooke: 15, 40, 44, 45, 60, 69, 102, 64, 114, 133, 38, 46, 86, 125. Robert, 2nd Baron: 8, 9*, 44, 51, 83, 114, Episcopacie: 60; The Nature of Truth: 60, 83. An Historical Account of the Noble Family of: 45

Grew, Nehemiah: 10, 128

Grey, R. (trans. Browne): 58

Greyhound, St. Paul's Churchyard: 40

Greyhounds: 40

Gribaldi, Matteo: 55

Gribbel, John: 44

Gribble, Mr., Clerk of Scrivener's Company: 44

Grieck, Claude de: 68

Grierson: C.: 58. Sir Herbert J. C.: 1, 9, 16, 18, 27, 31*, 35, 34, 44, 59, 60, 63, 68, 76, 77, 84, 86*, 102*, 108, 112, 110, 128, 132, 133*, 135, 138, 139, 141, 144, 145, 43, 64, 85, 88, 91, 93, 101, 109, 130, 131, 137, 148, 150; works by: John Milton: 60, 74, 48; M and Wordsworth: 60*, 95, 77; Criticism and Creation: 48

Griffin(s): 90, 144, 92, 73

Griffin: B.: 59. Edward, the Younger (pr.): 44, 55

Griffith of Oakham School: 20

Griffith: Capt.: 44. D. W.: 137. Elizabeth: 115; Essays Addressed to Young Married Women: 115. Dr. Matthew (1599?-1665): 9, 19, 44, 116, 128, 38, 91, 93, 55; sermon that M hated, The Fear of God and the King ...: 147; wrote The Samaritan Revived: 147

Grignion, C.: 97

Grigson, G.: 97

Grimaldi, F. M.: 4

Grimes, Ethog: 144

Grimeston, Edward: 128

Grimm, brothers: 64

Grimme, Hubert: 40

Grindal(l): Edmund: 40, 73, 143; and prophecying: 143; opposed Queen Elizabeth: 143. R.: 44

Grinder, Mary: 44

Grisar, H.: 71

Grismond, John II (pr., 1649?-64?): 44, 91

Grisons (Grizons): 44, 73. See also: Swiss Evangelical Cantons

Griswold, Rufus: 63

Groans of Kent, The: 59

Grocers of Norwich: 65

Grocyn, William: 40, 142, 3, 18, 64

Grolier Club (Catalogue): 44

Groningen (Groningham): 49, 73

Gronovius: Abraham: 117. (John) Frederick: 10, 44*

Gront-Houwelick: 65

Groombridge, W.: 58

Groome, George: 44

Groppa, A.: 6

Grosart, A. B.: 23, 44, 45, 68, 79, 83, 91, 64

Gross, Charles: 45

Grosse, Alexander: 93

Grosseteste, Robert: 32, 36. Chasteau d'Amour: 36

Grosvenor Street, London: 44

Grosvenor: Humphrey: 44. Sir Richard: 44

Grotesque: crudity of style and interpreation in Hume: 88. Passages appreciated by, misinterpreted by Bentley: 88. Style, Newton's dislike of: 88. Warton on: 88

Grotius, Hugo (Huig van de Groot): 1, 2, 6, 7, 15, 17, 28, 30, 40, 42, 44*, 54, 58, 65*, 68, 70, 73, 74, 76, 77, 84, 89, 103, 113, 116, 128, 129, 142, 3, 22*, 32*, 64, 36*, 93, 94, 109, 115, 130, 137, 149, 117*, 55. Works: Annotata ad Vetus Testamentum: 74; De Jure Belli: 91; Adamus Exul: 36*, 149*, 55, 77; Satan, Eve in: 149; temptation: 149; artistic defects: 149*

Groto, Luigi: 68

Grouchy, Nicolas de: 40

Groundsill Coppice: 45

Grout, Donald: 39

Grove Leaze, co. Oxon.: 44. See also: Groveleyes

Grove: George: 44, 100. H., influenced by, praises M: 58. Robert: 44. W.: 58

Groveleyes: 45. See also: Grove Leaze

Growte, Stephen: 120

Grub Street: 103. Journal: 58, 88, 117*

Grube, G. M. A.: 5

Gruber, I. D.: 44

Grueber, Herbert A. See Hawkins, Edward

Grundisburgh, co. Suffolk: 44

Grunebaum, G. E. von: 125

Grunewald, M.: 97

Gruter, Jan: 44. Gruter(ian): 73

Grynaeus, Simon: 10, 41, 73, 117

Gryphius: Andreas: 10. Christian: 44. Othon, Virgilii Centones: 74, 64

Gualter of Zurich, Rudolph: 44, 73

Guarded Mount: 49. See also: Bayona

Guardian angels: 93

Guards, of Paradise: 50

Guarini, Giovanni Battista: 1, 4, 6, 27, 44, 66, 70, 32, 64, 39, 101, 117. Il Pastor Fido: 55

Guarino: 40

Guasti, Cesare: 5, 60, 122

Guatama: 71

Guazzo: F.: 128. Stefano: 40, 114

Gudeman, Alfred: 21

Gudger, F. W.: 128

Gudii (Gudius), Marquardi: 44

Guerard, Albert: 87

Guerlac: Henry: 128. Rita Carey: 33

Guerra angelica, La: 65

Guerra degli angeli: 65

Guerra elementale: 65

Guerret, Elizabeth (Salmasius' maid): 44

Guest, Charles: 45

Gueus, le: 3

Guevara: 40. Antoinio de: 93

Guhrauer: 7

Guiana: 19, 49, 73, 144. See also: El Dorado

Guibert de Nogent: 40

Guicciardini: C.: 6, 40. Francesco: 40, 114, 145, 93; Historia d'Italia: 82

Guidaccerius, Agathius: 40

Guidiccioni: 120. Laelio: 6. Laura: 6

Guido: 90, 117

Guignards: 44

Guignebert, Charles: 113

Guild Hall Elegy upon...Bradshaw: 44, 91

Guild, William: 54, 79, 128, 93

Guildhall, London: 44, 45, 49, 73, 103

Guilford: 49

Guillaume, A.: 68

Guillemeau, Jacques: 16

Guillim: 3. John: 8, 44, 82; A Display of Heraldrie: 82

Guilt: 47. Man's: 31*. See also: Sin

Guiltspur Street: 44

Guimarea, Dom Joseph de (ambassador from Portugal): 44, 103

Guinea: 150. Nigritarum: 49

Guiney, Louis Imogen: 44

Guinicello (Guinizelli), Guido: 111, 120

Guinti: 88

Guion: 51

Guisborough School, York: 40

Guise: Duke of: 6. Edward: 45. Elizabeth: see Eyton, Eliz. Elizabeth (Newman): 45

Guisian of Paris, like a: 73

Guitar: 121

Guizot, F. P. G., Histoire de la Civilisation en France: 74

Gulielmi Sallustii Bartassii Hebdomas: 65

Gulliver (in Gulliver's Travels): 72

Gulliver's Travels: 71

Gumbledon, John: 142. Works: Christ Tempted: The Divel Conquered: 142; Two Sermons: First an Angel in a Vision: 142

Gunkel, Hermann: 113, 123

Gunning, Henry: 40

Gunpowder Plot: 20, 40, 44, 46, 72. Christian and pagan elements: 8

Guns: 40. Gun (sign): 44. Gunpowder, use of by rebel angels: 113

Gunter, Edmund: 64

Gunther: Anthon: 10, 44; see also: Oldenburg. Charles F.: 44. R. T.: 44, 128

Guntzer, Christopher: 44, 91

Guortemir (Guorthemirus): 73

Guorthigirniaum: 49. See also: Tiebi

Gurdon, John: 44

Gurnay, Edward: 40

Gurney: David: 115; A Sermon Preached December 5, 1792: 115. J. H.: 44

Gurteen, S. Humphreys: 111, 36

Gurwitsch, Aron: 39

Gusford. See Goodlesford

Gustavus Adolphus, King of Sweden: 10, 20, 38

Gusto: 146

Gutenberg, Johann: 40, 93

Guthkelch, A. C.: 81

Guthlac, St.: 36

Gutta serena: 16

Guttridge, G. H.: 115

Guy of Warwick (The Corrected History of Guy, Earl of Warwick (John Lane, M's father's friend): 44

Guy Fawkes' Day: 40, 103. See also: Fawkes

Guy: Harold A.: 93. Henry (H. G.): 44

Guyon, Sir: 60, 73, 113, 3

Guzman de Alfarache: 60, 88

Gwalter, Rudolf: 93

Gwinne, Matthew: 40

Gwreans an bys: 65

Gwynne, Nell: 103

Gyas: 2

Gyles, Edmund: 45

Gyll, Gordon J. W.: 44

Gymnasium: 40

Gypsies Metamorphosed (Jonson): 29

Gyraldus, L. Gregorius: 4. De Deis Gentium: 74

-H-

H., C. J.: 44

H., I.: 59, 99. See also: Heath, James

H., J.: 44, 59

H., Mr.: 44. See also: Hales, John

H., S. See Hickman, Spencer

Haak: Ericus: 10. Elizabeth: 10. Theodore: 7, 10*, 40, 44, 117, 91: Chelsea College, Danish Mission, Dutch Bible, English Parliament, Gaistliche und Weltliche Gedichte, Heidelberg, Palatine Collections, PL, Protestant Cantons of Switzerland, Royal Society, "1645" Group: 10*. Theodore, Sr.: 10

Haberdasher's Hall: 44

Habermann (Avenar, Avenarius), Johann: 40

Habington, Thomas: 93

Habits: virtues and vices as: 123. M's: 30, 40, 51, 137

Habor (modern Khabur): 49, 73

Hacker, John: 40

Hacket, Bp. John (1592-1670): 40, 44, 116, 103, 94; <u>Scrinia Reserato</u>: 91. E. Byrne: 44. Thomas: 44. Hacket's Speech in the House: 51

Hackluyt, Dr: 103

Hackney, London: 44

Hacon and Ricketts (publisher): 97

<u>Haddington Masque</u> (Jonson): 29

Haddington: 49

Haddon: 3. Clere: 64. Walter: 40, 73, 64

Hades: 90*, 72

Hadfield, P.: 93

Hadham, John: 141

Hadow, W. H.: 70

Hadrian: 3, 36, 64

Hadwen, W.: 58

Hadzor, co. Worcs.: 44

Haemon (Sophocles'): 70

Haemony: 1, 29, 73, 90, 72. Spiritual sense of: 143. Interpretations of: 104

Haemus: 49, 73

Hafnia: 49. See also: Copenhagen

Hagar: 73

Hagendahl, Harald: 93

Haggadah: 36

Haggard: Howard: 16. Rider: 64

Hagley: 70. Hagley Park: 97

Hagstrum, Jean: 79, 115, 25

Hague, the (Haga Comitis): 44*, 49, 103. Seen lately at the: 73

Haigh, A. E.: 92*

Hail: 128. Causes and kinds: 128

Hailes, Lord: 40

Haillan, Bernard Girard du: 40

Hain, Ludovicus: 40

Haine, William: 20

Haines, Charles G.: 93

Hair: Adam's: 118. Eve's: 118

Hake, Edward: 93

Hakewill: 132. Master: 45. George: 35, 40, 102, 114, 142, 145, 26, 32, 93, 101, 148; An Apologie or Declaration of the Power and Providence of God...: 142. W.: 44. William: 45

Hakluyt, John: 44; <u>Metropolitan Nuncio</u>: 91. Richard: 15, 19*, 40, 128, 82, 150, 55. <u>Hakluyt's Voyages</u>: 117. <u>Hakluyt Society, Publications</u> of: 44

Halakhah: 36

Halberstadt (Halberstad): 44, 49

Halcyon: 144

Hale: Mr.: 44. Sir Matthew: 44, 128, 142, 32. Will T.: 9, 51, 57, 144; Hale W. T., edition of <u>Of Reformation</u>: 66

Hales: Sir Edward: 44. James: 44. Sir James (judge, d. 1554): 44, 91. John W.: 9, 33, 40, 44, 51, 113, 114, 132, 93, 101, 148. Katherine: see Ewens, Katherine

Haley: Francis: 128. K. H. D.: 44

Half Moon (sign): 44

Halicarnassus: 44. Halicarnassian, the: 117

<u>Halieutica</u> (Oppian): 3

Haliewell. See Holywell

Halifax: Dorothy Evelyn Augusta Onslow, Lady: 44. Lord: 116

Halkett, Samuel and John Laing: 44

Hall-Stevenson, J.: 58

Hall: Mr. (pr.): 44. Dr. A. R.: 40, 44. The Younger: 41. Basil: 93. Clayton M.: 44. Edward (A.): 29, 40, 64. Frederic: 142; <u>Pedigree of the Devil</u>: 142. Bp. George: 93. Hubert: 45. J.: 44, 58, 99; engraver: 97; pamphleteer denounced by M: 80. James: 44. John E. (1627-56): 40, 44*, 70, 103, 114, 123, 91, 115; The Adieu: 115. Bp. Joseph: see separate entry. Robert: 91. Stephen: 45. Thomas: 44, 114. Vernon: 102. Vernon, Jr.: 122. W.: 33, 58

Hall, Bp. Joseph: 1, 8, 9*, 10, 15, 16, 17, 19, 20, 23, 24*, 30*, 37, 40, 41, 44*, 45, 51, 60, 66, 68*, 70, 79, 84, 103, 114, 123, 128, 136, 142, 144, 143, 87, 113, 132, 145, 147, 26, 32, 38, 62, 71, 82, 91*, 148, 88, 93*, 94, 130, 55. Remonstrates with the exiles: 147. On duties of clergy: 143. M's denunciation of: 80. Works: A Survey of that Foolish, Seditious, Scandalous, Prophane Libell, the Protestation Protested: 147; A Modest Confutation: 147; Characters of Virtues and Vices: 91; Episcopacy by Divine Right: 91; Invisible World Discovered: 142; Humble Remonstrance: 57, 91; Contemplations upon...the Holy Storie: 74; Contemplations upon... the New Testament: 74; Explication ...of the Whole Divine Scripture: 74; Cases of Conscience: 91; Defence: 91; Remains: 91; Resolutions and Decisions: 91; Short Answer: 91; Toothless Satires: 91. See also: Of Reformation; Animadversions; Apology

Hallam: 120, 132, 94. Arthur Henry: 87, 111, 137, 146; went to Spain with Tennyson: 87; attitude toward M: 87; on PL: 87; fame of discussed in In Memoriam: 87; "The Bride of the Lake": 87; "Timbuctoo": 87. Henry: 4, 33, 63, 87, 130; on M's sonnets: 87. I.: 58. West: 45

Hallard, J. H.: 64

Halleck, Reuben Post: 15

Hallel: 40

Haller: Adalbert von: 65. Malleville: 93. R. and M.: 139. William: 9*, 23, 37, 44*, 52, 58, 66, 79, 83, 102, 108, 110, 111, 113, 116, 123, 128, 143, 141, 144, 85, 91, 93, 101, 106, 109, 148; and Malleville: 54, 66, 110, 115; M and Puritanism: 143; reforming the church: 143; works: The Rise of Puritanism: 60, 83; Tracts on Liberty in the Puritan Revolution: 50. William and Godfrey Davis: 60

Hallesby, Ole K.: 93

Halley, Edmund: 10, 89. Observations of stars by: 89. Discovery of the great cluster in Hercules by: 89. Cited on eclipse of the sun: 89. Halley's comet: 89

Halliday: Dr.: 58. Bernard (bks.): 44

Halliwell, J. O.: 40, 64

Halloran, William: 25

Hallywell, Henry: 142. Melampronoea or Discourse of the Polity and Kingdon of Darkness: 142

Halton (Holton) co. Oxon.: 28, 44

Halton, Sir William: 45

Halvaker, co. Sussex: 44

Haly: Elizabeth Dixon: 44. Francis: 44. Nicholas: 44

Ham: 1, 90. See also: Cham

Hama: 3

Hamadryads: 90

Hamal (alpha arielis): 89

Hamann: 7. Johann Georg: 87

Hamartia: 68

Hamartigenia: 65

Hamartiology: 93

Hamartolus, Georgius: 68

Hamath: 49, 73, 144

Hambleton, Thomas: 44

Hamburg: 40, 44*, 103, 3

Hamburga (Hamburgum): 49

Hamel, J.: 19

Hamer, Douglas: 83

Hamerton, P. G.: 97

Hamet Basha: 44. See also: Ahmed IV

Hamey: Baldwin: 44*. Jeremy: 44*

Hamilton series: 45

Hamilton: A. C.: 69. Alexander: 115. Bernice: 93. Douglas: 16. Edith: 52. G. Rostrevor: 102. James Douglas, Duke of: 73. K. G.: 79. G. R.: 86, 102, 122, 141, 148. Marie P.: 110. Newburgh: 117. W.: 58*, 97; influenced by L'Allegro and Il Penseroso: 58. W. D.: 9, 40, 44*, 45*. Sir William: 40

Hamlet: 8, 31, 40, 45, 70, 118, 139, 71, 72, 131. The character: 5, 60, 113, 72, 88, 92

Hamley, E.: 58

Hammerle, K.: 128

Hammersmith: 40*, 62. Co. Middlesex: 44

Hammon: 90. See also: Ammon

Hammond: George: 142; *A Discourse of Angels*: 142. Henry (1605-60): 1, 44, 54, 73, 114, 22, 32, 91, 99, 101; *Paraphrase and Annotations upon... the New Testament*: 74; Letter of Resolution: 91. James: 117. Mason, "Concilia Deorum": 74. Col. Robert: 73, 38

Hamond, John: 40

Hamor: Ralph: 44. Susan: 44

Hampden: Miss: see Brome. Anne: see Pye, Anne. John: 45, 60, 103, 64

Hampshire: 45, 49. See also: Southampton

Hampson: Robert: 44. Sir Thomas: 44, 45. W.: 58

Hampstead, London: 44

Hampton Court: 44, 103. Conference: 40

Hampton: Christopher: 93. Henry: 44

Hanael: 41

Hanaper Officer: 44

Hancock: Daniel: 44. George: 44. John: 60. Robert: 116

Hand(s): 54. Symbol of unity: 128. Working with, M on: 80

Handel, George Frederick: 6, 15, 35, 58, 60, 88, 97, 115, 130, 64, 146, 149, 117. Oratorios from M, oratorio *L'Allegro*, influence of: 58

Handmaidens, chorus of: 92

Handwriting: of M: 28. Of Aubrey: 28. Of Elizabeth Minshull: 28. Of Edward Phillips: 28. Of John Phillips: 28. Of Wood: 28

Hanford, James Holly: 1, 4, 5, 6, 8, 9, 15, 16, 19, 20, 45, 64, 24*, 31, 33, 40, 41, 42, 44*, 52, 54, 57, 58, 59, 63*, 66, 68, 73, 77, 79, 83, 84, 100, 95, 98, 102, 104, 107, 108, 86*, 112, 110, 111, 113, 114, 122, 123, 125, 128, 132*, 133, 135, 136, 138, 141, 142, 144*, 14, 26, 43, 61, 91, 93, 101, 109, 146, 80, 143, 62, 82, 85, 92*, 106, 130*, 137*, 148*, 83, 140, 21, 48. PL occasionally heretical: 107. Biographical critic of M: 61. Duration of Samson's pain: 61. On suffering; 61. On M's religious background: 104. On character of Comus: 143. Works: *Studies in Shakespeare, Milton and Donne*: 142; "M and the return to humanism": 83; *A Milton Handbook*: 77, 83, 82, 48, 142; "The temptation motive in M": 83; "The Rosenbach M Documents": 82, 77; "The Chronology of M's Private Studies": 60, 82; *John M, Englishman*: 82; "The Dramtic Element in 'PL'": 60; "M and the Art of War": 82, 77

Hanford, J. N.: 134

Hanger, George: 44

Hania: 49. See also: Henault

Hanley, Thomas: 128

Hanmer: J. (sonnets of): 58. Meredith: 93. Sir Thomas, ed.: 135, 97

Hannay, Patrick: 21

Hanney, R. K.: 40

Hannibal: 120, 3

Hanport, John: 10

Hanse Towns: 44

Hanseaticae Civitates; 49

Hansley, Mr.: 44

Hanson: Anthony T.: 93. R. P. C.: 36, 39, 93; *Allegory and Event*: 74

Hanwell, co. Oxon.: 44, 45*

Happiness: 31, 47, 83. Of those that suffer: 116. As the result of the attainment of perfection: 83. M on: 80. See also: Joy; Felicity; Good, highest

Happy life (beata vita) defined: 81

Har: 25

Haraberezaiti, Mt.: 32

Haran: 19, 49, 73, 144

Harapha: 1, 4, 68*, 73, 103, 125*, 126, 72, 92*, 109, 55

Harbage, Alfred: 40, 44, 68, 108. "Census of Anglo-Latin Plays": 74

Harbardus: 44, 73

Harbison, E. H.: 39

Harbord: Sir Charles: 44, 45. William: 44

Harby, Mr.: 44

Harcourt: Agnes: see Cope, Agnes. Edward: 44. Sir Robert: 45. Sir George Simon, Earl of: 45, 44. William Edward, 2nd Viscount: 44

Hardcastle, S.: 58

Hardenberg, Friedrich von: 136

Hardening of heart: 93

Harder, J. H.: 63, 113

Harderus, Henricus: 65

Harding: Awdrey: 45. Davis P.: 20, 37*, 52, 56, 60, 68, 79, 81, 110, 118, 122, 123, 141, 32, 93, 101, 106, 21; "M and the Renaissance Ovid": 74. E. and S. (publishers): 44. Emily J.: 97. Thomas: 45

Hardinge: G.: 58; admires M: 58. N.: 58; admires M: 58

Hardman, Oscar: 93

Hardon, John A.: 93

Hardwick: 45

Hardwicke, Philip Yorke, 2nd Earl of: 44

Hardy: 15, 149. E. and S. (publishers): 44. John Edmund: 23, 29, 60, 79, 110, 128, 139, 93, 101, 21; see also: Brooks, Cleanth. N.: 59. Nathaniel: 54*. T.: 58. Thomas: 34, 76, 138, 93, 150. Sir Thomas Duffus: 45

Hardyng, John: 82, 93. <u>Chronicle</u>: 82

Hare: A. J. C.: 44. Francis, Bp. of Chichester: 44. Henry: see Coleraine, Lord Henry Hare. John, in <u>England's Proper and onely way</u>: 147. John (scrivener): 44. Julius Charles: 146. Richard (scrivener): 44

Harefield: 29, 40, 44, 49, 73. House: 103

Harewood: 49

Harflew: 49

Hargrave, Roger: 44

Hargreave, Gen.: 97

Harifeld: 44

Harington: family: 40. Sir John: 20, 40, 44, 66, 122, 135. Lucy: 40. (Harrington), William: 45*

Harison, Benjamin: 44

Harkness, Bruce: 44

Harleian: Library: 44. Charters: 44. <u>Harleian Miscellany</u>: 44. <u>Society Publications</u>: 44*, 45*

Harless, Adolph von: 7

Harley: G. D.: 58. Robert: 116; see also: Oxford. Sir Robert: 44

Harlot of Babylon: 54

Harlow, V. T.: 144

Harlowe: Pedaell: 44, 45. Robert: 45

Harman, Marian: 40

Harmodius (plural): 73

Harmonia: 90

Harmonics: 121

<u>Harmonious Vision, The</u> (D. C. Allen): 139

Harmony: 47, 54*, 121*, 146. Pythagorean-Platonic: 106. And poetry: 106. Personified: 121.

"Harnabie" (Farnaby): 40

Harnack, Adolph: 57, 107, 36, 93, 32. "Cosmopolitanism": 107. Estimate of Origen: 107. <u>History of Dogma</u>: 74

Haro, Luis de (prime minister of Spain): 44

Harold: 94

Haroutunian, Joseph: 115

Harp: 121*

Harper, Charles (pr.): 44

Harpies: 90, 72

Harrach, A.: 58

Harral, T.: 58

Harrawell, John: 45

Harrington: 51, 120, 94. Author of <u>A Word Concerning A House of Peers</u>: 8. Anne: 40. Lady Frances: 40. James: 9*, 16, 40, 44*, 52, 59, 60, 84, 103, 114, 38, 91, 115, 146, 117, 55; his model government: 147; and M: 147; M's interest in Harrington's model government: 147; Oceana: 147, 38, 91. Sir James: 44, 93. Sir John: 116, 128, 88; on court masque: 143. William: 44. See also: Harington

Harriot, Thomas: 40, 89, 114

Harris: family: 45. Mr.: 45. Mrs.: 44. Alice (Holloway): 45. B.: 44. Benjamin: 116. Gyles (Giles): 44, 45*. Henry: 45. J.: 58. James: 117. Jane: see Ayloffe, Jane. John: 45, 64. Judith: 45. Judith (Wallwin): 45. Lewis: 45. Richard: 45. Robert: 45; The Workes of: 45. Rowland: 44. Thaddeus Mason: 115; A Tribute of Respect, to the Memory of the Hon. James Boudoin, Esq.: 115. Victor: 145, 93, 148. William C.: 122. William O.: 37, 85, 93, 101. Sir William: 45. W. R.: 58

Harrison: 40, 51, 94. Archibald: 58, 122, 93. G. B.: 128. Frederick: 87. George: 44. Governor: see Addison, Galston. Jane: 123. Jane Ellen: 141. John: 40. Luke (pr.): 40. Ralph: 115; Rudiments of Eng. Grammar: 115. T. P.: 33, 21. Thomas: 38. Thomas (1606-60): 91. Col. Thomas (regicide): 44, 113. Thomas P., Jr.: 10, 33, 128, 64. William: 44, 45, 58

Harrod, W.: 58

Harrop, E. A.: 58

Harrow (sign): 44. See also: Symbolism

Harrowing of Hell (13th c. Eng. verse paraphrase of Gospel of Nicodemus): 74

Harsdörffer, Georg Philipp: 10

Harshness, rustick: 51

Harsnet: Bp. of Norwich: 33. Samuel: 40

Harsy, Antoine le: 122

Hart Hall: 45

Hart: H. C.: 128. Jeffrey: 110. John: 40, 135, 93. Philip: 117. S.: 97. W. H.: 44

Hart's Close, Edinburgh: 44

Harte, Walter: 44, 58

Hartford Convention in an Uproar, The: 115

Hartis, C. T.: 58

Hartley, David: 12

Hartlib, Samuel: 7*, 9, 10*, 27, 30, 40, 44*, 51, 60, 113, 114, 120, 128, 132, 3*, 142, 26, 53, 91, 93, 146, 55, 62, 130. M relation to: 51. Champion of Comenius: 94. Memoir of Hartlib (Dircks): 3

Hartman: Franz: 142; The Life of Paracelsus: 142. Geoffrey H.: 23, 81, 14*, 39, 21, 25

Hartmann, Moritz: 65

Hartop: Mrs.: 44. Jonathan: 44

Hartshorn Quay (or Key), London: 44, 45*

Hartt, Frederick: 106

Hartwell: K.: 102. K. E.: 144. K. S.: 100. Kathleen E.: 1, 9, 15, 20, 41, 63, 68, 107, 123, 36; stylistic influence of Lactantius upon M: 107; Lactantius and M: 82

Harum, David: 40

Harvard: College and Univ.: 40, 44*. Library: 44*, 45. Bulletin of: 44. Studies and Notes in Philology and Lit.: 44, 45

Harvengius, Philippus: 143. Christ as ladder: 143. Ladder of two woods: 143

Harvest: home: 89. Moon: 89

Harvey of Burgundy: 68

Harvey: Christopher: 79, 93. Rev. F. Tucker: 44. Francis: 40, 44. Gabriel: 20, 66, 83*, 102, 114, 123, 129, 32, 46, 88. John: 44, 58, 32, 93. R.: 59. Richard: 93. Thomas: 40, 44. W.: 97. William: 1, 16, 40, 44, 60, 79, 114, 128, 93, 142; Opera Omnia: 142

Harvye, Lucy. See Cotton, Lucy

Harward, Simon: 128

Harwich: 49

Harwood, Sir Edward: 40

Haseley: 45

Haselrig, Sir Arthur (member and president of Coucil of State): 44, 103, 38, 51, 91

Haskins, Charles H.: 128, 93

Haslefoot: Rebecca: 44. William: 44

Hasmolin: 142

Hasmoneans: 38

Haspecker, Josef: 93

Hass, William: 40

Hassall family: 44

Hassard, Robert: 44

Hassel: W. (artist of M portrait): 44. W. D.: 143

Hasted, Edward: 45

Hastings: 49. Marquis of: 44. Sir Francis: 45. James: 100; Encyclopedia of Religion and Ethics: 48. William: 44, 45

Hatch, Henry G.: 93

Hatche, Richard: 44

Hate: as a theme in PL: 48. Hatred: 47*, 51*. See also: Theme of Love

Hatfield House: 45

Hatfield Peverell, co. Essex: 44

Hathaway, B.: 6

Hatton, Lord (called Mr. Smith): 44. Charles: 44. Christopher: 44. John: 44; see also: Hutton. Sir William: 44, 45

Hatzfeld, H.: 27

Haug, Ralph: 44, 66

Haughfell, John: 44

Haughton Tower, co. Lancs.: 44

Haughton: 40. Family: 44. Mr.: 44. Edward: 93. Elizabeth: 44

Haulo, Robertus de: 121

Haun: Emile: 101. Eugene: 104

Haunted Palace, The: 136

Haunts of the Muses: 40

Hauptmann, Gerhart: 118. Versunkene Glocke: 149

Hauser, A.: 27

Hausted, Peter: 29, 40, 93

Hauteville, Jean de: 32

Hauvette, H.: 6

Hauwenreuter, Johann Ludwig: 40

Havana: 49

Havens: P. S.: 44. Raymond D.: 16, 44, 59, 68, 77, 86, 87, 98, 102, 113, 14, 71, 91, 92, 97, 130.

Haviland, Thomas P.: 115

Haward, Sir William: 44

Hawes: 133. Stephen: 37; Pastime of Pleasure: 37

Hawker: a poet: 94. Rev. Robert Stephen: 87

Hawkers, itinerant: 8

Hawkey, John: 88, 55

Hawkins: 121. Edward, Augustus W. Franks, Herbert A. Grueber: 44. Francis: 20. Henry: 15. Sir John: 40, 117. Sherman H.: 106. T.: 58. William: 40, 58

Hawks (falcons): 40. Hawking: 40

Hawley, Sir Joseph: 44

Haworth, Marcus: 81

Hawthorne, Nathaniel: 98, 136, 115, 137, 149. "Hawthorne and his Mosses": 98

Hay: Denys: 93. James: 40. Sophia: 64. W.: 58

Hayden: G.: 58. J.: 58. John: 33

Haydn: Franz Josef: 117. Hiram: 17, 69, 122, 93. Joseph: 15

Haydon, B. R.: 97

Hayes: John (pr., 1669-1705): 44, 91, 115; Rural Poems, Moral and Description: 115. S.: 58

Hayle, William: 44

Hayley Bond (M's): 44

Hayley: 149. A critic: 94. Richard: 44. William: 16, 44, 58*, 116, 133, 92, 97, 146*, 117*, 55, 25*; as epic theorist: 25; library of: 25; his M edition: 25; as Blake's patron: 25; on M: 58; works: Cowper's M: 146; Essay on Epic Poetry: 146; Life of M: 146

Hayman, F.: 97. And Gainsborough: 97

Haymo Halberstatensis: 68, 123

Hayne, Thomas: 68, 79, 93. The

General View of the Holy Scriptures: 109

Haynes, Lemuel: 115. Universal Salvation A Very Ancient Doctrine: 115

Hayois, L.: 58

Hays: Alexander: 44. James: 44. Patrick: 44

Hayward: Mr.: 44. Sir John: 73, 82, 93; Life and Raigne of King Edward the 6th: 82

Hayyoth: 142

Hazard: J.: 58. Paul: 93

Hazen, Charles Downer: 115

Hazlitt, William: 4, 16, 27, 33, 44, 58, 60, 81, 83, 86, 87, 105, 110, 111, 97, 130*, 137, 146*, 150. On Shakespeare and M: 87. Opinion of M's genius: 87. Preferred M's sonnets to Shakespeare's: 87. On M's Satan: 87. Bibliography of his M criticism: 146. Works: Character of M's Eve: 146; Character of the Excursion: 146; Coleridge's Literary Life: 146; Comus: 146; Fine Arts: 146; History of the Good Old Times: 146; Landor's Imaginary Conversations: 146; Lectures on the Eng. Comic Writer: 146; Lectures on the Eng. Poets: 146*; Notes of a Journey Through France and Italy: 146. On Different Sorts of Fame: 146; On M's Sonnets: 146; On M's Versification: 146; On Poetry in General: 146; On Posthumous Fame: 146; On the Question of Whether Pope Was a Poet: 146; On the Tendency of Sects: 146; Plain Speaker: 146; Round Table: 146. Schlegel on the Drama: 146; Select British Poets: 146; Sismondi's Lit. of the South: 146; Table Talk: 146

"He whom Heaven did call away" (attr. to M): 44

Headington: 45. Quarry and Shotover: 45

Headlam, A. C.: 36

Headley: H.: 58. John M.: 93. Headley's Select Specimens of Ancient Eng. Poetry: 88. His M notes: 88

Headly Hall: 45

Heads of Proposals (the Army's demands of Charles): 147

Heale, Rev. Mr.: 44

Healey: Sir Charles E. C. H.: see Didbin, Sir Lewis. John: 81, 123, 144, 93

Healing Question propounded and resolved (Sir Harry Vane): 147

Health: Mulcaster's concern for in education: 40; figure for order: 40, 128*; for truth: 128. M's: 30, 44*, 51, 137

Heard: G.: 99. W.: 58

Heare, heare, heare, heare (anonymous, outburst against the Independent tyrants): 147

Hearh, C. (engraver): 97

Hearing: 128

Hearne (Herne, Heron): Mr.: 45. Anthony: 45. Sir Edward: 45. George: 44, 45. John: 45. Richard: 45. Thomas: 40, 44, 45, 116, 117. William: 44*, 45*

Heath Grammar School: 42

Heath: James (1629-64): 44, 45, 116; Brief Chronicle: 91, 103. Sir John: 44, 120, 64. Richard: 30, 44, 73. Sir Robert: 40, 44, 45, 77; Paradoxical Assertions: 77. Sir Thomas: 40

Heathen: learning: 51. Ethnics, Gentiles: myths corruptions of Biblical truth: 123; heroes: 123; virtues of: 123*. Wisdom: 123; ignorant of true felicity and highest good: 123; gods: 123; princes: 123

Heav'n Field (Denisburn): 49

Heaven: 31*, 44, 47*, 50*, 76, 90, 103*, 107*, 111*, 118, 141, 143, 32*, 36*, 71, 72*, 146. Biblical setting of: 119. Nature of: 47*. Not described in De Doctrina: 107. Platonic: 107. Real: 107. Contrasted to Hell: 47, 102. Council in: 50, 102. Gates of: 102. Pavement of: 102. Poetic treatment of: 102. Rebellion and war in: 102, 93. Light from: 143. Ladder to in M's Scala: 143. New: 143. Development in M: 107*. Imagery of the: 8*. Sought apart from God: 47. Development in Origen: 107*. Differences between Origen's and M's: 107*. Four ways of conceiving in Origen and M: 107*. An intellectual state in Origen and M: 107*. Jewelled Heaven scoffed at by Origen: 107*. M's jewelled Heaven is poetic truth: 107*. Origen's and M's ideas of very similar: 107*. Platonic in Origen and M: 107*. A real place in PL and De Doctrina Christiana: 107*. On the Empyrean: 89. Dialogue in: 118. Books Descriptions of: 93.

Order in: 93. "Inner Heaven": 93. Frame and magnitude of: 96. See also: War in Heaven

Heavenly bodies, ancient beliefs as to movement of: 89

"Heavenly Man": 122. See also: Earthy man; Old man; New man; Adam equated with Christ; St. Paul

Heavitree: 45

Heba: 32

Hebe: 44, 73, 90, 3. See also: Youth

Hebel, J. William: 122

Heber: Bp.: 120. Richard: 23, 44, 120

Hebert: Arthur G.: 93. Jacques René: 60

Hebrew Wife (Selden): 30, 3

Hebrews (book): 92; see also: Bible. Hebraic theology: 136. M's conception of Hebraic diety: 136. Hebraism, in SA: 143*. Hebraism: see Judaism

Hebrews: 50, 126, 3, 32*, 99. Status of blind among: 16. The disbelief in the existence of the soul: 113. Attitude toward polygamy: 113. Music: 121. Poetry: 139. God: 71. Traces of, in M's language: 88. Lit. superior to Greek: 93. Language: 40*, 42*, 44, 51, 70, 103, 3, 72. Transliterations of: Adam, Eden, Eve, Messiah, Satan: 119. Variant translations based on: breathe, brooded, expanse, wind: 119. Grammar School Teaching of: 42*. M's study of: 20, 40, 44. Names of God: 41, 142. Poetry: 142. Verse, M's: 40. Poets: 30. Scriptures: 40. Sources of the myth of the Fall: 113. Christian theology in PL: 83.

Hebrides: 49, 73, 72. See also: Iles

Hebron (Chebron): 49, 73. Mount: 32

Hebrus: 144, 72. River: 44, 49, 73, 90

Hecaerge: 73, 3

Hecate: 1, 73, 90, 144, 25

Hecatompylos: 19, 49, 73, 144. See also: Hispahan

Heckscher, William C.: 123

Hecla, Mt.: 19

Hector: 1, 2, 17, 56, 60, 73, 90, 123. See also: Homer

Hecuba: 44, 73, 92

Hedd: 45

Hedda Gabler: 1. See also: Ibsen

Hedges, Sir Charles: 44

Hedio: 44, 73

Heer, Friedrich: 122

Heesen (Hassia): 49

Hegel: Fredrich: 7, 86, 113, 114, 139, 25. G. T. W.: 39. Georg: 72

Hegemonicon: 3

Hegendorff, Christopher: 20, 40

Hegenius: 44. See also: Hugenius

Hegesippus: 73

Heidegger: Johann Heinrich: 32, 93. Martin: 1, 39

Heidel, Alexander: 36, 64

Heidelberg (Heidelberga): town: 44, 49. Catechism: 40, 32. Univ.: 40

Heidenheim, Wolf: 40

Heider, Wolfgang: 40

Heidfeld, Hans: 40

Heidt, William G.: 142. Angelology of the Old Testament: 142

Heigham: Mr.: 45. Sir Thomas: 40, 44

Heilman: Professor: 131. R.: 23. Robert: 14. Robert B.: 128. Robert E.: 93

Heimann, Adelheid: 93

Heimbach, Peter: 16, 19, 28, 30, 31, 44*, 73, 108, 111, 128, 136, 144, 38, 91, 137, 3, 94. Letter of, mentioned: 55. M's letter(s) to: 16, 55

Heine, Heinrich: 136

Heinsius: Daniel: 40, 44*, 123, 92, 93, 99, 101, 117, 64. David: 10. Nicholas: 6*, 44*, 70, 103, 91, 64

Heinzel, Richard: 93

Heisenberg, Werner: 138

Heisig: 10

Hekalôth Rabbati: 142

Helder, Thomas (bks.): 44

Hele, John: 44

Helen of Troy: 2, 90, 92, 72, 70, 73

Helen(a): 144. See also: Pontia (Salmasius' maid)

Helena, St.: 73

Heliand (Old Saxon Biblical epic): 74, 36

Helicon: 56, 73, 90, 111, 72, 92

Heliocentric universe. See Copernicus

Heliodorus: 2, 40, 122, 133

Heliopolis (Thebae): 144, 143

Helios: 1, 90. See also: Sun

Helium: 89

Hell: 17*, 41, 44, 47*, 50*, 60*, 63, 73, 89, 98, 103, 107*, 76*, 111*, 113, 128*, 141, 142, 3, 143, 32, 36*, 71, 72*, 78, 146, 25. Description of: 47, 89, 76. Different conceptions of: 89. Satan Traverses: 143. A horrible dungeon: 50, 143. Mouth of in Queen Mary's Psalter: 143. Room for man in: 143. Hierarchy: 93. Music: 93. "Inner Hell": 93. Composition and nature of: 96. Entropy of: 96. Theories of: 109. Contrasted with the Garden of Eden: 48. Biblical setting of: 119. Council in: 50, 102. Gates of: 50, 102. Location of: 102, 142, 93, 120, 89. Causeway: 120, 143. Creativity: 120. Fear of: 47. Light: 120. 1st view of: 76. In Satan: 76. As forecast: 76. Contrast with Heaven: 47, 76, 102. Images for: 76. Related to War in Heaven: 76. Creation of: 93, 120. Torments: 93, 143. Fire: 93. Created before world in De Doctrina: 107*. External to world in De Doctrina: 107*. External to world in PL: 107*. Fire punitive rather than curative in M: 107*. A physical place in De Doctrina: 107*. Physical in Origen: 107*. Psychological: 107*. The punishment of loss: 107* Hell-hounds: 128

Hell-mouth: 19

Hell's triennial Parliament: 65

Helladius: 38

Helle: 90

Hellenic: thought: 51. Influence on M: 52. Hellenism: 70, 71. IN PL, SA: 143. Explanation of term: 71. See also: Greece

Hellespont: 19, 44, 49, 73

Helligelandt: 49

Helmer, N.: 109

Helmes, Master: 40

Helmholtz, H. L. F. von: 16

Helmingham, co. Suffolk: 44

Helmont: Franz M.: 117. Jean Baptiste van: 7, 114. Mercurius: 7

Helplessness, as theme in SA: 125*

Helvetia: 73, 3

Helvetius: 7. J. F.: 128

Helvicus, Christophorus: 73

Helvidius Priscus: 18, 73

Helwys, Thomas: 114, 147. A founder of the Baptists: 147. A Short Declaration of the mistery of iniquity: 147

Heman: 73

Hemans, F. D.: 58

Hemera: 90. See also: Day

Hemingius (Hemmingsen, Niels): 44, 54, 73, 93

Hemingway, Ernest: 35, 95, 109, 137

Hemphill, George Troxell: 66

Hemsterhuys: 3

Henaeus, Andreas: 65

Henault: 49. See also: Dell; Elversham; Esthambruges; Hania; Scaldis

Hench, Gerard: 44

Henderson: 120. Alexander: 51, 144, 38. G.: 58. S.: 58. T. F.: 44. T. S.: 58

Hendrickson, G. L.: 66

Hendry, George, on freedom and grace: 47

Henham, J.: 58

Heninger, S. K., Jr.: 100, 93, 25

Henley, co. Oxon.: 44. Henley-on-

Thames: 45

Henley: 45. J.: 58. Pauline: 44. Robert: 44, 45. S.: 58

Hennessy, George: 40

Henri: II: 93. IV: 83*. Charles, Prince of Tarentum: 44. See also: Henry

Henrietta Maria, Queen of Eng.: 6, 29, 33, 40, 44, 103, 116, 136, 109, 137, 21, 64

Henry: I: 73, 103. II: 51, 73. II of France: 33, 64. III of France: 64, 73; his Ordre du Saint Esprit: 38. IV: 45; of Germany: 52. IV, of France: 6, 64. V, of Eng.: 44. VI, of Eng.: 40, 45, 32, 64. VII, of Eng.: 40, 44, 45, 73. VIII: 29, 33, 40*, 42, 44, 51, 52, 18, 64, 73, 83*, 103, 113, 121, 116, 3, 39, 71, 131. Henry V (Shakespeare): 118, 3. Henry IV (Shakespeare): 3, 88, 131. See also: Henri

Henry de Bracton, De Legibus et Consuetudinibus Angliae: 83

Henry: Earl of Huntington: 40; Historiarum Libri VIII: 82. Earl of Northumberland: 40. Grandfather of Louis XIV of France: 44. Prince: 20, 40, 45, 116, 21; Prince of Wales: 39, 93, 64*. Of Nassau (Nassovius), Frederick-Henry: 73, 20, 44

Henry: G. W.: 128. H. T.: 126. J.: 58. L. (N.) H.: 44. Matthew: 115; A Method for Prayer: 115. Nathaniel H.: 44, 59, 107, 93; M's materialism derives from Hobbes, the Socinians, the Baptists: 107

Henshaw: George: 44. Bp. Joseph: 93

Heorot: 36

Hepburn, Ronald W.: 93

Hephaestus: 2, 90, 141, 92, 25

Hepple, N.: 58

Heptameron, The: 142

Heptaplomeres: 78

Hera y dela Varra: 65

Hera: 2, 90. See also: Juno

Heraclidae (Euripides): 70

Heraclides Ponticus, Allegoriae: 44

Heraclitus: Ponticus: 1, 40, 44. The Mythographer: 142

Heraclitus: 1, 4, 23, 73, 124, 88, 5. Logos, philosophy of: 48. Heraclitean: 125. Heraclitus Ridens: 116

Herald (Lycidas): 104

Herald. See Ryley, William

Heraldry: 40. M's knowledge of: 8

Heraldus, Mr.: 44

Heraud, John Abraham (protege of Southey): 87*. Miltonic Satan in works of: 87. The Descent into Hell: 87. Judgement of the Flood: 87

Herberstein, Sigismundus: 19

Herbert: Sir Edward, Lord Chief Justice: 44. Lord Edward of Cherbury: 10, 15, 30, 113, 114, 130, 86, 128, 132, 32. George: see separate entry. H. W., translations by: 58. Sir Henry: 29. Mrs.: 86. Magadalen: 23. Lady Mary: 29. Sir Thomas: 88. W.: 58. William: 45, 54, 87. Sir William of Swansey: 40

Herbert, George: 4, 8, 15*, 17, 23, 27, 37, 40, 42, 44, 35, 59, 68, 76, 79, 81*, 84, 86, 114, 125, 127, 128, 132, 145, 11, 39, 53, 72, 91, 93, 101, 109, 115, 64, 130, 131, 146, 55, 25. Influence on Vaughan: 81*. Works: Eucharistic poems, Temple, "Agonie," "Altar," "Banquet," "Churchporch," "Decay," "Dedication," "H. Communion," "Invitation," "Obedience," "Peace," "Pilgrimmage," "Sacrifice," "Superliminare": 81

Herbinus, Johannes: 32

Hercules, Great cluster in: 89

Hercules: 1, 2, 8, 27, 29, 44, 60, 68*, 70, 73, 90*, 122, 123*, 3, 32, 46, 72, 92*, 146, 25. As type and prototype of Christ: 79, 46. As emblem of heroic virtue: 123. Choice of: 123. Parallel with Samson: 123. Parallel with Christ: 123. Rebukes Comus: 143. Hercules' Pillars (Herculean Pillars, Herculeis Columnae): 49, 73, 3; see also: Cales; Gibralter

Hercynian Wilderness: 49, 73, 3

Herder: 7. Johann Gottfried von: 87, 32

Herdesianus, Henricus Petreus, Dedicatory epistle and Preface to Fracastoro's Joseph: 74

Herebort, Professor: 44

Hérédia, José-Maria de: 15

Heredity and human weakness: 31

Hereford: Mr.: 45. Mrs.: 44

Hereford: 45, 49. Public Library: 44

Herefordshire: 44, 45, 49

Herennius, C.: 20

<u>Heresiography</u> (Ephraim Pagitt): 147

Heresy: 9*, 51, 114. Definition of, M's: 107, 51. Heresies: 107*; held in common by M and Origen: 107*; in M: 141, 107*; Origen's listed by St. Jerome: 107*; M's: 109; M anticipates charges of: 107. Heretical ideas in Satan's speeches: 113. Imagery: 8

Herford, C. H.: 12, 111, 123, 135, 141, 39, 64

Hergest, William: 93

Hering: Fran. (sic): 40. Samuel: 114

Heriot, G. (poem on West Indies): 58

Herkless, John: 40

Herkules. See Hercules

Herles, Charles: 93

<u>Hermaica Gymnasmata</u>: 40

Hermann: 94. Of Reichenau: 93

Hermans, Jacobus: 83. M's idea of perfection like and unlike that of: 83

Hermaphroditism: 128

Hermas: 73, 83

Hermelink, Heinrich: 93

Hermeneutical principles, M's: 79

Hermes Trismegistus: 4, 40, 42, 52, 57, 73, 81, 112, 113, 114, 118, 142, 88, 93, 25. And Hermeticism: 128. <u>Pimander</u>: 142

Hermes: 1, 7, 57, 73, 90, 128, 3, 72, 92, 25. See also: Mercury

Hermesianax: 40

Hermetic: ideas: 93. Writings, rabbinical treatments of Greek ideas in: 41. Hermeticism: 5, 81, 113, 123, 72, 25

<u>Hermetica</u> (Ficino): 112, 36

Hermetica, etc.: 57

Hermione: 90, 92

Hermippus: 90

Hermit, M's friend in Naples: 44

Hermogenes: 3, 53, 71, 82, 88. Gen. to Constantius: 116. <u>Progymnasmata</u>: 20, 70, 73, 112

Hermolaus Barbarus: 40

Hermon (Senir): 49, 73

Hernando: 123. See also: Gratiani

Herne: Hierene: 29. Robert: 93. See also: Hearne

<u>Hero and Leander</u> (Marlowe): 134, 139, 71

Hero: 27*, 11*, 123*, 146. Feast: 123. Order between man and daemon: 123. Of PL: 123. As godlike: 123. Of poem: 123. Principal: 123. As aerial spirit: 123. As demigod: 123. As orator: 123. Definition of: 123. As purified soul: 123. As martyr and saint: 123. Parentage of: 123*. Nine Worthies: 123. In PL: sources for conception, his blindness, relation to father, role of Sin: 11. In SA: relation to Chorus, contradictions of role, sacrifice of, as a representation: 11. Heroic: 125; morality: as theme in SA: 125*; and practical grasp: 125; and the return to the community: 125; play: 145; tradition, revolution of: 123; couplet: 40; poems, directed primarily to military: 123; poetry: 70; see also: Community. Heroical love (amor nobilis): 122

Herod: 60, 125, 72. Antipater: 73, 38. Son of Antipater: 38. The Great: 73. Agrippa I: 73

Herodotus: 19, 40, 57, 60, 89, 90, 128, 144, 26, 32, 71, 82, 21

Heroic virtue: 60*, 123*. Distinction between philosophical and poetic ideals of: 123. Definition of: 123. Comprehends all other virtues: 123. Eminence of: 123. Splendor of: 123. Divine likeness essence of: 123. See also: Divine Image; Godlike man; Godlikeness

<u>Heroides</u> (Ovid): 20, 73

Heroism: 67, 37*, 46*, 93. False, of Satan: 37*. "Epic" heroic encounters: 37*. Abdiel's: 37*, 46. Loyal angels as heroes: 37*. And faith: 37*. Christian, non-physical: 37*. Of the epic voice: 37*. The reader's: 37*; see also: Reader. Demonic: 46. Revolutionary: 46. False: 45*. And poetry: 106. See also: Satan, as demonic hero; Son of God; Christian heroism; Heroic Virtue

Heron, Germain: 79. See also: Hearne

Herrick: 121, 120, 132. Marvin T.: 6, 40, 122, 123, 39. Robert: 35, 15, 59, 69, 77, 84, 86, 105, 128, 39, 91, 131, 150; <u>Devotional Poets</u> (ed. Newbolt): 77

Herring: Francis: 40. Michael: 44

Herringman, Henry (bks., pr., 1653-92): 44, 91

Herrtage, Sidney: 128

Herschel: Sir John: 89; quoted on globular clusters: 89; on Venus: 89. Sir William: work of in sideral astronomy: 89; observations of the Milky Way: 89; method of star gauging: 89; discovery of binary star systems by: 89; on the number of stars in the great cluster in Hercules: 89

Hersfeld (Herefeldt). See William VI

Herskovits, Melville J. and Frances S.: 118

Hertel, François: 65

Hertford, Earl of: 45

<u>Hertford, The History and Antiquities of the County of</u>: 45

Hertford: co. Essex: 44. Town: 49. Hertfordshire: 40, 45, 49

Hertz, Neil: 14

Herveus Burgidolensis: 123

Hervey: 130, 149. J.: 58

Hesdena: 49

Hesebon: 2, 49, 73, 144. See also: Seon's Realme

Hesiod: 1, 2, 4, 8, 19, 23, 27, 37, 40*, 44, 56, 57, 18, 64, 58, 60*, 68, 70, 73, 77, 89, 90*, 114, 118, 120, 122, 123, 129, 133, 141, 142, 3, 26, 32, 36, 53, 71, 72, 88, 93, 97, 130, 146, 148. Works: <u>Theogony</u>: 144; <u>Works and Days</u>: 74

Hesione: 92

Hesperides (Hesperian): 19, 49, 73, 90*, 144. Apples of: 123. Garden of the: 32. Hesperian Gardens: 118. Hesperean: 19. Hesperus: 1, 73, 89, 32; evening star: 90; in <u>Comus</u> and <u>Masque of Hymen</u>: 143; fair gardens of: 143. Hesperia: 73. See also: Spain

Hesse: Hermann: 39. Maurice, Landgrave of: 44. William (or Maurice), Landgrave of: 44. See also: William VI

Hessels, Jan. F.: 40

Hessus: 56. Helius Eobanus: 64

Hestia: 90. See also: Vesta

Heston: 44

Hesychius: 90, 123

Heterocosm: 146

Heth: 3

Hethe: 45

Hetherington: 120

Hethersett: 45

Hethfield: 49

Heton: Anne: 91. Martin (1552-1609): 91

Hetruria (Hetruscan): 73. See also: Italian

Hevelius, Johann: astronimical work of: 89. Publishes Horrox's treatise: 89

Heveningham, Mr.: 44

Hewett (Hewet): Sir John: 45. Margaret (Cope): 45. Sir Thomas: 45. See also: Huet

Hewler, Mr.: 45

Heworth Moor: 49, 73

Hewson, Col. Sir John (regicide, d. 1662): 44, 91

Hexaemeron: by Georgius Pisides: 65. By St. Ambrose: 65. By St. Basil: 65

Hexameron: 50. Hexaemeral lit.: 63, 102

Hexameter, suitable for translations: 58

Hexham (Hagustald): 49

Hexham, Henry: 40

Hexham's Mercantor: 19*

Hey, J.: 58

Heydon: Sir Christopher: 114. J. F.: 128. Joan: 44, 54, 114, 116, 142; Theomagia, or the Temple of Wisdom: 142

Heyford, Warren: 45

Heylin: 94. John: 88

Heylyn (Heylin), Peter: 15, 19*, 24*, 40, 44, 77*, 102, 114, 128, 144, 32, 93. Cosmography: 88, 77

Heywood: Francis: 45. Jasper: 40, 59. Thomas: 40, 41, 65, 77*, 108, 123, 133, 144, 36, 82, 93, 142*, 148. The Hierarchie of the Blessed Angels: 36, 65, 142

Heyworth, P. L.: 14

Hezekiah: 73, 123, 64

Hibbert, Samuel: 142. Sketches of the Philosophy of Apparitions: 142

Hibernia: 44. See also: Ireland

Hickes: 88. George: 116*

Hickey, Emily: 71

Hickman: Margaret: 45. Spencer (bks., 1670-72): 44, 91

Hicks: Sir Baptist: 40, 44. William: 44

Hidaspis River: 19

Hiding, M in: 44

Hidragorre, as epic machinery: 123. See also: Gratiani

Hieatt, A. Kent: 100, 64

Hierapolis: 49, 73

Hierarchie of the blessed Angells: 36 65, 142

Hierarchy: 54, 67, 122*, 140. Hell: 93. Sublunar world: 93. Religious and moral values of: 143. And M: 143. In Heaven: 93. Hierarchies, list of in PL: 41. See also: Scale of Nature

Hierocles: 44, 60, 114, 123

Hieroglyphics: 123

Hierome, St. See Jerome

Hieron: I of Syracus: 93. John: 40. Samuel: 54

Hieron: 73

Hieronymus: 100. See also: Jerome

Hierurgia Anglicana, use of staff: 104

Higden, Ranulph: 32, 93, 64

Higford, William: 54

Higgins: Christopher (Scotch pr.): 44. John: 40, 93. Mrs. Napier: 45

Higginson, J. J.: 33

High (complicated): 121

High: master at St. Paul's School: 40. Steward of the univ.: 40

High: Anglicans: 136. Church: 40, 87. Church Party: 51

High: Commission, Court of: 143, 94. Court of Justice: 9, 84, 103, 116. Court of Parliament: 116

High: Holborn: 44, 103, 94. Street: 45. Language, ideal of, Bentley's, the Richardsons': 88

Higher Middle Party: 51

Highet, Gilbert: 15, 21

Highgate, London: 44*

Highlands, Scotland: 44

Highmore: J.: 58. S.: 58

Higinus (Hyginus): 73. Julius: 128

Hilard: family: 45. (Hillard, Hilord), John: 45

Hilarius: 65, 113.

Hilary: 57, 78. St.: 102, 99*. Of Arles: 32, 36*; Metrum in Genesim: 36*. Of Poitiers, St.: 73, 77, 36, 93; Homilies on the Psalms: 36

Hildebert: 36; Theological Treatise: 36.

Hildebertus Cenomanensis: 65. "Sermones de Sanctis": 74. See also: Hildebert

Hildebrand: 36. St. Gregory VII: 52, 116

Hildebrandt, Franz: 93

Hilder, Thomas: 54, 93

Hilderbrand, Grace H.: 44

Hildersham, Arthur: 40

Hildreth, W.: 58

Hildyard, Rev. J.: 44

Hill of virtue: 123

Hill: 3. A.: 58. Aaron: 117. Abraham: 44. B. M.: 45. Birkbeck: 92. Dr. Claude: 44. D.: 97. D. M.: 105. Henry (pr.): 44. J., on PL: 58. Richard: 44, 58, 99. Thomas: 44, 45, 59, 77, 103, 128; Schoole of Skil: 77. Walter M.: 44. William: 44, 54

Hillard. See Hilard

Hillebrand, H. N.: 40

Hillel: 68

Hills, Henry (publisher): 10, 116, 97

Hillyard, Edward: 45

Hilord. See Hilard

Hilton: John: 121. Walter: 7, 97; the Scala Perfectionis: 143

Himelick, R.: 122

Himerides: 49, 73

Himes, J. A.: 113, 128, 129

Himinbjorg: 32

Hinchliffe: J.: 58. W., influenced by L'Allegro, quotes Lycidas: 58

Hind and the Panther: 71

Hinde, William: 93

Hinduism: 34. Hindus, and astronomy: 89

Hinguor, Danish leader: 44

Hinkle, Beatrice: 75

Hinnom, Valley (Vale) of (Gehenna, Tophet): 19, 49, 143, 144, 72. See also: Opprobrious Hill; Siloa; Soloman, garden of

Hinson. See Powell alias Hinson

Hinson: Anne (Powell): 45. Thomas: 45

Hinton, R. W. K.: 60

"Hints to a Young Author": 117

Hinxsey, North: 45

Hipparchus: 40, 89, 112, 100

Hippias Minor (Plato): 112

Hippias: 73, 123

Hippisley, Sir John: 44, 103

Hippius, Fabianus: 40

Hippocrates: 4, 16, 73, 112, 128, 3. Twins of: 144

Hippolytus of Rome: 60, 77, 107, 93. Four phase Logos: 107. Logos immanent within God develops into external Word: 107. The Word a creature: 107. Works attr. to Origen: 107. Works not known to M: 107. Philosophumena: 77

Hippolytus: 5

Hipponensian: 73

Hippotades: 73, 90

Hircania(n): 44, 144

Hirschberg, Julius: 16

Hirschhorn, Mrs. J. B.: 44

Hirst, Désirée: 93

Hispahan: 19, 49, 73. See also: Tauris; Hectompylos

Hispaniola: 49

Histoire entière et veritable du Proces de Charles Stuart: 44

Historia de Combustione Buceri et Fagii: 73

Historia regni Italici (Sigonius): 94

Historia Animalium (Aristotle): 3

Historia Apocrypha Virginis Deiparae: 123

Historia Orbis Terrae: 88

Historia Scholastica: 65

Historiae Parlimenti (attr. to M): 44

Historian Unmask'd: 116

Historians: 40, 51

Historiarum: 62

Historic Society of Lancashire and Cheshire, Transactions: 44

Historical and Poetical Medley, The: 117

Historical argument, rhetoric: 51

"Historical criticism": 86

Historical narrative: 51

Historical writing, M's views on: 44*

Historical Account of...two Corruptions of Scripture: 78*. See also: Two Letters

Historical Manuscripts: Commission: 40, 44. Reports of the Royal Commission on: 45

Historical Register of...Cambridge: 40*

Historical Society of Pennsylvania: 44

Historical-mindedness: 34

Historical: points of view in early commentaries, and in Warton: 88. Method of investigation the main result of 18th c. M annotation: 88. Sense lacking in Hume, in Bentley: 88. Approach in Pearce's treatment of M's errors, and of his language: 88. Arguments, Pearce prefers logical to: 88. Perspective, unsatisfactory sense of, in Thyer's notes, in Newton's comments: 88. And social setting of M's poetry examined by Warton: 88. Treatment of metrical problems, Todd's: 88

Historie of Heaven: 65

Historie of Tithes (Selden): 147

History: 17*, 19, 40, 51, 144, 11*, 96*, 25. Relation to poetry and theology: 123*. M's conception of God in: 113. Painting: 97*. The self and: 11. As providential: 11. As a labyrinth: 11. Images: 8*. In PL, PR: 11. And the image (idol): 11. Cyclical: 93. Linear: 93*. Lessons of: 93. And mythology: 48; see also: Myth; Mythology. Books: 40.

History of the Eng. Language, A (Baugh): 135

History of the Parliament of England. See Thomas, May

History of the Pestilence, The (Wither): 135

History of the Wicked Plots: 116

History of the Works of the Learned: 44, 88

History of the World (Raleigh): 65, 134, 88. See also: Sir Walter Raleigh

History of Alexander the Great (Pseudo-Callisthenes): 74

History of Britain (M's): 16, 20, 113, 116, 88, 55. M's account: 55. See also: Milton, John, Works

History of Classical Scholarship (Sandys): 3

History of Independency (Clement Walker): 103, 147

History of King Leir and his Three Daughters: 88

History of Parliament, Biographies of the members of the Commons House: 83

History of Passive Obedience Since the Reformation: 116

History of Sacrilege (Sir Henry Spelman): 147

History of St. Paul's School, A (McDonnell): 20

History of Thomas Ellwood, Written by Himself: 70, 3

History of Timur Bec (Cherifeddin Ali): 88

Histriomastrix, or a Scourge for all Stage-Players (William Prynne): 103, 121, 147, 71, 94

Hitchcock, Edward, The Religion of Geology: 87

Hitler, Adolf: 15, 60, 134, 136

Hittites: 32

Hive: Or a Collection of thoughts on Civil, Moral, Sentimental and Religious Subjects, The: 115

Hoadly: Benjamin, influenced by L'Allegro and Il Penseroso: 58, 115; The Measures of Submission to the Civil Magistrate Considered: 115. J., influenced by M: 58

Hoard, Samuel: 114, 93

Hoare, Richard: 44

Hoban. See Hobart

Hobart: family: 40, 44. Sir Henry: 40, 44, 45. Sir Herbert and family: 40. (Hoban), Nathaniel, Master in Chancery: 44, 45. Sir Robert H.: 44. Lt. Col. Sir Vere: 44

Hobbes, Thomas: 1, 6, 9*, 10, 12,

15*, 17, 18, 23, 27, 28, 35, 37, 40, 44*, 51, 56, 60*, 79, 83, 86, 89, 102, 103, 113, 114*, 116, 122, 123, 128, 134, 120, 132, 142, 144, 145, 147, 32, 39, 80, 93, 94, 137, 148, 150, 55, 64, 130. Claims reading of the classics a cause of the rebellion: 147. Compared with M on toleration: 147. On man's slavery: 147. On persecution: 147. On fables: 53. Works: Answer to Davenant's Preface to Gondibert: 74; The Leviathan: 142, 91; Behemoth: 91; De Corpore Politico: 147

Hobbinol (pastoral name for Gabriel Harvey): 83*

Hobhouse, T.: 58

Hoblyn, R.: 58

Hobson Street, Cambridge: 40

Hobson: Mr.: 44, 45. Capt. John (1597-1657): 28, 44, 59, 120, 91, 55. Lady Margaret (Ley): 44, 120. Thomas: 58, 128, 137; Duport's lines on: 40. Thomas (college carrier): 40*, 44, 121, 103. William: 44

Hobson: poems: see Milton, John, Works. Epitapns on: 132, 133; see also: Epitaphs on Hobson

Hoby, Sir Thomas: 60

Hochban, John I.: 93

Hodge: A. A.: 63. Charles: 63

Hodges: Hugh: 44. Richard: 45

Hodgkin, Thomas (pr.): 44

Hodgkinson: Henry: 44, 45. James (scrivener): 40, 44, 45

Hodgson: Leonard: 93. Ralph: 65

Hodnet (Hodnitt), co. Salop: 44

Hodson, William: 58, 93

Hodwell: 45

Hody, Humphrey: 18

Hoe, Robert: 44

Hoff, "Widow": 10

Hoffman: Charles Fenno: 98. F. J.: 23

Hoffmann: D.: 41. Ernst: 93

Hoffsten, Ernest G.: 40

Hofmannsthal, Hugo von: 39

Hofmannswaldau, Christian Hofmann von: 10

Hofsten, N. von: 128

Hog, William (Latin trans. of M): 58, 117. See also: Hogg

"Hog Latin": 40

Hogarth, William, The Analysis of Beauty: 97*, 146, 117

Hogg: T.: 58. William (Gulielmus Hogaeus): 73, 91, 94

Hogg's Instructor: 87

Hojeda, Diego de: 64

Holaday, Allan: 93

Holbeck, Martin: 40

Holbein: 18, 35, 90. H.: 97

Holborn, co. Middlesex: 44

Holborn, London: 44

Holbourne, Sir Robert: 91

Holbrook, co. Suffolk: 44

Holburne: Sir Thomas William, 5th Baronet of Menstrie: 44. Of Menstrie Museum of Art: 44

Holchar. See Houlker

Holcombe, Henry: 115. The 1st Fruits, in a Series of Letters: 115

Holcroft: Sir Henry: 44. T.: 58

Holden, John (bks.): 44

Holding: Dr.: 44. (Holling), Mr.: 44

Holdisworth, An Answer without a Question: 88

Holdsworth: E.: 58. Richard: 40*, 93

Hole, Richard: 58, 117

Holford, M.: 58

Holidays at St. Paul's School: 40

Holiness: 24, 123, 122*. See also: Divine Image

Holinshed, Raphael: 17, 40, 88, 93. Chronicles: 103, 82*

Holker. See Houlker

Holkham Bible Picture Book, creation,

Fall and redemption in, and PL: 143

Holland (Howland), part of Lincolnshire: 49

Holland (Low Countries): 44*, 49, 60, 103*, 150, 3. See also: Netherlands

Holland: Cornelius (regicide): 44. Earl of: 120. Henry Rich, 1st Earl of: 40, 44, 36, 93; works: Exposition of...Job: 74; Historie of Adam: 36. Lord: 103. Philemon: 19, 40, 128, 144, 93. Thomas: 40

Hollanda, Francisco de: 5

Hollander, John: 29, 14, 39, 93

Hollandse Mercurius: 44, 91

Hollar, Wenceslaus: 40

Hollengton, Josias: 44

Holles: 120. Frances: 40. John: 40

Hollingsworth, A. G. H.: 40, 44, 116

Hollins, John: 44

Hollis: J.: 53. Thomas: 44*, 116, 117, 55; admires M: 58. Thomas Brand: 44. Thomas, the Elder and Younger: 115. See also: Blackburne, F.

Holloway Road, London: 44

Holloway: Alice: see Harris, Alice. Alice (Darrell): 45. Alice (Leigh): 45. Charles: 44, 45. Christmas: 44, 45. Elizabeth (Powell): 44, 45. Francis: 45. Hewett: 44. John: 45, 86. "Necessity": 45. Sir Richard (judge): 44, 45. T. (engraver): 97. W.: 58

Holman, Philip: 45

Holmby (Holmeby): 49, 73

Holme: 49

Holmes: Abiel: 115; works: An Address Delivered before the American Antiquarian Society: 115; A Sermon, Preached at the Ordination of the Rev. Jonathan Whitaker: 115. E.: 105. Elizabeth: 81. (Homes), Nathaniel: 9, 38, 93. Nicholas: 44. Oliver Wendell: 137. R.: 58

Holsatia (Holstein). See Frederick III

Holste, Lukas. See Holstein, Lucas

Holstein, Denmark: 44

Holstein: 49, 3. Lucas (Holstenius, Librarian of the Vatican and Secretary to Cardinal Berberini): 6*, 7, 28, 30, 44*, 73, 26, 91, 87, 121, 94, 55

"Holy Sonnets" (Donne): 135

Holt: family: 45. Sir John: 40, 44. Ralph: 45. Richard: 44, 45. Robert: 45

Holton, co. Oxon.: 40, 44*, 45

Holy warfare: 122

"Holy Willie's Prayer": 71

Holy writ. See Bible

Holy Commonwealth: 44

Holy Community: 9*, 60

Holy Ghost: 71. See also: Holy Spirit; Trinity

Holy Land: 19, 103

Holy Scriptures: 63. See also: Bible

Holy Sepulcher: 72

Holy Spirit: 7*, 41, 42, 47*, 60*, 63*, 113, 144, 143, 22*, 32, 71, 25. Unimportance of in M's system: 113. How inspired: 143. In the Word: 143. Final judge: 143. And the regenerate: 143. Sacred Muse: 143. Office of: 143. Biblical authority for: 119. General operation of, in the Church, illumination of Scripture, in sacraments: 47. See also: Revelation

Holyband. See Desainliens

Holyday, Barton (Barten): 93

Holyhead: 144

Holyoke: Edward: 117. Francis (lexicographer): 44, 123

Holywell (Haliewell), co. Oxon.: 44

Holywood, John: 89, 114

Holzmann, Albert W.: 44

Holzschuler, Ludwig won: 118

Home rule: 51

Home, Henry (Lord Kames): 115

Homer II: 112

Homer, P.: 58

Homer: 1*, 2*, 4, 5*, 6, 8, 15*, 16, 17, 18, 19, 20, 23, 27, 28*, 30, 31,

34, 37, 40*, 41, 44*, 50, 51, 56*, 57, 58*, 59, 60*, 66, 70*, 73, 74, 76, 79, 81, 84, 86, 87, 89, 90*, 95, 98*, 100, 103, 105, 108, 111, 113, 114, 118*, 120, 122*, 123*, 126, 127, 128, 129*, 132*, 133, 136, 142, 144*, 145, 3*, 11, 26, 32*, 36, 39, 46*, 53, 62, 71, 72, 82, 88*, 92, 93, 94, 97, 101, 115*, 130*, 64, 146*, 149*, 148*, 150*, 117*, 25, 21*. As poeta doctus: 123. Thought no greater than M: 58*. And M compared: 146. Homeric mythology: 92. "Homeric" chain: see Chain. Homer (Chapman): 3. Works: Iliad: 2*, 35, 74, 77, 95, 46, 109, 115, 131,146*, 148*; structure of: 25; Odyssey: 2*, 74, 46*, 115, 146; Homeric Hymns: 90*. See also: Iliad; Odyssey; Achilles; Hector; Odysseus

Homes, Nathaniel. See Holmes, Nathaniel

Homilies: 40

Homosexuality: 141

Hondedei, Z.: 6

Hondius, Henrick. See Hexham

Hone: Joseph: 101. Ralph E.: 6, 44

Honerdus, Rochus: 117

Honestas: 123. See also: Honor

Honesty: 51. Honnete homme: 122

Honigmann, E. A. J.: 39

Honor: 122*, 51, 123*. As a subject of deliberate rhetoric: 123. As object of mananimity: 123. As constituent of happiness: 123. Lists: 40

Honoré d'Autun: 36. Elucidarium: 36

Honorius: Of Autun, staff as symbol: 104, 143, 93. Emperor: 21. Flavius: 73

Honyborne, Michael: 45

Honywood: Elizabeth: see Cotton, Eliz. Michael: 40, 64. Sir Robert: 44. Sir Thomas: 45

Hood: Edwin Paxton: 87; on M's sonnets: 87; on M's sublime universe: 87; on M's Satan: 87; on M and Dr. Johnson: 87; John Milton: The Patriot and Poet: 87. Thomas: 40

Hooke: 89. Richard: 93. Robert: 10

Hooker: 94, 130. Edward N.: 44, 93. Richard: 1, 9*, 15, 18, 17, 37, 40, 44, 52, 60, 66, 69, 73, 87, 102, 113, 114, 134, 32, 38, 39, 93*, 101, 146, 148, 150, 117; Laws of Ecclesiastical Polity: 37, 46; and M compared: 146. Thomas: 37, 93 Hooker, Thomas (pr.): 44

Hoole: 3. Charles: 20*, 40, 42, 56. John: 44, 58

Hooper, John: 73, 91

Hoopes: R. A.: 101. Robert: 17, 80, 93

Hope, Cape of: 73

Hope: 51*, 123*, 143. Tidings of: 143. And faith: 143. The ladder of: 143. In court masques: 143. Definition of: 123. Object of: 123

Hopeton, Lord: 136. And his shepherd: 136

Hopf, Constantin: 93

Hophni and Phine(h)as: 73

Hopkins Review: 44

Hopkins: C.: 58. Gerard Manley: 34, 40, 76, 81, 1, 15, 87*, 105, 84, 86, 95, 72, 130, 150; opinion of M: 87; sonnets of: 87; Miltonic elements in sonnets of: 87; interest in artistry of M's prosody: 87; interest in classic authors: 87; in classical tradition of Eng. lit.: 87; attitude toward M: 87; Sonnets: "Where art thou friend," "My love is lessen'd," "I must feed fancy," "You see that I have come to passion's end," "See how Spring opens with disabling cold," "Thou art indeed just, Lord": 87; anguish resulting from God's justice in his sonnets: 61. J. G.: 16. John: 40, 32, 91, 117. Matthew: 114, 142; The Discovery of Witches: 142. Richard: 44. Thomas: 44

Hopkinson: Francis: 115; works: Charity, Description of a Church, Dirtilla, The Battle of the Kegs, Ode on Music, The Miscellaneous Essays and Occasional Writings of Francis Hopkins, Esq.: 115. John: 32

Hopman, F.: 122

Hopper: Claude: 44. V. F.: 100

Hopson, Rachel: 120. John: see Hobson

Hopton, co. Suffolk: 44

Hopton: Elizabeth (Greere): 45. Robert: 45. Susanna: 81. Sybil: 45

Hopwood, C. H.: 45

Horace: 2*, 4, 6, 15, 17, 18, 20*, 27, 30, 31, 35, 40*, 44*, 47, 50, 56*, 57, 58, 59*, 60, 68, 70*, 73, 74, 79, 90*, 100, 103, 108, 112, 111, 114, 118, 121, 120, 122, 123, 125, 128, 132, 133, 145, 3, 26, 32, 53, 62, 71, 72, 82, 88, 92, 93, 94, 109, 115, 130, 131, 146, 64, 149, 117*, 21, 25. M's translations from: 58*. On decorum: 66. Works: "Quis multa gracilis," translated: 55; Art of Poetry: 39

Horatius: 123

Hore: family: 45. (Hoare), Thomas: 44, 45

Horing, William: 44. See also: Loring

Horizons: 128

Horlogium Hebraicum: 40

Horman, William: 40, 128

Horn: Caspar: 100. Georg: 93. Konrad: 40

Hornbook: 40

Horne: John: 114. Thomas: 44

Horneby: Joseph: 44. Nathaniel: 44

Hornechurch: 45

Horneck, Anthony: 10

Horney, Karen: 52

Hornius, G.: 88

Hornsey, London: 44

Horonaim: 49, 73, 144

Horoscope, M's: 128, 44

Horrell, J., on M: 80

Horror: 90, 136. Depends upon paradox: 136

Horrox, Jeremiah: 89*. Study of astronomy: 89. Acquaintance with Crabtree: 89. Work on Rudolphine Tables: 89. Investigation of Lunar Theory: 89. Detection of long inequality in Jupiter and Saturn: 89. Observation of transit of Venus, treatise of: 89. Treatise on defense of Kepler: 89. Scientific works: 89. Support of Copernicus: 89. Death: 89

Horseman: family: 45. Barnabus: 44, 45. Constance: 45. George: 45; see also: Furseman, George. John: 45. Nicholas: 45. Ralph (Raphael): 45. Samuel: 45

Horsepath Copse (Coppice): 44, 45

Horsepath, co. Oxon.: 44, 45

Horses: 40. Horseback riding: 40. Horse market: 40

Horsey, Sir George: 44, 45

Horsforth, co. York: 44

Horsley, J. C.: 97

Horsted: 49

Hortensius, Quintus: 73

Horton, co. Bucks.: 29, 40*, 44, 45, 51,

Horton: Kenneth T.: 115. Thomas: 40

Horton: 70, 113, 144, 103*, 112, 121, 3, 62, 71, 94, 109. M's stay at: 16, 19, 30, 40, 42, 44*, 113, 94

Hortus Adami: 65

Hortus Deliciarum: 143

Horus: 144, 72. Horus-Ra: 68

Horwood, Alfred J.: 16, 20, 40, 44, 63. A Commonplace Book of John Milton: 82

Hosea: 70, 73, 74. See also: Bible

Hosier, John: 44

Hoskins: Mr.: 44. Sir John (1634-1705): 10, 23, 145, 91. Martha: 44. William: 44

Hoskyns, John: 45. The Life, Letters, and Writings of: 45

Hosmer, J. K.: 9

Hospinian: 41

Hospital of St. James: 44

Hostels at Cambridge: 40

"Hot Gospellers": 103

Hotham: Charles (1615-72?): 7, 44, 91, 148. Durant: 7. Sir John: 7, 73, 144. Justice: 7

Hotman, Francis (François): 40, 73. Franco-Gallia: 82

Hotson, Leslie: 44

Hotspur: 1, 2

Hottinger: Johann: 1, 22. Prof. of theology: 10

Hotton, Rev. Godofred: 10, 44

Houbraken, Arnold (painter): 44

Hough, Graham: 122

Houghton (possible maiden name of M's maternal grandmother, Ellen Jeffries): 40

Houghton Library (Harvard): 44

Houghton Magna: 45

Houghton: Mr.: 44. Arthur A.: 91. John: 115; New Introduction to Eng. Grammar: 115. M. (engraver): 97. R. E. C.: 63

Houlker (Holchar, Holker), Thomas (attorney): 44, 45

Hounds-Law (Middlesex village): 49

Hounslow (Hunsloe), London: 44, 45*, 73

Hours at Home: 44

Hours: 2, 73, 90*. Dancing: 121

House bill to keep clergy out of secular affairs: 51

House of correction: 103

House of Commons: or, Debate in St. Gyle's Chapel, The: 117

House of Commons: 44, 51, 103. See also: Commons

House of Fame: 20, 111

House of Lords: 44, 51, 103*, 113. See also: Lords; Long Parliament

House, Humphrey: 12, 101

Houseman, James. See Huysman

Houses of Parliament, decoration of: 97

Houses, M's: 28*, 40, 94

Housman: A. E.: 12, 133, 141, 131, 150, 18, 35. John E.: 93

Hoveden: 3

Hovingh, P. F.: 36

How Doth the Holy City: 121

How: Samuel: 9, 79; Sufficiencie of the Spirits Teaching: 74. William (pr.): 40

Howard: Charles: 10, 40, 44; see also: Nottingham. Douglas: 64. Esme: 44, 58. Lady Frances: 39, 64. H.: 97. Henry: 128. Henry, Earl of Northampton: 114. Henry, Earl of Surrey: 56, 59, 64. J. J.: 44, 58. Katherine: 65. L.: 58. Leon: 23, 44, 107, 123, 143, 93, 115; M's retraction derived from Ramean logic: 107. Luke: 23. Margaret: see Cotton, Margaret. Lady Mary, Countess of Arundel: 45. N.: 58. Sir Robert: 44, 116, 130, 137. Theophilus: 44; see also: Suffolk, Earl of. Thomas, Earl of Arundel: 40, 44, 45, 64. de Walden, John Griffin, Baron, and Baron Braybrooke: 44. Lord William: 45, 116

Howarth: H.: 23. R. G.: 44; see also: Pepys

Howe, Samuel: 114

Howell: A. C.: 23, 93. A. G. F.: 5. Alexander: 44. Elizabeth (Powell): 44. James: 6, 8, 40, 44, 59, 120, 135, 145, 91; Epistoloe Ho-Elianae: 91. T. B.: 44. Thomas: 44, 45. Wilbur S.: 23, 40, 44, 123. William: 93

Howells, Elizabeth Lloyd: 44

Howes: Edmund: 93. John: 20, 97

Howgil, Francis: 7

Howitt: 94

Howland, John: 44

Howlet, Robert: 40

Howse, William: 44

Howson, J. S.: 44

Hoyle: C.: 58. F.: 34. Thomas (alderman of York, d. Jan. 30, 1650): 91, 103

Hoym, Count: 44

Hozeau: 89

Hrabanus Maurus: 40. See also: Raban

Hrothgar: 36

Huarte, John: 128

Hubba (Danish leader): 44

Hubba's Lowe, Chippenham: 44

Hubbard: Edith P.: 6, 44. John:

115; The American Reader: 115. Ruggles: 115

Hübener, Gustav: 102, 113

Hubert, Henri: 39

Hubner, Joachim: 10*

Hubris: 141*, 92. Definition of: 141. As phenomenon of consciousness: 141. The Greek sin: 141. And culture (science, arts): 141. And the Fall: 141. In relation to God: 141. In M's poetry, character: 141. See also: Satan; Power; Civilization; Processus Individuantionis; Hybris

Huckaby, C.: 85, 122

Huckell, J.: 58

Hucks, J.: 58

Huddesford, G.: 58

"Huddling": 40

Hudibras: 136

Hudson: Mrs.: 44. Rev. Mr.: 58. Dr. John: 44. Thomas: 122; Historie of Judith (trans. of Du Bartas Judit): 74

Hue and Cry after Cromwell, A: 59

Hueffer: family: 44. Francis: 59, 120

Hues, Robert: 40

Huet (Hewett): Beersheba (Bathsheba) Snelling: 44. Bp.: 32, 117. William: 44

Huetius (Huet, Pierre Daniel): 123

Hugenius (Hegenius): 44

Huggins: Richard: 45. Sir William: 7

Hugh: St.: 73. Of St. Victor: 24, 69, 79, 36, 32, 40, 42, 69, 77; staff as symbol: 104; works: "De Filia Jephthe," "De Scripturis," "Sermo LIX," "Sermo LXIII": 74; De Sacramentis: 74, 77, 36; Sum. Sent.: 77

Hughe, William: 93

Hughendon, co. Bucks.: 44

Hughes-Stanton, B.: 97

Hughes: Arthur: 128. Elizabeth: see Standard, Eliz. (Ashworth). G. R.: 44. H.: 58. J.: 58; influenced by L'Allegro and Il Penseroso, praises M: 58. John: 145. Merritt: see separate entry. Richard: 45. Thomas: 40, 44, 58, 114. William: 45

Hughes, Merritt Yerkes: 1, 5, 6, 15, 17, 18, 19, 23, 24, 29, 31, 33*, 37, 40, 44, 52, 56, 59*, 60, 63, 66, 68, 73, 74, 64, 75, 79, 81, 83, 95, 100, 102, 105, 107, 112, 110, 111, 116, 122, 123*, 125, 126, 127, 128*, 133, 134, 135, 142, 144, 143, 32, 53, 62, 91, 92, 93, 99, 101, 106, 109, 115, 137, 148, 21. On Hell: 143. On M's readers: 143. Works: ed. John Milton Complete Poems and Major Prose: 82, 48; "Christ...and the Renaissance Heroic Tradition": 74, 109; "M and the Symbol of Light": 74; PR, the Minor Poems, and SA: 74. See also: Milton, John, Complete Poems and Major Prose

Hugill, Lyla Guest: 44

Hugo of St. Victor. See Hugh of St. Victor

Hugo: 123, 133. Cardinalis (Hugo de Sancto Charo): 123. Victor: 1, 65, 113, 46, 131. See also: Tasso

Huguenots: 60. Huguenot Society Publications (and Proceedings): 40, 44

Hugwald, U.: 32

Huisman, Johannes A.: 100

Huizinga, Johan: 69, 122, 133, 39. And imagination in Middle Ages: 143

Hulbert, Viola Blackburn: 83

Hull: co. York: 44. Town: 49, 73

Hull: 103, 144. John: 93. R. F. C.: 64. T.: 58. William: 93

Hullah: 121

Hulme: F. W.: 97. T. E.: 12, 23, 76, 86, 108

Huloet, Richard: 40

Hulson: Diones: 44; see also: Partridge. John: 44

Hulton (Milton?), Mr.: 44

Hultzen, L. S.: 40

Human nature: M's conception of: 113. Feeling: 125*

Human Form Divine: 25

Humanism: 7*, 9*, 27, 34, 70, 83, 110, 144, 143. Classical in

Renaissance: 123*. Christian: 47, 11. Background of: 52. M's Christian: 143. And man's depravity: 143. Atheistical: 143. M as a: 52. Humanistic: education: 20*; see also: Education: humanistic theory: 51. Humanists: 51; responsible for curriculum at Paul's School: 20*. Humanitarian training: 8, 51

<u>Humanita del Figlivolo di Dio, La</u>: 117

Humanities: 40

Humanity: 47, 125. M's attitude toward and relations with: 137. The virtue of (communitas), in the Gorgias: 125. In Cicero: 125. M's treatment of: 125. And individual morality: 125. See also: Community; Heroic morality

Humbaba: 32

Humber (Abra) River: 44, 49, 73, 3

Humbert, Paul: 32

<u>Humble Advice and Earnest Desires of certain well-affected Ministers... of Oxon, and...Northampton</u> (Presbyterian protests): 147

<u>Humble Apology Of Some commonly called Anabaptists, The</u>: 116

<u>Humble Petition...Of Several Churches...in London, commonly (though falsly) called Anabaptists</u>: 147

<u>Humble Petition of the Brownists</u> (a plea for toleration): 147

<u>Humble Petition of Divers Well-affected</u>: 9

<u>Humble Petition of Many Thousands of Wives and Matrons, The</u>: 54

<u>Humble Petition of 1641</u>: 60

<u>Humble Proposals...for the... Propagation of the Gospel</u>: 9

<u>Humble Proposals of sundry Learned Divines</u>: 44

<u>Humble Proposals</u>: 59

<u>Humble Remonstrance, An</u>: 51, 103, 113, 136, 26

Humble: Anne: 120. George: 120. Sir William: 120

Hume: Alexander: 40, 44. David: 17, 37, 142, 32, 39, 71, 64, 115, 146, 117, 13; works: <u>Dialogues Concerning Natural Religion</u>: 142; <u>Essay on Natural Religion</u>: 142; <u>Essay on Miracles</u>: 142. J.: 58. Patrick: 1, 28, 37, 40, 41*, 57, 68, 73, 86, 102, 105, 116, 128, 142, 143, 145, 43, 88*, 91, 109, 117, 55; a schoolmaster: 94; <u>Annotations of M's PL</u>: 58, 142

Humfray, N.: 58

Humfrey: Job: 44. Richard: 123

Humiliation: in Messianic exemplar: 122. Christ's: 123*

Humility: 47, 83, 123, 143, 93. True: 143. And M: 143. Bernard, Benedict on: 143. 12 steps: 143. And love: 143. School of: 143. See also: Helplessness

Hummel, J. H.: 10

Humor: 66*, 92. Good: 51. M's: 8, 27, 40, 137. And realism valued by the Richardsons: 88. As relief in sublime passages, the Richardsons on: 88

Humours: 128*. In <u>Masque of Hymen</u>: 143. Theory: 8

Humpheys, A. R.: 86

Humphrey, Duke of Gloucester: 40

Humphrey, Laurence: 40

Humphreys: David: 115; <u>The Miscellaneous Works</u>: 115. Thomas: 44

Humphries: Rolfe: 104. Samuel: 44

Hungary: 49, 103

Hunger: 17, 31

Hungerford, Sir George: 44, 117

Hunnaeus: 40

Hunne, Richard (burned as a heretic): 147

Hunnis, William, <u>Life and Death of Joseph</u>: 74, 64

Hunnish: 51

Hunnius, Aegidius: 44, 73

Huns: 71

Hunsloe. See Hounslow

Hunt: Mr.: 44, 58. James: 114. John: 44, 45. Leigh: 16, 44, 58, 70, 86, 87, 133, 130, 146, 21; sonnets on lock of M's hair: 87; Shakespeare and M compared: 87; works: <u>An Answer to the Question What Is Poetry?</u>; <u>Autobiography</u>; <u>Conversation of Pope</u>;

Descent of Liberty; Don Giovanni; Essay on the Sonnet; Indicator; London Journal; Lord Byran and His Contemporaries; Milton; Mr. Moxon's Publications; Originality of M's Use of Proper Names; Wishing Cap Papers; Wordsworth and M: 146; On the Latin Poems of M, Some Account of the Origin and Nature of Masks: 146*; bibliography of his M criticism: 146. Prefaces: 146. R. W.: 44, 59. Richard: 45. Thomas: 116*. T. W.: 63

Hunter, Gleanings: 43

Hunter: Rev. Joseph: 40, 44*, 45, 58. William: 115; An Oration; Delivered in Trinity-Church, in Newport, on the 4th of July 1801: 115. William B.: 44, 60*, 123, 14, 39, 106, 48, 23, 75, 110, 128*, 142, 93, 115, 137; works: M on the Nature of Man: 48; "M on the Incarnation," "M's Arianism Reconsidered," "M's Theological Vocabulary": 74

Hunterian Museum, Glasgow: 44

Hunting of the Foxes (analysis of Independent strategy): 147

Huntingdon Literary Museum and Monthly Miscellany, The: 115

Huntingdon, Henry of: 73

Huntingdon: 3. City: 44. Huntingtonshire, co.: 44, 45

Huntingford, T.: 58

Huntington Library (Henry E.): 40, 44*. Huntington Library Quarterly: 44*. Huntington Library Bulletin: 44

Huntington: 49. Countess of: 29. Ferdinando Hastings, Earl of: 44. Henry W.: 44. Joseph: 115; A Plea Before the Venerable Ecclesiastical Council at Stockbridge: 115. Joshua: 115

Huntley: Mr.: 45. Frank L.: 128, 93; on M: 80. John: 44, 75, 123

Huntly, George: 33

Hunton, Philip (1604?-82): 44, 32. Kingship tract, A Treatise of Monarchy: 147, 91

Huon de Bordeaux: 32, 88

Huppé, Bernhard: 100

Hurd: 132. Bp. Richard: 4, 27, 33, 59, 68, 70, 88, 91, 117

Hurdidge, Francis (Hurdidgius Franciscus): 44

Hurdis, J.: 58*

Huré, J.: 100

Hurn, W.: 58

Hurst Castle: 103

Hurst: John: 44. Richard: 44

Hurwitz, S.: 141

Hus: 3

Husain, Itrat: 93

Husanus, Henricus: 65

Husband-wife relationship: 31

Husband, Edward (publisher): 44

Husbands, J.: 58

Huskinson, R. K.: 16

Huss(e), John: 51, 60, 73, 114

Husserl, Edmund: 39

Hussey: James: 44, 45. Thomas: 44

Hussie, Philip: 44

Hussites: 38

Hutcherson, Dudley R.: 110

Hutcheson, George: 74. Exposition of the Book of Job: 74

Hutchins: Edward: 68. George: 44. John: 44

Hutchinson: 121, 3, 94. Col.: 130. Anne: 23, 44. F. C.: 79. F. E.: 40, 44, 60, 81, 86, 110. G. Evelyn: 81. Mrs. Lucy: 38; Life of Col. Hutchinson: 37, 13. T.: 58. Thomas, on the Puritans in Massachusetts: 147

Hutchison, R. E.: 44

Huth: A. H.: 36. C. F.: 44

Hutter: 40

Hutton: Francis: 120. Henry: 40. J.: 4. James: 40. (Hatton), John (scrivener, M's father's servant): 44. Katherine: 120. Mary: 120. Richard: 44.

Huxley: 35, 94. Aldous: 142; on grace, predestination, salvation: 143; Ape and Essence: 142. Thomas Henry: 18, 58, 87, 113

Huygens: Christian: 10, 89, 128.

Constantyn: 10

Huysman, Jacob (Houseman, James, artist of M portrait): 44

Hyacinth: 1, 73, 90, 72

Hyades: 44

Hyaline: 128, 143

Hyas: 44, 73

Hybris: 68, 55. Eve's sin of: 31. See also: Hubris

Hydaspes: 49, 73, 144

Hydatius of Chaves: 93

Hyde Barton: 45

Hyde: Anne, Duchess of York: 45. (Hide), Miss: see Lowe, Mrs. Edward: 45, 103, 116, 38; see also: Clarendon, Earl of. Sir Nicholas: 44, 45. Lawrence (L. H.): 44. Sir Robert: 45, 116. Thomas: 40, 42. W.: 97. The, Ingatestone: 44

Hydra: 73, 90

Hyginus: 40, 90*

Hylas (son of Thiodamantaeus): 44, 73, 90

Hylkema: 7

Hyman: Lawrence W.: 110. S. E.: 141

<u>Hymen</u>: 29, 50, 73, 90, 143, 72

<u>Hymenaei</u> (Jonson): 29. Or <u>Masque of Hymen</u>: 143

<u>Hymen(a)eus</u>: 73

Hymettus: 49, 73, 3

<u>Hymn in Honor of Beauty</u> (Spenser): 70. <u>Hymne of Heavenly Beautie, An</u>: 12, 88. <u>Hymne of Heavenly Love</u>: 65*, 88

<u>Hymn on the Nativity</u>: 121

<u>Hymn to Aphrodite</u> (Sappho): 20

<u>Hymn to Cromwell, A</u>: 59

<u>Hymn to Jupiter</u> (Callimachus, trans. by Pitt): 88

Hymn: 121. Hymns: 40, 50. See also: Milton, John, PL VII

<u>Hymni nocturni</u>: 65

<u>Hymnus ante cibum</u>: 65

Hypanis: 49

Hyperborean: 44, 73, 32. People: 49. Heaven: 3. See also: Arctic

Hypercatalectic verses, Calton and Newton on: 88

"Hyperion" (Keats): 130

Hyperion(ios): 73, 90, 3. See also: Sun

Hyperius, Andreas Gerardus: 93

Hypostasis: 93. Meaning of: 96

Hypothesis, rhetorical term: 20. Hypothetical: counter-syllogisms: 51; enthymeme: 51

<u>Hypotyposis divini judicii</u>: 65

Hyrcania(n): 19, 49, 73. See also: Caucasus

Hyrcanus: I, John: 73. II, son of Alexander Janneaus: 38

Hyrcanus: 73

-I-

I., S. A.: 40

Iaccho (Bacchus): 73

Iago: 87

Ialdabaoth: 36

Iambic and Trochaic dimeters: 40

Iamblichus: 123, 142, 32, 93. <u>De Mysteriis Aegyptiorum, Chaldaeorum, Assyriorum</u>: 142

<u>I am the Resurrection</u>: 121

"I and my chimney": 98

Ianichius, Peter: 40

Iapetus: 1, 73, 90

Ibbitson, Robert (pr., 1646-61): 91

Iberia: 19. Iberian: 73; Dales: 49, 73

Ibis (Ibida): 73

Iblis: 1, 42, 123

Ibn Ezra: 1, 40, 41*, 63, 32; works: <u>Intro. to Pentateuch</u>: 41; <u>Yesod Mora</u>: 41. Abraham: 40, 22

Ibn Yunis: 89

Ibsen, Henrik: 1, 15, 111, 92. Peer Gynt: 149

Ibycus: 40

Icadius: 72

Icarius: 73

Icarus: 114, 141

Iccius: 49

Ice, origin: 128

Iceland: 19, 32

Iceni, the: 44

Icenorum, Stoam tuam: 73

Ickford, co. Bucks.: 44

Icombe: 45

Iconium: 49

Iconoclast: 11. In M's prose: 11. As basis of PL: 11. As Samson's final role: 11

Iconography: 29

Iconologia (Ripa): 29

Ictinus: 92

Id, actions in PL which derive from the: 118

Ida, Mt.: 2, 49, 73. See also: Crete; Ida

Ida: 49, 90. See also: Ida, Mount

Idaean(m): 73

Idatius of Chaves: 68

Idbury: 45

Idea of a University (Newman): 3

Idea of Law Charactered, The: 116

Idea of Nature in M's Poetry (Madsen): 111

Idea of Tyranny: 116

Idea: 51, 144; of creation: 93. Ideas: 5, 51*; properties and perception of: 96

Ideal: commonwealth: 51*. Environment: 51. Future curriculum: 51. Plan: 51. "Ideal Spectator," The: 70

Idealism: 141. Philosophic: 141

Ideality: poet's: 149. M's: 149

Idealization of harmony: 121

Idealization, the Richardsons', of M: 88

Ideals, classical and Christian: 51

Iden, Henry: 64

Idiotisme Lingua Grk.: 40

Idle River: 49

Idleness: 144

Idlestreet (Ilstreye), co. Herts.: 44

Idol(s): 60, 63. Poetic: 123

Idolatry: 47, 51, 122, 123, 11*, 143*, 46, 82. In SA: 11. In PL: 11*. The Church of Rome: 143. The Mass and: 143. Of stained windows: 143. And Reformation: 143. The new: 143. Foul: 143. In Judges: 143. Not tolerated: 143. Samson opposes: 143. Deteriorating influence of: 119. See also: Self-deification

Idumanian. See Chelmer

Idumanii: 73

Idumanius: 49

I duo primi Libri dell'Adamo: 65

Idyllic: features appreciated by the Richardsons: 88. Moods in Shakespeare, Peck on: 88

Ieremiel: 41

Ietzirah, Sefer (Hebraice Sepher Ietzira): 40

If that a sinner's sighs: 121. If ye love me: 121

Iffley, co. Oxon.: 44, 45

Ignatius: 57, 73, 125, 144, 44, 51. Loyola: 23. Of Antioch: 69; Epistle to the Philadelphians: 57, 82. Diaconus: 65, 36; Drama de Primi Parentis Lapsu: 36

"Ignavus satrapan," M's: 44

Ignesham: 49. See also: Benson

Ignis fatuus et ignis lambens: 128*

Ignoramus (Ruggles): 70

Ignorance: 47, 114*. Sectaries accused of: 114*. "Ignorance the mother of devotion": 114

Ignoto, son of Lady Roos: 44

Igraine (Iögernen): 44, 3

Ikonoklastes: 136. See also: Eikonoklastes

Il Penseroso: 58, 103, 113, 129, 72*. 55, 98, 112, 95, 100, 118, 144. Purpose in: 144. Together with L'Allegro: ascent, Melancholy, Mirth, music, speaker, stance, in, and structure of: 72. Imagery: 8. See also: L'Allegro

Ilarione da Verona: 74, 64. Crisias: 74

Ile-de-France, Paris: 44

Iles, Thomas: 45

Iliad: 2*, 8, 17, 27, 30, 50, 70, 111, 118, 133, 46, 71, 94, 130*. See also: Homer

Ilissus: 3. River: 44, 49, 73

Illaca: 73

Illinois, Univ. of: 44. Library of: 40

Illium (Ilion): 73, 90

Illumination: 47. See also: Holy Spirit

Illusion(s), demonic: 123, 125

Illustrated London News: 44

Illustration(s): rhetorical: 51, 97*. Of PL: 15, 97*. Of old editions referred to by Warton: 88. Development and techniques of book illustration: 97*. To Comus, SA, Minor Poems, L'Allegro, and Il Penseroso: 97*. Copious, from M and also in Dunster's edition: 88. No conclusions, only, in Hume: 88. Wealth of, in Warton's commentary: 88. Lack of adequate, in Addison's essays: 88. Warton's artistic manner of: 88. As a course of pictorial subjects: 97*

Illustrator(s): M's: 146. The task of the: 97. See also: Portraits; Milton, illustrations of

Illyria (Illiricum): 49, 73

Illyricus. See Flacius Illyricus

"I love thee not, Nell": 44

Ilstreye. See Idlestreet

Ilus: 73, 3

Image du Monde, L': 65

Image of Minds (Barclay): 3

Image Breaker. See Eikonoklastes

Image Unbroken: 103

Image(s): 69*, 11*, 143, 53, 96, 117*. Recreative vs. creative perception of: 118. Function of: 11. As double: 11. Of man: 11. Dr. Johnson's interpretation of: 11. Son as, Eve as: 11. Of God: 24*, 47, 81*, 93. Dumb: 143. And the unlearned: 143. Ulterior purpose: 143. Spiritual sense of: 143. And icons: 53. And discourse: 53. Divine: 48; see also: God's image and likeness in man. Of demonic: 47. See also: Discourse; Idolatry; Man; Rhetoric

Image, J.: 58

Imagery: conceptual: 110. Enameled: 110. Generic: 110. Light: 110. Nonvisual: 110. M's: 16, 34. In Dante and M: 143. Necessary in religion and poetry: 143. Style and: 141. Christian: see Symbolism

Imagery (continued): agricultural, alchemy, animal, the arts, astrology, astronomy, beauty, bee, beggars, Biblical, bird, blindness, body, books and learning, boyhood, building, business practice, Catholic religious, Christ, city life, classics, clothes, coin, color, comet, commerce, controversy, cooking/food, dance, darkness, dawn, deceit, derogatory, disease, drama, East Indian trade, engraving, eyes, family life, filth, fire, fishing, flowers, fly, folk lore, games/sports, geography, gloss, hands, hawkers, Heavens, heraldry, heretical religious, historical, horror, household, hunting, hypocrisy, insects, jewels, Jews, law, learning, light, literature, lower classes, mathematics, medicine, metals, middle classes, monarcy, money, motion, mountains, music, nobility, occupations, oratory, pagan, paintings, parenthood, physics, plague, poetry, political, professional classes, proverbs, religious, Royalist images, schooling, science, scriveners, sea, sexual, skin, slave, smell, sound, speech, stone, superstition, taste, teaching, touch, twins, virginity, visual images, voice, war, witches, writing: 8*. See also individual topics

Imagination: 5, 7*, 70, 79, 146*, 25. Fragmentation of: 25. Fallen: 25. And fancy: 128. Of M as applied to music: 121. Blake's theory of: 25. As Jesus: 55. M's towering, admired by Hume: 88. Bentley's lack of: 88. Pearce on the "fire of imagination": 88. M's mythological imagination: 46. Pearce on, as distinct from accuracy: 88; his ability to follow the workings of the: 88. The elder Richardson on M's fury: 88. Reader's, to be stimulated to activity, according to Richardson: 88. Richardson on, and originality: 88. On poetry enriching the, improving morally and making happy: 88. Valued by Thyer even though irregular: 88. Warburton an enthusiastic advocate of the: 88. Massey on: 88. Warton's, and logic: 88. Warton siding with the cause of: 88. As main agent in poetry: 88. Dunster's: 88. Poetic, valued by Dunster: 88. In sacred poetry used for advertising religion: 88

Imaginative: excellence, Dunster's instinctive appreciation of: 88. Traits, intellectual rather than, dealt with by Dunster: 88

Imaus: 144. Mt. (and mountains): 19, 49, 73. See also: Scythia; Tartaria

Imbonati, Carlo: 22

Imitated and plagerized: 44

Imitatio Dei: 72

"Imitation, An": 117

Imitation: 5, 146, 117*. 18th c. attitude towards: 58. Theory of: 11. Art of: 25. First Jacobean: 40. Of models as teaching method: 20*, 40, 51. Of ideas, of nature, poetic, of action, of classical authors, of Christ, of perfect hero, of Adam and Eve, icastic, phantastic, by dissembling orator and sophist: 123. See also: Satan, imitation of God

Imitations: Bentley demands too great literalness from: 88. The Richardsons' on complete assimilation in M's: 88. Peck on poetry as selective imitation: 88; emphasizing imitation, forgetting the poet's personality: 88. Newton sees supreme value of M's, in their artistic quality, comparing him to Virgil: 88. Of Homer, M's regarded as superior to originals: 88. M's, Todd on: 88

Immanence: 34*. Of God in nature: 121

Immanent: 96

Immature students: 51

Immediacy: 125

Immessen, Arnoldus: 65

Immorality: 47, 141, 71. M's (alleged in Italy): 44

Immortal Mentor, The: 115

Immortality of the Soul: 144

Immortality: 24, 47, 60, 113. Of verse: 70. See also: Life everlasting

Immutability of God: 93

Imogen (Inogen): 3, 44, 73

Impasse: 47

Imperial Dictionary of Biography: 44

Impersonation in letter and theme writing: 20

Impey, E. B.: 58

Impiety: 51

Impious practises: 51

Impossible, the: 51

Impression: 51. Poetry dependent on the, it produces on the mind, Thyer and Warton: 88

Impressionism in the notes of the Richardsons: 88

Impressions in the air: 128. See also: Comets; Meteors

Impressions: substitution of, of one sense to those of another: 88. Physical, periods of susceptibility to, (the Elizabethans, the Romantic Period, the Symbolists): 88

Imprimatur: 51

Improvisation: 121

Imputatio Fidei (John Goodwin): 147

In medias res: 50*

In obitum Praesulis Wintoniensis. See Elegy III

In ruinam camerae Papisticae (Gill the Younger): 20

In symbolum apostolorum: 65

In the cool of the evening: 65

In vita di Madonna Laura (Petrarch): 83

In Adventum Veris: 113, 26

In Librum Aristotelis de Arte Poetica Explicationes (Robortelli): 70

In Nomine: 103, 121

In Praise of the Tuscan Language: 111

In(n)ogen (Imogene): 73

Ina: 3. King: 73

Inaccuracy: forgiven by Thyer if poetic: 88. Newton's pedantic censure of, in M's poetry: 88

Inaudibility of sphere music: 121

Incarnation: 5, 9, 17, 50, 32, 71, 72*, 96. See also: Christ; Son of God; Nativity; Atonement

Incas: 19

Incentive, rhetorical: 51

Incest: 139. Mythology: 141

Incident: 92*

Incompatibility: 54

Incompleteness of representation, the stimulating effect of: 88

Incomprehensibility of God: 93

Incongruity: 124

Inconsistency: 51*. In the Richardsons' definition of poetry: 88. Inconsistencies: 50*. M's, misunderstood by Newton: 88. See also: Defects

Inconveniences of toleration: 103

Ind(e) (India): 73, 150. See also: India

Indebtedness. See individual entries on M's indebtedness to other sources

Indemnity, Act of. See Pardon

Indenture: of fine: 45. Of 1623: 40

Indepedency Stript and Whipt (Richard Osborne): 147

Independency Of England Endeavored to be Maintained (Marten): 147

Independency: 114*

Independent Chronicle (and Universal Advertister): 115, 117

Independent's Loyalty (Richard Osborne): 147

Independents: 7*, 9*, 44, 51*, 52, 103, 132, 147, 38*, 78*, 94. And Levellers in debate: 147. Clash with the proponents of Presbyterian state church: 147. Disturbing to the Presbyterians: 147. Leaders: 147. Lord Brooke's influence: 147. Numbers of: 147. As regicides prosecuted by the implacable Presbyterians: 147. Sentiment against Charles: 147. M's relation to: 52, 113. M's Independent tendencies: 147. M's peculiar independency: 147. M, outspoken as an: 147. M becomes an: 94. See also: Congregationalists

Inderwick, F. A.: 44*, 45; Records of the Inner Temple: 44

Index: verbal, made use of by Newton: 88. Roman Catholic: 117

Indexes: Index Expurgatorius: 103, 71. Index Ethicus: 44. Index Oeconomicus: 44. Index Politicus: 44. Index Theologius: 44. Index Legalis: 45. Index Poeticus (Buchler): 20. Index Poeticus (Farnaby): 20. Index of Prohibited Books: 82. Index Rhetoricus (Farnaby): 20. Indexes to M's Commonplace Book: 20. Index to Pindar (M's): 44

India (and West Indies): 44, 49, 73, 144, 3, 32, 150. East and West: 73. Astronomy in: 89. East (Ind, India Orientalis): 19*, 44, 49. India, West (India Occidentalis): 49. Indian: steep: 73; religion: 47; Ocean: 3, 32, 150; voyage: 3. Indies: 103, 32. See also: Agra; Banda; Malabar; Tidore; America; Cusco

Indiana Univ.: 44

Indians: 19, 3. West: 19

Indicopleustes, Cosmas: 32

Indicum Mare: 49. See also: Ethiopian; India

Indifference, M's to popular approval: 51

Indifferent things: 9*

Indignation: 51

Indirection, use of: 51

Inditement against Tythes (John Osborne): 147

Individual: liberty, appeal to love of: 51. The, and moral truth: 125;

see also: Wisdom; Community; Heroic morality; Inseparate. Individualism: in M: 71; as a factor in M's reform: 147. Individuality: 124; slow development of a sense of: 118; of style and language, Pearce's partiality for M's: 88; and appreciation of 17th c., of manner: 88; of M's manner described by the Richardsons: 88; of M's language emphasized by Warton: 88; Todd's ideal of: 88

Indra: 1

Inductive reasoning: 31, 51

Indulgence and Toleration Considered: 116

Indus River: 19, 49, 73, 32. See also: Ganges

Inegild: 3

Infallibility: 47. M's, Bentley on: 88. Pearce does not insist on M's: 88. On the part of M, not maintained by Hawkey: 88

Infant Jesus (sign), Dijon: 44

Inference: 51

Infernal Council: 113

Inferno (Dante): 70, 103

Inferno: 111

Infidels: 122, 3

Infinitude in PL: 40

Infinity: idea of: 83. Of universe: 128

Influence of M in English Poetry: 71

Influence: 51. Of M: 117

Information: 47. See also: Tree of knowledge

Infused virtues: 122

Ingatestone, co. Essex: 44

Inge: Dean: 112. William Ralph: 18, 114, 143; symbols and the supernatural: 143; on Christ: 143; and infallible Book and Church: 143; idea of progress: 143; and scale of virtues: 143

Ingegnieri, Angelo: 29

Ingeld: 36

Ingelo, Nathaniel: 79

Ingelow, J.: 58

Ingenuity, Warburton's valuation of: 88

Ingersoll: Charles Jared: 115; Inchiquin, The Jesuit's Letters: 115. R. G.: 71

Ingham, William: 44

Ingilby, Sir Henry: 44

Ingleby-Smith-Furnivall and John Munro: 44; Shakespeare Allusion-Book: 44

Inglis, J. B.: 44

Ingoldsby (city): 44

Ingoldsby, William: 144

Ingrafting: 63

Ingram, John K., A History of Slavery and Serfdom: 82

Ingratitude: 93

Ingria. See Charles X

Ingulf: 3

Initiative: 51

Injunction: 45

Innatism: 81

Inner Temple Masque (Browne): 29, 26

Inner Temple, London: 40, 44*, 45*, 103. Inner Temple Records: 45*. Inner Temple, Students Admitted to the: 45

Inner: affinity: 98. Light: 7*, 9, 83*

Innes, M. M.: 36

Innocence: 37, 67, 140*. Language of: 37. The reader and: 37. Of nature, the: 37. Presentation of: 37. Definition of: 37. State of: probable duration: 93; had it continued: 93

Innocency and Truth Justified (John Lilburne): 147

Innocent III, Pope: 73, 93

Innovation and tradition in Miltonic epic: 123

Inns of Court and Chancery, Antiquities of the: 45

Inns: in Bread Street Ward: 40. Of

Court: 44, 103

Ino: 90

Inocencia perdida, La: 65

Inquisition after Blood: 103

Inquisition for Blood, An (to the Parliament and the Army): 73

Inquisition: 27, 51, 3

Insanity: 8

Inscription: on statue of Charles I (attr. to M): 44. Inscriptions and mottoes in St. Paul's School: 20

Insects: 128*. Ants (domestic and civil habits), bee, beetle, cankerworm, caterpillar, gnat, flies, leech, lice, locust, spider (conjugal constancy, weaver), wasps, worms: 128

Insertion: 50*

Insight, universal: 51

Inspiration: 5*, 7, 44, 50*, 70*, 113, 125*, 146. Daughters of: 25. M's ideas on: 113. Divine (general in M's works): 30*. Human vs. divine: 125. And persuasion: 125. And style of Scriptures: 125. And "the flesh becomes word": 125. As theme in SA: 125*. And reason: 125. Christ's and Samson's compared: 125. Poetic: 106*. Places of: 106. Sources of: 106. Dangers of: 106*. Burdens of: 106. Warburton's valuation of sudden: 88. Degree of, Dunster tries to calculate M's: 88. See also: Endowment; Creative; Nature; Spontaneity; Muse, Milton's

Instance, specific: 51

Instincts, goodness of the natural: 113

Institor, H. and J. Sprenger: 128

Institute of Historical Research, Bulletin of: 44

Institutes (Calvin): 134, 71

Institutio Graecae Grammatices Compendaria (Camden): 20

Institutio Oratoria (Quintilian): 70, 118, 3

Institution of a Christian Prince (Erasmus): 3

Institutiones in Linguam Graecam (Clenard): 20

Institutum Christiani Hominis (Erasmus): 3

Instruction: 47, 51, 96. Function of poetry: 31

Instructions for Forreine Travel (Howell): 94

Instrument of Government: 103

Instrument: 121*. Instruments for mensuration: 40

Instrumental music: 121

Insurrection, resort to: 51

Integration, of mind and feelings in Bks. III and IV of PL: 118

Integrity: 24, 47

Intellectual: problems: 51. Pursuits: 51. Inquiry: 80. Liberty: 113. Virtues: 122. Life: 51. Newton interested in, and technical rather than emotional problems: 88. Acuteness, Warton's: 88. Tendency, Dunster's, suited to task of editing PR: 88. Keenness, Dunster's: 88. Rather than imaginative features studied by Dunster: 88. M's intellectual powers: 146

Intellectualis viseo Dei: 96

Intellectualism: 27. And didacticism of PR regarded by Thyer as due to the subject: 88

Intelligence: 31, 44, 51

Intelligencer, The: 116

Intelligencer: 44. See also: Parliamentary; Public

Intemperance: 17*. In wisdom: 123. Eve's: 17. Adam's: 17*

Intent, of epic: 123. See also: Cause, final; Epic

Intention: 53. Intentional Fallacy, The: 12, 76, 123; see also: Wimsatt, W. K. Intentionality, principles and function of: 96*

"Intercursus Magna": 44

Interest of England Stated (John Fell): 147

Interest Will Not Lie (Nedham): 147

Interest: 45, 51*. In justice and morality: 51

Interior monologue: 98

Interlude: 70

Internality, principle of: 71

International: friendship: 51. League and covenant: 103. Unity: 51

Interpenetration: 34

Interplay, of various poetic methods examined by Dunster: 88

Interpretation: 11*, 96. Arbitrary, Lofft's: 83. Nature of: 11. Space of: 11. Of the Bible: 11. The maze of: 11*. In SA, PR: 11. Lack of artistic, in Hume's treatment of language: 88. Too emotional, of elliptic constructions in Richardson's commentary: 88. Picturesque, preferred by the Richardsons to reliable: 88. Careful, in Thyer's notes: 88. Lack of artistic, in Callander's commentary: 88. Little, in David Steel's M notes: 88

Interpreter, The: 45

Interpreter's Dictionary of the Bible: 48

Interrogation. See Adam and Eve; Serpent

Interrogatory: 45

Interval: 121

Intolerance: 47

Intonation, Lofft on: 83

Introduction to the Classics (Anthony Blackwell): 88

Introduction to the History of Educational Theories (Browning): 3

Introduction to the Old English History, An: 116

Introduction to the Works of John Milton (Hiram Corson): 136

Introduction: 51*. See also: Exordium; Proem

Intuition: 17, 125. As inference from sense impressions: 118. Followed by discipline: 125. And persuasion: 125. Confirmed on tower: 125. Critical, preferred by the Richardsons to learning: 88. The same relying too much on: 88. And knowledge: 96

Invective, in the prose and poetry: 75

Inveges, Agostino: 32

Invented proofs: 51

Invention: of licensing: 51. Poetic: 70, 123. Rhetorical (inventio): 118, 20, 40

Inversions: 98

Inverted power: 136

Inviolability of Mt. Zion or Jerusalem: 41

Invocation(s): 70, 96*. Of Christ: 78

Invocative blocks: 100. See also: Proportional structure

Involvement: 47

Inwardness, M's: 137

Io: 1, 73, 92

Iogern: 73

Iolaus: 92

Ion (Plato): 44, 73, 112

Ionathan: 1. See also: Targum

Ionia: 49, 73. Ionian: 73. Ionian School of Gr. Philosophy: 41, 89. See also: Melesigenes

Ipres: 49

Ipswich: co. Suffolk: 44*. Town: 49. Wolsey's school at: 20. St. Paul's system: 40

Iraneus: 41

Irascible faculty: 123*

Irassa: 49, 73, 90

Irchenfield: 49

Ireland (Hibernia): 44*, 45, 49, 51, 103*, 144, 3

Ireland, W. H.: 58

Irenaeus, St., of Lyons: 15, 23, 44, 57, 68, 73, 79, 83, 102, 107, 113, 123, 3, 32, 36*, 72, 82, 91, 93, 48. Generation of Son a mystery: 107. Pre-existing Logos: 107. Recapitulation: 107. Subordinationist: 107. As witness: 144. Bank of: 144. Works: Demonstration of the Apostolic Teaching: 36; "Against Heresies": 36, 74

Irene (Johnson): 130

Ireneus: 100

Irenical writing: 114*

Irenicus, Francis: 44

Ireton, Bridget. See Bendish

Ireton: 51, 120. Bridget: see Bendish. Henry (regicide): 9*, 44, 60, 103, 38, 91, 51, 120; defends property rights: 147; opposes manhood suffrage: 147; and M on law of nature: 147; and M: 147

Iris: 73, 90

Irish (a game): 40

Irish: 103, 3. Channel: 103. Massacre: 51. Protestants, M's contribution to: 44. Rebels: 45. Sea (Vergivian, Vergivium Salum): 44, 49

Iron Age: 36

Ironmongers Company Records: 40

Ironsides: 7, 103. See also: Cromwell

Irony: 47, 59, 123, 124, 125*, 136, 46, 92*. Of redemption: 60. Of God: 113. In PR: structural; Satan as vehicle of; M's belief in; competition in: 125. Ironic figure, M as an: 52. See also: Satan; Time

Irrational: vagueness, Pearce on: 88. Richardsons on dreamy, irrational features in Shakespeare: 88. Impulses, Dunster on: 83

Irregularity: of metre appreciated by Hume: 88. Vigour sometimes found by Bentley to make up for: 88. Metrical, opposed by Bentley except at times, where it enhances M's vigour: 88. Of M's verse smoothed away by Bentley: 88. Metrical occasionally recognized by Pearce as deliberate: 88. Shakespeare regarded by the Richardsons as inferior to M becuase of his: 88. And eccentricity approved by the Richardsons if artistic: 88. Apparent, of verse explained by Peck as due to comprehensive and flexible structure: 88. Admissible if indicative of imaginative power and emotion (Thyer): 88. Picturesque, Warton on: 88. Value of, Dunster and Stillingfleet on: 88. In M, cases of, shown by Todd to be authentic: 88

Irrelevant matter, elimination of: 51

Irrevocabilitié du Test...Charles Stuart: 44

Irtis: 49

Irus: 2, 72

Irvine, Presbytery of: 44

Irving, E.: 87

Irwin: D.: 97. E.: 58. R.: 36

Isaac: 16, 68, 73, 127, 128, 32, 72. ben Gerson: 40. ben Joseph Salam: 40. Rabbi: 123. See also: Zohar

Isaacson, Henry: 93

Isabel of Burgundy: 32

Isabella: of Aragon: 29. Queen of Castile and Leon: 123

Isaiah di Trani: 41

Isaiah: 4, 44, 56, 73, 74, 90, 103, 118, 141, 142, 144, 126, 64, 3, 72, 146, 25. Fall of Lucifer: 61. The Second: 34. See also: Bible

Iscariot, Judas (pseudonym): 44

Isell, co. Cumberland: 44

Isham: Mr.: 44. Sir Charles: 44

Ishbosheth: 44

Ishmael: 73, 98, 72

Ishtar: 32

Isidore of Seville, St. (Isidorus Hispalensis): 40, 68, 73, 77, 90, 100, 102, 121, 123, 128*, 32, 36, 93, 143. Staff as symbol: 104. Works: <u>Allegoriae Quaedam Sacrae Scripturae</u>: 74*; <u>De Ortu et Obitu Patrum</u>: 74; <u>Etymologiarum</u>: 74, 77; <u>In Exodum</u>: 74; <u>Sent.</u>: 77; <u>Expositions of the Mystic Sacraments</u>: 36

Isis: 1, 19, 44, 73, 144, 72

Islam: 40. Islamic, tradition of the fallen angels: 123

Isle of Wight: 103

Isleworth: 45

Islington, London: 44

Islip, Simon: 40

Ismene: 92

Ismenian: 90. Steep: 49, 73. See also: Thebes

Ismeno: 123. See also: Tasso

Isna: 49

Isocrates: 56, 59, 122, 3, 71, 94,

146, 20*, 40*, 51, 18, 68, 73, 103, 112, 120, 123, 132, 26

Isola: Emma (Mrs. Edward Moxon): 44. Pietro della, "Il Sansone": 55

Isolation. See Alienation

Israel (Jews, Judah, Hebrew, Palestinus): 9*, 19, 40, 125, 44, 49, 3, 46, 72*. Israelites: 51, 3, 72*. See also: Canaan; Judah

Israel Potter: 98

Israel, Menasseh Ben: 44

Issachar: 44, 73

Issues, contemporary: 51

<u>Italia Liberata</u>: 130

<u>Italian Element in M's Verse</u> (Prince): 111, 135

Italian: commentaries referred to by Speght: 88. Culture, M's love for: 40. Expressions; derived from the, in M, Hume on: 88. The Richardsons: 88. Thyer: 88. Friend's, M's: 44. Journey (M's): 28*, 30*, 44, 132*, 26, 94*, 87, 113, 53, 136, 55*; influence on M: 132*, 55*; M's judgement of: 113; M's account: 55; M's itinerary: 55. Language: 30, 40, 44, 3*, 70, 103. M's study of and knowledge of: 20, 40, 44

Italian Literature: referred to in early Eng. commentaries: 88. Read by Peck: 88. Todd dealing with: 88. Effeminacy of condemned by Hume: 88. Bentley's references to: 88. The Richardsons dealing with: 88. Thyer's knowledge of: 88. Prolixity of, Thyer's objections to: 88. Newton's reading in: 88. Fantastic style of, censured by Newton: 88. Joseph Warton's knowledge of: 88. Thomas Warton's familiarty with: 88. Affectation and pomp of, disliked by Thomas Warton: 88. Dunster interested in: 88. Todd's references to: 88. Bowle's and Stillingfleet's allusions to: 88. Comedy: 70. Poems and poets: 40; M's: 130, 70, 94; M's debt to: 146. Italian rhythms: 40. Italianate smoothness, censured by Bentley: 88. Italian sonnet(s): 30, 59, 113, 121, 71, 55; disciplined manner of, praised by Newton: 88. Italianate poetry, M's: 40

<u>Italian Renaissance in England, The</u>: 112

Italian, miscellaneous: Italians, the: 70*, 103, 3, 40, 44. Merchants: 40. Music: 121. Nation: 3. Pronunciation of Latin: 51. Renaissance: 31. Tutors: 40

Italy: 8, 19, 30, 40, 44*, 51, 70, 98, 103*, 113, 132*, 49, 3*, 72. Influence of: 132*. See also: Ausonia; Hesperian; Italia; Florence; Rome

Itchingfield, co. Sussex: 44

"Ite Missa est": 126

<u>Iter ad Paradisum</u>: 32

"Iter Boreale": 45

Ithaca: 72

Ithuriel: 4, 42, 50, 56, 73, 111, 128, 123, 142, 71, 72, 140

Itinerarium (William of Worcester): 88

<u>Iuglers Discovered</u> (John Lilburne): 147

Ivan IV, the terrible: 60

Ivanovich, C.: 6

Iver: 45

Ives, Simon: 29, 39

Ivimey, Joseph: 44, 63, 87, 146. On M's prose: 87. Works: <u>John Milton: His Life and Times</u>: 87; <u>Religious and Political Opinions</u>: 87; "Animadversions on Dr. Johnson's Life of M": 87

Ivo Carnotensis: 68

Ivronia: 49

<u>Ivst Mans Ivstification</u> (John Lilburne): 147

Ivy tree, parable of: 143

Ixion: 44, 60, 73

Izard, Mr.: 45

-J-

J., T.: 88

J., W.: 44

Jabesh-Gilead: 49, 73

Jaboc: 144

Jacchaeus. See Jack

Jachin: 73

Jack, Gilbert: 40

Jackman: family: 45. (Jakeman), Alice: 45. Avis: 45. Elias: 45. Martin: 45. Michael: 45. Susan: 45. William: 45

Jackson: 98. Son and Company: 112. A. V. W.: 36. Anne: 45. Arthur: 54; Annotations upon...the Five Doctrinall, or Poeticall Books: 74. Edward: 16. Elizabeth (Towersey): 45, 59, 137. Gilbert: 45. Henry: 44, 117. Henry: 44, 117. J.: 58. J. E.: 45, 63; see also: Aubrey. Sir John: 33, 45. Thomas (Canon of Canterbury, Dean of Peterborough): 40, 67, 93. W.: 58. W. W.: 112. William: 45, 117. William A.: see Unger

Jacob: 16, 68, 73, 103, 127, 142, 144, 72, 130. His dream: 143. Vision at Ebenezer: 27. Jacob's Ladder: 27, 93. Jacob's staff: 40

Jacob and Joseph (13th c. Eng. poem): 74

Jacob: ben Asher (Baal ha-Turim): 41. ben Chaijim: 41. ben Chayyim: 40

Jacob: G.: 58. Giles: 70. Henry: 9

Jacobean(s): 27, 70. Drama: 139. Period: 88

Jacobite's Journal: 97

Jacobs: J.: 44. W. W.: 35

Jacquelin, Hélie: 74

Jacques: de Vitry: 40. de Vorigine, Legenda Aurea (trans. William Caxton): 74

Jacquot, Jean: 29, 39

Jaeger, Werner: 60, 66, 53

Jael: 73, 122

Jäger, J. W.: 10

Jaggard: Dorothy: 40. Isaac: 40, 64. William: 40, 44, 114

Jago, Richard: 58, 117

Jahaia, R. David, Meters of the Hebrews: 74

Jair: 68

Jakeman, Elias: 44. See also: Jackman

James I: 10, 16, 20, 19, 29, 33, 35, 40*, 42, 44, 45, 51, 52, 56, 59, 60, 73, 87, 103*, 108, 114*, 116*, 142, 147, 11, 143, 72, 32, 38, 39, 71, 26, 93, 94, 137, 21, 64, 13. And Church of Eng.: 147. And Puritan agitation: 147. And the Statute of Monopolies: 147. In Directions to Preachers warns against dangerous doctrines: 147. Proclamation Enjoining Conformity: 147. Wins Puritan disfavor: 147. On the Gospel: 143. Works: Proclamation Enjoining Conformity: 147; his trans. of Du Bartas' Uranie in Essayes of a Prentise: 74; Daemonologie: 142; James the 1st, The Progresses of...: 45. See also: Bible: Authorized Version

James, St.: 4, 44, 73, 127, 71. Epistle of: 3, 71. See also: Bible

James: Abp. of Armagh: 51. Of Edessa: 65

James: II: 16, 40, 44*, 51, 103, 116*, 71. V of Scotland: 44. Edward, Prince, "The Old Pretender": 116

James: Mr.: 44. C. W.: 59. Professor D. G.: 12, 130. E. O.: 36. Elinor: 116. Henry: 34, 37, 60, 86, 105, 118, 127, 133, 135, 138, 53, 72, 137, 150. M. R.: 123, 36. Margaret: 60, 144. Nicholas: 117. R. R.: 16. Richard: 40. Thomas: 40. Thomas C.: 115; The Country Meeting: 115. William: 40, 64, 133, 142, 137; A Pluralistic Universe: 142

Jameson: Mrs. Ann Brownell: 87; on M's attitude toward women: 87; Memoirs of the Loves of the Poets: 87. (Johnson), Capt. John: 44

Jamieson, J.: 58

Janavel: 120

Jane, Joseph: 16, 44*, 116. Eikon Aklastos: 91

Jansen, John (publisher). See Jansson

Jansen: Cornelius (Janssen, Cornelis), portrait painter: 20, 28, 44*, 103, 99*. Enikel: 93. Jansenism: 93

Janson: 3. H. W.: 128

Jansson, Atlas: 102, 144

Jansson: Mr.: 44. Jan (John, publisher): 10, 19, 44, 73, 128, 91, 93

Jantz, H.: 23

Janua linguarum: 40

Janua Linguae Latinae Reserata (Comenius): 3

Janua: 40, 51

Januas: 73

Janus: 60, 73, 90, 32

Japan: 49, 32. Japanese poetry, cross cultural comparison with: 118

Japhet: 1

Japheth: 1, 90, 144. Unwiser son of: 73. See also: Iapethus

Jaques, Robert: 45

Jarrell, Randall: 143. On modern critics: 143

Jarumannus: 3

Jason: 56, 73, 90, 123, 3

Jasper Sea, the: 89

Jastrow, M.: 41

Javan, Isles of: 49, 50, 73. See also: Tarsus

Javello, Crisostomo (Javellus, Chrysostom): 40, 73

Jayne: Joseph: 103. Sears: 29, 79, 122, 123, 39, 101, 21

Jeaffreson, J. C.: 44

Jealous Lovers, The: 62

Jealousy: 25. (Envy), of Son, Satan's: 50

Jeanes, Henry: 44, 123

Jeanne d'Arc: 60

Jeans, Sir James: 15, 113

Jebb: John: 117. Sir Richard C.: 51, 68, 120, 123, 132 85, 92*, 148, 150; and Hebraic spirit in SA: 143

Jedin, Hubert: 93

Jefferson, Thomas: 71, 82, 115*, 117. Works: *The Commonplace Book of Thomas Jefferson*: 82; *The Literary Bible of Thomas Jefferson*: 82

Jeffrey: 130. Family: 44. (Jeffery, Jeffray, Jeffreys), Agnes: 44. Anne Bode: 44. Bridget: 44. Christopher: 44. Edmund: 44. Edward: 44. Elizabeth: 44. Francis: 70, 87, 146. Grace: 44. Helen (Ellen, M's grandmother): 44. Henry (two or more): 44. Hester and John (M's 1st cousins): 28, 44; see also: Blackborrow. Hester (another): 44. Jane Pellet: 44. Joan (M's great-grandmother): 44. Joan (another): 44. John (M's great-grandfather): 44*. Juliana (Julyan): 44. Katharine: 44. Lettice: 44. Margaret (M's great-aunt): 44; see also: Truelove. Mary: 44. Matthew: 44. Paul (M's grandfather): 44*; his daughter: 44. Prowe: 44. Richard: 44. Richard (another) and his wife: 44. Robert: 44. Sarah (M's mother): 28*; see also: Milton. Sarah (another): 44. Thomas (more than one): 44. William: 44

Jeffreys, Sir George (judge): 44, 58, 116

Jeffries: family: 40. Ellen: 40. Margaret: 40. Paul: 40. Sarah: 40

Jeffryes (publisher): 97

JEGP: 44*

Jehoiada: 73

Jehoram: 73, 91

Jehosaphat: 73

Jehovah: 73, 103, 72, 25. See also: God; Urizen

Jehu (Iehu): 73, 91

Jehuda bar Simon, Rabbi: 123

Jehvern. See Oldenburg

Jekyll, J.: 58

Jemmat, C.: 58

Jeneper Hill. See Juniper

Jenison, Robert: 93

Jenissey: 49

Jenkes, Richard: 10

Jenkins: Mr.: 44. Judge: 45. Harold: 44, 100. John: 100. Sir Leoline: 44, 150. Rev. R. C.: 44

Jenkinson, Anthony: 19

Jennens, Charles: 58, 117

Jenner: C.: 58. David: 116. Sir Thomas: 44

Jenney, William: 44

Jennings: H. C. (trans. Dante): 58. J.: 58

Jennye, Edward: 44

Jenour, Hester: 45

Jentillot, M. (pretended envoy from France): 44

Jenyns, S.: 53

Jephepija: 41

Jephson: R., burlesques PL: 58. William: 44

Jephtha(h): 63, 73, 123, 141, 130

Jerahmeel, Chronicles of: 36*

Jeremiah ben Eleazar: 41

Jeremiah: 2, 30, 68, 73, 74, 122, 141, 3, 11, 62, 64, 72, 25. See also: Bible

Jericho: 44, 49, 73, 144, 72

Jerkers' Office (London): 44

Jermin, Michael: 93

Jeroboam: 144. I: 73. II: 73

Jerome, St.: 1, 4, 23, 40, 41, 44, 51, 54, 57, 60, 73, 18, 64, 77, 79, 107, 113, 123, 142, 32, 93*, 99, 106, 63, 68*, 74, 90, 100, 114, 125, 128, 144, 36, 71, 82, 88. St. Jerome's dream: 51. Letter to Heliodorus: 143. Attitude toward Origen: 107. Life: 107. Origen's heresies: 107. Responsibility for Origen's bad reputation: 107. And creation: 143. Works: "Ad Paulinum": 74; "Excerpta ex Commentarii in Jobum": 74; Ep. ad. Tit.: 77; Expositio Quatuor Evangeliorum: 74; In Danielem: 74; In Librum Job: 74; In Matthaeum: 74; In Novum Testamentum: 74; Preface to Chronicle of Eusebius: 74; "Preface to Job": 74; Quaestionum in Genesin: 74; Letters: 36; On Famous Men: 36. See also: Bible, Vulgate

Jerome: the Bohemian: 3. Of Prague: 73. Stephen: 93

Jeronimo: 45

Jerram, Charles S.: 16, 19, 33*, 53, 92, 21

Jersey, Isle of: 44

Jerusalem (Hierosolymae, Salem, Salymon): 19, 40, 44, 49, 144, 3, 32, 72, 21, 25. As Heavenly city: 25. Children of: 25. Exile of: 25. "The New": 72. As epic subject: 123. See also: Tasso

Jerusalem (Blake): 25*. Newton in: 25. As prohecy: 25. As synoptic poem: 25. Chapter prefaces: 25. And its audience: 25. Perspectives in: 25. Allegory of: 25. Los in: 25. Quest for vision: 25. Epic tradition: 25. Skofield in: 25. Dialectics in: 25. As comedy: 25. Conclusion of: 25. As a sequel to Milton: 25. The Art of: obscurity, style, innovation, inversional transformations: 25. Structure of: fourfold, mechanical form, organic form, symmetry in, prophecy, romance, fluidity, rearrangement of plates: 25. Themes in: return, garment, fulfillment, atonement: 25. Blake's designs for: 25; plates 1, 59, 95: 25. Compared with: Book of Revelation, Iliad, Miltonic structures, PR, Bible, Blake's early prophecies, Gerusalemme Liberata, Faerie Queene: 25

Jerusalem Delivered: 70, 111

Jeruschalmi, Simson (ben Samuel): 32

Jesse: 72

Jessey, Henry: 114, 38

Jessop: 16. Edmund: 7. William: 44

Jesuits: 27, 40, 42, 44, 51, 60, 103, 142, 3, 71, 94. Jesuit plot: 30

Jesus College, Cambrdige: 40*, 44, 45, 103

Jesus: 1, 20, 31, 44, 51, 57, 73, 95, 103, 112*, 141, 71, 25*. As revolutionary: 25. As orator: 25. Crucifixion: 25. Incarnation: 25. Garments: 25. Joseph as type of: 25. In Blake: resurrection of: 25; wrath of: 25; as archetypal man: 25; in PL, PR: 25; parabolic style of: 25; see also: Albion; Imagination; Jerusalem; Lamb of God; Los; Luvah; Milton, especially PR. "Who is called the son of Sirach": 73. See also: Christ; the Son

Jethro: 73

Jew: 45

Jewel, Bp. John: 40, 60, 38, 93, 117

Jewell: 142

Jewers, A. J.: 45

Jewin Street, London (M's house in): 44*, 103

Jewish Encyclopedia, The: 142

Jewish: Apocalyptic lit.: 41. Church: 51. Commentaries on Scripture: 40. Law: 51. Mysticism:

42. Psalters: 40

Jewitt, Orlando (engraver): 44

Jews: 8, 27, 40, 44, 51, 103, 107, 3, 71. Alexandrian: 107; theology of: 107. Captivity of: 143. Toleration of: 143. Conversion: 93. See also: Israelites

Jezebel (Jesabel): 73

Jhengiz Khan: 83

Jig: 121. Jigging: 51

Jiriczek, Otto L.: 20

Joab: 73

Joachim: Joseph: 39. Of Floris (Fiore, de Flore): 79, 38. Joachite beliefs concerning age of spirit: 38; see also: Joachim of Fiore. Friend of Heinsius: 44

Joad, C. E. M.: 142. Good and Evil: 142

Joannes Damascenus: 65. Joannes de Sacro Bosco: 3. Joannes Scotus: 3. Joannes Secundus: 40, 148. Joannes Philoponos: 65

Joannis de Luz, Fanum Divi: 49

Joannis Miltoni Sententiae Potestati Regiae Adversantis Refutatio: 116

Job: 1, 4, 44, 51, 52, 57, 60, 73, 74*, 76, 90, 103, 112, 122*, 123, 125, 126, 139, 141, 142, 144, 3, 26, 62, 72, 91, 92, 109. "Patient" mentioned: 80. Book of: 70, 132, 135, 30, 141, 72, 146, 48; as an epic model: 30; cited: 89; see also: An exposition ...upon the Book of Job (Caryl)

Jocasta: 92

Joccatra (Jactura): 49

Jochanan: 41

Jochums, Milford C.: 40, 128

Jögerne: 44. See also: Igraine

Johann Casimir, Administrator of the Palatinate: 10

Johannes Phocas: 90

Johannessen, K. L.: 6

Johannis Miltoni, Angli pro Populo Anglicano. See Milton, John, Works

John (Buckholdt) of Leyden: 114, 91

John the Baptist...or, A Necessity for Liberty of Conscience, as the only means under Heaven to Strengthen Children weake in faith (Henry Robinson): 147

John the Baptist: 44, 73, 126, 72, 25

John Milton: A Sketch of his Life and Writings (Bush): 135. See also: Milton

"John Milton in Westminster": 44. See also: Milton

John-a-Noaks: 45, 73

John-a-Stiles: 45, 73

John: of Antioch, Malalas: 73. Of the Cross, St.: 27, 79. Of Damascus, St.: 57, 32, 36, 93; Expositions of the Orthodox Faith: 36. Of Garland: 20. Of Gaunt: 38. Of Oxnead: 93. Of Salisbury: 20, 40, 83, 114. Patriarch of India: 32. Penry (Pierce): 83

John, Chrysostom, St.: 93*

John, St., of Patmos: 4, 44, 51, 126, 72, 25*. The Apocalypse of: 62

John, St., the evangelist: 60, 70, 111, 44, 73, 126, 72, 109. Quoted: 95. First epistle of: 99. In Greek: 40. Gospel for Christmas Day: 126. Gospel for Good Friday: 126. Gospel of: 40, 44, 74*, 126, 3, 99. See also: Triple Equation; Bible

John, St., the Evangelist, Church: 40

John: III, King of Poland: 44. IV, King of Portugal: 44*. XXII, Pope: 93, 64. Elector of Saxony: 83. Fisher, St.: see Fisher, J. Gabriel: 40. King: 34, 51, 73, 71, 91

John's St., College, Cambridge: 40

Johnson: 132, 3. Mr.: 44, 45. Ambrose: 45. B. J. and R. (publishers): 97. C. F.: 58. C. S.: 44. Charles: 44. Elizabeth: 44; her daughter, Elizabeth: 44. Francis: 7, 40, 100, 102, 128*, 142; Astronomical Thought in Renaissance Eng.: 142. George: 45. John: 44, 58. Joseph: 97, 146. Robert: 45, 145. Dr. Samuel: see separate entry. Thomas: 128. Thomas H. (publisher, pr., and bks., 1642-77): 44, 91, 37, 115. Wendell Stacy: 110. William: 45

Johnson, Dr. Samuel: 1, 4, 6, 8, 12, 15, 16, 17, 27*, 28, 29, 33, 34, 40, 41, 42, 44*, 50, 52, 56, 58*, 59, 35, 64, 60, 68, 70, 73, 76, 77, 79, 81, 83, 84, 86*, 87*, 95, 98, 100, 102, 105*, 107, 108, 110, 113, 114, 118,

116*, 120, 123, 124, 127, 128, 129, 133, 134, 135, 139, 141, 142, 138, 145, 147, 11, 26, 39, 71, 72, 85, 88*, 92*, 93, 94*, 97, 101, 105, 115, 130*, 131, 137, 146*, 149, 148*, 150*, 117*, 55, 140, 21, 13. Compared with M: 87. Attitude toward the sonnet: 87. On religious poetry: 87. Atttitude toward M: 87. Reaction to his opinion of M: 87. Influence of Life of Milton: 87. Ultra-Toryism of: 87. Accused of misinterpreting M: 87. Notions of prosody criticized: 87. Dislikes M's politics: 58. On Lycidas, Samson: 58. On M: 58. On M's sonnets" 58, 87, 146. On PL: 58, 146. Thought PL orthodox: 107. On dangers of free press in Life of Milton: 147. Literal failure of Lycidas: 61. Romantic assessment of: 146. Opinions on: Comus, L'Allegro, Il Penseroso, Lycidas, on M's Latin and minor poems, on M's rhyme: 146. Works: Rambler articles on M: 109; Rasselas: 109; Lives of the Eng. Poets: 142. Lives of the Poets: 146; Life of Milton: 146, 87, 109, 58, 95

Johnson's Almanac, for the Year 1810: 115

Johnston: Archibald: 44. Arthur: 64, 117*

Joinville, Jean Sire de: 32

Joliff, Humphrey: 44

Jolley, Thomas: 44

Jonah: 123, 32, 72. Prototype of Christ: 46. Book of: 19

Jonah's Cry out of the Whales belly (John Lilburne): 147

Jonas: Arngrimus: 19. Jodocus: 40. Leah: 122

Jonathan: 40, 73. ben Uzziel: 73, 123. The Targoum: 113

Jones: 3. Anne (Fettiplace): 45. Arthur: 45. Charles M., "M's Brief Epic": 74. Charles W.: 112, 122. Rev. C. P.: 44. E.: 15. Eleanor (Pope): 45. Elizabeth: see Greenwood, Eliz. Ernest: 35. Francis: 40, 44. Frederick: 14. H.: 58. H. S. V.: 60, 122. H. W.: 23. Henry: 45. Howard Mumford: 115

Jones (continued): Inigo: 20, 27, 29*, 139, 39*, 88, 97, 64, 55, 21. James: 44. John, of Balliol College: 58. John, Bp. of Cork: 58. John, "an uneducated youth": 58. John (Johanes): 44, 45, 128. Mary (Powell): 45. Michael: 44. The Rev. Morgan: 88. Peter (M's father's servant): 40, 44. Col. Philip: 44. R.: 59, 94. R. M.: 7. Richard: 112, 134. Richard (master of St. Paul's): 40. Richard, 3rd Viscount and 1st Earl Ranelagh (M's student): 20, 30, 44, 73. Richard Foster: 7, 9, 16, 23, 37, 44, 116, 77, 144, 145, 93. Rufus: 79. S.: 58. Thomas: 97. Sir Thomas, Chief Justice: 44. Thomas Mason: 87. Thomas W.: 44. Sir William: 58, 117. Walter: 45. William: 40, 44, 45, 79

Jones Bequest, Victoria and Albert Museum: 44

Jones-Davies, M.-T.: 39, 64

Jones, T. Gwynn ("Tudor Welshmen's English"): 83

Jonson, Ben: 1, 4, 15, 17, 19, 20*, 23, 27, 29*, 31, 33, 35, 40*, 42, 44, 45, 50, 58, 59, 60, 68, 69, 70*, 73, 75, 76, 79, 81, 84, 86, 89, 90, 102, 103, 104, 105, 108, 114, 120, 124, 127, 128, 129, 132, 133, 134, 135*, 136, 142, 145*, 3, 143, 26, 32, 39*, 46, 53, 62, 71, 72, 82, 88, 91, 94, 97, 64*, 130, 131, 137, 146, 148, 150, 117, 55, 21. Style of: 143. Folio of 1640: 143. On decorum: 66. Structure of court masque: 104. Influence on M: 104. Works: Masque of Hymen: 143; The Silent Woman: 82; Volpone: 82

Jonston, John (Jonstonus, Johannes): 40, 77, 128*. History: 77

Jophiel: 41

Jordan River: 19, 49, 73, 144, 72*. See also: Paneas

Jordan: family: 45. Friar of Severac: 32. John: 44, 45, 58. W. K.: 9*, 60, 102, 116. William: 65, 77, 36, 93, 64; Creation of the World: 36

Jordans, co. Bucks.: 44

Jordon-Smith, Paul: 122

Jorgensen, P. A.: 23

Jortin: 57, 88. John: 58, 117

Jose ben Kisma, Rabbi: 38

Joseph and Potiphar's Wife: 25

Joseph, Sister Miriam: 15, 23, 60, 86

Joseph: 40, 63, 73, 127, 71, 72. Joseph (another): 73. Joseph's dream: 136. Of Castile: 40. Of Exeter: 133. Son of Abraham: 72. The patriarch: 123

Josephus, Flavius: 128, 22, 38, 93, 148, 13, 1, 17, 19, 41, 68*, 73, 42, 60, 112, 114, 123, 32, 36, 88, 99. Works: Against Apion: 74; Antiquities of the Jews: 74, 36, 144; Workes (trans. Thomas Lodge): 74

Joses, Rabbi: 73

Joshua ben Karcha, Rabbi: 123

Joshua: 51, 68, 73, 123, 127, 3, 32, 72, 25. Prototype of Christ: 46. In Gibeon: 50

Josiah: 73, 143, 72

Josippon: 41, 42

Josippus ("Iosippum"): 73

Joubert, Laurent: 40

Jougoria: 49

Jourdan, Silvester: 32

Journal étranger, Le: 117

Journal of a Visit to London and the Continent: 98

Journal of English Literary History, A: 48

Journal of Hist. of Medicine: 44

"Journal of Melville's Voyage in a Clipper Ship": 98

Journal of Sacred Literature, The: 87

Journal up the Straits: 98

Journals of the House of Lords: 44. See also: Lords

Journals of House of Commons: 44*, 59. See also: Commons

Jove (Jupiter): 1*, 44*, 50, 57, 60*, 73, 90*, 112, 3, 11, 71, 72*. Son of: 73. See also: Zeus; Jupiter

Jovian: Or, An Answer to Julian the Apostate: 116

Jovianus, Joannes. See Pontanus

Jovius, Paulus: 44, 82. Historia Sui Temporis: 82

Jowers, John: 44

Jowett: 3, 64. B.: 68, 81, 112, 64. Benjamin: works: The Dialogues of Plato: 48; The Dialogues of "Phaedo": 57

Joy, Frederick W.: 44

Joy: 47, 51, 90. Theme of, in PL and in passim: 104. See also: Happiness

Joyce: George: 44. James: 1, 12, 15, 23, 34, 60, 86, 100, 64, 105, 118, 139*, 39, 93, 101, 106, 150; works: Dubliners: 25; A Portrait of the Artist: 95; Finnegans Wake: 60; Ulysses: 60

Joyeuse, Duc de: 29

Joyner, William: 45. See also: Lyde alias Joyner

Jubal: 4, 121, 127

Jubilees, Book of: 24

Jubye, Edward: 68

Judaea: 68

Judah (Jew, Judea): 49, 51, 73, 143, 72, 25. See also: Israel

Judah ben David Hayyuj: 40

Judaism: 107, 36. Unimportance to "Cosmopolitans": 107

Judas: 4, 44, 45, 68, 71, 72, 91. See also: Iscariot

Judge(s): 45. Fallibility in religion: 51. Judging over again: 51

Judge, Divine. See Son of God

Judge's Head (sign): 44

Judgement of Martin Bucer (Milton): 112, 113, 147, 103. See also: Milton, John, Works

Judges, book of: 118, 126, 92. See also: Bible

Judgment and Decree of the Univ. of Oxford: 44, 116

Judgment of an Anonymous Writer: 116

Judgment of Doctor Rainoldes, The (Usher): 51, 57, 94, 26

Judgment: 25, 50, 51*. Day of: 143. Divine: 122. Last: 63. Judgments, analytic: 96. See also: Last Judgement; Man; Son of God

Judicial rhetoric: 20, 123

"Judicious," the: 70

Judith (9th-10th c. Anglo-Saxon epic): 74

Judith: 122

Judson, A. C., The Life of Edmund Spenser: 83

Juga: 49. See also: Ustiug

Jugge, Richard: 40

Julian: 51, 32. The Apostate: 51, 73, 114, 116*, 3. Julian, the Apostate: 116*; compared with Pro Populo Anglicano Defensio: 116*

Julian's Arts: 116

Juliana of Norwich: 1, 7

Juliana: 36

Julianus of Halicarnassus: 74

Jülich. See Charles X; Frederick William

Juliers: 49

Julius Caesar (Shakespeare): 97, 130

Julius: Africanus: 93. II, Pope: 52. Great (Caesar): 2, 73, 72

Julia Domna: 64

Jung-Stelling: 7

Jung: Carl Gustav: 1, 12, 15*, 27, 60, 75*, 76, 118, 123, 64, 128, 86, 141*, 32, 131. L.: 36. Moses: 41

Jungius, Joachim: 7, 10

Jungle, The (Upton Sinclair): 118

Junilius: Africanus: 77

Junior-year studies: 40

Juniores sophistae: 40

Juniper (Jeneper) Hill, co. Oxon.: 44

Junius-Tremellius, Latin version of Bible. See Bible

Junius: 44, 103, 114. Adrian (Hadrianus): 40. F.: 94, 99. Franciscus: 74, 32*, 93, 55, 103, 123, 43, 40, 41, 42, 64, 68, 73. MS.: 36. Junius Manuscript (ed. George Philip Krapp: 74; see also: Biblia Sacra; Bible. Franz: 44. Patrick (Patricius): 22; see also: Young. Thomas: 44; see also: Young

Juno: 2, 44, 56, 57, 89, 90*, 3, 32. Relation to heroes: 123. As epic machinery: 123. Temple of: 143. In Masque of Hymen: 143. Juno sat cross-legged: 73

Jupiter: 1*, 2, 17, 44*, 56*, 57, 60, 89, 111, 144, 3, 32, 72. See also: Jove

Jus Caesaris Et Ecclesiae vere Dictae: 116

Jus Divinum Ministerii: 91

Jus Populi (attr. to M): 44

Jus Regiminis: 116

Jus Regium: 116

Jusserand, Jean Jules: 44, 60

Just man: 51

Just Rebuke Of a Late Unmannerly Libel: 116

Just Vindication of Learning: 116. Compared with Areopagetica: 116

Justa Edovardo King Naufragium: 33*, 44, 53

Justice Advanced: 44

Justice: 9*, 24, 47, 45, 50*, 51*, 90, 122*, 123*, 125*, 36*. Theme of in Lycidas: 104. Love for: 51. Administration of: 51. Appeals to people's sense of: 125. As a masque figure: 125. Of God: 35, 93

Justification: 63, 122, 93. By faith: 123, 93. Of God's ways: 123. By works: 93

Justification of Separation from the Church of England (John Robinson): 147

Justin: 40*, 56, 90. II: 73. Martyr (Justinius), St.: 40, 44, 57, 60, 73, 74, 77, 83, 113, 114, 107, 142, 3, 32, 36, 71, 93; angels have bodies and take nourishment: 107; chiliast: 107; God incomprehensible: 107; Greeks borrowed from Moses: 107; Logos: 107; subordinationism: 107; works: Fragments: 36; First Apology, Second Apology: 57, 74; Dialogue with Trypho: 74, 36, 82

Justina, Queen of Valentinian: 44

Justinian I (Empteror, Flavius): 40, 44, 45, 73, 103, 111, 123, 3, 71, 93, 82. Code of: 51

Justinianus: 73

Justinius: 20

Justinus, Marcus Junianus: 73

Justling Rocks: 49. See also: Bosporus

Justus Jonas: 57

Jutland: 49. Jutlanders: 3

Juvarra: 27

Juvenal: 8, 15, 19, 40*, 44, 54, 56, 59, 73, 90, 114, 18, 64, 88, 91, 146

Juvencus: 44, 65, 90, 3, 149. Gaius: 74, 36; Evangeliorum Libri Quatuor: 74, 36. Hispanus: 77

Juxon: Thomas: 40. Bp. of London (William): 33, 40, 44, 73, 103

-K-

K., H. (Harry Kitching?): 44

Kabbala(h), the: 86, 113*, 7, 71, 78. Influence on M: 113*. Fludd's relation to: 113. Kabbalists: 71. See also: Cabbala

Kabuki drama of Japan: 118

Kaesgrave, co. Suffolk: 44

Kaf: 32

Kafka, Franz: 1, 35, 11

Kain und Abel Spiel: 65

Kairos. See Time

Kalender of Shepherdes: 128

Kallen, H. M., Job as a Greek Tragedy: 74

Kalussia: 49

Kalussien: 49

Kamer, Lord: 97

Kamerau, Gustav: 93

Kames: Lord: 39. Henry Home, Lord: 117. Lt. Henry Home: 58

Kana, syllabary of Japan: 118

Kant, Immanuel: 5, 12, 86, 113, 121, 136, 71, 149

Karelia. See Charles X

Karl: Prince Elector Palatine: 10. Ludwig, Prince Elector Palatine: 10*. Landgraf von Heesen-Kassel: 10

Karlstadt: 7

Karppe, S.: 113

Kassubia. See Charles X; Frederick William

Katharsis: 92*

Katherine of Aragon: 40

Katzenelnbogen (Cutzenellebogen). See William VI

Kauffman, Angelica: 97

Kaufmann, U. Milo: 79

Kautzsch, E.: 41

Kaw-we-Naki: 41

Kaye: Archdeacon: 44. Canon A. E.: 44

Kazin, Alfred: 60

Keach, Benjamin: 79

Keasar, Robert: 44

Keate: Gilbert: 44; influenced by PL: 58. W.: 58

Keatinge: 3

Keatinge's Washington Almanac For the Year of Our Lord 1806: 115

Keats, John: 1, 8, 15, 18, 23, 44, 52, 56, 58*, 73, 35, 83, 84, 36, 87*, 95, 105, 110, 118, 120, 132, 133*, 134, 138, 139, 14*, 26, 46, 71, 88, 109, 130, 137, 146*, 64, 150, 55, 25. Borrowings from M: 58. Influenced by L'Allegro: 58. On M: 58. Wherein like M: 58. Sonnets of: 87. Blank verse of: 87. Attitude toward M, M's art: 87. Annotations to Burton's Anatomy of Melancholy: 146. Annotations to PL: 146*. "Negative capability": 146. Others' reminiscences of: 146. Keats Memorial House, Hampstead: 44. Power: 146. Works: Letters (quoted): 95, 146*; Ode; 146; Ode to Apollo I: 146; "On Retribution, or the Chieftan's Daughter": 146; Sonnets: 146; Lamia: 149. "On Seeing a Lock of Milton's Hair": 87; Hyperion: 87, 146; Hyperion (1st and 2nd versions): 133; Ode on Indolence: 133; Ode to a Nightengale: 133; Sleep and Poetry: 133; Keats, John, Memorial Volume: 44

Keble Hall: 44

Keble: John: 87, 111, 94; attitude toward M: 87; sonnets in Miltonic tradition: 87; on "primary" and "secondary" poets: 87. Joseph: 44, 58. Richard: 45

Keck: 40. Mr.: 45. Anthony: 45. Samuel: 45

Keckermann, Bartholomew: 40*, 32, 93,

123, 128

Kecwich, Samuel: 44

Kederminster: 94

Keech (Keeth), William: 44

Kegor: 49

Keightley, Thomas: 1, 16, 33, 40, 41*, 44, 59, 63, 70, 73, 87, 83, 102, 128, 142, 120, 121, 132, 144, 93, 21. Opinion of M: 87. M's influence on: 87. On M's Puritanism: 87. M's belief in characters in PL: 87. An Account of the Life, Opinions, and Writings of John Milton: 87, 142

Keil, Heinrich: 40

Keills, John: 32

Keith, A. L.: 110

Kellaway's Buildings: 45

Keller: Helen: 16. Ludwig: 7

Kellet: A.: 58. E. E.: 44, 105, 111

Kelley, F. Joseph: 110

Kelley, Maurice: 1, 9, 23, 24, 37, 40, 44*, 52, 54, 59, 69, 75, 79, 83, 86, 100, 102, 107*, 116, 122, 123, 128, 142, 144, 14, 22, 85, 91, 93, 101, 106, 137, 148, 64, 140*, 48. Christ dies body and soul: 107*. De Doctrina Christiana as aid in interpreting PL: 107*. Explains retraction: 107*. "God" means "angels" in PL: 107*. God's invisibility not result of his nature but of man's frailty: 107*. M contradicts himself about the Spirit: 107*. M is consistent concerning Absolute God: 107*. M's Muse is the Father: 107*. PL and De Doctrina Christiana synchronous works: 107*. PL differs from De Doctrina Christiana regarding Christ's mediatorial function: 107*. PL differs from De Doctrina Christiana regarding sacerdotal function of the Son: 107*. PL occasionally heretical: 107*. Rejects Saurat's theory of the retraction: 107*. Satan and Beelzebub one person in De Doctrina Christiana: 107*. Wolleb and Ames: 107*. Works: "M and Machiavelli's Discorsi": 82; M's Arianism again Considered": 60, 74; "Daniel Skinner, Lord Preston, and M's Commonplace Book": 82; This Great Argument: 60, 74, 142, 82, 109, 48; "Addendum: The Later Career of Daniel Skinner": 82

Kellingworth, G.: 117

Kelly, J. N. D.: 74, 36, 93*. Early Christian Doctrines: 74

Kelpius, Johann: 7

"Kel.sen.": 44, 45

Kelton, Arthur: 93

Kemble, J. P.: 58

Kemke, Joannes: 40

Kemp: Lysander: 44, 59. Robert: 44. Thomas: 45

Kempe: Edward: 40. Martin: 10. William: 20, 40

Kempis, Thomas à: 7, 122, 39

Ken, T.: 58

Kendall: George: 114. Lyle H., Jr.: 44. William: 44, 58

Kendon, Frank, churches as Bibles: 143

Kendrick: J.: 97. Sir Thomas: 93

Kenet: 49

Kenilworth, Illinois: 44

Kennedy: Mr.: 44. C. R.: 58. George: 37. J.: 58. John Fitzgerald: 137. R.: 58. W. D.: 97

Kenner, Hugh: 34

Kennet, White: 44*, 45, 88

Kenney, J.: 58

Kensington, London: 44, 45

Kent, History of: 45

Kent: Mr.: 44. Elizabeth Grey, Countess of: 44. James: 44, 45. William: 12, 27, 70, 97

Kent: 44, 45*, 49, 103, 3, 92. Home of the Sidneys: 83

Kepers, J.: 79

Kepharjel: 41

Kepler, Johannes (or John): 1, 7, 8, 16, 40, 77, 100, 89*, 114, 128, 144, 93, 146, 142, 149. Visits Tycho Brahe: 89. Appointment at Prague: 89. Rudolphine Tables: 89. Financial and domestic troubles: 89. Publishes "The New Astronomy": 89. Investigations of laws of planetary motion: 89. Kepler's Laws: 89. Definition of: 89. Estimate of the distance of the stars: 39. Letter to Galileo on discovery of Jupiter's moon: 89. Death: 89. Appreciation of: 89. Characteristics: 89. "Epitome of the Copernican System" of inhibited: 89. Ast. Nova (trans. Salusbury): 77

Ker: U. P.: 141. Professor William P.: 58, 60, 132, 133, 36, 88, 92, 109, 150; and M's great mistake: 143. See also: Dryden

Kerdic: Shoar: 49. Kerdics League: 49. Kerdicsford (Chardford, Nazaleod): 49

Kerensky, Aleksandr Feodorovich: 60

Kerényi, K.: 141

"Keri": 40, 41, 3

Kerman, Joseph: 39

Kermode, Frank: 15, 17, 23, 37, 67, 81, 86*, 110, 122, 123, 125, 39, 53, 101, 115, 146, 25. On PL: 104. Coherent patterns in lit.: 61. Reality and control in Lycidas: 61. Works: "M's Hero": 60; The Living M: 60, 48

Kern, Fritz, Kinship and Laws in the Middle Age: 83

Kernodle, G. R.: 39

Kersey, John: 40

Kerslake, Thomas (bks.): 44, 43

Kerub: 142. See also: Cherubim

Kesteven: 49

Keswick Hall, near Norwich: 44

Ketiv: 41

Kett: Francis: 93. H.: 58

Ketton: 45

Ketuvim: 41

Ketzel, Wolfgang: 65

Kew: 40

Key of History: 40

Key of Solomon the King: 142

Key(s): 121, 143. Doctrine of the: 143. Key (sign), London: 44

Keyes, Clinton W.: 91

Keylaway, Robert: 45

Keymer: family: 45. Christopher: 45. Clement: 45. Elizabeth: see Ewens, Eliz. Henry: 45. William: 44*, 45*

Keynes: Edward: 45. Elizabeth: see Ewens, Eliz. Geoffrey: 45, 135

Khan: 19

Khetiv. See Qere and Khetiv

Kidd, B. J.: 116

Kiddall, Marmaduke: 120

Kiddell, H., on M: 58

Kidder, Bp. Richard: 32

Kidgell, J. (parodies Young): 58

Kidwelly, co. Caermarthen: 44, 45

Kieffer, Erhard: 44. See also: Kiesser

Kierkegaard, Soren: 15, 47, 124, 125, 14*, 39, 48. Treatment of Fall and original sin: 48. The Concept of Dread: 48. On the convenient and the eternal; on love and fear; on the object of faith; on Christ and Truth; on pretensions to religion: 47

Kiesser (Kieffer), Erhard: 44, 91

Kiffin, William: 114

Kilby: Mr.: 44. Richard: 93, 64

Kilcolman, Ireland: 44

Killigrew: Lady: 44. Simon: 45. Thomas: 44. Sir William: 44

Killing No Murder (M mentioned in): 44, 103, 116

Killingworth, William: 44

Kimber, Isaac: 44

Kimchi: 1, 22. David: 40, 41*, 73. Joseph: 40. Moses: 40, 41, 42

Kimedonicius, Jacobus: 93

Kimpel, Ben F.: 110

Kinaston. See Kingston

Kinde, Mr.: 44

Kinderzuct: 65

Kindlemarshe, Mrs.: 44

Kindness: 51

King (now Hobson) Street, London: 40

King Arthur (Dryden), Scott's introduction to: 70

King Henry IV: 131. See also: Henry IV (Shakespeare)

King Lear: 38. King Lear: 130, 131

King William and Queen Mary Conquerors: 116

King: Mr.: 40. Sir Andrew: 10. Edward ("Lycidas"): see separate entry. Edward, Bp. of Elphin (uncle of "Lycidas"): 44. Edward (1726-97): 44; see also: Kingston, Earl of. Col. Edward: 44. Geoffrey: 40. Gregory: 40. Bp. Henry (H.): 33, 40, 45, 58, 59, 79, 84, 86, 26, 64, 93, 21. J. M.: 97. John: 40, 44, 45, 54, 114, 64. Bp. John: 93. Capt. John: 44. Sir John Dashwood: 44. L. W.: 41. Raphael (bks.): 44. Richard John: 44. Roger: 40. Stephen: 44. Abp. William: 12, 44, 58

King, Edward (fellow of Christ's): 4, 27, 29, 30, 33, 40*, 44*, 52, 84, 89, 111, 112, 126, 132, 144, 26, 32, 38, 64, 53, 71, 72, 88, 91, 94, 101, 109, 137, 148, 55, 21. Preferred over M for fellowship: 103. Death of, as Lycidas: 61. Drowned in 1637, model for Lycidas: 61, 103. See also: Lycidas

"King of Glory": 41

King's Cabinet: 144. King's Cabinet Opened (attr. to M): 44

King's College and Chapel, Cambridge: 40, 44

King's College School: 87

King's College, Aberdeen: 40

King's College, Oxford: 44

King's Ditch, Cambridge: 40

King's Gate, London: 44

King's Head (bookshop): 44

King's Langley: 45

King's Newnham: 45

King's Peace, The: 45

King's Prayer (in Eikon Basilike): 30

Kingdom, the: 141. Of Christ: 9*, 114, 103, 3; see also: Christ. Of evil: 47. Of God: see Heaven

Kingdom's Faithful and Impartial Scout: 44

Kingdom's Scout: 91

Kingless England, swords for: 147

Kings: 9*, 15, 30, 51*. M on the treatment of: 51. M hater of: 146. M' attitude toward: 113 King's: Bench: 44, 45. Evil: 16. Music: 29. Person: 51. Power, M summarizes the limitations of under the Eng. constitution: 147. Supremacie: 51. Kingship: 51*, 83*, 147*; M epitomizes the weakness of: 147; M feels kingship inconsistent with Christianity: 147; army view of: 147; attacks by Levelllers on in 1646: 147; Cromwell on: 147; M's view on: 147*; Prynne on: 147; Prebyterian agitation for in 1649: 147; restoration of: 147; theories of, in Mum and the Sothsegger: 83*; divine origin of: 83; theory of, on the Continent: 83; theory of, in Eng.: 83; Stigel's influence on: 83; Stigel's explanation of: 83; as tyranny: 83; duties of: 83; necessity for: 83; Stigel's theories of: 83. See also: Monarchy

Kings of Judah, example of: 51

Kings Book: 40. See also: Eikon Basilike

Kings Parade, Cambridge: 40

Kingsford: 3

Kingsgate: 44

Kingsley, Charles: 87, 18. On Spasmodic poetry: 87. Defense of Puritans: 87. On M's Puritanism: 87. Plays and Puritans: 87

Kingsmill, Thomas: 40

Kingston (town): 49

Kingston upon Hull, co. York: 44

Kingston-upon-Thames: 45

Kingston: (Kinaston): Anne Powell: 44, 45. Edward King, 1st Earl of: 44. Thomas: 44, 45

Kingu: 36

Kinloch, Tom F.: 93

Kinneresford: 49

Kinsalensis: 49

Kintyre, Scotland: 44

Kinwith: 49

Kiow (Kyovia): 49

Kipling, Rudyard: 40, 53, 112, 136, 137

Kirby: E. W.: 9. George (composer): 44

Kircher: 113, 121. A.: 4. Athanasius: 142, 32, 88; Oedipus Aegyptiacus: 142

Kiriathaim: 49, 73

Kirk: Bridget: see Pye, Bridget. G. S.: 64. Bp. Kenneth E.: 93. R. E. G. and E. F.: 40. Rudolf: 60, 72, 128. Thomas: 45, 92, 97

Kirkconnel, Watson: 15, 17, 118, 122, 123, 128, 32, 36, 64, 101. Celestial Cycle: 74, 95

Kirkman, Francis (bks.): 44

Kirkpatrick, James: 117

Kirkwood, G. M. T.: 44

Kirtlington, co. Notts.: 44

Kirton, co. Suffolk: 44

Kirton, Joshua: 10

Kishon: 49

Kissling, R. C.: 5

Kitab al-'Unvan: 65

Kitchin, George: 44

Kitching, Henry: 44

Kitto Bible: 99. See also: Bible

Kitto: H. D. F.: 148, 6. J. V.: 44

Kittredge, G. L.: 58, 142. Witchcraft in Old and New England: 142

Kivette, Ruth Montgomery: 137

Klähr: 3

Klatzkin, Jac.: 41

Klausner, Joseph: 93

Klein, Robert: 5, 39

Klibansky, Raymond: 93

Klingender, F. D.: 97

Klockus, Joannes, Christiados: 74, 64

Klopstock, Friedrich Gottlieb: 65, 74, 115, 146, 117, 13, 7, 64, 130. And M compared: 146

Kluckhohn, Clyde: 118

Kmosko, M.: 123

Knagg, Henry: 120

Knappen, Marshall Mason: 9, 54, 60, 83, 102

Knapton, co. York: 44, 45

Knapton: James (bks.): 44. John (bks.): 44. Paul (bks.): 44

Knattingley. See Knottingley

Knausts, Heinrich: 65

Kneller, Sir Godfrey (painter): 44, 97

Knewstub, John: 114

Knight: 40. Charles (publisher): 44. Douglas: 37. G. Wilson: 12, 15, 23, 27, 34, 60*, 76, 83, 102, 110, 128, 108, 141*, 14, 39, 93, 21, 130; The Burning Oracle: 109. Harold: 93. Henry C.: 115; The Cypriad in Two Cantos: With Other Poems and Translations: 115. Richard Payne: 58, 146; An Analytical Inquiry into the Principles of Taste: 88. Samuel: 20, 40, 58. W. F. Jackson: 56

Knightley: Jane: 45. Mary (Upton): 45. Richard: 44*, 45*

Knights of Round Table: 103

Knights, L. C.: 86*, 95, 108, 144, 93. On sensibility: 104

Knipe, E.: 58

Knipperdolling, Bernard: 91

Knoepfler, Aloisius: 40

Knole, Sevenoaks: 44

Knolles, Richard: 19, 40, 44

Knollys: Hanserd: 9, 114, 38; radicalist: 147. William: 40

Knott, Edward (pseud.): 114

Knottingley (Knattingley), co. York: 44, 45

Knowable, what is: 96

Knowledge of Things Unknowne: 128

Knowledge: 7, 17*, 24*, 31*, 47*, 51*, 52*, 67, 83, 124*, 125*, 128, 139, 143, 106*. And the poet: 106*. And reason: 106. Of God: 139. PR as drama of: 52. Self knowledge: 125. Two competing theories of: 125. As power: 125*. Four stages of: 125. And Christ's descent into self: 125*. And persuasion: 125. As love: 125. Of God: 125. As common to all: 125. And Satan's descent into self: 125. Limits of: 128. Vain curiosity: 128. As key to salvation: 143. Within bounds: 143. True wisdom: 143. Sum of: 143. Temperance of: 93. Theory and elements of: 96*. In Everyman: 72. See also: Adam and Eve, knowledge; Tree of Knowledge; Wisdom

Knowles: Sir Francis: 44. J. D.: 44. John: 97, 148

Knowlton, Edgar C.: 68, 69, 92, 93

Knowsley Masque (Salusbury): 29

Knowsley, John: 40

Knox, John: 7, 40, 44, 47, 51, 52, 60, 68, 73, 103, 116, 143, 147, 3, 71, 99*. The right of people to overthrow existing government in interest of their religion: 147. On life of spirit: 143. Works: A Letter to the Queen Regent of Scotland, in which he justifies religious revolution: 147; The Admonition of John Knox to the Commonality of Scotland: 147; Book of Common Order: 126; "A Confession of all Estates and Time": 126; Prayers, etc, subjoyned to Calvin's Cathechism: 126; Exposition upon Matthew IV: 74

Knox: Samuel: 115; A Compendious System of Rhetoric: 115. Vicisimus: 58, 117, 115; The Spirit of Despotism: 115

Kobylanski, Ilzi Faustyn: 65

Koch, Hugo: 93

Kocher, Paul H.: 128*, 93

Kodinos, Georgios. See Codinus, Georgius

Koebner, Richard: 39

Koepfel. See Capito

Koestler, Arthur: 93, 101

Koetschau, Paul: 41

Kölner Anglistische Arbeiten: 44

Komensky, Jan Amos: 40. See also: Comenius

Kommos: 92*

Konarnum: 49

Konavalov (Konovolov), Aleksandr Ivanovich: 60

König, J. V.: 10

Kooiman, Willem J.: 93

Koonce, B. G.: 62

Kophon prosopon: 72

Köping, Sweden: 44

Koran: 15, 41, 113

Körner: 7

Kostlin, Julius: 93

Kowaka-mai (Japanese quasi-epic): 118

Kraft, J. D.: 10

Kraft, Kaspar: 40

Kramer, Samuel Noah: 65, 36, 64

Kranidas, Thomas: 37, 54, 75, 123, 101, 106. On M: 104

Krantor: 4

Krapp, G. P: 64

Krause, Erich: 123

Krieger, Murray: 23, 14. Prior notion and poetry: 61

Kristeller, Paul Oskar: 5, 60, 69, 81, 122, 123, 39, 93, 101, 21. Classics and Renaissance Thought: 74

Kronos. See Saturn

Kropotkin, Peter A.: 60

Krosse Keyes. See Cross Keys

Krouse: F. Michael: 4, 6, 27, 52, 79, 123, 125, 143, 26, 37, 80, 93, 39, 85, 101, 137; Samson's faith: 143; Greek tragedy in Renaissance: 143; M's Samson: 74.

Kruegerus, Jacobus: 44

Kubla Khan: 136, 88

Kudos (glory): 122. See also: Honor

Küeffer, Johan: 10

Kuen-Lun: 32

Kuhl, E. P.: 59

Kuhn, H.: 100

Kuhnmuench, O. J.: 36

Kuhns, Oscar: 111

Kunz, C. F.: 15. George F.: 128

Kurth, Burton O.: 122, 123. M and Christian Heroism: 74

Kurtz, Benjamin P., and Charles M. Gayley, Methods and Materials of Literary Criticism: 74

Kyd, T.: 15, 58, 108

Kyle: 49

Kymeus, Johannes: 65

Kynaston, Sir Francis: 42, 88. Herbert: 64

-L-

L., E.: 44. See also: Howells, Elizabeth Lloyd

L., F. (pr., 1541-57): 44. Francis Leach: 91

L., I.: 59

L., J. M. C.: 44

L., R.: 91

L., Sir W.: 44

L., W.: 54. Virtues of women, men: 54

Labadie, Jean (de): 30, 44, 73, 112, 62, 91, 137

Labeo: 44. Labeo(nem), Attius: 73

Labor: 24*, 47, 50*. See also: Composition, revision. Laborers: 83

Labouchere, Henry, 1st Baron Taunton: 44

La Boulaye, France: 44

Labriolle, Pierre de: 81

Labyrinth: 11*. The meaning of: 11*. Of language: 11. As form of history: 11. And "last judgement": 11. In PR: 11

Lacan, Jacques: 11

Lacedaemon: 73, 3. Lacedaemonian(s): 73

Lacey, Thomas A.: 93

Laches: 121

Lachesis: 44

Lachisum (Lachish): 73

Lachisus: 49

Lacock, co. Wilts.: 44

Laconic(k): 73

Lacroix, Paul: 29

Lacrymae Adami: 65

Lactantius Placidus: 57

Lactantius, Firmianus: 1, 15, 17, 18, 20, 24, 40, 44, 56, 57*, 60, 68, 73, 74, 77, 90, 102, 107, 113, 114, 121, 128, 142, 3, 32, 38, 71, 93, 101, 115, 149, 64, 55, 21. M's knowledge and use of: 57*. Chiliasm: 107. Son antedates creation: 107. Works: Opera: 82*, Epitome of the Divine Institutes: 74; "Treatise on the Anger of God": 74; Divinae Institutiones: 57*, 74, 77; De Ave Phoenice: 57; De Ira Dei: 57; De Opificio Dei: 57; Epitome: 57, 77

Lacy: Mr.: 44. W.: 58

Ladd, Joseph Brown: 115; The Poems of Arouet: 115

Ladder: 143. And Christ: 143. Of 2 woods: 143. In Ambrose: 143. In Zeno: 143. And 15 step of: 143. Honorius: 143. In Hilton's Scala: 143. In Calvin: 143. Scala coeli: 143

Ladewig, Th.: 100

Ladies' Magazine, The: 115

Ladiscay: 49

Ladislas, King of Bohemia: 60

Ladner, G. B.: 39

Ladon: 19, 73, 49, 90

Lady (in Comus): 1*, 29*, 40, 73, 112, 143, 72*. And reason in Comus: 143. Invincibility of: 143. Character of: 143. As a symbol: 143. Importance of dance with Father: 104. Relationship to Nature: 104. Response to Comus: 104. Moral attitude of: 104. As allegorical image: 104

Lady Day: 40. Lady Day Quarter: 40

Lady MacBeth: 72. See also: MacBeth

Lady Margaret: preacher: 40. Professorship of divinity: 40

"Lady of Christ's passage": 30, 40, 44, 94

Lady's Pocket Library, The: 115

Lady's Weekley Miscellany, The: 115

Laelius, Caius: 73, 3

Laertes: 90. Perellius: 56

Laerties: 73

Laertius, Diogenes: 70, 73, 112, 3, 71

Lafayette, Marquis de: 60

Lafontaine, Henry Cart de: 40, 120

Laforque, Jules: 1, 86

Laquerre, L.: 97

Laherne. See Laugharne

Lahor(e): 49, 73, 19. See also: Agra

Laing: D.: 9, 132. Malcolm: 58, 88. John: see Halkett. Samuel: see Halkett

Laird, John: 12

Laistner, M. L. W.: 36

Laity: 9*

L'Allegro: 98*, 103, 113, 121, 144, 143, 55. Imagery in: 143. Style of: 143. Purpose in: 144. See also: Milton, John, Works

"L'Allegro el Il Penseroso in Sonno; or, The Power of Sleep": 117

Lake country: 58

Lake: Bp. Arthur: 93. K.: 57. John: 116. Sir Thomas: 64

Lakes, Osmunl: 64

Lamartine, Alphonse de: 44, 65, 111, 113

Lamb, Charles: 23, 44, 50, 58*, 87, 132, 91, 97, 130, 137, 146. Annotations to M's Poetical Work: 146. Bibliography of his M criticism: 146. Letters: 146. Others' reminiscences of: 146. Works: Characters of Dramatic Writers: 146; Elia: 146; Last Essays of Elia: 146; Miscellany: 146; On the Custom of Hissing at the Theatres: 146; On the Tragedies of Shakespeare: 146; Review of Moxon's Sonnets: 146; Review of the Excursion: 146; Scraps of Criticism: 146; The Sister's Expostulation: 146; Specimens of English Dramatic Poets: 146; Table Talk: 146; To the Poet Cowper: 146

Lamb: John: 44. Thomas: 116

Lamb: 3. Of God: 25

Lambard, William: 40, 82. Archeion: 82

Lambarde, Mr.: 44

Lambe: John: 114. T.: 58

Lambech, Peter: 44

Lambert: 120. Francois: 93. Gen. John: 44, 51, 73, 103, 116, 38. Of Hersfeld: 93. William: 45

Lambeth: 49, 73. Palace: 103. Palace Library: 40, 44. Palace MS.: 45

Lambinus, Dionysius: 40, 44

Lambley, Kathleen: 40

Lamboll, George: 44

Lambourne: Ann: 44. Thomas: 44

Lame Giles His Haultings (William Prynne): 147

Lamech: 16

Lamennais, Felicité de: 111

Lamentations: 74

Lami, G.: 6

Lamia (snake): 128. "Lamia" (Keats): 134

Lamont, W. M.: 59

Lamotte-Houdart: 149

Lampas: 49

Lampe, G. W. H.: 79, 93. And K. J. Woolcombe, Typology: 74

Lampert, Evgueny: 93

Lampridius, Aelius: 73

Lampsacus (Lampsacenum): 73

Lampton, W. J.: 58

Lancashire (Lancaster co.): 44, 45, 49. Lancaster, co. or town: 44, 45, 51. Duchy of: 44

Lancashire and Cheshire Historic Society, Transactions of: 44. Publications of Record Society of: 45. Lancashire and Cheshire Inquisitions: 45

Lancaster, House of: 44. Lancaster and Cheshire, Remains...Connected with: 44

Lancaster: H. C.: 63. N.: 58. Walter B.: 16. William: 44

Lance, G.: 97

Lancelot, Claude: 40

Lancelot: 73, 122, 123

Lancetta, Troilo: 65, 77, 32, 149

Land tenure: 45

Land's End. See Belerium

Landaff: 49, 73

Landguard Fort, co. Suffolk: 44

Landi, Stephano: 6, 137

Landino, Cristofero: 60, 111. Works: Dante con Pespositione di Cristofero Landino: 60; Disputationes Camaldulenses: 60

Lando, Ortensio: 23, 114

Landor, Walter Savage: 15, 16, 58*, 73, 86, 87*, 102, 105, 111, 113, 118, 129, 132, 144, 88, 130, 137, 146*, 150, 55, 21, 138. Admires M: 58. On M's sonnets: 53, 87. Response to M: 87. On M's "Piedmont" sonnet": 87. Admired M's artistry: 87. Interest in classical authors: 87. Attitude toward M: 87. On Shakespeare's sonnets: 87. On PL: 87. Works: Imaginary Conversations: 87; "To the President of the French Republic": 87; Gebir, influence of PL on: 87; bibliography of his M criticism: 146; Abbé Delille and Walter Landor: 146; Andrew Marvel and Bishop Parker: 146; Archdeacon Hare and Walter Landor: 146; Eng. Hexameters: 146; Gibbon: 146; Joan of Arc: 146; M: 146; M and Andrew Marvel: 146; Old Fashioned Verse: 146; Poems of Catullus: 146. Popery: 146; Second Conversation: Southey and Landor: 146*; Southey and Landor: 146*; Third Conversation: M and Andrew Marvel: 146; To Eliza Lynn: 146; To Rev. C. C. Southey: 146; To the Author of Festus: 146; To the Author of the Plaint of Freedom: 146; To the President: 146; To the Nightengale: 146; Written on M's Defence: 146

Landowners: 51

Landscapes, Warton on melancholy as an integral element of beauty in: 88

Landseer, E.: 97

Landy, M. K.: 122

Lane: Mr.: 44; see also: Jane. J. W.: 45. John: 40, 44*, 45; Works: The Corrected History of Sir Guy, Earl of Warwick: 44; "Tritons Triumph to the Twelve Months": 44. Lady: 40. Thomas: 44. W.: 44. Rev. William: 44

Laneham, Robert: 20

Lanfranc of Canterbury: 68

Lang: Andrew: 33, 76, 118, 148, 64. August: 93, 64. Paul Henry: 100

Langbaine, Gerard: 40, 44, 115

Langbaum, Robert: 53

Langborne, Ward: 40

Langdon-Davies, John: 93

Langdon: Ida: 5, 17, 31, 60, 66, 75, 102, 108, 112, 122, 123. S.: 36

Langer, Susanne: 12, 23, 76

Langford: Samuel: 44. Thomas: 101

Langfors, Arthur: 93

Langho (Whaley): 49

Langhorne, Dr. John: 44, 58*, 117, 3

Langland: 133. J.: 129. William: 60, 102, 36, 25; Piers Plowman: 36

Langley: C.: 59. J.: 128. John, High Master: 20, 44. Peter: 44, 45. S.: 58. Samuel: 40. Thomas: 44

Langoémagog (Giant's Leap): 49

Langston: Mr.: 45. Peter: 45

Langton: E.: 141. Edward: 142, 93; works: Satan, a Portrait: 142; Supernatural: the Doctrine of Spirits, Angels, and Demons, from the Middles Ages until the Present Time: 142. William: 64

Langtrae, co. Oxon.: 44

Language(s): 67, 70, 11*, 143, 117. Of religion: 143. Drills: 51. Logical imprecision in: 118. Barrier: 47. Double meaning of: 11*. After the Fall: 11*. Before the Fall: 11*. Continental vernacular: 40. Taught in London ca. 1625: 40. See also: Decorum; Style

Languages: taught in London ca. 1625: 40. Used by M: 40, 44, 51. M's study of: 137, 20*

Language(s) used by M: 40, 44, 51. M's study of: 137, 20*. M on: 51. Of M's as affected by his knowledge of music of religion: 143. In Comus, Lycidas, of PL, SA, PR: 11*. Language and Style in Milton (ed. Emma and Shawcross): 135

Languedoc: 44, 49, 73

Languet, Hubert: 44. Thomas: 93

Langus (Lange), Johann: 73

Lanier: 149. Nicholas: 29, 40, 39, 120. Sidney: 128. Thomas: 40

Lansberg, Philip van: 114. Lansberg Tables: 89

Lansdowne, George Granville, Lord: 117

Lanson, G.: 6, 18

Laocoon: 56. Lessing's: 88

Laodicea: 49. Laodicean(s): 73

Laodun: 49

Laparelli, Marcantonio: 65

Lapide, Cornelius à: 24*, 68, 32, 99*. Works: Commentaria in Quatuor Prophetus Maiores: 74; Commentarius in Josue, Judicum, Ruth: 74; Commentarius in Quatuor Evangelia: 74; In Pentateuchum: 74. See also: Steen, C.

Lapini, Frosino, Letiöne...della Poesia: 74

Lapland: 19, 49, 73, 103. Witches: 144

Laporelli, Marcantonio, Christiade: 74, 64

Lapp, J. C.: 123

Lapsus et reparatio hominis: 65

Lapsus Adae: 65

Lapworth. See Lupworth

Lardner, W. D.: 58

Lares: 142, 144

Lark: 25

Larkey, S. V.: 128

Larkin: J. F.: 20, 40. P. A.: 44

Lars: 90

Larson: M.: 102. Martin Alfred: 54, 63, 68, 86, 113, 144; works: "M's Essential Relationship to Puritanism and Stoicism": 60; The Modernity of Milton: 60

L'Arte Poetica (Minturno): 70

Lascaris, Constantin: 40

Lasco (Lasko): Albertus Alasco, Baron of: 40, 44. P.: 44

Laslett, Peter: 32

Lassels, R.: 6

Last Booke of John Smith (John Smyth): 147

Last Day, The: 58

Last Day: 72

Last Judgment: 72*, 25. Imminent: 93. Signs of: 93. Literalistic conceptions: 93. See also: Eschatology

Last Speech and Behavior of William Late Lord Russell, The: 116

Last Supper: 72

Last, G. H. (bks.): 44

Late George Apley (J. P. Marquand): 118

Lateran: 49. Council of: 73

Latham: Miss: 35. Mr.: 44. R. E.: 36

Lathom, Paul: 116

Lathrop: Gordon: 16. H. B.: 145. Joseph: 115; works: Discourses on the Mode and Subjects of Christian Baptism: 115; A Miscellaneous Collection of Original Pieces: 115

Lathwood: 44

Lathy, T. P.: 58

Latian music: 44

Latimer, apb. Hugh: 18, 15, 27, 44, 51, 73, 143, 38, 82, 91. Value of preaching: 143; and scala coeli: 143

Latin classics: 70. Comedy: 70. Language of: 70, 3*. Thesaurus: 103. Tragedy: 70. Eloquence: 3. Dunster regards M's terseness as derived from the: 88

Latin poems: 18, 20, 40, 44, 58. Read in Svogliati Academy: 44. M's: 130, 70, 129, 88, 146*, 117*.

Discussed: 55. Works: Ad Ioannem Rousium, preface, quoted: 55; Ad Patrem: 55; Elegy I, IV, V, VI, VII: 55; Epitaphium Damonis: 55; Mansus, mentioned: 55

Latin Bible: allusions to: adhere: 119; fire and ice: 119; minims: 119; palpable darkness; peccant: 119; play: 119; substance: 119

Latin Dictionary: 16

Latin Elegies: 136

Latin Grammar (Lily): 3

Latin Secretaryship to the Commonwealth, M's appointment to: 51.

Latin, M's study and use of: 20*, 30, 40*, 117*. As M's literary language: 132*. The Richardsons praising M's "pure Latin": 88. Latin Poems of J. M.: 112, 113

Latin: 40*, 44*, 51, 98, 103*, 132*, 72, 88. Latinate style: 40. Latinism: 70. See also: Classical

Latini, Brunetto: 93. See also: Brunetto

Latins, making: 73

Latins, the: 70, 3

Latinus, King: 56

Latium (Latialis): 49, 3

Latius...Caesar: 73

Latmus: 44, 49, 3

Latona: 73, 90, 3

Latria: 40

Lattimore, Richmond: 1, 76

Laubmann, G.: 57

Laud, William (Abp. of Canterbury): 1, 7, 10, 15, 20, 27, 64, 33*, 40*, 42, 44, 51, 57, 59, 60, 91, 93, 117, 66, 73, 87, 103, 113, 114, 116, 126, 132, 134, 136, 145, 143, 26, 32, 38, 62, 71, 94. Attempt to check rising Puritan clamor: 147. Discipline of: 143. And Sherfield: 143

Lauder, Rev. William: 44, 73, 129, 144, 32, 36, 88, 94, 97, 130, 146, 149, 117*, 55. Attack on M; imitates PL: 58

Laudun, Pierre de: 1, 4, 100

Laufener, Adam-und Eva-Spiel: 65

Laugharne (Laherne): 44

Laughing Mercury: 103

Laughter: 8. Of God: 93

Laughton, Thomas: 40

Laundresses: 40

Laura (Petrarch's): 83, 111, 103, 3, 44, 70, 73, 64

Laureate of Peace: 12

Laurel as an emblem of admiration: 83

Laurence: Mr. (Academy of): 44. Apb.: 88. St.: 73. Edward and Henry: 28. J.: 58

Laurentian Library: 44

Laurentin, René: 93

Laurentius, Andreas: 128

"Laurentius Anatomica": 40

Laurie: 3

Laurifiers: 40

Laus Asini: 40

"Laus Pisonis": 21

Lausanne (Lausanna): 44, 49

Lausus: 2

Lavater: Johann Caspar: 65, 90, 97, 25. Ludwig: 7, 142; Of Ghosts and Spirits: 142

Laverna: 73

Lavinia: 17, 60, 73, 90, 3

"Lavinia Walking," (attr. to M): 44

Lavinius, Father Petrus: 32

Lavoix, Henry: 100

Law books, M's: 45

Law Dictionary, or the Interpreter, A. (Cowel): 45

Law Dictionary, A (Tomlins): 45

Law Merchant, Select Cases Concerning the: 45

Law: D. G.: 44. William: 7, 83, 142, 32, 146

Law: 9*, 31, 51*, 60, 83*, 113, 122, 144, 11*, 143*. Four kinds: 128. As exemplified in music: 121. M's rejection of the moral: 113. Civil: 9*. Licensing: 51. Moral: 9*, 31. Mosaic: 63*, 46. Positive: 9, 83. And Gospel: 9*. Of falling bodies: 89. Of God, Moses: 9*. Of nations: 9. In M's prose: 11. In PL: 11. As a source of contradictions: 11. The keys and the sword: 143. On preaching: 143. Natural: 93. International: 93. Hierarchy of laws: 93. Of Nature: 9*, 60. Of Nature, Secondary: 9*. Of the Spirit: 9*. Studies: 40. In SA: 125. And inspiration: 125. Christian: 46. M's references to: 40. M's decision against entering: 40. Relation between positive and natural law in M's philosophy: 147

Lawes: Henry (1596-1662): 27, 28, 29*, 33, 40*, 44*, 59, 73, 84, 100, 121*, 120, 87, 103, 126, 135, 136, 111*, 26, 32*, 53, 62, 82, 88, 91, 101, 109, 130, 137, 148, 64, 94, 117, 55, 21; see also: M's Sonnet XIII. Jerome: 44. William: 29, 40, 59, 103, 120, 39

Lawiers Logike (Fraunce): 20

Lawler, D.: 58

Lawlor, J. J.: 150

Lawrence: 121, 130. D. H.: 15*, 34, 35, 37, 86, 95, 127, 132, 133, 109, 137; Lady Chatterley's Lover: 95. Edward: 44*, 30, 59, 120*, 26, 38, 137, 55; see also: M's Sonnet XX. H.: 59, 94. Henry (1600-64), President of Council of State: 10, 30, 44, 59, 142*, 102, 120, 91, 93; works: Militia Spiritualis, etc.: 142. John: 44, 120, 117. Major Richard: 44. Sir T.: 97. T. E.: 64. Thomas (author of Mercurius Centralis): 44. William: 44

Lawry, Jon S.: 32, 106. Pagan and Christian allusions in Lycidas: 61

Laws of Ecclesiastical Polity (Hooker): 134

Laws, The (Plato): 51, 121, 3, 112*, 3

Laws: as proof: 51. Conflict in: 51

Lawson: Mr.: 44; see also: Dawson. George: 102. John: 93. Sir W.: 28. Sir Wilfred: 44

Lawyers: 9, 45, 51. Attack on: 40

Laxton: 45

Lay of the Last Minstrel (Scott): 94

Lay preaching: 114

Lay Monastery: 58

Lay: 121

Layard, C. P.: 58

Lazarus: 72

Le Blanc, Jean-Bernard: 117

Le Bossu, René: 122, 109. Traité du Poëme Epique: 74

Le Brun, Charles: 27

La Chesnaye: 29

Le Clerc, Jean: 117

Le Cordier, Helie: 74, 64. L'Illustre Souffrant, ou Job: 74

La Fontaine: 70

Le Gallienne, R.: 58

Le Grice, C. V.: 58

Le Laboureur, Louis: 64: works: Charlesmagne: 74; Magdalaine Pénitente: 74

Le Loyer, Pierre: 128, 142; Discours et Histoires des Spectres: 142

Le Mesurier, T.: 58

La Milletière, Theophile Brachet de: 114

La Mothe le Vayer, François de: 44, 145

Le Moyne, Pierre, Saint Louys: 74, 122

Le Neve, John: 45

Le Noir, Philippe, Emanuel: 74, 64

Le Non-Conformiste Anglois Dan Ses Ecris: 116

La Pensée de Milton: 71

La Peyrère, Isaac de: 32

La Primaudaye, Pierre de II: 114, 128*, 93

La Pujade, Antoine: Christiade; Mariade; Muse Chrestienne: 74, 64

La Rochefoucauld: 70

Le Roy: Adrien: 40. Henri: 114. Louis: 32, 93

La Sylva de Medrano: 88

La Wall, Charles H.: 16

Lea, Henry Charles: 44

Leach: 3. A. F.: 20*, 40, 57*, 144; "M as Schoolboy and Schoolmaster": 57. Francis (pr.): 44, 91

Lead, Jane: 7, 10

Leadam, I. S.: 45

Leader, C.: 97

Leadership (Humanistic ideal of): 8, 31, 40, 51, 122*, 123. Principle in PL: 147. M's conception of: 147

League of Smalkald: 60

League: 143. Satan's with man: 143

Leah: 111

Leapor, M.: 58

Lear (Leir), King: 60, 73, 87, 92. See also: King Lear

Lear, Floyd S.: 143. St. Isidore and medieval science: 143

Learned: the: 51. Men: 51. Expressions, Bentley's partiality for: 88. Character of M's poetry making indispensable the study of his sources, according to the Richardsons: 88

Learning: 51*, 114*, 117, 129, 146. Purpose of: 40. Origin and descent of: 114. Rational apology for, criticism of: 114*. As vain philosophy: 114*. Religious criticism of: 114*. In divinity: 114*. M's love of: 30. Bible only adequate basis for: 40. Range of: Hume's, Bentley's, Pearce's, the Richardsons', Peck's, Paterson's, Thyer's, Jortin's, Meadowcourt's, Newton's, Callander's, Massey's, Joseph Warton's, Thomas Warton's, Lofft's, Dunster's, Todd's, Bowle's, Stillingfleet's: 88. Considered by Richardsons less useful than critical intuition: 88. And subject of PL regarded by Paterson as its principle features: 88. M's, overemphasized by Paterson: 88. Preferred by Newton to Shakespeare's imaginative excellence: 88. See also: Commonplace Book; Influences

Leary, Lewis: 115

Leather, M.: 58

<u>Leaves of Grass</u>: 71

Leavis, F. R.: 1, 4, 12, 15, 34, 37, 60, 77, 84, 86, 105*, 123, 95, 124, 136, 145, 101, 110, 133, 130, 131, 146, 48. <u>Revaluation</u>: 109

Lebanon: 49, 73, 32. See also: Adonis

Lechmere: Edmund: 93. Sir Nicholas: 44

Lechner, Sister Joan Marie, <u>Renaissance Concepts of the Commonplaces</u>: 82

Lecky, W. E. H.: 142, 71

Lecler, Joseph: 93

LeClercq, Pieter: 117

LeComte, Edward S.: 1, 12, 23, 29, 59, 75, 128, 14, 93, 58, 101. On M: 80. Symbolism in Lycidas: 104

Leconfiel: Charles Henry Wyndham, 3rd Baron: 44. Hugh Archibald Wyndham, 4th Baron: 44

Leconte de Lisle: 65

Lecoy de la Marche, Albert: 40

<u>Lectio</u>: 40

Lectius, Jocobus, <u>Jonah</u>: 74, 64

Lector principalis: 40

<u>Lector</u>: 40

Lectqrae: 40

Lecturer: 40. Lectures: 40, 98

<u>Lectures and Notes on Shakespeare and Other Eng. Poets</u>: 83

Lectures on the Eng. Poets (Hazlitt): 83

Leda: 2

Ledbury: 45

Ledoux, C. N.: 97

Lee River: 49, 73

Lee, co. Bucks.: 44

Lee: family: 45. Mr. (pr.): 44. (Lea, Leigh, Ley), Mr.: 45. Alice: see Holloway, Alice Leigh. Anne (Cope): 45. Frances (Cope): 45. F. G.: 87. Francis: 7, 10. Sir Francis: 45. Sir Francis, Baron Dunmore: 45. Isaac: 44. Sir J.: 45. John: 44, 45. Lady Margaret: 44, 103; see also: Hobson. Mary (Egerton): 45. Myles: 44. Nathaniel: 27, 116. Sir Robert: 44,

45*. S.: 129. Sir Sidney: 44, 135. Sir Thomas: 45. William (pr.): 44, 91. Sir William: 45

Lee: 2, 130

Leech: David: 64. John: 40, 44, 64

Leeds (Loydes), co. Yorks.: 44, 49

Leeds: Sir John: 44. Sir Thomas: 44

Leeke: Sir Francis: 44. Rev. W.: 44

Lees: Elizabeth: 44. John: 44. Johnson: 44

Leeth, Scotland: 44

LeFeure, Tannequi: 117

Leeuw, G. van der: 141

Lefèvre d'Etaples, Jacques: 93

Leff, Gordon: 93

Lefkowitz, Murray: 59, 39

Legacies: from Bradshaw: 44. From Wentworth: 44

<u>Legacy of the Ancient World</u>, De Burgh in: 3

Legal Index (attr. to M): 44

Legalism: 34, 47. See also: Moralism; Self-righteousness; Virtue; Works

<u>Legall Fundamentall Liberties of the People of England</u> (John Lilburne): 147

Legatt, Mr.: 44

Legé, A.: 97

<u>Legend of Good Women</u> (Chaucer): 88

<u>Legend of Sir Nicholas Throckmorton</u>: 88

<u>Legenda d'Adamo ed Eva</u>: 65, 123

Legendary: atmosphere, valued by Hume: 88. Events appreciated by Hume: 88. Beauty and grandeur admired by the Richardsons: 88. Lore studied by Peck: 88

Léger, Jean: 120

Legg(e), Col. William: 73

Legh, Gerard: 40

Leghorn (Lyvorne, Legorn, Liburnum, Ligorn), Italy: 44, 3

Legislation: 51. Exercise in arguments for or against a law: 20. Legislators: 51; Eng.: 51. Legislature: 51

"Legislator of the Heavens" (Kepler): 89

Legouis: Emile: 4, 12, 68, 83, 132, 139, 35. Pierre: 44

Legrand: Anthony: 60. Antoine: 93. Philippe: 70

Leibnitz, Gottfried, Wilhelm von: 7, 10, 12, 40, 42, 39, 146

Leicester (Caerleir): 44, 49, 3. See also: Lestershire

Leicester, Earl of: 83

Leicestershire: 45. Leicester(shire), <u>The History and Antiquities</u>: 45

Leida, Marquis of: 44

Leiden (Leida, Lugdunum): 49

Leigh-Hunt, Trevor R.: 44

Leigh: family: 44. (Lee), Mr.: 44. Edward (Eduard): 40, 67, 102, 114, 142, 22, 32, 93, 99, 148; <u>Annotations on Five Poetical Books</u>: 74; works: <u>Annotations upon all the New Testament</u>: 142. Sir Francis: 44; see also: Chichester, Earl of. Sir James: 40; see also: Marlborough. John: 44. John (another, pr.): 44. Richard (b. 1649): 40, 44, 60, 116, 117; works: <u>Transproser Rehearsed</u>: 91; <u>Censure of Dryden</u>: 91. <u>Susanna</u>: 44. Thomas: 40, 58

Leighton: Alexander: 9. Sir William: 40, 44, 103, 121; Feares and Lamentations: 126

Leipnitz, G. W. See Leibnitz

Leipzig, Germany: 44

Leishman, J. B.: 86, 105, 110, 14

Leisure: 70. M's ideas on, use of: 30

Leitch, W. L.: 97

Lekprevik's Psalter: 42

Leland: 132, 130. John: 142; <u>View of the Principal Deistical Writers</u>: 142

Lely, Sir Peter: 44

Leman, Lake: 44, 3

Lemannus: 49

Lemmi, C. W.: 69, 144

Lemnius, Livinus: 93

Lemnos (Lemnian): 2, 44, 49, 73, 144

Lemoine, H.: 53

Lemon: Mark: 44. Robert: 63, 55. Robert, the Elder and the Younger: 44

L'Empereur, Constantine: 22

Lemures: 73, 90, 144

Len Len: 45

Length: 92. In vowels and syllables: 118

Lenin, Nikolai: 60, 125

Lennox: 49. C.: 58

Lens, Bernard: 44, 97

Lenten term: 40

Lenth. See Lenthall

Lenthall: Mr.: 45. Sir John: 44, 45. P.: 44. William, Speaker of Parliament: 44*, 45*

Lentulo, Scipio: 40

Lentulo-Grantham: 40

Lentulus: Publius: 24. Senator of Berne: 10

Leo Afer: 57. John, Africae Descriptio: 82. John

Leo: 44, 3. I: 73. III, Emperor: 73. VI, Emperor of Byzantium: 73; Constitutiones, in Leunclavius' Iuris Graeco-Romani: 82. Pope: 36. X, Pope: 73, 116, 93, 64. The Hebrew: 40, 128. The Great, St.: 99

Leogecia: 49

Leon: Harry Joshua: 33, 64*. Moses de: 93

Leonard's, St., College, St. Andrew's Univ.: 40

Leonardo: de Pisa: 40. da Vinci: 5, 6, 29, 40, 90, 114, 71, 93, 149. William Ellery: 64

Leone Ebreo: 79, 60

Leonicerus: 40

Leonidas of Tarentum: 64

Leonids: 89

Leonora (Roman singer): 132

Leonora Baroni: 121. M's love affair with: 87. Legend of: 87

Leontius: 73, 144. Of Antioch: 73

Leopardi: 130

Leopold: Prince and Archduke of Austria: 44. Son of Ferdinand II: 6

Leopolis: 49

Lepos: 73

Lermaeus, Gabrielis: 65

Lerna: 49, 73, 3

Lerner, L. D.: 81, 86, 105, 128, 53. "Miltonic Simile": 74

Lernutius, Janus: 65

Les Jardins (Delille): 70

Lesbos (Lesbian Shore): 49. Lesbian: 73; artificers: 45. See also: Hebrus

Lesley (Leslie), Bp. John: 93

Leslie: C. R.: 97. Charles: 116, 117. J.: 58

Lesly, John: 93

Lesno: 3

Lesser evil, as deliberative argument: 97

Lesser fine arts: 70

Lesser Bear: 89

Lessing, Gotthuld Ephraim: 10, 139, 88, 97, 130, 149.

Lessius, Leonardus: 32

Lestershire: 49

Lestrange: Anne: see Cope, Ann Paston. Sir N: 45

L'Estrange: 51. Hamon: 44, 103, 91; Smectymnuo-Mastix: 91. Sir Roger (1616-1704): 9, 16, 44*, 98, 103, 116*, 38, 91*, 93, 148; works: L'Estrange's Narrative of the Plot: 116; attacks M again in Treason Arraigned: 147, 91; berates M in L'Estrange His Apology: 147, 116, 91; singles out M in No Blinde Guides: 147, 91; taunts M in Be Merry and

Wise, Or a Seasonable Word: 147, 91; *Considerations*: 91; *Double Your Guards*: 91; *Physician Cure Thyself*: 91; *Sir Politique*: 91

LesFarques, Bernard, *David*: 74, 64

Letany (Dr. John Bastwick): 147

Letchworth, T.: 58

Lethe: 44, 49, 73, 90

"Lethe" satire: 44

Lethington, William Maitland of: 73

Leto: 56, 90. See also: Latona

Letourneur: 149

Letter Intercepted: 44, 91

Letter-writing formularies: 20*

Letters and Journals (Byron): 70

Letters from an American Farmer: 71

Letters of a Late Eminent Prelate: 12

Letters on the Improvement of the Mind: 98

Letters on Toleration: 73

Letters, various: from a Dissenter to His Friend: 116. From Gen. Ludlow to Dr. Hollingworth compared with *Eikonoklastes*: 116. From Maj. Gen. Ludlow to Sir E. S. A. compared with *Eikonoklastes*: 116. From Oxford: 116. Out of Suffolk: 116. To a Friend: 116. To a Gentleman at Brussels: 116. To a member of Parliament: 116. To Mr. Samuel Johnson: 116. To Mr. Secretary Trenchard: 116. To the Author of a Late Paper: 116. Written to My Lord Russel in Newgate: 116. Letters of State: 116. *Of the Ministers of the City of London* (campaign of London ministers against toleration): 147. *To the Earle of Manchester* (a royalist rebuke): 147. To the Rev. Mr. T. Warton: 88. To Wilson (Wordsworth): 70. Concerning Poetical Translations: 88

Letters: M's writings of, official, and reception of, etc.: 30, 44*. Familiar: 55. *To a Gentleman in the Country* (attr. to M): 44. To George Wither (attr. to M): 44. To Peter Heimback: 16, 133. To Count Palavicini de Saluces (attr. to M): 44. To Philaris (M's): 16, 20

Lettice, J. (translations by): 58

Lettres sur les Anglais: 12

Leucippus: 114. Leucippean: 73

Leucoma, early prescription for: 16

Leucothea: 73, 90, 104

Leunclavius, Johannes: 73. *Iuris Graeco-Romani...Tomi Duo*: 82

Leusden, John: 22

Leutha: 25

Leutze, Emmanuel (connected somehow with M portrait): 44

Levant: 144. Company: 44

Leveen, Jacob: 123

Leveller, The: 9

Levellers: 7, 9*, 44, 45, 52, 60, 103, 114, 147*, 32, 38*, 94. In 1645, leaders for toleration: 147. In 1646, drive for secular freedoms: 147. For press liberty: 147. In 1647, petition of, and agitation against kingship: 147. In 1648, debate with army Independents: 147*. In 1648, distrust of Cromwell: 147. On manhood suffrage: 147. On interpretation of history: 147. Philosophy of, contrasted with that of Independents: 147. Religious psychology of, contrasted with that of Independents: 147*. In 1649, oppose Cromwell in *The Second Part of Englands New-Chaines*: 147*

Lever: Christopher: 93. J. W.: 44, 36. Ralph: 40

Levi (Levites): 73

Levi ben Gerson (Gersonides): 40, 41*

Lévi-Strauss, Claude: 118, 39

Leviathan: 17, 51, 60, 73, 103, 144, 143, 36, 72, 97, 130. Satan as: 123. Prototype of Satan: 46. Symbol of Hell: 46

Levin: Harry: 69, 32. Meyer: 108

Lévis, Justine de: 44

Levison, Wilhelm: 93

Levita. See Elias the Levite

Levites: 71. Levitical: 73

Leviticus: 44, 118. Book of, quoted: 95. See also: Bible

Levron, J.: 99

Levy, Gertrude: 125

Lewalski, Barbara Kiefer: 37, 52, 75, 79, 81, 104, 110, 122, 123, 32, 36, 39, 85, 93, 101, 106, 21, 64. Analyzes Christ's temptation on highest pinnacle: 61. Christ's crucifixion and death analogized in storm: 61. On the narrator of PR: 61. Works: "Authorship of Ancient Bounds": 74; "M on Learning": 74; "Structure and the Symbolism of Vision in...PL XI-XII": 74; "Theme and Structure in PR": 74

Lewes, Jeremiah: 44. Walter: 44

Lewes, Song of (ed. by Kingsford): 3

Lewis: 58. A. G.: 58. Anthony John: 44; see also: Medina Celi of Andalusia. C. Day: 1, 56, 86, 108. Clarrisa O.: 44. C. S.: see separate entry. Elizabeth: 44. Rev. G.: 44. G. S.: 24. John: 93. Martha: 44. Mary: 44. Park: 16. R.: 58. Thomas: 44. W.: 23. Wyndham: 35. Zechariah: 115; An Oration on the Apparent, and the Real Political Situation of the U. S.: 115

Lewis, Clive Staples: 1*, 12, 15, 17, 23, 27, 34*, 37, 52*, 54, 56, 60, 66, 68, 69, 75, 76, 81, 86*, 95, 98, 102, 105, 107, 110, 112, 111, 118, 84, 122, 123, 124, 126, 127, 128, 133, 134, 136, 138*, 139, 141*, 142*, 14, 143, 22, 26, 32, 36, 39, 53, 85, 93, 99, 101, 106, 130*, 131, 137, 146, 148, 150, 64, 140*, 48. Definition of orthodoxy: 107. Fall results from pride and disobedience: 107. Heresies in PL insignificant: 107. M's theology important: 107. PL orthodox: 107. "Small heresies": 107. Hierarchy of values: 143. On Satan's character: 143. On PL: 104. Works: Preface to PL: 95, 142, 109, 48; Out of the Silent Planet: 142; Perelandra: 142; Screwtape Letters: 142

Lewisham: 40

Lewisohn, Adolph: 44

Lewkenor, Lewis: 128

Lex aeterna: 69*

Lex Rex: 44. See also: Rutherford

Lexicon(s): 51, 57. Lexicon Graeco-Lat.: 40. Lexicon Latinograecum Vetus: 123. Lexicon, M's latin: 94. Lexicons and Grammar of Oriental languages in 16th c.: 41. Lexicon Platonicum: 112

Ley: James, Earl of Marlborough: 28, 44, 59, 120; see also: Marlborough. John: 73. Lady Margaret: 28, 44, 59, 73, 87, 71, 120, 26, 91, 94, 55, 87; friendship with M: 87; sonnet on: 26, 87; see also M's Sonnet X. Lady Mary (Petty): 44; see also: Marlborough. Lady Phoebe: 120. Roger: 44

Leybourn: Robert (pr. and bks., 1645-61): 44, 91. William (pr. and bks., 1645-65): 44, 91

Leyden, J.: 58

Leyden: 44*, 3. Univ. of: 40, 103, 94

Lhuyd, Humphrey: 144

Libanius (Labanius): 73, 90

Libation-Bearers: 111

Libbe, Richard: 44

Libbie (auctioneer): 44

Libecchio: 73, 144

Libel: 51

Liber de Causis: 112

Liber in Genesin: 65

Liber. See Bacchus

Liber: M.: 113. Pater: 73

Liberal arts, the basis of education: 20

Liberalism, M's: 129

Liberals: 51

Liberating children: 51

Libert (Libbert), James: 45

Libertines: 51

Liberty (masque figure, in Lycidas): 29

Liberty of Conscience, the Magistrates Interest: 116

Liberty of Prophesying, The: 116

Liberty: Christian: 9*, 51, 54. Civil: 51*. Natural: 9*. Private or Domestic: 9*, 30*, 51. Religious: 9*, 30, 51. And marriage: 54. Of the press: 9*, 30, 51. Of conscience: 51. Of speech: 51. Of worship: 51. Individual, in poetry, the Richardsons on: 88. And License: 109. Modern conceptions of: 102

Liberty: 9*, 30*, 51*, 90, 113*, 143, 96. M's passion for: 113, 58. His general conception of: 113*, 129, 102, 25. Intellectual: 113. Moral: 113. Political: 30, 9*, 113. Priests, enemies of: 113. Established by Christ: 113. As birthright under God: 143. And corrupt nations: 143

Libitina: 73

Libna(h): 73

Libra: 89, 90

Libraria communis: 40

Libraries: 40

Library of Congress: 44

Library, M's: 44*, 55

Library: 44*. *Library Journal*: 44

Libri Theologici, etc.: 91

Liburnum: 49, 73

Libya (Libia, Lybia): 19, 44, 49, 73. Libyan (Lybian) sands: 73. Libycos leones: 73

License: 47, 51. Licensing: 44*, 51*; of musical instruments: 121; M's view on: 30*. Licensing Act: 116*, 78. Licensing Acts: of 1640: 55; of 1643: 55. Licenses, Poetical: regarded as due to lack of scholarship: 88; of the Elizabethans: 88

Licentiousness: hatred of: 51. Of the Royalists: 51

Lichas: 73, 90

Lichfield, co. Staffs.: 44, 49

Lichtenstein, Aharon: 81

Licinius: 73. Archias: 70

Lickbarrow, I.: 58

Liddle, Alice : 35

Lidley (Liddell), Mr.: 117

Lieb, Michael: 106

Liebert: 7

Liegenhain. See William VI

Life and Death of Mrs. Mary Frith: 44

Life and Death of Vane: 91

Life and Reign of King Charles (attr. to M): 44, 91

Life and Times (Wood): 45*

Life everlasting: 47

Life of Adam: 65. *Life of Adam and Eve*: 24*

Life of Colet (Knight): 20, 112

Life of Lycurgus (Plutarch): 3

Life of Plato: by Olympiodorus: 112. By Diogenes Laertius: 112

Life of Ramus (Freigius): 20

Life of Socrates (Diogenes Laertius): 112

Life of William Lord Russell: 116

Life, M's: earliest life of M: 45. By Edward Allam or himself: 44. *Life of Milton* (Samuel Johnson): 147, 130. *Life of John Milton, The* (Masson): 20; 51*, 116, 3*, 130. *Life of Milton, The*: (E. Phillips): 70, 20, 3. *Life of Milton, The* (Toland): 70, 116. *Life of Milton, Collections for the* (Aubrey): 70

Life: 44

Lifeboat (film): 95

Liganburgh: 49

Ligeia: 73, 90

Ligeris: 49

Light Shining in Buckingham-Shire (Gerrard Winstanley): 147

Light Shining in Darkness, and the Darkness Comprehending it Not: 115

Light: 60*, 63, 70*, 89, 107, 113, 128*, 144, 143. Nature of: 40. Refraction of: 89. Transmition of: 89. Undulatory theory of: 89. Velocity of: 89. Linked with Logos: 107. Creation of before the sun: 119. In connection with M's monism: 110. Imagery: 110. Creation: 128. Male and female: 128. Movement: 128. Pre-solar: 128. Three kinds: 128. And darkness symbolism: 128. Of torches: 143. Sacred influence: 143. M's reaction to: 16. Symbolism of: 81*. M's invocation to: 113. Probable source in Fludd: 113. See also: God as Light; Son of God as Light

Lightfoot(e): John: 40*, 41, 42, 68, 123, 22, 32, 93, 99; works: *Harmony of the Foure Evangelists*: 74; *Harmony ... of the Old Testament*: 74. Thomas: 40

Lighthouse, Anne: 44

Lighting, in masques: 29*

Lightning: 128*. Causes and kinds: 128

Likeness: 124. Of God: 24

Likes (similia), argument from: 123

Lilburne, John: 8, 9*, 33, 44*, 45, 59, 60, 103, 108, 113, 116, 147*, 32, 38, 91. Against Bps. against crown: 147. And Reformation: 147. A secular reformer: 147. A zealous Independent: 147. Contrasted with M: 147*. Hated by the Presybterians: 147. Leader of the secular radicals in 1646: 147. Loses faith in Cromwell: 147. On economic change: 147. Opposes the established church: 147. Persecuted for his beliefs: 147. Philosophy of economic reform: 147. Political philosophy: 147. Rejects philosophy of Diggers: 147. Views on tithes: 147. Works: against Commons in Rash Oaths Unwarrantable: 147; against kind and lords in The Just Man's Justification: 147; against the lords in The Grand Plea: 147; attacks kingship in Regall Tyrannie: 147. Berates tyrants in A Whip for the House of Lords: 147; for free press in Englands New Chaines Discovered: 147; gives an account of his imprisonment in The Copy of a Letter from Lt. Col. J. L. to a friend: 147; his democratic doctrine stated in Innocency and Truth Justified: 147; in Legal Fundamental Liberties: 147; in Free-Man's Freedome: 147; on free press in Preamble to Englands Birth Right: 147; on the repression of printing in The Second Part of Englands New Chaines: 147; protests in England's Birth Right Justified; replies to Diggers with Legall Fundamental Liberties: 147; states his political faith in The Free-Mans Freedome Vindicated: 147; supports cause of toleration in Oppressed Mans Oppressions declared: 147; Just Mans Justification: 147; Londons Liberty in Chains: 147; The Legal Fundamental Liberties of the People of England: 147; The peoples Prerogative: 147; The Iuglers Discovered: 147; to Cromwell in Jonah's Cry out of the Whale's belly: 147

Lilburne, (John), Overton (Richard), Prince, (Tho.), The Second Part of England's New-Chaines: 147*

Lilburne, Col. Robert: 44

Lilburns Ghost: 9

Lile, Mr.: 103

Lilies Rules Construed: 20

Lilith: 24, 113, 123

Lilja: 65

Liljegren, S. B.: 6, 9, 44, 133, 138, 60, 86, 102, 113, 132, 130, 141, 88, 91

Lille, Alain de: 32

Lilly: John (pr.): 44. M. L.: 58. William (astrologer): 20, 40, 44, 45, 114, 128, 58, 142; works: The World's Catastrophe: 142; Monarchy or No Monarchy: 91

Lily: John: 82. (Lilye), William (1st master of Paul's): 20, 18, 27, 40*, 73, 3; his Latin grammar: 20*, 126

Limbo: 17, 73, 102, 111, 72. And suicide, M on: 80. Of Vanity: 2, 51, 67, 70, 128

Lime Street: 45

Limehouse: 44

Limentani, U.: 39

Limery, M.: 40

Linacre (Linaker), Thomas: 18, 40, 73, 112, 3, 64

Linche, R.: 59

Lincoln (Lincolnshire): co. and city: 44, 45, 49. Bp. of: see William, John. College, Cambridge: 44, 45. College, Oxford: 44, 45. Grammar School: 40, 112. Archives Committee: 44

Lincoln: Abraham: 40, 72, 137. Levi: 115; Letters to the People By a Farmer: 115

Lincoln's Inn, London: 44, 45*, 103. Admission Register: 45. The Black Books of: 45. The Records of the Honorable Society of: 45

Lindenberger, Herbert: 14

Lindisfarne (Holy Island): 49

Lindsay: A. D.: 9, 112, 148. Sir David: 93. Frederic: 142. Thomas M.: 60

Lindsey: 49. Earl of: see Bertie, Montague

Linear B syllabary of Greek: 118

Lines Written by A Young Man, After He

Was Seized With a Consumption: 115

Linq, Nicholas: 128, 93

Lingelsheim: 10

Linguae Latinae Dictionarium: 44

Linguae Romanae Dictionarium Luculentum Novum: 44

Linguistic arts of the trivium: 20

Linn: John Blair: 115*; works: Miscellaneous Works Prose and Poetical: 115; The Powers of Genius: 115. William: 115

Linnell, J.: 97

Linschoten: 19

Linton. See Newton Lincoln

Linus: 70, 73, 128, 3, 32

Lionardi, A.: 5

Lipenus, Martinus: 68

Lipiner, Siegfried: 65

Lippe, Graf von der: 10

Lippershey, Hans: 89

Lipscomb: A. A.: 16. W.: 58

Lipsius, Justus (Joest Lips): 40, 69, 73, 114, 123, 145*, 64, 93, 148, 122. Works: De constantia: 60; Manuductionis ad Stoicam philosophiam: 60

Lisbon, Portugal: 44

Lisideius: 70

Lisle: 94. Lord: 103. H. M.: 58. John: 44, 45. Philip Sidney, Viscount: 44, 51

Lister: Joseph: 16. T.: 58

Liston, co. Middlesex: 44

Liszt, Franz: 39

Literae ab Olivario...Sueciae: 44

Literae Humaniores: 42

Literae Rabbinicae: 41

Literalism: 47. As form of Biblical interpretation: 68*. Meaning, combination of metaphorical with, Warton on: 88

Literary Cabinet: 115

Literary Criticism in the Renaissance (Spingarn): 70

Literary Essays Contributed to the Edenburgh Review: 83

Literary Gazette: 63

Literary Magazine and American Register, The: 115*

Literary Miscellany Or Monthly Review, The: 115

Literary Miscellany, The: 115

Literary Studies (Bagehot): 83

Literary World, The: 98

Literary: aims, M's: 129*. Criticism: 51, 141. Judgment: 51; limitations of: 141; meanings in: 141; and psychology: 141. Oratorical ideals of M and the ancients: 20*. Sources, M's use of: 137. Method: 47; see also: accommodation. Painting: 97*. Scholarship: 67. Talent, M's: 30. Theory: 17, 30

Literature: of Knowledge and Power: 146. M on: 51. Influence of imitation: 20. Elizabethan Puritan's attack on: 31. Renaissance criticism of: 31. Service rendered by: 70. Older English: commentaries of: 88; quotations from, in early commentaries: 88; Hume's references to: 88; Bentley's knowledge of: 88; Pearce's examination of: 88; the Richardsons on: 88; Peck dealing with: 88; Thyer's knowledge of: 88; Warburton's familiarity with: 88; Newton familiar chiefly with more conventional tracks in: 88; Callander on: 88; referred to by Massey: 88; Warton's knowledge of, and references to: 88; author of Letter to Warton out of sympathy with: 88; Dunster's interest in: 88; Todd's wide reading in: 88; illustrations from: 88; Bowle's study of: 88. Rabbinical: see Rabbinical. Spanish, Portuguese: see Spanish; Portuguese. Italian: see Italian. Greek and Latin: see Classical. French: see French

Literis Antiquae Britanniae, De: 104

Liternum: 49, 73

Lithuania: 44

Little: Rev. Mr.: 44. Marguerite: 6, 40, 44. R. Ernest: 44 Little Britain, London: 44

Little Burstead, co. Essex: 44

Little Genesis: 65

Little Girl Lost, The: 25

Little Iliad: 74

Little Nonsuch: 91

Little St. Bartholomew's, London: 44

Little Turnstile: 44

Littlemore: 45

Littlesbery, Sir William (alias Horne): 40

Littleton, His Treatise of Tenures: 45

Littleton: Dr.: 28. Adam (lexicographer): 40, 44. Sir Charles: 44. Elizabeth: see Willoughby, Eliz. Sir John: 45. Sergeant: 44. Sir Thomas: 40, 45, 73

Littré, Maximilien, Paul and Emile: 27

Lituania (Lettow): 49

Liturgia Mozarabica: 68

Liturgy (Liturgies): 9, 51, 67, 78

Lively, Edward: 40, 42, 93

Liver: 128

Liverpool, co. Lancs.: 44

Lives (Plutarch): 3

Lives and Characters of the Eng. Dramatick Poets: 116

Lives and Characters of the Eng. Poets (Giles Jacob): 70

Lives and Opinions of Eminent Philosophers (Diogenes Laertius): 112, 3

Lives of the Most Famous Eng. Poets (Winstantley): 116

Lives of the Poets (Johnson): 29, 83, 3, 94

Livesey, Sir Michael (regicide): 44

Living conditions at Cambridge: 40

Living soul: 24

Living Age: 44, 63

Livingston: Brockholst: 115; Democracy: An Epic Poem: 115. Luther S.: 44. William: 115; Philosophic Solitude: 115

Livius, Titus. See Livy

Livonia: 49

"Livre Anglais," Paris: 44

Livre de la Passion (14th c. French poem): 74

Livy (Titus Livius): 18, 40, 44, 73, 90, 120, 123, 128, 3, 82, 88, 93, 146, 117, 91. History of Rome: 74

LL, N.: 44

Llangahangell: 45

Lledrod (Lledred): 45. See also: Mount and Lledrod

Llethered. See Mount and Lledrod

Lloyd: A. H.: 40. C., sonnets of: 58. David: 44, 58, 116. George: 40. Humphrey: 88. James: 44, 58. Lodowick (bks. and pr., 1648-71): 91, 7, 93. Sir Marmaduke: 29. Michael: 29, 101, 79. Morgan: 7. Sir Richard (judge): 44, 58*. R., on M: 58. Robert: 117. William, Bp. of St. Asaph: 10, 44

Llwyd, R.: 58

Loans to and bonds from: Cope: 44*. Powell: 44*. Robert Warcupp: 44

Lobbying: 51. Lobbyists: 51

Local assemblies: powers of: 51. M on: 51. Provisions for: 51. M's proposal of: 147

Local government: advantages of scheme for: 51. Subordination of: 51

Locatelli, S.: 6

Loci communes: 40, 96

Lock: J.: 97. Matthew: 40

Locke: Miss: 58. J. Courtenay: 150. John: 2, 12, 15, 23, 40, 86, 116, 147, 3, 26, 32, 39, 142, 53, 91, 94, 115*, 130, 137, 146, 117, 13; compared with M on: toleration issue: 147; liberty of thought: 147; law of nature theory: 147; works: An Essay Concerning Human Understanding: 142; The Works: 142; Posthumous Works of John Locke: 82. Matthew: 39. W.: 97

Lockhart, Sir William: 10, 44, 94, 130

Lockman, John: 58, 117

Lockwood, Laura E.: 15, 19, 58, 63,

70, 144, 3, 14. Lexicon to the Eng. Poetical Works of John Milton: 57

Lockyer: Rev. Nicholas: 44. Robert (d. 1649): 91

Locrian: remnants (those): 73, 112, 3, 71. Spear: 73

Locrians, Epizephyrian: 3

Locrine: 90

Locris: 49

Locustae (Fletcher): 26

Locustae, vel Pietas Jesuitica: 65

Locusts, or Apollyonists: 65

Locusts: 19

Lodestone: 128

Lodge Copse: 44, 45

Lodge: Mr.: 45, 120. Anne: 60. Sir Oliver: 136. Thomas: 19, 40, 44, 45, 59, 58, 79, 128*, 145, 93, 64; works: Defence of Poetry: 74; Learned Summary upon the Famous Poeme of...Bartas: 74; see also: Du Bartas; Guillaume, Second Semaine; Josephus, Workes. Lodge's Looking Glasse for London: 88

Lods, A.: 113

Loe: Barrister: 44. William: 40, 93

Loesser, Arthur: 39

Loetscher, F. W.: 79

Loewe, H.: 123, 36

Loewenberg, A.: 6

Lofft, Capel: 1, 44, 58*, 88*

Lofoot: 49

Loftus, Edmond: 44. Thomas: 64

Logan: Josias: 19. M.: 58

Logarithms: 40

Loggan, David: 40

Loggin: family: 45. (Loggan, Loggyn, Loggins), Mr.: 45. John: 45. Robert: 45. Thomas: 44, 45

Loggyn, Jeremiah: 44

Logic (Ramus): 70

Logic: 20*, 40*, 50, 51, 53, 96. Study of: 114*. Aim of: 40. And arts of discourse: 53. Definition vs. description: 53. Likeness: 53. And narrative order: 53*. M's handbook: 53. Narrator's: 96. Ramistic: 96. Chopping: 40. Rhetoric: 40. Logical: argument, division, method, order, outline, support: 51; proof: 51*, 123; argumentation preferred by Pearce to historical illustration: 88; discipline, Warton's contrasted with the Richardsons' lack of consistent logic: 88. Logic (Milton): 112*

Logicke, "or Second part of Logonomia." See Logonomia

Logomontanus: 89

Logonomia Anglica (Gill the Elder): 20*, 29*, 40, 112, 26

Logonomia: 20

Logos: 5, 41, 60, 107*, 126, 71, 25. In Clement of Alexandria: 107*. Four levels of manifestation: 107*. In Hippolytus of Rome, a creature: 107*. Idea of: 107*. Immanent in God, externalized as the Word: 107*. Immanent Logos develops into external Word: 107*. Invisible: 107*. In Irenaeus of Lyons, Logos is thought preexistent: 107*. In Justin Martyr: 107*. Linked with light: 107*. The literal begetting: 107*. Made visible as Son at metaphorical begetting: 107*. In Melito of Sardis, preexistent: 107*. In M, invisible: 107*. In Origen, Philo: 107*. The self-creation: 107*. Speaks for God in PL: 107*. Speaks to Adam in Eden: 107*. In Titian: 107*. In Tertullian, derived from Wisdom: 107*. In Theophilus of Antioch, 1st born of God: 107*. Three-stage: 107*. Unknown to angels prior to metaphorical begetting: 107*. In M: begetting of, self created, speaks to pagans: 107. See also: Word

Logres (Loëgria): 49, 73

Lohfink, Norbert: 93

Loire River, France: 44

L'Oiseau, J. de Tourval: 40

Lok, H.: 59

Loki: 1

Lollard(s): 73, 3, 38. Persecution: 83

Lomas, Mrs. S. C. See Cromwell, Oliver

Lomazzo: 27. Antonio: 5

Lombard Street, London: 44, 103

Lombard, Peter: 24*, 44, 68, 73, 102, 32

Lombard: 142. Laws: 3

Lombardo, Marco: 111

Lombards ("Lumbard"): 44, 73, 3

Loménie, Louis Henry, Comte de: 44

Londina Illustrata: 40

London, William (bks., 1653-60): 44, 128, 91

London: 8*, 19, 20, 30*, 40*, 44, 45*, 49, 51, 103*, 3*, 21. Commissary Court: 40. Corporation of: 45. Polyglot: 22. Book trade: 40. Bridge: 44. City Companies: 40. Visitation of: 45. Tower: 44. Provincial synod: 103. Lane: 44. House: 40. Fields: 44. Directory: 45. Court of Alderman: 40. M's visits to, return to: 94. See also: Augusta

London: London, A Survey...(Stowe): 20. London Carcanet, The: 98. London Chronicle: 44, 60. London Daily News: 44. "London 1802": 45. London Gazette: 44. London in 1638, The Inhabitants of: 45. London Journal; see Hunt. London Magazine, The: 44, 115, 146, 117. London Marriage Licenses (Joseph Foster): 40. London Printer His Lamentation: 44. London Quarterly Review: 63. London Society of Antiquaries: 44. London Times: 44*. See also: Times. London Times Literary Supplement: 44*. London Topographical Record: 44

Londonderry, Ireland: 44, 49, 73. See also: Derriensis; Londinoderriensis Portus

Londons Liberty in Chains (John Lilburne): 147

Lonely God, The: 65

Long poems, not written by Gray-Collins-Warton group: 58

Long Combe: 44

Long Crendon: 45

Long Lane: 44, 45

Long Parliament: 51, 103*, 113, 109, 55. M and: 147

Long: Charles: 44. J. D.: 58. Sir James: 10. Percy W.: 83. R.: 58. Thomas: 44, 116*

Longchamp, Bp. of Ely, William: 73

Longe, J.: 54

Longfellow, Henry Wadsworth: 16, 58, 111, 137.

Longford, Earl of: 44

Longhena, Baldassare: 27. S. Maria della Salute: 27

Longinus: Caesare: 142; Trinum Magicum: 142. Dionysius Cassius: 1, 2*, 5*, 20, 31, 56, 58, 60, 70, 73, 112, 123, 35, 145, 3, 39, 53, 82, 88, 115, 130, 146, 150, 117

Longland, Charles: 44

Longman and Law (publishers): 97

Longobards: 44. Longobardis: 73

Longolius: 20

Longonis Portus: 49

Longrove, Robert: 44

Longtown, co. Cumberland: 44

Longus: 122, 64

Longworth, T. Clifton: 93

Loofs, Friedrich: works: "Kenosis": 74; Nestorius: 74

Looking Glasse for London: 88

Lookup, John: 44

Loom: 25

Loomis, Roger Sherman: 123

Looten, C.: 44

Lop (desert): 144

Lope de Vega: 77, 64

Loporovient: 49

Lorca, F. Garcia: 65

Lord keeper of the great seal: 45

Lord Chancellor: 45

"Lord Chancellor's Original, Of the": 44

Lord Chief Justice: 44. Lord Chief Justice Scroggs his Speech in the Kings-Bench, The: 116

Lord Hay's Masque (Campion): 29

<u>Lord Jeffrey and Wordsworth</u> (Beatty): 70

Lord Mayor of London: 44. Lord Mayor's Court: 45

Lord-Bishops: 51

Lord: Elizabeth: 44. Francis: 44. George de F.: 93

Lord's Prayer: 40, 126, 72

Lord's Sacraments: 51

Lord's Supper: 51, 126, 78

Lords and Commons: 51

<u>Lords Bishops None of the Lord's Bishops</u> (attr. to M): 44

Lords: 51, 83. House of: 44, 45. <u>Journal</u> of House of: 40, 44, 45

Loredano: 77. Family: 6. Giovanni Francesco: 6, 65, 32. L.: 6

Lorenzo delle Colombe: 5. Loret(t)o: 49, 73

Lorenzo: Prince of Tuscany: 44. M.: 6

Loria: 113

Lorich(ius), Reinhard: 20, 40

Lorimer, H. L.: 64

Loring, Mr.: 44. See also: Horing

Lorrain (Lotharingia): 49. Lorrainers: 73

Lorrain, C.: 6

Los Angeles <u>Examiner</u>: 44

Los: 146, 25*. As visionary-prophet, poet-artist, imagination, creator, logos; spectre of, sons of, perspective of, daughters of, errors of, messangers of, purgation of, reign of; and trial of Satan, regenerated: 25. <u>Los, The Song of</u>: 25

Lossky, Vladimir: 93

Lot: 2, 73, 72

Lotharius: 73

Lothbury, London: 44

Lothian (Laudian): 49

Lotichus Joannes Petrus, <u>Holofernes</u>: 74, 64

Lottin, Odon: 93

Lotto, Lorenzo: 123

Loudon, Synod of: 44

Loudun (Laodun): 73

Louis: King: 3. St.: 123. VIII: 73. XI: 73, 114. XIII, King of France: 44, 73, 64. XIV of France: 10, 27, 44*, 52, 60, 73, 103, 116, 123, 150

Louise de Savoy, Queen: 64

Loukovitch, K.: 6

Lounds, Mr.: 44

Lounsbury, Thomas (R.): 87, 93

Louthan, D.: 23

Loutherbourg, P. de ("Eidophusikon"): 58

Louvain: 40, 49, 73

Louvre, Paris: 44

Louw, W. E. G.: 65

Love: Charles: 115; <u>A Poem on the Death of General George Washington</u>: 115. Christopher: 44, 142; <u>The Ministry of Angels to the Heirs of Salvation</u>: 142. Nicholas: 44, 93. Richard: 40

Love: 47*, 51*, 67, 69*, 90, 113, 122*, 124*, 143*, 93*, 25. And service as source of perfection: 83*. Conjugal: 54*. Profane and sacred: 143*. Abounding: 143. Immortal: 143. Divine: 47, 143. God's gift: 93. Its nature: 93. A passion: 93. And obedience: 93. Adam's idea of: 48. Contrasted with hate: 48. Divine and human: 48. The emotional principle of PL: 48. The supremacy of over evil: 48. The theme of: 48. M's conception of: 113. Among the angels: 113. As epic theme: 123. Reason and freedom: 47. Human necessity of: 47. Disordered by Fall: 47. Motivation to Pilgrimage: 47. As heroic virtue: 123. As charity: 123. Etymology of heroes from: 123. And knowledge: 125. As theme in SA: 125. And power: 125. M on: 30*, 31. Experiences, M's: 44. Romantic, M on: 80. And sex, M's experience with and attitude toward: 137. See also: Cupid; Charity; Friendship; Lust; Zeal; Christ; Community; Heaven; Sex

<u>Love Freed for Ignorance and Folly</u> (Jonson): 29

Love Restored (Jonson): 29

Loveden, Walter: 44

Lovejoy, Arthur O.: 6, 15, 17, 23, 31, 52, 63, 68, 69, 108, 77, 100, 102, 118, 118, 128, 141, 144, 143, 36, 36, 93, 137, 148, 140. And way to perfection: 143. Christian myth and Christian theology compared: 61. Works: M and the Paradox of the Fortunate Fall: 109, 48, 60; The Great Chain of Being: 60

Lovekin, Richard (nephew of M's 3rd wife): 44

Lovelace: 120. Lord: 44, 45. Richard: 16, 84, 109

Lovell: A.: 44. E.: 58. R.: 58

Lovering, Mr.: 40

Lovers Made Men (Jonson): 29

Lovers' Infiniteness (John Donne): 131

Loves Triumph through Callipolis (Jonson): 29*

Lovibond, E.: 58

Low Church: 40

Low Countries: 44*. See also: Netherlands; Holland; United Provinces

Low, Samuel: 115. Poems: 115

Lowder: 83

Lowdermilk, W. H. and Company: 44

Lowe: Mr.: 45. Mrs. (Hyde): 45. Sir Edward: 45. George: 45. J.: 58. J. H.: 1, 36. Jane (Drake): 45. Jane (Wright): 45. Oliver (father's servant): 44. Wright: 45

Lowell: 130. James Russell: 86, 111, 94, 115, 137; sonnets of: 58. John: 115

Lowenhaupt, W. H.: 113, 144*

Lower classes: 113

Lower Holloway. See Holloway

Lower Middle Party: 51

Lower: Thomas: 44. William: 44

Lowes, John Livingston: 12, 27, 57, 58, 98, 122, 144

Lowestoft, co. Suffolk: 44

Lowin, George: 44

Lowinsky: Edward: 39. T.: 97

Löwith, Karl: 93

Lowndes, William Thomas: 44

Lowth, Robert, Bp. of London: 40, 115, 25. A Short Introduction to Eng. Grammar With Critical Notes: 115

Lowther, Robert: 10*

Loxo: 73

Loy, J. R.: 23

Loyal Protestant: 116

Loyalty of Popish Principles Examin'd, The: 116

Loyalty: 51, 123. To Protestantism: 51. See also: Patriotism; Fealty

Loyer, Pierre le: 123

Loyola, Ignatius: 18, 23, 27, 40, 52, 81, 116, 145. With his Jesuits: 73

Loyolite (Loiolitam): 73

Lua (a goddess): 40, 73

Lubac, Henri de: 39, 93

Lübbing, Dr. H.: 44*

Lübeck: 44

Lubin, Eilhard: 40

Lublino, Samuele: 40

Luca (Lucomnis Urbs): 49

Luca, Franciscus: 68, 99*

Lucan: Marcus Annaeus: 1, 2, 19, 40, 50, 58, 70, 73, 74, 90, 111, 122, 128, 145, 32, 88, 64, 130, 115, 117; De bello Civili: 95; works: Pharsalia: 60; The Civil War: 60, 74, 95.

Lucanus, Ocellus: 32

Lucaris, Cyril: 40

Lucas: C.: 58. D. W.: 21. de Borgo: 40. E. V.: 58; see also: Lamb, Charles. F. L.: 1, 44, 132, 136. Of Tuy: 93. Perceval: 44*, 45

Lucca (Diodati's birthplace, M's visit to): 30, 44, 73, 103, 3. See also: Luca

Lucha Mikrokozma: 65

Lucian: 18, 2, 20, 40, 44, 57, 60, 73, 90, 114, 123, 3, 64, 82, 88, 93, 117. "Heracles": 74

Lucifer en Beelsebub: 65

Luciter in Starlight: 65

Lucifer Vieillissant: 65

Lucifer: 1*, 44, 60, 68, 73, 90, 103, 107, 111, 123*, 141*, 142, 143, 36*, 71, 72, 25. Crown offered to: 143. Released: 143. The morning star: 89. Name, envy, pride, rebellion of: 36. Dante's Lucifer: 70. See also: Demonic; Satan; Prometheus; Devil; War in Heaven

Lucifer: 87. By Anatole France: 65. By Noel: 65. By Santayana: 65. By Vondel: 65*, 70, 94, 130. See also: Satan

Lucifero: 65

Lucifers mit seiner gesellschaft val: 65

Lucilius: 73

Lucina: 73, 90

Lucks, Henry A.: 93

Lucretius: 1, 13, 5, 15, 40, 44, 57, 58, 60, 69, 73, 74, 90, 112, 111, 118, 121, 123, 128, 133, 139, 142, 145, 3, 26, 32, 36*, 72, 88, 94, 101, 130, 131, 146, 148, 150, 117. *De Rerum Natura*: 36. M's copy of: 40

Lucrine Bay: 49, 73

Lucullus: 6

Lucumo: 3

Lucumonis: 73

Lucy: (Harington, Russel), Countess of Bedford: 40*. C.: 97. Sir Thomas: 114. Fairfax: 44. Luke: 44

Ludgate: 44, 45, 49. Hill, London: 44, 103

Ludlow Masque: 104*. See also: Comus

Ludlow: "Ludlow, Major General": 116*. *Ludlow No Lyar*, compared with *Eikonoklastes*: 116. Ludlow's *Memoirs*: 116

Ludlow: Edmund: 10, 44, 59, 116. Edward: 44

Ludlow: 49, 51, 73, 136, 72, 94. A symbol: 143. Castle: 29*, 40, 44, 103, 88, 94, 21

Ludolphus of Saxony: 99

Ludovicus Pius: 73

Ludus Coventriae: 65, 123, 36*, 99

Ludus Literarius (Brinsley): 20*

Ludwig: Elector Palatine: 10. Philipp von Simmern: 10. W.: 59

Luis de Camoens: 77

Luke: 71, 99. Gospel of: 40, 44, 57, 74*, 118, 126, 135, 3, 71; see also: Bible

Lukenor, co. Oxon.: 44

Lull, Ramon: 10

Lullaby: 121

Lullius, Raymond: 73

Lully: 7. Raimon: 40

Lum, Peter: 128

Luminalia (Davenant): 29

Lummenaeus, Jacbous Cornelius: 68

Luna: 25. Juan de: 40

Lund: 44

Lungo, I. del: 6

Lupercalia: 73

Lupis, A.: 6

Lupo, Thomas (composer): 44

Lupton: Donald: 93. J. H.: 20, 112; *The Tythe-Takers Cart Overthrown*: 147. Thomas: 128

Lupworth: (Lapworth), Anne: see Lyde alias Joyner, Anne. Edward: 45. Margery: 45

Luria, Isaac: 93

Luserna: 49

Lusher, George: 44, 45

Lushington, Thomas: 93

Lusitania: 44

Lust, la demoiselle de Cristal: 65

Lust: 47, 113, 122, 93. As the Fall: 113

Lustratio: 70. See also: Catharsis

Lute: 40, 121*

Lutetia. See Paris

Luther, Martin: 4, 7, 9*, 10, 15, 18, 27, 40, 41, 42, 44, 47, 51, 52, 54, 60*, 67, 68, 70, 73, 74, 77, 79, 86, 103, 83, 102, 114, 116, 120, 122, 123, 128, 141, 142, 147, 3, 11, 143, 22, 32*, 36, 38*, 71*, 82, 93*, 99, 101, 115, 146, 148, 48, 13, 25. And the Word: 143. And the Protestant revolt: 147. View of knowledge: 96. On: literature and theology; hatred of God; incarnation; growth in grace; fear of punishment: 47. On man as God's image: 48. Works: Against the Armed Man Cochlaeus: 60; Liber contra Rusticos: 82; Appeal to the German Nobility: 60; Tischreden: 77; Colloquia Mensalia (Tischreden, trans. Henne Bell): 74; Table Talk: 77; Prefaces to...Luther's Bible, (ed. T. A. Reaiwin): 74; Works: 48; Commentary (Lectures) on...Genesis: 74, 36, 48; "Old Testament Prefaces," "Preface to the Book of Job," "Prefaces to...Apocryphal Books": 74

Lutherans: 44, 73, 71. Lutheranism: 38, 78

Lutrin: 2, 130. See also: Boileau

Lutterworth: 44, 45

Lüttgens: 10

Luttrell, Narcissus: 40

Lutwich, Edward: 44

Lutwin: 65

Lutz, Renharius: 22

Luvah: 25

Luxury: Hume's love of, of style: 88. Of style, appreciated by Warton: 88. And grandeur valued by Todd: 88

Luyken, C.: 97

Luz: 73, 144, 143

Lyaeus: 73, 3

Lycaeum: 51. See also: Lyceum

Lycaeus: 49, 73, 90

Lycambes: 73

Lycaon: 73. Lycaonius: 73

Lycéc: 40

Lyceum: 49, 73, 3. See also: Lycaeum

Lycia: 49

Lycidas: 1, 103, 112, 98, 102, 90, 87, 95, 104*, 111, 113, 118, 129*, 144, 11*, 143*, 72*, 80, 88*, 101*, 55. Animadversions: 80. Expression of M's early optimism: 80. Imagery: 8. Of Reformation, analyzed: 80. Savonarola: 80. "Two-handed engine": 80; meaning of: 104; attempts to explain: 80. Digressions in: 101. Textual changes in: 101. Three part structure of: 101. Un- rhymed lines in: 101. Christianity consolation, immortality, judgments, methexis, mortality, stance in, structure of: 72*. Poet's desire in: 11. And Orpheus: 11, 144. Compared to Comus: 11. Purpose, unity of, 143. And church reform: 143*. And prophecy: 143. And poetic symphony: 143. Theme of divine justice: 104. Tonal, tempo and structural patterns in: 104. Christian imagery in: 104. As drama: 104. Biblical references in: 104. Imaginative unity in: 104. Criticism of Eng. Church: 104. Renaissance-Puritan elements in: 87. As a touchstone of poetic taste: 87. Tennyson's recitation of: 87. Concept of fate, fame in: 87. Its pastoralism: 129. Its sources: 129. Emotional responsiveness: 104. As a rustic poem: 126. Dolphins, the Wolf: 144. Geography in: 144. Personal feeling in: 144. See also: Milton, John, Works

Lycidas (not the work): 3. As character: 72*

Lycisca: 73

Lycophron: 1, 40, 44, 58, 73. Lycophron: 94

Lycosthenes (Conrad Wolffhart): 20, 40

Lycurgus (Licurgus): 44, 60, 73, 112, 114, 3, 82

Lycus: 92

Lyde: alias Joyner, Anne: 45. Alias Joyner, Anne (Beauforest): 45. Alias Joyner, Anne (Lupworth): 45. Alias Joyner, Edward: 44, 45. Alias Joyner, Richard: 45. Alias Joyner, Robert: 45. Alias Joyner, William: 45

Lydgate, John: 15, 67, 68, 123, 32, 36, 131, 133, 88. The Fall of Princes: 36

Lydia: 19, 44, 49. Lydian: airs: 3; mood in music: 40, 73; "mode": 70, 121

Lyff of Adam and Eve: 36

Lygdamus: 64

Lyly, John: 63, 128, 88, 131, 15, 18

Lyman, Asa: 115. The American Reader: 115

Lymnos: 144

Lynceus: 44, 73

Lynch: Kathleen: 108. L. E. M.: 79, 81

Lynchhill Coppice: 45

Lynde: Edmund: 120. Elizabeth: 120

Lyndesay, Sir David: 65

Lynn, William: 45

Lynne, Walter: 40

Lynt, co. Wilts.: 44, 45

Lynwric Ap Grano: 88

Lyon: Charles: 44. T.: 9

Lyones (Lyonesse): 49, 73

Lyons: 44, 49. 3. See also: Sonnet XVIII

Lyra, Nicholaus: 22

Lyre: 121

Lyric: 27, 146*, 149*, 70. Poems, M's: 146*. Strains in PL: 149*. Source, movement, freedom, checking, range of: 149. Three stages: 149. Epic uplift: 149. Influence of, in France and Germany: 149. Influence of in England: 149*. Lyrical poetry, function of: 70. Lyrics: 50, 58

Lyrical Ballads: 12, 117. By Wordsworth, Advertisement to: 70; Preface to (1800): 70

Lyster (Lister), Sir Matthew: 44, 45

Lystra: 49

Lyttleton: Charles: 44. Lord George: 58*, 117; on M: 58. Lord Thomas, praises M: 58

Lytton: Frances: 45. See also: Cope, Frances. Sir Rowland: 45

Lyvorne: 44. See also: Leghorn

-M-

M., A. (Abraham Miller, pr., 1646-53): 91

M., B.: 44, 73

M., G. (George Miller, pr., 1625- 46): 44, 91

M., I.: 44

M., J. R.: 44

M., J.: 44. See also: Martin, John

M., R. S.: 44

M., R.: 44*

M., S.: 44

M., W.: 44

M.S. to A.S.: 9

Mab: 73

Mabb, Thomas (pr., 1650-65): 91

Mabber, James: 44

Mabbot(t): Gilbert: 44, 103, 91. Thomas O.: 20, 40, 44*, 59, 63, 128; ed. Supplement to Columbia Ed. (with French, and Kelley): 44

Mabe. See Mylor and Mabe

Mabe, co. Cornwall: 44

Mabol. See Mabbot(t), Gilbert

Macarius: 73

Macaulay: 3. Mrs. Catherine: 117. Col.: 44. Macaulay: 3. Col.: 44. Mrs. Catherine: 117. G. C.: 58. Rose: 83, 133, 26, 92, 137; Milton: 83. Thomas Babington, Baron, 1st Lord: 1, 4, 9, 27, 29, 34, 37, 40, 44, 58, 60, 63, 73, 76, 83, 86, 87*, 105, 107, 110, 111, 114, 136, 141, 143, 71, 92, 94, 97, 109, 130, 148, 55; on M's power of suggestion: 143; Review of De Doctrina Christiana: 107; effect of PL on: 87; attitude toward M: 87; on M's sonnets: 87; hostile reviews of religious epics: 87; on M's Puritanism: 87; on style of M and John Martin: 87; attitude toward John Martin: 87; works: "Milton": 87; "A Conversation between Mr. A. Cowley and Mr. J. Milton": 87

Macbeth: 60, 70, 73, 135, 72, 94. Lady Macbeth: 136

Macbeth: 8, 31, 34, 40, 70, 136, 139, 71, 72, 88, 130

Maccabaeus, Judas: 73, 123

Maccabees: 2, 74

Macclesfield: 40

Macconell, Capt. Samuel: 44

M'Donald, A.: 58

Macdonald: 3. Hugh: 44; see also: Andrew Marvell. Margaret: 12

Macdonell: 120

M'Dougall: 35

Macdowell, Mr.: 44

Macé de la Charite: 65, 64

Macedo: 44. José Agostinho de: 65

Macedon: 19, 73, 3

Macedonia (AEmathia, Emathia): 49. Macedonias: 32

Macfee, William: 115

Macgreggor, Malcolm. See Mason, William

Machaerus: 73

Machaon: 73

Machaut, Guillaume de: 32

Machen, Arthur: 33

Macherus: 49

<u>Machiavelli</u> (Macaulay): 3

Machiavelli, Niccolo: 18, 40, 44, 52, 59, 60, 73, 86, 111, 120, 123, 32, 38, 39, 46, 93, 145, 55. Works: <u>Dell' Arte della Guerra</u>: 82; <u>Discorsi</u>: 82*; <u>The Prince</u>: 32. Machiavellianism: 60

Machinery, epic: 122*

Macie: Mr.: 45. John: 44

Mack: Jesse F.: 9, 113, 116. M.: 23. Maynard: 12, 79, 101

Mackail, John W.: 1, 5, 16, 56, 102, 87, 132, 133, 88, 54, 130. On M's art: 87. <u>The Springs of Helicon</u>: 87, 132

Mackay, J.: 58

Mackenzie, Phyllis: 115. W. A.: 16

Mackie, D. M.: 6

Mackinnon: Flora Isabel: 142; <u>The Philosophical Writings of Henry More</u>: 142. James: 93

Mackintosh: Sir James: 44. Robert: 93

Macklem, Michael: 93

Macklin, C.: 97

Macksey, Richard: 39

Maclean, Hugh: 21

Macleane, Douglas: 44

Maclise, D.: 97

Maclure, Miller: 122

Macmillan Company: 45, 112

Macmurray, J.: 15

Macock, John (pr.): 44

Macpherson, James: 87, 88, 149. Influenced by M: 58

Macray, William Dunn: 40, 44

Macready, William: 98

Macrobius: 40, 60, 90, 121, 123, 128, 38, 82, 88, 130, 93

Macrocosm: 71

Macropedius, Georgius: 20, 40, 65

Macropsia: 139

MacCaffrey, Isabel Gamble: 17, 23, 37*, 60, 66, 75, 79, 81, 86, 105, 110, 118, 123, 32, 39, 53, 85, 93, 101, 106, 48. <u>PL as "Myth"</u>: 48. Fallen and unfallen worlds, ambivalence of a perfect Eden: 61. Myth and theology in PL: 61. On the simultaneous physical, spiritual nature of M's images: 61. Sense of frustration and tension in SA: 61. Use of images of darkness and light: 61

MacCarthy, Desmond: 133

MacCulloch, John A.: 93

MacCullum, Hugh R.: 37, 79, 110, 14, 93, 101, 106. "M and Figurative Interpretation of the Bible": 74

MacDonald, George: 16

MacEachen, Dugal B., on Tennyson's sonnet: 87

MacKellar, Walter: 79, 102, 112, 21, 3, 15, 19, 20, 40*, 44. Ed. <u>Latin Poems</u>: 44*

MacKendrick, Paul: 33

MacKenna, Stephen: 79

MacKensie, Donald: 40

MacKenzie: Donald C.: 44. Sir

George: 116, 145, 117. Phyllis: 60, 110, 14

MacKinney, Loren: 128

MacKinnon, M. H. M.: 148

MacLachlan, H. John: 44, 148. _Socinianism_: 74

MacLaurin, J.: 9

MacLeish, Archibald: 108, 137. _J.B._: 74

MacLennan, W. G.: 93

Mad Dog Rebellion: 147

Madách, Imre: 65

Madame Bovary: 1. See also: Flaubert, Gustave

Madan: Falconer F.: 40, 44*, 60, 86, 91. Francis F.: 116. S.: 58

Madden: F.: 23. W. B.: 58

Maddox Street, London: 44

Maden, Richard: 93

Maderna, Carlo: 6, 27

Madian: 49, 73

Madison, James: 51, 115

Madness: 92

Madras, India (Fort St. George): 44

Madrid: 44, 103

Madrigal: 40, 121*

Madsen, William G.: 23, 29, 52, 66, 81, 110, 111, 32, 104, 53, 93, 101, 140. On Lycidas: 104. Christ and Samson contrasted: 61. On saintly patience and human action: 61. "Earth the Shadow of Heaven": 74

Maecenas, Gaius Cilnius: 73, 21

Maehly, J.: 88

Maenads: 90

Maenal(i)us: 49, 73, 90

Maeonia. See Lydia

Maeonides: 16, 49, 60, 73, 90, 3. See also: Melesigenes; Homer

Maeotis (sea of Azov; Tauric Pool): 19, 49, 73. See also: Pontus

Maes German (Guid-crue): 49

Maestlin: 89

Maestricht (Trajectum): 44

Maeterlinck: 35

Maffei, Andrea: 117

Magalotti, Lorenzo: 117

Magdalen College, Oxford: 40, 44, 45

Magdalene College, Cambridge: 40, 45

Magdeburg. See Frederick William

Magellan: 15, 19, 73, 144. Straits: 49

Magellanic clouds, the: 89

Maggi: 70

Maggs Brothers (bks.s): 44*. _Milton Catalogue_: 91

Magi: 72. Gifts of: 123

Magic: 7*, 29, 69

Maginn, William: 87

Magirus, Johannes: 40, 123, 32

Magistrates: power over church: 9*, 51. Civil power: 9*, 51

Magistry, Supreme: 51

Magius, Hieronymus: 123

Magna Bibliotheca Veterum Patrum, Ed. Margarinus de la Bigne: 74

Magna Carta: 60, 103, 116, 3, 82

Magnanimity: 51, 60*, 122*, 123, 125. See also: Honor; Self-knowledge; Merit

Magnentius, Flavius Popilius: 73

Magnesia: 49, 73

Magnetick Lady, The (Jonson): 20, 29

Magnificat: 72. _Magnificat_ (St. Luke): 126, 139

Magnificence: 122. See also: Magnanimity

Magnifying the facts: 51

Maguire, T. H.: 44

Mahaffy, J. P.: 92

Mahanaim: 49, 73

Mahazuel: 142

Mahnke, Dietrich: 93

Mahomed IV, Grand Seignior or Sultan of Turkish Empire: 38

Mahomet Han, Grand Signior: 44

Mahomet: 19, 60

Mahoney, John L.: 93

Mahood, M. M.: 17, 23, 76, 79, 81, 110, 125, 139, 128, 101. Poetry and Humanism: 74, 48

Maia: 73

Maidenhead Court, London: 44

Maimonides, Moses: 40, 41, 73, 36, 93. Guide for the Perplexed: 74, 36

Main, D. M.: 58

Mainz (Moguntia): Germany: 44. Elector of: 10

Mair, G. H.: 23, 79, 122

Maire, Jean le: 10

Maisières, Maury Thibaut de: 15, 65, 122, 102. Poèms Inspirés du Début de la Genèse: 74

Maitland Club, Miscellany: 40

Maitland, William: 60

Maizeaux, Pierre des: 117

Majesty, classical, simplicity and grace, the Richardsons on: 88

Major, John (Joannes), M.: 65, 14, 93, 64

"Making Latin": 40

Making of the greater man: 83*

Makylmenaeus (MacIlmaine), Roland: 40

Malabar: 19, 49, 73. See also: Decan; India (East)

Malacarne, Professor: 70

Malacca: 19, 150

Malachi: 73, 74, 126

Malalas: 65. John: 88

Malapertius, Carolus: 117

Malatesta (Malatesti), Antonio: 6, 30, 44, 73, 137

Malay Archipelago: 150

Malbon, Mr.: 45

Malchim (Malakim): 142

Malcolm III: 73

Malcolm, J. P., London Redivivum: 44

Maldon, co. Essex: 44, 49. See also: Camalodunum

Maldonat, John (Maldonatatus, Johannes): 73, 142, 99*. Traicté des Anges et Demons: 142

Male supremacy: 25

Mâle, Emile: 27, 143. Creation by the Son: 143. Art in Middle Ages: 143. Gothic Image: 74

Malebolge: 111

Malebranche, Nicolas de: 40

Malenfant, M. de: 44

Malestrand: 49

Malherbe: Chretien Guillaume de: 94. F. de: 4

Malinowski, Bronislaw: 76

Malipiero: Federico: 65, 77. G. F.: 6

Malkin, Benjamin: 25

Mallarmé, S.: 88, 130

Mallet: David: 12, 58, 117; influenced by M: 58. Michael: 91

Malleus Maleficarum: 142

Mallory: Mary: see Cope, Mary. Nicholas: 45

Malmesbury, William of: 73, 123, 3

Malmesbury: co. Wilts.: 44. (Maidulfsburg) town: 49

Malone, Edmund: 28, 44, 58, 150

Maloney, Michael F.: 110

Malorate, Augustine: 143

Malory: 132, 133. Anna: 10. Ralph: 10. Sir Thomas: 27, 60, 76, 93, 137; Morte D'Arthur: 74, 46

Malraux, Andre, La Conditione Humaine: 35

Malthus, Thomas: 72

Malvenda, Thomas: 32

Malvezzi, Virgilio: 44, 73

Malym, William: 40

Mammon: 1, 2, 4, 31, 50, 51, 56, 60, 70, 73, 76, 98, 103, 107, 112, 111, 123*, 124, 127, 128, 141, 142, 3, 46, 71, 72, 109, 130, 55, 140. Becomes stoop-shouldered in Heaven: 107

Mamre: 49

Man: Mr.: 44. Audrey: see Brome, Audrey. E. H.: 118. John: 44. Paul de: 39. Robert: 45

Man (Island): 49, 144. See also: Mevanian Island

Man: 8, 17*, 24*, 31*, 41, 47*, 50*, 54*, 63*, 107, 113, 144*, 143, 36*. Creation of: 50, 144, 93, 107. Little lower than angels: 107. Manifests God's goodness: 107. As part of God: 113. As epic subject: 122, 123. Soul: 144. In nature: 144. His reason: 144; discoursive reasoning: 93. Biblical theory of: 48. His chief end: 47. Judgment of himself: 47. Takes place of fallen angels: 50. Undifferentiated term: 17. God's respect for: 47. The concept of: 48. Christian doctrine of: 48. Dignity of: 48. As the image of God (divine similitude): 48, 93. Created upright by God, in God's image: 119, 93. How knowledge of God gained by: 119. His will, frailty, loneliness: 144. Depravity of: 144, 36. In Paradise: 17, 143. Mortality of: 36*. M's concept of the nature of: 80. Response to music: 93. Relation to angels and animals: 93. Associated with circle, turbulent sea: 93. His proper study: 93. Fall of: 149, 46*; in PL: 104; Adam: 149*; Eve: 149; question of unfairness: 149; difficulty in plot: 149. In Mask: 104. His rank: 93. Superior to woman: 93. See also: Free will; Adam; Adam and Eve; Fall; Atonement

<u>Man and Superman</u>: 65

<u>Man in the Moon</u>: 103

<u>Man Wholly Mortal</u>: 44

<u>Man's Fall and Exaltation</u>: 115

Manardus, Joannes: 64

Manasseh: 73

Manasses: 65. Constantinus: 44

Manchester Square, London: 44

Manchester: co., Lancashire: 44, 49. Earl of: 143. Edward Montagu, 2nd Earl of: 44

Mancinelli (Mancinellus), Antonio: 20, 40

Mancini, P.: 6

Mandelslo: 19

Mandeville: Bernard de: 136, 115. Lord Henry: 45. Sir John: 15, 19, 37, 128, 32

Mandonnet, R. P.: 79

"Mane citus lectum fuge," (Milton): 44, 121

Manelli, F.: 6

Manes: 73, 90

Manetti, B.: 6

Manfred: 111

Mani: 71. <u>Epistula Fundamenti</u>: 36

Manicheism: 112. Manichaean controversy: 71. Maniche(an)s: 73, 139, 32. Manicheanism: 60, 114, 32, 36*, 71, 146. Manichee(ism) in PL: 31, 34, 47

Manierre, William B.: 115

<u>Manifestation</u>, statement of Leveller principles: 147

Manilius, (Gaius): 40, 44, 73, 89, 114, 3, 117

<u>Mankind</u>: 60

Manley: John Matthews: 60. Thomas (translator): 44, 59, 64; <u>Affliction and Deliverance of the Saints</u>: 74

Manlius Capitolinus, Marcus: 73, 130

Mann: Edward: 44. Thomas: 6, 125, 142, 39; <u>Doctor Faustus</u>: 142

Manna: 128

Manner, according to Newton more important in poetry than matter: 88

"Manner of Proceeding...in Chancery": 44

Mannering, Thomas: 40

Manners: Lady: 58. John: see Roos

Manners: 40. Books on: 40. And morals, Lily's code of: 20

Mannheim: Karl: 60. R.: 23

Manning: Miss: 16. Anne: 87, 137; works: The Maiden and Married Life of Mary Powell: 87; Deborah's Diary: 87. F.: 58. Owen: 44. Thomas: 40

Manningham, Richard: 40

Mannix, John Bernard: 16

Manoa: 1, 4, 53*, 70, 73, 125*, 128, 132, 144, 143, 72*, 92*, 109, 55. His role assumed by Chorus: 125. Character of: 132. Prayer and obedience: 143. Sacrifice: 143. Assured by Samson: 143. His consolation: 143. In judgment upon Samson: 72. In offer of catharsis: 72. In tragic enlightenment: 72

Manoah: 103

<u>Mans Mortallite</u> (Richard Overton): 44, 113*, 147, 91

Mansart: 27

Manschreck, Clyde L.: 93

Mansell, John: 40

Mansfield: A. S.: 44. Arthur: 44. Katherine: 8

Manso, Giovanni Baptista, Marquis of Villa: 6*, 15, 28, 30*, 44, 70, 84, 108, 120, 26, 94, 137, 146, 117, 64, 55, 21*, 136, 3, 109, 111, 128, 132, 59, 103

Manson, William: 93

Mant, R.: 58

Manton, Thomas: 44, 59, 99*. <u>Christs Temptation</u>: 74

Mantova, Domenico: 120

Mantua: 49, 3. Italy: 44. City of Lombardy: 49

Mantuan, Giovanni Battista Spagnoli: 44, 45, 74, 32, 83, 64, 3, 26, 101, 117, 21, 20, 4, 40, 44. Works: <u>Parthenice</u> (1502, ed. J. B. Ascensius): 74; <u>Parthenice Mariana</u>: 74

<u>Manuductio ad Artem Rhetoricam</u> (Vicars): 20

Manuel II: 40

Manuscripts, Cambridge: Peck's use of: 88. Mentioned by Pearce: 88. Used by Peck to study M's corrections: 88. Employed by Peck to prove M's artificiality. And for studying M's corrections: 88. Examined and made use of by Newton: 88. Used by Warton: 88. Identified by Todd: 88

Manuscripts, M's. See Milton, Manuscripts

Manuzio (Manutius), Aldo: 18, 40

Manwarden, Mr.: 44

Manwaring: Edward: 117. (Mainwaring), George: 45. Ralph (Randulph): 45. Roger: 73

Manwearing family: 45

Manwood, Thomas: 64

Manysidedness: of M's manner, the Richardsons on: 88. Of the Richardsons' sensibility: 88

Manzoni, Alesandro: 5

Maori myth of a dual Deity: 136

Map(s): 19, 40, 128, 144*. M's use of: 144*. M recommends: 144. And M's poetic inspiration: 144. Making: 40. Of London: 40

Maplet, John: 128*

Mapletoft, John: 10

Maraldi: 89

Marandé, Léonard de: 93

Marat, Jean Paul: 60, 115

Marazzuoli, Marco: 137

Marbecke, John: 68, 64. Works: <u>Holie Historie of King David</u>: 74; <u>Lyves of Holy Sainctes</u>: 74

Marbury, Mr.: 44, 45

Marcel, Gabriel: 5

Marcelli: 60

Marcellina: 44

Marcellinus: 32, 93

Marcellus: 1

Marceon, St., College: 40

"March into Virginia, The": 98

Marchand: Leslie A.: 44. (Marchant), John: 88; on M: 58

Marchbaldington: 45

Marchioness of Winchester: 62

Marchland (Marshland), co. Norfolk: 44

Marcile, Theodore: 123

Marcion: 44, 142, 3, 32, 36

Marck, Johannes van: 93

Marckl d. Mad Ethiou: 44

Marco Polo: 143. Voyages of: 143

Marcus: 142. Aurelius (Antonius): 40, 73, 3, 71, 88, 93

Mardall, in Shrewsbury: 44

Mardi: 98*

Marduk: 36

Mare Liberum: 103

Mare Street, London: 44

Marenzio, Luca: 6, 44, 121

Mareotis: 49. Mareoti(da)s: 73

Maresca, T. E.: 59

Maresius: 44. Samuel: 93

Mareuil, Pierre de: 117

Margaret Moses, St., Church: 40

Margaret, St., Fish Street: 40

Margaret: daughter of James I: 40. Of Nevarre: 112. "Old": 44. Teresa, Sister: 111

Margate: 44

Margiana: 19, 49, 73, 144. See also: Arachosia

Margites: 3

Margoliouth, H. M.: 44, 81*. See also: Marvell, Andrew

Marian exiles: 40, 83. Marian Exiles (the) (Garrett): 83

Mariana, Juan de: 44, 116

Mariani, Valerio: 5, 6

Marianus: Angelus: 7. Scotus: 93

Marie Antoinette: 25

Marie-Magdeleine (Desmaret): 70

Mariet, Thomas: 91

Marigny, J. Carpentier de: 44, 91

Marigo, Aristide: 5

Marilla, E. L.: 52, 110, 123, 137.

Milton and Modern Man: 48

Marinaro: 73

Marini (Giambattista). See Marino

Marino (Marini), Giambattista: 6, 23, 50, 70, 73, 122, 39, 53, 1, 65, 132, 64, 21, 128, 88, 149, 117. Works: Sospetto d'Herode (quoted, speech of Satan): 149; L'Adone: 74; Gerusalemme Distrutta: 60; La Strage degl'Innocenti: 60, 74. See also: Crashaw, Richard (translator)

Mario, Antonio: 64

Mariokh: 41

Mariolatry: 93

Mariology: 93

Mariottini, Felice: 117

Maritain, Jacques: 60, 76, 81

Marius: Gaius: 73. Of Cologne: 32. Victor: 77, 102

Mark Lane, London: 44

Mark Twain: 137

Mark. See Frederick William

Mark: 99. Gospel of: 3

Markets at Cambridge: 40

Markham (error for Marchmont): 91

Markham: Gervase: 40. Col. Henry: 44

Markland: 88. A.: 58

Marks Hall, Essex: 40

Marks: Carol L., "Thomas Traherne's Commonplace Book": 82. H. F.: 44

Marlborough: Sir James Leigh (Ley), Earl of: 35, 44, 103. Lady Mary (Petty) Lee: 44

Marleborow (Marlbrigia): 49

Marler, Thomas: 44

Marlianus, John Bartholomew (Marliani, Joannes Bartholomaeus): 40, 44

Marlorat, Augustin(e): 67, 38, 93, 99

Marlow: 45

Marlowe, Christopher: 1, 4, 15*, 19, 23, 27, 34, 35, 44, 18, 52, 58, 60, 86, 103, 108, 87, 114, 128, 129, 105, 64, 132, 134, 139, 141, 145, 3, 14,

26, 39, 82, 93, 101, 109, 130, 146, 149, 150, 55. Works: 35, Hero and Leander: 69; Dr. Faustus: 35, 126, 109, 149; Jew of Malta: 35; Tamburlaine: 35, 149

Marmion, Shakerly: 5

Marmoleso, Don Francisco Fernandez: 44

Marmontel: 94

Marnham (Marnhead), North and South, co. Nottingham: 44, 45

Maro. See Virgil

Marocco (Morocco): 49, 73. See also: Almansor

Marolles, Michel de, Traité du Poëme Epique: 74

Maronilla: 73

Marot, Clement: 33, 40, 64

Marple Hall, Cheshire: 44

Marprelate, tracts, the: 60. In Elizabeth's time, most effective Puritan pamphleteer: 147. Angers the Puritans: 147

Marprelate, Martin: 44, 147, 91, 114, 38

Marquand, J. P.: 118

Marquardt, W. F.: 40

Marquis de Grandvin: 98

Marriage of Heaven and Hell (Blake): 130, 25. Criticism of Swedenberg: 25. Criticism of M: 25. Structure, themes, "argument" of: 25. And Revelation: 25. Time perspectives: 25. And Bible of Hell: 25. Voice of the devil in: 25. Representation of Hell: 25

Marriage song: 50

Marriage: 8, 9*, 17*, 24*, 41, 54*, 63, 69*, 102, 113, 144, 46, 109*. Devil's jealousy of: 102. The Fathers on: 113. Paul on: 113. M's views on: 137, 55, 32, 113*, 71, 48. M's ideal of: 147. Puritan views of: 66; essence of: 93; marital chastity: 93; and divorce, M's attitude toward: 137, 117. Marriage relationships: abused by man after the Fall: 119; enjoyed by man before the Fall: 119

Marriages (Milton's): 137, 136, 44*, 84. His 1st: 84; Phillips' account: 55; anonymous biographer's account: 55; date: 55. His 2nd: 84; and wife's death: 94; Phillips' account: 55. His 3rd: Phillips' account: 55, 94. See also: Milton, Mary Powell; Milton, Elizabeth Minshull; Katherine Woodcock

Marriot: John: 58. Richard (bks., 1645-79): 91

Marriott: Sir James A. R.: 9, 58. T.: 58

Marris, Sir William: 64

Marryat, Capt.: 136

Mars: 2, 44, 89, 90, 111. Son... of: 73

Mars' Hill speech, Paul's: 51

Marseilles: 44

Marsh: M. de la: 44. Edward Garrard: 25. Henry (bks.): 44. John: 44, 93. John Fitchett: 40, 44*, 45. Thomas: 40

Marsh's Library, Dublin: 44

Marshall: E. H.: 19. Elizabeth: see Milton, Elizabeth Marshall. J. T.: 92. John (bks., 1645-47): 91, 115. Richard (apprentice scrivener): 44. Stephen (1594-1655): 9, 44, 51, 144, 38*, 91, 93; sermons by: 38*. T. F.: 97. W. Calder: 97. William (artist): 44, 137, 55. William (pr.): 44. William H.: 85, 140

Marshland, co. Norfolk: 44, 45. See also: Marchland

Marsili, Giovanni: 44

Marsiliers, Pierre de: 40

Marsilius of Padua: 83, 93. Defensor Pacis: 82

Marston Moor: 116. Battle: 113

Marston Sicca (Dry Marston): 45

Marston: 45, 133. John: 29, 44, 84, 146; The Scourge of Villanie: 82

Marsyas: 44, 111

Mart, Richard: 44

Martel: 10

Martello, Carlo: 111

Marten, Sir Henry (regicide): 9, 44, 45, 103, 38, 94, 147. Works: outspoken in The Parliament Proceedings justified: 147; The Independency of England Endeavored to be maintained: 147

Martha, C.: 4

Martha: 72

Martial music: 121

Martial: 18, 19, 20, 40*, 44, 59, 70, 73, 90, 120, 91, 64

Martianus Capella: 121, 123, 128, 88

Martin Ludgate, St., Church: 40

Martin-Achard, Robert: 93

Martin: Burns: 44, 132, 86, 93. Charles F.: 45. E.: 97. John: 23, 27, 98, 87*, 97*; influence abroad: 97; and Gandy, Turner: 97; art works based on Miltonic subjects: 87; mezzotints for PL: 87; collaborated with Edwin Atherstone: 87; natural Sublime in paintings of: 87; manner compared with M's: 87; Macaulay's attitude toward: 87; works: <u>The Characters of Fees</u>; <u>Adam's First Sight of Eve</u>: 87; <u>The Expulsion of Adam and Eve</u>: 87; <u>Belshazzar's Feast</u>: 87. John (bks., 1549-80): 44, 91. John (pr.): 44. L. C.: 44, 79, 81, 141, 143; see also: Vaughan, H. Sarah: 44. T.: 58

Martin: St.: 73, 143. V, Pope: 73, 116

Martin's St. in the Fields Church: 40

Martindale, Adam: 44

Martini: Father: 32. Gregorius: 123

Martinias, Hebrew Grammar: 20, 42

Martinias, Matthias: 40, 123

<u>Martins Eccho</u> (Richard Overton): 147

Martini(us): Martin: 73, 3. Martinus: 44. Petrus: 40 Martinus: Cornelius: 40. Jacobus: 40. Petrus: 40

Marturin, C. R.: 97

Martyn: Henry: see Marten. John: see <u>Grub-Street Journal</u>. W. Carlos: 63. William: 40

Martyr(s): 27, 51, 144. As hero: 123. Martyrdom: 27, 51, 122*

Martyr: Justin: 103, 115. Peter (of Vermigli): 19, 73, 55

Martz, Louis L.: 23, 29, 37, 52*, 79, 122, 145, 32, 36, 104, 35, 93, 101, 106*, 115, 21. On PL: 104. "Paradise Regained: The Meditative Combat": 74

Marulic, Marko, <u>Davideis</u>: 74, 64

Marullus: 40

Marvell, Andrew: 1, 4, 9, 10, 16, 17, 23, 27, 28, 30, 35, 37, 40, 44*, 45, 58, 59, 73, 79, 81, 84, 86*, 100, 103*, 105, 118, 116, 120, 127, 132, 136, 145*, 11, 26, 32, 38, 39, 46, 53, 72, 91*, 64, 94, 101, 106, 109, 130, 131*, 137, 146, 148, 150, 117, 21, 55. Works: "Appleton House": 109; "Garden": 81, 145; "Horatian Ode": 81, 145*; <u>First Anniversary of the Government under Oliver Cromwell</u>: 145; <u>Hortus</u>: 145; <u>Poem upon the Death of Oliver Cromwell</u>: 145; Thoughts in a Garden: 35; <u>Rehearsal Transprosed</u>: 145; <u>Tom May's Death</u>: 145

Marvell: Rev. Andrew (poet's father): 44, 120. Henry: 16

Marvellous, Christian. See Wonder

Marvelous, the: 69

Marvin, Capt. John: 44

Marx, Karl: 35, 52, 60, 25. Marxism: 1

Mary (ship): 44

<u>Mary of Burgundy, Hours of</u>: 97

Mary Aldermary, St., Church: 40

Mary Bow, St., Church: 40

Mary Magdalen, St., Church: 40

Mary: 70, 73, 125, 3, 71, 72*. Virgin: 4, 17, 44, 51, 113, 122, 36, 32; see also: Eve. In Luke 10:39: 60. Of Bethany: 72. Magdalen(e): 27, 44, 72. Princesses: 1516-58: 91; 1631-60: 91. I, Queen: 18, 40, 44, 45, 60, 73, 64, 103; and John Knox: 147. II, Queen: 40. Queen of Scots: 60, 116, 128. Stuart: 73. Daughter of James I (Princess of Orange): 40, 44. Tudor: 93. Countess of Pembroke: 40. Of Modena, Duchess of York and later Queen of James II: 44. Of Guise: 60

Mary's St., College, St. Andrew's Univ.: 40

<u>Maryland Gazette, The</u>: 115

Masaccio: 97, 109

Mascall: Eric L.: 93. Leonard: 128

Masefield, John, <u>Cargoes</u>: 8

Masenio, Jacopo (Masenius, Jacbobus):

117*, 65, 77. Sarcotis: 74

Maseres, Francis (editor): 44, 58

Masham, Sir William (member and President of Council of State): 44

Masius: Andreas (Maseus, Andreus): 40, 74, 32. Dilacus: 40

Mask of Comus: 136. "Mask Presented at Ludlow Castle, A": see Comus. Use of structural patterns: 104 Purpose of masque: 104. Framework of: 104. Concept of Nature: 104. As drama: 104. Transformations in: 104. Imaginative unity of: 104. Key words: 104. Different versions of: 104. Christian imagery in: 104. Pelagian traits in: 104. Theme of divine rescue: 104. Biblical references in: 104. Concept of man: 104. See also: Milton, Works

Mask(s): 50, 70, 92. The Mask: 94. See also: Ludlow Mask; Masque; Mask of Comus

Masked, Richard: 44

Masochism: 47

Mason: Charles: 44, 64. Dorothy: 128. Sir Edmund: 44. George: 70. James: 58. John: 44, 54, 58, 117, 64. Robert: 64. William: 58*, 70, 117; influenced by L'Allegro and Il Penseroso: 58; on Samson: 58. Rev. William: 44

Masorah. See Massorah

Masoreth(s): 73

Masque of Beauty (Jonson): 29

Masque of Blackness (Jonson): 29

Masque of Flowers (anonymous): 29

Masque of Lords (Campion): 29

Masque of Queens (Jonson): 29

Masque(s): 15, 27, 29*, 121, 136, 145, 143, 46, 146*, 55, 21*. M and: 137. Introduced from Italy: 136. Character of: 143. Theme of Comus: 143. In the 18th c.: 58

Masque, A. See Comus

Masques and Triumphs, Of (Bacon): 136

Mass: 143. As symbol: 143

Massachusetts Historical Society: 44

Massachusetts Magazine, Or Monthly Museum of Knowledge and Rational Entertainment, The: 115*

Massachusetts Mercury, The: 115

Massacre: 2

Masseket Azilut: 142

Massenius: 94

Massey: Nehemiah: 44. William: 37, 88, 117; Remarks on PL: 58

Massic cups: 3

Massicus: 49. Massic(a): 73

Massie, Joshua: 44

Massilia (Marseilles): 49

Massinger, Philip: 59, 68, 70, 84, 86, 128, 88, 13, 120, 130

Massingham, Hugh: 93

Masson, Professor David: 1, 6*, 7, 9*, 15, 16*, 19, 20, 23, 28, 29, 33, 34, 35, 40*, 41*, 44*, 45*, 51*, 54, 57, 59*, 63, 68, 70, 73, 75, 77, 83, 86, 89, 102, 105, 110, 71, 88, 91*, 135, 92, 94, 87*, 113*, 114, 116, 128, 129, 132*, 136, 133, 141, 142, 144, 14, 22, 62, 109, 130, 137, 148*, 150, 117, 21, 48, 3*, 120. On Shakespeare's sonnets: 87. On M's Satan: 87. On Puritans, M's Puritanism: 87. Considered M great prose writer: 87. Attitude toward M: 87. Works: The Life of Milton: 60, 74, 77, 83, 87, 43, 82; The Poetical Works of John Milton: 60, 43

Massorah: 40, 41, 42. Massoreths: 40, 41. Massoretic text: 40

Master in Chancery: 45

"Master of Sentences." See Lombard, Peter

Master of the Rolls: 44

Master of Ballantrae, The: 136

Master: Diana (Whorwood): 45. Sir Edward: 45

Master's degree, M's: 40

Masterman Ready: 15

Masterman, J. H. B.: 63, 86, 92

Masters, M's private: 40

Masters: E. L.: 58. M. K.: 58. Robert: 40

Matchiavel Junior: 116

Material: 92*

Materialism: 34, 47, 107. Commodianus: 107. Gregory Thaumaturgus: 107. In M: 113. In Fludd: 113

Mathematics: 40*. Arts of the quadrivium: 20. As related to music: 121*. M's study of: 40, 44. M's interest in: 113

Mather: Cotton: 71, 149; on the Puritan ideas: 147. Increase: 142, 71, 115; <u>Angelographia</u>: 142. Samuel: 37, 93

Mathewes, Augustine (pr.): 44

Mathews, Mr.: 44

Mathias Mechovita: 128

Mathias, T. J.: 146

Matilda: 70, 111

Matins: 126

Matisse, H.: 97

Matoré, G.: 23

Matriculation charge: 40

Matrimony: 72. See also: Marriage

Matrona: 113

Matter: 63*, 89, 107*, 113*, 128*, 72*. Distribution of, according to ancient philosophies: 89. Weight of invisible, demonstrated by Galileo: 89. Speculations and discoveries concerning properties of: 89. All things of one: 107*. Ex Deo: 107*. Holy: 107*. Invisible and formless: 107*. In M: 107*. Perversion of: 128. Unity of: 128. Original: 144. M's theory of: 71. Pre-existent: 93. Essentially indestructible: 107*. In Origen: 107*. And M: 107*; everything of one: 107; ex Deo: 107; holy: 107; indestructible: 107; invisible and formless: 107; theory of indestructibility of: 41; M's belief in divinity of: 113*. Origen, Augustine on: 113. Satan's heretical views on: 113. Nature of before creation: 41. Medieval Jewish ideas of eternity: 41. See also subentries under titles of poems

Matteson, Susanna Adeline: 115

Matthaeus, Monachus: 44, 73

Matthew: 40, 139, 112, 99. St., and gospel of: 40, 139, 44, 50, 3, 71. Of Westminster (fictitious chronicler): 73, 3, 93; see also: Matthew of Paris. Of Paris: 82. Sir Tobie: 81

Matthews: family: 44. A. G.: 44. Arthur D.: 44. Honor: 93. G. F.: 45. J. and G. F.: 44

Matthias, Jacobus: 44

Matthiessen, F. O.: 98

Mattingly, Garret: 39

Mattithiah Gaon: 41

Matuta: 90. See also: Leucothea

Maude, T.: 58

Maugars, A.: 6

Maugham, W. Somerset, <u>A Writer's Notebook</u>: 95

Maundrell: Mr.: 2, 44, 45. Henry: 45

Maundy: Mary (Mrs. Thomas): 44. Thomas (goldsmith): 44

Maunsell, Andrew: 128

Maupas, Charles: 40

Mauretania: 32

Maurice: Frederick Denison: 87, 143; considered M not sectarian: 87; on stages of M's life: 87; Apostles' Creed: 143. Henry: 116. (Mauritius), John: 44. Landgrave of Hess: 40. Maurice, of Nassau, Prince of Orange: 40, 44, 123, 21. T.: 58

Mauriciados, Des...Fűrsten Mauritzen ...dapffere Kriegsthaten: 123

Mauricus: 73

Mauritania, Africa: 44. Mauritanian (Maurusius): 73

Mauritius (Mauricius): 73

Maurois, Andre: 18

Maurus, Rabanus: 67, 68, 32, 99

Maury, Paul: 100

Mausbach, Joseph: 144

Mauss, Marcel: 39

Mavor: Ivan: 44. W.: 58

Mawbey, J.: 58

Mawer, J.: 58

Mawman, J. (publisher): 97

Maxey: Anthony: 93. Thomas (pr., 1640-56): 91

Maximian: 44, 73

Maximilian: I, Emperor: 73. Duke of Bavaria: 10

Maximin I: 73

Maxims: 51

Maximus von Phillipe: 73

Maxwell: A.: 34, 58. J. C.: 1, 29, 59, 134, 137; works: "'Gods' in PL": 60; "M's Knowledge of Aeschylus: The Argument from Parallel Passages": 60. John: 32

May, Thomas: 9, 10, 44, 144*, 145, 93, 117, 55. And Eikonoklastes: 144*. Courtiers and clergy: 144. King enemy of Parliament and people: 144. King and Papists: 144. Citizens and Parliament: 144. King and Strafford: 144. King's expeditions: 144. Crown jewels: 144. History of the Long Parliament: 144

Maya: 47

Mayart, Samuel: 44

Maydwell: Mr.: 44, 45. Lawrence: 45

Mayence, Synod of: 36

Mayer, John: 67, 143, 93, 99*. Commentary upon...Job, David, and Solomon: 74

Mayerne-Turquet, Theodore de: 16

Mayerson: C.: 4. Caroline W.: 14, 101

Mayhew, Jonathan: 115*, 117. Works: Christian Sobriety: 115; A Discourse Concerning Unlimited Submission and Non Resistance to the Higher Powers: 115; Objections Considered: 115; Of the True Value, Use and End of Life: 115; The Right and Duty of Private Judgment Asserted: 115; Seven Sermons Upon the Following Subjects: 115; The Snare Broken: 115; Upon the Necessity of Yielding a Practical Obedience to the Gospel: 115

Mayhews, Thomas: 44

Maynard, Thomas (consul to Portugal): 44

Mayne: F.: 58. Jasper: 44

Mayor, J. E. B.: 40

Maypole in Strand, London: 44

Mazarin, Cardinal Jules: 6, 44*, 59, 103, 120, 136, 94, 64

Mazocchi, D. See Mazzocchi, Domenico

Mazovia: 49

Mazzaro, Jerome: 39

Mazzaroth (Sirius): 89

Mazzeo, Joseph Anthony: 5, 1, 6, 23, 60, 75, 100, 122, 39, 93

Mazzocchi: Domenico: 6, 29, 64. Virgilio: 137, 64

Mazzoni: 70, 112, 3. Giacomo: 66, 73, 120, 53, 92. Guido: 60. J. (Jacopo): 23, 69, 122, 21, 111, 123; Difesa della Comedia di Dante: 74

McAdam, Edward L., Jr.: 44

McBain, Howard Lee: 115

McCain, J. W.: 44

McCarthy: Joseph: 137. Mary: 15

McClung. See Evans

McClure, N. E.: 40

McColley, Grant: 1, 15, 17, 19, 23, 24, 34, 44, 68, 60, 75, 86, 100, 144*, 107, 128*, 141, 142, 143, 36, 101, 102*, 110, 122, 32, 93, 106, 80, 109. Bible as M's major source: 107. M and the book of Enoch: 107. Works: "M's Bible in Heaven and Rupert of St. Heribert": 60; "PL": An Account of Its Growth and Major Origins: 60, 142

McConnaughty, J. L.: 40

McCrea, N. G.: 20

McCrie, Thomas: 40

McCutcheon, R. P.: 44

McDiarmid, J.: 68

McDonnell, Sir Michael F. J.: 20*, 40, 44

McDonough, Thomas M.: 93

McEuen, K. A.: 128

McGiffert, A. C.: 83

McGovern, J. B.: 44

McGowan, Margaret: 29

McGregor, M. F.: 68

McIlwain, Charles H.: 60

McIntyre, John: 93

McKenzie, G.: 23

McKeon, Richard: 122

McKerrow, R. B.: 40, 44, 68

McKillop, A. D.: 58

McLachlan, Herbert: 141, 93

McLane, Paul E.: 83

McLaughlin, Elizabeth T., "Milton and Thomas Ellwood": 82

McLelland, Joseph C.: 93

McMahon, A. Philip: 83

McManaway, James G.: 40, 44

McNamee, M. B.: 122

McNeill, John T.: 93

McNeir, W. F.: 122

McQueen, B. (pr.): 44

Mead: G. R. S.: 39. Rev. Joseph: 1, 40*, 42, 44, 22, 134, 32, 117; account books of, geography, history, logic, rhetoric texts of, letters of: 40; M and: 22; early influence on M: 147. Lucia Ames: 44. See also: Mede

Meadow, Philip: 38

Meadowcourt: 88. Richard: 117

Meadows, Philip (diplomatist): 16, 44*, 103, 94

Meagher, P. K.: 93

Meakin, William: 44

Mean: 121

Meander: 49, 73

Meanesborow: 49

Meaning: levels of: 47. Hume's analysis of shades of: 88. And etymology, Hume on: 88. And rhythm, the Richardsons on: 88. And sound, the Richardsons on: 88. And word-order, the Richardsons on: 88. Combination of literal with metaphorical, Warton on: 88

<u>Means to Remove Hirelings</u> (Milton): 112, 111. See also: Milton, Works

Means: 51

Mearne, Samuel (bks.): 44

Measurable music: 121

<u>Measure for Measure</u>: 88

Measure: 121

Meather Cannock. See Merthyr-Cynog

Mecca: 19, 49. Those who have travelled to: 73

<u>Mechanick Exercises</u> (Moxon): 135

Mechanists: 142

Mechizedek. See Melchisedech

"Mecubals": 142

Mede (Mead), Joseph: 7, 9, 128, 142, 114, 38, 93. Works: <u>The Apostasy of these Latter Times</u>: 142; <u>The Works</u>: 142; <u>Clavis Apocalyptica</u>: 94. See also: Mead

Medea: 54, 56, 73, 3, 72, 92, 25. <u>Medea</u>: 90

Medes: 19

Media: 19, 49, 73. See also: Atropatia

Medical lore: 123*. See also: Remedies; Diseases

Medical Library Association, <u>Bulletin</u> of: 44

Medicean codex: 44

Medici Chapel: 27*

Medici: family: 7, 6, 44. Catherine de': 64. Cosimo de', the Elder: 5, 64. Francesco de': 44. Lorenzo de': 5, 39, 64, 149. Mary (Marie) de, Queen of France: 6, 44, 64. House of: 103

Medicine: 40. State of in M's time: 16*

Medieval: 27. Culture: 51. Training: 51. Mysticism: 42. Ornithology: 41. Habits explained in Speght's Chaucer commentary: 88. Matters, references to, Bentley's, Richardsons': 88. Life, Sir Isaac Newton (quoted), Peck, Paterson on: 88. School education carried through to Renaissance: 20. Writers, Bp. Newton's knowledge of: 88. Interests, Callander's, Warton's: 88. Romance, elements of, mixed with classical features, Warton on: 88. Reading, Bowle's, Stillingfleet's, parallels in Todd: 88. Medievalism:

132, 71*. See also: Gothic; Romance

Medina: 19. J. B.: 97*; and the baroque: 97; and Biblical iconography: 97; and decorative painting: 97; and landscape: 97

Medini Celi, Anthony John Lewis, Duke of: 44

Meditation(s): 71. Augustinian: 81*. Ignatian: 81. Handbooks of: 81. Relation to contemplation: 81. Meditative: blank-verse poetry: 58*. Meditative genre: 81

Meditations (St. Bernard): 131

Meditations on the Lord's Prayer: 40

Mediterranean: 49, 103

Medmenham: 45

Medocium. See Meadows

Medonius: 44

Medusa: 60, 73, 90, 142

Medway: 49, 73, 103

Meen, H.: 58

Meetkerke, Edward à: 64

Megaera: 73, 90

Meggott, Richard: 44, 116

Meijer, E. J.: 97

Mein Kampf (Hitler): 134

Mela: 3. Pomponius: 19, 40, 73

Melanchaetes: 73

Melancholia (Dürer): 88

Melancholy: 7, 90, 114, 144*, 72, 97. And Il Penseroso, Comus, PL: 144. Personal note on PL: 144. As an integral element of beauty in landscapes, Warton on: 88. Meanings of the word in the 17th c.: 109. M's: 144. 18th c. lit. of: 58. See also: "Graveyard poetry" for 18th c. lit. of; Il Penseroso

Melanchthon (Melanchton), Philip (in German, Scharzerd): 40*, 44, 73, 77, 83, 114, 123, 22, 32, 93*, 79, 101. Works: Commentarius de anima: 60; Commentary on Genesis: 60; In Doct. Phy. 1567: 77

Melanchthon-Sturmius pattern of grammar school education: 40

Melbourne: 40, 44

Melchisedec(h): 45, 68, 73, 32

Melcombe: 45

Melditch, co. Cambridge: 44, 45

Meldreth: 45

Meleager: 73, 64

Melesigenes: 49, 73, 90, 3. See also: Maeonides

Melete: 20

Meliboea: 49. Melibaean: 73

Meliboeus: 73, 72

Melicertes: 90. Mask: 104

Melind(e): 19, 49, 144, 73. See also: Mombaza

Melius Inquirendum: 116

Mellers, Wilfrid: 6, 39

Mellish, John: 40

Mellius de Sousa, Joannes: 65, 64. Works: De Reparatione Humana: 74; In Librum Job: 74

Mellther Kennocke. See Merthyr-Cynog

Melody: 121

Melpomene, music: 44, 103

Melqart: 68

Melros: 49

Melton: Sir John (Sixfold Politician): 44. John (astrologer): 44

Melun: 49

Melville: Allan: 98. Andrew: 40, 114. Elisabeth Shaw: 98. James: 40. Herman: 128, 136, 115; works: Moby Dick: 115; M referred to by: 98*. Maria Gansevoort: 98. Richard: 40

Memling: 90

Memmius Gaius: 73

Memmius Gemellus, Gaius: 73

Memnon: 44, 73, 90

Memnonian: 73

Memoires of the Lives, Actions, Sufferings and Deaths: 116

Memorabilia (Xenophon): 112

Memorable Deeds and Sayings, The (Valerius Maximus): 20

Memoria (fifth part of rhetoric): 20

Memorial of God's Last Twenty-nine Years Wonders: 116

Memorials (Barksdale): 45

Memorials of St. Margaret's Church, Westminster: 44

Memorizing as a method of teaching: 20, 51

Memory, Dame: 70

Memory: 128. Function of: 96*. Basis of all learning: 40, 51. Power of: 81*. M's: 44. Poet's: 50. See also: Brain; Anamnesis

Memphian: 73

Memphis (Alcairo): 19, 49, 144. Basha of: 44

Mempricius: 57

Menachem: 41

Menage, Giles: 44

Menahem ben Saruk: 40

Menaka, F.: 102

Menalcas: 44, 73

Menander: 4, 57, 70, 73

Menapia: 49

Menard, Pierre: 39

Menasseh ben Israel: 7, 52, 38

Menbidj, Agapius: 65

Mendelson, E. M.: 39

Mendoza, Juan Gonzalez de: 19

Menelaus: 90, 92

Menenius Agrippa: 128

Menexenus (Plato): 112

Mennes, Sir John and James Smith: 44

Menno Simons: 114

Meno (Plato): 112

Menochius: 58

Menoetes: 2

Menstrie, co. Clackmannanshire: 44

Mensuration (geometry and astronomy): 40

Mental regeneration: 51

Ments: 49

Menzies, W.: 68, 81, 85, 93, 125

Meozzi, Antero: 111

Mephibosheth: 142

Mephistopheles: 60, 113, 142, 72. In Goethe and Marlowe: 142

Merbeck, John: 40

Mercator (Kremer), Gerhard(us): 1, 19, 24, 40, 77, 102, 128, 139, 144*, 32, 93, 101. Verity on: 144. Africa: 144. Winds: 144. _Atlas_: 144, 77

Mercer: John: 77, 43. T.: 58

Mercera: 44. See also: Salmasius, Madame

Mercers' Chapel, London: 44

Mercers' Company: 20*, 40

Mercerus, John (Joannes): 41, 123. _In Jobum_: 74

Merchant Adventurers, Company of: 44, 103

Merchant Taylors': Company: 40, 44. School: 20, 40, 42, 44, 103, 3

Merchant: F. I.: 145. M.: 97

Merchants: English Company of: 44. English in Italy, Hamburg: 44

Mercia: 49. Mercians: 3

Mercier, P.: 97

Mercreds-Burnamsted: 49

Mercuries: 103

Mercurius Academicus: 103. _Mercurius Anti-pragmaticus_: 103. _Mercurius Aquaticus_: 103. _Mercurias Aulicus_: 103. "Mercurius Britanicus": 40, 44, 73, 103. _Mercurius Civicus_: 103. _Mercurius Clericus_: 103. _Mercurius Democritus_: 103. _Mercurius Diabolicus_: 103. _Mercurius Elenctitus_: 103. _Mercurius Fumigosus_: 103. _Mercurius Librarius_: 44, 91. _Mercurius Melancholicus_: 103. _Mercurius Mastix_: 103. _Mercurius Militaris_: 44. _Mercurius_

Politicus (attr. to M): 44*, 59, 103*, 116, 91*, 94. Mercurius Pragmaticus: 44, 103, 91. Mercurius Publicus: 44, 116, 91. Mercurius Trismegistus: see Hermes Trimegistus

Mercury (as masque figure): 29, 44

Mercury Vindicated from the Alchemists at Court (Jonson): 29

Mercury: 56, 73, 89, 90, 3. See also: Hermes

Mercy (figure in "Nativity Ode"): 29

Mercy vs. Justice: 60*

Mercy: 47, 50, 51, 36*, 25. Oil of: 123. Of God: 93

Meredith: Edward: 116. George: 1, 54, 58, 65, 87, 113, 132, 134, 71, 72, 137; works: "Lucifer in Starlight": 87; "Poetry of Milton": 87; Modern Love: 132. John: 44

Meres: Francis: 59, 114, 71, 64; Palladis Tamia: 74. John: 44

Meresig: 49

Mereswar: 49

Merian: Mrs. (Lady): 44. Matthias: 10

Meriba: 49

Mericke, William: 44

Meridian: 89

Merit: 31, 107, 122*, 123*. Source of nobility: 123. Vanity of human: 123. Angels achieve rank through: 107. Dependent on goodness: 123. See also: Goodness; Reward

Meriton, George: 93

Merivale, Patricia: 137

Merleau-Ponty (Maurice): 11, 39

Merlin: 44, 103, 3, 25

Mermaid Tavern: 44, 103

Meroe: 49, 144, 73

Merope: 92

Meroz: 49, 51, 73

Merrett, Christopher: 10

Merrick, J.: 58

Merrill: R. V.: 60, 128. Zachary: 44

Merriman, Roger Bigelow: 60

Merry Wives of Windsor (Shakespeare): 20

Merry, R.: 58

Mersenne: Marin: 1, 6, 10*, 24*, 77, 102, 114, 142, 128; Opera Omnia, Questiones Celeberrimae in Genesim: 142. Peter: 100

Merthyr-Cynog (Meather Cannock, Mellther Kennocke, etc.), co. Brecknock: 44, 45

Merton (Merantun): 45, 49

Merton College, Oxford: 40, 45

Merton: E. S.: 128. Robert K.: 77

Mertun: 49

Meru, Mt.: 32

Mervyn, James: 44

Meryell (Myriell), Henry: 20

Mesopotamia: 19, 49, 144, 32, 150. See also: Euphrates

Messalina: 73

Messena: 49, 73

Messenger in SA: 92*

Messenger, Ernst C.: 93

Messiah (anonymous): 58

Messiah: 2*, 41, 60, 143, 36, 71, 72. Foretold: 143. Birth related: 143. See also: Christ; Son of God; the Son; Trinity

Messianic kingdom: 123*. Messianic expectations: 93; see also: Eschatology

Messina, Straits of: 49. See also: Scylla

Metalogicus (John of Salisbury): 20

Metamorphoses (Ovid): 20, 29, 111, 118

Metamorphoses: 122. Of Satan: 123*. As image of virtue or vice: 123*

Metaphor(s): 31, 47, 51, 69*, 76*, 79, 53. Distinguished from type: 79. "Sacred": 79. M's definition of: 79. Having musical significance: 121. Bentley opposed to unconventional: 88. Pearce on legitimacy: 88. Metaphorical meaning, combination of literal with, Warton on: 88. See also: Accommodation; Images

Metaphrastes (The Metaphrast), Simeon: 73

Metaphysical Poetry, On (James Smith): 131

Metaphysical Poetry: Donne to Butler (Grierson): 131

Metaphysical: poets: 36. Poetry: 132*. Metaphysicals: 27. Metaphysical Society (The): 87. Metaphysical conception of music: 121. Metaphysical school, Warton on eccentricities of: 88

Metaphysics (Aristotle): 5, 112

Metaphysics: 40*, 51. In M's On Time, PL: 40. As 2nd-year subject: 40

Metastasio, Pietro: 39, 117

Metcalfe, Robert: 40, 42

Metellus, Caecilius: 16

Meteors: 89, 128. Causes and kinds: 128. Meteoric showers: 89

Meteorum Liber: 65

Meth, Ezekiel: 7

Methexis: 72*. See also subentries under titles of poems

Method of composing, M's: 44

Method of righteousness: 123

Method of the Doctrine of the Christian Religion (Ussher): 134

Method: 70. Epistemological, historiographic, and Ramistic: 96

Methodists: 7, 78

Methodius: 23, 77, 107; chiliasm: 107; fragments: 74. Of Olympus, St.: 36, 93; From the Discourse on the Resurrection: 36

Methodology: 123

Methods and Aims in the Study of Lit. (Cooper): 70

Methodus conficiendarum epistolarum (Celtes): 20

Methodus conscribendi epistolas (Hegendorff): 20

Methodus de conscribendis epistolis (Macropedius): 20

Methuselah: 32

Meton, the Metonic circle: 89

Metonymy, defined and illustrated: 118. Of objects and actions: 118

Metre: 70. See also: Verse

Metrical analysis: 125

Metrical Paraphrase of the Old Testament: 36

Metrics: 55*

Metrodorus: 128

Metropolitan Museum of Art, N.Y.: 44

Metropolitan Nuncio: 44, 103, 91

Metropolitan Railway, London: 44

Metrum in Genesim: 65

Metz: C.: 97. Rudolf: 113, 144

Meun, Jean de: 18, 32

Meurer: 64

Meurier, Gabriel: 40

Meursius (De Meurs), Jan: 44, 117

Meuse (Mosa) River: 44

Mevanian Islands: 49. See also: Man (Island)

Mews, London: 44

Mexia, Pedro: 60, 143, 128, 93. On ages of world: 143

Mexico: 19, 49, 150

Meyer Tobias: 89

Meyler, W.: 58

Meynell, Alice: 87

Meysey Hampton, co. Gloucestershire: 44

Mezen: 49. See also: Slobotca

Mezentius: 2, 20

Mezentius: 73, 113, 123. See also: Virgil

Micah: 73

Micaiah: 3

Michael Angelo. See Michelangelo

Michael, Archangel: 1, 2, 4, 17*, 19, 31, 41*, 44, 50*, 52, 56, 57, 60*, 63*, 70, 73, 76, 89, 98, 102, 103, 112, 111, 113, 123*, 124, 127*, 128*, 46, 141, 142*, 144, 143*, 32*, 36, 71, 72*, 96*, 109*, 130, 140*, 55. And PL: involvement with Adam: 104; narratives of: 104; tonal and tempo patterns of: 104; account of Moses' establishing Law: 126; his sword: 143; advice to Adam: 143; prophet of glad tidings: 143; and true religion: 143; reveals future: 143; speech in PL: 46; prophecy of: 140*. See also: Angels; War in Heaven

Michaëlis de Vasconcellos, Sra.: 64

Michaelis, Sebastien: 142

Michaelmas term: 40, 45

Michel: Lawrence: 39. P. H.: 5

Michelangelo, Buonarroti: 5, 6, 15, 27*, 40, 52, 76, 111, 120, 46, 136, 139, 97, 137, 146*, 117, 13, 25, 88, 149, 64. 16th sonnet: 109

Michelet, Jules: 18, 39

Michell: Francis: 44. (Mychel), Sir John: 44, 45. R.: 58. William: 44, 45

Mickiewicz, A.: 58

Mickle, W. J.: 58, 149, 117

Micklem, Nathaniel: 93

Mico: Samuel: 44. William: 44

Microcosm: 24, 69, 71, 93. See also: Cosmic identities

<u>Microcosme</u>: 65

"Microcosmus, Theodorus" (fictitious pr.): 44, 91

Micrometer, the: 89

Microscope: 128

Micyllus, Jacobus: 20, 40

Midas: 90

Middelburg: 44, 73

"Middle": 92

Middle class: 40. Education: 40

Middle Ages: 27, 40, 70, 103, 143*, 72, 92. Faith in: 143. The earth in: 143. And pattern of time: 143*

Middle Hill, Broadway, co. Worcs.: 44

Middle Basin (Raysing, Reasing, Resing, etc.): 44, 45

Middle Temple: London: 44, 45*. <u>Records</u>: 45*. Lane: 40

Middle-Angles: 49

Middle-Burrough (Medioburgena): 49

Middlebrook, Samuel. See Grebanier

<u>Middlesex, The Visitation of in</u>: 45

Middlesex: 45*, 49. Earl of: 45; see also: Cranfield, Lionel. Lord, on Pope: 58. Pedigrees: 45. Sessions Rolls: 44

Middleton Stony: 45

<u>Middleton, Thomas, The Works of</u>: 45

Middleton: 45, 49. Mr.: 44. Chrystopher: 65. Conyers: 32. Henry (pr.): 44. Richard: 93. Sir Thomas: 44, 35, 45, 86, 108, 114. Thomas: 45, 60

Midgard, Mt.: 32

Midgley, Robert: 44

Midlands: 44

Midrash(im) Rabbah: 40, 41, 42, 123, 36*. Works: <u>Deuteronomy Rabba</u>; <u>Ecclesiastes Rabba</u>; <u>Esther Rabba</u>; <u>Exodus Rabba</u>; <u>Genesis Rabba</u>; <u>Leviticus Rabba</u>; <u>Numbers Rabba</u>; <u>Song of Songs Rabba</u>: 36

<u>Midsummer Night's Dream</u>: 139, 26

Midsummer: Day: 40. Eve: 58. Term: 40

Midwestern Univ. Museum Association: 44

Midwife: 128

Midwim: 45

<u>Might Overcoming Right</u> (John Geree): 147

Migne, J. P.: 57, 116, 128. <u>Patrologiae</u>: <u>Opera Omnia Boetii</u>: 82

Migraine headaches: 40

Milan (Mediolanum): 44, 103, 3, 49

Milan, Duke of: 29

Milbourne, Luke: 116

Milburn, R. L. P.: 93

Milde and Mabee. See Mylor and Mabe

Mildmay: Sir Henry (master of king's Jewel House): 44. Mary: see Fane, Mary, Countess of Westmoreland. Preacher: 40. Sir Walter: 40

Mildred's, St., Church: 40

Mile-End Green: 49. See also: Sonnet XI

Milegast: 73

Miles: London innkeeper: 103. Miles's Coffee House: 51. Luke: 44. Josephine: 60, 76, 110, 128. J. (James): 23

Miles: 91

Milesia(n): 73

Miletus: 49

Military: Council: 51. Practice: 40, 51

Militia, Committee for: 44

Milito of Sardis: 107. Pre- existing Logos: 107

Miliukov, Pavel Nikolayevich: 60

Milk Street, Shrewsbury: 40, 44

Milky Way, the: 89*, 128. Extent, width, form, structure of: 89. Computation of stars, uneven distribution of stars, unfathomable abysses, remoteness of stars in: 89. In M's poetry: 89

Mill. See Symbolism

Mill: James, on liberty of thought and discussion: 147. John Stuart: 27, 44, 148

Millan (Mediolanum). See Milan

Millar: Andrew (publisher): 44. J.: 36

Millenarians: 9*, 113. M's relations to: 113. Millenarianism: 60, 107, 114, 38*, 93

Millenary Petition (a Puritan view): 147

Millennium: 7, 9*. Idea of: 52

Miller and Mabee. See Mylor and Mabe

Miller: Mr.: 44. Lady A. R.: 58; see also: Batheaston. David: 21. Dorothy D.: 93. Draper: 44. Edna: 44. Ella (editor): 44, 45. Frank J.: 56. George: 44, 45. Henry: 137. James: 58. Johann: 10. John C.: 115. John: 44. John (1754): 58. John (1863), Aeneid: 58. Milton: 60, 122, 123, 21. Perry: 9, 23, 37, 40, 79, 83, 115. R. D.: 99. Richard: 44. Sonia: 44. William: 118

Miller's Tale, The (Chaucer): 134

Milles, Thomas: 60, 116, 128*, 93

Millieus, Antonius, Moyses Viator: 74

Milligan, Burton H.: 115

Millington: 28, 59, 94. Book-dealer: 103. Edward: 44, 116, 55. Gilbert: 44

Mills: Elijah H.: 115; An Oration Pronounced at Northampton: 115. Laurens J.: 40. W.: 58

Milman, H. H.: 58, 146

Milne, Doreen J.: 116

Milner-Gibson-Cullum, Gery: 44

Milner, George: 87. On Tennyson's "Montenegro" and M's "Piedmont": 87

Milnes, R. M.: 44, 87. Timbucktoo compared to M's poetry: 87

Miltiades: 44, 123

Milton (Tillyard): 134

Milton and the Aristotelian Definition of Tragedy (Bywater): 70

Milton and the Puritan Dilemma (Barker): 134

Milton and Forbidden Knowledge: 26

Milton and Wordsworth (Grierson): 134, 139

Milton Handbook, A (Hanford): 134, 135, 136, 45, 83

Milton Memorial Lectures: 144

Milton Restor'd and Bentley Depos'd: 88, 117

Milton, manuscripts of lit. works, legal documents, papers, etc.: 44*. Memorial Lectures (ed. by Ames): 70, 63. Milton papers (Hamilton): 3. Milton papers (Stevens): 3. Portrait of himself (alleged): 44

Milton family: 44*. Medical history of: 113. Phillips' account: 55. Mr.: 44. Mrs.: 44. "Milton" pseudonym: 44

Milton: Agnes (M's great-grandmother): 40, 44. Alice: 44

Milton: Ann: 52. Anne (M's sister): 16, 40, 44, 84, 103, 94; marriage to Edward Phillips: 55; her daughter Anne: 44; see also: Phillips, Anne. Anne (M's daughter): 16, 28*, 44*, 103*, 137, 150, 55, 94. Anne (M's brother's daughter): 44. Anne (b. 1578): 40, 44, 89

Milton: Sir Christopher (M's brother): 9, 15, 16, 20, 28*, 40, 44*, 45*, 56, 84, 113, 132, 91, 137, 55, 94; his son, Christopher: 44. Christopher Milton (others): 44. Christopher (Uncle): 40

Milton, Deborah Clarke (M's youngest daughter): 16, 28*, 44, 63, 84, 86, 103, 136, 137, 150, 55, 94. See also: Clarke, Abraham

Milton: Elizabeth (d. 1582): 40, 44. Elizabeth Caswell: 44. Elizabeth Haughton (M's grandmother): 44. Elizabeth Minshull (M's 3rd wife): 40, 44*, 45, 63, 73, 84, 137, 150, 55, 94

Milton, Francis: 44

Milton, Henry (M's great-grandfather): 40, 44

Milton, Isabel. See Milton, Elizabeth

Milton, James (scrivener): 44

Milton, Jane (b. 1584): 40

Milton, John (poet). See end of Milton surnames below.

Milton, John (M's father): 9, 15, 28*, 29, 30*, 40*, 44*, 45, 59, 60, 73, 84, 103*, 113, 121, 126, 132, 136, 26, 91, 137, 117, 55, 21, 94; attributed writings, depositions, investment activities, musical compositions, real estate, connections with Scriveners' Company: 44*. Phillips' account: 55. John (M's son, 1651-52): 16, 28*, 44*, 59, 103, 137, 55. John (son of M's brother, Christopher): 44. John (Major, quartermaster to Pennington): 44, 59. John (miscellaneous, two different ones): 45

Milton: Katherine Woodcock (M's 2nd wife): 44*, 84, 137, 16, 30, 150, 55, 94; see also: Sonnet XXIII. Katherine (M's daughter): 28, 44, 120, 137, 55

Milton: Mary (M's daughter): 28*, 44*, 63, 103*, 137, 150, 55, 94; quoted by Elizabeth Fisher: 55. Mary (daughter of M's brother, Christopher): 44*. Mary Powell (M's 1st wife): 16, 44*, 45, 63, 68, 84, 103*, 137, 94; Phillips' account of M's marriage: 55; anonymous biographer's account of M's marriage: 55; death, Phillips' account: 55; see also: Powell; Doctrine and Discipline

Milton, Martha Fleetwood (later Coward, daughter-in-law of brother Christopher): 44*

Milton: Mathewe (sic): 40. Prudence: 44. Richard: 64. Richard (M's grandfather): 28, 40, 44*, 94. Richard (M's nephew): 23, 44*. Richard (father's apprentice): 44, 103

Milton: Robert: 44. Rowland: 44. Samuel: 44. Sara(h) Jeffrey (M's mother): 16, 4, 30, 40, 44*, 45, 73, 84, 103, 137, 55. Sarah (M's sister): 40, 44. Sarah (M's brother's daughter): 44

Milton: Tabitha (M's sister): 16, 40, 44. Thomas (M's nephew, son of Christopher): 16, 28, 44*. Thomasine Webber (wife of Christopher): 44. Thomasine (daughter of M's brother, Christopher): 44, 45 William: 44. Daughter of Henry Milton: 44

Milton, John (poet): The following entries are partial, yet representative. Readers should consult individual topics throughout the Index for particular subjects and references. Works with a biographical emphasis include the following: 16*, 20*, 28*, 40*, 44*, 45*, 26*, 55*, 84*, 94*, 103*, 108*, 72*, 109*, 113*, 116*, 147*

Milton (early life). Ancestry: 94. Birthplace: 94. Baptism: 44. Birth and education: 44. Early home influence: 136. Presbyterian influences: 94. Little of religious fanaticism in him or his family: 113. Early recognition of his genius: 113. Family: 113; father: 94, 113; grandfather: 113. Stages of life: 87; youth of: 9, 87; early life: 87; youth and youthful characteristics: 137; at St. Paul's School: 44, 94; early studies: 8, 94.

Milton (middle years). Middle years: 35, 87. Pensioner of Christ's Cambridge: 44, 94; at Cambridge: 9, 113. College punishment: 94. Takes B.A. and M.A. Degrees: 94. Journey to Italy: 6*, 94; endangered by the Inquisition in Italy: 136. Hammersmith Period: 53. Lives in Aldersgate: 9, 94. Education of nephews: 94

Milton (later years). M and his age: 10*, 18*, 144, 137, 146. His religion: 136; not a puritan: 136. Almost a free-thinker: 136. A Royalist: 108, 147. From Presbyterianism to Independency: 147, 94. Political views and government service: 113, 137. As a democratic reformer: 147. Champions birthright of Eng. people: 147. Joins the Hon. Artillery Co.: 136. As orator, statesman: 20. Care of his father: 136. United of private, political, literary life: 113. Supports the Parliamentary cause, local assemblies, franchise: 147. As Latin Secretary: 9, 45, 51, 25. Ordered to answer Salmasius: 136. Violent attack on him: 136. At work on Latin-Eng. Dictionary: 136. Saves Sir William Davenant: 136. High point of public life: 61. Marriages: 8, 9, 54*, 94. Domestic unhappiness: 8, 9, 54*, 94. His children: 87, 94. Defends Cromwell's ejection of Parliament: 13. Refuses King Charles' offer of reinstallment: 136. Fallen on evil days: 136. His monetary losses: 94. Life after Restoration: 84. His 2nd peril after the Restoration: 113. His return to literature: 113

Milton (character and qualities). True character: 9, 144, 51; controversy regarding true character: 144. Personal characteristics: 51. Personal appearance and habits: 94. Affability: 136. Aloofness: 146. Amiable and normal: 87. Anti-heroism: 45. Austerity and innocence: 137. Capacity for admiration: 137. Cheerfulness: 44. Cold and austere: 87. Condemns greed: 53*. Constancy: 146. Conventionality: 146. Devotion to poetry and music: 137. Disposition: 94. Distrust of the masses: 147. Egotism and pride: 141, 113*, 146. Emotional responsiveness: 104. Erudition: 146. Faith in virtue: 143. Frigility: 146. Genial charm: 136. Grandeur: 146. Humanity: 146, 25. Humor: 146; deficiency of: 87.

(character and qualities continued) Iconoclast: 146. Impulsiveness: 136. Independence: 137; of mind: 87, 143; of character and method: 143, 94. Lack of feeling: 146. Enjoyment and knowledge of music: 137, 112. Masters passions: 129. Mental isolation: 94. Metabolic genius: 136. Modesty: 146. Morality: 146. Originality: 144. Patriotism: 9, 51. Piety: 94. Platonism: 13. Poetic nature of: 87. Practicality: 51. Proficient public speaker: 8. Range of excellence: 13. Religious: character and sincerity: 51; zeal: 146. Religious and moral idealism: 137. Rebellious nature of: 87. Sagacity: 51. Self-control and discipline: 51. Selfhood: 25. Sense of detachment: 61. Seriousness: 146. Shallowness: 146. Shortcomings: 146. Skepticism: 114. Stoicism: 141. Temperament: 136; Hebraistic: 87. Toleration: 94, 146. Uniqueness: 13. Varied qualities of: 87. Vastness of mind: 146

Milton (character, miscellaneous). M and atomism: 32. M's purpose: 143. Social relations: 137. Relations with people and attitude toward humanity: 137. Value of M's vision: 143. Vocation: 53*, 94. Desire for fame sublimated in <u>Lycidas</u>: 136. Life of the spirit: 143. Dissillusionment: 113, 143. His spiritual pride embodied and sublimated in the Satan of PL: 136

Milton (health). Medical history: 128*. Albinism, arthritis, eyestrain, flatulence, glaucoma, gout, infant mortality in family, melancholia, self-medication, syphillis: 128; blindness: 20, 128

Milton (his attitudes, views, ideas on, of). Chronology: 32. Civil magistrates: 51. Classical learning and classicism: 7, 89, 80, 137. Dancing and theatre going: 137. Philosophy of marriage and divorce: 66, 54*, 136. The Dutch: 51. England: 137. Fame: 137. Happiness: 80. Himself: 51, 137. Knowledge and work: 32. Man's nature: 80. Marriage (ends of, sexuality, spirituality, authority in, unity): 54*. Military science, training: 51. Misogyny: 144, 146. Money: 137. Music: 51. Nature of government: 51. Natural knowledge: 51. Natural law: 32. Natural rights: 32. Orthodoxy: 144. Partial rotation: 51. "Patriotic piety": 136. Profane, licentious men: 51. Reading: 51. Restoring monarchy: 51. Right of kings: 51. Right reason: 80. Romantic love: 80. Scientific inquiry: 80. Sensuality: 141. Tyrants: 51. Utopian schemes: 80. War: 137. Women: 141, 80, 94, 137

Milton (political activities, views). Political philosophy: 51. Antiprelatical pamphlets: 53. Political principles: 13. Controversies conerning: 87. Controversy harmful to: 87. M thought of as: a democrat: 87; not a democrat: 87; as a republican. Views of as a republican and democrat: 87. Activities defended: 87; attacked: 144. On civil liberty: 51, 94. On civil power: 87. On advantages of free commonwealth: 51. On authority: 7. On censorship and licensing: 51*. Unmistakably the democrat in various parts of The Tenure of Kings: 147. The Tenure vs. Charles I: 147. Plan of governmental organization: 51. Plan of ideal commonwealth: 51. M's and Canne's views of monarchy compared: 144*. Opinion of Hall: 144. Answers Digby: 144

Milton (education). Theory and practice as an educator: 137. On religious education: 51. M and learning: 143, 80, 94. Reasons for reading: 143. On academies: 51

Milton (religion, theology). Christianity of: 141. Christ and God: 137. On Christ's Kingdom and teaching: 51. On Christian liberty and tradition: 51. Problem with Christ and nature: 61. Knowledge and use of the Fathers: 57*. On God's justice: 114. On Ways of God: 147. M an Old Testament Christian: 147. Hebraism of M: 25. M and rabbinical exegesis: 22*. Transliteration of Hebrew: 22. M's biblicism: 114*. Attitude toward Bible: 137. Idea of creation: 32. On destruction of Paradise: 32. On original perfection: 32. Subconscious disbelief in Genesis story: 87. M's heresies: 137, 22*. Knowledge of, borrowings from, Lactantius: 57*. "Error not heresy": 107. Interpretation of scripture: 25. Use of typological interpretation: 32. Independence and originality in theological speculation: 22*. Method and theory of Biblical criticism: 22*. M's scriptural via media: 114. Religious views: 6*, 9*, 57*, 94. Possible mystical element in M's religion: 137

(religion, theology, continued). Free -will: 136, 80. Fate and Foreknowledge: 80. Predestination: 80. Refutation of Predestination: 22. On peace and salvation: 80. Man's prime responsibility: 80. "Limbo" and suicide: 80. Salvation: 80. Ambivalence toward Incarnation: 61. On Covenants: 32. Working with hands: 80. Attitude towards the church and its organization: 137, 51, 104. On the liturgy: 136. Ideas of worship: 32. On church history: 51. Attitude towards Episcopacy: 136; opposition to: 51. Puritanism of: 25, 141. Theory of Church and State: 94. Attitude towards Catholics and papacy: 61, 51; and Romanism: 136. On papal censorship: 51. Reformation: 51; on the origin of Protestantism: 51. On religious reform: 51. His legal theology: 114. His religious liberty, freedoms: 136, 51. Distrust of early theologians: 107. Beliefs tried by early creeds: 107. M and Socinians: 22. M and gnosticism: 141. His symbol of the Almighty a "cause of atheism": 136. Conviction of imminent overthrow of evil: 80

Milton (and poetry/prose). Poetical character: 146. Priest of poetry: 146. M as poet: ideal, religious, revolutionary, epic, musical, mythic, pastoral, philosophical, picturesque: 146. As satirist: 45. Poet of the sublime: 87, 97*, 136. Insensitive to the plastic arts: 136. Poetry his vocation: 94. His purpose in poetry: 61. Poet's inner conflict displayed: 61. His rhythmic style instinct with his egotism: 136

Milton (on poetry). Idea of decorum: 25, 146. Poetry not detached from life: 137. Poetry, theory and practice: 9, 137, 94. Views on inspiration: 137. And sacred muse: 143. Poetry and virtuous action: 61. On the poet as preacher: 61

Milton (his poetry/prose). Praised: 58*. Excellence in genres: 146. Metrical skill: 87. Rhetorical skill: 146. Abound in metaphors and similes: 143. Attitudes toward nature in poetry: 94. Cyclical rhythm of light and darkness in M's poetry: 61. Colocation of words: 146. Descriptive talent: 146. Diction: 94. Double epithets: 146. Fancy: 146. Gusto: 146. Harmony: 146. Ignores great painters: 146. Interest in prosody: 87. Images of unity in: 66*. Imagination: 146. Immitation of musical forms: 61. Inimitability: 146. Language: 146. Liberation of: 146. Metrics: 146. "Modern" element in: 87. Marginal glosses: 136. Method of writing: 144. M's narrative style: 136. Style of his poetry: 144, 146. Obscurity: 146. Originality: 146. Organic unity: 146. Orthography: 146. Pictoral power: 129*. Pronouns: 146. Proper names: 146*. Rhythmical use of antithetical elements: 61. Rhetorical technique: 51*. Sublimity: 146*. Tendency to personify abstractions: 136. Unchangeable order of words: 13. Unpremeditated verse: 146. Use of comic notes: 104. Versification: 146*. Vocabulary: 94. See also: Poetry of John Milton

(poetry/prose, miscellaneous). Originally proposed a great patriotic poem: 136. Consideration of Arthurian poem: 137. Euripedes preferred by M: 13. Latin verse: 13. Lectures on M's poetry: 13. Marginalia in Minor Poems: 13*.

Marginalia in Hayley's Life of M: 13. His prose neglected: 87. Revival of interest in prose: 87. Robert Fletcher's edition of M's prose: 87; importance of: 87. John Mitford's edition of poetry and prose: 87. M's prose defended: 87. Style of M's prose: 94*

Milton (debts to, and comparisons with, other writers). M and the classical tradition: 32*; and pagan mythology: 144; sources: 137. Preferred to Homer: 87; ranked with Homer and Virgil: 58*; compared to Virgil: 104. And Renaissance works concerning paradise, Renaissance commentators, patristic writing, Catholic and Protestant Commentators, writers of celestial cycle, Medieval lit., Puritan leaders, works of geography, political writers: 32. Moses Bar Cephas: 32. Marius Victor: 32. Compared to Shakespeare: 87*, 136, 13; influenced by Shakespeare: 104. Compared to Dante: 13, 32, 111*. Debt to Spenser: 25. Jeremy Taylor: 13. Debt to Lord Brooke: 144. Andrewes, Aquinas, Aristotle, Avitus, Bacon, Bodin, Boemus, Drayton, Filmer, Goodwin, Grotius, Hakewill, Hall, Hobbes, Keckermann, Lightfoot, Loredana, Machiavelli, More, Pope, Purchas, Raleigh, Ross, Ussher, Vondel, Weemse, Wolseley: 32; H. Vaughan: 80. See also: Addison, Burton, Byron, Chapman, Chatterton, Coleridge, Cowley, Dante, Demosthenes, Dryden, Haak, Homer, Hooker, Klopstock, Newton, Plato, Pope, Shakespeare, Sidney, P., Southey, Spenser, Tasso, Taylor, Virgil, Wordsworth, and other individual authors

Milton (reputation among writers). Rank among Eng. poets 58*. A precursor of Modernism: 136. Relative popularity of his works: 97. Cultural impact of: 25. Victorian attitude toward: 86, 136. Late Victorian dissatisfaction with: 87. Actively admired by late Victorian poets: 87. Rejection of M's thought by late Victorians: 87. Condemned by some critics: 143. M's "Heaven" and the Victorian imagination: 136

Milton (general reputation). "A Power among Powers": 136. Reputation: 25. Popularity: 87*. Obscurity: 25. Detractors: 146. Early admiration for M: 86. Traditional prejudice against character and ideas: 86. Rejection of his thought and art: 87. Charges against M's character: 86. Defense of character: 86. Renewed interest in his ideas: 86. Misconceptions regarding: 144. Prestige: 51

Milton (reputation as). Antiquarian: 95. Awakener: 25, 146. Character in Blake's "Milton": 25. Christian humanist: 80*, 143. Christian poet: 51. Courtier: 136. Epicure: 146. Genius: 146, 136, 94. Egocentric genius: 136. Historian: 3. Libertarian: 146. Man: 146. Manipulative poet: 25. No mystic: 136. Non-conformist: 146. Patriot: 146. Pedant: 146. Philosopher: 146. Polemicist: 75. Political: 75. Political revolutionary: 61. Prophet: 25. Prototype of classical spirit: 55. Radical sectary in the making: 147. Reflected in his Satan: 87. Reformer: 145. Revolutionary artist: 46. Symbol of Reformation and Glorious Revolution: 87. Thinker: 146

Milton (influence on subsequent artists). Victorian period: 87*. 19th c. painters: 87. Eng. poetry: 86*, 97. Continental poetry: 97. See also individual writers

Milton (illustrators). See Portraits; Barry; Blake; Flaxman; Fuseli; Hogarth; Palmer; Romney; and other individual artists

Milton (editors). See Bentley; Birch; Newton, T.; Symmons; Todd; Warton; and other individual editors

Milton (biographers). See Birch; Carpenter; DeQuincey; Fenton; Hayley; Ivimay; Johnson; Mitford; Mortimer; Phillips, E.; Richardson, J.; Symmons; Todd; Williams; and other individual writers

-WORKS-

Milton, John (works). For full listing, see entries below, individual titles, and specific topics.

Accedence Commenc't Grammar (1669): 20, 28, 40, 44*, 73, 112, 116, 3, 91, 55

Ad Eandem: 73

Ad Ioannem Rousium (To John Rouse): 9, 30, 40, 44, 70, 73, 133, 82, 91, 117, 55, 21

Ad Leonaram Romae Canentem: 70, 44, 101, 73, 112, 14, 132, 46, 137

Ad Patrem: 4, 6, 8, 9, 20, 27, 30, 40, 42, 44, 45, 59, 70*, 73, 74, 112, 121, 128, 129, 132, 133, 136, 144, 3, 26, 38, 39, 53, 62, 71, 72, 82, 91, 106, 109, 137, 148*, 55, 21

Ad Salsillum, Poetam Romanum: 44, 73

Animadversions Remonstrant's Defence

(1641): 8*, 9*, 15, 19, 28, 30*, 40, 44*, 50, 57, 59, 60, 63, 66, 68, 70*, 73, 75, 83, 84, 103, 112, 113, 123, 128*, 129, 132, 133, 136, 141, 144, 147, 3, 26, 38, 43, 46, 62, 78, 80, 82*, 85, 88, 91*, 94, 117, 55

Apologus de Rustico et Hero: 20, 40, 44

An Apology (Smectymnuus), 1642: 1, 8*, 9*, 12, 15, 16, 17, 19, 20, 28*, 29, 30*, 31, 33, 40, 41, 42, 44*, 45, 52, 57, 59, 60, 70*, 73, 74, 75, 83, 84, 103, 112*, 111, 113, 128*, 132, 133, 136*, 144, 145*, 147, 3*, 22, 26, 39, 43, 53, 62, 71, 78, 91*, 92, 101, 109, 146, 148*, 117, 55*, 25

Apology against a Pamphlet (1641): 70*, 66*, 73, 113*, 123, 129, 144, 38, 62, 82*, 94, 106

Arcades: 1, 4, 8, 17, 29*, 40, 42, 44, 58, 59, 70, 73, 79, 87, 109, 137, 146, 148*, 117, 55, 21, 103, 113, 121, 128, 132, 133, 135, 136, 145, 3, 14, 26, 38, 39, 46, 72*, 82, 91, 92, 106

Areopagitica (1644): 1, 6, 7, 8*, 9*, 12, 15, 17, 18, 19, 51*, 20, 27, 28*, 30, 31, 37, 40, 41, 42, 44*, 52*, 54, 57*, 58, 59, 60*, 66, 67, 68, 70*, 73, 75, 76, 79, 83, 84, 87, 93, 102, 103, 112*, 111, 113*, 121, 123, 128, 129, 132, 133, 134, 136, 139, 141, 144, 145, 147*, 3*, 11*, 26, 36, 38*, 39, 43, 46, 53, 61, 62, 71*, 72, 78, 80, 82*, 85, 91*, 92, 94, 101, 106, 109, 130, 137, 146*, 149, 148*, 150, 117*, 55*, 21, 48

Art of Logic (Artis Logicae), 1672: 8, 9, 17, 20*, 28, 37, 40, 42, 44*, 63, 70, 73, 103, 112*, 122, 123*, 11, 53*, 82, 91, 94, 146, 148, 55, 21

Articles of Peace (1650), Observations on: 8, 9, 28, 40, 44, 103, 55

At a Solemn Music: 4, 8, 9, 40, 44, 70, 73, 75, 89, 121, 124, 126, 132, 134, 136, 14, 26, 38, 39, 72*, 88, 101, 106, 109, 137, 146, 148*, 117, 55

At a Vacation Exercise in the College: 4, 8, 15, 17, 20, 30, 40*, 44, 50, 70, 73, 77, 86, 87, 112, 124, 128, 129, 132, 133*, 134, 144, 145, 3, 26, 38, 39, 46, 72, 91, 92, 101, 130, 137, 146, 148, 55, 21, 13

"Being Religious by Deputy": 137

Bridgewater Manuscript, The: 101, 117

Brief Notes: 8, 9, 28, 30, 44*, 51, 73, 103, 82, 73, 128, 147, 43, 82, 91

Cambridge (Trinity) Manuscript: 63, 77*, 145, 36, 38, 53, 85, 88*, 101, 148*, 117*, 55*, 21

Canzone: 30, 44, 59, 132, 3. Italian: 132

Carmina Elegiaca: 44, 148

Character of the Long Parliament (1681): 28, 44, 59, 116, 91, 117, 55

Christian Doctrine: 1, 8, 9*, 12, 15*, 16, 17*, 19, 20, 27, 28, 30*, 31*, 34*, 37*, 40, 41*, 42, 44*, 50*, 54, 57, 52*, 59, 60*, 66, 67, 68, 70*, 73, 74*, 75, 76, 77, 79, 83*, 86, 87*, 95, 100, 102*, 103, 104, 107*, 112, 111, 113, 116, 118, 122*, 123*, 124, 126, 127, 128*, 129*, 132*, 133, 134, 136, 142*, 143*, 144, 145, 147*, 3*, 11, 14, 22*, 26, 71*, 72, 78*, 82*, 85*, 91, 92*, 94, 96, 97*, 101, 106*, 109, 130*, 137*, 146, 149*, 148*, 150*, 117, 55, 140, 48*, 25. Columbia Univ.'s photostate of MS.: 43

Colasterion (1645): 8*, 9, 17, 28, 30, 44*, 54, 59, 66, 70, 73, 79, 103, 112, 113, 128, 132, 144, 147, 3, 26, 43, 62, 82, 91*, 109, 55, 48

Commonplace Books: 9*, 16, 17, 19, 20, 28, 40, 42, 44*, 45, 57*, 60, 63, 70, 73, 74, 75, 112, 111, 113, 121, 128, 132, 135, 144, 147, 3, 26, 38, 71, 94, 150, 55

Comus: 1*, 4*, 6, 8*, 12*, 9*, 15*, 17, 18, 19, 20, 27*, 28, 29*, 30, 31, 37, 40, 42, 44*, 50*, 52*, 57*, 58*, 59, 60, 63, 67, 68, 69*, 70*, 73, 74, 75, 76*, 79, 84, 86, 87, 95, 100, 103, 104*, 112, 111, 113*, 118, 121, 122, 123, 124, 125, 126, 128*, 129*, 132*, 133*, 134*, 135*, 136*, 142, 144*, 145*, 147, 3, 11*, 14*, 143*, 26*, 38, 39*, 46*, 53*, 62, 71*, 82*, 88*, 91, 92, 94, 101*, 109, 130*, 131, 137*, 146*, 149, 148*, 150, 117*, 25*, 55*, 21*, 13

A Declaration, or Letters Patents... (1674): 16, 28, 44, 73, 82

Declaration against Spain: 60, 123, 82, 91

Defence of English People (Pro Populo Anglicano Defensio), 1651: 1, 8*, 9*, 15, 16*, 20, 28*, 30*, 40, 41, 42, 44*, 51, 52, 59, 60, 66, 70*, 73, 74, 71, 82*, 58, 85, 91*, 92, 94, 84, 86, 103*, 113*, 116*, 112, 123, 128*, 132*, 136, 147*, 3*, 26, 38*, 43, 62, 146, 148, 150, 117*, 55

Defence of Himself (Pro Se), 1655: 8*, 9*, 19, 20, 28, 30*, 40, 44*, 59, 66, 70, 73, 75, 112, 113, 128*, 132, 147, 26, 38, 62, 82*, 91, 94, 106, 109, 130, 137, 146, 55

Defensio Secunda (Second Defence of English People), 1654: 6, 8*, 9*, 15, 16, 17, 19, 46, 20, 28*, 29, 30*, 40, 42, 44*, 51, 52, 59*, 60, 66, 68, 70*, 73, 74, 61, 84, 102, 103, 112, 111, 113*, 122, 123, 128*, 53, 129, 132*, 133, 134, 136, 39, 141, 144, 145*, 147*, 3*, 11, 14, 26, 38*, 62, 71, 82*, 85, 91*, 92, 94, 101, 106, 109, 137, 146, 148, 55*, 21, 25

De Idea Platonica quaemadmodum Aristoteles Intellexit: 40, 42, 44, 57, 70, 73, 75, 76, 112, 132, 72, 46, 148

Dictionary. See Thesaurus, M's

Doctrine and Discipline (1643): 1, 8*, 9*, 15*, 17, 18, 19, 20, 28*, 30*, 31, 37, 40, 41, 42, 44*, 50, 51, 52, 54*, 59, 60, 63, 66, 68, 70, 73, 76, 79, 84, 83, 86, 102, 103, 112*, 113*, 116, 122, 123, 128*, 132*, 134, 135, 136*, 139, 144, 145, 147, 3*, 11, 14, 22, 26, 36, 38, 43*, 53, 62, 71, 82*, 91*, 92, 94, 101, 109, 137, 146, 148, 150, 117, 55, 48, 25. Divorce tracts: 113, 117

Eikonoklastes (1649): 8*, 9*, 15, 16, 17, 19, 20, 28, 30*, 34, 40, 41, 44*, 59, 60, 66, 70*, 73, 74, 83, 84, 86, 103*, 112, 113, 116*, 121, 122, 123, 128*, 129, 132, 135, 136, 144*, 147, 3*, 11, 26, 38*, 43, 46, 53, 62, 78, 82*, 85, 91*, 92, 94, 101, 109, 130, 137, 146, 150, 117, 55

The Elegies: 59*, 70*, 113, 145*, 55*. Liber Elegiarum: 148. Latin: 129, 150. Elegy I: 4, 8, 30*, 40, 44, 73, 132, 133, 3*, 26, 46, 72, 82, 137, 148, 117, 55, 21*, 13. Elegy II: 40, 44, 73, 132, 133, 26, 72, 21. Elegy III: "In Obitum Praesulis Wintoniensis": 4, 40, 44, 73, 112, 126, 132, 26, 38, 72, 82, 91, 148, 117, 21*. Elegy IV: 9, 20, 30, 40*, 73, 112, 128, 26, 38, 62, 72, 82, 91, 137, 148, 55, 21. Elegy V: 30, 40, 44, 73, 112, 104, 113, 128, 132, 133, 26, 46, 61, 72, 82, 137, 148*, 55, 21*. Elegy VI: "Ad Carolum Diodatum": 4, 9, 29, 30, 40, 44, 73, 75, 112, 132*, 133, 11, 26, 38, 53, 61, 62, 72, 82, 91, 101, 109, 137, 148*, 55, 21. Elegy VII: "Anno Aetatis Undevigesimo": 4, 9, 30, 40, 44, 73, 112, 128, 132, 26, 71, 72, 137, 148*, 55

An Epitaph on the Marchioness of Winchester: 4, 29, 40, 44, 73, 132, 133, 144, 72, 91, 137, 146, 148, 55

Epitaphium Damonis: 4, 6, 8, 9, 12, 15, 17, 20, 30*, 33, 40, 44*, 57, 59, 60, 70, 73, 112, 111, 121, 128, 129, 132*, 133, 136, 144, 145, 3, 26, 38, 46, 53, 71, 82, 91, 94, 109, 137, 149, 148*, 117, 21*, 55

Fifth Ode of Horace: 40, 44, 73, 117

History of Britain (1670): 1, 4, 8, 9, 15, 16, 17, 19, 20, 28*, 30, 31, 40, 44*, 57, 82*, 146, 55*, 58, 60, 66, 70*, 73, 88, 91, 92, 94, 137, 117, 84, 113, 116, 123, 128, 132*, 133, 135, 136, 144, 145, 3*, 26, 38, 46, 62

History of Muscovia: 8, 19, 28, 44, 45, 73, 128, 132, 136, 144, 3, 82*, 94, 55

Il Penseroso: 1, 4*, 8, 17, 18, 19, 27, 28, 37, 40*, 42, 44, 51, 52*, 57, 58*, 60, 68, 70*, 73, 74, 75, 76, 79, 95, 98, 103, 112, 87, 113, 118, 128, 129, 132, 133*, 134, 144, 142, 145, 3, 14*, 26, 38, 39, 62, 71, 72*, 82, 88, 91, 92, 94*, 101, 106, 109*, 130, 131, 137, 146*, 149, 148*, 150, 117*, 55, 21*, 13, 25. See also: L'Allegro

In Effigiei Eius Sculptorem (On the Engraver): 44, 73, 88

In Inventorum Bombardae (On the Inventor of Gunpowder): 40, 44, 73, 117

In Obitum Praesulis Eliensis (Bp. of Ely): 4, 15, 40, 44, 73, 132, 133, 14, 38, 62, 148

In Obitum Procancellarii Medici (Death of Vice-Chancellor): 40, 44, 73, 128, 132, 133, 21

In Proditionem Bombardicam (Gunpowder Plot): 8, 44, 73, 117

In Quintum Novembris: 15, 19, 20, 40, 59, 73, 75, 76, 86, 122, 123, 128, 132, 133, 136, 144, 26, 62, 71, 82, 137, 148, 55, 21

Judgement of Martin Bucer (1645): 9, 17, 20, 28, 30, 40, 51, 42, 44*, 54*, 59, 60, 66, 70, 73, 103, 112, 113, 128, 132, 135, 147, 3, 26, 38, 43, 46, 62, 82, 91, 94, 109, 55

Juvenilia: 70

L'Allegro: 1, 4*, 8*, 16, 17, 18, 19, 20, 27, 28, 29*, 35, 40*, 42, 44, 51, 52*, 58*, 60, 70*, 73, 74, 79, 87, 98, 103, 113, 121, 128, 129*, 132, 3, 133, 134, 143, 144, 145, 14*, 26, 38, 39, 53, 62, 71, 72*, 82, 88*, 91, 94*, 106, 109*, 130, 131, 137*, 146*, 149, 148*, 117*, 55, 21*, 13, 25. See also: Il Penseroso

Letters (general): 44*, 30*, 132*, 53*, 117, 146. Letter to Peter Heimbach: 79. Letter to Thomas Young, July 21, 1628: 74. Letter to Dati: 148

Letters (familiar): 4, 8, 15, 16*, 17, 20, 28*, 30*, 33, 40*, 42*, 70*, 73, 44*, 59, 112, 3*, 129, 132*, 144, 92, 94, 55, 82, 91

Letters of State (Phillips ed. 1694): 28, 30*, 44*, 59, 73, 123, 82, 91, 148, 150, 55. State Papers: 82

Letter to a Friend: 8, 9, 28, 33, 40, 44, 45, 51, 59, 70, 73, 128, 3, 38, 91, 109, 73, 147

Letter to General Monk: 45, 78, 82

Likeliest Means (1659): 8, 9*, 16, 20, 28, 30*, 31, 40, 44*, 50, 52, 59, 60, 63, 68, 70, 73, 51, 79, 83, 112, 111, 113, 116, 123, 128, 132, 147, 3, 11, 26, 38, 43, 46, 71, 78, 82*, 85, 91, 94, 117, 115, 55, 48

Literae Pseudo-Senatus: 44*, 117

Lycidas: 1, 4*, 6, 8, 9, 15, 16, 18, 20, 19, 17, 27*, 28, 29, 30, 33, 40*, 33, 44*, 52*, 57, 58*, 59, 60, 63, 66, 70, 73, 74, 75, 76, 79, 84, 87, 95, 98, 102, 103, 104*, 112, 111, 113, 118, 126, 128*, 129*, 132*, 133*, 134, 135*, 136, 143*, 144, 145, 3, 11*, 14*, 26*, 32, 38*, 39, 46, 53*, 71, 72*, 78, 80, 82, 85, 88*, 91, 92, 94, 101*, 109*, 130*, 131, 137*, 146*, 148*, 150, 117*, 55*, 21*, 13, 25

Mansus (Manso): 6, 15, 17, 20, 28, 30, 40, 44, 70, 73, 74, 77, 111, 122, 128, 132*, 133, 134, 145, 3, 26, 46, 62, 137, 148, 117, 55, 21*

Naturam Non Pati Senium (That Nature is not Subject to Old Age): 4, 40, 44, 70, 73, 128, 132, 133, 91, 109, 137, 148

Notes for: "Samson Hybristes": 123. "Christus Patiens": 123. Tragedy and heroic poem on King Alfred: 123

Observations on the Articles of Peace (1649): 9, 59, 60, 70, 73, 103, 132, 147, 38, 43, 82*, 91

Of Education (1644): 8, 9*, 12, 15, 18, 20, 28, 30, 17, 31, 40*, 42, 44*, 51, 52, 58, 60, 66, 68, 70*, 73, 76, 83, 98, 103, 112*, 111, 113, 121, 122, 123, 128, 129, 134, 136, 144, 145, 147, 11, 26, 38, 53*, 62, 71, 72, 78, 82*, 85, 91, 92, 101, 106, 109, 130, 137, 146*, 148, 150, 117*, 55, 21, 25, 94

Of Prelatical Episcopacy (1641): 8, 9, 15, 28, 30, 40, 41, 44*, 57, 60, 63, 66, 68, 70, 73, 76, 83, 103, 113, 123, 128, 144*, 147, 3, 26, 38, 43, 71, 78, 82, 91, 117, 55, 94

Of Reformation (1641): 4, 8*, 9*, 12, 15, 28*, 30, 33, 37, 40, 44*, 51*, 52, 57, 59, 60, 63, 66, 70, 73, 74, 75, 76, 79, 83, 84, 86, 102, 103, 112, 111, 113, 116, 122, 123, 128*, 129, 134, 135, 136, 142, 144*, 145, 3, 26, 38*, 43, 46, 53*, 62, 71, 78, 80, 82*, 91*, 109, 137, 146, 148, 117, 55, 94

Of True Religion (1673): 8, 9, 16, 28, 30, 44, 60, 63, 73, 84, 83, 103, 113, 116, 123, 132, 134, 136, 147, 3, 26, 43, 53, 71, 78, 82*, 85, 91, 94, 55, 94

On the Death of A Fair Infant Dying of a Cough: 4, 8, 28, 29, 40, 44, 59, 73, 112, 128, 132, 26, 62, 72, 82, 101, 130, 146, 148, 117, 55, 21*

Song: On May Morning: 40, 44, 58, 59, 73, 132, 133, 26, 71, 72, 137, 146, 148, 117, 55

On the Morning of Christ's Nativity: 1, 4, 8, 9*, 15, 17, 19, 29, 30, 40*, 44, 52, 57, 58, 59, 60, 63, 58, 70, 73, 74, 75, 76, 79, 84, 86, 87, 89, 98, 100, 102, 104, 112, 121, 123, 126, 128*, 129, 132*, 133, 134, 144, 145, 11, 14, 26*, 32, 36, 38, 39, 46, 53*, 61, 62, 71, 72*, 78, 82, 85, 88, 91, 94, 101*, 106, 109*, 130, 131, 137, 146, 148*, 150, 117, 55, 21*, 13

On the New Forcers of Conscience under the Long Parliament: 8, 9, 40, 44, 59*, 83, 113, 147, 3, 26, 78, 82, 91, 146, 55

On Shakespeare: 40, 44, 59, 70, 73, 112, 132, 133, 3, 14, 62, 72, 91, 137, 146, 148, 55

On Time: 9, 37, 40, 44, 59, 73, 75, 112, 132, 133, 14, 26, 38, 71, 72, 148, 117, 55

On the University Carrier: 4, 44, 73, 121, 128, 14, 82, 91, 137, 146, 117, 55, 13

Outlines for Tragedies: 82

Paradise Lost (general): 1*, 2*, 4*, 6*, 8*, 9, 12*, 15*, 37*, 118*, 41*, 44*, 45, 50*, 51, 16*, 17*, 18*, 19*, 20, 27*, 28*, 29, 30*, 31*, 35*, 40*, 52, 54*, 57*, 67, 58*, 59*, 60*, 63, 66*, 68, 69, 70*, 73, 74*, 79*, 81*, 75, 83*, 84, 86*, 89*, 87*, 98*, 102*, 104*, 103*, 107*, 112*, 104*, 110, 113*, 114*, 116, 122*, 125*, 126, 127*, 128*, 129*, 132*, 133*, 134*, 135*, 136*, 141*, 142*, 143*, 144*, 145*, 147*, 3*, 11*, 14*, 22*, 26*, 32*, 36*, 38*, 39*, 43, 46*, 53*, 62*, 71*, 72*, 78*, 80*, 82*, 85*, 88*, 91*, 92*, 94*, 96*, 97*, 101*, 130*, 131*, 137*, 146*, 149*, 148*, 150*,

117*, 55*, 140*, 21*, 48*, 13*, 25*, 109*

Paradise Lost: Book I: 2*, 37*, 41*, 50*, 57*, 127*, 14, 104, 105*, 140*. Book II: 2*, 37*, 41*, 50*, 57, 127*, 14, 140*, 104, 105*. Book III: 2*, 37*, 41*, 50*, 57, 127*, 14*, 140*, 104, 105*. Book IV: 2*, 37*, 41*, 50*, 105*, 127*, 14*, 140*. Book V: 2*, 105*, 37*, 41*, 50*, 57, 127*, 61*, 140*. Book VI: 2*, 37*, 104, 105*, 41, 50*, 127*, 14*, 140*. Book VII: 2*, 37*, 41*, 50*, 105*, 57, 127*, 14*, 140. Book VIII: 2*, 37*, 41*, 50*, 57, 105*, 127*, 14*, 140*. Book IX: 2*, 37*, 41*, 50*, 127*, 14*, 105*, 140*. Book X: 2*, 37*, 41*, 50*, 105*, 127*, 14*, 140*, 105*. Book XI: 2*, 37*, 41*, 50*, 105*, 127*, 14*, 140*. Book XII: 2*, 37*, 41*, 50*, 57, 127*, 14*, 140*, 83, 104*, 105*

Paradise Regained: 1*, 4*, 6, 8*, 9, 12, 15*, 17, 18, 19*, 20, 27*, 28, 29, 30*, 31*, 35, 37, 40, 44*, 50, 51, 52, 57*, 58*, 59, 60*, 63, 66, 68, 70*, 73, 75, 76, 79*, 81*, 83, 86, 87*, 95, 100, 103, 104, 107, 112*, 111, 113*, 114*, 116, 118, 122*, 123*, 124, 126*, 128*, 129, 132*, 133, 134*, 135, 136, 141*, 142, 143, 144*, 145*, 147*, 3, 11*, 14*, 26*, 32, 36, 38*, 39, 46*, 53, 62*, 71*, 72*, 78*, 80*, 82*, 85*, 88*, 91*, 92, 94*, 97*, 101*, 106*, 109*, 130*, 131, 44, 98, 100, 102, 137*, 148*, 150, 117*, 55*, 140, 21*, 13, 25*. Presentation copy of: 44

The Passion: 4, 8, 15, 27, 29, 30, 40, 44, 50, 70, 73, 74, 75, 122, 123, 126, 128, 129, 76, 132, 133, 134, 26, 53, 71, 72, 91, 92, 101, 109, 130, 137, 146, 148, 117, 55, 13

Philosophus ad Regem Quendam (A Philosopher to a Certain King): 20, 40, 44, 91

Postcript, A: 56

Present Means and Brief Delineation: 28, 44, 73, 147, 14

Prolusions (general): 4, 8*, 9, 17, 18, 19*, 20, 28*, 30*, 37, 40*, 44*, 52*, 60, 66, 70*, 73, 74, 84, 147*, 112*, 113, 128*, 129, 132*, 133, 134*, 136, 26, 53*, 82, 91, 92

Prolusions: Prolusion I: 66, 76, 128, 132, 133, 134, 144, 82, 109, 148, 55. Prolusion II: 17, 52, 112, 121, 128, 133, 132, 134, 144, 3, 14, 26, 109, 148, 55. Prolusion III: 9, 17, 112, 128, 132, 134, 3, 26, 82, 109, 148, 55. Prolusion IV: 9, 132, 134, 148. Prolusion V: 112, 128, 134, 38. Prolusion VI: 112, 128, 132, 133, 134, 144, 3, 26, 82, 137, 148, 55. Prolusion VII: 9, 18, 52, 76, 112, 128*, 132, 148, 133, 134*, 62, 142, 3, 82, 38, 101, 106, 109, 137

Psalms (general): 15, 132, 146, 117, 55. Paraphrases of: 132, 91, 94. Psalms I-VIII: 73, 38, 85, 55. Psalms LXXX-LXXXVIII: 73, 55. Psalm I: 55. Psalm II: 75, 55. Psalm III: 55. Psalm IV: 55. Psalm V: 55. Psalm VI: 55. Psalm VII: 55, 13. Psalm VIII (M trans.): 55, 13. Psalm LXXX: 85, 55. Psalm LXXXI: 85, 55. Psalm LXXXII: 38, 85, 55, 13. Psalm LXXXIII: 85, 55. Psalm LXXXIV: 85, 55. Psalm LXXXV: 85, 55. Psalm LXXXVI: 85, 55. Psalm LXXXVII: 85, 55. Psalm LXXXVIII: 85, 55. A Paraphrase on Psalm CXIV: 44, 73, 75, 72, 55. Psalm CXIV: 30, 40, 42, 44, 73. Psalm CXXXVI: 40, 44, 73, 72, 101, 55. Psalm 144: 101

Readie and Easie Way (1660): 8*, 9*, 15, 16, 19, 27, 28, 30*, 40, 44*, 50, 51, 52, 146, 148, 59, 60, 63, 70, 73, 79, 82*, 85, 91*, 94, 106, 137, 83, 84, 103, 113, 116, 123, 128, 129, 132, 136, 144, 147*, 3, 11, 26, 38, 43, 46, 62, 71, 78, 117, 55

Reason of Church-Government (1642): 6, 8*, 9*, 12, 15*, 17, 19, 20, 27, 28*, 30*, 31, 33, 37, 40, 41, 42, 44*, 50, 52, 57, 58, 59, 60*, 63, 66, 67, 70*, 73, 74, 75, 113*, 116, 122, 123, 76, 77, 79, 81, 83, 100, 102, 103, 107, 112*, 111, 128*, 129*, 132*, 133, 134, 135, 136, 144*, 145, 147*, 3*, 26*, 36, 38*, 43, 46, 53*, 61, 62, 71, 72, 78, 82*, 85, 88, 91*, 92, 101*, 106*, 94, 109, 130, 137, 146*, 149, 148*, 117, 55*, 21, 48, 25

Rehearsal Transpros'd (attr. to M): 116, 145

Samson Agonistes: 1*, 2*, 4*, 6*, 8*, 12, 15, 16*, 17*, 18, 19, 20, 27*, 28, 30, 31, 37, 40, 44*, 50*, 52*, 57, 58*, 60, 63, 67, 68*, 70*, 73, 74, 76, 79*, 81, 83, 84, 86, 87*, 95, 98*, 103*, 104, 105, 112*, 111, 113*, 118, 116, 122, 123*, 126*, 127, 128*, 129*, 132*, 133*, 134, 135, 136*, 145*, 141, 143*, 144*, 3*, 11*, 14*, 26*, 36, 38, 39, 53, 62, 71*, 72*, 78, 80*, 82*, 85*, 88*, 91*, 94*, 101*, 106, 109*, 130*, 131, 137*, 146*, 148*, 150, 117*, 55*, 140, 21*, 13, 25

Second Defence. See Defensio Secunda

Sonnets (general): 15, 58*, 63, 70*, 73*, 87*, 112, 111, 113, 120*, 129, 135*, 60, 145, 26*, 53, 91, 92, 94*, 130, 146*, 117, 55*. Italian: 30, 113, 121, 72, 150, 55

Sonnet I: "O Nightingale": 9, 30, 40, 44, 59, 87, 120, 132, 26, 39, 71,

72, 137, 148, 55

Sonnet II: Donna leggiadra (Beautiful Lady): 40, 44, 59, 120, 129, 55

Sonnet III: "Qual in colle aspro" (As on a Rugged Mountain): 40, 59, 120, 26, 72, 148, 55

Sonnet IV: Diodati, e te'l diro (Diodati, and I Will Say It): 40, 44, 59, 112, 120, 128, 137, 55

Sonnet V: "Per certo i bei vostri' occhi" (In Truth Your Fair Eyes): 40, 59, 120, 128, 148, 55

Sonnet VI: "Giovane piano, e semplicetto amante" (Young, "Gentle ...): 40, 59, 120, 26, 72, 148, 55

Sonnet VII: "How Soon Hath Time": 8, 9, 30, 40, 44, 59*, 120, 128, 132, 3, 26, 38, 62, 72, 91, 137, 148*, 55, 21

Sonnet VIII: "When the Assault was Intended to the City": 8, 30, 44, 59, 103, 120, 62, 82, 91, 137, 55

Sonnet IX: "Lady that in the Prime": 8, 44, 59*, 76, 120, 14, 26, 101, 137, 55

Sonnet X: To the Lady Margaret Ley: 8, 40, 44, 59*, 87, 120, 26, 55

Sonnet XI: On the Detraction which followed upon my writing: 8, 30, 40, 44, 59*, 66, 113, 120, 3, 55

Sonnet XII: On the same ("A Book was writ of late..."): 8, 30, 44, 59*, 66, 87, 112, 120, 132, 26, 82, 148, 55

Sonnet XIII: To my Friend, Mr. Henry Lawes, on His Airs: 29, 44, 59*, 87, 120, 26, 39, 62, 55, 13

Sonnet XIV: On the Religious Memory of Mrs. C. Thomason: 44, 59, 112, 120, 14, 82, 137, 55

Sonnet XV: On the Lord General Fairfax: 28, 44, 59*, 120, 132, 147, 26, 38, 62, 82, 137, 55, 94

Sonnet XVI: To the Lord General Cromwell: 8, 28, 44, 59*, 60, 103, 120, 132, 3, 26, 38, 82, 137, 148, 55

Sonnet XVII: To Sir Henry Vane: 28, 44, 59*, 87, 120, 132, 38, 82, 91, 55

Sonnet XVIII: On the Late Massacre in Piemont: 44, 59*, 75, 87*, 103, 120, 141, 26, 82, 137, 148, 55

Sonnet XIX: "When I consider...": 30, 40, 59*, 87, 120, 126, 132, 3, 11, 14, 26, 38, 72, 82, 148, 55, 21

Sonnet XX: "Lawrence of Virtuous Father": 8, 30, 40, 44, 59*, 120, 3, 14, 26, 38, 137, 55, 21

Sonnet XXI: "Cyriack, Whose Grandsire ...": 30, 40, 44, 59, 87, 120, 128, 3, 14, 82, 137

Sonnet XXII: To Mr. Cyriack Skinner upon his Blindness: 8, 28, 30, 44, 59*, 70, 87, 120, 128, 3, 26, 62, 82, 137, 55

Sonnet XXIII: "Methought I saw...": 8, 30, 44, 59*, 75, 87, 120, 14, 26, 36, 101, 131, 137, 148, 55, 21

<u>Tenure of Kings and Magistrates</u> (1649): 8, 9*, 15, 16, 28, 30, 40, 44*, 91*, 92, 45, 51*, 52, 59, 71, 78, 82*, 85, 60*, 63, 66, 70, 73, 76, 79, 11, 38*, 39, 43, 62, 145, 84, 102, 103, 112, 111, 113, 116*, 123, 129, 132, 135, 136, 147*, 144*, 26, 3, 101, 106, 130, 137, 146, 148, 117, 55, 94

<u>Tetrachordon</u> (1645): 8*, 9*, 15, 17, 28, 30, 37, 40, 41, 42, 44*, 51, 52, 54*, 57, 59*, 63, 66, 70*, 73, 76, 88, 91, 92, 94, 109, 130, 84, 83, 87, 102, 103, 112*, 111, 113*, 124, 128*, 132, 136, 144, 147, 3*, 26, 36, 38, 39, 43*, 46, 62, 82*, 94, 137, 148, 150, 55, 48

<u>Theme on Early Rising</u>: 82

<u>Thesaurus</u>, Greek (M's): 28, 44. <u>Dictionary</u>, Latin (M's): 28*, 44. <u>Latin Grammar</u>: 94. <u>Latin Lexicon</u>: 94

<u>Treatise of Civil Power</u> (1659): 8, 9*, 16, 28, 30*, 44*, 50, 51, 52*, 57, 59, 63, 70, 73, 74, 79, 102, 103, 113, 116, 122, 147, 3, 26, 38, 43, 46, 62, 71, 78, 85, 91, 106, 137, 148, 117, 55

<u>Upon the Circumcision</u>: 9, 15, 30, 40, 44, 73, 87, 112, 126, 132, 134, 14, 53, 62, 72, 109, 146, 148, 55

Verses found with the Commonplace Book: 44

Verses, Latin, from <u>Pro Populo Anglicano Defensio</u>: 58, 103*. See also above: Defence of English People

Milton, MSS.: Partial listings appear under individual MS. titles. Also consult the extensive catalog in book 44*.

Milton, <u>Attributed Works</u>: 44*. Among those listed are the following, some of which also appear under their respective titles in the Index: "Advice to a Painter"; Alarum to the ...Armies; "Argument or Debate in Law"; "Bellipotems Virgo";

Canterbury's Dream; Cupid's Funeral Pile; De Tribus Impostoribus; Declaration against the Dutch; Discourse Showing...Three Kingdoms; epigram on Pope Urban VIII; epitaph on Elizabeth Swettenham; Epistola ad Pollionem; "Exit Tyrannus"; "Extempore upon a Faggot"; "Fair Mirror of Foul Times"; Grand Case of Conscience; Great Britain's Ruin Plotted; "He Whom Heaven did call away"; Historiae Parliamenti; inscription on statue of Charles I; King's Cabinet Opened; Legal Index; Letter to a Gentleman in the Country; Life and Reign of King Charles; Lords Bishops none of the Lord's Bishops; Man Wholly Mortal (passage in); News from Hell, Rome, and Inns of Court; Novae Solymae; "On Day Break"; "On Mel Heliconium"; "Our Lives are albums"; Panegyrici Cromwello Scripti; Plain English; Poems of William Drummond (alleged contributor as editor); "Prayer of Patience" ("I am old and blind"); Pro Populo adversus Tyrannos; Proposals of Certain Expedients; Reasons Why the Supreme Authority; The Rehearsal Transpros'd; Responsio ad Apologiam Anonymi; Right of the People over Tyrants; Sabaudiensis...Narratio; Satyr Against Hypocrites; Scriptum Parlamenti; sentence in Mercurius Politicus; Sovereign Right...of the People over Tyrants; Theatrum Poetarum; Treatise of Magistracy; "Upon a Fly"

Milton, Works (specific editions). Complete Poems and Major Prose, ed. Merrit Y. Hughes: 74. The Complete Prose Works, ed. Don M. Wolfe, et al., Yale ed.: 82*. English Poems by John Milton, ed. Brown: 70. Poems (1645): 81, 91*, 137; Poems of Mr. John Milton Both English and Latin, Compos'd at several times. Printed by his true Copies. The Songs were set to Musick by Mr. Henry Lawes...(January 2, 1646): 73, 53, 62; Poems upon Several Occasions...With a small Tractate of Education To Mr. Hartlib. London... (1673, pub. Thomas Dring): 73, 91; Poems upon Several Occasions, English, Latin and Italian, ed. Warton: 70. Prose Works: 70. Editions of Collected Works: 97*

Milton, John (various works concerning). Original Papers Illustrative of the Life and Writings of JM: 45. The Life of JM (Masson): 45. The Prose Works of JM (Bohn, ed.): 45. The Works of JM (Columbia, ed.): 45*. M, A Sheaf of Gleanings: 45. "Papers connected with the Affairs of M and his Family": 45. "A New Letter by JM": 45. M and Plato: 112. "M and Plato's Timaeus": 112. M and the Renaissance Ovid (Harding): 20. M and Rustication (Rand): 70. M books: 44. "M's Hell" (Broadbent): 111

Milton co., Oxon.: 44

Milton controversy: 53. See also: Eliot, T. S.

Milton elm: 44

Milton Gallery. See Fuseli

"Milton gateway": 44, 45. See also: Forest Hill

Milton, Great: 45

Milton (Blake): 25*. Epigraph to, purpose of, M's shadow, perspectives in, criticism of Swedenborg, copies of, innovation in, in relation to Jerusalem, theme of return: 25. In relation to PR, and Bible, as "prelude" poem, M entering Blake's foot: 25. Los in, structure of, relation to history, M and Ololon joining, themes in: 25; M's descent: 25*. Satan in, inspired by Comus, M struggling with Virgin, Ololon's descent, Ololon's role, conclusion of, preface to, union of poets, Bard as character, levels of exegesis: 25. Blake in, as radical comedy, limits of poetry, as prophecy, as dramatic poem, relation to audience, as living theatre, in relation to earlier prophecies, call to action, didacticism of: 25. Alteration of, thematic action, irony in, providence in, echoes of Revelation, M's expulsion, nadir of, obscurity in, epiphany in: 25. As self- consuming artifact, as theophany, ambiguity in, paradox in, temporal values in: 25. Bard's Song in: 25*; obscurities in, effect on audience, as prophecy, characterization in, and Four Zoas, and Genesis, and PL, and Revelation, quarrel in, structure of, subversive tactics of, action, theme, syntax, grammar of, logic, irony in: 25. Blake's designs for plates 4, 16, 18, 40, 42, 50: 25

Milton, Man and Thinker (Saurat): 134, 136, 71, 88

"Milton stone" (Forest Hill): 44, 45

Milton's Blindness (Brown): 20

"Milton's Cipher and the Harleian Library": 44

Milton's Corrections to the Minor Poems (Lockwood): 70

Milton's Grand Style (Ricks): 111

Milton's Knowledge of Music: by Hadow: 70. By Spaeth: 70

Milton's Lament for Damon and his other Latin Poems: 112

Milton's PL (Diekhoff): 134

Milton's Rabbinical Readings: 78

Milton's Samson and the Christian Tradition: 26

"Milton's Schoolmasters" (Clark): 20

Milton's Sublimity Asserted: 58

"Milton's Use of Latin Formularies" (Wright): 20

"Milton's Well": 44

Miltoni Defensio: 28

Miltonic Setting, The (Tillyard): 134, 135, 131

Miltonic: flavor in words of earlier origin, perceived by Paterson: 88. Expressions, misinterpretation of, giving rise to new shades of meaning: 88. "Miltonic controversy": 44. Universe: 87; in PL, attracted writers of Miltonic religious epics: 87; described: 87; in Montgomery's "A View of Heaven": 87; its sublimity: 87; in PR, grandeur and spaciousness of: 87

"Miltonicus": 117

Miltonist: 73, 103, 91

Mime: 70

Mimesis: 72

Mimnermus of Colophon: 40

Mimus: 112

Mincius: 1, 49, 73

Mind: 96*. Right frame of: 51. M's subconscious: 136

Minden: 44. See also: Frederick William

Mineka, Francis E., "Critical Reception of...De Doctrina Christiana": 74, 87

Minerals and metals: 128*. Gunpowder, marble, mercury, nitre, pearl (engendered of dew in shellfish), Philosopher's stone, ruby, salt, saltpeter, brass, brimstone, carbuncle, chrysolite, chrystal (formed from hail), diamond, elixir (see also: gold), evanthum, gold, aurum potabile, in Heaven and Hell, solar metal, sapphire, silver, sulpher, topaz: 128

Minerva: 2, 56, 60, 73, 90*, 144, 25

Mingzeis, Alexander: 93

Minhah: 40

Mining: 128, 93

Ministering spirit, angel as: 123

Ministers: 63, 143. Silenced: 143. To preach the Word: 143. False: 143. In baptism: 143. Parish: 51. Puritan: 51. Ministry: 9*, 47, 51, 53. Of redemption as heroic norm: 123. See also: Milton, John, his vocation; Exaltation; Humiliation

Ministry, education for and rejection of: 30

Minkowski, H.: 23

Minor poems: 58*, 83, 88*, 117*, 55*. Dated: 55. Early volume: 55. M's, ed. by Warton: see Warton. See also individual titles

Minor premise: premise, and omission of: 51

Minos: 44, 73, 111, 123

Minotaur: 111

Minsheu (Minshew), John: 40, 73

Minshull: family: 44. Anne (Mrs. Thomas): 44. Anne Boote (Mrs. Randle): 44. Anne Dawson (Lighthouse, wife of Thomas): 44. Dorothy Goldsmith: 44. Edward: 44. Elizabeth (M's 3rd wife): 16, 28*, 40, 44*, 103, 136, 43, 146; see also: Milton, Elizabeth Minshull. Ellen Goldsmith: 44. Margery Rawlinson: 44. Mary: 44. (Minshal), Randle (M's father-in-law): 28, 44. Richard: 44; and his son, Richard: 44. Thomas: 44

Minturno, Antonio Sebastiano: 1, 4, 6, 31, 52, 70*, 120, 123, 101. Arte Poetica: 74

Mintz, Samuel I: 44, 93

Minucius Felix Marcus: 57, 36, 101. Octavius: 57, 36

Minutes of the Life of Mr. John Milton (Aubrey): 134

Mira, the wonderful: 89

Mirabeau, Count de: 117, 37

Mirabilis Annus (1661); 128

Mirac: 89

Miracle plays: 35, 92. And Morality plays: 149

Miracle(s): 63, 122, 123, 132, 142, 78, 93. M's idea of: 132. Belief in, during the Middle Ages: 71. See also: Marvellous; Wonder

Miranda: 72

Mirandola, Pico della: 7, 6, 18, 40, 42, 100, 112, 32

Miriam Joseph, Sister: 37, 123, 93

Mirk's Festial: 36

Mirror (of Justices): 73

Mirror for Magistrates: 15, 60, 11

Mirror in mensuration: 40

"Mirror" literature: 133. M and: 102

Mirror of Alchimy: 128

Mirror of Lit.: 146

Mirror of Taste and Dramatic Censor, The: 115

Mirrour of the World: 65

Mirth: figure: 29, 90, 144, 72. Garden of: 32. See also: Euphrosyne; Il Penseroso

Misanthrope, The: 1. See also: Moliere

Miscegenation: 128. An effect of the Fall: 128

Miscellanea: 44. Miscellanea Genealogica et Heraldica: 44, 45*

Miscellaneous accumulation of material in Paterson's commentary and "The State of innocence": 83. See also: Encyclopaedic

Miscellaneous Letters and Essays: 116

Miscellaneous Works of Charles Blount, Esq., The: 116

Misere mei, Deus: 126

Misery: 47, 51. Of man's condition: 123

Mishna: 36

Misogyny: 92, 137

Mispa (Mizpah): 49, 73

Mist: 128*. Causes and kinds: 128

"Mistagog: Poetic": 40

Mistére du Viel Testament, Le: 65, 68, 77

Misteri de Adam y Eva: 65

Mists' Weekly Journal: 44

Mitatron: 41

Mitcham, co. Surrey: 44

Mitchell: C.: 97. Maria: 128. Stewart: 44. W. Fraser: 51, 79, 145, 15

Miter (Mitre): Court, London: 44. Sign, London: 44. Tavern, London: 44. Tavern, Cambridge: 40

Mitford series: 45

Mitford: 70, 94. John: 33, 40, 44, 58, 87, 146; ed. Prose Works: 44. Nancy: 39. W.: 58

Mitford's Essay upon the Harmony of Language: 88

Mithra: 1, 71

Mitton (coat of arms): 40

Mitytenensis, Zacharias: 32

Mixed style: condemned by Newton: 88. Equals romance and classicism, Todd on: 88

Mixed Essays, Irish Essays and Others (Arnold): 83

Mixolydian mode: 121

Mizaldus, Antonius: 65

Mnemonic systems: 67

Mnemosyne: 90, 121

Mnesis, nymph: 44

Mnestheus: 2

Moab: 49, 73, 144. Moabites: 41. See also: Seon's Realme

Mobidity: 47

Moby Dick: 98. Moby Dick: 98*, 136

Mock: funeral, M's: 44. Heroic: 122. Maxim: 51

Mocket, Richard: 40

Models: 51

Modena, D. of: 6

Moderation: 51, 93. Hume's theoretical appreciation of, and ease: 88. Warton's occasional taste for classicist: 88

Moderator: 40

Modern Language Association (MLA): 44

Modern Language Notes: 44*, 48

Modern Language Quarterly: 44

Modern Language Review: 44*, 150

Modern Painters (Ruskin): 111

Modern Pharisees, The: 116

Modern Philology: 44*

Modern: causes hindering the Reformation: 51. Man, relation of M's works to: 30*. Theorists: 51

Modes of persuasion: 51

Modes: musical (moods): 40. Greek: 121*

Modest Confutation (Hall): 9, 30*, 103, 136, 147, 26, 91

Modest Narrative of Intelligence: 147

Modest Plea for an Equal Common-Wealth (William Sprigg): 147

Modestinus, Herennius: 54, 73

Modestus (nickname): 44

Modesty: 51

"Modi of Parliament": 3

Modiford, James: 44

Modin: 49, 73

Modoin, Bishop: 18

Modona (Modena): 49, 73

Modulation: 121

Modus Transferendi Status: 45

Mody, J. R. P.: 68

Moffatt, James: 143, 93

Moffet, T.: 59

Mogila: 49

Mogul: 1, 19, 45, 73

Mohammed: the Prophet: 123. Mohammedan(s): 103, 71. Mohammedanism: 71

Mohl, Ruth: 60, 111. The Three Estates in Medieval and Renaissance Literature: 82

Mohun: Elizabeth: see Cope, Eliz. Walter: 45

Moir, D. M.: 58

Moira: 93

Moisant de Brieux, Jacques: 64

Moldavia: 49

Mole River: 49, 73

Molech. See Moloch

Molgomsay (Mongozey): 49. See also: Tawze

Molière, Jean Baptiste Poquelin: 1, 27, 44, 136, 94

Molina, Luis: 32

Molinaeus: 40. Petrus: 65

Molineux, Sir Richard, Viscount: 44, 45

Molinism: 93

Molins, W.: 44

Mollenhott, Virginia R.: 101

Mollerus, Fredericus: 65

Mollyner, Lawrence: 44

Molmenti, P.: 6

Moloch (Biblical Molech): 1, 2, 4, 19, 29, 50, 57, 60, 73, 98, 104, 111, 123*, 124, 127, 142, 144, 143, 46, 71, 72, 109, 130, 55, 140*, 146

Moloney, Michael F.: 40, 93

Moluccae Insulae: 49. See also: Amboyna; Ternate; Tidore

Moluccas: 19, 150

Moly: 1, 29, 90, 144, 72. The "divine herb": 136

Molyneux: Max: 40. Sir Thomas: 10. William: 10

Mombaza: 19, 49, 73, 144. See also: Melind; Quiloa

Momigliano, Attilio: 111

Mommsen, Theodor E.: 93

Momus: 60, 73

Mona antiqua restaurata: 88

Mona: 73. Isle of: 144

"Monachos mentiti Daemones": 117

Monachus, Georgius: 113

Monarche, The: 65

Monarchia, De (Dante): 70, 111

Monarchies, Four. See Four Monarchies

Monarchists. See Royalists

Monarchy Triumphing Over Traiterous Republicans: 116

Monarchy: 9*, 51*, 83*, 113. M's distrust of: 147. M's attitude toward: 113

Monarder, Nicholas: 44

Monastics, meaning of perfection to, and objections to the perfection of: 83

Monboddo, Lord James Burnet: 56, 58, 88, 146, 117*. On M: 58

Monck: George: see Albemarle. M.: 58

Mond, Émile: 44

Monde antediluvien, Le: 65

Mondo creato, Il: 65

Monergism: 71. Monergist: 71

Monet, Claude: 27

Money-Kyrle, R.: 39

Money, M and: 137

Monin, Joannes Edoardus du: 65

Monism: 15, 47, 110

Monitor: 44

Monk, Lt. Gen. George: 16, 44, 45, 51, 59, 103*, 116, 120, 132, 136, 147, 38, 91*, 55, 94. See also: Albermarle, Duke of; Present Means, A Letter to a Friend; Ready and Easy Way

Monkish learning: 40

Monmouth, James Scott, Duke of: 44, 116

Monmouth: 45, 49. Monmouthshire: 49

Monodic (style of music): 121

Monodies: 58, 92

"Monophysitism," in Encyclopedia of Religion and Ethics (ed. James Hastings): 74

Monoux: Alec: see Cope, Alice. Sir Henry: 45

Monroe: 3

Mons Scandali: 144

Monson, Willian, Viscount (regicide): 44

Monsters: 128

Monstrous birth: 128

Montagne, F. C.: 16

Montagu House, London: 44

Montagu: Duke of: 97. Henry, 1st Earl of Manchester: 114, 93. Lady Mary: 58; praises PL: 58. (Montague), Bp. Richard: 114, 40, 93. Walter: 114. Zacheus: 93

Montague (Montacutium), Edward: 73

Montague: John: 40. Margarett Prescott: 16. Sidney: 44. Sir William: 44

Montaigne, Michel de: 1, 4, 15, 19, 40, 44, 56, 60, 18, 102, 114*, 125, 128, 141, 136, 145, 3, 32, 39, 72, 93, 64

Montalban (Montaubon): 49, 73

Montalbán, Jean Pérez de: 68

Montalto: 6

Montanists: 73. Montanism: 38

Montano, Edward J.: 93

Montanus: 38. Benedictus Arias: 68*, 123

Montausier, Marquis de: 60

Montchrestien, Antoine de: 64. Susane: 74

Montecuccoli, R.: 6

Montefiore, C. G.: 36

Montelion: 103

Montemayor, Jorge de: 40, 70, 64

Montesquieu, Baron de: 58, 115

Monteverdi, Claudio: 6*, 40, 44, 121 39, 64, 137, 55

Montezuma (Motezuma): 19, 73

Montfaucon: 97

Montfort (Momfort), Simon de, Earl of Leicester: 73

Montgomery: Hugh: 44; see also: Mount Alexander. Sir James: 16, 58, 87. Robert: 65, 87*; influenced by M: 58; religious poetry criticized by Maginn and Macaulay: 87; natural Sublime in poetry of: 87; Miltonic Satan in poetry of: 87; works: Omnipresence of the Diety: 87; The Messiah: 87; Satan: 87; "A Vision of Hell": 87; "A Vision of Heaven": 87; "The Crucifixion": 87; "A Dream of Worlds": 87. Walter A.: 21

Montgomeryshire: 44, 49, 144

Monthly Anthology and Boston Review, The: 115*

Monthly Magazine and American Review, The: 115

Monthly Magazine: 117

Monthly Mirror: 44

Monthly Register, Magazine, and Review of the U. S., The: 115

Monthly Review: 63, 88, 146

Montmorency, J. G. de: 16

Montolieu, Mrs.: 58

Montpellier: 40. Medical school of: 16

Montreulx, Nicholas de: 64. Jesus Christ en l'Authel: 74

Montrose (Montrossius), James Graham, 1st Marquis and 5th Earl of: 73, 103, 44

Monts: 44. See also: Charles X; Frederick William

Moody: 130. E.: 58. Ernest Addison: 40. Lester D.: 54. William Vaughn: 40, 44, 58, 59, 68, 70, 143, 137, 148; ed. Works: 44

Moolhuizen, J. J., Vondels Lucifer en Milton Verloren Paradijs: 95

Moon: G. W.: 58. Washington: 44

Moon: 89*, 90, 128*, 144*. Annual equation, atmosphere absent, classical name of, craters in, density of, distance from the earth, earth in contrast with, harvest, hunter's, magnitude, measurement of time by, motion of, mountain ranges of, the modes, orbit of, perturbation, phases of, plains of, revolution, rotation, surface of, synodical period of, regarded as exhalations from the earth, variation: 89. Eclipses of: 89, 128. Properties and influences, spots, world in: 128. Poetical allusions to, M's allusions to, the moon goddess, symbolical of Astarte or Ashtoreth, an object of worship, superstitions regarding, the laboring moon, lunatic, moon-struck: 89. See also: Diana

Moore Park: 40

Moore-Smith, G. C.: 44, 63, 45

Moore: family: 44*, 45. Mr.: 40, 44, 45. A.: 58, 97. Alexander: 136. Lady Alice: 45. Andrew: 19. Anne Agar (M's niece): 44. C. A.: 44, 58, 113, 128, 71. Cecil: 31. David (M's nephew): 44. E.: 122. Rev. E. R.: 44. Edmund F.: 44. Elizabeth Blunden: 44. Sir Francis: 45. G. F.: 40, 41, 68. H.: 58. J.: 58. John, Bp. of Norwich: 116. J. R.: 44. John: 102, 116. John Robert: 44, 45*, 116. Mary: 45. Olin H., "Infernal Council": 74. Richard: 44. Sarah: 44; see also: Dashwood. Thomas: 58, 87, 146. Sir Thomas (M's grandfather): 44, 45. Thomas the Elder: 54. W.: 58

Moorefields, London: 44

Moorgate: 44

Mopsus: 44, 73, 128

Moral: liberty: 113. Choice: 123. Adages: 40. Regeneration: 51. Themes: 40. Hume on, importance of PL: 88. The Richardsons on, improvement caused by poetry: 88. Their identification of easy pleasure and purifying moral experience: 88. Id. on poetry being valuable apart from moral problems but the best poetry improving man's moral character: 88. Law: 25. Philosophy (ethics): 40, 51

Moralia (Plutarch): 3

Moralism: 47. See also: Legalism

Moralistic: treatment of M's characters in Hume: 88. Attitude dropped by Hume with regard to Satan: 88. View in Paterson: 88. See also: Didacticism; Decorum

Moralists, The: 12

Morality: M's discussion of assertion of own: 30*, 51. And education in the Renaissance: 20*. Christian: 51. Thyer opposes Shaftesbury's description of, and reason as the principal qualities of M's poetry: 88. Morality plays: 60*, 132, 145

Moralizing in 18th c. poetry: 58*

Morals: by Plutarch: 29. By Seneca: 71

Morals: 20*, 51

Morand: Paul: 86. P. P.: 34*

Moray, Sir Robert: 10

Mordaunt: Henry, Earl Peterborough: 45. Penelope, Countess of Peterborough: 45

Mordell, Albert: 60

More: Mr. (father of Alexander): 44. (Morus), Alexander: 9, 15, 16, 17, 28*, 30*, 44*, 45, 59, 66, 70, 84, 103, 113, 128, 3, 26, 62, 82, 93, 64, 137, 55; works: Laus Christi Nascentis: 74; Cry of the Royal Blood: 82; see also: Morus. Anne (afterwards, Donne): 131; sonnet to: 131. Cresacre: 44. Sir George: 93. Hannah: 139. See other entries under More

More, Henry: 1, 7, 15, 23, 41, 44, 54, 58, 60, 65, 77, 79, 81, 83, 87, 100, 102, 112, 113, 114*, 123, 132, 142*, 32, 36, 71, 93*, 99, 64, 130, 137, 148, 55; admired Origen: 107; angelology of: 142; works: Antidote against Atheism: 142; Antidote against Idolatry: 142; Collection of Several Philosophical Writings: 142; Enchiridium Metaphysicum: 142; Enthusiasmus Triumphatus: 142; An Explanation of the Grande Mystery of Godliness: 74, 142; Conjectura Cabbalistica: 142, 144, 36; Immortality of the Soul: 142*; Enchiridion Ethicum: 60; The Second Lash of Alazonomastix: 60; Illustration of Daniel and... Revelation: 74; Philosophical Poems: 142; Sadducismus Triumphatus: 142; Demo. Plat.: 77; Psychozoia: 77; Antimonopsychia: 77; Psychathanasia: 77

More: John: 93. Sir Jonas: 10. Paul Elmer: 18, 4, 31, 52, 60, 138, 71, 130, 137, 83, 98, 110, 111, 118, 124, 132, 141; art and ideas in Lycidas: 61. Sir Thomas: 7, 10, 15, 18, 20, 40, 42, 44, 52*, 60, 66, 73, 87, 112, 128, 129, 132, 3, 22, 32, 38, 82, 91, 115. W.: 33

Morea: 49, 73. Morea: 49

Moreau, Pierre: 142

Moreh: 49, 144. Plain of: 73

Morel: F.: 64. Guillaume: 40. L.: 58

Morello, Teodorico: 40

Morer, Richard: 45

Moréri, Louis: 117

Mores Gentium: 40

Morgan Pierpont Library: 40, 44

Morgan: Edmund: 54. Griffith: 40. J. Pierpont: 44. Joseph: 123. N.: 58. Penelope E.: 44. Lady S.: 6. W.: 58

Morgante, An Italian romance (Il Morgante Maggiore): 73

Morhof(f): 130. Daniel George: 44

Morian, friend of Comenian group: 10

Moribus, Carmen de: 40

Morice, J.: 44

Morillon, Julien-Gatien: 64. Works: Joseph: 74; Livre de Job: 74

Morine Coast: 49

Morisan: Bernard: 40

Morison, Samuel Eliot: 40, 115

Morisot, Claude Barthelemy: 44, 60

Morland, Sir Samuel: 10, 16, 44*, 59, 120, 142, 94. The Urim of Conscience: 142

Morlet, Pierre: 40

Morley: E.: 63. George: 44, 116. Henry: 44. Col. Herbert: 44. Thomas (composer): 40, 44, 100, 121*. William: 44. William D.: 44

Mornaeus, Mr.: 44

Mornay, Philippe de: 114, 148

Morning Chronicle, The: 146

Morning Post, The: 146

Morning: morn: 90. Morning star in M's poetry: 89. Morning and evening stars: 89. See also: Aurora; Venus

Morocco: 19, 44, 45

Morpheus: 73, 90

Morrell, Thomas: 117

Morrice (dance): 121

Morrice: Secretary: 103. J., Iliad: 58. Sir William: 44, 91

Morris: 3, 94. J. W.: 63, 102. John: 40. Mary: see Smith, Mary (Morrison). Reginald Owen: 100. Richard: 117. William: 18, 27, 87, 97, 64; attitude toward M: 87; Earthly Paradise: 58

Morrison: Mrs.: 44. Mary: 45. (Alias Morris), Mary: see Smith, Mary

Morritt family of Rokeby: 44

Morse: family: 44. C. J.: 59. J. Mitchell: 21. Jedidiah: 115; A Sermon, Delivered May 18th, 1808, at the Ordination of the Rev. Joshua Huntington: 115. Katherine: 16

Morshead, E. D. A.: 58

Mort, Mr.: 44, 45

Mortalism (mortalists): 9, 44, 60, 63, 102, 113*, 114, 132, 93, 137. M's: 107. Proscribed in 42 articles of 1553: 107. The "mortalists": 113*

Mortality, Bills of: 40

Mortgage: 45

Mortimer: Charles E.: 146. Dr. Cromwell: 44. J. H.: 97*. Roger: 122

Mortlock, Henry (bks.): 44

Morton: R. P.: 97. S. W.: 58. Bp. Thomas: 67, 93

Morton's Academy for Dissenters: 44

Morus: 8, 44, 132, 71, 91*, 94. See also: More, Alexander

Morwyng, Peter: 36

Morysine, Rycharde: 20, 40

Moryson, Fynes: 55

Mosa: 49, 73

Mosaic law: 44, 102, 103, 3, 143, 32, 71; abrogated: 93; cosmology: 89. Mosaic covenant: 11

Mosby, J. N.: 58

Moschus: 4, 33, 40, 90, 93, 64*, 130, 148

Moscow (Mosco): 19, 44, 49, 103, 150

Moscua River: 49. See also: Moscow

Moseley (Mosley), Humphrey (bks., pr., publisher): 44, 59, 103, 132, 91, 55, 94

Mosellanus, Petrus: 20, 40

Moser, Hans Joachim: 100

Moses bar Cepha: 1, 77, 32, 88. De Par.: 77

Moses ha-Nakdan: 41

Moses: 1, 2, 4, 5, 15, 41, 44, 51, 60, 68, 73, 87, 102, 103, 112, 122, 125, 127, 139, 142, 143, 144, 3*, 11, 32*, 46, 71, 72, 82, 91, 106, 25. As prototype of Christ: 46. Law of: 54. Moses-Adam Apocalypse, Coptic fragment of: 123. In the Mass: 143. As prophet of Christ: 143. Deuteronomic code: 82*. Links with Satan: 25. See also: Satan as Moses; Son of God as prophet

Mosier, Richard D.: 115

Moss, Howard: 14

Mosse: Francis: 44. G. L., M's mortalism derived from 17th c. source: 107. George: 10. (Moses), Miles: 93

Mossom, Bp. Robert: 93

Most Humble Supplication (a Baptist manifesto): 147

Mostyn, Thomas: 44

Motet: 121

Mother Hubbard's Tale (Spenser): 88

Mother, references to by M: 40

Motherwell, W.: 58

Motion: 121

Motive: 51. Motivation: for pilgrimage: 47; see also: Drama. Motivating interests: 51

Motley: 149

Mott, F. L.: 79

Motter, T. H. V.: 40

Moule, G. (bks.): 44

Moulin, du: 113. Family: 44. Lewis: 44. Mary: 44. Pierre: 103, 116, 44*, 136, 93; see also: Du

Moulin, Peter; Molinaeus. Pierre (father of M's antagonist): 44

Moulton: Mrs. (Archdale): 45. H. R.: 45*. Richard: 44. Richard G., Book of Job: 74, 148. Robert: 45

Moultrie, J.: 58

Moundeford, Richard: 64

Mounson, Sir William: 128

Mount and Lledrod (Lledred, Lletnered, Lethered) co., Cardigan: 44, 45

Mount of God: 39

Mount Alexander, Hugh Montgomery, Earl of: 44

Mount: Amara: 50, 144. Atlas: 56. Calvary: 144. Carmel: 144. Casius: 144. Etna: 55. Hermon: 144. Ida: 56. Lebanon: 144. Niphates: 56. Olivet: 144. Purgatory: 111. Rhodope: 144. St. Michael: 144. Senir: 144. Sinai: 144. Sion: 56

Mountagu, Edward: 44. See also: Sandwich

Mountague: Sir Edward: 45. Sydney: 45

Mountain, old Bp. (Geo. Montaigne): 73

Mountains: 19. Welsh: 40. M on: 19. See also: Imagery

Mountfort, D.: 58

Mouse-trap, the Cross as: 93

Mouth: 143. Dumb mouths: 143. Sword out of: 143. The Lord's: 143. Deliver sheep from: 143. And cursed speaking: 143. See also: Preaching; Word of God

Movat, James: 40

Moving pictures, dialogue in: 118

Mower to the Glow-worms, The (Andrew Marvell): 131

Mowinckel, Sigmund: 93

Mowntney, Mr.: 44

Mowson, J.: 97

Moxon: Edward: 146. Joseph: 135

Moyce, Katherine: 44

Mozambique (Mozambic): 19, 49, 73, 144

Mozart, Wolfgang Amadeus: 79, 39, 46, 64, 146

Mozley, J. H.: 33

Mr. Blackall's Reasons For Not Replying: 116

Mr. Hunt's Postscript: 116. Compared with Pro Populo Anglicano Defensio: 116

Mr. John Milton's Character of the Long Parliament: 116

Mr. L'Estrange Refuted with his own Arguments: 116

"M.S. Found in a Bottle" (Poe): 136

Much's Land: 44

Muckingford, co. Essex: 44

Muddiman: J. B. (pseudonym for J. B. Williams): 44. J. G.: 44

Mudge, Eugene Tenbroeck: 115

Mueller: J. S.: 97. Johann: 40. M.: 6

Muellerus, Vitus: 40

Muenster, Sebastian: 40

Mugalla (Sheromugaly): 49

Muggleton, Lodowick: 7, 23, 114, 142

Mugliston, W.: 58

Muiopotmos (Spenser): 70, 88

Muir: Edwin: 15. Kenneth: 60, 79, 86, 105, 123, 134, 64; John Milton: 74

Muirhead, John H.: 112

Mulberry trees: 44. M and Mulberry Tree Legend: 87

Mulcaster, Richard, Highmaster of Paul's: 20, 40*, 42, 135, 137, 132, 3. R., Leben und Werke (Klähr): 3

Mulciber: 1, 56, 60, 73, 89, 90, 124, 128, 72, 92, 109, 130. See also: Vulcan

Mulgrave, Edmund Sheffield, Earl of: 44, 133

Mulhauson. See Swiss Ev. Cantons

Mull, M.: 105

Mullahy, Patrick: 47. On freedom: 47

Mullally, Joseph Patrick: 40

Müller, Mahler: 65

Mullinger, James Bass: 40*, 22

Multi-language books and word lists: 40

Multitude: 93. Distrust of: 51

<u>Mum and the Sothsegger</u>: 83*

Mumford, Lewis: 98

Mumpsimus: 40

Munby, A. N. L.: 15

Mundane shell: 25

Mundane Universe: 89

Munday, Anthony: 40, 93. See also: Mundy

<u>Mundorum Explicatio</u>: 65*

<u>Mundus Alter et Idem</u>: 30, 40, 73

Mundy: Anthony: 40, 93, 114. F. N. C.: 58. Peter: 44

Munford, W.: 58

Munger, Harold N., Jr.: 44

Munkacsy, Michael: 16

Munkácsy, Mihály: 137

Munnings, J. S.: 58

Münster, Peace of: 103

Munster, Sebastian: 19, 41, 123, 128, 22. Munster's <u>Cosmographia</u>: 88

Munz, Peter: 93

Münzer, Thomas: 7, 60

Muraena: 73

Muralt: 10

Murchel, Israel: 40

Murcia: 44

<u>Murder in the Cathedral</u>: 72

Murdock, Kenneth B.: 79, 115

Murena: 3

Muret, Marc Antoine: 40, 44

Muretus, M. A.: 145

Murmell, Joannes: 40

Murphy: Arthur: 58, 117. Gwendolyn: 45, 128

Murray: A. T.: 118, 122. Gilbert: 18, 56, 58, 60, 77, 133, 138, 92, 64, 21. Henry A.: 98. John O. F.: 93. Lindley: 98, 115; works: <u>English Grammar</u>: 115; <u>The English Reader</u>: 115; <u>Introduction to the Eng. Reader</u>: 115; <u>Sequel to the Eng. Reader</u>: 115. Patrick: 146. Peter and Linda: 27. Sir Robert: 7. Robert H.: 93. Thomas: 40. W. A.: 75, 131, 145

Murry, J. Middleton: 1, 4, 84, 132, 133, 130, 60, 105

Murschelius (Israel): 20

Murtola, Gasparo: 6, 15, 65, 77. <u>Della Creatione del Mondo</u>: 74

Musaeus: 40, 73, 90, 3, 72. Translated: 58

Muscle, Mr.: 44

Muscovy: 103. Grand Duke of: 103. Company: 19

Musculus, Wolfgang: 41, 44, 63, 73, 102, 123, 128, 142, 93, 99

Muse(s): 8, 41, 42, 44, 60, 90*, 111, 121, 124, 127, 70*, 136, 72, 146. M's: 63*, 144, 106*, 137. Period when M's Muse failed him: 136. Identification a theological problem: 107. As logos: 107. The Heavenly: 70, 72. See also: Urania

<u>Muse's Looking Glass</u>: 26

<u>Muse's Method</u> (Summers): 111

Musgrave: Mrs.: 44. G.: 58

Musgrove, S.: 34, 102, 138, 141, 131, 137

<u>Music of spheres</u>: 17, 89, 93

<u>Music</u>: 34, 40*, 44*, 51, 70*, 113, 121*, 72*. M and: 137. Degrees in: 40. For the Italian poems: 40. Function of: 70*. And mead: 40. The new: 40. Tutors at Cambridge: 40. Vocal: 40. Books: 121. Harmony, symbol of activity of God: 46. Painting and poetry, the Richardsons on: 88. Peck on M's knowledge of, influencing his versification: 88. During creation: 93. Throughout universe: 93. In Hell: 93. During Fall: 93. Response to: 93. Its effect: 93. And prosody: 96. M's love of, Richardson's account: 55. See also: Milton, knowledge of Music

Musical: form of in SA: 125*. Adaptations: 117. Imagery: 55

Musicians: 40. London Company of: 40

Mussato, Albertino: 32. "Epistola Fratris Joanhin": 74

Mussell, Tristram: 44

Mussolini, Benito: 60

Mustard, W. P.: 64

Musurgia Universalis: 121

Musurus, Marcus: 123

Mutability: 93. Of Adam: 48

Mutius, Macarius: 64. <u>De Triumpho Christi</u>: 74

Mutschmann, Heinrich: 16, 19, 20, 44*, 113, 128, 132, 88, 108. Works: <u>Der andere Milton</u>: 60; "Die Beweggrunde zu Miltons Festlandreise": 60

Mutual hypostatic union: 107

Mutuality. See Community

Muzzrelli: 6

Mycale: 49, 73

Mychell, J. See Michell, J.

Myers: 94. Ernest: 16, 58. L. H.: 134. Louis L.: 93

Mylius: Mrs.: 44. Hermann: 7, 10, 30*, 44*, 45, 59, 73, 62, 55

Mylor (Miller, Milde) and Mabe (Mabee) co., Cornwall: 44, 45

Mynch Court: 45

Mynde, the: 45

Mynors, R. A. B.: 40

Myopia (possible cause of M's blindness): 16

Myrick, Kenneth: 60, 110

Myriell: Henry: 40. Thomas: 40, 44, 121, 93; <u>Tristitiae Remedium</u>: 126

Myrmidons: 44, 73, 3

Mysia(ns): 44, 3

<u>Mystére d'Adam, Le</u>: 65, 36

<u>Mystére de la Passion, Le</u>: 65

<u>Mysteries of Love and Eloquence</u> (Phillips): 103, 94

Mystery plays: 15, 69. Mystery cycles: 123

Mystery: 92, 25. And suggestion: 88. Mysteries: of religion: 114*; divine: 144

Mysticism: 7*, 60, 113, 114*, 125, 78. M and: 137. Combined with Puritanism, Warton on: 88. Avoidance of: 118. M's freedom from in M's attitude towards music: 121*. Mystics: 7*

Mytens, Daniel (painter, M portrait): 44

Myth(s): 118, 124*, 125, 143, 32*, 46, 96, 146. And legend: 143. Definition of: 118. PL as: 118. Regularities in: 118. Intractability of: 118. Satan and: 125. Of the "two brothers": 125. Of Appolonian difference and Dionysiac identification: 125. M's "new": 125. In <u>Comus</u>, <u>Lycidas</u>, PR: 11. In PL: 11, 48. Of Samson: 11. And golden age: 32*. And Genesis: 32, 48. M's use of: 32*. Greek: 32. Relation of paradise to: 32. In criticism: 32. Biblical and classical: 46. Revolutionary: 46. Arcadian: 46. And plot distinguished: 48. And history: 48. Mythic: the: 69; theory of the world: 48; battle against evil: 125; quest: 125; logic: 125; "way of death": 125. See also: Knowledge; Mythology

<u>Mythology and the Renaissance Tradition</u> (Douglas Bush): 139

Mythology: 7, 8*, 51, 121, 53, 25, 48. And Scripture: 144. In simile: 53. Hume fond of: 88. Callander's knowledge of: 88. Mythological interest, M's: 60. See also: Folklore; Imagery

Mytton family: 44

-N-

N., N.: 116. See also: More, A.

N., T. See Newcomb, Thomas

Naaman: 144

Nabal: 73

Nabholz, Dr. Johannes: 44

Naboth: 44. Naboth's vineyard: 73

Nachet, A.: 16

Nachmanides: 41

Nacton, co. Suffolk: 44

Nadeau, Raymond E.: 40. Works: "The Progymnasmata of Aphthonius in Translation": 32; "A Renaissance Schoolmaster on Practice": 82

Naevius, Gnaeus: 73

Nag Hammadi Library: 36

Nagay (Mangat): 49

Nagler, A. M.: 39

Nahor-ben David, Isaac Sagi: 16

Naiads (as masque figures): 29, 90*. Naiad(es): 73

Naisus: 49

Nakedness: 54

Nalson, John: 116

Namancos: 19, 49, 73, 144. See also: Bayona; Guarded Mount

Name and Nature of Poetry, The: 12

Name-calling in forensic oratory: 31

Names: 53. Significance and understanding of: 96*. Proper, Spenser's, chosen to suit his characters: 88

Nanquier, Simon: 64

Nantes: 49. Council of: 44, 73

Nantwich (Namptwich), co. Cheshire: 44*, 45

Naogeorgus, Thomas: 65

Napier: G.: 58. John: 40, 102. Logarithms: 89

Naples (Neapolis): 44*, 49, 73, 103, 3, 94; see also: Parthenope. Revolt in 1647: 60. M's visit to: 6*, 30

Napoleon, Bonaparte: 60, 136, 115, 25

Naramzie, Sea of: 49

Naramzy, Point of: 49

Narcissus: 56, 44, 73, 90, 104, 11, 36, 72, 106, 25. Narcissism: 139

Nardi, Bruno: 5

Narim: 49

Narragansett Club (Publications of): 44

<u>Narration</u> (Henry Burton): 147. An account of his persecution: 147

Narration: 51*

<u>Narrative of Arthur Gordon Pym</u> (Poe): 136

Narrative: 53, 25. Voice: 117. In theme writing: 20. False characters speak (falsely) in: 31. As validation: 53*. And argument: 53*. As basis for reference in PL: 53. Verification in books XI-XII: 53*. And structure: 53. Process and structure of: 96*

Narrator: logic and function of: 96*. In PL: role of: 104; tonal and tempo patterns of: 104

Narulum: 49

Narv: 49

Naseby: 44, 49, 103, 116, 94. The Battle of: 73

Nash: 79, Ralph: 79, 101. (Nashe), Thomas: 135, 93, 41, 59, 60, 68, 77, 86, 142, 145, 32, 82; works: <u>Pierce Penniless</u>: 142; <u>Pierce Penniless</u> (ed. Collier): 77

Nasir Eddin: 89

Naso. See Ovid

Nason, G.: 58

Nassau: 44. House of: 51

Nathan, Robert: 137

Nation: 51*

<u>National Era</u>: 44

National Gallery, London: 44

National Portrait Gallery, London: 44

National Synod, Westminster: 103

National: subjects of Selden's annotations: 88. Setting of M's poetry, Peck on: 83. History: 97. Covenant: 103. Reputation, interest in: 51. Weaknesses: 51. Welfare: 51

Nationalism: 19, 51. M's: 60

<u>Nativity of Presbytery</u> (a Mar-Priest pamphlet): 147

Nativity, Ode on the Morning of Christ's. See "On the Morning of

Christ's Nativity"

Nativity: 103, 72. Nature's reaction: 93. Legends of: 93. M's view: 93

Natura naturans and naturata: 93

Natura Brevium: 45

Natural law: tradition of: 93. M on: 93. And divine law: 128

Natural vs. spiritual: 60

Natural Frailty of Princes Considered: 116

Natural History (Pliny): 121, 3

Natural: philosophy: 40. Accents: 51, 114*. History: 123; and epic poetry: 128. Man: 123. Theology: 93. Religion: see Nature

Naturalism: 27

Nature: 5*, 8*, 9*, 17*, 20, 27*, 51, 52, 69, 70*, 90, 113, 58, 122*, 128, 132, 104, 141, 143, 72*, 93*, 137, 148, 25. As cycle: 25. Natural religion: 25. And grace: 128, 148. And sin: 128. Book of God's works: 128, 93, 81. Decay of: 128, 93. Perversion of: 128. Idea of: 132. Dualism in: 143. Man's nature: 143. Order of, involved in Fall: 46. M as interpretor of: 149. Traditional view: 93. Obedient to God: 93. Levels of: 93; see also: Scale of Nature. As straight line: 93. As circle: 93. Phases of: 149*. Vastness of: 149. Sentiment for: 149. Concept of (Mask): 104. M's feeling for: 113. Disorder of, after the Fall: 113. Owes its birth to some prior agent: 123. As musical: 121*. M and: 147, 137, 16. Primitive, tendency of the Richardsons toward: 88. Jortin on: 88. Warton's delight in, and knowledge of: 88. Self evident in: 96. Knowledge and definition of: 96*. Conception of: 149, 104. Scheme of creation: 149. Ptolemaic: 149; reasons for Ptolemaic: 149; reasons against Ptolemaic: 149. Figure of: 29. Imitation of: 69*. Vitalism in: 118. Law(s) of: 69*, 102, 93, 54. Light of: 9*. Link of: 17*. As massa perditionis: 69. Redemption of: 69*. Regnum naturae: 69. And spirit: 69*, 9*. See also: Endowment, creative; Inspiration; Animals; Birds; Imagery; Natural theology

Naudé, Gabriel: 6, 114, 93

Nauert, C. G.: 39

Nauplios, The: 70

Nausea, F.: 128

Nausicaa: 56

Navagero, Andrea: 64

Navigation: 40. Act: 66, 103. And the constellations: 89

Navy Commissioners: 44

Nayler, James: 38

Naylor, H. Darnley: 56

Nazareth: 49, 73. Nazarite(s): 73, 143, 72

Nazianzen, Gregory (Nazianzenus, Gregorius): 44, 74, 95, 92, 21, 142, 65, 72. Works: Christ Suffering: 82; "Oratio XXIV": 74

Neaera: 73, 90

Neal: 94. D.: 9, praises PL: 58

Neale: C. M.: 40. J. E.: 39

Neapolis. See Naples

Nebaioth: 73

Nebo: 49, 73, 144. See also: Abarim

Nebraska, University of: 44

Nebuchadnezzar: 19, 41, 60, 73, 142

Nebulae: 89

Necessity: 2, 73, 90, 123, 144, 48. Irrelevant to deliberative rhetoric: 123. God not subject to: 113

Neckam (Nequam), Alexander: 128*, 32

Necromancy: 114

Nectanebo: 73

Nectar: 90

Nedham. See Needham

Needham: Francis: 44. (Nedham), Marchmont (Marchamont): 28, 44, 59, 103*, 91*, 117, 55, 94, 38, 115; works: possibly wrote A New discovery of Old England: 147; replies to the army in A Plea for the King and Kingdome: 147; Interest Will Not Lie: 147. Walter: 44

Needler: Benjamin: 54. H.: 58

Needlework: 70

Neele, H.: 58

Negation: 25. Method of: 123*. See also: Contraries

Negative: instances, avoidance of: 51. M's grasp of: 125. As poetic argument: 125. Theology: 93

Negotiation de la Paix: 44

Negri, P. G.: 6

Negus, Empire of (Abassin): 19, 49, 73, 144. See also: Emperor, the; Amara; Ethiop

Nehemia(h): 73

Neile, Sir Paul: 10

Neiman, Frazer: 59, 14

Nelson: 97. Benjamin N., The Idea of Usury: 82. J. C.: 122. James G.: 115. Lowry, Jr.: 6, 39, 101, 21. William: 60

Nemesianus: 64*

Nemesis: 141

Nemesius: 128. Of Emesa: 93

Nemmers, E. E.: 79

Nemo, Capt.: 60

Nennius: 73, 82, 93

Neocaesarea: 49. Council of: 73, 44, 113

Neo-classicism: 17, 70, 132. See also: Italians, the

Neo-Christian: 34

Neo-Latin poetry: 40

Neologisms, M's: 88

Neoplatonism: 7*, 40, 54, 60*, 79*, 112, 113, 118, 121, 123, 125, 144, 32, 38, 39, 72*, 25. Neoplatonic: 125. Neoplatonists: 70, 71. Separation between one and many: 107. See also: Platonism, Florentine

Neo-Plinyism: 128

Neoportus: 49

Neo-Ptolemaic: 139
Neoptolemus: 56, 123. See also: Quintus Smyrnaeus

Neo-Reformation theology: 47

Neostoicism: 60, 113

Neothan, Abbot: 3

Nepenthes: 90, 144

Nephews, M educates his: 94

Nephilim: 123. See also: Giants, Biblical

Nepos, Cornelius: 40

Neptune: 2, 44, 56, 57, 73, 89, 90*, 104, 3, 72. As epic machinery: 123. See also: Camoens; Homer

Nereids: 90

Nereus: 73, 90, 104

Nero: Emperor: 44, 60, 116, 144, 3, 71, 64. Claudius: 91

Neronian sense: 73

Nessus: 73

Nestle, Eberhard: 40

Nestor: 56, 123. See also: Homer

Nestorius: 74. Nestorians: 71. "Nestorianism," in Encyclopedia of Religion and Ethics (ed. James Hastings): 74

Netherby: 94. Hall, co. Cumberland: 44

Nethercot, Arthur H.: 44, 59, 91

Netherlands: 44, 49, 103. See also: Low Countries; Dutch; Belgia; Belgium

Nettenburg: 10

Nettlebed Academy: 78

Nettleship: Henry: 56. Richard Lewis: 66

Nettleton, Christopher: 44

Neueste aus der anmuthigen Gelehrsamkeit, Das: 117

Neumann: E.: 141. Joshua: 128

Neuse, Richard: 39. On Mask: 104

Neuvecelle, J.: 6

Neve, Philip: 44, 49, 117*. Praises M: 58

Nevill(e): Lady Adelyn: 44. Graham: 93. (Nevile), Henry (1620-94): 10, 30, 44*, 54, 73, 88, 91, 115, 117

Neville: 51. Judge: 44*.

Nevin, John: 44

Nevizzano, Giovanni: 54

Nevo, Ruth: 122

New leader: 35

New man: 122. See also: Old man; Heavenly man; Earthly man; Adam-Christ parallel; St. Paul

New science: 128. Changing man's estimate of himself: 80. See also: Copernicus

New Atlantis: 73, 112

New College (Oxford): 44, 45

New Colophon: 44

New Criticism: 1, 118, 53

"New critics": 86

New Discovery, A (Hoole): 20. A New Discovery of the Old Art of Teaching School: 3

New England (Nova Anglia): 19, 44, 49

New England Almanack, The: 115

New England Courant, The: 115

New England Diary and Almanac, 1809, The: 115

New England Historical and Genealogical Register: 44

New England Primer, The: 115

New England Quarterly Magazine, The: 115

New England Weekly Journal, The: 115

New English Dictionary: 44, 45, 95

New English Grammar, A (Howell): 135

New Exchange, London: 44

New Foundling Hospital for Wit: 44

New Greek Comedy, The (Legrand): 70

New Greek Comedy: 70

New Hampshire: 45

New Haven (Franciscopolis): 49

New Haven Gazette and the Connecticut Magazine, The: 115

New Inn (Jonson): 94

New Inn: 45

New Jerusalem: 32, 71. See also: Heaven

New Laokoon, The (Babbitt): 70

New Memoirs of the Life and Poetical Works of Mr. John Milton (Francis Peck): 88. See also: Peck, Francis

New Model Army: 116, 147

New Monthly Magazine: 63

New Movement: 63*

New Orleans: 44

New Palace Yard: 103. Westminster: 44

New Propositions from the Armie (London Independents support army's policies): 147

New Quere (John Saltmarsh): 147

New Shakespeare Society Transactions: 45

New Star of the North...(Gill the Younger): 20

New Statesman and Nation: 44

New Testament: 44, 70, 123*, 103, 142, 3, 143, 71, 72. Authority of: 51. II Peter, Jude, Revelation: 123. Source of art: 143. New Testament, Greek: 40. New Testament, Syriac: 41. See also: Keys; Word of God

New Version of Paradise Lost, A: 105, 88

New Years Gift (urges an elective king): 147

New Years Gift for the Parliament and Armie (Gerrard Winstanley): 147

New York City: 44. New York Magazine Or Literary Repository, The: 115. New York Public Library: 44*, 45. New York Society Library: 98. New York Sun: 87; on Huxley's use of PL in New York lectures: 87. New York Times: 44; Book Review: 44. New York Tribune: 87; on Huxley's use of PL in lectures: 87. New York Univ.: 44

"New Zealot to the Sun, the": 98

Newberry Library Bulletin: 44

Newbolt, Sir Henry: 16

Newburn, battle of: 44

Newbury, co. Berks.: 44

Newbury, John: 35

Newcastle: 49, 73, 103. William Cavendish, Marquess and Duke of: 44, 73

Newcomb (Newcome), Thomas (pr., 1649-81): 44*, 51, 58, 91; influenced by M: 58; on PL: 58. Henry: 40

Newcomen, Matthew (1610?-69): 44, 51, 91, 93. See also: Smectymnuus

Newcourt, Richard: 40

Newenham, F.: 97

Newes, The: 116

Newgate, London: 44, 103. Prison: 44

Newhall, co. Cheshire: 44

Newington Green Academy: 44

Newlin: Claude M.: 115. Thomas: 44

Newman: 133, 3, 130. Family: 45. Alice: 45. Arthur: 45. Elizabeth: 45. Elizabeth: see Guise, Eliz. Elizabeth (Osbaston): 45. Francis: 45. Francis W.: 58, 64. Henry: 45. Jane: 45. Cardinal John Henry: 15, 34, 58, 86, 87, 18, 74, 113, 71, 150; attitude toward M: 87; sonnets, Miltonic: 87; on M's Satan: 87; friend of Hurrell Froude: 87; on SA: 87; works: "On the Characteristics of True Poetry": 37; Arians of the 4th Century: 74. Mary: see: Chilcott, Mary; Powell; Mary. Osbaston: 45. Robert: 45. Thomas: 40. Venus (Weedon): 45

Newmarket: 40, 49, 73. Road: 40

Newmeyer, Edna: 93. "Beza and Milton": 74

Newnham Courtney: 45. Newnham Regis: 45

Newport, William. See Nieuport

Newport: 49, 73; see also: Neoportus. Newport Grammar School (Essex): 42

News from Hell, Rome and Inns of Court (attr. to M): 44

News Published for the Satisfaction: 44

Newsham, Thomas: 44

Newsletters: 40

Newstead, Christopher: 93

Newton (Milton) Hall, co. Essex: 44, 45

Newton Lincoln, co. York: 44

Newton: 141*, 149. A. E.: 16. Sir Isaac: 5, 6, 7, 12, 15, 16, 23, 40, 89, 114, 118, 136, 142, 32, 39, 88, 97, 115, 146*, 25; commentary on Revelation: 25; Blake's criticism of: 25; inferiority to Shakespeare and M: 13; and M compared: 146. Rev. John: 44. Martin (stationer): 44

Newton, Bp. Thomas: 1, 4, 15, 20, 28, 33*, 37, 41, 44, 59, 60, 68, 73, 56*, 86, 87, 102, 105*, 110, 113, 120, 118, 127, 128, 134, 138, 142, 144, 43, 92, 88*, 93, 97, 99, 94, 101, 106, 109, 146, 150, 117*, 55. Young Tennyson's knowledge of Newton's Life of M: 87. Ed. of Life of Milton: 133, 44. Dissertations on the Prophecies: 57. PR: 57. See also: Milton, PL

Nicaea: 49, 73, 139. Bps. of: 139. See also: Nice

Nicandor (Nicander): 40, 73, 128, 3

Nicanor, Lysimachus: 9, 73

Nicator, Seleucus: 19

Niccholes, Alexander: 54

Niccolini, F.: 6

Nice (Nicaea): 44, 3, 94; see also: Nice. Nicene Council: 27, 44. Nicene Creed: 74, 126, 78

Nicephorus: 44. Phocas: 73

Nicetas: 40, 70, 89, 3, 74. Choniates or Acominatus: 73, 82; Imperii Graeci Historia: 82

Nichol, Dr.: 89

Nicholas Acon, St., Church: 40

Nicholas Papers (ed. Warner, G. F.): 44. 45

Nicholas: of Cusa (Cardinal): 74, 79, 83, 100, 39, 93, 32. Of Lyra: 74, 36, 32; Postilla: 74; see also: Lyra, Nicholaus de. Of Methone: 93

Nicholas: Sir Edward (Secretary of State): 44*. Henry: 7. John: 44

Nicholl: John: 40. W. G.: 97

Nicholls, Robert: 44

Nichols: J.: 58. James: 40. John: 29, 40, 44, 45, 39, 117. Josias: 93

Nicholson: Mr.: 45. Otto (Otho), Examiner in Chancery: 44. Richard:

40. Watson: 44

Nichomachus. See Nicomachus

Nickalls, J. L.: 23

Nicklaes, Henry: 114

Nickolls: John (ed. John Milton, Original Letters...Cromwell): 44. John, Jr.: 44

Nicocles or The Cyprians (Isocrates): 20

Nicol, Pierre. See Evelyn, John

Nicolai, N.: 44

Nicolas, Edward: 38

Nicoll, Allardyce: 39

Nicolson: B.: 97. Marjorie Hope: 1, 5, 9, 15, 18, 19, 23, 41, 44, 52, 54, 87, 60, 69, 76, 77, 79, 59, 86, 87, 100, 102, 112, 110, 142, 144, 32, 36, 128*, 71, 93, 101, 137, 146, 21, 48; on Adam's despair: 61; M's interest in astronomy: 61; pagan and Christian elements combine: 61; on cult of literary sublimity: 87; on natural sublime: 87; works: The Conway Letters: 142; Science and Imagination: 48; The Breaking of the Circle: 48

Nicomachean Ethics (Aristotle): 52, 70, 112, 3

Nicomachus: 73, 121

Nicot: 40

Nidda (Widda). See William VI

Nider: 142

Niebuhr: H. R.: 143; on Gnostics: 143. Reinhold: 15, 47*; On: mutability, atonement, the kingdom of Heaven, moral pride, finiteness and infiniteness, papal pretension, knowledge and fanaticism, forgiveness: 47. The Nature and Destiny of Man: 48

Nieman, Fraser: 137

Niemicrovia: 49

Nieremberg: Eusebius, S. J.: 123. Juan Eusebio (Nierembergius, Johannes E.): 44, 67

Niesel, Wilhelm: 93

Nietzche, Friedrich: 18, 15, 54, 60, 113, 141, 11, 39, 71, 72. On creative genius: 136

Nieuport (Neuportius), William (ambassador): 44*, 30, 73

Niger: 19, 49, 73

Night Thoughts (Young): 88

Night: 1, 89, 90*, 144, 143, 71. As character: 72. In Comus and Masque of Hymen: 143. Marriage and revelry in: 143. And Chaos: 143. Dark and dreadful: 143. See also: Chaos

Nightingale, a Conversation Poem, The (Coleridge): 70

Nightingale, Lady Elizabeth: 97

Nightingale: 144, 146. Mask: 104. Nightingale's song: 121

Nigritas. See More, A.

Nike: 72

Nile (Nilus): 19, 49, 44, 114, 144, 32, 3. See also: Negus

Nilus Abbas: 68

Nimeguen, English embassy at: 150

Nîmes, France: 44

Nimrod: 1, 19, 60, 73, 102, 112, 111, 122, 123, 127, 144, 143, 32, 130, 146. His sin: 143. Ruler of Babylon: 143. As tyrant: 143

Nin-ti: 36

Nine degrees: 93

Nine Psalms Done Into Meter: 42

Nine-day cycles, Satan's: 100

Nineteen Propositions: 73

Ninevee (Ninos): 49, 44

Nineveh: 19*, 73, 144

Ninos (Ninevee): 44, 49

Ninth sphere (crystalline): 89

Ninus: 19, 73, 144

Niphates, Mt. (Assyrian Mount, Specular Mt.): 19, 49, 73, 32, 72, 144. See also: Taurus

Nisibis: 19, 49, 73, 144

Nisroc(h): 73, 142, 72, 140

Nisus: 2

Niwanbirig: 49

Nixon, Anthony: 102

Nizolius, Marius: 20, 40

Nizzoli, Giovanni: 117

Njegosh, Petar P.: 65

"No bishop, no king": 40

No Blind Guides, etc. (L'Estrange): 103, 116, 147

No Drol, But a Rational Account: 147

No More Addresses: 73

No Papist nor Presbyterian: But the modest Proposalls of Some well-affected and Free-born People (pamphlet on toleration): 147

Noah: 1, 17, 27, 44, 50, 68, 102, 103, 111, 123, 127, 128, 144, 143, 32*, 36, 72*, 106. To Abraham, second age: 143. Drunkenness of: 36

Nobiles: 40

Nobility: argument from: 123*. As constituent of happiness: 123

Noble Voice, The (Van Doren): 83

Noble: James Ashcroft: 58, 87; on M's Piedmont sonnet: 87. Mark: 44. Oliver: 115; Some Strictures upon the Sacred Story Recorded in the Book of Esther: 115. T.: 58. William B.: 143; on faith: 143

Nobles (in masques): 29

Noci, Carlo: 21

Nock, A. D.: 36

Nocken: 65

Nocturnal upon St. Lucy's Day (John Donne): 131

Noël, Lady Penelope: 20

Noel: Francis (pr.): 44. Manz: 65. Philip: 44

Nogarola, Lodovico: 32

Noh drama of Japan: 118

Noise, in musical sense: 121

Nol. See Cromwell

Nomentanus, Crescentius Johannes: 73

Nominalism: 71

Non sequitur: 51

Non-artistic proof: 51*

Non-conformity: 47. Nonconformists: 27, 40, 51

Non-literary aims of Selden's notes to Polyolbion: 88

Non-scribers: 44

Non-technical modes of persuasion: 51

Nonesuch: 97

Nonius, Marcellus: 128

Nonnus: 90, 88

Nook, S. A.: 16

Noon-day, in M's poetry: 89

Noon, hour of: 17

Noonday devil: 93

Norbury, Mrs.: 44

Norden: Eduard: 100. John: 40, 45, 93

Nordenskiold, A. E.: 19, 144

Nordstrom, Johan: 18

Nores, Jason de (Giasone di): 122

Norfolk co.: 44, 45, 49, 73

Norgate, T. S.: 58

Noriberga: 49

Norica: 49

Normal human nature, M's conception of: 113

Norman Conquest: 44, 60, 103

Norman Hills, co. Suffolk: 44

Norman Isles: 73, 3, 49

Normandy: 49, 51

Normans: 103, 3

Norris: John: 40, 114, 142, 32; The Theory and Regulation of Love: 142. (Norres), Sir William: 44, 45

Norse legends: 97

North American Review: 44, 63, 115

North Cadbury, co. Somerset: 44

North Sea: 49

North: Arthur: 44. B.: 58. C. R.:

123. Dudley, 3rd Baron: 114.
Elizabeth: 83. F. J.: 144. George:
108. H. F.: 5. Sir Thomas: 40

Northampton, co. and city: 44, 49,
103. Northamptonshire: 45, 49. Earl
of: 45

Northbrooke, John: 93

Northcote, J.: 97

Northeast Passage: 19*. And north-
west passage: 150

Northern Passion (14th c. Eng. poem):
74

Northern Subscribers' Plea: 44

Northmore, Thomas: 58, 115.
Washington, or Liberty Restored: 115

Northumberland (Northumbria): 45, 49

Northumberland: Algernon Percy, 10th
Earl of: 44. Henry Percy, Earl of:
44. Duke of (John Dudley): 73, 91

Norton, co. Staffs.: 44

Norton: Bonham: 40. Sir Gregory:
91. John (pr.): 40. Thomas: 40.
William (pr.): 40

Norumbega: 19, 49, 73, 144

Norway (Norwegia): 19, 44, 49.
Norwegian: 51; stateliness: 3. See
also: Frederick III

Norwich (tune): 40, 121

Norwich A: 36. Norwich B: 36

Norwich, co. Norfolk: 44, 49.
Grammar School: 20, 40

Norwood: 89. G.: 92

Norwoods Manor, Sproughton: 44

Nos Anciens et leurs Oeuvres (ed.
Crosnier): 44

Nosce teipsum: 93

Nostoi: 74

Nostradam, César de: 64. Perles ou
les Larmes de la Saincte Magdeleine:
74

Nostradamus: 114

Notary, John (pr.): 40

Notation, argument from: 123. See
also: Argument; Etymology

Note of fine: 45

Note-Books (Samuel Butler): 131

Notes and Lectures on Shakespeare
(Coleridge): 70

Notes and Queries for Somerset and
Dorset: 45

Notes and Queries: 44*, 45, 87

Notestein, Wallace: 45, 142. A
History of Witchcraft in England: 142

Nott: Eliphalet: 115; The Addresses,
Delivered to the Candidates for the
Baccalaureate: 115. K.: 15, 86.
S.: 58

Nottingham, Charles Howard, 1st Earl
of: 44

Nottingham: 44, 45*, 49, 103;
Nottinghamshire: 49; Nottinghamshire,
Annals of: 45. Nottinghamshire, The
Antiquities of: 45

Notus: 73, 90, 144

Nouvelle Biographie Universelle: 40

Nouvelles Ordinaires de Londres: 44,
103

Nova Solyma: 7, 91

Nova Zembla: 19

Novae Solymae (attr. to M): 44. See
also: Gott

Novalis: 7

Novarra: 89

Novatian, subordinationists: 107.
Novatians: 73

Novel, as destructive of literary
formality: 118

Novogardia: 49

Novogrod: 49

Novum Organum (Bacon): 112, 134

Novus Atlas: 144

Now my task: 121

Nowell: Alexander: 40. Lawrence:
40

Nox: 90. See also: Night

Noy(e), William: 40, 143

Noyer-Weidner, A: 100

Noyes: Alfred: 16, 58. George R.:

44

Nugent, R.: 58

Numa (Pompilius): 73, 128

Number symbolism: 100*. In Augustin, Dante, Plato, Virgil: 100. Of the beast (666): 93. See also: Pythagorean theories; Progressio Quaternaria; Significant form

Numbers, Book of: 95. See also: Bible

Numbers (music and arithemtic): 40, 121

Numenius: 93

Numeration in petties: 40

Numerical structure. See Symmetrical structure

Numerology: 40, 93, 25. See also: Three Eras; Four Monarchies; Six Ages; Harmony; Pythagorean-Platonic

Numidia: 49

Numidian poets: 19

Nunc dimittis: 126. Nunc Dimittis (St. Luke): 139

Nuova Musica: 40

Nuremberg: 44. Polyglot: 22. Nuremberg Chronicle: 143. See also: Frederick William

Nurse, for M's son, John: 44

Nurture: 47

Nussbaum, Frederick: 128

Nüssler: 10

Nuttall: 97. G.: 23. Geoffrey F.: 93. P. A.: 45

Nye: Philip: 9, 44, 59, 114, 120. Russel Blaine: 115

Nygren: Bp. Anders: 93. Gotthard: 93

Nymphs: 90*. Of Severn: 29

Nyseian Isle (Nysa Ile): 19, 49, 73, 144, 32, 72. See also: Triton

Nysnovogorod: 49

-O-

O., J. (John Owen): 91

O., R. (pr.): 44

Oakeham, Mr.: 44

Oakeley: Richard: 44. Samuel: 44

Oakes Hall, Fonsbury: 44

Oakham: co., Rutland: 44. School: 20

Oakley, Francis: 93

Oakley, Mr.: 45

Oat: 121

Oates, Titus: 44, 116

Oath(s): 45, 63

Oatlands (Coway Stakes): 49

Ob, River: 19, 49, 73

Obduracy, characteristic of the reprobate: 123

Obedience: 17, 31, 83, 122*, 123*, 124, 143*. To authority: 60. The essence of M's religion: 121. Christian: 143. To God: 143. Fundamental law: 143. Voluntary: 143. Basis of felicity: 143. And ideal: 143. And love: 93. As a moral principle in PL: 48. See also: Disobedience; Justice; Law

Obediential power of God: 93

Oberon, the Fairy Prince (Jonson): 29

Oberuferer Paradiesspiel: 65

Objection: 51*

Objective world: 96*

Objectivity, elements of: 96

Objects of experience, myth and thought: 96*

Oblation: 126. In Prayer Books of Edward VI: 126. In Scottish Prayer Book of 1637: 126

Obrecht, Jacobus: 100

O'Brien: Elmer: 101. G. W.: 23. Henry: 44. K.: 58. Mary: 117

Obscenity, M and: 137

Obscurity. See Blake; Milton; Poetry; Prophecy

Obsequies to the Memorie of Mr. Edward King: 33

Observations on the Fairie Queene, by

T. Warton: 88

Observations on the Peace of Kilkenny: 94

Observations on the Original of Government: 115

Observations on Mr. Johnson's Remarks: 116

Observations upon some of his Majesty's late Answers and Expresses (Henry Parker, attr. to M): 44, 147

Observations, etc.: 103

Observator, The: 116. Observator, Observ'd, The: 116

Observer, The: 117

Obsopaeus, Vincent: 40

Obstacles to heroic enterprise: 123*

Obstructions: 51

Obstructors to Justice (John Goodwin): 103, 116, 147

Occa River: 49

Occam, William of: 15, 114

Occasion: 51, 123. See also: Cause

Occleve, Thomas: 133

Occultism: 113, 142*. Profusion of: 142*. M's knowledge of: 142. Occult science: 114*

Occupations of residents of Bread Street Ward ca. 1625: 40

Ocean, the (appreciated and not appreciated): 58

Oceana (Harrington): 51, 103, 147

Oceanus: 57, 73, 90, 92. Mask: 104

Ochino, Bernardino: 113, 114, 93, 55, 148

Ochtertyne: 44

Ocnus: 73, 128

Octave: 121

Octavian, Lord: 60, 64

Octavius Caesar: 51

Octodurus: 49

Oddington: 45

Ode(s): English: 27. Models for: 30. Greek: 40. Latin: 40. See also: Latin poems

Ode on the Nativity, the. See Milton, John, Works

Ode on Immortality (Wordsworth): 94

Ode to Horror: 58

Odeberg, Hugo: 41

Odell, Jonathan: 115. The American Times: 115

Odemira, Count (envoy from Portugal): 44

Oderisi (Oderigi) da Gubbio: 111

Odets, Clifford: 108

Odingsells, Charles: 93

Odo of Cluny (Occupatio): 74, 64

Odrysian: 73

Odysseus: 56*, 60, 90, 123, 72, 25. Analogies with Satan: 123*. See also: Ulysses; Homer

Odyssey (Homer): 2*, 17, 50, 70, 112, 111, 118, 133, 136, 3, 26, 46*, 72, 130. See also: In medias res; Homer

Odyssey (Pope): 88

Oechalia (Oealia): 49, 73

Oecolampadius, Joannes: 74, 114. In Job: 74

OED. See: Oxford English Dictionary

Oedipean night (Oedipodioniam... noctem): 73

Oedipus at Colonus: 26, 130

Oedipus Rex (Sophocles): 70, 11, 71, 131

Oedipus: 1, 2, 52, 68, 70, 90, 125, 3, 46, 72, 92*

Oengus Celi-De: 65

Oesterley, W. O. E. (and Box, G. H.): 142, 36, 93. A Short Survey of the Lit. of Rabbinical and Medieval Judaism: 142

Oeta (Trachinia Rupes): 49, 73

Of the Kingdom of Christ (Bucer): 112

Of the Reformation of the English Church: 51

Of Civil Power: 30*. See also:

Milton, John, Works

Of Education (Milton): 98, 112*, 111, 103, 55. Presentation copy of: 44. See also: Milton, John, Works

"Of Masques and Triumphs" (Bacon): 29

Of Patience and Submission to Authority: 116

Of Prelatical Episcopacy: 83, 103, 144*, 87. M's account: 55. Reply to: 144. Date of: 144. Irenaeus discredited: 143. Bps. as witnesses; ranks of Bps.: 144. Used by Lord Brooke: 144

Of Reformation (M): 112, 111, 118, 129, 80, 144*, 55, 83, 116, 103, 102. Prayer analyzed: 80. Refutation of Digby's Speech: 144*. Dramatic character of: 144. See also: Milton, John, Works

Of Resisting the Lawfull Magistrates upon Colour of Religion: 60

Of Studies (Bacon): 3

Of True Religion, Heresy, Schism: 83, 103, 116. Phillips' account: 55

Of Verbal Criticism: 114

Offa the Mercian: 3

Offa's Dyke: 49

Offemont. See Daubray

O'Farrell, Nellie McNeill: 44

"Office and Jurisdiction of a Constable": 44

Office of a Constable: 44

"Office of a Marshal": 44

"Office of a Vice-Constable": 44

Officer: 126, 72. Officers of St. Paul's School: 40

Official: church: 51. Incompetent: 51. Tenure of: 51

Offley: family: 45. Little: 45. (Oflye), Robert: 45. (Ofley), Thomas: 44, 45*

Offlye. See Offley

Offor, George: 44

Og: 73

Ogden: C. K.: 39. H. V. S.: 1, 17, 23, 110, 36, 101, 106, 21. J.: 58. John Cosens: 115; *An Address Delivered at the Opening of Portsmouth Academy*: 115. Uzal: 115, 117; *Antidote to Deism*: *The Deist Unmasked*: 115

Ogg, David: 116

Ogilby, John: 40, 56, 97. See also: Ogilvie

Ogilvie (Ogilby), John: 58*, 117

Ogilvy, J. D. A.: 36

Oglander, Sir John: 44, 120. His son, John: 44

Ogygium: 73

"Oh had I Wings": 121

"Oh, Woe is me": 121

Ohio State University: 44

Ojetti, Ugo: 44

Okeham School in Rutlandshire: 40

Okes, Mary (pr., 1643-45): 91

Olai, Wilhelmus Worm: 44

Olaus Magnus: 19, 44, 57, 114, 128*, 53

Olave's, St., Parish: 40

Old and New Chains, etc: 103

Old and New Schoolmaster (Lamb): 3

Old Bachelor, The: 115

Old Bailey, London: 44

Old Covenant: 71

Old English: 40. Materials: 40

"Old English Edition": 44

Old Exchange, London: 40, 44, 103

Old Fish Street: 40

Old Looking-Glass for the Laity and Clergy of all Denominations, An: 115. See also: Considerations Touching

Old Maid, The: 117

"Old Man": 122. See also: New man; Heavenly man; Adam-Christ parallel; St. Paul

Old Parliamentary History: 44

Old Saxon Genesis: 65

"Old Soldier of the King": 103

Old State Paper Office: 103

Old Street, London: 44

Old Testament: 44, 103, 113, 116, 123*, 142, 3, 71, 72. M and the: 136. Important to Cosmopolitanism: 107. See also: Bible

Old Wives Tale (Peele): 29, 94, 26, 94. See also: Peele, George

Oldenburg, Germany: 44. See also: Oldenburg, Anthon Gunther; Frederick III

Oldenburg: 49, 3. Anthon Gunther, Count of, and Lord of Delmenhorst, Jehvern, Kniphausen, etc.: 10, 44*, 55. Heinrich (Henry): 7, 10*, 16, 28, 30, 44*, 73, 113, 59, 38, 91, 137, 148, 103, 120, 94; letter to, quoted: 55

Oldfather: C. H.: 144. W. A.: 41

Oldham, Sir John: 71

Oldisworth, W.: 58

Oldmixon, John, History of England: 44

Oldsworth, Michael: 64

Oldys, William: 44, 94

Olevian, Kaspar (Caspar): 40, 41, 32

Oligarchy: 9

Olinger, Paulus: 65

Oliphant, R.: 58

Olissipo (Ulyssipo): 49

Oliver. See Cromwell

Oliver: (Olivier), Isaac: 17, 33. Leslie M.: 44. Peter: 115, 117

Oliver's Secretary: 45

Olivier, Sir Laurence: 118

Ololon: 146, 25. Compared with Sabrina: 25. As river of life: 25. And the Lady in Comus: 25. As multitudes: 25. See also: Comus

Olson, Albert H.: 93

Olympia: 49, 72. Olympias: 73, 90, 128. Olympian: gods: 50; games: 73, 71; hill: 73. Olympic games: 71. Olympiads: 72. See also: Olympus

Olympiodorus: 73, 74, 112. Commentarium in Beatun Job: 74. See also: Niceta

Olympius: 73

Olympus (Olympian Hill): 2, 19, 44, 49, 90, 103, 3, 32, 72*. See also: Gods of Olympus

Oman: C.: 6. John W.: 93

Omar Khayyam: 60, 89, 136

O'Meara, John J.: 81

Omission of words: 98

Omnipotence: 47, 93. See also: God

Omnipresence (as an attribute of God): 113, 93

Omniscience: 93. See also: Foreknowledge

Omond, T. S.: 58

Omoo: 98

On the Approach of Spring: 103

"On the Death of a Fair Infant" (M): 55. See also: M, John, Works

On the Death of Satyrus: 71

"On the Late Massacre in Piemont" (M): 103. See also: M, John, Works

"On the Library at Cambridge": 44

On the Morning of Christ's Nativity, Ode: 102, 112, 87, 98, 89, 100, 121, 72*, 101*, 104, 55. Theme of: 104. Role of invocation to muse: 126. Demons lose powers at Christ's coming: 107. Methexis, Nature, present tense; stances in: 72. Structure of: 72. Alexandrine in, antecdents of, catalogue of gods in: 101. Historical process in, 3 part structure of: 101, stanza of: 101. PL, affinities with: 101. Comments on to Charles Diodati: 61

On the New Forces of Conscience: 83

On the Origin of Evil: 65

On the Poetry of Pope: 12

On the Soul of the World: 3. See also: "Locrian remnants"

On the Sublime (Longinus): 70, 112, 3

On Being Human (More): 111

"On Day Break" (attr. to M): 44

On Grammarians (Suetonius): 20

"On Mel Heliconium" (attr. to M): 44

<u>On Modern Gardening</u> (Walpole): 70

"On Mrs. Catherine Thomason" (M's sonnet written to): 112, 94. See also: Milton, John, Works

"On Shakespeare": 112, 55. See also: Milton, John, Works On Plants (Theophrastus): 3

<u>On Stones</u> (Theophrastus): 3

"On Time" (M): 112. See also: M, John, Works

"On Translating Homer": 98

<u>On University Education</u>: 71

"On Worthy Master Shakespeare" (M). See "On Shakespeare"

<u>Ondergang der eerste wereld</u>: 65

Oneal: 73

Onega: 49

<u>Oneirocritica</u>: 44

Onesimus: 73

Ong, W. J., SJ: 23*, 37, 110, 123, 135, 53, 82. <u>Ramus and Talon Inventory</u>: 82

Onkelos (the Targumist): 1, 24, 40, 41, 73, 113, 123

Onomatopoeia: 118

Onslow: Arthur, Speaker of House of Commons: 44*, 55, 88. Arthur George, 3rd Earl of: 44. George, Earl of: 44. Thomas, 2nd Earl of: 44. Sir William Arthur Bampfylde, 6th Earl of: 44. William Hillier, 4th Earl of: 44

Ontology: 113*. Ontological propositions: 96

Oothoon: 25

Opel: 7

Open Trust Myth: 78

<u>Opera Christiana</u> (ed. Georgius Fabricius): 74

<u>Opera Luducra</u>: 40

Opera: 27, 29, 121, 145, 92

Ophanim: 142. See also: Cherubim

Ophion: 60, 73, 90

Ophioneus: 60, 123

Ophir: 19, 49, 73, 144. See also: Chersonese; Sofala

Ophis: 60

Ophites: 113, 36

Ophiuchi: 89

Ophiucus: 56, 73, 89, 128

Ophiusa: 19, 49, 73

Ophthalmology, state of in M's time: 16

Opie; A.: 58. John: 146

Opinion of Council of State and M's: 44

Opinion, freedom of: 31

Opinions: 51

Opitz: 7, 10

Opler, Morris Edward: 118

Oporinus, Johann: 73

Oppian(us): 58, 40, 44, 73, 128, 3, 88, 64

Oppius, Gaius: 128

Opponencies: 40

Opponens: 40

Opponents: 51

Opportunity: 51

Opposing at St. Paul's School: 40

Oppositio: 40

Opposition: 51. Emotional: 51

<u>Oppressed Mans Oppresions declared</u> (John Lilburne): 147

Oppression: 51

Opprobrious Hill (Hill of Scandal; Offensive Mountain): 49

Ops: 57, 60, 73, 90. See also: Rhea

Optatus, St.: 116

Optic nerve, paralysis of, possible cause of M's blindness: 16

Optics: 128

Optimism: 47, 143. M's: 137. Unfounded: 143

Opus Posthumum: 116

Oracle (of God) = God: 107. Oracles: 144; cessation of: 93 Orage, A. R.: 113, 136

Oram, S. M.: 53

Orange, France: 44. Council of: 36

Orange: Princess Mary of: 10. Prince William of: 10

Oras, Ants: 1, 44, 60, 128, 85, 93, 64, 101, 21. <u>M's Early Editors and Commentators</u>: 109

<u>Oratio Caini</u>: 65

Oratio Eristica: 40

Oratio: 40

Oration: 40, 51. Latin composition of: 40. Political: 51

<u>Orationes</u> (St. Basil): 65

<u>Orationes Historicae</u> (Stephanus): 40

<u>Oratiuncula ad puerum Jesum</u> (Colet): 20

<u>Orator</u> (Cicero): 20, 40, 70

Orator: requirements of: 30, 40. In debate with Abdiel: 123. As hero: 123, Satan as: 123. In addressing his followers; the gods of the Abyss: 123. M's idea of: 25. Like God: 25. Oratorical and Literary Ideals of M and the ancients: 20, 31. Orators: 51; univ., public: 40. See also: Poet

<u>Oratoriae Libri Duo</u> (Butler): 20

Oratory: 40, 25. Patterns of, ideology of, mixture of styles in: 25. The practice exercises: 20, 31. Kinship with poetry: 31. And virtuous action: 31

Orbilius: 73. Reference of Horace to: 20

Orc: 25

Orcades (Orkney): 44, 49, 73. See also: Orkney Islands

Orchard: M.: 142. T. N.: 40, 128, 129

Orchestra: 121

<u>Orchestra</u> (Davies): 29, 134

Orcus: 44, 73, 90, 3

Ord, Thomas: 44

Ordalium: 73

Order (a masque figure): 29

<u>Order Book of Council</u>: 103

Order: 51*, 124*. In Heaven, of creation: 93. Of universe: 93; see also: Scale of Nature. Inverted after Fall: 93. And love: 93. Violation of: 124*. Elizabethan conception of: 102

Ordericus, Vitalis: 93

<u>Orders of the Council</u>: 30

Orders: 142*. Dionysian: 142. See also: Angels; Degrees

<u>Ordinale de Origine Mundi</u>: 36

<u>Ordinance for the Suppression of Blaphemies and Heresies</u>: 71

<u>Ordinance for Printing</u>: 55

<u>Ordinance Survey Atlas of England and Wales</u>: 45

Ordination of ministers: 114*

<u>Ordo senioritatis</u>: 40

Oreads: 90

Oreb: 18, 73, 144, 3

Orestano, F.: 6

<u>Orestes</u> (Euripides): 70

Orestes: 56, 60, 90, 92

Orestis aemule: 73

<u>Orfeo</u> (Politian): 29

Orford, Horace Walpole, 4th Earl of: 44

Organ (musical instrument, M and): 40, 44, 121*

Organic whole, Warton's treatment of M's works as one: 33

Organization: 51

Orgel, Stephen: 29, 39*, 64, 21. On court masque: 104. On drama in Mask: 104

Orgies: of <u>Comus</u>: 143. Of Chemos: 143

Orgilia: 49, 73

Orgonte: 123. See also: Gratiani

Oriana: 44, 121

Oriel College, Oxford: 40, 44, 45

Oriental languages: 40, 3

Orientus of Auch: 36. _Commonitorium_: 36

Oriet, Didier(t)e: 64. Works: _Esther_: 74; _Susanne_: 74

Origen: 5, 18, 9, 15, 24, 30, 40, 41, 44, 57, 60, 65, 66, 68, 69, 70, 73, 74, 77, 79, 86, 100, 102, 112, 107*, 113, 114, 123, 125, 128, 142, 144, 3, 32, 36*, 38, 39, 82, 93*, 99, 64. Accomodation, Adam's sin is mankind's, "all in all": 107. Angels: achieve rank through merit, concerned with men's affairs, created before the world, feast with men, not ranked hierarchically: 107. Azazel, Beelzebub, Belial: 107. Character of: 107. Christ: as judge, as 2nd Adam, dies body and soul: 107. Clement of Alexandria his teacher: 107. Demons: power of, achieve rank through merit, change shape at will, eventually pardoned, lose power at Christ's coming, powerless against good men, ruled through fear by the Son, take on animal bodies; demonic suggestion: 107. Evil nonexistent until thought becomes action: 107. Fall multiple: 107. Father and Son not of same essence; father martyred: 107. Generation begins with Wisdom: 107. God: did not make demons, inaudible, permits evil, his foreknowledge does not influence future events, uses demons to tempt and punish men: 107

Origen (continued): Gods of nations are demons: 107. Good spirits and men: 107. Greek gods as demons: 107. Gregory Thaumaturgus his most famous pupil: 107. Heaven: four ways of conceiving, how developed, an intellectual state, jeweled, strictures against, Platonic: 107. Hell: fires curative rather than punitive, physical, psychological: 107. Heresies: importance of, listed by St. Jerome, held in common with M: 107. Hippolytus of Rome, thought to have written the works: 107. Life and works: 107. Literary output: 107. Logos: invisible, speaks to pagans: 107. Mammon: 107. Man: but little lower than angels, created to manifest God's goodness: 107. Matter: everything of one, ex Deo, holy, indestructible, invisible and formless: 107. M, influence upon: 107. Mutual hypostatic union: 107.

Not a millinarian: 107. Pantaenus, may have studied under: 107. Prov. VIII interpreted: 107. Reason is choice: 107. Representative: of a climate of opinion, of early Christian thought: 107. Rule(s): of judgment, for interpreting Scripture: 107. Satan: as light, author of evil, falls through pride, in serpent, his glory turned to dust, his eminence in Heaven, thinks his power his own: 107. Self mutilation: 107. Sleep of the soul: 107. Son: metaphysical begetting, anointed through merit, as mediator before Fall, anointing the 2nd State of his development, a second God: 107. Spirit: 107. Studied with Plotinus under Ammanius Saccas: 107. Theanthropos: 107.

Theologian: importance as, respects, theological terms invented by: 107. Traducianism, uncertain about: 107. Universe, cyclic: 107. Virtue, cloistered: 107. Word feminine: 107. World: training school for virtue, use of Word: 107. Writings available to M, M influenced by, why M drawn to, M cites Origen as lay preacher: 107. Origen's knife: 107. Works: _De principiis_ and _Contra Celsum_ remarkable for organization: 107; _De Principiis_: 74; _Contra Celsum_: 60, 74, 107, 36; _Homilies on Genisi_: 36; _On Principles_: 36; _Peri Archon_: 74; _In Ezech_.: 77; _Enarrationes in Job_: 74; _Homiliae in Jesu Nave_: 74; "Homilia XIV, item de Balaam": 74; _In Exodum, Homilia VI_: 74; _In Job_: 74*; "Selecta in Job": 74

Origenes: 7, 88. Origenism: 93

Origin of evil: 83

Origin of the question: 51

Original Letters and Papers...to Oliver Cromwell (ed. Nickolls): 44

Original Sin: 9*, 51, 113, 71, 93. Doctrine of not in SA: 113. See also: Depravity; Fall; Self-deification; Sin, original

Originality: 70, 146. Of M's thought: 113. The Richardsons on, and imagination: 88. Richardsons on, as opposed to authority: 88. Warburton on: 88. Newton's lack of, his respect for M's: 88. Todd's ideal of: 88. Of opinion, lack of, in Todd: 88

Origines Juridiciales: 45

Origins of Modern Science (Butterfield): 134

Origo mundi: 65

Oriokh: 41

Orion: 19, 73, 89, 3. Constellations of: 89. Great nebula in: 89

Orithyia: 90

Orkney Islands (Orcades): 19, 44. Orkneys: 3

Orlando Furioso: 70, 118, 135, 26. Trans. by Harington: 135. See also: Ariosto

Orlando: 123. See also: Ariosto; Boiardo

Orleans: 49. Gaston Jean Baptiste, Duke of: 44, 91

Ormerod, George: 44, 45

Ormond(e): Earl of: 103. George Butler, Earl of: 44. James Arthur Norman Butler, Marquis and 2nd Duke of: 44, 45, 116. James Butler, 15th Earl and Marquis of Bath (1610-88): 55

Ormonde, Marquis of, Report on Manuscripts of: 44

Ormus: 19*, 49, 73. See also: Balsara

Ormuz and Amurath: 133

Ormuz: 150

Ormuzd: 71

Ornithoparcus, Andreas: 40

Ornstein, Robert: 93

Orontes River: 19, 49, 144. See also: Antioch; Daphne; Hamath

Orosius: 3, 38, 82. Paulus: 93

Orpheus: 1, 40, 44, 51, 57, 60, 70, 73, 79, 90*, 103, 112, 121*, 128, 144, 3, 11, 32, 46, 72*, 88, 106, 130.; see also: David and Orpheus. Orphic poetry: 73. *Hymn to Pan*: 106; see also: David and Orpheus. Orphic societies: 92. *Orphic Hymns*: 90*

Orphism: 48

Orsino, Fabio: 64

Ortega y Gasset, José: 60

Ortelius, Abraham: 1, 19*, 24, 40, 73, 128, 144*, 32. Galicia, Magellan, Sabrina, Mona, Belerium, Namancos, Pelorus, Palestine, Imaus, Arabia, Serbonian Bog, Abyssinia: 144. Maps and history, merits of, and places compared with Elen, grave of Daphne: 144. Works: *Theatre of the World*: 144; *Atlas*: 102

Orten, Mr.: 40

Orthodoxy: 113. M's: 141. M's rejection of: 113

Orthoepia Anglicana (Daines): 135

Orthography in Shakespeare and Elizabethan Drama (Partridge): 135

Orthography: 40

Orton: H.: 68. John: 44

Orus: 73

Orvell (Orwell): Edward: 44

Orwell, George: 15, 34, 72

Os novissimos do homem: 65

Osbaston: Elizabeth: see Newman, Elizabeth. Henry: 45

Osbert, King of Eng.: 44

Osboldston, Mr.: 44

Osborn(e): Francis: 54*, 114, 142, 93; *The Works*: 142. James M.: 44, 81. Louise B.: 45. Dorothy, The Letters of: 45. L. B.: 23. Francis: 38. John: 147; *An Inditement against Tythes*: 147. Richard: 147; works: a caustic plea in *The Independent's Loyalty*: 147; satirizes the army leaders in *Independency Stript and Whipt*: 147. Thomas: 40, 88

Osburga: 3

Osee: 60

Osgood: Charles Grosvenor: 19, 44, 56, 63, 77, 79, 110, 129, 141, 144, 143, 148; works: *The Classical Mythology of M's English Poems*: 57, 60; *The Voice of England*: 82; *The Works of Edmund Spenser*: *Minor Poems*: 60. S.: 16

Osiander: Andreas: 93. Lucas: 93

Osiris: 1, 19, 73, 90, 139, 144, 3, 72. Myth: 60

Oslac: 3

Osorius, Hieronymus: 123

Ossa: 2, 49. See also: Pelion

Ossian: 58, 89, 88

Ostend: 44, 49

Ostrowski-Sachs, Margarete: 141

Oswestre (Maserfield): 49

Oswi: 3

Otanes: 73

Otford (Ottanford): 49

Otfried (Otfrid of Weissenburg); 64. Evangelienbuch: 74, 36

Othello: 134, 139, 136, 88

Othello: 70, 118, 92

Othniel: 68

Otho, Prince of Saxony: 44, 64

Otis, James: 115

Ottley, R. L.: 68

Otto: Ottonus (Hottonus): 73. Prince of Hesse: 44. Of Freising, Bp. (Ottonem Frinsingensem): 73, 93. Carl: 60

Ottoman Empire: 31. Ottomans: 3. Ottoman tyrant: 44

Otway: 132. F.: 58. Thomas: 27, 58, 117

Oudin, César: 40

Oughtred, William: 10

Ouglitts (Ouglets): 49

Oulton: Richard (pr.): 44, 55. W. C.: 58

"Our Lives are Albums" (attr. to M): 44

Our Modern Demagogue's Modesty and Honesty: 116

Ouse (Oose, Usa) River: 44, 49, 73, 3

Ouseley, T. J.: 16

Ousia: 93

Ousley: 121

Oustzilma: 49

Out-cryes of oppressed Commons (Lilburne and Overton): 147

Outcry of the London Prentices: 44

Outlawry: 45

Outler, Albert C.: 81

Outline: 51. Of PL, of tragedies: 50

Outside shell of the world: 128

Overall, Bp. John of Norwich: 116, 32

Overbury: Sir Nicholas: 29. Sir Thomas: 40, 128, 64, 137

Overey, Edward: 44

Overman, Thomas: 45

Oversoul: 47

Overton, Richard: 103

Overton: 94. Col.: 120. Henry (bks., 1629-48): 91. Richard: 9*, 44*, 103, 113*, 114, 147*, 38, 71, 91, 93; writer: 147; considers secular freedom: 147; works: Arraignment of Mr. Persecution (on censorship in, plea for toleration of Catholics, elaborates on toleration principles, shows his hatred of tithe-gathering): 147; A Defiance Against All Arbitrary Usurpations (estimates value of liberty of the press, shows his development as a political theorist): 147; Mans Mortallitie (is accused of heresy for having written): 147; An Alarum To the House of Lords (plea for political liberty): 147; A Sacred Synodicall Decretall (characterizes the Presbyterians): 147; Martins Eccho (defends liberty in): 147; An Arrow Against All Tyrants (writes of his imprisonment): 147. Gen. Robert: 44, 73, 38, 93, 137

Ovid, Publius Ovidius Naso: 1, 2, 4, 6, 8, 15*, 18, 19, 20*, 23, 27, 29, 40*, 44*, 56*, 57, 59, 60, 68, 69, 70, 73, 81, 87, 89, 90*, 103, 108, 118, 120, 121, 111, 122, 123, 127, 128, 132, 133, 136, 139, 141, 142, 144, 145, 3, 14, 26, 32, 36, 39, 53, 62, 72, 88, 93, 97, 64*, 101, 106, 109, 130, 137, 146*, 149, 148, 150, 117*, 140, 21*, 13, 25. Definition of chaos in: 89. translations of: 58. Influence on M: 104. Works: Metamorphoses: 57, 74, 36, 46; XV Books of P. Ovidius Naso, Metamorphoses (trans. Arthur Golding, 1587): 74; Metamorphoses (trans. George Sandys, 1632): 74

Owen: Mr.: 51. Mrs.: 44. David: 60; works: Anti-Pareus: 60; Puritano-Jesuitismus: 60. E.: 128. Galyn: 88. Goronwy: 117. Rev. John: 9, 40, 44, 59, 114, 116, 120, 22, 32, 38*, 71, 93. John, Great Skeptical Dramas: 74. Rev. Josiah: 44. Thomas: 44. Wilfred: 86

Owiga: 49

Owst, Gerald R.: 68, 93

Oxen (juniors): 40

Oxenbridge: Daniel: 44. John: 44

Oxenden, Henry: 64. *Jobus Triumphans*: 74

Oxenstiern, Count: 103

Oxenstierna: 7

Oxford (Salter): 45

Oxford and Cambridge Miscellany (ed. Fenton): 44

Oxford and Cambridge Review: 44

Oxford Aulicus: 147

Oxford Bibliographical Society: 44

Oxford Edition of M's Works: 44

Oxford English Dictionary (*OED*): 1, 40, 44, 150

Oxford Gazette: 103

Oxford Historical Society: 45. *Publications*: 44

Oxford Justices: 45

Oxford Movement: 87

Oxford Reformers (Seebohm): 3

Oxford: 40, 44*, 45*, 49, 51, 103, 112, 3, 94, 97; see also: Articles of Oxford. Castle: 45

Oxford Univ.: 29, 40, 44*, 45*, 51, 58*, 103*, 113, 21. Convocation and Decree: 116. M's opinion of: 30. M popular at: 58. Miniature M: 70. Medicine taught at: 16. Univ. Press: 112. University Library: 40

Oxford, "Gentlemen of," *New Version of PL*: 58. PL in prose: 58. Supposed author of *The State of Innocence*: 88. Author equals: Semicolon: 88; George Smith Green: 88

Oxford, John (Edward) Harley, Earl of: 44

Oxford, Survey of the Antiquities of: 45*

Oxford, The Parliamentary History of the County of: 45

Oxford, The Siege of: 45

Oxfordshire: 44*, 45*, 49, 103. Assessment Rolls: 45. Record Society: 45. *The Natural History of*: 45. *The Victoria County, History of*: 45. Visitation of: 45*

Oxinden: Henry: 40. James: 40

"Oxonian": 44

Oxus: 19, 49, 73. River: 144. See also: Sogdiana

-P-

P., J.: 116, 44. See also: J. Phillips

P., R.: 116

P., T. (pr.): 44. Error for "T. C.": 91. Thomas Power: 117

P., W.: 116

Pacifism: 141

Paciuolo, Luca: 40

Pacius: 40

Packer Collegiate Institute, Brooklyn: 44

Packer: Mr.: 44. John: 45. Philip: 44

Packington, Lady Dorothy: 54

Pacorus, King: 19

Padan-Aram: 49, 73, 143

Padan-Aran: 144

Padelford, Frederic M., "Robert Aylett": 74, 83, 122

Padiglione, C.: 6

Padlachia: 49

Padua, Marsiglio: 55

Padua: 40, 44. Medical School of: 16. Univ. of: 44

Paean: 73

Paedobaptism: 71

Paeninas Alpes: 73

Pafort, Eloise: 40

Pagan and Christian Creeds: 71

Pagan(s): 27, 51. Mythology: 70. Divinities: 19. Cosmology: 121. Definition of: 71. Renaissance: 71. Learning, M's attitude toward: 137. M on beauties of pagan world: 61. Paganism: 144*; idolatry: 144*; decline of: 144; M's catalog of: 144; source of catalog in PL: 144;

part of literary background: 144*; Egyptian, Greek and Roman: 144*; Gentile: 144*

Paganini, Nicolò: 39

Page: Mr.: 44. B. S.: 79. D. L.: 64. Graland: 44, 45. John (T.): 44, 45. R. (engraver, M portrait): 44. Thomas Nelson: 111

Pageant: 70. Pageantry: 51

Pagel, W.: 34

Paget: John: 9. Margery Goldsmith: 44. Dr. Nathan: 7, 16, 28, 44, 63, 84, 86, 103, 128, 150, 55, 94. Thomas: 44

Pagitt, Ephraim (1575-1647): 7, 9, 44, 103, 114, 147, 93, 101, 55. Heresiography (a pamphlet on M's heresy): 91; 147

Pagliano, Duke of: 44

Pagnine's Hebrew Lexicon: 42

Pagnini, Luca Antonio: 123

Pagnino, Santi: 40

Pagninus: 41

Pain, Philip: 115. Daily Meditations: 115

Pain: 2

Paine: J.: 97. Robert Treat: 115; works: Adams and Liberty: 115; The Works, in Verse and Prose, of the Late Robert Treat Paine: 115. Thomas (pr., bks., 1630-49): 44, 60, 71, 91, 115, 55; works: The Age of Reason: 115; Common Sense: 115

Painting: 40, 70. The Richardsons on, music and poetry: 88. And poetry, Dryden and Peck on: 88. Revolt of angels in: 123. Ancient, studied by Warton: 88. M's references to: 137. Painter's point of view in the artistic analyses of the Richardsons: 88. Portrait is painter's attitude of the same: 88

Palace Yard, London: 103

Palaemon: 90

Palaeography, Genealogy, and Topography: 45

Palaephatus, De Fabulis: 74

Palamabron: 146, 25*. See also: Milton, John

Palatine: 49. Mount: 73. Count: 73. Palatinate: 49, 103. Palatine Catechism: see Heidelberg Catechism

Palavicini de Saluces, Count: 44

Paleario, Aonio (Palearius, Aonius): 65, 55

Palermitana, La: 65

Pales: 1, 73, 90

Palestine (Philistia): 19, 44, 49, 144, 3, 32. Setting of: 119. See also: Philistines

Palestrina, Giovanni da: 87

Paley, William: 93, 13

Palfreyman, Thomas: 93

Palgrave, Francis T.: 87, 128, 36

Palingenius, Marcellus: 65. Zodiac of Life: 46

Palisca, Claude: 39

Palissy, Bernard: 10

Palke, John: 40

Pall Mall, London: 44, 103

Palladian oil: 73, 3

Palladio: 27. Andrea: 39

Palladium: 73

Palladius, Rutilius: 44, 3, 32

Pallas (Titan): 2

Pallas: 89, 90; see also: Minerva. Athena: 2, 56, 73

Pallavicine, Mr.: 44

Pallavicino: 1, 88

Palm: Sunday: 72. Tree(s): 144. Tree (sign), London: 44

Palma: 49. See also: Canaries

Palmer (Spenser): 3

Palmer: Mr.: see Castlemain. A. H.: 97. A. S.: 92. Elihu: 115; Principles of Nature, Or a Development of the Moral Causes of Happiness and Misery Among the Human Species: 115. G. H.: 58. Sir Geoffrey, Attorney General: 44. Henrietta R.: 93. Herbert (1601-47): 9, 10, 30, 44, 59, 103, 120, 147, 55; attacks M's heresy: 147; works: Glass of God's Providence: 91; justifies the war in Scripture and Reason: 147; supports

Paradeisspiel aus Vordenberg: 65

Paradice Regain'd (anonymous): 58

Paradice, Alice: 44

Paradine: Mary: 45. Thomas: 44, 45

Paradis perdu, Le: 65

Paradise: 24, 31, 50*, 49, 70*, 81*, 83, 89, 102, 103, 112, 111*, 132, 141, 143, 144*, 3, 72*. As whole earth: 32. Destruction of: 32. Description and extent: 32, 87. And celestial paradise: 32. First and final: 101. Interior reality: 101. True paradise within: 143, 93, 96. Riches, fleeting joys, the reality of: 143. A myth: 142. Significance of in PL: 132. Image of in world mythology: 118. Relation of earthly to Heavenly: 102. Location of: 32*; after deluge: 101. Garden in Eden as: 32. Symbolic interpretation of: 32*. Continued existence of: 32. Legends of: 32. Symbolized by university: 32 See also: Heaven; Tree of Knowledge; Tree of Life; Adam and Eve; Eve; Rivers of paradise; Garden; Guards; Eden; Adam and PL

"Paradise of Bachelors, the": 98

Paradise of Fools: 76, 39, 103, 111, 72, 117, 80. Locality of: 89. See also: Limbo

Paradise Lost. The following entries are partial, yet representative. Readers should consult individual topics throughout the Index for particular subjects and references. See also: Milton, John, Works

Paradise Lost (themes and topics). Ambition: 144. Ascent: 72*. Choice: 72*; in Book IX: 104. Concept of Man: 104; man's inherent weakness and potential greatness: 80. Concept of Nature: 104. Curiosity: 114*. Creation: 81*, 148; of world: 143; of Heavens and earth: 89. Death: 104. Divine giving: 104. Discipline and liberty: 134. Glory: 52. Hero: 129, 134, 146; M as hero of PL: 113; "New hero": 72*. Hierarchy of values: 143. Human condition: 52. Joy: 104. Jungian myth: 60. Knowledge, purpose of: 80. Leadership principle in PL: 25. Loss: 104. Making of a greater man: 83. Matter as a mode of spirit: 13. Melancholy: 144*. Mind over emotions essential: 80. Nonentities, final dissolution of: 80. Presentation of Evil: 52. Platonic Idea: 107. Recoil: 72*. Redemption: 104. Rule of judgment: 107. Scala naturae: 144; chain of being: 52, 107, 134. Self-indictment of moral and intellectual irresponsibility: 80. Spiritual regeneration: 104, 134. Temperance: 144. Tutelage: 72*. Utopian ventures, rejection of: 80. Vain philosophy: 114*. Vain wisdom and false philosophy: 80. World is training school for virtue: 107. Wrath: 104

Paradise Lost (as a poem, structure and poetics). Epic tradition: 25, 11, 129*; as anti-epic: 25; compared with ancient and Renaissance epics: 83; cosmological epic: 89; epic catalogues: 146; radiates from epic notion: 149*; contained epic: 72. Structure: 11*, 46*, 53*, 85, 25, 72*, 146, 55; as logical structure: 52; metaphorical structure: 60; idea of: 55*; irony of structure and style: 60; structural patterns: 104*; defective in plan: 146; plan and arrangement: 143, 13; early plans for: 50, 25; aesthetic pattern: 148; artistic construction of: 113; perfection in form: 146, 143. Sublimity of: 87, 146; sculpturesque quality: 146; tragic dimensions: 25; grandeur of: 146; harmony of: 146; vastness of scale: 89, 143; splendid works of art admired: 87; simplicity of: 146; merits: 146. Subject (theme): 146, 13; as a "prelude poem": 25; autobiographical passages: 55; impossible material for poetry: 149; difficulties of subject: 146; central purpose for writing: 80, 143; as radical strategy: 53*; related to M's prose: 11*; as prayer and as pastoral: 11; a psychological camera obscura: 136; as mimesis of the argument: 60; nature of parallels with De Doctrina: 63; unconscious meaning of: 63; "Two Episodes" anticipate the central problem: 80; subject real and nominal: 102; argument: 67; crisis: 101; moral of: 146; ethical signficance: 129*; subject matter reflected in the sonnets: 87. Imagery: 8*

(as a poem, structure and poetics--continued) Structural system of: 96*. Preface: 25. Muse: 146. Prologues: 146; function of: 81; rhetorical functions: 60. Invocations: 148, 53*; epic: 129. Title: 146. 10 book division, importance of: 81. Verse paragraphs: 101. Comparisons: 129. Anticapatory devices: 101. Division of time: 143*. 3 movements of: 143. Cosmic scenes and views: 87. Key words: 104. Narratives in: 104. Scenario: 145. Book I summarized: 80; contextual relations between I and II: 80. Books XI and XII: 104, 53*, 146; Lazarhouse: 85; links with V: 104; 3 voices in XI: 104; key words of XII: 104; influence

nature: 32. M's conception of: 106*. As Garden: 79. And pagan nature: 106. Mount of Paradise: 32. And the forbidden fruit: 106. Ruin of: 32

Paradise Lost (and Eve). Eve: 85, 146*. Her dream: 146; Eve and Satan as toad: 80. Narcissism: 146. Sin: 80; temptation: 134, 146; Fall: 148. Lament: 146. Treated with moral severity: 146. Her jealousy: 80. Her confession to Adam: 126. Her sin and Adam's interpreted: 80. Her plight compared with Dalila's: 80. Reproof of: 80. See especially: Eve

Paradise Lost (and God). God: 81*, 87. Kingdom of, M's early expectations: 80. And light: 107. His design: 72*; providence and plan for man: 80. Father and Son not same essence: 107. Justification of God in PL: 72*. A "school divine": 146*. Creates good from evil: 107; knows evil, permits evil: 107. Attributes of, invisible, His foreknowledge does not influence future events, His holy rest: 107. Commands Son to create: 107; Logos is God's voice: 107. Relationship to man in PL: 87

Paradise Lost (and Heaven). Heaven: 146. Council in: 148. Empyrian: 89. War in: 79, 81, 80, 53*, 146*. Golden ladder, method of communication between Heaven and New Universe: 89; the passage down to Paradise: 89. See especially: Heaven

Paradise Lost (and Hell). Hell: 89, 81*, 148, 146*. External to world: 107. Location of: 102. Pandemonium: 87, 80, 146; Utopian philosophy: 80; leaders in: 80; panic, its effects: 80. Debate in: 80, 148. Communication between Hell and New Universe: 89. The viaduct from Hell: 89. Chaos, as "norm of reference": 53*. Limbo: 81; condemned souls guilty of errors of innocence: 80. Paradise of Fools: 80, 146

Paradise Lost (Satan). Satan: 79, 81*, 126, 85, 146*, 137, 148, 25*, 134*. As hero: 146; democratic statesman: 80; allegorical figure: 134; as "dictator type": 134; light: 107. Altercation with other angels: 80. Grandeur of: 146; humanity of: 146. Compared with: God: 146; Bonaparte: 146; Prometheus: 146. Falls through pride: 107, 25; thinks his power his own: 107. Absurdity of: 134. Pre-eminence in Heaven: 107. Identifies Son from the first: 80. Rebels at time of metaphorical begetting of Son: 107. Attitude and Fall compared with Adam's: 107. Explusion from Heaven: 80, 25; his revolt: 148. His aim: 13. His morality: 146. Disobedience compared with Adam and Eve's: 134. Directed to Paradise by Uriel: 80.

(Satan--continued) On Mt. Niphates: 146. As toad at Eve's ear: 80. Flees from Gabriel: 80. Doomed on divine scales: 80; reads celestial sign: 80. His journey: 25; his metamorphosis: 146. His glory turned to dust: 107. His vision: 53. Reaction to his and Adam's "falls": 80. Tempts Christ in hope of finding human imperfections in the Son of God: 80. Satan not here: 137. Why Satan could not have been made completely contemptible: 137*. Is the devil an ass?: 137. His use of liturgy: 126. Satan in illustrations: 87

Paradise Lost (criticism, effect and influence). PL viewed as divine poem, blasphemous poem: 146. Out of date: 83. Inspirations equalled only by Shakespeare: 136*. Critics on "crisis": 134. Religious criticism: 107. Importance of sound interpretation: 83; meaning often misunderstood: 83. Effect on 17th c. mind: 87. Model for Miltonic religious epics: 87. And Montgomery's "A Vision of Heaven": 87. PL in 18th c.: 55. 18th c. interpretations: 83. Early American reputation: 55. The Romantics: 146; Romantic interpretations: 83. The Victorians: 83; influence on 19th c. artists: 87; early 19th c. view of: 87; late-Victorian change in attitude toward: 87*; imitations of in 19th c.: 87; decline in popularity of: 87. Early 20th c. interpretations: 83; in 20th c. generally: 55; modern criticism: 32; modern attitude: 86*; decline of interest in: 87; review of criticism: 80.

Paradise Lost (criticism, effect and influence--continued). Effect of PL on Macaulay: 87; Eng. thought: 87; on laboring classes: 87; of religious content on reading public: 87. Bagehot on realism of Satanic council scene: 87; on "begat" passage: 87. John Dennis on sublimity of PL: 87. Natural sublime in: 87. Hopkins on counterpoint in verses of: 87. Goethe's Faust and PL: 87. And Blake's Jerusalem: 25*. Huxley's use of: 87. Tennyson's knowledge and recitations of PL: 87. Once favorite reading of Darwin: 87. Influence on theology and theodicy: 87

Paradise Lost (miscellaneous, as a poem). Treatment of heroic: 148. Supernatural action: 148. No principal character: 146. Obscene poem: 146. Perspective in: 146. As reference: 53*. Homologation: 53.

Mythology in: 53; mythical elements: 46. In relation to Comus: 11. In relation to PR: 25; companion piece to: 80. In relation to SA: 113, 11; Samson compared with Adam: 80; his denunciation of Dalila compared with Adam's of Eve: 80. Contextual relationships among the 3 major poems: 80. Unification of component parts of 3 major poems: 80. PL, PR, SA as a trilogy: 80. Use of history in: 11; PL and history: 144; of the world: 148; 6 ages of history in: 101; historical process in: 101*. Fable and characters: 87. Anticipation of PL in M's early works: 113. Largely a political poem: 113. As history of an Ubermensch: 87

Paradise Lost (miscellaneous). PL and its age: 146; M's culture: 144. Defense of: 146. Man but little lower than angels: 107. Matter, nature of: 107. Methexis: 72*. Philosophical interest in poem analyzed: 80. M's use of: Arabia, Bel, Babel, Egyptian gods, pyramids, Nyseian Isle, Palestine, winds, serpents, cranes, pygmies, fig tree, vulture's flight, Jeraboam's idolatry, Serbonian Bog: 144. Role of PL in Miltonic research: 141. Episodes exemplify man's obligation to fight evil: 80. PL condemned: 87. Judgment scene in Book X: 104. Vision of Book XI: 104. Relation of visions and narrative in Books XI and XII: 53*. Illustrations to PL: 97*. Implication in PL for modern man: 80

Paradise Lost (and critics of/on). Addison: 130*. Bush, Macaulay, Marvell, Saurat, Shelley, Toland: 130. Eliot, Hanford, Lewis, Raleigh, Richardsons, Stoll, Tillyard, Williams: 130*. Browning, Elizabeth: 87. Coleridge: 130. DeQuincey: 87. Harrison, Frederic: 87. Johnson: 130*. Keightley: 87. Landor: 87, 130. Pattison: 87

Paradise Lost (publications, editions, text, reception). Date: 55. 1667 and 1674 editions: 104. Publication: 55, 146. Payment: 13. Reception: 55. Presentation copy: 44. Task to read: 146. Phillips' account: 55. Ellwood's account: 55. Early editions and translations: 55. Preface: 55. 18th c. editions: 55. Sorelli's translation: 37. Blake's, Fuseli's, and Martin's illustrations: 87. 2nd edition, prized by Tennyson: 87. M's satisfaction with PL: 50. Disillusionment: 80

Paradise Lost (French trans. by St. Maur): 88.

PL, A Preface to (C. S. Lewis): 136

Paradise Lost and the 17th Century Reader (Rajan): 134

Paradise Lost and Its Critics (Waldock): 134, 139, 136

Paradise Lost and Paradise Regained by the Wonderful Works in God: 117

Paradise Lost in Our Time (Bush): 83, 139

Paradise Lost, Explanatory Remarks on: 45

Paradise Regained: The following entries are partial, yet representative. Readers should consult individual topics throughout the Index for particular subjects and references.

Paradise Regained (and religion, theology, the Bible, and the Church). Baptism: 80, 25. Ecclesiastical details: 114. Efficacy of Christian ideals: 80. Freedom of dogma: 113. Radical theology: 25. Reflects Protestant movement in Eng. in 1630's and 1640's: 80. Spiritual significance of man: 80. Holkham Bible: 143. Book of Job: 146. "Word" in: 72*. Projects restoration of Paradise: 80. Images of Christ and Satan: 52. Son of God, concept of: 81. Christ's victory: 143. Motivation of Satan: 99*. Demons lose power at Christ's coming: 107. Motivation of God: 99; God's designs: 72. Motivation of Christ: 99. Belial: 85. Rome and Parthia: 85. Andrew and Simon: 85

Paradise Regained (and the Son). Nature and office of the Son: 148. His childhood: 107. Baptized: 80. Adam equated with: 99. His temptation and Samson's compared: 80. In the wilderness: 80. Interest in spiritual uplift: 80. Fortified against all temptations: 80. Tempted as a man: 99*. Fasting of: 99. Length of temptation: 99. Accused by Satan of ignorance of the world: 80. Denounces the Romans: 80. Faith in His divine origin challenged by Satan: 80. Rejects personal glory: 80. Resists Satan's attempts at seduction and reasserts original purpose: 80. Shows no human weakness: 80. Satan tempts Him with food: 80. Rejects glory of war: 80. His victory: 143, 101. Acknowledged divine at conclusion of temptation: 142, 99

Paradise Regained (and Satan). Degenerate in PR: 87. Disguise of:

99. His rhetoric, character, Socinianism: 146; portrayed as skeptical Socinian: 13. Attends Christ's baptism: 80

Paradise Regained (and temptation). Temptation(s): 47, 125*, 46, 80, 146, 148*, 25. Number and order of: 99*, 119. Precedents for: 101; use of the tradition: 99. God's purpose in temptation: 85. Hunger as thematic link: 85. Encounter with Satan in wilderness: 80, 93; wild beast and wilderness: 99. Satan accuses Christ of ignorance of the world: 80; challenges Christ's faith in His divine origin: 80. Satan's challenges symbolize evil threatening society: 80. By violence: 99; with reckless despair: 80. Summarized: 80. Of the world, flesh, and devil (triple equation): 99*. Temptations of the 1st and 3rd days: distrust and presumption: 85.

(temptation--continued) Of bread (dic ut lapides): 99*; of appetite: 125; banquet: 146. Of the kingdoms (regna omni mundi): 99*; glory of war, knowledge: 80, 146; of Athens: 148. Temptations of the 2nd day, knowledge: 85*. Temptations of pleasure, riches, power: 85*, 80. Violent storm, Satan's attempt to frighten Christ: 80, 85. Of the tower (mitte te deorsum): 99*; dares Christ to defy natural laws: 80; the pinnacle: 125, 101, 25. Irony in temptations: 101. Fails to find human weakness in Christ: 80. Renunciation of: 101

Paradise Regained (construction). Ellwood's and Phillips' accounts: 55. Execution of superior to PL: 13. Written at Chalfont St. Giles: 87. Biographical element in: 87

Paradise Regained (general). M's admiration for: 146. Offensiveness of: 146; perfection of: 146. Defense of: 146. Quoted by Sir Walter Raleigh: 87. Hopkins' interest in: 87. Sources: 46, 55; Italian influence: 55; romance elements: 46

Paradise Regained (in relation to). Blake's Milton and Jerusalem: 25. SA: 11, 25. PL: 129, 11, 25; sequel to PL: 85; companion piece to PL: 80; emphasis compared with that of PL: 85. Trilogy of M's 3 major poems: 80

Paradise Regained (structure and poetry of). Structure and poetry of: 46, 72*, 146, 148. Epic tradition: 25; brief epic: 88, 72. Proem: 25. Outline: 55. Thematic structure: 85. Structural functions of rituals and liturgical sections (Baptism, use of Canticles, lament and prayer of Apostles, Mary's meditation, final anthem of angels, relation to Nicene Creed, similarity to canticles of praise, references and suggestions to liturgy): 126. Panoramas: 87. Dramatic element: 25; drama of knowledge: 52. Rhetoric: 72*. Meditative voice in: 81. Poetry of: 146. Style: 81*. Stances: 57*. Recoil in: 72. Typology: 25. Descriptions: 146. Dialectic: 72*. Perspectives: 25. Interiority: 25. Imagery: 8*. Conclusion: 46, 146

Paradise Regained (themes and various topics). Theme of PR: 29, 113, 46; aims summarized: 80. Presents problems facing modern man: 80. Presents prerequisites for a nearly ideal modern society: 80. M regards intellectual confusion as menace to society: 80. Stoicism in: 101. Romantic myth: 146. As source for Miltonic religious epics: 87; imitation of cosmic scenes: 87. Universe of PR: grandeur and spaciousness: 87. Rejection of classics: 25. Theme of return: 25. "Bread" in: 72*. Dreams in: 72. Judgements: 72. Magnaminity: 72. Methexis in: 72*. "New Hero" of: 72*. A withdrawal: 143. And history: 11. Illustrations to: 97*

Paradise Regained (anonymous): 58

Paradise Regained: the Tradition and the Poem (Elizabeth Pope): 139

"Paradise within thee": 83

Paradiso (Dante): 70, 3

Paradiso Perso, Il: 88, 117

Paradisus Amissus (Hogg): 94

Paradisus, sive Nuptiae: 65

Paradox: 114*, 96, 109*. Of humility, of fortunate Fall: 93

Paraenetick for...Christian Liberty: 9, 27

Parallax: 89. Bessel stellar parallax: 89. Of alpha centauri: 89. Solar: 89

Parallelism: 63, 98. Parallelisms: 13; literary, used by Bentley for textual reconstruction: 88

Parallels, literary, untrustworthy: 41

Paraphrase of St. Paul's Epistles: 78

Paraphrase: 20

Parcae: 73

Parcall, James: 45

Pardee, Benjamin: 115. Two Orations, and Poetry on Different Subjects: 115

Pardon (M's): 44. Prayer of: 123

Pardon (Oblivion), Act of: 44

Parentage (M's): 30. See also: Milton, John, Life

Parentheses: 98. Parenthetical constructions in M's works, Pearce on: 88

Parergon: 144

Pareus (Paraeus): 1, 24*, 30, 44, 54, 128, 3, 72, 92. In S. Matthaei Evangelium: 74. David: 50, 60, 73, 123, 37, 44, 67, 68, 77, 22, 32, 38, 82, 99*, 25. Johannes Philippus: 40. Phillip: 10, 41, 60, 70

Parey, Ambrose: 113

Parham, co. Suffolk: 44, 45

Parifioli, Lorenzo: 65

Parigi, Alfonso: 29

Paris (Priam's son): 90, 92. Judgement of: 122, 123

Paris: Mr.: 58. Gaston, Trois Versions Rimées de l'Evangile de Nicodème: 74; see also: Coutances, André de. Joane: see Cotton, Joane. Matthew: 73, 93

Paris: 44, 49, 56, 103, 3. M in: 44. Medical school of: 16. Parliament of: 44

Parish: clerk: 40. Clergy: 51. Minister: 51. Register Society: 44; Publications of the: 45

Parish: Elijah: 115; An Eulogy on John Hubbard: 115. John E.: 37, 60, 123, 93, 101; "Unrecognized Pun in Paradise Regained": 74

Parison or auditory balance: 118

Pariukh: 41

Parival, Jean Nicholas de, History of This Iron Age (trans. by Harris): 44

Park: T.: 58, 97; sonnets of: 58. Thomas: 91

"Park" (St. James?): 44

Parke-Bernet Galleries: 44

Parker Chronicle: 36

Parker Society Publications: 40

Parker: Mr.: 44. Bp.: 88. B.: 58. Henry: 9, 44, 60, 144, 147, 32, 93; expresses his view on power of kings: 147; Observation upon some of his Majesties late Answers: 147. James: 20. John: 44, 91. Martin: 93. Matthew: 40. Peter (pr.): 44, 103. R. W.: 114. Bp. Samuel (1640-88): 16, 40, 44*, 116, 142, 145, 91; works: A Free and Impartial Censure of the Platonick Philosophie: 142; Reproof: 91. T. H. L., on Calvin's preaching: 143. T. M., on religion and politics: 143. Theodore: 44. Thomas: 45. William: 44, 45. William Riley: 4, 6, 9*, 20, 27, 40, 44*, 52, 59*, 60, 66, 68*, 84, 86, 102, 116, 123, 126, 133, 144, 143, 53, 62, 85, 93, 64, 101, 106, 137*, 148*, 21*; Greek spirit in SA: 143; Samson's suffering: 143; "M's Early Literary Program": 74

Parkes, William: 45

Parkhurst: Ferdinando: 93. John: 38

Parkinson: James: 44, 116. John: 128, 32. Richard: see Martindale, Adam

Parkman, Francis: 98

Parks George B.: 19, 44. William: 115

Parlamentum of Feendis: 65

Parliament Arraigned (a royalist tract): 147

Parliament(s): 9*, 30*, 44*, 45*, 51*, 60*, 83, 103*, 113, 144*, 143, 94. Houses of: 97. And the engine: 143. Religious authority of: 143. M's definition of: 147. M's respect for: 51. M's praise of: 136. "Nineteen Propositions of": 60. Nominated: 9*. Of 1659: 103. Of Restoration: 103. Long: 9*, 60. The Rump: 60. Short: 9. Oxford: 9. Richard's: 9. See also: Milton, Character of the Long Parliament

Parliamentary History of the County of Oxford. See Oxford

Parliamentary Intelligencer: 44, 116, 91

Parma, Italy: 44

Parma, Ranuccio (Farnese) II, Duke of: 44

Parmenides: 141

Parmigianino (Parmigiano): 27, 97. "Madonna del Collo Lungo": 27

Parnassus, Mt.: 44, 49, 70, 73, 111, 3, 97. Parnassian fount: 3

Parnell, Thomas: 58, 117. Admires M: 58. Influenced by L'Allegro: 58

Parochial Antiquities...of Ambrosden: 45

Parochial Collections: 45*

Parodos: 92*

Parody: 15, 123. Demonic: 46*; see also: Punning. Dialectical: 46

Paronomasia, Richardson on: 88

Parousia. See Eschatology

Parr: 120. Elnathan: 102, 93, 101. Queen Catherine: 45

Parry, Henry: 40, 123

Parsifal: 60. Parisfal: 149

Parsons: Bartholemew: 54. Edward S.: 28, 40, 44, 45, 63, 86. Howard: 44. J.: 97. P.: 58. Robert: 114, 116, 93. William: 44, 58

Part: unexpectedly used as meaning the whole: 83. In music: 121. Of speech: use of one for another: 98, 114; Peck, and Newton on: 88. Part-Singing: 121

Parthenia: 58. Parthenia Sacra: 72

Parthenon: 5

Parthenope: 90. Tomb of: 49.

Parthanope: 73. See also: Naples

Parthia: 49, 72. Parthian: horsemen (Parthus eques): 73; Empire: 38. Parthians: 19*, 73, 125

Partial rotation: 51

Partial: 121

Participation mystique: 141

Partition: 51

Partridge: A. C.: 135. Diones (Hulson): 44. Edward, on Jonson's masques: 104

Party: 51. Broad Church: 51. High Church: 51. Presbyterian: 51. Radical: 51. Root-and-Branch: 51. M's party influence shown by works: 13

Parva Naturalia (Aristotle): 3

Pascal: 113, 130. Blaise: 5, 10, 34, 44, 47, 72, 93, 94; Pensées: 74, 81. M.: 44

Paschal: 72

Paschasius: St.: 4. Radbertus (Radburtus): 68; Expositio in... Matthaei: 74

Pascoli: 120

Pasham: 49

Pasor: George: 40. Matthias: 10, 40

Pasquale, Luigi: 64

Pasquetti, G.: 6

Pasquier: 40

Pasquin, A.: 97

Pasquine in a Traunce: 88

Passerin d'Entrèves, A.: 5, 93

Passero, Felice: 65, 77. L'Essamerone: 74

Passion: 69*, 113. The Passion: 129, 132, 133, 134, 72. Legitimacy of: 113. Imagery of: 8. Nature's reaction: 93. Protestant view of: 93. The Passion: 129. Of Christ: 81*. Passion (10th c. French poem): 74. Passion (12th c. French poem): 74. Passion of Our Lord (13th c. Eng. poem): 74

Passionate Pilgrim: 132, 94

Passive: obedience: 60. Resistance: 60

Passport (M's): 44

Past: the past: 51. Causes: 51. History of Eng.: 51

Paston: Anne: see Cope, Anne. Sir W.: 45

Pastor Fido (Guarini): 70

Pastor(s): 47, 51

Pastor, L. F. von: 6

Pastoral tradition: "On the Morning of Christ's Nativity": 55. "Lycidas": 55

Pastoral: 17, 27*, 35*, 40, 76, 110, 122, 11. Music: 121. Poetry: 146.

Conventionalizing influence of the: 58. Names: 83. Pastoral Poetry: 129; Pastoralism: 21*

Patch, Howard (Rollin): 23, 110, 123, 32

Patent Rolls: 45. Calandar of: 45

Pater Liber: 40

Pater Noster: 40. Paternoster Row: 40, 44

Pater, Walter: 18, 52, 86, 87, 132, 88, 39

Paterius: 68

Paterson: Dr. J.: 58, 105; Commentary on PL: 58. James: 88, 117

Path, T. E.: 37

Pathetic: appeals: 51. Proof: 51*, 123. Fallacy: 93

Pathos: 98

Patience: 17*, 122*, 123*, 93. The competition in: 125. And fortitude: 125. Divine and human: 125. In PR, and as theme in SA: 125. And inspiration: 125. See also: Endurance; Martyrdom; Fortitude

Patin, Gui, Lettres: 44

Patmore, Coventry: 58, 87*, 130. Interest in classical authors: 87. On conscience artistry, versification: 87. Attitude toward M: 87. On the sonnet: 87. The Unknown Eros: 87

Paton, George W.: 93

Patriarch, the, at Jerusalem: 3

Patriarcha: 116. Patriarcha Non Monarcha: 116

Patriarchat: 51

Patriarchs: 113

Patricius, Franciscus: 7, 40

Patrick: Father or Dr.: 44. J. Max: 9, 58, 29, 44, 75, 118, 128, 64. John Merton: 75. Simon, Bp. of Ely: 44, 68, 91

Patrides, C. A.: 36, 39, 53, 79, 101, 106, 110, 122, 123, 137, 148. Works: "M and Arianism: 60; "M and Protestant Theory of the Atonement": 60; "PL and the Theory of Accommodation: 60

Patriotism (M's): 30, 47, 51*. Patriots: 51

Patripassians: 71

Patrizi, Francesco: 40, 39, 64

Patroclus: 73, 123

Patrologia Graeca: 116

Patrologia, The: 142

Patrologiae Latinae: 143

Pattee, Fred Lewis: 115

Patten: G.: 97. William: 68

Pattern: 143*. Hero: 123. Protestant in Lycidas: 143. In PL and Geneva Bible: 143*. Of time in PL: 143

Patterson: Frank Allen: 1*, 16, 40, 44, 45, 51, 52, 56, 59, 69, 73, 79, 83, 133, 148, 135, 144, 102, 48; on M: 80; see also: The Works of JM, Columbia U. P. Frank E.: 64. Robert Leet: 110

Pattinson, Thomas: 44

Pattison, Mark: 9, 33, 40, 42, 44, 51, 59, 63, 68, 83, 86, 87*, 102, 105, 113, 120, 128, 144, 132, 71, 85, 92, 64, 130, 137, 150, 21, 48. On Lycidas: 58, 87. Editor of sonnets, biographer of M: 55. On nature of the sonnet: 37. Concerning M: M's Piedmont sonnet, 3 periods of M's life, on M's theology, on M's attitude toward the Bible: 87. Works: Milton: 87; The Sonnets of John Milton: 87

Pau, France: 44

Paul: 51, 72. Adrian: 3. St.: 1, 4, 5, 17*, 18, 27, 30, 34, 37, 44, 54, 56, 60, 67, 70, 73, 68, 79*, 95, 102, 113, 114*, 116, 122, 123, 125, 126, 127, 141, 142, 3, 32, 36*, 39, 82*, 92, 109, 150; doctrines of: 38; Epistles of: 74; Mars' Hill speech: 51. St. (Bp. of Constantinople): 73. John: 40. III, Pope: 40. IV, Pope: 64. V, Pope: 27, 40

Paul's Alley: 45

Paul's, St., Cathedral: 40, 73

Paul's, St., School: 40*, 3

"Paules Pigeons": 20

Paulet: family: 40. Charles, Duke of Bolton: 40. Jane (Savage), Marchioness of Winchester: 62, 55. John: 40; see also: Winchester, Marquis of

Pauli: 7, 10

Paulinus: of Beziers: 36; *Epigramma*: 36. Of Nola: 68.

Paulucci, Lorenzo (Venetian resident): 44

Paululus, Robertus, staff as symbol: 104

Paulus: Diaconus, *Historia Miscella*: 82. Emilius: 73; on divorce: 136. Jovius: 3

Pauluzzi, Lorenzo: 114

Pauly (Pavly), Jean de: 40, 113

Pauncefote (Pauncefoot), Tracy, Reigstrar: 44*

Pauperis, in forma: 45

Pausanias: 40, 112, 64, 90*, 123

Pauses: at line endings: 118. The Richardsons on: 88. Importance of metrical, Newton on: 88

Pausilipi: 73

Pausilipum: 49

Pauw (Pauui), Adrian (de) (Dutch Ambassador): 30, 44, 59, 103, 73

Pavia: 49, 103

Pavone, Francesco: 40

Pax vobiscum: 126

Payne: J. F.: 44. John: 44. Knight R.: 97. R.: 45. Sibilla: 40

Payson, Seth: 115. *A Sermon Preached at Concord, June 6th, 1799*: 115

Peace: 51*. Corrupting: 47. M on: 80. Universal during Nativity: 93. As masque figure: 29. Of mind: 47

Peach: Mr.: 44. Mrs.: 44

Peacham: 121. Henry: 44, 56, 123, 39, 93. Henry (the elder): 15, 114, 23; works: *Garden of Eloquence*: 74; *Paradox*: 91. Henry (the Younger): 15, 40

Peacock: 133. George: 40, 44. T. L.: 86

Pearce: 88*, 94. Roy Harvey: 23, 115. W.: 58. Zachary: 1, 17, 35, 60, 86, 105*, 118, 128, 134, 135, 138, 150, 117*, 55; on M's minor poems: 58

Pearl, The: 15, 110

"Pearl Poet," works: *Cleanness*: 74; *Patience*: 74; *Pearl*: 74; *Sir Gawaine*: 74

Pearsall Smith, L.: 109

Pearse, Mr.: 44

Pearson: Arthur: 16. Edward: 44. J. and Company (book dealers): 44. John: 64, 148. Martin: see Peerson. Susanna: 58. Sarah (Powell): 45. See also: Peirson

Peasants' War: 60

Pease, Theodore Calvin: 9, 60

Pecchiai, P.: 6

Pech de Calages, Marie de, *Judith*: 74, 64

Pecheux, Mother Mary Christopher: 75, 123, 36, 101, 93

Pechora (Petsora, Petzora): 19, 49. See also: Pustozera; Vaiguts

Pechter, Edward: 37

Peck(e): Mr.: 44, 45. Christopher: 44, 45. Edward: 44, 45. Francis: 16, 33*, 40, 44*, 58, 60, 73, 123, 88*, 117*, 55; on M: 58. H. W.: 63, 83, 144, 97, 130; "The Theme of PL": 83. Susanna: 44, 45. Thomas: 45

Peckham: (Willoughby), wife of Sir George: 44, 45. Dorothy (Powtrell): 45. Sir George: 44*, 45. M.: 97

Pecten: 121

Pedantry: 114*. Bentley, Paterson's: 88. Found by the Richardsons to handicap common sense: 88. Thyer free from: 88. Newton's learned, attacked by Marchant: 88

Pedridan: 49

Pedro, Infante Dom: 32

Peed: Mr.: 44. John: 44

Peel, Sir Robert: 87

Peele, George: 4, 29, 103, 108, 129, 39, 88, 64, 146, 117, 55. Works: Old Wives' Tale: 94; Arraignment: 35. See also: Old Wives' Tale

Peerage of England, The: 45

Peers, C.: 58

Peerson (Pearson), Martin (composer): 44

Pegasus (Pegasean): 44, 73, 90, 112, 3, 72

Pegge, Richard: 40

Pegnitz Society: 7

Péguy, Charles: 65

Peignot: 102

Peile, John D.: 40*, 44, 45

Peirce, Mr.: 44

Peiresc, N. C. F. de: 6

Peirs, Dr., Vice-Chancellor of Cambridge: 44

Peirson: Richard (also his son, Richard): 44. (Pearson), Sarah: 44

Pekin: 19

Pelagian(s): 73, 71. Controversy: 71. Traits: in <u>Mask</u>: 104; in PL: 104. Pelagianism: 114, 93, 32, 36, 71. Semi-Pelagianism: 36

Pelagius: 36, 71, 93. <u>On Romans</u>: 36

Pelbartus of Temesvar: 36. <u>Pomerium Sermonum</u>: 36

Pelegromius, Simon: 40

Peletier, Jacques: 40

Peleus: 90, 92

Pelham Street, Spitalfields: 44

Pelham, Sir William: 45

Pelides: 73

Pelikan, Jaroslav: 93

Pelion: 2, 49, 73

Pell: Mrs.: 10. John: 10*, 44. John, Jr.: 10

Pellean: 49. Conqueror (Alexander the Great): 73

Pelleas (Pellenore): 73

Pellegrini: 1

Pellet, Jane. See Jeffrey

Pelletier, Richard: 14

Pellican(us) (Kuersner), Conrad: 40, 22, 82, 93

Pellikan, Konrad: 93. See also: Pellican(us)

Pelling, Edward: 44, 116

Pelopidae: 90

Pelops: 44, 60, 73, 90, 3, 92

Pelorus: 19, 49, 73, 144. See also: AEtna

Pels, Peter: 44, 91

Pember, Edward Henry: 111

Pemberton, H.: 58, 86, 105

Pemberton's <u>Observations on Poetry</u>: 88

Pemble, William: 114, 128, 32

Pembroke College, Cambridge: 40, 44, 45

Pembroke College, Oxford: 40, 45

Pembroke: Earl of: 40, 44, 45, 120; marriage of to Mary Sidney: 73. Mary Herbert, Countess of: 91, 64

Pembroke's Inn: 40

Pembruge, Anthony: 44

Pen: 49

<u>Penates</u> : 29, 73

Penbray, co. Carmarthen: 44

Pendant World: 143*. New-created: 143. As a star: 143. Satan sees: 143. Sin and Death invade: 143

Pendlebury: Anne Milton (daughter of Christopher): 44. Collins: 44. Rev. John: 44

Pendleton, John W.: 44

Pendomer (Pendower): 45

Pendower, co. Somerset: 44

Penelope(ia): 73

Penelope: 90, 72

Penetential Psalms: 126

Peneus: 49, 73

Penguies, Count de. See de Meneses

Penho: 49

Penian Alps: 103

Penington. See Pennington

<u>Penitence of Adam</u>: 65

Penn: John: 58, 117. William: 83, 114, 116, 103

Pennant, T.: 58

Penney, Norman: 7

Pennie, J. F.: 58

Pennine (Poenine) Alps: 44

Pennington: family: 94. Mrs.: 58. Edgar Legare: 115. Isaac: 7, 44, 83; his father: 44

Pennsylvania Gazette, The: 115

Pennsylvania Historical Society: 44

Pennsylvania Magazine, Or American Monthly Museum, The: 115

Penny, Mrs. Frank: 44

Penrose, T.: 58

Penruddock, Sir John: 91

Pensée de Milton, La: 112

Penshurst (home of the Sidneys): 83

Pensioner: 40

Pentateuch: 44, 73, 74, 3. Importance to "Cosmopolitanism": 107

Pentecost: 72. Reversal of: 47

Pentheus: 73, 114, 72, 92

Penticross, W.: 58

Penuel: 49, 73

Penyston: Elizabeth: see Ayloffe, Eliz. Thomas: 45

People: the: 51, 9*, 113*, 147*. Good of, will of: 9*. Power of: 9*, 51. M's distrust of the: 113. Classes of, in England during the Revolution: 147. In the pamphlets of 1648-49: 147. M's conception of: 147*. Lilburne on: 147. Presbyterians and royalists on: 147. Sedgewick's idea of: 147. The People vs. the officers (Leveller view): 147. People's rights, menace to: 51

Peoples Prerogative (John Lilburne): 147

Peoples Right Briefly Asserted (John Redingstone): 147

Peor: 73, 144

Pepin: 121. Of Herstal: 73. King of the Franks (father of Charlemagne): 73, 116

Pepper, Henry: 115. Juvenile Essays; Or, A Collection of Poems: 115

Pepys Ballads: 68

Pepys: Samuel: 7, 10, 16, 40, 44, 86, 103, 120, 38, 82, 88, 91, 109, 130, 150. W. W.: 58

Perachon: 64. Naissance de Jésus-Christ: 74. See also: More, Alexander

Peraea: 73

Perceiver, nature of the: 96

Perception: in children, distortion of by belief: 118. Principles and function of: 96*

Perceval (Percival), H. M.: 68, 92

Percivale, Sir: 60

Percussion instruments: 121

Percy, Bp. T., sonnets of: 58

Percy: Algernon: see Northumberland. Earl of: 44. Sir Henry: 73, 114. Henry: 114; see also: Northumberland.

Percyvall, Richard: 40

Perea: 49

Pereira: 24*. Antonio: 64

Perelandra (C. S. Lewis): 118

Pererius, Benedictus: 1, 40, 60, 77, 102, 142, 32*

Pereslave: 49

Peretto, Francesco: 40

Perez: Gonzalo: 56. Juan de Montalban: 40

Perfect-Cursed-Blessed Man: 65

Perfect man, the: 33*

Perfect Diurnall: 44, 59, 103, 91

Perfect Looking Glasse for All Estates, A: 20

Perfect Narrative of the...High Court of Justice: 44

Perfect System of Divinity: 44. See also: De Doctrina

Perfect Weekly Account: 9

Perfect, Dr.: 58

Perfectibilitarianism: in M's works: 83*. In the Old and New Testaments: 83. In Baptist and Quaker Doctrine: 83. In 19th c. beliefs: 83

Perfection: 83*, 143*, 122. Heroic: 122. M's concept of: 83. M's use of the term in PL and PR, his minor poems, and prose works: 83. Ladder of: 143. And humility: 143. Striving for: 143. Unattainability of: 143. As basic symbol: 143. Of creation: 93

Pergamum: 49

Peri Hupsous: 37

Peri Kosmou: 65

Peri: Giovandomenico: 55. Jacopo: 6, 39

Pericles: 73, 3, 146. Periclean Athens: 71

Periegetes (Dionysius): 3

Periodization schemes: 93

Perionio, Joachimo: 40

Peripatetics: 70, 73, 112, 142, 71

Peripeteia: 100*, 122, 123, 132, 92. See also: Aristotle

Peripeteia: 72

Periphrases: 58

Perkins, William: 9, 15, 40, 41, 54*, 60, 73, 79, 102, 114, 134, 142, 144, 143, 32, 38, 93*, 99*. The keys: 143. And Sword: 143. And prophecy: 143. On faith: 143. Works: A Discourse of the Damned Art of Witchcraft: 142; The Works: 142; Combate betweene Christ and the Devill: 74*; Foundation of Christian Religion: 74

Perkinson, Richard: 100

Perl, Carl Johann: 100

Permia: 49

Permission, divine: 122, 123

Permissive, evil: 122, 93. See also: Free will

Pern(e), Andrew: 73

Peroratio: 40

Perpetual: council, objections to: 51. Grand council: need of; M on: 51. Senate: argument for: 51; M on: 147. Parliament, M on: 147

Perraud, François: 142. Demonologie ou Traitté des Demons et Sorciers: 142. See also: Perrault

Perrault: 2, 130. Charles: 65, 64, 150

Perret, Jacques: 100

Perrier: M. E.: 89. P.: see Vidier, A.

Perrin, François, Sennachérib: 74, 64

Perrinchief, Richard: 40, 44, 116

Perron, Cardinal of: 44

Perrot, South: 45

Perrott, Sir James: 93

Perry: Anne Davidson: 52. Henry: 44, 45. Nicholas: 45. Ralph Barton: 143; Puritanism and Democracy: 83

Perryn, Henry: 45

Perse School, Cambridge: 40

Perse(iae): 73

Persecution for Religion Judg'd and Condemned (a Baptist liberty of conscience tract): 147

Persecution, during the late Middle Ages: 71

Perseids, the: 89

Persephone: 27, 73, 90. See also: Proserpina

Persepolis: 19, 49, 73, 144

Perseus: 89, 90, 114. Great cluster in: 89

Perseverance, final: 63

Persia (Achaemenius, Persis): 19*, 44, 49, 144, 3, 32, 150. Astronomy in: 89. Persians: 40, 42, 32. Persian: astrology: 42; wisdom: 3. Persian Bay (Gulf): 49, 150. See also: Ormus; Bactria; Ecbatan; Hispahan; Tauris; Casbeen

Persius: 20, 40, 44, 56, 73, 121, 145, 64, 94

Person, David: 114, 128*, 93

Personal Heresy, The: 12

Personal Narrative (Edwards): 71

Personal: and contemporary elements

of PL ignored by Hume: 88. Attacks on Bentley in "A Friendly Letter": 88. Grudges against Bentley, Pearce's: 88. Character of Richardsons' and Bentley's commentaries: 88. Element of SA exceptionally valued by Newton: 88. Feature of M's poetry, Warton on: 88. Interplay between, and literary elements in M, Warton on: 88. As distinct from artistic life: 88

Personality: analogy of: 47. M's works dealt with by Hume apart from his: 88. Peck almost forgets the author's, emphasizing imitation: 88. Newton on M's: 88. Warton on M's, as revealed in his poetry: 88. And habits: Aubrey's account; Phillips' account: 55. Anonymous biographer's account: 55

Personification: 70, 118. An unfriendly critique: 118. A questionable example: 118. See also: Allegory

Personified abstractions, odes to: 58

Persons of Godhead: 93

Perspectiva communi: 40

Persuasion: 51, 31*. As theme in PR: 125*. Heroic poem as means of: 123. Ethical, modes of, arguments, devices, passages, preaching, purpose, speakers, value, writing: 51. Persuasiveness: 51

Perth Grammar School: 40

Pertha: 49

Peru (Peruana Regna): 19, 49. Peruvian realms: 3. See also: Austria; Cusco; Guiana; India, West

Perversion. See Creation; Demonic

<u>Pervigilium Veneris</u>: 132

Peryer, George (scrivener): 44

<u>Pesikta</u>: 36. <u>Pesikta Rabbati</u>: 41, 57

Pessimism: 141, 144, 47, 132. In PL: 48. In M: 132

Pestalozzi: 3

Pestilence: 2

Pet and Jackman voyage: 19

Petau, Denis. See Petavius

Petavius: (Denis Petau, Dionysius): 40, 41, 44, 73, 93, 128

Petegorsky, D. W.: 9, 108

Peter College, London: 40

<u>Peter Ramus and the Educational Reformation of the 16th C.</u>: 112

Peter: St.: 1, 4, 44, 54, 73, 111, 126, 127, 3, 72*. Comestor: 93. Damian: 111; <u>Collectanea in Vetiis Testamentum</u>: 74. John: 17, 23, 34, 37*, 60, 66, 81, 86*, 123, 100, 105, 110, 118, 122, 36, 85, 115, 146; <u>A Critique of PL</u>: 48. Lombard: 77, 82, 93; Sent.: 77. Martyr: 63, 102, 142*, 3, 30, 44, 51, 71, 82, 148; works: <u>Commentaries</u>: 142; <u>Commentarie upon...Judges</u>: 74, 82; <u>Commentary on I Corinthians 7</u>: 82; <u>Common Places</u>: 142, 82; <u>Most Fruitful and Learned Commentaries upon Judges</u>: 142; see also: Vermigli. Of Abano: 142. Of Blois: 93; <u>Compendium in Job</u>: 74. The Vulnerable (Cluny): 41

"Peter's Palace Hall": 44

Peter's Pence: 82

Peterborough Cathedral: 40

Peterborough, Earl of. See Mordaunt

Peterhouse (St. Peters) College, Cambridge: 40, 103

Peters: Rev. Mr.: 97. Hugh (1598-1660): 7, 44, 113, 114, 147, 91; sermons by: 38; left-wing leader in the Revolution: 147; admonishes Parliament on London's poverty: 147; influence of, on Cromwell: 147; preaches against kingship: 147; recommends excommunication for Williams: 147; writes of the despair of the Commonwealth supporters: 147. J. R.: 68. Nicholaus: 40

Petis de la Croix: 88

Petiscus: 44, 3

Petit, Herbert H.: 93

<u>Petition concerning Religion</u> (a protest of the harsh measures against the Puritans): 147

<u>Petition for the Prelates</u>: 9

<u>Petition of Rights</u>: 132

Petition: 45, 51, 54. City: 73. Of Right: 51, 103. To compound, M's: 44

Petitot, Jean (painter, M portrait): 44

Petkum, Simon de (Danish resident): 44

Petra: 49, 73

Petrarch, Francesco: 1, 4, 5, 6, 15, 18, 20, 27, 29, 30, 31, 33*, 40, 44, 41, 51, 58, 59*, 60, 70, 73, 76, 83, 87*, 103, 111, 114, 120*, 122, 123, 132, 133, 136, 145, 3, 39, 62, 72, 82, 94, 93, 64*, 109, 130, 137, 146, 150, 88, 117, 55, 21, 13. Petrarchan: conceit: 40; rhyme scheme: 27. Works: Africa: 74; De Familiari: 74; Ecloque: 74; Sonnets: 55; Sonnet 108: 82

Petre, Catherine. See Powell, Catherine

Petremand, Thierry: 64. Judith (verse paraphrase): 74

Petri Molinaei, P. F.: 116

Petrocchi, Giorgio: 23, 60

Petronius, Arbiter (Gaius): 1, 40, 58, 73, 123. Another friend of Herod: 73

Petrov, Vasili Petrovich: 117

Petrus: Cantor: 40. de Riga: 65. Hispanus: 40

Petsora: 73, 150

Pett: Peter: 44. Phineas: 44

Pettegrove, James P.: 81

Petter, George: 93

Pettet, E. C.: 59, 81

Petti, Anthony G.: 93

Pettie, George: 54

Petties (schools): 40

Pettigrew, Richard C.: 115

Pettikum (Petkum), Simon de (Danish envoy): 44

Pettislego: 49

Pettit, Edward: 116

Pettus, Sir John: 128, 93, 150

Petty school (M's): 40

Petty Bag, Clerk of the: 45

Petty France, London (M's home in Westminster): 44*, 94, 103

Petty: John: 44. Mary: see Marlborough. Maximilian: 91. Sir William: 9, 10, 44, 114, 91, 115, 148

Peucer: 128

Pevensey: 49. See also: Andredchester

Pevsner, Nikolaus: 27

Peyer, Henry: 44

Peyrére, Isaac de la: 52

Peyton: Robert, Examiner in Chancery: 44. Thomas: 65, 77, 142, 32, 36, 93; Glasse of Time in the Second Age: 74, 142, 36, 149

Pfochen, Sebastien: 22

Pforzheimer: Arthur (and Mrs. Arthur): 44. Carl H., Library: see Unger, Emma, and W. A. Jackson

Phaeacians: 90, 32

Phaedo (Plato): 29, 104, 112, 111, 113, 121, 3

Phaedra: 92

Phaedrus (Plato): 5, 20, 112*, 134, 3

Phaer, Thomas: 20, 40

Phaethon: 56, 73, 90, 141

Phaeton: 72

Phalanx, the Macedonian: 40

Phalaris (tyrant): 20, 73, 60

Phalereus: 70, 112, 3, 53, 82. Demetrius: 73

Phaleucian (Phalaecian): 73

Phallus. See Symbolism

Phanes: 90

Phanocles: 40

Phantom editor, Bentley's: 88

Pharaoh: 113, 144, 72. Pharaoh's daughter: 1

Pharisees: 44, 3, 71. Pharisaism: see Self-righteousness

Pharpar: 19, 49. River: 144. See also: Abbana; Damascus

Phavorinus (Varinus, Bp. of Nocera): 123

Phelip, J. S.: 44

Phelps: Gilbert: 86. R.: 58. W. L.: 58

<u>Phenomena</u> (Aratus): 3

Phenomena, definition, knowledge, and organization of: 96*

Phenomenological vision: 96

Pherecrates: 121

Pherecydes: 60, 74, 123, 92

Pheretiales: 73

Phidias: 72, 92

<u>Philadelphia Repertory</u>: 115

<u>Philadelphia Repository and Weekly Register</u>: 115

Philadelphia, Pennsylvania: 44

Philadelphists: 7

Philalethes (pseudonym): 44

Philammon: 90

Philaras, Leonard: 16, 28, 30*, 31, 44*, 59, 73, 103, 113, 120, 128, 3, 137, 134

Philarcheus: 117

Philastrius: 68

Philebus: 5, 112

Philemon: 70, 73

Philetas: 40, 54

Philip: E. C.: 44. W.: 40

Philip: I of Austria and Holland: 44. II, King of Spain: 60, 82, 64. IV, of Spain: 44*, 103, 71. The Evangelist: 73. Of Harveng: 69. Landgrave of Hesse: 64. II, King of Macedonia: 40, 73, 120, 3, 72. Of Neri: 27

Philipon, Marie M.: 93

Philippi (AEmathia Urbs): 49, 73, 72

Philippians: 74

Philippicus: 73

Philipps, R.: 58

Philippson, Johann (Joannes): 40. See also: Sleidanus

Philippis Presbyterius, <u>In Historiam Job</u>: 74

Philips. See also: Phillips

Philips: 3. Sir Ambrose: 44, 64. J. T.: 20. Katherine, "In Memory of Mrs. E. H.": 21. Richard: 44. (Phelips), Sir Robert: 116

Philistia: 72*. See also: SA

Philistian: 49

Philistines: 49, 51. Enemies, rulers over Israel: 143. And Samson: 143. The lords of: 143. See also: Palestine; Philistian

Philistines: 68*, 112, 3

Phillimore, J. S.: 18

Phillip, J.: 97

Phillips-Aubrey: 40

Phillips dictionary: 40

Phillips-Kersey dictionary: 40

Phillips: Mr.: 45. Mrs. (Pye): 45. Anne (M's sister, later Agar): 28, 40, 44*, 45, 103. Anne (M's niece): 40, 44, 55, 21. Catherine Prowde: 44. Edmund (Edward): 44, 84. Edward (M's brother-in-law): 28, 33, 40, 44*; marriage to Anne Milton: 55. Edward (M's nephew): 1, 6, 9, 15, 16, 20, 28*, 30, 33, 40*, 41, 42, 44*, 45, 50, 51, 60, 63, 70*, 73, 74, 81, 86, 89, 100, 114, 121, 132, 77, 58, 59*, 102, 103*, 112, 111, 113, 116, 120, 123, 128, 135, 136, 138, 144, 145, 22, 26, 36, 43, 62, 82, 85, 88, 91, 93, 146, 148, 150, 117, 21, 94*, 92, 97, 55*; as biographer: 55*; works: <u>Illustrious Shepherdess and Imperious Brother</u>: 91; <u>Tractatulus</u>: 91; see also: Buchler; Milton, John, <u>Letters of State</u> (ed. Phillips). Edward, of Braden Heath: 44. Edward, of Pembroke College, Oxford: 40. Edward and John: 19, 86, 116, 137. Elizabeth (M's niece): 44, 55. Francis: 44.

Phillips: James E.: 93. Jerome: 93. John (M's nephew): 15, 16, 20, 28*, 40, 44*, 45, 58*, 59, 63, 73, 103, 135, 136, 94, 139, 39, 91, 150, 55, 121, 115, 117, 128; makes little use of M's minor poems: 58; Responsio: 91. John, <u>The Splendid Shilling</u>: 55. Katherine (mother of elder Edward): 40, 44. Philip Lee: 144. Richard: 44, 45. Robert: 44. S.: 58. Sir Thomas: 44, 45. William: 58, 87, 44; <u>Mt. Sinai</u>: 87

Phillis: 90

Philo-Bent: 117

Philo-Spec: 117

Philo: Philo Byblius: 57. Philo Judaeus: 1, 5, 15, 60, 63, 65, 69, 73, 77, 79, 100, 112, 114, 121, 123, 124, 125, 128, 32*; God: 107; gods of nations are demons: 107; Greeks borrowed their ideas from Moses: 107; Logos, defined: 107; philosophy important to Christianity: 107; teachings, spread of, acceptable to Christians: 107; theological system: 107. Philo of Byzantium: 70

Philo: 24*, 102, 36*, 93. Works: Questions and Answers on Genesis: 36; De Opificio: 74, 36; De Vita Contemplativa: 74; Legum Allegoria: 36

Philoctetes: 92. Sonnet on: 58

Philodemius Eleutherius: 9

Philodemus: 5

Philolaus: 112

Philological Quarterly: 44

Philological: tendency of Hume's notes: 88. Professionalism in Pearce: 88. Pedantry, Paterson's: 88

Philomel(a): 44, 73, 72, 90

"Philo-Milton Petriburgensis": 117

Philoponos, Johannes: 73, 32

Philosopher(s): 51. Ancient: 40. Philosopher's Stone: 7, 89. Philosopher King: 40

Philosophers Banquet, The: 128

Philosophical Dictionary: 111

Philosophical Transactions of the Royal Society: 44, 88

Philosophical: poetry: 58*. Terms: 40. Conceptions of heroic virtue: 122

Philosophus ad regem quendam: 73, 72

Philosophy: 7, 17*, 30, 31, 40, 51, 121, 144, 25. In grammar school: 40. Of education: 51. And art: as basis of: 149*; trend of modern thought: 149. See also: Cosmology; Ethical philosophy; Political theory; Theology

Philostratus (Flavius): 90, 123, 134, 142, 64, 146, 117

Philpot, C.: 58

Philyra: 3. Philyrean: 73

Philyreius. See Chiron

Phimostomus: 44, 73

Phine(h)as: 73

Phineus: 16, 30, 44, 60, 73, 90, 3

Phipps, John: 40

Phips, William: 115

Phison River: 32

Phleget(h)on(tius): 73

Phlegethon: 90

Phlegra: 49, 73, 90

Phlegraean Fields: 19, 144

Phlegyas: 111

Phoclydes: 40

Phoebus: 1, 56, 70*, 73, 121, 3. Lycidas: 104. See also: Apollo

Phoenicia: 49. Phoenicians: 73, 144, 32. See also: Assyria

Phoenix (Amyntorides): 19, 44, 57, 73, 90, 144, 143, 106

Phoenix, or Solemn League and Covenant: 116

Phoenix: 36

Phonetic: transcriptions of Eng. words: 20. Features of M's language, Peck on: 88. Value of M's spellings sometimes neglected by Newton: 88. Point of view, combined with artistic considerations, Lofft's: 88. Points, Todd on: 88

Phosphenes: 16

Photinians: 71. Photinianism: 22

Photinus: 22

Photius: 44, 73, 123, 144

Photophobia (theory as to M's): 16

Phrases Oratoriae (Farnaby): 20

Phrases: 40

Phrasidamus: 64

Phrica (Phrix): 73

Phrixus: 90

Phrygia(n): 49, 73. "Mode": 70, 121

Phyllis (Phillis): 73

Physic: 40

Physical Observations on Arabia Petraea (Dr. Shaw): 88

Physical: appearance (M's): 44. Astronomy, basis of, in Kepler's works: 89. Exercise: 40, 51. Love (when legitimate): 113. Sensitiveness, periods of great: 88

"Physicks" (i.e., natural philosophy): 40

Physician Cure thy Self: 116. See also: R. L'Estrange

Physician: 128. As atheist, as Christ, as magistrate or minister: 128

Physician's Tale (Chaucer): 3

Physics: 40*

Physiologus: 19, 73, 114, 128. Physiologus: 53

Piaget, Jean: 118

Pianezza, Marquis of: 59, 120

Pianoforte: 121

"Piazza, the": 98

Piazzetta, G. B.: 97

Pibrac (Du Faur): 40

Picard, Jeremie (Jeremy): 44, 59, 63*, 89, 102, 82, 55

Picasso, Pablo: 72

Piccard, Ch.: 141

Piccarda: 111

Piccini, G.: 6

Piccoli, R.: 14

Piccolomini: Pius II, Aeneas Sylvius: 40. Alessandro: 60, 123. Francesco: 40, 123

Piccotti, G. B.: 64

Pichon, R.: 57

Pickering (Picheringum): Sir Gilbert: 44, 73, 38. William (publisher): 40, 44, 87; see also: Milton, John, Works; Pickering and Chatto

Pickering and Chatto (bks.s): 44. Pickering ed. of Works: 44. See also: Milton, John, Works

Pickersgill, F. R.: 97

Pico: Gian Francesco: 114. della Mirandola, Giovanni: 5, 27, 60, 79, 81, 113, 114, 121, 69, 123, 142, 11, 32, 38, 39, 72, 93, 64, 101, 148, 106; works: Commentary on Benivieni's "Canzone d'Amore": 60; De hominis dignitate, Heptaplus, De ente et uno: 60; see also: Mirandola. The Younger: 66; works: De Rerum Praenotione: 74; Examen Vanitatis Doctrinae Gentium: 74

Pictor (Pictorius), George: 142. Works: Theologica Mythologica: 74; An Introductory Discourse on the Nature of Spirits: 142

Picts: Pictish invasions: 3. Pictland: 49

Picture of the Councel of State (by leading Levellers): 147

Picture of the Good Old Cause: 44, 103, 116, 91

Picture of Human Life. See Pinax

Picturesque: the: 97. Picturesqueness: of interpretion preferred by the Richardsons to reliability: 88; appreciated by Warton, Todd: 88

Piedmont (Piemont), Italy: 44, 103, 49. M's official correspondence regarding: 16. Piedmontese: 103, 123; massacre of the: 94; see also: Savoy

Pieper, Josef: 93

Pierce Penilesse (Nash): 135

Pierce: Mr. (sculptor): 44. Claude A.: 93. William, John Penry: 83

Pieria: 3. Pierian (Pierides): 44, 73

Pierius, Christianus (Coloniensus): 64. Jonas Propheta: 74

Piero della Francesca: 125

Piero di Cosimo: 15, 39

Pierpont Morgan Library: 20. See also: Morgan

Pierpont: John: 115; The Portrait, A Poem Delivered Before the Washington Benevolent Society: 115

Pierre de Saint-Louis: 64

Pierre: 98*

Pierrepont, Anne. See Roos

<u>Piers Plowman, Vision and Creed of</u> (William Langland): 73, 77, 83, 128, 71, 117

Pierson: David: 91. John: 91; see also: Bramhall, John. Martin: see Peerson

Pierus: 49

<u>Pietas et Gratulatio Collegii Cantabrigiensis Apud Novanglos</u>: 115

Piety: 121*, 123, 125*, 141. Related to faith and justice in PR: 125. Related to temperance and Platonic vision of the Good: 125. As beginning and end of wisdom: 125. And perception: 125. Of proper relationship: 125. In SA: 125. And lamentation: 125. Pietists: 7. See also: Faith; Holiness; Zeal; Martyrdom; Virtues

Piggot: Mr.: 44. Samuel: 44

Piggott, John: 116

Pigmies: 19. See also: Pygmies

Pigna, Giovanni Battista: 122, 129. Works: <u>Gli Heroici</u>: 74; <u>Romanzi</u>: 74

Pignerole, Peace of: 103, 94

Pike, Josiah (apprentice scrivener): 44

Pikolous: 1

<u>Pilae reciprocatio</u>: 40

Pilate, Pontius: 60

Pilfrance: 44

Pilgrim(s): fathers: 7. Brownists the forerunners of: 147. Distrust of Williams: 147. Harmony among at Amsterdam: 147. Join the Amsterdam Separatists: 147. More democratic than Puritans: 147. Poverty of: 147. Robinson beloved leader of: 147. Settle in Plymouth: 147. Pilgrimage: 47; in Comus: 143

<u>Pilgrim's Progress</u>: 17, 31

Pilkington: Rev. Mr.: 44. Mrs.: 44. James: 40. Rev. Matthew: 44

Pillars of Hercules: 103

Pillot: 40

Pilon, Germain: 64

"Pilot of the Galilean Lake": 143. And Samson: 143

Pimenta, Nicholas: 15

Pinarolium: 49

<u>Pinax</u> (Cebes): 112, 3

Pindar: 1, 4, 5, 6, 15, 18, 27, 30, 40*, 44, 58, 59, 60, 66, 68, 70, 74, 90*, 103, 120, 123, 132, 133, 141, 3, 32, 62, 88, 101, 146, 148, 150, 21, 94. Thought inferior to M: 58. M's notes in 1620 edition of: 40. <u>Lycidas</u> influenced by Pindaric Ode: 58

Pindemonte, Ippolito: 70

Pineda, Joannes (Juan): 74, 32. <u>In Job</u>: 74

Pinega: 49. See also: Duina

Pinkerton, J.: 58

Pinnard, H.: 93

Pinto, Vivian De Sola: 23, 44, 81, 86, 128

<u>Pious Annotations Upon the Holy Bible</u> (preface attr. to M): 44

Pipe-smoking (M's): 44

Pipe: roll: 45. Organ: 121. Pastoral: 121

Piper, D. T.: 44

Piranesi, Carceri Series: 27

Piranesi, G. B.: 97

Pirene (Pyrenen): 73

<u>Pirke de Rabbi Eliezer</u>: 24*, 41, 36*

Pirrepont: Henry: see Dorchester. Robert: 44

Pirton Bynfield, co. Oxon.: 44

Pisa: 44, 49, 3

Piscator: J. P.: 22. John (Joannes): 40, 41, 74, 123, 99; <u>Commentariorum in Omnes Libros Veteris Testimenti</u>: 74

Pisgah: 19, 144. Vision: 96*

Pisida: 49. Pisidian: 49, 73

Pisidias (George Pisidias): 77

Piso: 44, 21. Caius: 82. Lucius Calpurnius (surnamed Frugi): 73. Lucius Calpurnis Caesonius: 73

Pison. See Phison River

<u>Pistis Sophia</u>: 142, 41

Pistorius, Johannis: 40

Pitch: 121. Importance of to sound patterns: 118

Pitiscus, Bartholemew: 40

Pitkin, Hannah: 39

Pitman, John: 115. A Poem on the Social State and its Future Progress: 115

Pits, John: 44

Pitt: C.: 58, 105, 88. Moses (bks., pr.): 44. Mr. (clothier): 44. Moyses: 28. Robert: 117. W.: 97. William: 25, 13

Pittheus: 44

Pitti Palace: 27

Pitti: Alessandro: 44. Giulio: 44

Pittman, J. H.: 128

Pitts: Philip: 44, 45. Simon: 44. Thomas: 44. W.: 97

Pity: 51, 123, 25*

Pius II: 32, 64. Pius IV: 73. Pius V: 86, 136. XII: 32

Pivareu, St., College: 40

Placaeus of Saumur (Josua Laplace): 73

Place, dialectics and frames of: 96

Place: de Grève, Paris: 44. du Salin, Paris: 44

Placentius: 40

Placita Philosophorum (Plutarch): 112

Plagiarism: 70

Plagiary Exposed: 116

Plague: 44. The: 136. Of 1665: 93. At Cambridge: 40. In London: 40, 44. The Great: 94

Plain and Easy Introduction to Practical Music: 121

Plain English (attr. to M): 44, 103, 116, 91. By John Redingston, M accused of writing: 147

Plain-dealing: a game: 40. A song: 121

Plaine Pathway to the French Tongue: 40

Plainsong: 40

Plaintiff: 45

Plan: of being: 113. Ideal, logical, of censorship, education, rhetorical: 51

Plancius, Peter: 40, 73

Planets: 89, 128*, 144. The aspects and motions of: 89. Orbits, starry dance of: 89. Aspects, creation, light, malignance of Saturn, movements, sustenance: 128. See also: Moon; Sun

Plans for poems (M's): 44*. Plan Five, for tragedy: 50*

Plantin, Christophe: 40

Plastic art: 70

Platagenet, Thomas, Earl of Lancaster: 73

Platitudes: 51

Platner, criticism of Hermann: 94

Plato: 2, 4*, 5, 6, 7, 8, 9, 12, 15*, 17, 18*, 19, 20, 24, 27, 29, 30, 31, 37*, 40*, 41, 44, 51, 52*, 54*, 56, 57, 58, 59, 60*, 67, 68, 69, 70*, 73, 74, 77, 81, 37, 90*, 100, 102, 103, 105, 104, 108, 112, 111, 113, 114*, 121*, 116, 120, 122, 123*, 124, 125*, 129, 132*, 134, 135, 141, 142, 144, 145*, 3*, 26, 32, 36, 38, 39*, 46, 53, 62, 71*, 85, 82*, 88, 93, 64, 101, 109, 115, 130, 131, 146*, 149, 148*, 117, 48, 25. On limit and decorum: 66. Influence on M's "nonentities": 80. "Myth of Er": 80. Idea of perfection defined by: 83. And M compared: 146. M's debt to: 146, 104. Epistomology: 48. Philosophy: 48. The opposition of theorectical interest between Plato and M: 48. M's reference to: 112. Plato's restrictions, utopian conception: 51. Dualism of God and the world: 107. Influence upon "Cosmopolitanism": 107. Theory of ideas in M's technique: 110. Works: Timaeus (God makes use of demigods in creation): 107, 60, 125, 48; The Dialogue: 142, 82; Charmides: 112, 125; Gorgias: 60, 125; Laws: 60, 125, 147, 82; Phaedo: 60, 125, 57, 81, 48; Phaedrus: 37, 60, 125, 48; Republic: 37, 60*, 74, 89, 125, 48; Sophist: 37, 60; Symposium: 37, 60, 109; Theatetus: 125; Cratylus: 37, 60; Apology: 74; Philebus: 125. Clitophon: 112. See also: Lovejoy; Jowett

Platonic: 27*, 124*, 125*. Idea: 76, 103. Philosopher king: 125.

Tripartite soul: 125. Theory of knowledge: 125. Unity of obeying and ruling: 125. "Way of death": 125. Love: 137. Anthropology of alienation: 48. Doctrine of human soul: 48. Idealism: 48. Virtues: 51. See also: Temperance; Virtues

Platonic Tradition in Anglo-Saxon Philosophy: 112

Platonic-Christian: 139

Platonick Song of the Soul: 65

Platonische Renaissance in England, Die: 112

Platonism: 60*, 81*, 123, 142, 139, 32, 71, 125, 72*, 88, 146, 21*. In Eng.: 81. In M: 142. Basic in M: 143. In Comus: 143. Florentine: 72; see also: Neoplatonism. Platonism in the Poetry of John Milton: 112

Platonismus in der Englischen Renaissance vor und bei Thomas Eliot: 112

Platonists: 71, 88

Platt: Frederic, "Perfection," Encyclopedia of Religion and Ethics: 83. William: 44, 45

Plattes, Gabriel: 10

Plautus: 18, 20, 40, 44, 70, 73, 103, 128, 82, 88, 101, 137, 21

Playfere, Thomas: 42, 93

Playford, co. Suffolk: 44

Playford, John: 29, 44

Plays: 51. Playwriters: 51

Plea for the King and Kingdom (Marchmont Nedham): 147

Plea for Non-Scribers (Subscribers): 44. See also: Gee, Edward

Plea: 45, 51

Pleading, direct: 51

Pleadwell, Capt. F. L.: 44

Pleasure Reconciled to Virtue (Jonson): 29, 134, 26*. And relation to Comus: 143

Pleasure: 51. The elder Richardson's identification of superficial, with purifying moral experience: 88. And instruction as the objects of epic poetry, Thyer on: 88. Contempt of, as heroic virtue: 123. And instruction in poetry, Newton on: 88

Plectrum: 121

Plede per le manare nulla: 45

Pléiade, The: 40, 90

Pleiades: 73, 89*, 132. Brilliancy, motion, names, scintillation of: 89. In Greek mythology, number of stars in, nebula in: 89. "Lost Pleiad," the; "Sweet influences" of: 89. Time of appearance: 89

Pleione(s): 73

Plenitude: 139

Plenty: 90

Pleonasms, Hume on: 88

Plesco (Vobsco): 49

Pleurreus, Stephen: 64. Aeneis Sacra: 74

Pleydenwurf, Wilhelm: 93

Plimouth: 49

Plimpton Collection at Columbia Univ.: 20

Pliny: 1, 4, 15, 19*, 20, 40, 44, 57, 89, 90*, 103, 113, 121, 123*, 144*, 3, 82, 88, 130. Fig tree, Ptolemaic system, winds, dolphins, serpents, cranes and pygmies, nightengale: 144. Griffins, phoenix, halcyons, moly, Meroe, Taprobane: 144. Natural History and PL: 144*. Naturalis Historia: 57. Pliny the Elder: 73, 114, 64. Pliny the Younger: 73, 114, 145

Plockhoy, Peter Corneliszoon: 147. Suggests method for settling religious disputes: 147. Writes The Way to the Peace and Settlement of these Nations (a plea for voiding of tithes): 147

Plomer, Henry R.: 40, 44, 59

Plot (Mythos, Fable): 123*, 92*

Plot Discovered (attr. to M): 44

Plot, R.: 45

Plotinism: 60

Plotinus: 1, 5, 7*, 15, 18, 34, 40, 79, 81, 112, 114, 121, 123, 124, 125, 144, 32, 71, 82, 93, 64, 101. Enneads: 74

Plots against M by Italian Jesuits: 44

Plow. See Symbolism

Plummer, A.: 36

Plumptre: E. H.: 58. J.: 117

Pluralities and Nonresidency, Of: 59

Plurality of worlds: 114, 128

Plutarch: 1, 2, 4, 5, 6, 18, 19, 20, 29, 31, 40*, 44, 51, 54, 59, 68, 70, 73, 79, 90*, 112, 114, 121, 120, 123, 125, 128*, 133, 141, 142, 144, 145, 3, 11, 26, 39, 71, 82, 93, 64, 130. Works: De Defectu Oraculorum (influence of, on M's passages treating of oracles): 57; On Isis and Osiris: 60; Moralia: 60; Moralia and PL: 144; De musica: 50; Life of Caesar: 60; Lives (trans. Thomas North): 74; Morals (trans. Philemon Holland): 74

Pluto: 2, 44, 57, 73, 90, 111, 3, 72, 91

Plutocrats: 51

Plutonian Hall: 90

Plutus: 73, 3

Plymouth: 45

PMLA: 44*, 45

Pococke, Edward: 40, 41, 42, 22

Podgoursky, Count Ivan N.: 44

Podhajecy: 49

Podobedov, A.: 117

Podolia (Padolia): 49

Poe: Dr.: 45. Edgar Allan: 35, 136, 115, 137, 148; The Maelstrom: 35. Dr. Leonard: 44, 45

Poemandres: 124

Poemata de Mosaicae historiae: 65*

Poemata dogmatica: 65

Poemata ex Recensione Adami Siberi (Stigel): 83

Poemata sacra: 65

Poemata Miltoni Manuscripta, etc.: 149

Poems (William Drummond; M possibly contributed as an editor?): 44

Poems of John Milton: 112

Poems of Mr. John Milton (Cleanth Brooks and John E. Hardy): 139

Poems on Affairs of State: 44, 116

Poems Moral and Divine: 115

Poems Upon Several Occasions (M, ed by T. Warton): 88. See also: Warton

Poems, M's early, published: 94

Poems, M's liked by children: 58

Poems: 1645: 9, 28*, 30, 44*. Presentation copy of: 44

Poems: 1673: 28, 44*

Poenine. See Pennine

Poet(s): 50, 70*, 40, 51. Greek: 51. "Poets Majore": 40. And meditation: 75. As amanuensis: 25. As hero: 75. In relation to his audience: 25. And the "monomyth": 75. As visionary: 25. As shaman: 75. Colderidge's idea of: 146. M's idea of: 146, 25, 87. As prophet: 146, 25. As fallen creator: 75. As fictional character: 53. And the source of inspiration: 75*. And prophet: 53. As prophet, king, and priest: 75. Staged in Lycidas: 53. And the concept of "play": 75. Satan as: 53. And the creative process: 75*. Raphael as: 53. And climate: 70. As interpreter, orator: 25. And criticism: 70. Blake's idea of: 25. Orphic: 25. As citizen: 70. Like God: 25. As legislator: 25. The bad, ideal, mediocre, training of the: 70*. As teacher, audience of, character of, in propria persona: 70. Admired and quoted by Gill the Elder: 20. M as a: 52*. M as poet prophet: 87. M's poetic ambitions: 46. See also: Bard

The Poet (M's views on): 30*, 31, 40

Poetae Minores Graeci (Winterton): 20

Poetarum Scotorum Musae Sacrae: 117

Poetasters, indictment of: 30

Poetic style: 70. Latin poems: 55; On the Death; Vacation Exercise; On the Morning; The Passion; Song on May Morning; L'Allegro; Il Penseroso; Comus; Lycidas: 55. Punctuation, classical allusion, epic simile, dual nature, suspended sense, in 18th c., spelling: 55. Italian sonnets, Eng. sonnets, Psalms, PL, SA, PR, diction, discussed, blank verse, syntax: 55

Poetic: talent (M's): 44. Theory: 69*, 146; M's: 30*, 31*, 102; and practice, M's: 137*. Treatment, thesis susceptible of: 20. Tributes from friends: 44

Poetic universe: 100. Astronomy: 100. Astronomical dialogue, dial of the moon: 100. Postlapsarian world: 100. Pre-lapsarian world: 100*. Zodiacal watch: 100

Poetic: achievement (M's view of his own): 30*. Aspirations or ambitions of M: 30*, 113. Motives for giving up poetry for politics: 113

Poetic: conceptions of heroic virtue: 122. Diction: 76, 98. Ecstacy: 51. Imitation: 59*. Justice: 17*. Objective: 69. Scene: 69. Sense, the Richardsons on M having to be understood in a: 88. Structure: 69

Poetica d'Aristotele (Castlevetro): 70, 3

Poetica Stromata: 45

Poetical works (M's): 117*. See also: Milton, John, Works

Poetical Decameron (Collier): 94

Poetical Sketches: 25

"Poeticall Dictionary": 40

Poetics (Aristotle): 70*, 112, 111, 118, 3. Trans. by Potts: 131

Poetics (Scaliger): 70

Poetics: 70, 111, 123*

Poetizing tendency of M: 121

Poetria (John of Garland): 20

Poetry and Humanism (M. M. Mahood): 139

Poetry as a Means of Grace (Osgood): 134

Poetry: 17*, 30, 31*, 40, 51, 63*, 87, 129*. Renaissance, conception of: 102. Eulogy of: 70. Laws of: 70. Minor types of: 70. Subject matter of: 70. Objective vs. subjective: 87. "Two schools" of: 87. Function of: 70. And religion: 70. And rhetoric: 70. And truth: 70, 53*. And fact: 70. And history: 69, 70. And logic: 70, 53. And music: 70, 121. And passion, philosophy, prose: 70. Theory of: 112, 53*. As game, allegory, classes of: 146. And the Church: 53. As song: 121. Success of M's poetry: 141. Failures of M's poetry: 141. Egotism in, ethical concerns of, and learning, an overflowing: 146

Poetry: Dunster's immature theory of: 88. Sacred, Dunster on: 88. Newton's quantitative standards in appreciating: 88. And painting: 146. And philosophy: 146. And religion: 146. A waking dream: 146. M's salvation in poetry: 136. As selective imitation: 88. Thyer's conventional theory of, his didacticism and religious bias: 88. Meadowcourt on, as instruction made attractive by decoration: 88. Newton wants it to conform to common sense and the Bible, and to give pleasure: 88. Serious, meditative, Warton on: 88. The imagination as the main agent in, Warton on: 88. Richardsons on, equals ornament: 88. Richardsons inconsistent in their defintion of: 88. Richardsons on, and moral problems, and prose as differing apart from metre: 88. Richardsons on, music and poetry: 88. M's definition of, by Peck: 88. Peck on truth in, on painting and: 88. Distinct from fact, according to Pearce: 88. Broad-minded conception of, in the Richardsons' commentary: 88. Survey of character of M's, in the Richardsons' commentary: 88. Style of, differs definitely from that of prose, according to the Richardsons: 88. The Richardsons on, and religion, and enriching the imagination, improving morally and making happy: 88

Poetry, definitions of: Blake's: 146. Coleridge's: 146. Fuseli's: 146. Hazlitt's: 146. Hunt's: 146. M's: 146*, 13. Shelley's: 146. Wordsworth's: 146

Poetry: Romantic: 25. Obscurity: 25. And action: 25. Function of: 25. And revolution: 25. Of allusion: 25. Of contests: 25

Poetry of John Milton: 89, 101, 55. Irregularity in: 101. Mannerism in: 101. Mosaic Law in: 101. Pattern and process in: 101. Spatial treatment in: 101. Evolution theory portrayed in: 89. Composition of influenced by the seasons: 89. Characteristics of: 89. Scholarship of: 89. How religious beliefs are used in: 102*. M's renunciation of: 94. Classical elements in: 55. Essence of M's poetry: 143. Criticized by writers: 97. Use of Bible in poetry and prose: 43. M returns to: 94. Christian heroism in: 101. Humanism in: 101. Liberty in: 101. Warfare in: 101. Continuity in: 101*. Contraries in: 101*. Decorum in: 101. Discipline and energy in: 101. Inspired 19th c. artists: 55. Subjective nature of; 87. Cosmic elements in: 87. Early poems: 87. Puritan spirit in early poems: 87. Problem of fate and free will in: 87. M's early experience with: 20*. Own early poetry: 44. M's high style in: 52. M's view of: 52. M's ideas on: 129*. M's views on poetic inspiration: 137

Poggietto, Cardinal: 111

Poggio (Bracciolione): 18, 40, 3

Pohle, Joseph: 93

Pöhmer, J. A.: 10

Poimandres: 35

Point of view, importance of in narration: 118

Pointon, Marcia: 39

Points, in musical notation: 121

Poiret, Pierre: 40

Poison Tree, A: 25

Poison: 128. Of Romish doctrine: 143

Pokius, William: 44

Poland (Polonia): 44, 49, 103, 3. King of: 120. Polanders: 51. Polish Prince: 44. Polish Brethren: see Socinians; Socinianism

Polanus: 128. Amandus: 47, 123*, 93

Polar Circles: 49

Polarisation, discovery of: 89

Pole (Poole), Cardinal Reginald: 40, 73, 93

Pole: 49

Poleman, Joachim: 7

Policies: 51. Root-and Branch: 51. Of those in power: 51

Policy: 51*. Of censorship: 51. Of licensing: 51

Polignac, Cardinal de: 58, 117

Politian (Angiolo Poliziano): 29, 40, 149

Political: conservatism, of author of Milton Restor'd: 88. Conservatism, Newton's, Warton's: 83. Attitude, Marchant's: 83. Beliefs: 117*. M's political convictions of 1660: 147. M's political judgements: 147. M's political activities, criticized: 58, 84

Political: controversies: 51. Discourse of Episcopacy: 51. Freedom: 51. Orations: 51. Pride: 51. Societies: 51. Structure: 51. Politicians: 51

Political: economy: 13. Evil: 113. M's conception of: 113. Freedom, M's religious interpreation of man's: 147, 51. Ideas: 55*; in M: 113*; in Augustine: 113; liberty: 55, 113; M on: 113; in anti-episcopal pamphlets: 55; popular sovereignty: 55; discipline: 55; regicide: 55; republicanism: 55; in Ready and Easy Way: 55; in PL: 55; in PR: 55. Philosophy, M's: 147. Theory: 51; M's and relations with government: 137. Views, M's: 28

Politics (Aristotle): 70, 121, 3

Politics: 31, 40, 51, 146. Poet's relation to: 123. Felicity as end of: 123

Poliziano, Angelo: 6, 44, 3, 39, 64

Pollak, O.: 6

Pollard: A. W.: 44, 135, 39. John: 45. Leonard: 93

Pollentius: 44, 73

Pollio: 44

Pollitt, Joe D.: 115

Pollock: Sir Frederick (on Tennyson's emulation of M): 87, 93. Thomas C.: 44, 56

Pollok: R.: 58. Robert: 65, 87*; natural Sublime in poetry of: 87; Satan in poetry of: 87. The Course of Time: 87

Pollux: 90, 122

Polo, Marco: 19, 128

Polus: 112

Polwhele, R.: 58*

Polyaenus: 40, 44

Polyandrus, Johannes: 54

Polybius (Greek historian): 1, 4, 40, 44, 73, 3, 32, 88, 93, 64, 115

Polycarp (Polycarpus), St.: 44, 73, 123, 144, 93. And Ignatius: 44

Polychronius: 74

Polyclitus: 132

Polycrates: 73

Polydamas: 44, 73

Polydamna: 90, 144

Polydeuces: 90

Polydore Virgil: 133

Polydore: 3

Polydorus: 2

Polygamy: 113, 136, 71, 93. M on: 113. Among the ancients: 113. Justified in De Doctrina Christiana: 136

Polyneices: 92

Polyolbion (Drayton): 88

Polypheme: 2

Polyphemus: 2, 44, 56, 73

Polyphonic music: 121

Polypragmaticus, Johannes. See Milton

Polypus. See Symbolism

Pomarius: 41

Pomerania: 49. See also: Charles X; Frederick William

Pomisania: 49

Pommer, Henry F.: 115

Pommerich, E.: 122

Pommier, Amelee: 65

Pomona: 1, 73, 90

Pomp, affect, on the Italian model, disliked by Warton: 88

Pompeius, Cnaeus: 3

Pompen, F. A.: 113

Pompey: 44, 122, 123, 62. Gnaeus Pompejus Magnus: 73

Pomponatius: 142

Pomponazzi, Pietro: 18, 114, 22, 93, 64

Pomponius Mela: 90, 32, 88

Pona, Cavalier Fran.: 65

Ponder, Nathaniel (bks., 1669-96): 91

Ponent: 144

Ponge, F.: 23

Pontano, Giovanni: 40, 59, 64

Pontanus: Jacobus: 40. Joannes Jovianus: 40, 65. Ludovicus: 64

Ponte, S. Angelo: 27

Pontia: 30, 128. (Bontia, alias Helen), Eng. maid of Salmasius: 44*, 73

Pontianus: 112

Pontic: 44

Ponticus, Heraclides: 55

Pontiew: 49

Pontifex, Mark: 79

Pontific College: 3

Pontoppidan: 128

Pontormo, Jacopo da: 27

Pontus: 90. Pontic: 49. Black Sea: 19, 49, 73

Poole: Mr.: 44. Dorothy (Pye): 45. Sir Edward: 45. Joshua: 44, 93; English Parnassus: 58, 91. Matthew: 54, 68, 22, 99; Annotations upon the Old and New Testament: 74

Pooley, W.: 58

Poolman, Mrs. E.: 44

Poor Richard Revived: Or Barber and Southwick's Almanack, For the Year of Our Lord, 1798: 115

Poor Robin: 44*

Poor, Henry W.: 44

Pope at Work: 12

Pope, the: 44, 47, 51. Protestant attitude toward: 51. Dread of: 143. As Antichrist: 143, 93. And usurper: 143. Throne of: 143. And ivy tree: 143. As father of falsehood: 143. Popery: 51, 114, 78. Popish: places: 51; religion: 51

Pope, Alexander: 12*, 15*, 16, 17, 19, 28, 35, 37, 44, 52, 56, 58*, 60, 68, 70, 73, 75, 86*, 87, 98, 100, 102, 105, 110, 120, 123, 124, 127, 136, 139, 141, 142, 14, 32, 39, 71, 72, 88*, 92, 93, 97, 94, 64, 109, 115*, 130, 137, 146*, 148, 150, 117*, 55, 21, 13, 132, 133, 3. Borrows from M: 58*. Followers of, not hostile to M: 58*. Influenced by M: 58. On M: 58. Thought inferior to M: 58. Compared with M: 146. The theme of PL as stated by: 83. Works:

Correspondence (ed. Sherburn): 12; Dunciad, The: 12, 82, 115; Epistles to Several Persons (Moral Essays): 12; Essay on Criticism: 12, 53; Essay on Man: 35, 141, 142, 109. Rape of the Lock, The: 12, 142; Satires: 12; Windsor Forest: 12, 115; Epistle to Augustus: 35

Pope: Arthur: 44. Eleanor: see Jones, Eleanor. Elizabeth: 26. Elizabeth Marie: 4, 17, 19, 52, 68, 81, 84, 123, 124, 128, 139, 93, 137; PR: The Tradition and the Poem: 74. Mary: 44. Mary Elizabeth: 85. W.: 58

Pope's Head Alley, London: 44

Popham, Edward: 44

Popish: Club: 44. Plot: 116

Popple, William: 44

Popular: approval: 51. Assemblies, advantages from creation of: 51. Creation of: 51. Distrust of: 51. Evil of: 51. Defects of: 51. Music: 121

Popularity of M: 58

Porcine Orations: 40

Porcupine, Alias the Hedge-Hog: Or Fox Turned Preacher, The: 115

Pordage: John: 7, 114, 142*; works: Innocence Appearing through Mists of Pretended Guilt: 142; Theologia Mystica: 142. Samuel: 60, 65*, 114, 142, 32, 36, 64; Mundorum Explicatio: 142, 36

Porden, W.: 58

Porphyry, Bp. of Gaza, life of: 125

Porphyry: 5, 7, 40, 73, 112, 114, 123, 142, 32, 64. Works: De Divinus atque Daemonibus: 142; De Sacrificio et Magia: 142; De antro nymphorum: 46

Porrino, G.: 59, 120

Port Folio, The: 115*

Porta Lucis (cabalistic): 40

Porta: Giovanni Battista della: 40. Malatesta: 123

Portal, A.: 58

Portalié, Eugène: 81

Portascith: 49

Portents: 144, 93. As testimony: 123*

Porter: A. M.: 58. John: 44

Porteus, B.: 58

Portia: 60

Portland: Duchess of: 44. Duke of, Report of Manuscripts of: 44. William Arthur Henry Cavendish Bentinck, 7th Duke of: 44

Portman, M. V.: 118

Portmann, Adolph: 118

Porto Longo, Spain: 44

Portonaris, Francesco: 40

Portoricus: 49

Portraits (M's): 28, 40, 44*, 146, 20, 55. See also: Ashfield; Bargrave; Bayfordbury; Cooper; Leutze; Flatman; Lamb; Faithorne; Hassel; Marshall; Jansen; Mytens; Onslow; Petitot; Richardson; Simon. See listings in Book 44*, Volume V

Portsmouth Collection: 78

Portsmouth: 49, 73

Portty, Richard: 44

Portugal (Lusitania): 44, 49, 103, 150. See also: John IV, King of Portugal; Sa de Menezes; Guimaraes; Alfonso V; Spain. Revolt in 1640: 60. Portuguese: 19, 40, 44, 150; literature: 88

Portumnus: 73

Portus, Aemilius: 40

Pory: Sir John: 19, 29, 40. Robert (1608?-68): 20, 40, 91

Poseidon: 2, 90. See also: Neptune

Posidonius: 4, 114

Posie of Prayers: 40

Posing of Accidence: 40

Positions (Mulcaster): 3

Positive thinking: 47

Positivism: 87, 142

Posnania: 49

Posselius, Johannes: 40

Possentesburg: 49

Possevino: Antonio, Tractatio de Poesi et Pictura Ethnica: 74. Giovanni Battista: 123

Possible, the: 51

"Possible and the impossible" use of: 51

Possidonus: 5, 128

Post Boy, The: 116

Post Man, The: 116

Post-Reformation Church: 51

Post, C. R.: 92

Postel, Guillaume: 40, 69, 93. Postellus, Gulielmo: 32

Potentates: 142

Pott, C.: 6

Potteius: 117

Potten: 45

Potter, author of Antiquities of Greece: 88

Potter: Mr.: 44. Charles: 40. Christopher: 40. Francis: 10. George R.: 44, 79, 115. Roland: 58*, 93, 117; on M: 58

Potterne: 45

Potts, L. J.: 131

Poulain de la Barre, Francois: 54

Poulet, Georges: 14, 39

Poulter, Mrs.: 44

Poultney, Sir William: 91

Poultry, London: 44

Pound, Ezra: 1, 23, 34, 44, 81, 86*, 105, 118, 124, 136, 138, 141, 39, 101, 130, 25

Poussin: 133. Nicholas: 6, 134, 146

Povensa: 49

Povey: Mr.: 44. Justinian: 91. Thomas: 10

Powel: Gabriel: 93. Griffin: 40

Powell Bond: 44

Powell-alias-Hinson, Sir William: 44, 45

Powell-alias-Hinson suit against All-Souls College: 44

Powell: family: 30, 44*, 45, 132, 150, 117, 55. Genealogy: 45. Mr.: 45. Miss: see Shuter, Mrs. Agnes: 45. Ambrose: 45. Mrs. Ann: 45. Anne: 45, 113. Anne: see Hinson, Anne. Anne: see Kingston, Anne. Anne (Moulton): 9, 44*, 45*. Anne (several, unidentified: 44. Anthony: 44. Archdale: 45.

Powell: Barbara (Cary): 45. Benjamin: 45. C. L.: 9, 28, 43, 71, 91. Catharine (Petre): 45. Chilton Latham: 54, 102, 93. Edmund (Edmond): 45. Sir Edward: 45, 45*. Elizabeth: 44, 45; see also: Holloway. Frances: 45. Francis: 45. George: 45.

Powell: Henry, M. P.: 44. James: 45. Jane: see Brokesby, Jane. Sir John: 8, 44, 45. John (judge): 44, 45. John (another): 44. Katherine (Young): 45. Lt. Capt.: 103. Marian: 45. Marie: 45.

Powell, Mary (1st Mrs. John Milton): M's 1st wife: 9, 15, 16, 28*, 30, 31, 35, 54, 59, 66, 84, 86, 87, 103, 45, 87, 113*, 120, 132, 136, 26, 38, 62, 71, 91, 93, 109, 146, 149, 148, 150, 137, 144; Leaves M: 94, 92, 113. Reconciled to M: 94, 113, 84. Death of: 94. M's marriage with: 132, 113, 94. Domestic unhappiness: 94. His children born: 94. See also: Milton, Mary Powell

Powell: Mary: see Jones, Mary. Mary (Newman): 45. Lady Mary (Vanlore): 45. Richard (M's father-in-law): 9, 28*, 40, 44*, 45*, 86, 103, 136, 137, 55, 94. Richard J. (M's brother-in-law): 44*, 84. Mrs. Richard: 103. Robert: 44. Sarah: see Pearson, Sarah. Sarah (Warburton): 45. Thomas: 45*. Vavasour: 114. William: 44, 45. Capt. William: 45. Winifred: 45. Winifred (Throgmorton): 45. Yeldard: 45

Powell's Buildings, London: 44

Power of Kings from God: 116

Power of Kings: 116

Power of Parliaments in the Case of Succession: 116

Power Age, The: 136

Power: Thomas: 91. William: 40

Power: 47, 51*, 141*, 92, 146. Ambivalence of symbol: 141. In the Church: 141. Represented by Christ, Satan: 141. In M: 141. M on power of kings: 51. See also:

Civilization

Powers of the Soul: 81*

Powers, Hiram: 98

Powers: 142

Powicke: F. J.: 132. F. M.: 15

Powis, Sir Thomas: 44

Powle: 44

Powlett, Thomas: 44

Powtrell: Dorothy: see Peckham, Dorothy. Walter: 45

Powys: Llewelyn: 60. T. F.: 35

Practicability: 51

Practical: appeal: 51. Ends: 51. Ideal: 51. Knowledge: 51. Means: 51

Practice: 51. Influence of artistic, and friends on the elder Richardsons' criticism: 88. Warton's literary, influences his critical work: 88. Dunster's theory differs from his critical: 88. Practices: educational: 51; of magistrates, condemned: 51

Practise of Christian: 40

Practise of Pietie: 40

Prae-existence: 58

Praedicatio: 40

Praeexercitamenta rhetoricae. See Progymnasmata

Praelectio: 40

Praelector: 40

Praeneste: 49

Praetorius, Michael: 40

Praevaricator: 40

Pragmaticus. See Needham, Marchamont

Pragmatographia: 15

Praise of Folly. See Erasmus

Praise: 51. And dispraise, themes in: 20. Praises for M from: Denham: 44; Dorset and Dryden: 44; Stubbe: 44

Prantl, Karl von: 40

Prat, Fernand: 79, 142. The Theology of St. Paul: 142

Pratensis, Felix: 40, 41

Pratt: Dr. Dallas: 44. E.: 58. S. N. ("Courtney Melmoth"): 58. Samuel Jackson: 115; The Sublime and Beautiful of Scripture: 115

Praxeas: 73

Prayer in Time of Captivity, A (in Eikon Basilike): 30

Prayer-Book: 15, 40. Book of Common: 44. 1549 edition: 40. Various Prayer-Book(s): 104; use of staff: 104; Scottish: 126. First of Edward VI, Collect for Burial of the Dead: 126. See also: Book of Common Prayer

Prayer: 7, 24, 47*, 93. "Prayer of Patience" (attr. to M): 44. Prayers by Colet and Erasmus: 20. Prayer of Humble Access: 126

Praz, Mario: 23, 27, 87, 128, 134, 141, 144, 97, 64, 131. The Hero in the Eclipse: 87

Preachers: 51. Preaching: 51; Christian: 51; persuasive: 51; to bind and loose: 143; as necessary for salvation: 143; Christ's sceptor and sword: 142; primary office of ministers: 143. See also: Word of God

Pre-Adamites: 44

Precamur sancte Domine: 121

Precationes...Hebraica, Graceca, et Latina (1528): 40

Precedency: 51. Precedents: 51

Precept: 51. Precepts and examples, study of: 20*, 31

Predestination: 7, 9, 47, 114*, 71, 60, 63, 81, 113, 122, 132, 36, 93. M on: 80. See also: Freedom

Predicament(s): 73, 40. Infernal: 123

Predication, limits and logic of: 96*

Preface to Paradise Lost (Lewis): 111, 134

Prefixes and suffixes: 98

Prejudices: 51

Prelacy. See Episcopacy

Prelates: 51*. M's attack on: 147. Prelate-martyrs: 51

Prelatical Episcopacy: 113, 132

Prelatry (M's views on): 30*, 51

Prelections on authors, teaching by: 20

Preliar: 141

Prelude: 26. Wordsworth: 3

Premierfait, Laurent de: 68

Premises: 51. Basic: 51. Minor: 51. Statement of: 51

Prendergast, J. P.: 44

Prendeville, J.: 88

Prentis, Rev. T. D.: 44

Prentiss, Charles: 115. Works: A Collection of Fugitive Essays, in Prose and Verse: 115; New England Freedom: A Poem Delivered Before the Washington Benevolent Society: 115

Pre-Raphaelites: 87, 97. Attitude toward M: 87

Pre-Reformation Church: 51

Prerogative and Privilege Represented in a Sermon: 116

Prerogative Court of Canterbury: 44, 45*. See also: Principal Probate Registry

Presbyter, Jack (nickname?): 44

Presbyterian: 113*. Covenant, M signed: 147. Bias: 51. Antipathy: 51. Belief: 51. Benefits: 51. Discipline: 51. Doctrine: 51. Party: 51. Predicament: 51. Establishment of Scotland: 103

Presbyterians(ism): 7, 8, 9*, 28*, 30, 44*, 51*, 52, 54, 60*, 103*, 114*, 132, 147*, 38*, 71, 78*, 94. M's relation to: 94. M's antipathy toward: 147. M's outburst against, on prerogatives of crown: 147. Against concept of toleration: 147. Agitate for reconciliation with king: 147. Agitate for state church: 147. Appeal for suppression of sects: 147. Arminius and creed of: 147. Censorship of: 147. Church organization of: 147. Distrust democratic notions: 147. Edwards leading pamphleteer of: 147; see also: Edwards. In Parliament, wish to disband Cromwell's army: 147. In practice reject Calvin: 147. Justify Parliamentary cause: 147. M an enemy of: 147, 55*. M declares for creed of: 147. M denounces program of: 147. M rejects creed of: 147. Ministers of, attack M's diverse tenets: 147. Ministers attack toleration: 147. Ministers of, for the king: 147. Ministers of, in Eng.: 147. Prosecute regicides: 147. Target of M in The Tenure: 147

Presbyters: 51, 103

Presbytery: 3

Prescience. See Foreknowledge

Prescott, William H.: 16

Present Means and Brief Delineation of a Free Commonwealth, The: 51

Present State of Engl. Language: 70

Present State of Europe: 116

Presentation, poetry as presentation vs. telling: 118

Press: 51. Eng.: 51. Free: 51

Prester John: 19, 32

Prestige, George L.: 93

Preston Capes: 45

Preston Cromarch: 45

Preston: John: 37, 40, 44, 54, 114, 32, 93. Sir Richard Graham, Viscount: 44; see also: Graham, Sir Richard. W.: 58

Preston: 44, 103

Prestwich, Rev. John: 44

Prestwich's Respublica: 44

Presumption: 47, 51, 114, 125. Praefidentia, contrary of fiducia or trust: 123

Pretension: 47

Preternatural in epic and tragedy: 149

Pretorius, Bernardus: 64

Prevenient grace: 93. See also: Grace

Prewet, Mr.: 44, 45

Pre-existent: "idea": 93. Matter: 93 Priam: 2, 56

Priapus: 73, 144

Price: Alan: 128. Daniel: 93. Gabriel: 93. H.: 58. James H.: 115; Miscellany, in Verse and Prose:

115. John: 44, 147; works: berates the Presbyterians in _Clerico-Classicum_: 147; writes Pulpit Incendiary (pamphlet against the king): 147. Martin: 25. Richard: 115. U.: 97. William: 93

Pride and Prejudice: 12

Pride, Thomas: 103, 38

Pride: 47, 50, 113, 122, 125, 143, 36*, 93, 25, 51. National: 51. Personal: 51. Political: 51. Religious: 51. Demonic: 47. Human: 47. M's: 17, 30*, 113*. As theme of PL: 83. As cause of Satan's revolt: 50. Satan's: 50, 113. As motive of Fall: 113. Sin of: 143. Satan descends through: 143. As basis of Satan's kingdom: 143. Its all-inclusive nature: 93. Of rebel angels: 93. Of man: 93. See also: Self-righteousness

Pride's Purge: 51, 147

Prideaux: 44. Edmund, Attorney General: 44, 45. Humphrey: 144. Bp. John: 40, 93, 64. Mathias: 93. Sir W. S.: 44

Priest(s): education of: 40. Eng. Catholic in Italy: 44

Priesthood, decided against by M: 40. M's hatred of: 113

Priestley: J. B.: 108. Joseph: 115, 13. William (elder): 44. William (Younger): 44. Mrs. William: 44

Primaudaye, Pierre de la: 15, 60, 100, 102

Prime, John: 93

Primero (a game): 40

Primers: 40

Primitive: thought patterns, relevance of to lit.: 118. Nature, the Richardsons' predilection for: 88. Art: 97

Primitivism: 50

Primogeniture: 83

Primum Mobile: 71. _Primum Mobile_, the: 89, 128

Prince of Darkness: 111. See also: Satan

Prince of Wales: 40

Prince Arthur: 65

Prince, education of: 40

Prince: E. T.: 111. Frank Templeton: 1, 6, 15, 23, 27, 37, 52, 56, 59, 60, 81, 86*, 105, 120, 122, 127, 135, 14, 26, 85, 64, 101, 150; _Italian Element in M's Verse_: 74. Thomas: 44, 45

Prince's Arms (bookshop): 44

Princely Pelican: 91

Princeton Univ.: 44. Library: 44. Press: 112

Principal: 45. Coppice: 45. Probate Registry: 44

Principalities: 142

Principia Mathematica: 78

Principles of Christian Religion, The (Ussher): 134

Principles of Taste (Knight), M's marginalia in: 13

Printemps d'yver, Le: 40

Printers: M's: 55. Lists of ca. 1560: 40. At Cambridge: 40

Printing: 51. Control of: 51. Acts: 103. Commissioners for Regulation of: 44. In 17th c.: 50. Printing-publishing locations: 40

Priolo, Benjamin: 44

Prior: Matthew: 44, 58*, 88, 115, 117; criticism by: 94; influenced by M, praises PL: 58. O. H.: 128. William: 44

Priscian: 20*, 30, 40, 44, 73

Prison: 45. M in: 44*

Pritchard: James B.: 64. John P.: 68, 100, 144, 36; "Fathers of the Church": 74. Paul: 57

Pritius. See Milton, Literae Pseudosenatus

Private person: 122. See also: Public person

Private tutor: 40

Private Correspondence and Academic Exercises: 112, 134. See also: Milton, Works

Privation, principle of: 40

Privie Counsels. See Privy Council

Priviledges of the People (Joseph

Warr): 147

Privileges, Committee for: 44

Privy Council: 40, 44, 51

Privy Seal: 45

Prix de Rome: 97

Prizes at St. Paul's School: 40

Pro se Defensio (M): 112, 147, 94. See also: Milton, John, Works

Pro A Lincinio Archio Poetica Oratio: 62

Pro Populo Adversus Tyranno: 44. See also: Milton, John, Works

Pro Populo Adversus Tyrannos: 44, 116. Compared with The Tenure of Kings and Magistrates: 116

Pro Populo Anglicano Defensio: 116*, 136, 94. Compared with Mr. Hunt's Postscript and Julian the Apostate: 116*. See also: Milton, John, Works

Pro Rege et Populo Anglicano, etc.: 103. See also: Rowland, J.

Proaemium: 121

Proairesis: 51. Moral choice: 123

Proba: 44, 3. Valeria Faltonia: 65, 74, 32, 36; Cento: 36, 74

Probability: 122. Probabilities: 51. "Probability" in plot: 70; in plot and character: 123*

Probationary Odes: 58

Problemata: 40

Problems (Aristotle): 128, 121

Problems: 40. Intellectual: 51

Probus: 1, 4

Process: 53*

Processus Belial: 36

Processus Individuationis: 141*. Greek type: 141. Jewish type: 141. Ambivalent reactions to: 141. Inflation: 141. Regression: 141

Proclamation: 45. Proclamation against M: 44, 91. Proclamations, Royal: 51

Proclomation For Calling in, and suppressing two Books written by John Milton: 116

Proclus: 7, 40, 73, 90, 112, 121, 123, 125, 142, 32, 93, 64. Works: In Platonicum Alcibiadem de Anima atque Daemone: 142; Manual of Literature: 74; The Elements of Theology: 142

Procne: 90

Procopius (Byzantine historian): 44, 68, 73, 74. Official: 73. Procopius of Caesarea: 82; works: De Bello Persico: 82; Historiarum Libri VIII: 82. Of Gaza: 55, 123, 32

Procrustes: 1, 60, 123

Proctor: Robert: 40. Sherwin: 150

Proctors: 40

Proculeius: 60

Prodicus: 123

Prodigal son, parable of: 72

Prodromus: Petrus: 65. Theodorus: 68

Proem: 51. See also: Exordium, introduction

Proemium to the 4 Justitiaei (Cook): 88

Professional life: 51. Professions: 51

Progress: 51, 132, 143. Belief in: 132. A delusion: 143. Conflicting ideas of: 143. Discredited: 143

Progresse of the Soule (Donne): 118

Progressio Quaternaria: 100*. Inverted: 100*

Progressive Revelation: 9*

Progymnasma scholasticum (Stockwood): 20

Progymnasmata (Greek name for exercises in prose theme writing): 20, 82

Progymnasmata: by Aphthonius. By Hermogenes: 20*. By Theon: 20

Prohibition(s): 51. Reason for future: 31

Projet du plan de la création: 65

Prolepsis: 123

Prolixity, Thyer opposed to Italian, finding it dulls the mind: 88

Prologos: 92*

Prologue: 50

Prologues and Invocations: to PL: 31. Comus: 143

Prolusio: 40

Prolusion(s): 3*, 40, 113, 129, 134*, 26, 62. And 17th c. academic life: 134. Criticism and curriculum: 134. M on learning: 134. Of M: Prolusion II, III, V, VI, VII: 112; see also: Milton, John, Works; Imagery

Prometheus (Aeschylus): 130

Prometheus Bound: 1, 70, 26

Prometheus Desmotes: 141

Prometheus Lyomenos: 141

Prometheus Unbound (Shelley): 130

Prometheus: 1*, 2, 17, 34, 44, 56, 60, 68, 73, 90, 95, 114, 121, 128, 141*, 3, 32, 72, 92*, 146. And M's Satan: 141. As hero: 141. As sinner: 141. And Christ: 141. And Lucifer: 141. And Satan: 141*. And hubris: 141. As symbol of human existence and civilization: 141. Interpretion of myth: 141. Development of myth: 141. Romantic conception of: 141. In lit.: 141

Promise, object of faith: 123*. Promised Land: 72. Promised Seed: 96

Promos and Cassandra (Whetstone): 70

Promptorium (1499): 40

Pronouns (inconsistency): 50

Pronunciation: 51, 117. Of early Eng.: 20. Pearce on classical and Elizabethan, of proper names: 88. Sympson on stage: 88. M's, and his spellings: 88. Aubrey's testimony on M's, adduced by Lofft: 88. By Lofft: 88. Todd on spellings and: 88. See also: Phonetic

Pronuntiatio or actio, part four of rhetoric: 20

Proof-Reading in the 16th, 17th and 18th c. (Simpson, P.): 135

Proof: 31, 51*. Deductive: 51. Ethical: 51*. Inductive: 51. Logical: 51*. Method of: 51. Non-artistic: 51*. Pathetic: 51*. Proposition, more proof: 51. Proofs, artificial: 123. See also: Modes of persuasion

Proofreading: 50

Propert, John L.: 44

Propertius, Sextus: 1, 4, 15, 20, 40, 44, 90, 114, 123, 128, 64*, 148, 117, 21

Property, risks to: 51

Properzi, Daniele: 65

Prophecies of Daniel: 78

Prophecy: 7, 51, 114*, 11, 25. Education by, nature of, design of, Blake's conception of, Newton's conception of, Swedenburg's conception of, structure of, treatises on, and oratory: 25. And history, tradition of, and vision, and mythology, time dimensions of, explication of, and imagination, not prediction, failing of, obscurity of: 25. And poetry: 53*. Prophecying: 142; meaning of: 143; supported by Grindal: 143

Prophet: 25. As creator: 25. As interpreter: 25. Stance of: 25. Relation to audience: 25. Rage of: 25. Prophets: education of: 40; the Hebrew: 141

Propitiation, The: 115

Proportion: 51, 121*. Rule of: 40

Proportional structure, epic blocks: 100*. Invocative blocks: 100

Proposal for Correcting, Improving and Ascertaining the Engl. Tongue (Swift): 3

Proposals of Certaine Expedients (attr. to M): 9, 44

Propositio confirmatio: 40

Proposition: 51*. Statement of: 51. Of poem: 123. See also: Statement

Propositions and conclusions (a tolerationist demand by the Baptists): 147

Propriety, in poetic characters: 123. See also: Decorum

Prose style (M's): 55*. Todd on: 88. Miscellaneous, discussed: 55. Latin exercises: 55. Latin letters: 55. Anti-episcopal pamphlets: 55. See also: Individual works

Prose works (M's): 55*, 129*. Autobiography in: 129. Presentation copy of: 44*. Their form: 129. Idealism of: 129. Translations: 58. Writing: 40. Works: 146*, 117*; 18th c. interest in: 58; M's account: 55; early editions: 55. See also: Individual titles

Proserpina (Proserpine): 1, 19, 27, 44, 73, 90*, 102, 112, 144, 3, 32, 72, 25

Prosody: of the 18th c., M's influence on: 58*. Eng. metrical: 40. Greek metrical: 40. Hebrew metrical: 40. Latin metrical and prose: 40. M's criticized: 58. Rules of, studied: 20. See also: Verse

Prosopopoeia: 20

Prosper, of Aquitaine, St.: 65, 73, 36, 93. Carmen de Providentia Divina: 36

Prosper: 74. De Promissionibus et Praedictionibus Dei: 74*

Prosperity: 51

Prospero: 72

Prosperus Aquitanus. See Prosper, of Aquitaine

Protagoras (Plato): 112

Protagoras: 20, 51, 73, 112, 121, 123, 3

Protector, the (Edward Seymour, Duke of Somerset): 73

Protector, Lord: 146. Protectorate: 9*, 51, 103. Protectoratists: 51

Protesilaos: 123

Protestant: 51*, 103, 3. Controlled in religion by State: 51. Churches abroad: 51. Countries: 51. Martyrs: 51. Thinking: 51. Reformation: 50*. Reformers: 71. League, proposed by Philip Sidney: 83. Protestants: 103, 3. Individualism, dynamics of: 147*; M's: 147; outcome of, as an intellectual method: 147

Protestantism: 7, 8, 27, 44, 51*, 60, 103, 142, 143*, 53, 72. Devotion to: 51. Loyalty to: 51. Nature of: 51. Origin of: 51. Conflict of, with Catholicism in the 16th c.: 83*. Ethic of: 60. Radical: 52*. Jesuit attack on: 142. Dependence on Scholastic doctrine: 142. And secular power: 143. Basic doctrine of: 143. And Calvin: 143. And Geneva Bible: 143. Essential ideas in: 143. Protestant Bible: 143

Protestation Protested (Henry Burton): 147

Proteus: 73, 90, 104, 128, 3. Proteus Myth: 57

Protevangelium: 123, 32*, 93. Protevangelium: 93

Prothalamion (Spenser): 130

Prothema: 40

Protoparentum crimen et poena: 65

Protoplastus: 65

Prototypes, heroic, classical and Biblical: 123*

Proudfit, Alexander: 115. The Ruin and Recovery of Man: 115

Proust, Marcel: 23, 34, 35, 54, 86, 135, 139, 39

Provence, France: 44

Proverb, in theme writing: 20

Proverbs: 44, 74, 112, 139, 3

Proverbs: 92. Proberbs viii: M's interpretation: 107; Origen's interpretation: 107. Orthodox interpretation: 107; source of invocation to Book VIII of PL: 107. See also: Bible

Providence, colony of: 51

Providence: 17*, 31*, 51, 122*, 123, 93, 25. M's justification of: 52*. Providential view of history: 93*. See also: God

Providentia (Catelina): 49. See also: Tortuga

Provincia: 49

Provincial states: 51

Provocation: 125

Prowde: family: 44. Catherine: see Phillips. Richard: 44. Thomas: 44

Prowett, S.: 97

Prudence: 51, 122*, 123. Prudent foresight: 51. Prudent spirit: 51

Prudentius Clemens, Aurelius: 20, 44, 57, 65, 68, 74, 3, 36, 82, 32, 88, 149. Works: Hamartigenia: 36, 149; Peristephanon: 74, 82; Dittochaeon: 149; Psychomachia: 74, 149

Prufrock, J. Alfred: 72

Prunières, H.: 6

Prussia (Borussia): 44, 49

Prutenic(k) tables: 73, 89, 128

Prynne, William: 9*, 13, 20, 33*, 44*, 51, 59, 60, 66, 68, 73, 84, 85, 87, 103, 121, 116, 120, 147*, 39, 71, 91, 55. Attacks M's divorce theory: 147. Attacks the prelates: 147. Calvinist disciple: 147. For reconciliation with Charles: 147. Historical and political arguments: 147. Protests inconsistency of the Independents: 147. Struggle against the Independents: 147. Views on tithes: 147. Works: A Fresh Discovery (attacks Lilburne in): 147, 91; and license of the press: 147; A Fresh Discovery of some Prodigious New Wandring-Blasing-Stars (on liberty of conscience): 147; Breife Memento (shows that the Presbyterians again favored the king): 147; Histrio-Mastix (causes his imprisonment): 147, 88, 82, 94; A Serious and Faithful Representation (does not defend the king): 147; Lame Giles His Haultings (attacks the Laudian tenets): 147; Divorce at Pleasure (pamphlet against M): 147; Twelve Considerable Questions: 91; Mount Orguil: 91; Republicans and Others: 91; Sword of Magistracy: 91; True Narrative: 91

Przybylski, Jacek Idzi: 117

Psallein: 121

Psalm paraphrases: 40, 44, 132, 94. M's trans and paraphrases of, in general: 15, 20, 28, 30, 44, 50, 94. See also: Milton, John, Works

Psalms: 2, 40, 44, 74*, 90, 121, 139, 144, 3, 132, 39, 72, 99, 48, 106, 55. Psalms 1648: 9, 16. Psalm II (attr. trans. M): 44. Psalm XXII: 126*; for Good Friday: 126; Venite of Morning Prayer: 126; Jubilate Deo of Morning Prayer: 126; Cantate Domino of Evening Prayer: 126*. Psalmbooks: 40. Psalter: 40, 67. Psalter, Anglican: 40. Psalter, Hebrew: 44. Psalter, Jewish: 40. Psalter (Ravenscroft): 121

Psellus, Michael Constantine: 60, 112, 123, 142*, 93. Works: De Daemanibus: 142; De Operatione Daemonum Dialogs: 142; Dialogue on the Operation of Daemons: 142; Traicte Par Dialogue de L'Energie ou Operations des Diables: 142

Pseudo-hero, Satan as: 123

Pseudo-pilgrims: 47. See also: Apostasy; Apostates

Pseudo-Basil: 24*, 32. See also: Basil, St.

Pseudo-Bede: 36. Commentaries on the Pentateuch: 36

Pseudo-Bonaventure: 36, 99. Mirrour of the Blessed Lyff of Jesus Christ: 36

Pseudo-Callisthenes: 128

Pseudo-Chrysostom: 99

Pseudo-Clementine Homilies, Son is substance but not essence of God, Son self-originated: 107

Pseudo-Dionysius: 41, 38, 39. See also: Dionysius the Areopagite

Pseudo-Eustathius: 128

Pseudo-Jerome: 99

Pseudo-Rashi: 41

Pseudo-Tertullian: 36. Against all the Heresies: 36

Pseudopigrapha: 24

Psyche: 1, 29, 73, 104, 112, 3, 72, 25

Psyche: 65, 90

Psychoanalysis: 47, 113

Psychology: 17*, 113*, 25. Psychological: element: 92; method, Hume's lack of: 88; examination of M's sentence structure by Pearce: 88; approach to lit. of the Richardsons due to their personal practice of art and friendship with writers: 88; analyses of sentence structure, their: 88; probability in PL, the Richardsons on: 88; features of style, Peck on: 88; valuation of poetry, Thyer's: 88. inquisitiveness, Newton usually lacks, yet gives a psychological explanation of the value of classical tradition: 88; method, Warton's: 88; combined by Dunster with aesthetic and biographical methods: 88; and artistic considerations applied by Dunster to chronological problems: 88; treatment of style in Stillingfleet's notes, rudiments of: 88

Psychomachia: 65, 79. And Samson's soul-struggled: 126

Psychopannychism: 22, 93. Psychopannychites: 142

Psychotic thought patterns similarity to those of children and primitives: 118

Ptolemaeus (Kings of Egypt): Ptolemaeus Euergetes (i.e., "benefactor"), Ptolemy III: 73. Ptolemaeus (Euergetes II) Physcon (i.e., "fat paunch"): 73. Ptolemaeus Auletes (i.e., "flute player"): 73

Ptolemy, Lucius Claudius: 4, 6, 15, 19, 40, 89*, 144, 32, 71, 72, 94. Ptolemaic system: 27, 71, 94, 89*, 109; described: 89; additions in the Middle Ages: 89; harmonious sound associated with the revolution of the sphere: 89; description of substance and fuction of the spheres: 89; the universe circumscribed and within the power of man's mental capacity: 89; eccentric, epicycle and others expedients in: 89; multiplication of spheres: 89; supremacy of the sun in: 89; the stars in: 89; shattered by Copernican system: 89; Raphael's remarks on: 102; status of in 17th c.: 102; why used by M: 102; and the Geometric universe: 128*; and PL: 61. Geographia: 144

Public Faith of Alexander More: 30

Public Intelligencer: 44, 103, 91

Public Record Office: 40, 44. A Guide to: 45. Lists and Indexes: 45. "P. R. O. Research: The Equity Side of Chancery, 1558-1714": 45

Public: 51. Affairs: 51. Controversies: 51. Events: 51. Good: 51, 122. Leadership: 51. Life: 51. Men: 51. Mind: 51. Office: 51. Officer: 92*. Opinion: 51. Orator (univ.): 40. Purpose: 51. Person: 122; see also: Private person; Leadership; Sovereignty. Question: 51. Schools of the univ.: 40. Speaking, M on: 51

Publications of the Modern Language Association of America (PMLA): 48

Publius (Publilius), Syrus: 40

Puccini, Giacoma: 125

Puckering: Sir Henry Newton: 44, 59. Sir Thomas: 40

Puclekerke: 49

Pudicitia: 90

Pudsey, William: 44

Puech, H. C.: 36

Puente, Luis dela: 93

Pufendorf (Samuel von): 7, 44

Pularonis Insula: 49. See also: Banda

Pulci, Luigi: 19, 114, 64, 21

Pullein, S.: 58

Pulley, William: 93

Pulleyn, Octavian (bks.): 44

Pulpit Incendiary (John Price): 147

Pulse: 128

Pump Court: 45

Puncheon portrait of M: 44

Punctuaction: Hume's misreading of M's: 88. Bentley's treatment of M's: 88. Pearce on M's: 88. Haukey tries to restore M's original: 88. David Steel of M's: 88. Lofft on: 88. Lofft's system of, too elaborate and arbitrary: 88

Punic Coast: 49, 73

Punishment: 47, 122, 20, 40. Corporal, of schoolboys: 20, 40. Of burning for females, abolished by act of Parliament, fear of: 147. See also: Merit; Reward

Punjab: 19

Puns: 15, 98, 117. Hume's dislike of: 88. Richardson's and Sir Walter Raleigh's defence of: 88. Punning: 46

Pupils, M gives up his: 94. Letters to, names of: 30

Purbach: 89

Purbeck: 49

Purcell, Henry: 40, 121, 39, 130

Purchas, Samuel: 1, 10, 15, 19*, 24*, 40, 44, 50, 57*, 102, 110, 128, 32*, 36, 82, 88, 93, 150, 142, 55, 77. Pagan gods: 144*. Moloch, Chemosh, Thammuz, Dagon: 144. Accounts of creation: 144. First act of creation: 144. Light: 144. Man: 144. Eden: 144. Mt. Amara: 144. Works: Pilgrimage: 57, 77, 144, 36; Pilgrimes: 57, 82

Purdy, A. C.: 79

Purefoy, Col. William (member and President of Council of State): 44

Purfoote, T.: 40

Purgatorio (Dante): 70

Purgatory: 111, 143, 71, 93. Idea repugnant to M: 107; Mount of: 32

Purification, origin of: 41

Purified soul, hero as: 123

Puritan(s): 7, 27*, 31, 40, 44, 51, 60*, 83, 87*, 103*, 113, 121, 136, 147*, 71, 94, 150. Origin on term: 87. Attack on lit.: 31. Revolution: 60*, 25. Sympathies of Spenser: 83. Sympathies of Sidney: 83. Attitude toward music: 121. Tradition, M's relationship to: 94. Renaissance: 71. Autobiography: 106. Admonition to Parliament, appeal for civil protection: 147. Commercial efficiency of: 147. Contradictions in personalities of: 147. Creed of, diverse effects of: 147, 113. Demand redress of church grievances: 147. Distrust democracy: 147. Economic philosophy of: 147. Emphasize private virtues: 147. Fanaticism of: 147. Habits of: 147. Intolerance of: 147. Persecute the Separatists: 147. Prosperous settlers of Massachusetts Bay: 147. Provoke anger of James: 147. Psychology of: 147. Ridiculed: 87. As stern people: 87. Traditional view of: 87. Anglican reaction to: 87. Typical Royalist view of: 87. Enemies of art and culture: 87.

Concept of church government: 87. Misrepresented: 87. Failure of: 113. Represented by Samson: 113. Readers of the Bible: 147. Resist the Crown: 147. Habit to reason politically from God downward to humanity: 147. Puritan leader emerges: 147. See also: Puritanism

Puritanism: 7, 9*, 27*, 52, 54*, 60, 83*, 87*, 114*, 132, 139, 141, 144*, 143, 72, 109. Puritan ministers: 51. And church reform: 143. Concept of history: 144. Taste of: 144. Faith of: 144. View of Belial and Satan: 144*. And Bible: 144. And the Word: 143. And democracy: 143. Conformity and uniformity in: 71*. Definition of: 71, 143. M's relation to: 52*, 60, 87, 113, 146, 71; of M's later poetry, Warton opposed to: 88; combined with mysticism, Warton on: 88; Warton's antagonism to, attacked in Letter to Warton: 88; M as: 87*; Victorian approaches to M's: 87; key to M's life and work: 87; a stern, narrow discipline: 87; uncritical view of: 87; historical view of: 87; grotesque side of: 87; M the genius of: 87. In PL: 83. In SA: 52*. See also: Milton, attitude towards: Baptists, Congregationalists, Fifth Monarchists, Independents, Levellers, Millenarians, Puritans, Presbyterians, Quakers, Ranters, Seekers, Socinians

Purity: 36

Purity: 69*, 123, 51. Of M's life: 44

Purley, Mr.: 44

Purple Island, The (Fletcher): 1, 65, 134, 26

Purpose, M's: 50

Pursglove, William: 19

Pursuit(s): 2. Intellectual: 51

Purves, J.: 59

Purye, Nicholas: 45

Pusey, Edward: 87

Pustozera: 49

Puteanus: 146. Erycius (Hendrik van der Putten): 29, 40, 64, 117; Comus: 55. James: 44

Putnam, C. J.: 21

Putney Debates: 9

Putney Projects (Wildman): 147. Attacks the Proposal of the Army: 147

Putney: 44

Puttenham, George: 1, 4, 15, 20, 23, 33, 56, 59, 60, 66, 69, 79, 100, 135, 142, 145, 93, 21. The Art of English Poesie: 142, 74

Puttick and Simpson (bks.s): 44

Puy, H. du: 129

Puytendre, Louis de: 44

Pye: family: 45. Miss: see Phillips, Mrs. Anne (Hampden): 45. Bridget (Kirk): 45. Charles (engraver): 44. Dorothy: see Poole, Dorothy. Edmund: 45. Sir Edmund: 45. Mrs. H.: 58. Hampden: 45. Henry James: 45, 58, 117.

Pye: Joan (Rudhall): 45. John: 44*, 45*. Sir John: 45. Letice: 45. Mary: see Speake, Mary. Mary (Croker): 45. Rebecca (Raynton): 45. Richard: 45. Sir Robert: 44*, 45*, 103, 94. Sir Roger: 45. T.: 58. Thomas: 45. Sir Walter: 45. William: 45. Sir William: 45

Pygmies: 90, 144. See also: Pigmies

Pyle, Fitzroy: 40, 59, 14

Pym, John: 9, 10, 33, 59, 60

Pynchon, William: 148

Pynfold, Robert: 44

Pynson, Richard: 40

Pyramids: 19, 89, 144

Pyramus: 73

Pyre, J. F. A.: 87

Pyrene: 44, 49

Pyrrha: 1, 56, 73, 90, 72

Pyrrho: 114*

Pyrrhonists (Pironicks): 60. Pyrrhonism: 72

Pyrrhus: 73, 120, 123, 3

Pythagoras: 4, 7, 20, 34, 40, 44, 51, 52, 57, 60, 73, 89, 100*, 112, 114, 121*, 123, 125, 128, 142, 145, 3, 32, 39, 71, 72, 88, 92, 93, 64, 25. Influence upon "Cosmopolitanism": 107. Pythagorean: 125; theories: 100*; system: 121; ideas: 38; platonic doctrine: 136; see also: Progressio Quaternaria. Pythagoreans: 88

Pythian: 90, 3. Apollo: 112. Fields: 49, 73; see also: Delphos. Oracle: 3. Vale: 19

Pythias: 123

Pythius. See Apollo

Python: 60, 73, 90, 123

-Q-

<u>Qain</u>: 65

Qere and Khetiv (Ketiv): 41, 22

Quack doctors: 8

Quadragesimal: 51

Quadrants: 40

<u>Quadriregio, Il</u>: 65

Quadrivium: 40, 103, 3. Mathematical arts of the: 20

Quadrumvirate of Angels: 41

Quaestio: 40

<u>Quaestiones Naturales</u> (Seneca): 3

Quakers: 7*, 9, 44, 51, 83*, 103, 132, 147, 94, 38. Against tithes and the ministry: 147. Persecuted under Cromwell: 147. Tolerant of Catholics: 147. M's approval of: 83. M's acquaintance with: 83. M and the: 132. Quakerism: 114*. See also: Friends

Quality: a performer: 40. Of tone: 121

Quantitative: Eng. verse: 40. Standards in Newton's appreciation of poetry: 88

Quantity: a performer: 40. Logical: 123. Mathematical: 123. In verse, Newton's misapplication of principle of: 88

Quaritch, Bernard (bks.): 40, 44

Quarles: Francis: 15, 40, 68, 74, 114, 144*, 92, 93*, 64, 101, 115, 117; works: <u>Histoirie of Samson</u> and SA: 144*, 74*; realism of: 144; Samson's mission: 144; Delila's stratagems: 144; mentioned, as source for SA: 55; <u>Feast for Wormes...the History of Jonah</u>: 74; <u>Hadassa...the History of Queene Ester</u>: 74; <u>Job Militant</u>: 74*. James: 45. Martha: see Doyley, Martha

<u>Quarrel of the Ancients and Moderns</u>: 150

<u>Quarrel of Adam and Eve</u>: 118

Quarry Copse: 44, 45

Quarter of 1637 (Comus): 29*

<u>Quarterly Review</u>: 44, 63, 146

Quartos: 135. "Good quartos": 135. Shakespeare: see <u>Richard II</u>

Quasimodo, Salvatore: 111

Quasten, Johannes, credits Origen with invention of theological terms: 107

Quatbrig: 49

<u>Quebec</u>: 58

Queen Anne's Mansions, Petty France: 44

<u>Queen Elizabeth's Bishops</u>: 9

Queen Mary's cushion: 128

Queen Regent (Mary of Guise): 73

Queen Street, London: 44

Queen's Bench: 45

Queen's College, Belfast: 44

Queen's College, Cambridge: 40*, 45, 103

Queen's College, Oxford: 40, 45

"Queens Walk" Harefield: 29

Queenhithe (Queene-Hithe), London: 44, 49. See also: Charing Cross

Quell, Gottfried: 93

Quennell, Peter: 52

Querela Temporum: 116

Queries of Highest Consideration (Roger Williams): 147

Querilly, France: 44

Questions: 51

Quick: 3. Oliver C.: 93. R. H.: 40

Quierzy, Synod of: 36

Quies: 90

Quietism: 141

Quietists: 7

Quill: 121

Quiller-Couch, Sir Arthur: 16, 132, 133, 144

Quillet, C.: 53

Quiloa: 19, 49, 73, 144. See also: Mozambique

Quincy, Josiah, Jr.: 115. Observations on the Act of Parliament Commonly Called the Boston Port-Bill: 115

Quinn: Dennis B.: 93. E. C.: 36

Quinquarboreis, Joannes: 40

Quintessence: 128. See also: Elements

Quintianus, Joannes F.: 65, 117

Quintilian, Fabius (Roman rhetorician): 1, 5, 18, 20*, 31, 40*, 44, 51, 56, 59, 57, 70, 73, 118, 120, 123, 145, 3*, 26, 53, 82, 115, 130, 146, 117, 21, 94, 88

Quintius: 73, 3. Lucius Cincinnatus (Roman gen. and statesman): 73

Quintus Smyrnaeus: 90, 123

Quirini Arx: 49

Quirinus (Romulus): 73, 90

Quirt, Capt.: 1

Quispel, G.: 36

Quistorp, Heinrich: 93

Quistorpius, Joannes, Annotationes in Omnes Libros Biblicos: 74

Quiting, Arnold: 65

Quixote, Don: 1

"Quod cum coelicolis habitus" (on William Staple, attr. to M): 44

Quomodo: 45

Quotation: 51. Excessive, in Warton's edition attacked in Letter to Warton: 88. Quoting previous decisions: 51. See also: Illustration

Qvarnström, Gunnar: 100, 106

-R-

R., W.: 117. See also: Rawlins, William

Raab, Felix, The Eng. Face of Machiavelli: A Changing Interpretation: 82

Rabadan, Mahomet: 123

Raban Maur (Rabanus Maurus): 40, 74, 123, 36. Works: Commentary on Genesis: 36; Allegoriae in Universam Sacram Scripturam: 74; Commentaria in Exodum: 74; Commentaria in... Judicum: 74; Commentaria in Libros Quattuor Regum: 74; Commentariorum in Matthaeum: 74; De Universo: 74; Enarrationum in Librum Numerorum: 74

Rabba(n) (city): 49, 73

Rabba: 144

Rabbah barbar Hana: 128

Rabbinical: books: 40. Commentators on Scriptures: 40, 41, 144. Expressions, in M, Todd on: 88. Hebrew: 40, 42. Interest, M's: 60. Lit.: 60, 88. Texts available to M in translation: 41

Rabbis: 15, 40, 141, 22*. The Jewish: 141. M's knowledge of: 141. And rabbinical writings: 22*

Rabelais, Francois: 1, 15, 40, 87, 114, 136, 3, 39, 18, 64

Raben, Joseph: 111

Rabirius, Gaius: 73

Rabshakeh: 44. See also: M. Needham

Raby, F. J. E.: 74, 133, 36, 64.

History of Christian Latin Poetry: 74

Rachel: 60, 72

Racheli, A.: 122

Racine, Jean Baptiste: 5, 6*, 15, 100, 97, 94, 101, 130, 117, 133. Translated: 58; see also: Symmetrical structure. Louis: 117

Rack, Edmund: 115

Rackham: Arthur: 27, 97. H.: 23

Racovians: 103. Racovian Catechisme: 44, 59, 74, 22, 78

Radbertus, St. Paschasius: 99, 64

Radcliffe, A.: 58

Radclyffe (engraving from M portrait): 20

Radek: 35

Rader, J. L.: 128

Radiant point: 39

Radical party: 51

Radicalism (M's : 25

Radices Graece Lingua: 40

Radici Libini: 40

Radnorshire: 49

Radzinowicz, Mary A. Nevins: 122, 93

Raffaelle. See Raphael (Sanzio)

Raffaelo Sanzio. See Raphael (Sanzio)

Ragg: Lonsdale: 123. Laura: 123. Thomas, The Deity: 87

Rahab: 68, 73, 36, 25*

Rahere: 103

Rahner: Hugo: 93. Karl: 93

Raimbach, A.: 97

Raimond (Ramon Lull): 114

Raimondi, E.: 5

Raimundis comitibus: 73

Rain: 128*. Causes and kinds: 128

Rainborough, Thomas: 9, 60, 148

Rainbow: 123. Causes and kinds: 128

Raine, Kathleen: 12, 25

Raines, Richard: 44

Rainolds (Reynolds), Dr. John: 44, 51, 73, 94, 91, 30, 40

Rainsborough, property rights with scriptural reasoning: 147

Raiziss, S.: 23

Rajan, Balachandra: 1, 12, 15, 23, 34, 52, 54, 56, 59, 60, 66, 75, 76, 81, 86*, 100, 105, 110, 122, 123, 127, 128, 141*, 142, 36, 53, 85, 93, 106, 137, 146, 140. PL and the 17th c. Reader: 95, 142

Rákóczy, Prince (George the 2nd of Transylvania): 10, 44

Rakow, Poland: 44

Raleigh: Miss: see Elloway, Mrs. Anne (Chamberlaine): 45. Bridget: see Cope, Bridget. Carew: 45. Sir Edward: 45. W.: 68, 105, 110, 141. Sir Walter (1861-1922): 1, 15, 23, 34, 35, 102, 103, 107, 133, 134, 59, 138, 88, 150, 148, 60, 93, 130*, 140; on Shakespeare's sonnets, M's Satan, Dr. Johnson: 87; defends M's prose: 87; on M's Puritanism: 107; comments on PL: 83, 55, 87, 30; M's political activities defended: 87; on decline of Satan's popularity: 87; conception of PL: 87; attitude toward M's artistry: 87; PL, a monument to dead ideas: 87, 123; Milton: 87, 142, 109, 48

Raleigh, Sir Walter (1552-1618): 1, 15, 19*, 24*, 27, 18, 28, 35, 40, 44*, 52, 54, 56, 59, 60, 63, 65, 69, 76, 77, 86*, 87*, 90, 100, 102, 103, 113, 114, 116, 120, 122, 124, 123*, 132*, 134, 142, 144*, 145, 147, 3, 32*, 36, 88, 92, 93*, 64, 101, 115, 130, 137, 146, 148, 117, 48, 13. On: site of Eden, Flood, Nimrod, law, Satan, Arimaspi, Busiris, history: 144. On pagan gods: 144*. On: 1st act of creation, light, sun, firmament, man, Adam, starts: 144. His style and M's: 144. Reputation: 144. On God: 144. Works: Cabinet Council: 28, 144, 55; History of the World: 74, 55, 144*, 77, 36, 82; 12th Book of Ocean to Cynthia: 35; Pilgrim to Pilgrim: 35

Ralph: J.: 58. James: 115*; works: The Muses's Address to the King: 115; Night: A Poem: 115; Sawney: 115

Ram, constellation of: 44

Ramah: 49

Ramath-Lechi: 49, 73, 92

Rambler, The: 130, 117

Rambouillet, Marquise de: 40, 44

Rami Dialecticae Libri Duo Cum Commentariis (Downham): 112

Ramiel: 41, 73, 142

Ramoth: 49, 73

Rams (masters?): 40

Ramsay: A.: 58. Allan: 117. Andrew: 74, 77, 117; Poemata Sacra: 74. George: 40. Robert L.: 51, 60, 68, 113, 132, 64, 130. Sir William: 89

Ramsey: Andrew: 65, 64. Mary P.: 93. Paul: 93

Ramus-Hood geometry: 40

Ramus, Peter: 1, 10, 20*, 23*, 30, 37, 40*, 44, 70, 18, 103, 112, 114, 116, 123*, 135, 145, 3, 39, 72, 82, 91, 96, 137, 55. And Ramism: 123*; M's Ramism: 53*. Ramist rhetoric and logic: 20, 40. Ramists: 60. See also: Logic

Ranch, Hieronymus Justesen: 68

Ranconnet, Tresor de la Langue Francoise: 40

Rand: 3. E. K.: 20, 40, 56, 70, 108, 113, 132, 64, 18, 148, 21; and steps to perfection: 143. William: 44

Randall: Giles: 114, 32. Helen W.: 116. John: 93. John Herman, Jr.: 81

Randol, John: 93

Randolph: Mr.: 44, 45. Ambrose: 44. Edmund: 44, 45, 115. Robert: 44. Thomas: 40, 44, 59, 84, 113, 120, 145, 26, 52, 83, 54; _Journal_: 82

Ranelagh: Earl of: 28. Lady: 28, 103

Ranelagh: Lady (mother of Viscount): 44, 73, 120, 113, 94. Lady Catherine: 44, 55. Richard Jones, Viscount and Earl of: 44. Viscountess: 16, 30

Rank: 54

Ranke, L. von: 6

Rankley, A.: 97

Rannie (or Rennie?), J.: 58

Rans, Geoffrey: 29

Ransom theory: 93

Ransom, John Crowe: 23, 52, 86, 105, 124, 125, 14, 53, 64, 101, 130*

Ranters: 7, 114, 38

Ranton: 45

Rape of the Lock (Pope): 130

Rape of Lucrece (Shakespeare): 70

Rape of Proserpine (Claudian): 94

Rapha: 92

Raphael (angel): 1, 2, 4, 6, 17*, 31*, 40, 41*, 50*, 52, 54, 56, 57, 60*, 63, 67*, 70, 73, 76, 87, 89*, 98, 102*, 103, 111*, 123, 124*, 125, 112*, 113, 127*, 128*, 136, 141, 142, 144, 3, 32*, 36, 46, 71, 72*, 88, 96*, 97, 109*, 130*, 146, 117, 140*, 25. As a character in PL: discussed: 55; source: 55. His dialogues: 48. "Scale-of-being" lecture: 48. Appearance of: 119. Narrative of: 50, 104. Speech in PL: 46. Commission to, narrates war in Heaven, rebuke to Adam: 50. Doctrine of accommodation: 126. The "affable Arch Angel": 136

Raphael (Raffaelo), Sanzio: 15, 130

Raphah: 123. See also: Rephaim; Giants, Biblical

Rapidity of speech, and character, the Richardsons on: 88

Rapin, René: 1, 4, 17, 58, 145, 64

Rapisardi, Mario: 65

Rapture: 72

Raschi. See Rashi

Rash Oaths Unwarrantable (John Lilburne): 147

Rashdall, Hastings: 3, 36, 93

Rashi (Rabbi Solomon Bar Isaac): 1, 24*, 40, 41*, 42, 63, 113, 128, 144, 14, 22*, 32, 36*. _Commentary on the Pentateuch, on Genesis_: 36*. See also: Solomon ben Isaac

Rastell, John: 13, 40, 93

Ratchford, Fannie: 44

Ratcliffe, H.: 58

Rathbone, Isabel E.: 93

Ratio Constitutae Nuper Reipublicae: 44

Ratio Studiorum (Jesuits): 40

Ratiocinative method of Addison's essays: 88

Rational Theology...in the 17th c. (Tulloch): 112

Rationalism: 53, 20, 40, 143. Often identifiable with solid but misapplied common sense: 88. Traces of, in Warton: 88. Greek: 43. Christian: 20, 40. In Biblical interpretation: 68. Triumph of: 143. Dogma of progress: 143. In our time: 143. Definition of: 71. Bentley's: 88; simplication and regularization of M's syntax due to his: 88. Rationalist philosophy: 20

Rationalists: 9*

Rationality: 24. Of PL: 118. As an element of God's image in man: 48. And freedom: 43. Of man: 48

Rationalizing: 51

Ratisbon: 44, 103

Ratpus. See Rapture

Ratzevil, Prince: 44

Rauschenbusch, Walter: 47. On kingdom of evil: 47

Rautzau: 128

Rava, A.: 6

Ravaillac, François: 44

Ravel, C. du: 58

Raven: Charles E; : 59, 143; folly and wickedness of man: 143; the Christian and modern cosmology: 143; and date of creation: 143; on vastness of universe: 143. John: 44

Ravencroft, John: 40

Ravenna: 49, 73

Ravensberg (Ravenstein). See Frederick William

Ravenscroft, Thomas (composer): 40, 44, 121, 126. Compendium of church music: 126. _Whole Book of Psalms_: 126, 20, 44. Ravenscroft collection: 103

Ravensworth, Lord: 58

Raventlow, Chancellor: 10

Ravisius, Joannes. See Textor

Ravitz, Abe C.: 115

Ravius, Christian: 10

Rawdon Papers (ed. E. Berwick): 44

Rawlings, H.: 87; on the unconscious meaning in PL: 87; "The Transfigured Theology of 'PL'": 87

Rawlins: Caleb: 44, 45. William (pr.): 44

Rawlinson: Bp. Alfred E. J.: 93. John: 93. Margery: 44. Richard: 10, 45. W. G.: 97. William: 44

Rawly, Edward: 45

Raworth: John (pr.): 44. Ruth (pr.): 44

Ray: Don E.: 143; on Christ and Greek culture: 143. John: 40, 32, 93

Raymond (of) Sabunde. See Sebonde

Raymond: Dora Neill: 44*, 45, 116, 91*, 137. Edward: 44*, 45*. George: 44. J.: 6. John: 45. Klibansky; _Philosophy and History: Essays Presented to Ernst Cassier_: 48. Sir Thomas: 44

Rayne, co. Essex: 44

Raynham, co. Norfolk: 44

Raynsford, R.: 58

Raynton: Nicholas: 45. Rebecca: see Pye, Rebecca

Raziel: 123, 142

Re, Arundell del: 40

Rea: Francis: 30, 44. John: 44

Reactionary Essays on Poetry and Ideas (Allen Tate), _Notes on Donne_: 131

Read: A. W.: 44. H.: 105. Sir Herbert: 1, 23, 52, 60, 86, 132, 130. John: 75

Reade: J. E.: 65. Edmund: 87; works: _Cain the Wanderer_: 87; The Fall from Paradise: 87; _The Revolt of the Angels_: 87. Simon: 114. Thomas: 44

Reader(s): 40. Self-education of: 67. Affective criticism, analysis of responses, etc.: 37*. Experience and perception of: 96*. Reader's imagination, Richardson's demand of stimulus for the: 88. Encouraged to grow in self-knowledge; encouraged in Satan's rhetoric; his psychology and

Adam and Eve's; his search for cause; his comprehension of the state of innocence; as a hero; his freedom of will; his response to the crucifixion; his apprehension of the meaning of history: 37

Reading, co. Berks.: 44*, 49

Reading, John: 44*, 45

Reading: 103. Select: 70. Part of curriculum: 40, 51. For confirmation: 98

Readings on the Paradiso (Vernon): 111

Ready and Easy Way...: 3*, 103, 113, 116, 129, 55. M's use of the term "Perfection" in: 83. See also: Imagery; Milton, John, Works

Real Presence, doctrine of: 71

Real Treasure for the Pious Mind, A: 115

Realism: 27, 118, 141. Absence of in descriptions of the prelapsarian world: 118. Political: 141. And heroism: 141. Medieval: 71. And humor appreciated by the Richardsons: 88. Absurd, indulged in by the Richardsons: 88

Reality: 143. Ideas and seals of: 96*. Processive theory of: 48

Reason: 9*, 17*, 29, 31*, 37*, 40, 47, 51, 54*, 60*, 63, 83, 98, 102, 113*, 114*, 124*, 128, 143, 144, 11, 46, 96*, 25, 48. Samson fails to heed: 143. Enslaved after Fall: 46. Subordinate to revelation: 46. Demonic: 45. The law of God: 71. "Right," M on: 80, 48. Thyer opposes Shaftesbury's description of, and morality as the principle qualities of M's poetry: 88. The voice of: 51. Discursive and instinctive distinguished: 102. Effects of sin on: 102. In all men: 143. In Comus, Masque of Hymen: 143. Enthroned: 143. Christian definition of: 48. As God's image in man: 48. The nature of: 48. Fallen: 25. Is choice, M on: 107. And experience as source of perfection: 83. And learning, regenerate or unregenerate: 114*. As a masque figure: 29. Adam tempted by: 37*. And rhetoric: 37*. In religion, place of: 114*. In marriage, divorce, etc.: 54*. And passion: 100, 113*. Theme of in M: 113*, 55. In Renaissance thought: 113. Reasoning: 51*. See also: Wisdom; Knowledge and Reason; Right Reason

Reason of Church Government: 8*, 102, 103, 112*, 113, 100, 111, 116, 129*, 55. Presentation copy of: 44. M's account: 55. M's use of the term "Perfection" in: 83. Poetry written with aid of spirit: 107. See also: Imagery; Milton, John, Works

Reasonableness of Christianity: 78

Reasoning Apostate: 116

Reasons Humbly Offered for the Liberty of Unlicens'd Printing: 116

Reasons Why the Supreme Authority (attr. to M): 44

Reau, Louis: 93. Iconographie: 74

Rebec: 40

Rebecca(h): 73

Rebeck: 121

Rebellion in Heaven: 31*

Rebellion: 45, 122*

Rebora, P.: 6

Rebuffus, Pierre: 73

Recanati, Menahan ben Benjamin: 142

Recapitulation: 51. Theory: 93. Theory of Irenaeus of Lyons: 107

Recentes (freshmen): 40

Receuil de Traites de Paix: 44

Receuil Genevois d'Art: 44

Recitative: 121

Reck, Josef: 60

Recognition (anagnorisis): 123. See also: Aristotle

Recognizance: 45. Recognizance Rolls: 44

Reconciliation: 47. See also: Christ; Redemption; Salvation; Son of God

Reconsiderations (Kellett): 111

Record Intepreter, The: 45

Recordability: 96

Recorde, Robert: 40, 110, 128

Recorder (musical instrument): 40, 121

Recovery of Man: 117

Recreation: 40, 51, 144. M's views on: 40

Recrimination: 47

Recusant Rolls: 40

Red Cross Knight: 56, 72

Red Cross Street, London: 44

Red Fairy Book: 131

Red Lion: alley: 45. Court: 45. Fields, London: 44, 103. Inn: 68

Red Rover, The: 98

Red Sea (Erythrean Sea, Rubrum Mare): 19, 44, 49, 73, 143, 32, 72

Redburn: 98*

Redding (Ridding) Copse: 44, 45

Redding, C.: 58

Redeemed. See Three classes of men

Redemptio nostra: 65

Redemption: 17, 31, 47, 113, 144, 32*, 36*, 46, 25. As the return of reason: 113. Of fallen angels: 93. Of man: see Atonement. See also: Christ; Reconciliation; Salvation; Son of God; Atonement

Redgrave: R.: 97. R. and S.: 97

Redingstone, John: 9, 147. Works: Democratic tone in The Peoples Right Briefly Asserted: 147. In Plain English, tells how the king has undermined the safety of the people: 147

Redlich, H. F.: 6

Rednall, Robert: 44

Redon, Odilon: 5

Reductio ad absurdum: 51, 123

Reduction, eidetic: 96

Reed (musical): 121

Reed: Mr.: 44, 45. Amy L.: 144. Henry: 16. Isaac: 88. James: 58. Joseph: 117

Reese, Gustave: 100

Reeve, John: 58, 114

Reeves, Mr., Justice: 44, 59

Reflections upon the Roman Commonwealth: 78

Reform: 51*. Deadlock in: 51. Educational: 51. M's campaign for: 80

Reformation (general): 7*, 9*, 27, 34, 47, 51*, 87, 103, 113, 143*, 71, 48. Ecclesiastical: 9*. And liberty: 9*. And Renaissance scholarship: 47. Counter: 7. In Eng., Germany: 7. Not mentioned in PL: 113. In Lycidas: 143*. Two extremes of: 143. Apparent failure of: 143. And Scripture: 143. M and: 147, 80. See also: Word of God

Reformation in Eng.: 113, 132*, 133

Reformation, The (Ogg): 134

Reformed Catholique: 116

Reformed: churches: 51. Sister-churches: 51

Reformer: short-sighted: 51. Of a kingdom, the: 51

Reforms: 51. Root and Branch: 51

Refraction: 89. Refracting telescope, principle of: 89

Refugees: 103

Refutation (rhetorical exercise): 20, 51*. Methods of: 123

Regall Tyrannie (John Lilburne, attack on kingship): 147

Regan (Shakespeare's character): 87

Regemorter, Ahasuerus. See Glisson, F.

Regeneration: 7, 9*, 51, 63, 122*, 123*, 132*, 143, 25. Doctrine of: 132*. Preordained: 143. Through Christ: 143. Nature of: 143. Samson's: 143. Theme of spiritual in PL: 104; as theme of PL: 33. And the poet: 75. Heaven: 75*. On Earth: 75. And the name "Christ": 75. And the "greater Man": 75. In Hell: 75*. See also: Salvation; Divine image; Restoration; Grace

Regensburger Prophetenspiel: 65

Reggia: 27

Regicide(s): 44, 51. M's views on: 30

Regii Sanguinis Clamor ad Coelum (Cry of the Royal Blood): 59, 103, 113, 116, 132, 136, 106, 26, 55, 94. See also: Du Moulin, P.

Regime: of the prelates: 51.

Stuart: 51

Regimen Sanitatis Salerni: 128

Regiomontanus (Johann Mueller): 40, 89

Register van Holland en Westuriesland: 44

Register: 121

Registrar of court: 44

Regius, Raphael: 20

Regola de la Lingua Thoscana MS.: 40

Regosin, Richard: 67

Regulation: of printing: 51. Order for: 51

Regulus: 123., Regulus, Marcus Attilius: 73

Rehearsal Transpros'd, The: 116, 145. The 2nd Part: 116

Rehearsal, The: 103, 116

Rehoboam (Roboam): 73, 128

Reichenau library: 36

Reid: A.: 58. J. K. S.: 23. W. H.: 58

Reigate, co. Surrey: 44

Reik, Theodor: 139

Reinarch, Solomon: 1

Reincarnation in Zohar: 113

Reinhold, Erasmus: 128. Tabulae Prutenicae: 8

Reinking, Chancellor: 10

Reinolds, John: 64

Reinoso, Felix Jose(f): 55, 64, 117

Reisch, Gregor: 16, 128

Reisig, Jan Hendrick: 117

Reiteration, use of: 51

Rejection: of world: 47. Of natural depravity and predestination: 52. Method of, in PR: 123*

Rejoinder: 45

Reland, Hadrian: 32

Relation (a performer): 40

Relation of a Journey: 26

Relation of Kingdoms: 40

Relation of M to his time: 121

"Relations" (news): 40

Relativism: 47

Relativity: of value of words recognized by Pearce: 88. Of characterization, Newton's occasional insight into: 88

Reliance, carnal (fiducia carnalis): 123

Reliance, M's upon proof texts: 107; see also: Trust

Relics: 44*, 47, 87. M's hair, 87. M's rib bone: 44, 87. M's bed, clothing, dishes, spectacles, watch: 44

Religio Medici (Browne): 135, 71

Religion of Protestants: 78

Religion: 20, 30*, 31, 44, 47, 51, 113*, 144*, 143*, And the demonic: 47. Committee of: 51. M's: 44. Defence of true: 51. Formalism in: 51. Under the Gospel: 51. Under the law: 51. Retreat from: 147*. Without philosophy: 143. And ethical values: 143. Specious outward forms: 143. And poetry: 143; the Richardsons on: 88; Thyer on, as a vehicle of: 88. Dunster on imagination as means of advertising: 88

Religions (Eastern): 47. See also: Indian religion; Brahamnism; Buddhism

Religious: appeal, controversy, democracy, discipline, doctrine, emotions, factionalism: 51. Feelings: 51. Freedom: 51*. Ideals: 51. Ideas: 55*. Liberty commonwealth essential to: 51. Lit.: 40. Enemies of: 51. Loss of: 51. Struggles for: 51. Nature: 51. Offenses, discussed: 51. Organization: 51. Peace: 51. Poetry: 58*. Problems: 51. Reverance: 51. Teaching: 51; in education, M's views: 20. Tolerance: 51. Observances and education in schools: 20. Toleration approved by Parliament: 51. Calvinism: 55. In anti-episcopal pamphlets: 55. On the Trinity: 55. Ministry: 55. Individualism: 55. Changes in: 55. Arianism in Christian Doctrine: 55. M and Catholicism: 55. in Of True Religion: 55. On the crucifixion: 55

Religious views (M's): 137*, 28*. Beliefs: 117*, 30*, 31, 102, 113*. Thought, forces governing: 107. Troubles: 51. Tracts: 40. Poet, M valued by Hume as a: 88. Prejudices in dealing with M's characters, Hume's: 88. Feeling, Hume's enables him to appreciate PL: 88. Considerations of the Richardsons: 88; character of PL, their praise of: 88. Poem, PL, as praised by Paterson: 88. Tendencies in M, unorthodox, Thyer on: 88. Prejudices: Warburton's, Newton's, Heylin's: 88. Views, Newton's occasionally liberal: 88. Conservatism, Warton's: 88. Bias, Gillies's: 88. Tendency, Dunster's: 88. Poetry, Dunster on: 88. Dunster on desirability of writing it in an austere style: 88. In Comus: 55. In PL, PR, discussed: 55. Chastity: 55. Manicheean heresey: 55. Arminianism: 55. Creation: 55. Influence: 55. Orthodoxy: 146. Milton: A dissenter, views of, ideas of neglected, ideas of ridiculed, Arianism, latitudinarian practices, ideas concerning Sabbath, ideas concerning polygamy, Victorian attitude toward religious beliefs, theological concepts outdated, attitude toward literal reading of Bible, conception of God: 87

Religious epics (Miltonic): 87*. Appearance of: 87. Vogue of during 19th c.: 87. 4 greatest exemplar of: 87. M's influence on: 87*. Writers of: 87. Setting and characters of described: 87. Popularity of: 87. Criticism of: 87. Geographical descriptions in: 87. Scenes from Bible in: 87. The Sublime in: 87. Miltonic Satan in: 87

<u>Remaines of Gentilisme and Judaisme</u>: 45

<u>Remains</u> (A. H. Hallam): 111

<u>Remarkable Providences</u>: 71

<u>Remarks and Collections of Thomas Hearne</u>: 116

<u>Remarks on Antiquities...in Italy</u>: 98

<u>Remarks upon M's PL</u> (W. Massey): 88

Rembrandt: 90

Remedies: 128*. Aloes, antidotes, corrosive, crocus, electuary, euphrasy, eyesalve, herbs, learned from animals, leech, lettuce, manna, myrrh, natural, purgative, rue, rhubarb, salve, surgery, tartar, vinegar, vitriol: 128

Remedy, doctrine of: 17*

Remembering, art of: 20

Remi de Beauvais: 64. <u>Magdeleine</u>: 74

Remmius: Palaemon: 40. Abraham: 64

Remnant, the: 51. Theology of: 81

Remnis: 49

Remonstrance (by the army): 147

<u>Remonstrance of Many Thousand Citizens ...to their owne House of Commons</u>: 147

<u>Remonstrant's Defence</u>: 41

<u>Remonstrants</u> (Arminians): 40, 78*

Remus: 73

Remy, Nicholas: 142

Rena: Mr.: 44. Vincenzo dell: 44

<u>Renaissance in Italy</u> (Symonds): 3

Renaissance: 7, 3, 27*, 34, 40, 42, 51, 70*, 103, 112*, 132*, 72, 78. Renaissance concepts: chain of being: 80; Christian humanism: 80; despair: 80; fatal sin: 80; good and evil contending against each other: 80; original man endowed with wisdom: 80; source of all human failure: 80. Literary commentarites of the, influencing Eng. scholarship: 88 Literary canons of: 132. Thought of: 132*. Renaissance man, M as a: 52. Renaissance-Puritan elements in M: 87. Views of poetry: 31. Cosmology: 41. Spirit of in M: 87. Epic: 46. Literary theory: 46. Tragedy: 46

Renan, Ernest: 18, 142. Works: <u>Livre de Job</u>: 74; <u>Vie de Jesus</u>: 142

Renaudot, Eusebius: 128

Reni, Guido: 120, 88

Rennie, J.: 58

Reno, vale of: 144

Renouard, P. V.: 15

Renovation: 63*, 123. See also: Regeneration; Restoration of man

Rentius, Nicolaus (Cola di Rienzi): 73

<u>Renunciation and Declaration of the Ministers of Congregational Churches</u>: 116

Renwick, W. L.: 68, 132

Renzulli, Michele: 111

Repayring of the Breach: 60

Repeal: 51

Rependune (Repton): 49

Repentance: 47, 63, 123*. See also: Faith; Regeneration

Repertorio del mundo: 65

Repetition: 98, 11. M's: 50*. In Keats, in PL, in Young: 58. Hume opposed to M's, of whole lines: 88. Bentley dislikes: 83. Pearce on, combined with gradation: 88. Pearce on variation in: 88. Peck on: 88. Paterson on: 88. Newton's excessive dislike of: 88

Rephaim: 123. See also: Giants, Biblical

Replication: 45

Reply of Two of the Brethren (John Goodwin, demanding that sects and schisms be allowed): 9, 147

Reply to the Answer to... Observations upon some of his Majesty's Late Answers and Expresses (attr. to M): 44

Reports and certificates: 45

Repository and Ladies' Weekly Museum, The: 115

Representative: civil government: 51. Government, changes required to establish: 51. Representatives of the people: 51

Reprobate. See Three classes of men

Reprobation: 71

Reproduction: 128

Reproof to the Rehearsal Transprosed: 116

Republic (Plato): 29, 52, 112*, 121, 3

Republic: conducive to virtue: 51. Differences from monarchy: 51. Scheme for conduct of: 51. Success of: 51. Superiority of: 51. See also: Commonwealth

Republican Letters (of State), M's: 44

Republican: experiement, weakness of: 51. Government, incompetence to succeed in: 51. M's willingness for modification of: 51. Institutions, love of: 51. Ideals, defined: 80

Republicans: 51, 103. Republicanism: 38, 146*; Warton opposed to M's: 88

Reputation: 51*, 117*. National: 51. M's: in 17th c.: 55; in colonial American: 55; in 18th c., discussed: 55; in 19th c.: 55; European: 136

Requests: Court of: 45*; _Select Cases in_: 45. Proceedings: 45

Requiem: 65

"Requiem for Soliders Lost in Ocean Transport, A": 98

Resbury, Richard: 114

Rescue: 47. And redemption, theme of divine: in _Mask_, PL: 104

Residences (M's): 30, 40, 44*. At Cambridge: 40. See also: Aldersgate Street; Chalfont St. Giles; Horton; Petty France

Resistance (passive and active): 47

Resonant: 121

Respect: 51*. For man: 47; see also: God

Respiration: 128

Respondens: 40

"Responding to the question" at Christ's College, Cambridge: 44*

Responsibility of tutor: 40

Responsibility: 47, 124*. See also: Freedom

Responsio ad Apologiam Anonymi (attr. to M): 44

Responsio: 40

Responsions: 40

Restitution to the Royal Author: 116

Restoration. See Reconciliation

Restoration, the: 9, 27, 30*, 31, 34, 51, 60, 70, 103*, 132, 92, 150, 94, 113, 121, 136. Effect on M of: 132. London: 150. M argues against: 55. Lies concealed at: 94

Restoration: of episcopacy: 51. Of monarchy, dangers of: 51. Of man: 123*; see also: Regeneration

Restoring order in the state: 51

Resurrection: 47, 63, 113, 143, 32, 72*, 25. Of the body: 93

Retardation by emphasizing details: 88

Retardation of M disproved: 40

Retina, detachment of, possible cause of M's blindness: 16

Retired Mans Meditations (Sir Harry Vane): 147

Retraction: 107, 113*, 132. God's: 113*. In Fludd: 113. Doctrine of: 132. Theory: 93. M: 107

Return to source of being: Christ and Satan compared: 125. And knowledge: 125. Of Christ: 125*. And image of God: 125. Of Samson: 125*. Christ and Samson compared: 125. See also: Eliade; Withdrawal

Retz, Cardinal de: 59

Reubenites: 73

Reuchlin, Johann: 7, 40, 42, 113, 114, 123, 142, 22, 93, 64. De Arte Cabalistica: 142

Reusner, Nicolaus: 40

Revel (town): 49

Revelation (Apocalypse): 44, 47, 50, 76, 118, 132, 139, 87, 72, 92, 3, 11, 46, 78, 96, 25. Apocalyptic descriptions in: 87. Sublime poetry of: 87. Source of liberty: 46. M's belief in a double: 113. See also: Accommodation; Holy Spirit; Scripture; Apocalypse; Bible; Prophecy

Revelation: 67, 74, 126*. Book of, quoted: 95. See also: Bible

Revelations, as tragedy: 30

Revels Office: 29

Revels, explanation of: 29

Revenge as heroic motif: 123*

Revenue, burden of raising: 51

Reverence for the Christian ministry: 51

Review of English Studies: 44*, 45, 131

Review of Etchings of a Whaling Cruise and Sailor's Life and Sailor's Yarns: 98

Revision (of PL): 50*

Revius, Jacob: 93

Revolt of Islam, The (Shelley): 131

Révolte des Anges, La: 65

Revolution: and aethetics: 25. Blake's concept of: 25. See also: Civil wars; American Revolution; French Revolution; Puritan Revolution

Revue de Synthèse Historique: 44

Revue des Revues: 44

Reward: 122*, 123*. See also: Merit

Reynardson series: 45

Reynell, W. H.: 58

Reyner, Edmund: 54

Reynes, John: 40

Reynolds, Dr.: 26. See also: Rainolds

Reynolds: Bp. Edward: 37, 40, 45, 54, 59, 102, 114, 120, 93; Sermon Touching the Use of Humane Learning: 74. Henry: 15, 27, 76, 100, 106. J.: 97. John: 44, 142; Concerning the State and Oeconomy of the Angelical Worlds: 142. Sir Joshua: 44, 70, 146. Myra: 58. S. H.: 58. Samuel: 44

Rezan: 49

Rhadamanthus: 73, 123

Rhamus: 128

Rhé: 45

Rhea: 60, 73, 90, 144

Rhee (Reana): 49

Rhee, Isle of (Insula Reana): 73

Rhegius, Urbanus: 93

Rheita: 89

Rhemes: 49

Rhene (Rhine): 73

Rheno: 49

Rhesus: 123

Rheticus: 77

Rhetoric (Aristotle): 20, 70, 3

Rhetoric: 70*, 122, 123, 109. Study of: 114. Art of: 51. Classical:

51. Deliberative: 51. Principles of: 51. 17th c.: 51. Relation to character: 123. M's use of: 123. In infernal oratory: 123*. Capable of good or evil use: 123. As inimical poetry: 53. Rhetorical hesitation: 53. And "vehemence": 53. And dialectic: 109. Books on: 109. General theory and practice of: 20*, 31*, 40*, 51. Satan's: 37. God's: 37. And original sin: 37. And Ramism: 37. Of PL: 15*. See also: Discourse; Demonstrative rhetoric; Dianoia; Deliberative rhetoric; Orator

Rhetorica (Talaeus): 20

Rhetorica ad C. Herennium: 123

Rhetoricae Libri Duo (Butler's abridgement of Talaeus): 20

Rhetorical Grammar (J. Walker): 88

Rhetorical: age: 51. Blemish: 51. Criticism: 51. Elements: 51. Form: 51. Incentive: 51. Plan: 51. Point of view: 51. Practice: 51. Principles: 51. Skill: 51. Syllogism: 51. Theory, classical: 51. Tradition: 51. Work: 51. Figures as irrational: 118. Tendency of Bentley's style: 88

Rhetorician: 51. Rhetorician's art: 51

Rhine River: 19, 49

Rhine. See Charles X

Rhoades, J.: 58

Rhode Island: 103. Historical Society Collections: 44. Almanac, The: 115. Literary Repository, The: 115

Rhodes: 49, 3. R.: 97. Samuel: 44. T.: 58. Tabitha: 44

Rhodians (Rhodienses): 73, 3

Rhodius, Mr.: 44

Rhodon: 77

Rhodope: 49, 73, 90, 103, 3, 72

Rhombus: 44

Rhone River: 40

Rhyme: 146, 25. Condemnation of: 30. M constricted by: 40. Rhymes: condemned by Bentley: 88; Peck on M's: 88; Peck opposed to Dryden's depreciation of M's: 88

Rhymer, Thomas: 39

Rhythm: 98. In PL: 118, 121. The Richardsons on: 88; feel the connection between meaning and: 88. Peck on flexibility of in Il Penseroso and L'Allegro: 88. Lofft on M's: 88

Riario, Cardinel Pietro

Rib: 54. Adam's extra: 128

Ribbeck: 64

Ribla: 49

Ribner, Irving: 128, 39

Ribton-Turner, C. J., A History of Vagrants and Vagrancy: 82

Rical: 49

Ricchieri, Lodovico di Rovigo: 40

Ricci, Seymour de, Book Collectors Guide: 44

Riccio (Rizzio), David: 73. See also: Rizzio

Ricciotti, G.: 6

Riccoboni, Luigi: 68, 70

Riccobonus, Antonius: 123

Rice: Eugene R., Jr.: 122, 39, 93; Renaissance Idea of Wisdom: 74. Warner G.: 18, 125, 99

Rich Young Ruler, the parable of the: 83

Rich: Mr.: 44. Barnaby: 93. E. P.: 58. Sir Henry: 40. Lady Isabella: 44. Robert, Master in Chancery: 44, 45

Richard the Redeles: 83

Richard II (Shakespeare): 135

Richard III (Shakespeare): 70, 111

Richard: Andrew: 44. Elie: 44. Lewis: 39

Richard: Prince: 45. Richard II: 40, 60, 73, 83*, 103, 82*. Richard III: 103, 3. Of Cirencester: 93. Of Middleton: 77; Clarissimi Theologi: 77. Of St. Victor: 7

Richard's: Parliament: 51. Protectorate: 51

Richards: G.: 58. I. A.: 12, 23, 34, 35, 118, 124, 125, 133, 39, 101, 130, 131, 21. Coleridge on Imagination: 35; Science and Poetry:

35. Thomas: 44, 45

Richardson: 3. Mr.: 103. A. S.: 16. Charles: 93. Christopher: 44. J. S.: 115; An Oration, Delivered in St. Michael's Church: 115. Jonathan (father and son): 1, 10, 16, 28*, 37, 40, 44*, 45, 56, 58, 59, 63, 127, 132, 136, 14, 68, 84, 87, 86, 102, 105*, 111, 114, 73, 88*, 91, 97, 101, 130*, 137, 146, 150, 25, 55; Senior: 87, 117*; Junior: 25; praises M: 58; on M's temper: 87; M delightful company: 87; mentioned: 55; quoted: 55; Explanatory Notes and Remarks On M's "PL": 57, 87, 109. Richard: 117*. Samuel: 9, 147, 146, 117; justifies the Independents in An Answer to the London Ministers Letter: 147. Sir Thomas: 40, 44, 143. William: 58, 115; An Oration, Pronounced at Groton, July 4, 1801: 115

Riche: Sir Henry: 44. Isabel Cope: 44

Richelet, Nicolas, Preface to Ronsard's Hercule Chrestien: 74

Richelieu, Cardinal: 10, 40, 103, 136

Richmond, co. Surrey: 44

Richmond: 40. Charles Stuart, 3rd Duke of 3rd creation: 44. Duchess of: 44. Julia: 97

Richter: Christian: 65. George: 10, 44; Letters: 91. H. and J.: 97. J. G.: 91. Johann Paul: 146

Ricius, Paulus: 40

Rickards, G. K.: 58

Ricketts, C.: 97

Rickey, Mary Ellen: 81

Rickman, T. C.: 58

Rickmansworth: 45

Ricks, Christopher: 17, 37, 60, 67, 75, 86*, 104, 110, 111, 14, 32, 53, 101. M's Grand Style: 74, 109

Rickword, Edgell: 133

Ridding. See Redding

Ridding, Richard: 40, 44, 21

Riddle: 143. In Lycidas: 143

Ride through Stourhead: 58

Rider-Holyoke Dictionary: 40

Rider: John: 40. Matthew: 116

Ridiard: (Riddiard), Mary: 45. Sarah: 45. Thomas: 45

Ridicule: as theme in SA: 125*. Assisting reason, inspiration and helplessness: 125. Samson's final purge of folly: 125

Ridiculous, the, in PL: 123, 124*

Riding masters: 40

Ridley: E.: 58. Nicholas, Bp. of Rochester and London: 44, 51, 73, 91, 103. W. (engraver): 44

Rieger, James: 14

Riegl, A.: 27

Riemann, K. W. Hugo: 100

Rienzo, Cola di: 18

Rieu, E. V.: 36, 64

Riff: 44, 3

Riffe, N. L., "M in the 18th c. Periodicals: 'Hail wedded love'": 109

Riga, Peter: 44, 49, 65

Rigaer Prophetenspiel: 65

Rigaud, S. F.: 97

Right and Might Well Met (John Goodwin, justifies the army's right to purge): 147

Right ascension: 89

Right Reason: 52, 60, 122*, 123. M and the concept of: 52. "Right reason," M on: 80. "Right Reason" in PL: 83. See also: Reason

Righteousness: 24, 47

Rights of the Crown of England: 116

Rights of the Kingdom (John Sadler): 73

Rights of the People over Tyrants (attr. to M): 44

Rights: menaced by King's Council: 51. Of the people: 51. Of others: 51

Rigor of M's attitude toward law: 121

Riley: 88. John: 44

Rilke, R. M.: 5, 105

Rimbaud: 88

Rimbault, E. F.: 44

Rime: 50, 53*, 70. See also: Blank verse; Couplet; Lyrics

Rimmon: 19, 73, 144

Rinaker, Clarissa: 41, 53

Rinaldi, Odorico: 93

Rinaldo: 60, 123. See also: Tasso

Ring, Max, John Milton and His Time: 87

Ringmere: 49

Rintrah: 145, 25*. And Satan: 25. See also: Milton (Blake's)

Riolan, J.: 142

Ripa, Cesare: 27, 29, 39, 123, 97

Riphaean Mountains: 49

Ripley Castle, co. York: 44

Ripley, George: 128. "Believe It or Not": 44

Ripun: 49

Rise and Progress of Present Taste in Parks: 117

Rise of Puritanism, The (Haller): 134

Rise, Growth and Danger of Socinianisme: 71

Rising motion: as uncreative symbol: 75*. As creative symbol: 75*. See also: Falling motion

Ritchie, David G.: 93

Rite de passage: 96

Ritschl, Albrecht: 7, 114

Ritso, G.: 58

Ritual, Warton fond of ancient ecclesiastical: 88

Ritwyse, John: 40

Rival Friends (Hausted): 29

Rivalry: 47, 51

Rive: Count of: 44. Edmund: 40

River of Bliss: 89

Rivers of Paradise: 32*. Symbolic meaning of: 32. See also: Euphrates; Gihon; Phison; Tigris

Rivers: Mr. (student): 44. George: 40. "Nizel" (Nigel?): 40. Robert: 45

Rivet: (Rivetus), Andrew (Andre): 1, 45, 114, 40, 44, 73, 32, 22, 82, 123, 3; works: Praelectiones, "De Mutuo": 82; Commentary on Chapter I of Exodus: 82. R.: 148

Rivière, Jean: 93

Rivington: 97. C. R.: 40. Mr.: see Stationer's Register

Rivinus: 88

Rix, Herbert: 44

Rizzio, David: 73, 103, 137

Rochester-Castle: 73

Roach, Richard: 7

Road to Xanadu, The: 12

Roads from London ca. 1625: 40

Roan (Rothomagus), town: 49

Roane: Martha: 44. Robert: 44

Robb, Nesca, A.: 79, 93

Robbie, H. J.: 44

Robbins: Caroline: 44, 115. Frank Egleston: 15, 63, 75, 77, 122, 144, 93

Robert Bellarmine, St. See Bellarmine

Robert: Earl of Manchester: 40. Son of James I: 40. The Bruce: see Bruce. Of Auxerre: 93. Of Gloucester: 40. I.: 97. Of Naples (king): 64

Robertello, F.: 6

Roberts: Mr.: 44, 45. Alexander: 79. Ann: 45. Arthur: 120. Barnes: 45. Daniel: 115; Some Remarks on Modern Arianism: 115. Donald R.: 6, 124, 14. Edward: 44. Francis: 22, 99. George: 44, 45*. Hugh: 93. J.: 58. Kenneth: 16. Mary: 45. Mary (Glover): 45. Michael, Examiner in Chancery: 44. Nicholas: 44. Richard: 45. Samuel: 87; aversion to M: 87; on M's treatment of Mary Powell: 87; Milton Unmasked: 87. Thomas: 44, 45. W.: 58. W. Rhys: 18, 51. William H.: 58, 117; influenced by PL: 58

Robertson: Anne S.: 44. Bp. Archibald: 93. D., Esq.: 58. D., of Edinburgh: 58. D. W.: 37. Donald S. (Professor): 35, 44, 133.

J. G.: 44, 116. J. M.: 34, 71. Dr. James: 88. Jean: 20. Leonard, Master in Chancery: 44. Thomas: 20, 40

Robin Goodfellow: 144

"Robin-Hood Society": 58

Robin, P. Ansell: 128*

Robins, Harry F.: 59, 60, 75, 86, 110, 128, 143, 93, 101. If This Be Heresy: 74

Robinson Crusoe: 136, 92

Robinson: 40, 97. Mr.: 44, 45, 58. Bookseller: 44. Crabbe: 68. Edward: 45. Fred N.: 79. H. M.: 139. H. Wheeler: 93; The Christian Doctrine of Man: 48. Henry: 9, 60, 147, 91, 148; attacks the Covenant: 147; works: A Short Discourse Between Monarchial and Aristocratical Government (analyzes new government): 147; John the Baptist...or, a Necessity for Liberty of Conscience as the only Means under Heaven to Strengthen Children Weake in Faith: 147. Henry Crabb: 58, 145*, 150, 13, 25; on Blake, Thelwall, Wordsworth: 58. Humphrey (bks., pr.): 29, 44.

Robinson: J. H., The Mind in the Making: 83. John: 7, 9*, 44, 45*, 54, 114, 147, 93, 148; ideas for social action in the Puritan Revolution: 147; leader of the Pilgrims in the New World: 147; stand on church function: 147; A Justification of Separation from the Church of Eng.: 147. John A. T.: 93. Luke: 44. M. ("Perdita"): 58*. M. F.: 39. Robert: 40. T.: 58. T. H.: 97. Sir Tancred, M. D.: 44. Thomas: 44, 64; Life and Death of Mary Magdalen: 74. William H. (bks.): 44

Robortelli: 70

Robortello, Francisco (Francesco): 40, 74. In Librum Aristotelis: 74

Robotham, John: 54

Robson: C. A.: 100. W. W.: 81, 122, 101; on poetic success of PR: 61

Roch, John: 44

Rochdale, co. Lancs.: 44

Roche: Giles de la (French privateer): 44, 150. Robert: 54

Rochel: 49. See also: Rhee

Rochelle: 45, 73

Rochester, Bp. of: 136

Rochester: 45, 49. 2nd Earl of, John Wilmot: 23, 44, 145, 146

Rock-Savage, Cheshire: 40. Thomas, Viscount of: 44

Rock: Daniel (on medieval Eng. church): 104. Thomas (pr.): 44

Rococo: 27, 97*

Rocque, John: 40

Rodd: Horatio (print seller, M portrait): 44. T.: 44. Thomas: 44

Roderick, R. (sonnet by): 58

Rodney, Mr.: 44, 45

Rodolf, King of Germany. See Rudolf

Rodolph: 73

Rodolphus: 3

Roe Copse: 44

Roe: Lady Eleanor: 45. Sir Thomas: 10, 40, 45

Roeder, Ralph: 52

Roemer, Olaus: 89. Astronomical work of: 89

Roerelius, Andrew: 10

Roersch, Alphonse: 40

Roffet: 58

Roffy, Bp. Young of Rochester: 83

Roger: 3. Earl of Rutland: 40. Of Wendover: 93. Eugene: 32

Rogero (Ruggiero): 123. See also: Ariosto; Boiardo

Rogers: 130. Miss: 58. Mr.: 44. C.: 58. Daniel: 40, 54; Matrimonial Honor (1642): 91. Francis: see Ewens, Frances. George Alfred: 44. John: 7, 9*, 44, 38, 93. Kenneth: 44. Lambert: 44. Nehemiah: 93.

Rogers: Neville: 14. Richard: 40, 68, 123, 143, 148; and Christian means: 143. Samuel: 44, 58, 146. Thomas: 116. Thorold (historian): 147. Timothy: 93. William: 44, 115; An Oration, Delivered July 4, 1789: 115

Rohan, Duke of: 103

Rohde, E. S.: 15, 128

Róheim, Géza: 1

Rojas y Zorilla, Francisco de: 23, 68

Rokeby, co. York: 44

Rolandi, U.: 5

Rolfe: Edwin: 108. W. J.: 14

Rolim de Moura, Francisco Child: 65, 64

Roll, G.: 65

Rolland, R.: 6

Rolle: Lord, of Stevenstone: 44. John: 45. Richard: 7, 114, 123

Rolli: Mr.: 44. Paolo: 58, 105, 117

Rollin, Charles: 117

Rollins, Hyder E.: 44, 68, 128. And Herschel Baker, The Renaissance in England: 82

Rolls: 44

Rolt: C.: 97. R.: 58

Roman de la Rose: 76, 79, 32, 130

Roman(s): 44, 3, 103. Church: 150. Empire: 44, 103, 3. Democracy of: 51. Difficulty in competing with: 30. Extent of power: 19. Methods of fighting: 19. Treatment of blind by: 16. Edicts, fashions, lyrist, Pontiff: 3. Senate: 51. Languages: 40. Law: 54. History: 8. Numerals: 40

Roman Catholic Church: 40, 103, 113, 71, 87. Rule: 51. M's hatred of: 113. Roman Catholics: 73*; attitude toward M: 87, 103. Romanism: 103, 136, 139. Romanists: and diabolic doctrine: 143; and kingdom of Antichrist: 143; practices denounced: 143. Romish clergy: 3. See also: Catholicism

Romance language tutor (M's): 40

Romance(s): 122*, 123, 145*, 46, 117, 25, 17, 19, 30, 70*, 44. Humanists' attack on: 93. Newton objects to style of: 88. Mixture of medieval, with classical features, Warton on: 88. And classicist style, misture of, Todd on: 88. M's taste for: 70. Chastity taught in: 30. Elements in PR: 46. Hume's style showing elements of: 88. Condemend by Hume as fiction: 88. Bentley's condemnation of: 88. Pearce's sympathy with vague suggestiveness and: 88. The Richardsons theoretically opposed to: 88. Peck interested in: 88. Meadowcourt opposed to: 88. Newton objects to: 88

Romano, Giulio: 27, 97

Romans, l'Abbé: 58

Romans, Epistle to: 44, 74, 135, 3. See also: Bible

Romantic: art: 97. Artists: 97. Mode: 69*. Movement: 87, 97, 149; importance of Natural Sublime: 87. Revival, the: 136; adumbrated in M annotation: 88

Romanticism: 7*, 53*, 143, 109. As opposed to Classicism: 87. In Comus: 143. And Satan: 143. Walter Pater's definition of: 88. English, a period of universal sensitivity to physical impressions: 88. Romantics, the: 34, 97

Romantics: 97*. Romanticism: 7*. Romantic artists, movement: 97 Rome (Roma, Roman Empire): 30, 29, 40, 44*, 45, 49, 51, 70, 103, 111, 144, 145, 3*, 32, 72*, 97, 150, 21, 94. Education in schools of Eng. and: 20. Church of: 3. Moral degradation in: 71. M's visit to: 6*, 19, 30. See also: Roman

Romei: 102. Annibale: 5, 79

Romeo: 70 Romeo and Juliet: 40, 70, 26

Romescot: 82

Rommen: H. A.: 128. Heinrich: 93

Romney: George: 97*, 146, 117, 25. J.: 97. (Romeny), Sir William: 44

Romswinckel, Peter George: 44

Romualdez, Antonio V.: 93

Romulus: 44, 73, 90, 3

Rondet, Henri: 93

Ronga, L.: 6

Ronsard, Pierre de: 1, 5, 15, 33, 40, 58, 120, 122, 123, 93, 64, 115, 94. Works: Franciade: 74; Hercule Chrestien: 74

Ronssi: 44

Rood Lane: 45

Rooke, Lawrence: 10

Rooms, M's at Cambridge: 40

Rooney, W.: 23

Roos: Anne Pierrepont, Lady: 44. John Manners, 9th Earl of and 1st Duke of Rutland: 44

Rooses, Max: 128

Root-and-Branch: Bill: 51, 60, 103. Measures, members, parties, policies, reforms: 51. Petition: 147

Rope of sand: 128

Roper: Abel (bks., 1638-79): 44, 91. William: 52

Rosa, Salvator: 6, 88, 117

Rosalinde: 83*

Roscius Amerinus(i.e., from Ameria, a town in Umbria): 73

Roscoe: W.: 97; influence by PL: 58. W. S.: 58

Roscommon: 2, 130. Wentworth Dillon, 4th Earl of: 91, 117; see also: Rochester. Earl of: 58*

Rose(s): Rose (sign): 44. And marriage, revelry: 143. Summer's: 143. And Crown (sign): 44, 103. And Crown (bookshop): 44. Island: 49, 103. Of Bohemia, the: 40. Of Heaven, the: 70. Tavern, Cambridge: 40

Rose: father's house: 44. M's property, Bread Street, London: 44*

Rose: Edward J.: 25. H. J.: 21. J. B.: 58. M.: 36. R. H.: 115; _Sketches in Verse_: 115

Rosedale, H. F.: 16, 63, 102

Roselli, Alessandro: 68

Rosen, Edward: 44

Rosenau, M. J.: 16

Rosenbach Company: 44*

Rosenbach, Dr. A. S. W.: 44, 98

Rosenblum, R.: 97

Roses, War of: 122

Rosicrucians: 7*, 114, 142

Rosinus, J.: 128

Rospiglioni, G.: 6

Rospigliosi: family: 6. Giulio: 44, 64, 137. See also: Clement IX, Pope

Ross, Ireland: 44

Ross: A.: 99. Abraham: 142; _An Exposition of the Fourteene First Chapters of Genesis_: 142. Alexander (1591-1654): 1, 40, 44, 65, 77, 100, 102, 114, 123, 128, 142, 144, 143, 32, 36, 93, 64, 101, 106, 117; Christ the ladder: 143; works: _Christiados_: 74; _Pansebeia_: 91, 77; _Mystagogus Poeticus_: 74; _Virgilius Evangelisans_: 74; _The New Planet No Planet_: 77, 55; _Leviathan Drawn out with a Hook_: 142; _Abridgement_: 77*; _Questions and Answers upon Genesis_: 36; see also: Wolleb (Wollebius). Cary: 5. David M.: 93. (Ros, Roos), Lord John (Manners): 28, 44; see also: Roos. Jolyon: 44. Malcolm Mackensie: 1, 15, 23, 27, 66, 75, 79, 81, 86, 102, 110, 126, 141, 93, 64, 101, 148; on M's ambivalence toward the Incarnation: 61; works: "M and the Protestant Aesthetic": 60; _M's Royalism_: 60. W.: 97. W. O.: 36. William D.: 51, 122; on old-fashioned duty: 143

Rosse: Mr.: 44. Alexander: 44. Lord John: 103

Rossetti: Christina: 65, 87, 143; attitude toward M: 87; and glassy sea: 143. Dante Gabriel: 27, 58, 87*, 97; visit to M's Chalfont-St. Giles residence: 87; on cartoons for Houses of Parliament: 87; sonnets: 87; opinion of M's sonnets: 87; attitude toward M: 87; _The House of Life_: 87. William M.: 16, 87

Rossi: C. F.: 97

Rossiter, C.: 97

Rosso Fiorentino: 97

Rost Islands: 49

Rostagni, Augusto: 5

Rostove: 49

Röstvig, Maren-Sofie: 100*

Roswitha: 64. Works: _Maria_: 74; _Non-Dramatic Works_ (ed. Sister Mary Gonsalva Wiegand): 74

Rota Club: 16, 44, 51, 103. M's relation to: 51. See also: Harrington, James

Rota: 120. Berardino: 59, 64

Rotation in office, discussed: 51

Roth: Cecil: 79. Leon: 93

Rotherham, Thomas: 40

Rotherham: Library: 40. School: 20

Rotherhithe: 40

Rothmann, Christopher: 77. Brahe, Opera: 77

Rothwell: Henry (father's servant): 44. Henry (scrivener, pr.): 44. John (pr., publisher): 10, 44, 55. John, Jr. (bks., 1633-60): 91

Rotrou, M.: 44

Rotterdam: 44, 150

Rouai, François: 44

Roubillac, Louis François (painter, M portrait): 44, 97

Rouch, A.: 97

Rouen, France: 44, 103

Rougemont, Denis de: 142. The Devil's Share: 142

Rough, W.: 58

Round numbers: 50

Round Table, (mensa): 44

Round: 121

Roundheads: 103, 150

Rouquet, J.: 97

Rous(e): 51. The Elder: 93. Ode to: 132. F. P. (M. P. for Truro): 94. Francis, Speaker of Parliament: 7, 42, 44, 54, 38. John: 44*, 45, 103, 92. John (1574-1652): 30, 40, 44, 70, 52, 91; ode to: 132. Margaret: see Brome, Margaret. W. H. D.: 81

Rousseau: Jean Jacques: 52, 113, 132, 139, 141, 3, 26, 32, 71, 97, 146, 149, 117, 94. Theodore, Jr.: 44

Rousset, Jean: 39

Rout: 2

Routh: Bernard: 117. J.: 92

Routledge, G. (publisher): 97

Rovai, Francesco: 6, 44. Lost poem to: 44

Rowe Coppice: 45

Rowe: E.: 58; influenced by M: 58; knows M's minor poems: 58. Elizabeth Singer: 117. Major F. G. C.: 44. N.: 58, 97. Sir Nicholas: 44, 91. Owen: 44. T.: 58. Sir Thomas: 40. Sir William: 44

Rowland: Francis: 45. Henry: 88; author of Mona antiqua restaurata: 88. John (1606-60): 44*, 103, 91; works: Pro Rege et Populo Anglicano Apologia: 91; Polemica: 91

Rowlands Castle, co. Hants.: 44

Rowlands, Richard: 40

Rowley: Harold H.: 93. Samuel: 68. Uriah: 44. William: 44

Rowse, A. L.: 44

Rowton, M. B.: 64

Roxburghe Ballads: 68

Royal and Other Innocent Blood, etc: 103, 116

Royal Academy: 97*

Royal American Magazine, The: 115

Royal Blood Crying to Heaven: 121

Royal Commission for Promoting Fine Arts in the U.K.: 97

Royal Commission on Historical Manuscripts, reports of: 44*

Royal Exchange: 40, 44

Royal Guard: 116

Royal Image. See Eikon Basilike

Royal injunctions: 40

Royal Library, St. James' Palace (King's Library): 40, 44

Royal Martyr: 116

Royal Proclamation, August 13, 1660: 103

Royal Society of Lit.: 44, 63

Royal Society: 7, 15, 16, 40, 113, 128, 142, 11, 32, 44, 38. See also: Philosophical Transactions

Royal tutors: 40

Royalism (M's): 60, 147. M embattled in the Royalist whirlwind: 147

Royalists: 9, 44, 51*, 103. Licentiousness of: 51. Pamphleteer for restoration of the king: 147

Royalty, shameful desire to readmit: 51

Roybold, William (bks., 1651-60): 91

Roycroft, Thomas (pr., 1651-77): 44, 91

Roydon, Matthew: 64

Royer, B. F.: 16

Royston warden: 103

Royston: Mrs.: 44. Richard (pr., bks., 1629-86): 44, 91. Thornalls: 97. Warden: 103

Rubel, V. L.: 15

Rubens, Peter Paul: 40, 90, 103, 129, 97, 137, 133, 146. Frontispiece: 77

Rubinstein, Anton: 39

Rubio, Antonio: 40

Rucellai: Bernardo: 64. Cosimo: 64

Rudd: Anthony: 40, 44*, 45. Joan: 44

Rudder, Samuel: 44

Rudhall: Joan: see Pye, Joan. William: 45

Rudiard: James: 45. Mary: 45

Rudimenta grammatices et docendi methodis (Wolsey): 20

Rudolf: (Rodolf), King of Germany: 44, 53. Rudolf von Ems: 65, 32, 93

Rudolphine tables: 89

Rudwin, Maximilian: 93

Rudyerd (Rudyard), Sir Benjamin: 60, 38

Rue: 72

Ruff, Jacob: 65

Rufinus of Aquileia (translator of Origen): 107, 93, 36. Does not much alter Origen's works according to Cadiou: 107

Rugeley: G.: 58. Mary: see Agar, Mary

Rügen. See Charles X

Ruggieri, Archbishop: 111

Ruggle(s), George: 40, 70

Rugoff, M. A.: 128

Ruhe, Edward L.: 44*

Ruines of Time, The (Spenser): 20, 70, 83. Spenser's expression of admiration for Rosalinde in: 83. His admiration for Dudley family in: 83

Ruiz, Juan, Archpriest of Hita: 122

Ruland, Martin: 40

Rule of Reason, The (Wilson): 20

Rule, merit deserves to: 31. Rule of judgment (M): 107

Rulers, greed of: 83

Rules: for writing Latin verse: 40. The Richardsons' dislike of fixed: 88. Tyher on, handicapping and excess dulling the mind: 88

Rulice (Rulitius), John: 10

Rumor: 90

Rump Parliament: 44, 51, 103, 55. M and: 147. Dissolved by Cromwell: 147. And the state church: 147. And Toleration: 147. Restored, M and: 147

Run-on lines, the Richardsons on: 88

Runciman, A.: 97

Rundrum, Alan: 146

Runic letters (Old Eng.): 40

Runyon, Damon: 101

Rupert: 77; works: De Victoria Verbi Dei: 77; De Trin...In Ezech.: 77. Prince, Count Palatine: 10, 33, 44, 45, 73, 103. Of St. Heribert: 60, 68*. Saint: 143

Rupertus: 24*. Abbas: 99; works: In Evangelium S. Joannis: 74; Super Matthaeum: 74. Of Deutz: 32. Tuitiensis (abbot): 1, 65, 123, 36. Tutiensus: 102

Rupilius, Publius: 73

Rupp, E. Gordon: 93

Ruptures of the Commonwealth: 30, 132

Rural Magazine, Or Vermont Repository, The: 115

Rural. See Country-side

Rusca, Antonio: 60

Rush, Richard: 44

Rusher, P.: 58

Rushmere, co. Suffolk: 44

Rushton, E.: 58

Rushworth, John: 44

Rusk, Ralph L.: 115

Ruskin, John: 15, 27, 33, 87, 112, 88, 130, 58, 111, 118, 150, 94. On M's Satan: 87. On M's influence on Puritan mind: 87. On M's characters in PL: 87. St. Peter benign bishop: 143

Russell: Mr. (M's tailor): 44, 150. Benjamin: 115; An Address Delivered Before the Massachusetts Charitable Mechanick Association: 115. Bertrand: 12, 34, 76, 141, 143; science and the universe: 143. H. K.: 128. John: 58, 116. Richard: see Grub-street Journal. T. (sonnets of): 58. Thomas: 79, 120. (Russel), William Lord: 116*

Russia: 19*, 31, 44, 45, 103, 3, 150. Sea: 49. Russians: 3. See also: Muscovy; Moscow; Alexis I

Rust: Eric C.: 79, 93. Rev. George: 44, 142, 93; works: A Discourse of the Use of Reason in Matters of Religion: 142; Letter of Resolution Concerning Origen: 142

Rustic music: 121

Rustication: 30. Episode in M's: 40, 44

Rutgers Univ.: 44*

Rutherford, Mark, author of: 133

Rutherford, Samuel: 7, 9*, 44, 59, 79, 102, 114, 116, 120, 26, 32, 93, 101

Ruthven, K. K.: 39

Rutilians: 73

Rutland co.: 44

Rutland: Frances Montagu, Countess of: 44. John Manners, 8th Earl of: 44; 9th Earl of: see Roos

Rutli, Oath on the: 97

Rutt, J. T.: 44, 58

Rutter, Michael: 45

Rutupiae (Richborrow, Haven Trutulensis): 49

Rutupian Sea: 44, 3

Rutupina: 73

Ruvius. See Rubio

Ruvo: 49

Ruysbroeck: 7

Ruysdael, J.: 97

Ruyter, Admiral: 103

Ryan: E.: 58. Franklin W., Usury and Usury Laws: 82. John K.: 81, 93

Rycaut, Sir Paul: 44, 38

Ryder, Edward: 44

Rydinge Coppice: 45

Rye House Plot: 116*

Rye, the: 45

Ryff, Peter: 40, 59

Rylands, W. W. (engraver): 44

Ryle, Herbert E.: 123

Ryley: (Riley), W.: 45. William, Norroy King at Arms: 44

Rymer, Thomas: 17, 145, 130, 146, 117

Rysbrack: M.: 97. John Michael (sculptor, M portraits): 44

Ryther: (Ryder), Jane: see Whorwood, Jane. Sir John: 44

Ryves, Bruno: 44

-S-

S., A.: 44. See also: Samwell, A.

S., G.: 44, 116. Britain's Triumph: 91. See also: Starkey

S., H.: 44

S., I., M.: 44

S., I.: 116

S., Lord. See Scudamore, Viscount

S., M. (pr.): 44, 59. See also: Simmons, Matthew

S., R.: 117

S., S. See Simmons

Sa de Meneses, Don João Roderiguez, Count de Penguies (Portuguese ambassador): 44

Sá de Miranda, Francisco: 64

Saadia Gaon: 40, 41

Saba: 144

Sabaudia (Allobrogum Ducatas): 49. See also: Piedmont

Sabaudiensis...Narratio (attr. to M): 44

Sabbatai Zevi: 38

Sabbath: 9*, 63

Sabbatini, Nicolo: 39

Sabean (Sabaean): 49, 73. See also: Arabia

Sabellianism: 60, 73. Sebellians: 71

Sabellicus, Marcantonio Coccio: 93

Sabie, Francis: 65, 64. Adams Complaint: 74

Sabin, Joseph: 44

Sabine(s): 73

Sabine, George H.: 1, 4, 9, 40, 60, 79, 64, 108

Sabini: 49

Sabinus. See Sabine, George

Sabol, A. J.: 39

Sabrina Fair: 121

Sabrina: 1, 29*, 73, 90, 144, 143, 72*. As allegorical figure: 104. M's sources for: 104. Summoned: 143. A virgin: 143

Sabunde, Raymond (of). See Sebonde

Sacchi, Andrea: 27

Sacer est vates: 40

Sachs: Curt: 100. Hans: 65, 68, 129

Sachse: 7

Sackton, Alexander: 125

Sackville: Sir Lionel, Sackville-West, 2nd Baron: 44. Richard: 91. Thomas: 88

Sacrament(s): 7, 47, 51, 123, 46, 93, 69. The 7, of the church: 71. M's doctrine of the: 79. Sacramentalism: 96

Sacre de la femme, Le: 65

Sacred music: 121

Sacred theologian: 51

Sacred Decretall (Richard Overton, satirizes the Presbyterians): 147

Sacred Philosophy of the Holy Scripture, The (Gill the Elder): 20*, 40

Sacrifice: 51, 11*, 46. Origin of: 41. In SA: 125. And ritual: 125. Within the labyrinth: 11. In Comus, PR: 11. Willing: 11. Of the Word: 11. Of Samson: 11

Sacro Bosco (John of Holywood, Sacrobosco), John: 44, 40, 89, 128

Sadi (Persian poet): 94

Sadism: 47

Sadleir, Anne: 16, 44, 115

Sadler: Mr.: 44. John: 44, 38. M. T.: 58. William: 44, 45

Safford, Manchester: 44

Sages, education of: 40

Saggio di Critica sul Paradiso Perduto di Giovanni Milton (Scolari): 70

Said, Edward: 11, 39

Saillens, Emile: 59, 137

Sainliens. See Desainliens

St. Agnes Eve: 139

St. Albans: 40, 73

St. Aldate's: 45

St. Ambrose: 65

St. Andrew's Church, Cambridge: 40. St. Andrew's Church, Holborn, London: 44, 45. St. Andrew's, Holborn, parish: 44. St. Andrew's by the Wardrobe, parish: 44, 45. St. Andrew's Street, Cambridge: 40

St. Angelo: 49. Castle: 73

St. Anne, Blackfriars: church: 44. parish: 44

St. Anthony's School: 20, 42

St. Augustine: 65, 76, 139, 71, 64, 131, 149, 25. Philosophy of: 71. System of, suitable to a dogmatic church: 71*. City of God, quoted: 149. See also: Soliloquies

St. Avitus, De Mosaicae Historiae

Gestis, etc.: 149; temptation scene: 149

St. Bart's, London: 103

St. Bartholomew's Massacre: 83. St. Bartholomew Sunday: 44. St. Bartholomew's day: 103. St. Bartholomew's Close, London: 44. St. Bartholomew's Eve: 40. St. Bartholomew's the Less, London: 44

St. Basil: 65

St. Benet Sherehog, church and parish: 44

St. Benet's Church, Cambridge: 40

St. Bernard: 70, 71, 131

St. Bonaventura: 76

St. Botolph: Aldersgate, London: 44. Parish: 44, 45. St. Botolph's (Buttols, Buttolphes), parish and street: 44, 45

St. Bride's Churchyard: 44, 103, 94

St. Bridget's Churchyard: 44

St. Buttolphes. See St. Botolph's

St. Buttols. See St. Botolph's

St. Catharine's College, Cambridge: 40, 45

St. Clement Danes Church (and parish): 44. St. Clement Danes, Strand, London: 44. St. Clement's Churchyard: 44, 45.

St. Clement's, Oxford: 44, 45

St. David's: 44

St. Dennis, Cornwall: 44

St. Dionis Backchurch: 45

St. Dionysious: 110

St. Dunstan-in-the-East, London: 44, 45

St. Dunstan-in-the-West, London: 44

St. Dunstan's, London: 103 St. Dunstan's, London: 103. St. Dunstan's, Fleet Street, London: 44

St. Ebb(e)'s: 45

St. Edmond's Church, London: 103, 143. And Henry Sherfield: 143. Window defaced: 143

St. Edmund's Hall, Oxford: 44, 45

St. Ephrem: 65

St. Evremond, Charles de Marguetel de Saint-Denis, Seigneur de: 44, 70

St. Faith's, London: 103

St. Francis of Assisi: 103

St. Gall, Switzerland: 44. See also: Swiss Evangelical Cantons

St. George, Order of: 103. St. George's Chapel, Windsor: 40, 45. St. George's, Southwark, London: 44

St. Giles, Cripplegate, London: 44*, 94. St. Giles Cripplegate, M's grave in church, and parish: 44. St. Giles, London: 103. St. Giles in the Fields, London: 44, 45. St. Giles without Cripplegate: 44

St. Gregory: 64. St. Gregory by St. Paul's: 45

St. Hilarius Arelatensis: 65. St. Hilarius of Poitiers: 65

St. Hugh: 49, 73

St. Ives: 45

St. James chapel: 103. St. James (Clerkenwell): 45. St. James' Library: 44 St. James' Library: 44. St. James' Palace: 44. St. James Palace Library: 40

St. James' Park, London: 44, 51. See also: "Park"

St. Jerome: 51, 65, 64, 149, 25

St. John: 51, 70, 112, 25, 94; Apocalypse of: 62. St. John, eyesalve mentioned by: 16. St. John, J. A. (ed. Milton, Prose Works): 44, 45, 87, 128; defended M's political activities: 87. St. John, John: 58. St. John ed Luz (port): 44. St. John Chrysostom: 65. St. John of Jerusalem Tavern: 44. St. John, Oliver: 44, 91. St. John Zachary's (Zecharies) Church, London: 44.

St. John's: 44. St. John's College, Cambridge: 40*, 45. St. John's College, Oxford: 44. St. John's Gate, Clerkenwell, London: 44. St. John's Street, Clerkenwell, London: 44. St. John's Street, Dijon: 44

St. Lawrence: 64. St. Lawrence parish and church, Reading: 44

St. Louis, Missouri: 44

St. Luke: 139, 64. St. Luke, Gospel of: 132

St. Margaret, Ipswich: 44. St. Margaret's Church, Westminster: 44, 103

St. Martin-in-the-Fields: 40, 44. St. Martin-in-the-Fields, church and parish: 44*, 45

St. Martin's Lane Academy: 97. St. Martin's Church, Oxford: 44, 45. St. Martins le Grand: 44, 49, 103. St. Martins Lane: 150

St. Mary, Aldermary Church, London: 40, 44. St. Mary-le-Bow, London: 40, 44. St. Mary Hall, Oxford: 44. St. Mary Magadalene: 45. St. Mary Matfelon, Whitechapel, London: 44. St. Mary of the Arches, parish: 44, 45. St. Mary the Virgin, Aldermanbury, London: 44

St. Mary's Church, Cambridge: 40*, 44. St. Mary's Church, Oxford: 40, 45. St. Mary's Hall, Oxford: 40, 45

St. Maur, Raymond de (Nicolas Francois Dupre de St. Maur): 117; supposed and real: 88

St. Michael's Church, Cambridge: 40, 45

St. Nicholas (town): 49. St. Nicholas, Ipswich: 44. St. Nicholas, Ipswich, parish register, ed. Cookson: 44

St. Paul: Elizabeth de: 45. Ursula de: 45

St. Paul: 51, 70, 76, 112, 132, 139, 71, 64, 13, 25. St. Paul, Triumph de: 44, 45

St. Paul's Cathedral and close: 20, 27, 29, 44*, 45, 49, 103, 112, 121. St. Paul's churchyard: 103, 44*. St. Paul's converts: 51

St. Paul's Cross, London: 40

St. Paul's School: 20*, 29, 40*, 42, 44*, 56, 57*, 103, 121, 136, 62, 137, 21

St. Peter, Collegiate Church of, Westminster: 40; see also: Westminster Abbey. St. Peter and St. Mary (Stowmarket) Church: 44. St. Peter at Paul's Wharf, parish: 44

St. Peter: 64. Lycidas: 104

St. Peter's, Cornhill, London: 44. St. Peter's in the East (Oxford): 45. St. Peter's, Rome: 103

St. Pierre: 149

St. Prosperus Aquitanus: 65

St. Radegund: 45

St. Salvator's College: 40

St. Saphronius: 32

St. Saviour's Church, Southwark: 40

St. Sepulchre Church, Cambridge: 40. St. Sepulchre's, London: 44

St. Simeon Stylites: 71

St. Simeon: 122

St. Simon: 4

St. Stephen: 111. St. Stephen's, Brannell: 44. St. Stephen's, Coleman Street, London: 44. St. Stephen's Walbrook, church: 44

St. Swithin's Church, London: 44, 40. Parish: 40

St. Thomas: 73, 49. St. Thomas Apostle's Church: 44, 49

St. Valerie: 49

St. Victor, Paul de: 141

Saint-Amant, Marc-Antoine de Gérard: 74, 64. Works: Joseph et Ses Frères: 74; Moyse Sauvé: 74

Saint-Gelais, Mellin de: 122, 64

Saint-Martin: 73. Saint-Martin, Sieur du: 64; Nature Naissante: 74. St. Martin, Ludgate, London (parish): 44

Saint(s): 7, 9*, 47, 122, 103. Privileges of: 9*. As hero: 123. See also: Holiness; Sanctification; Martyrdom; Individual names

Saint-Lucy, Pierre de: 64

Saint-Peres, Jean de: 64. Works: Tobie: 74; Vie de Joseph: 74

Sainte-Garde, Bernouin: 64

Sainte-Marthe, S. de: 58

Saints Paradise (Gerrard Winstanley): 147

Saintsbury, George: 5, 35, 16, 44, 56, 58*, 77, 86, 87, 100, 64, 130. On M's narrowness: 87. Cambridge History: 77

Saito, Kakuaki: 118

Saladin: 123

Salamanca: 49, 73

Salamanders: 142

Salamis: 49

Salandra, Serafino della: 60, 65*, 32, 64

Salary (M's): 44*

Salaville, J. B.: 117

Sale of land to Sir Matthew Lyster: 44

Salem: (1) Island near Greece; (2) place west of Jordan; (3) Jerusalem: 49, 73

Salerno: 40. Medical school of: 16

Salianus, Jacobus: 4, 63, 32

Salignacus, Bernardus: 40

Salisbury Cathedral: 103

Salisbury, Manuscripts of the Marquis of: 45

Salisbury: Earl of: 44, 45. E. E. (and his wife): 40. John of: 18*. Thomas: 142; Galileus Galileus His System: 142. William: 44

Salishan Indians: 118

Salkeld, John: 102, 114, 142, 32, 93, 109. Works: A Treatise of Angels: 60, 142; A Treatise of Paradise: 60, 142

Sallust: 20, 40*, 44*, 56, 70, 73, 84, 123, 145, 3, 26, 82, 146, 117

Salmacis: 73

Salmanassar: 73

Salmasius (Claude Saumaise, antagonist of M, nicknamed Alastor, Ammon, Pan, Jove, Jupiter, Scribonius): 1, 8, 15, 19, 20, 28*, 30*, 40, 42, 44*, 45, 51, 52, 66, 70, 73, 84, 36, 113, 114, 116*, 120, 121, 123, 128*, 132, 136, 147, 3, 38, 43, 62, 71, 82*, 93, 64, 115, 130, 137, 146*, 150, 117, 94. His violent agitation of mind: 134. And Queen Christina: 30*. Defeat of; death of; defense of tyrants undertaken by; only opponent of M's worth answering; a sophist: 30. Works: Defensio Regia: 43, 82, 91*; Salmasius his Dissection and Confutation: 91; Responsio: 91; Phillips' account: 55; controversy discussed: 55. See also: Saumaise, Claude

Salmasius: Madame Anne Mercier, wife of Claudius (nicknamed Mercera, Xantippe): 44* Claudius (son of Salmasius): 44

Salmon, William: 16

Salmoneus: 56, 73, 141

Salmurium (Saumur): 49

Salmydessian: 44

Salomon: 29

Salsbury (Sarum, Searesbirig): 49

Salsilli (Salzilli), Giovanni: 6, 28, 30, 35, 44

Salt (meaning wit): 8

Saltair na Rann: 65

Salter, H. S.: 45*

Salters Hall: 40

Saltmarsh, John (d. 1647): 7, 9, 44, 59, 60, 79, 114, 147*, 32, 38, 91. Puritan protagonist: 147. Works: The Smoke in the Temple (argues for toleration, design of reconciliation): 147; A New Quere (doubts the haste of setting up a state church): 147; Shadows Flying Away: 147*; Groans for Liberty: 91

Saltonstall, Wye: 45

Salus Britannica: 116

Salusbury: John: 29. Thomas, Galileus Galileus His System: 142

Saluste, Guillaume de, Sieur du Bartas: 65*, 32. See also: Bartas

Salutati, Coluccio: 18, 60

Salvation: 47, 50, 123, 25, 51, 122*, 143. M on: 80. History and necessities of: 96*. Inseperable from beatitude: 123. Plan of: 143. Assurance of: 143. Steps to: 143. Through Christ: 143. Protestant doctrine of: 143. And works: 143. By grace: 143. To all: 143. Essential conditions to: 143. See also: Christ; Reconciliation; Redemption; Son of God

Salvian of Marseilles: 93

Salvianus: 65

Salviati: D. of: 6. F.: 6

Salvini: Antonio: 117. (Salvino), S.: 6, 44

Salway, Major: 45

Salzburger Paradiesspiel: 65

Salzilli, Giovanni. See Salsilli, Giovanni

Samael: 142

Samarchand: 19, 49, 144. City: 73

Samaria (Samritidae Orae): 49, 73

Samaria liberata: 50

Samaritan Revived (Matthew Griffith, favors restitution of kingship): 147

Samaritan(s): 42, 73, 3. Chronicle: 73. Pentateuch: 40

Sambiasi, Scipione: 21

Sambix, John à (publisher): 44, 91

Samian master: 3. See also: Pythagoras

Sammael: 41, 42, 36

Samnites: 73

Samoed: 73

Samoedia (Samoed Shore): 19, 49

Samogitia: 49

Samos: 19, 49, 73. See also: Delos

Samoyed: 144

Sampson: Alden: 16, 130; Studies in M: 83. Ezra: 115; works: Beauties of the Bible: 115; The Sham-Patriot Unmasked: 115. M. W.: 92

Samson Agonistes (ed. by Churton Collins): 70

Samson Agonistes: The following entries are partial, yet representative. Readers should consult individual topics throughout the Index for particular subjects and references.

Samson Agonistes (form, elements, themes of poem). Themes, aims, meaning: 68*, 80, 146; theme of divine rescue: 104; blindness theme: 101; freedom from dogma: 113. Form: 55. As tragedy: 148; tragic effect: 101; tragic quality: 35; Christian tragedy: 148; imitation of Greek drama: 13; relationship to Greek tragedy: 68. Comedy in: 101. As a play: 11; dramatic structure of: 68*; "interior drama" in: 101.

Samson Agonistes (form, elements, themes of poem continued). Political satire: 68. SA as sacrament: 126. As allegory: 68*. Anti-feminisim in: 68. Hellenism and Hebraism in: 68, 146. Christianity in: 72*, 101. God champion in: 72*. Imagery: 8*.

Samson Agonistes (form, elements, themes of poem continued). Versification: 146; metrics: 146; rhyme: 146; poetic style: 55. Development: 148; and structure: 11, 72. Chorus: 126, 85*, 101, 146, 55; prayer for absolution: 126; G. M. Hopkins on choruses: 87; metrics of chorus: 13. Autobiographical elements: 68, 146, 148. Catharsis: 72*, 148. Sources: 68, 55; Italian influence: 55. Biblical account: 148. And Geneva Bible: 143*. Preface to: 146, 55. Sublimity: 146. Diction: 146. Literalism in: 68. Dialectic in: 72.

Samson Agonistes (form, elements, themes of continued). M's use of term "Perfection" in: 83. Irony: 72*. "New hero" in: 72. Violence in: 11. Tropology in: 68. Rationalism in: 68. The "intimate impulse" of: 11. Compared to Comus, PL and PR: 11. Stances in: 72

Samson Agonistes (Samson, character of). Character: 1, 44, 51, 56, 60, 68*, 70, 103, 112, 128*, 144, 143*, 32, 71, 72*, 80*, 91, 109*, 94*, 146, 55. Type of Christ: 68*, 93; mission as Christ's representative: 80; the "greater man" in: 83. As tragic hero, historical personage, folk-hero: 68*.

Samson Agonistes (Samson, character of continued). Resigned to destiny: 80; renounces self in divine mission: 80; God's favor to: 143; conscious agent of God: 143. His role: 11*; in defiance of Philistia: 72; in judgement of Israel: 72; hero of Israel: 143; in defense of God: 72; in attack against Dalilah: 72; his invective against Dalilah and Adam's against Eve compared: 80; his work of faith: 85. Example of lustfullness: 68*.

Samson Agonistes (Samson, character of continued). In the prologos: 72. Compared with Adam: 80; their "falls": 80. Temptations: his and Christ's compared: 80; his testing: 126. Sinful pride of: 143, 85. Separation from world: 143. As a fool: 143. Dalilah: 143. His severe punishment: 143. Conversion to good: 85*. Rejection of evil: 85*. Confession of sin: 126, 85. Contrition: 126, 85*. Spiritual regeneration: 143. Significance of his final act: 80. Triumphant death: 143

<u>Samson Agonistes</u> (other characters). Dalilah: 11, 101, 143, 85*, 146; compared with Eve: 80. Harapha: 85, 101, 146. Manoa: 11, 101, 85*, 146; his speech in relation to Burial of the Dead: 126. proposes ransoming Samson: 80

<u>Samson Agonistes</u> (text). Presentation copy of: 44. Phillips' account: 55. Text: 55. Dating: 148, 55. Editions: 68. Disparagement of by critics: 68

<u>Samson Agonistes</u> (miscellaneous). Triple equation in: 101. Typological reading of: 101. Man's obligation to uphold spiritual obligations: 80. Relationship of poem to modern man: 80. M's patriotism and republican ideals: 80. Conceptual relation among the 3 major poems: 80. SA and history: 11. Model for Arnold's "Sohrab and Rustum": 87. Interest in prosody: 87. Southey's Thalaba compared with SA: 87. Bridges' imitation of: 87. Trends in interpretation of SA: 80

Samuel bar Nachman: 41

Samuel, Irene: 23, 31, 37, 52, 60, 66, 75, 100, 110, 118, 125, 128, 53, 137, 48, 123, 14, 32, 62, 93, 101, 140, 21. <u>Plato and Milton</u>: 60, 74

Samuel, Mr.: 44

Samuel: 70, 73, 3, 91, 40, 68. <u>1st Book of</u>: 74. <u>2nd Book of</u>: 74. See also: Bible

"Samuels Funerall": 45 Samwell, Anthony: 44. See also: S., A.

San Francisco, California: 44

San(c)ta Clara, Franciscus a: 73

Sanchez, Francisco: 114

Sancroft, William (1617-93), Abp. of Canterbury: 44, 116, 91

Sancta Crux: 49

Sanctification: 122, 123. See also: Saint; Holiness; Regeneration

Sanctity: 123. See also: Holiness

Sanctius, Gasparus: 74, 64. <u>In Librum Job</u>: 74

Sanctum Dominicum: 49

Sandals. See symbolism

Sandars, Nancy K.: 64

Sanday, W.: 36

Sandelands, Andrew: 40

Sandelands: Andrew: 40. Mrs. Andrew and family: 44

Sander, Nicholas: 79

Sanderlin, George: 87

Sanders: Mrs.: 44. (Saunders), Anne: see Cope, Ann. Deborah: 45. Jane: see Cope, Jane (Spencer). John: 45. Nicholas: 93. Robert: 45. Valentine: 45. William: 45. See also: Saunders

Sanderson: Mr.: 45. John: 40, 44. Robert: 40, 44. Robert, Bp. of Lincoln: 93, 64. Sir William: 44; <u>Complete History</u>: 91

Sandford: 45. Mr.: 44. John: 40

Sandimer: 49

Sandler, Florence: 25

Sandrinelli, Bernardo: 68

Sandwell: 45

Sandwich: 49; see also: Rutupiae. Earl of: 44. Edward Montagu, 1st Earl of: 44

Sandys: George: 1, 6, 15, 19*, 20, 40, 56, 57, 59, 18, 60, 69, 123, 128, 144, 26, 32, 39, 72, 93, 101, 106, 150, 55; works: <u>A Relation of a Journey</u>: 144; on allegorical signficiance of Moly: 104; <u>Ovid's Metamorphosis Englished</u>: 88; <u>Psalm paraphrases</u>: 126; <u>Travailes</u>: 57, 88.

Sandys: John Edwin: 22, 92, 64. Lady: 44. Sir Miles: 114, 93. Sir William: 44, 45

Sandys: 3. Family: 44. Ann: 44. Bp.: 147; wrote To Burghley and Leicester: 147. Sir Edwin, Abp. (brother of George): 68, 73, 143, 93; rejects purgatory: 143; on grace for all: 143; and Scripture: 143.

Sanford: family: 45. (Sandford), Mr.: 45. Francis: 45. Henry: 45. John: 93. Thomas: 45. William: 45

Sanguinet, Estiene de: 74, 64. <u>Dodécade de l'Evangile</u>: 74

Sanhedrin: 51, 73

Sankey: Benjamin T., Jr.: 60. John: 44

Sanmase, Monsieur. See Salmasius

Sannazaro: Giacomo: 21. (Sannazarro), Jacopo: 1, 4, 6, 29, 74, 120, 123, 26, 53, 88, 64*, 101; works: Arcadia: 74; De Partu Virginis: 74, 149

Sanservino, Roberto: 21

Sansom, J.: 58

Sansovino, Francesco: 60

Santayana, George: 15, 18, 58, 65, 112, 144, 143. Poetry and religion: 143. World unsaved: 143. Fall a myth: 143

Santi, Raphael: 46

Sanxon: 68

Saphon, Mt.: 32

Sapia: 111

Sapience: 60, 139

Sapphira: 73

Sappho: 5, 20, 40, 121

Saracen(s) (Sarasin, Sarazens): 73, 103

Saracen's Head in (Bread Street): 40, 44

"Saragossa, The Maid of": 97 Sarah: 68, 72, 91. Wife of Sabbatai Zevi: 38

Saravia, Andrian: 40

Sarbiewski, Maciez Kasimierz: 40

Sarcasm, use of: 51

Sarcotis: 65

Sardanapulus: 44, 73, 123

Sardinia: 44

Sardis: 49, 73

Sarepta: 49, 73

Sargant, W. L. (of Oakham School): 20

Sargent: 149

Sarmatiae: 144

Sarmatian(s): 44, 49, 73

Sarpedon: 56, 73

Sarpi, Pietro (Fra Paolo): 6, 51, 123, 82, 55. Historia del Concilio Tridentino: 82*

Sarra: 73

Sarrafin: 128

Sarravius: Mr.: 44. Claudius: 44

Sarsden: 45

Sarto, A. del: 6

Sarton, George: 123

Sartorius: 73

Sartre, Jean-Paul: 14, 72, 101

Sarum: 45, 73

Sasek, Lawrence A.: 37, 60, 79, 122, 101, 106, 140, 21

Sassetti, Filippo, Sopra Dante: 74

Sassone, Adriana: 64

Sassoon, S.: 58

Sassuolo: 60

Satan (Devil): 1*, 2*, 4*, 8, 16, 17*, 19*, 31*, 40, 41*, 42, 44, 50*, 51, 54*, 57, 60*, 63*, 67*, 68, 70*, 73, 76*, 87*, 89*, 98*, 102*, 103, 104, 111*, 113*, 114*, 118, 123*, 124*, 125*, 126, 127*, 128*, 129*, 132*, 136*, 141*, 142*, 143, 144*, 3, 11*, 32*, 36*, 62*, 71*, 72*, 80*, 92, 96, 106*, 109*, 130*, 146, 117*, 140*, 25*.

Satan (character, in general): 37*, 52*, 75, 87, 113*, 129, 132*, 97*, 55. Ambiguity in character: 141. Ambition: 144. Appearance: 50, 97*; beauty: 125. Associated with: Athenians of Acts, Belshazzar, Dives, Esau, Herod, Judas Iscariot, Nebuchadnezzar, the Pharisees, the 2nd Advent of Christ, the unrepentant thief on the cross: 119. Aspiring mind: 87; aspiration: 75*. Attractions of: 87. Author of evil: 107; meaning of evil in regard to: 52. Consistency of characterization: 52. Cosmological characterization: 128. Deceiver: 75*; his guile: 123*. Deliverer: 75. Demonic hero: 46; demonic heroism: 141. Depravity: 141. Despiser of low temptations of the world: 125. Doubt: 125.

Satan (character, in general continued). Exhibits characteristics of Lucifer in Isaiah: 123. False understanding: 46; knowledge of: 125. Foreknowledge of: 128; his field of vision: 39; prophetic perception of: 25; Hell within him: 76. As Hellish Hate: 48. Historian: 125. Human qualities of: 87. Intention: 76. Inventor: 75. As lover: 11. Nature: 144. Negative creative power: 128, uncreator: 75*. As old man: 11. As opacity: 146, 25. As poet: 121. Politician: 106; as state: 25. Power: 125*, 144. Pride: 141. Rationalist: 125. Representative of endless evil: 83.

Satan (character, in general continued). Revealed by speech: 119; as a liar by Christ: 119. Rhetoric: 37; too eloquent to be in Hell: 136. Roles: in Adam's Fall: 123*; in Old and New Testaments: 36. Search for glory and transcendence: 52. As Selfhood: 146, 25; Self: 125*; victim of Self: 125*. Sense of evil: 129. Separated ego: 46. And the serpent in Genesis: 123; disguised as serpent: 50, 36*. Sincerity: 125. Sources of character: 55; prototypes: 46. As spectre: 146. Sublime being: 87. Subtlety of: 143. Tempter: 106*. Tyrant: 113, 146. His will: 37. Language: 67.

Satan (activites, actions). Pattern of assault: 75*, two strategic objectives of: 125. Action in opening books: 76. Journey through Chaos: 75, 87, 76, 89, 72, 106; pact with Chaos: 46. Summoning his legions (painting): 97*. In Hell, after Fall: 72; speech in Hell: 50, 76. With Sin and Death: 11, 123, 72, 97*.

Satan (activities, actions). End declared good by: 119. His shield: 89. Passage through the Spheres: 89. With gods of the Abyss: 123. Lands in the Sun: 89, 72; address to Sun: 89. Arrival at Golden Stairs: 89. Reconnoiters world: 89, 143. Disguised as Cherub: 41, 36. Flight down to Earth: 89. By Limbo: 72. Disguises: 46, 99*. And Uriel: 17, 106. Starts at touch of Ithuriel's spear: 97. Transformations: 11. At entrance to Paradise: 76. In the Garden of Eden: 17, 89, 72. Motives for tempting Eve: 35; and for tempting Man: 36. Return to Hell: 89. Causes tempests: 128

Satan (before expulsion from Heaven). Before Fall: 89, 36. Origin of: 113. As brother of Christ: 125. Pre-eminence in Heaven: 107. Achieves rank through merit: 107. Pride and the Fall: 113, 129, 36, 107, 143, 87. Motives for Rebellion: 107, 36, 99*. Thinks his power his own: 107. As light: 107. Warned of his fate: 89. Angelic prediction as to Fall: 89. Rebellion of: 113; 36*, 89. Meeting with Michael on battlefield: 89. Battle in Heaven: 17, 89, 72*. Fall: 113, 129, 36. Flight: 89. Expulsion: 89

Satan (compared and contrasted with). Alchemists: 128; astrologers: 128; cannon: 76; comets: 128; dragon: 128; dragon of Revelation: 123*. Contrast with: Christ: 76; Gabriel: 76, 106. As cormorant, lion, tiger, toad, wolf: 128. Griffin: 144. Leviathan: 46, 97. Light: 107, 106. Moses and Pharoah: 106. As Ophion: 76. As Sun: 76, 128. As serpent: 128, 107. As whale: 128. As wandering fire and mist: 128. Vulture: 128, 144. As Passion: 113. Satan of PL compared with Satan of PR: 87

Satan (historical views). Medieval Satan compared with M's: 87; Ruskin on Medieval Satan: 87. In 17th c.: 141. 17th and 18th c. reaction to: 87. Conventional treatment of: 141. Romantic school concerning: 141, 52. Effect on Victorians: 87; their admiration for: 87; late Victorian view of: 87; decline of interest in: 87. 19th c. reaction to: 87. Anti-satanist school: 141. In Heraud's "The Judgement of the Flood" and "Descent into Hell": 87. In Bailey's "A Spiritual Legend": 87. Effect on Landor: 87

Satan (miscellaneous). Failure of: 143. Kingdom of: 143. Problem of: 123. Imitation of God: 123. Judged in the serpent: 123*. His degradation: 37*, 129, 62. Depicted: 129. Destroyed: 143. His progress: 143. Source of obscenity: 46; the obscene world of: 75*. Tragedy of: 62. And prelacy: 75. And imprisonment: 73*. And time: 76, 125. Glory turned to dust: 107. Failure of in tempting Christ foreshadowed: 119. Language of Scripture perverted by: 119. Swedenborg's view of: 25. Reign of: 25. Agents of: 144. In contemporary pamphlets: 144*. Satan and kingdom: 125. Paintings concerning: 97*.

Satan (Milton, audience, readers). M's attitude toward: 113*; M's sympathy for: 87; M's character reflected in: 87; M's portrayal of: 87; poetic effect of: 141*. Hero: 76, 83, 87, 106; as ironic hero: 52. Not hero of PL: 113, 129. Alienation of sympathy from: 118. Sataninst interpretations of PL: 118. Anti-satanist interpretations: 141.

Satan (Milton, audience, readers continued). Satan in PR: 132; upon the Annunciation; upon the Bread and Word; upon glory and Israel; upon nature and wealth; upon Sonship and wisdom; at the Temple: 72. M's handling in PL: 137. Blake's: 146. In Miltonic religious epics: 87. In Montgomery's "Satan," "Messiah," intellectual stature of, Faustian nature of: 87

Satan. See also: Devil; Christ; Prometheus; Power; Lucifer; Marriage of Heaven and Hell; Milton (Blake); Urizen; Serpent; Demonic; Fallen Angels; War in Heaven

Satan and Comus: 101. And interior paradise: 101. Language of: 101. See also: Christ

Satan Exalted Sat (frontispiece): 98

Satan, A Libretto (Cranch): 65

Satan, A Poem (Montgomery): 65

Satan's shapes: 77. See also: Nash(e), Thomas

Sataniada, La: 65

Satanism: 146

Satanist(s): 31, 132. Reading of PL: 106

Satanomachia: 65

Satchwell, R. W.: 97

Satire: 8, 15, 53. On women: 92. M as as satirist: 75. See also: Vehemence

Satires (Donne): 12

Satisfaction theory: 93

Satomail: 36

Sattler, Robert: 16

Saturday Review (English): 44

Saturday Review of Lit.: 44

Saturday Review: 44

Saturn: 1, 44, 57, 60, 73, 89, 90*, 144, 32, 71, 72

Saturnalia: 44

Saturninus, Lucius Appuleius: 73

Satyr against Hypocrites (attr. to M): 28, 44, 94

Satyr plays: 92

Satyr: 90

Satyrae: 65

Sauer, J.: 100

Saul of Tarsus: 51

Saul: 4, 60, 73, 139

Saulnier, V. Louis: 100

Saumaise: (Salmasius), Claude: 9, 16, 103*, 26, 93. Mme. Claude de: 103, 136. See also: Salmasius

Saumur (Salmurium, Salmuriensem): 3. France: 44*, 73

Saunder, Nicholas of Ewell: 40

Saunders: Herbert W.: 20. J. L.: 122. (Sanders), Valentine, Six Clerk: 44

Saurat, Professor Denis: 1, 4, 5, 9, 15, 16*, 23, 24, 27, 35, 34*, 40, 41*, 42, 44, 52, 57, 58, 60, 63*, 68, 73, 75, 76, 77, 84, 86*, 102, 112, 110, 118, 123, 127, 128, 132*, 136, 142, 138*, 43, 71, 85, 88, 92, 144, 22, 26, 133, 141*, 93, 99, 106, 109, 130*, 137, 148, 140. Absolute made relative with difficulty, Christ does not die, Fall the result of sensuality, God is absolute, matter derived from Son, matter develops unaided into beings, matter produced of the Son, M deprives God of his attributes, M's ideas on the creation derived from Fludd: 107. M's thought in PL important: 107. PL unorthodox: 107. Retraction: 107. On M: 80. Works: La pensée de Milton: 57, 60; Milton et le matérialisme chrétien en Angleterre: 60; M: Man and Thinker: 60*, 74, 142

Saurius, Francis: 142

Savage: Professor Henry L.: 44. Jane: 4, 40; see also: Winchester, Marchioness of. R.: 58. Sir Thomas: 40

Savell, Peter: 44

Savile, George: 117

Savile: Sir Henry: 40, 145. Thomas: 65, 93

Savilian, Dr. Wallis: 89

Saville, Lord: 33

Saviolo, Vincent: 40

Saviotti, A.: 6

Savonarola, Girolamo (Hieronimo): 18, 103, 73, 128, 38, 122. On "two handed engine": 80. Oracolo della Renovatione della Chrisa: 82

Savoy, London: 44

Savoy: Duke of (Emanuel): 10, 103, 120, 94. France: see Charles Emmanuel II; Piedmont

Sawbridge: George (pr., bks., 1647-81): 91. Thomas (bks., 1669-92): 44, 91

Sawtry, co. Huntington: 44, 45

Sawyer: Charles (bks.): 44. Hester: 45. Sir Robert: 44

Saxl, Fritz: 60

Saxo Grammaticus: 1, 57

Saxon: 44, 3. Letter: 40. Annalist: 3. Invasions: 3. Kings: 3. Phalanxes: 3. Poems: 3. Shore: 49

Saxony: 49. Duke of: 73. Elector of: 10. Maurice, Duke of: 91

Say: S.: 58*; influenced by M: 58; praises <u>Lycidas</u>: 58. Samuel: 88, 117. William: 44

Saybrook: 45

Sayce, R. A.: 44, 105, 122, 123, 64. <u>French Biblical Epic in the 17th c.</u>: 74

Saye and Sele, William Fiennes, Viscount of: 44*, 51, 120 44*, 51, 120

Sayer, Mr. (Bishop?): 44

Sayers: Dorothy: 34, 111, 32, 109. F.: 58

Sayes Court (and House), Chertsey: 44

Sayle, C. E.: 44

Saywell, John (bks., 1646-58): 91

Scacchus, Fortunatus: 123

Scaevola: Gaius Mucius: 123. Quintus Mucius: 123

Scaglione, Aldo D.: 93

Scaino: 70

<u>Scala naturae</u>: 144

<u>Scala Coeli</u>. See Ladder

<u>Scala Humiltatis</u>: 143

Scaldis: 49

Scale: 121. Of being(s): 24, 113; theme of in M, in Fludd: 113. Of nature: 93; see also: Chain of being

Scales of God: 17

Scales, Richard: 44

Scaliger: 42, 44, 70, 133, 130, 149, 94. Joseph Justus: 44, 40, 52, 22, 93, 64. Julius Caesar: 1, 2, 4, 44, 142, 6, 31, 33, 18, 40*, 56, 60, 73, 100, 122, 64, 146, 21; <u>Poetices</u>: 74

Scandinavia. See Seaton, Ethel

Scandinavian mythology in 18th c. poetry: 58

Scapegoat: 41, 11

Scapula, Johannes: 40

Scarborough, Sir Charles. See Scarburg

Scarborow (Scarborough): 49, 73

Scarburg, Sir Charles: 10, 16, 40

Scarfe, Francis: 86

Scarisbing, F. S.: 58

<u>Scarlet Letter, The</u>: 136

Scartazzini: 111

<u>Scelta di Prose di Dati</u>: 111

<u>Scena tragica</u>: 65

Scenery: 92

Sceptics. See Skeptics

Sceva the Jew: 73

Scève, Maurice: 5, 65, 100. <u>Microcosme</u>: 74

Schaef, Gerard (Dutch agent): 44. See also: Dutch agents

Schaffhausen. See Swiss Evangelical Cantons

Schäfke, Rudolf: 100

Schaller, Jakob: <u>Dissertatio</u>: 91. James: 44

Schanzer, Ernest: 23, 60, 93

Schaper, Carl: 100

Schapiro, Meyer: 93

Scharf, George: 44

Schärf, Riwkah: 141

Scharl, Emmeron: 93

Scharpe, Henry: 44

Schasz, J. A.: 65

Schaumburg (Schaunburg). See William VI

Schechter, Solomon: 93

Schedel, Hartmann: 93

Schedule of activities (M's): 44

Schegkius, Iacobus: 40

Scheibler, Christoph: 40, 32

Scheiner, Christoph: 16, 89

Schellerup, H. H. F. C.: 100

Schelling: F. E.: 108. F. W. J. von: 7, 12, 113, 14

Schemes, meaning and parts: 20

Schenkendorf: 7

Scherer, Edmond: 87, 98, 130. On M: 87, 94. On Renaissance-Puritan elements in M: 87

Scherillo, M.: 64

Scherpbier, H.: 44

Schickhard, William (Wilhelmus): 40, 41, 22. Jus Regium Hebraeorum: 82

Schickler, Baron F. de: 40

Schiff, G.: 97

Schiller, Friedrich von: 87, 97, 141, 146. M a "sentimental" poet: 87. Compared with Miller: 87. On Shakespeare: 87. "On Naive and Sentimental Poetry": 87

Schindler, Valentine: 1, 40, 41, 22*

Schindler's Hebrew Lexicon: 42

Schipper: 120

Schirmer, W. F.: 18

Schism: 114, 144. Schisms: 51. Schismaticks: 51

Schismatick Sifted (John Vicars): 147

Schlegel: Augustus William von: 136, 13. Friedrich von: 37, 150; on Romantic poetry vs. Classical poetry: 87. The Schlegels: 7, 87; on Shakespeare's sonnets: 87

Schleiermacher: 7. F. E. D.: 142

Schlesinger, Arthur M., comment of, on the perfectibility of man: 83

Schleswig-Holstein: 44. See also: Frederick III

Schlezer, John Frederick: 44

Schloegl, Nivard: 40

Schloer: Anna: see Malory. Christian: 10. Christopher Ernest: 10*. Frederick: 10*. Godofred, Jr. and Sr.: 10. Johann Christoph: 10. Johannes Fredericus: 10

Schmalkland League: 83

Schmaltz, Valentin. See Smalcius, Valentin

Schmidt: Alexander: 88. Carl: 41. Sebastian: 68

Schneider: 7. H. W., The Puritan Mind: 83

Schneidew(e)in, Johann: 73

Schoffler, H.: 113

Schofield, W. H.: 64

Schola Salericana: 40

Schola Salernitas: 128

Scholae in liberales artes (Ramus): 20

Scholar(s): education of: 40, 51. Scholarship: 51. Scholar-on-horseback: 40

Scholarly: procedure, M's idea of: 40. Part of the curriculum: 51

Scholasticism: 7, 15, 27, 34, 40, 47, 114*, 142. Influence on Puritans: 142*. Influence on: Salkeld, Agrippa, Fludd, M: 142. M's hatred of: 20, 30, 52. Scholastic philosophy: 70, 132. Scholastics: 40

Scholderer, Victor: 91

Scholem, Gerschom G.: 93

Scholemaster, The (Ascham): 20, 3

Scholes, Percy A.: 93

Scholfield, John: 25

Scholz, Janos: 39

Schomberg: A. C.: 58. G. A.: 58

Schonaeus, Cornelius: 40

Schonberg, Harold: 39

Schoner, Lazarus: 40

Schonheyder, Johannes Henricus: 117

School Laws (attr. to M): 44

School(s): 51. Bacon on, M on: 80. In London: 40. Schoolmen: 145. Schoolmasters, regulation of: 40; M's references to: 112. Schoolteaching, M's, Phillips' account: 55. School plays: 20. Schoolbook stock: 40

Schoolmaster in Picardy, A (H. B. Binns): 136

Schools of Medieval England (Leach): 3

Schools, Athenian: 40

Schoonhoven, Floris von: 64

Schopenhauer, Arthur: 1, 7, 113, 14, 39, 71

Schöpfung der Hölle: 65

Schöpfung, Die: 65

Schöpfung, fal und erlösung: 65

Schoppe, Caspar: 40

Schoppius: 10

Schorer, Mark: 81, 142. Works: William Blake: 142; The Politics of Vision: 142

Schorus, Antonius: 40

Schrade, Leo: 39

Schreiber, William I.: 40

Schroeder, Kurt: 112

Schroeter: 89

Schubert: 149

Schultetus: 40

Schultz, Howard: 17, 23, 37, 59, 74, 75, 122, 123, 128, 125, 26, 85, 93, 101, 106. Works: "Christ and Antichrist in Paradise Regained": 74; M and Forbidden Knowledge: 74

Schulz, Max F.: 115

Schumaker, Wayne: 86

Schumann, Clara: 39

Schutz, John A.: 115

Schuyler, Philip John and Madame: 115

Schwab, Moise: 142. Vocabulaire de l'Angelologie: 142

Schwarzenburg, Friedrich, Cardinal Prince of: 44

Schweitzer, Albert: 47, 143, 137. And ethical reform: 143. And life in God: 143. On: evil, love, thought, superman, essence of Christianity: 47

Schwenkfeld: 7

Schwiebert, E. G.: 93

Science: 15*, 47, 143. Sciences: 51; and triumph: 143; natural: 51; a spiritual desert: 143; and progress: 143; its fruits: 143; changing man's estimate of himself: 80. Scientific inquiry: 80. Applied by Lofft to the study of lit.: 88. M's knowledge of: 137. M's poetic method with: 128*

Scienza Nuova, La (Vico): 139

Scilcester: 49

Scioppius, Kaspar: 44, 94

Scipio: 123, 128, 3, 71. Africanus: 90, 122, 62, 125. Africanus (the Elder) Publius Comelius: 73. Aemilianus Africanus Numantinus (the Younger): 73

Scipioni, Alberto: 44, 94

Scire facias, writ of: 45

Sclater: Richard: 44. William: 40, 114; the elder: 93

Scobell (Scobel): Henry: 9, 44*, 45, 59. Richard: 44

Scoggin's Priest: 40

Scolari, Filippo: 70

Scone: 103

Scor, Anthony: 40

Scorn of ceremonies: 51

Scorpio: 89

Scot: Michael: 128. Patrick: 114. Reginald: 41, 77, 114, 123, 128, 142*, 88; anti-Scot: 142; works: Discourse of Devils and Spirits: 142; The Discoverie of Witchcraft: 142, 77. Thomas (regicide): 24, 44

Scotch (Scots): 44, 103, 3. Gratitude to the: 51. Borders: 49. Protest (1606): 40. "Scotch Storie," M's: 44. War: 44

Scotisms: 3

Scotland (and Scots): 44*, 49, 51, 103; see also: Caledonia. King of: see Charles II. Scottish: army: 51; commissioners: 51; education: 40; National Portrait Gallery: 44; preachers: 51; plan of Presbyterians: 147

Scotland Yard, London: 44

Scots, Confession of: 27

Scott-Craig, T. S. K.: 23, 52, 63, 79, 128, 123

Scott, Fred Newton, Anniversary Papers: 44.

Scott: 35, 51, 3. Mr.: 44. Arthur: 40. D.: 97. Edward: 44. George: 45. Hew: 40. John: 117. J. N.: 58. James: 58. James Brown, Law, the State, and the International Community: 83. John: 40, 44, 58*. John Anthony: 20. Mary Augusta: 40. Robert (bks.): 44. Thomas (d. 1660): 44, 58, 91, 93. W.: 58. Sir Walter: 23, 27, 35, 57, 112, 56, 70, 87, 120, 128, 136, 142, 97, 137, 146, 94; works: Ivanhoe: 95; The Bride of Lammermoor: 142. William: 115; Lessons in Elocution: 115

Scotus: 51. Alexander: 40. Johannes Duns: 31, 68, 73, 113, 114, 142, 70, 123, 3, 11, 71; Arbor Metaphysica: 40. Erigena (Johannes Scotus Erigena): 112

Scoular, Kitty: 39

Scourges of God: 93

Scrade, L.: 6

Scribes: 40

"Scribing quack": 44

Scribner's Sons, Charles: 44

Scribonius (nickname for Salmasius): 44, 128. See also: Salmasius

Scrinia Reserata: 116

Script type: 40

Scriptores Rerum Mythicarum Latini Tres (ed. G. H. Bode): 74

Scriptum Dom. Protectoris (Declaration ...against the Spaniards): 44

Scriptum Parlamenti (attr. to M): 44

Scriptural ideas developed in Apocryphal lit.: 41. See also: Biblical

Scripture and Reason (Herbert Palmer): 9, 30, 147

Scripture and Reason pleaded for Defensive Arms: 73

Scripture(s): 7*, 47*, 51*, 57, 103, 3*. Acceptance of: 51. Authority of: 51, 9*. Bulk of testimony from: 51. Interpretation of: 51, 9*. M's familiarity with: 51. Religious judgment based on: 51. Sole interpreter of itself: 51. Source of authority: 51. Plainness of: 9. M and the concept of: 52, 31. Familiarity of M's readers with: 102. Relation of learning: 102. Use of by M: 102. See also: Accommodation; Holy Spirit; Bible

Scrivener (anonymous): 44, 45

Scrivener, F. H. A.: 135

Scrivener's Company: 40, 44*, 45

Scriver, Christian: 123

Scriveyn, Adam: 40

Scroggs, Sir William, Lord Chief Justice: 116

Scroop's Court: 44, 45

Scroope, Adrian: 44

Scrutiny: 15

Scrymegeour, Henry: 40

Scryven, Mr. (perhaps master scrivener): 44

Scudamore: Mr.: 45. Lord: 89, 103. John, Lord, 1st Viscount (of Sligo): 40, 44, 73, 55, 94. Mary: 44. Richard: 40, 44. Thomas, Viscount of Sligo: 30; see also: Scudamore, John (wrongly called Thomas)

Scudder: Harold H.: 110. Henry: 10. Horace E.: see Keats, John

Scudéry, Georges de, Alaric: 74

Scull: Mr.: 45. Mrs.: 44

Sculpture: 70. M's references to: 137

Scultetus, Abraham: 91

Scylla (Whirlpool): 44, 49, 56, 70, 73, 90, 144, 71, 72. Mask: 104. See also: Charybdis

Scythia: 49. Scythian Shores: 3; see also: Imaus. Scythians: 19, 73, 32

Sea gods: 90

Sea of Jasper: 143

Seabury, Samuel: 115. A View of the Controversy between Great Britain and her Colonies: 115

Seafarer, The: 36

Seager, H. W.: 128

Seal, family (M's): 40

Seal, Great, of Eng.: 44

Seal: Spread Eagle: 40. Two- headed Eagle: 44

Seals, M's portrait in: 44*

Sealts, Merton: 98

Seamen, John Eugene: 122

Searle: Mr.: 44. George: 44

Season for writing (M's): 50

Seasonable Memorial in Some Historical Notes: 116

Seasonable Reflections, On a Late Pamphlet: 116

Seasons (Thomson): 94

Seasons, the: 89

Seaton: Alexander: 40. Ethel: 19, 23, 44, 14, 93. T.: 58

Seav'nburg: 49. See also: Fisburg

Sebbi of Seward: 3

Sebonde, Raymond de: 93

Seccombe, Thomas: 44, 58

Sechem: 144, 49. (Shechem, Sichem), Vulgate form of: 73

Secker: Thomas, Archbisoph of Canterbury: 44, 54. William: 32

Seckinton (Secandune): 49

Second Admonition to Parliament (Thomas Cartright): 147. Summarizes main currents of the rising Puritan Protest: 147

"Second Anniversary" (John Donne): 131

Second Corinthians: 99

Second Defense of King Charles I: 116

Second Defense: 111, 113*, 129, 55. Autobiographical passages, quoted: 55*. Presentation copy of: 44*. Imagery of: 8*. See also: Milton, John, Works, Defensio Secunda

Second Part of England's New-Chaines (Lilburne, Overton, and Prince): 147*

Second Part of Englands New-Chaines Discovered (William Walwyn): 147

"Second Shepherd's Play": 44, 126

Second Treatise on Civil Government: 26

Second: Age: 143. Second Bishops' War: 51, 60, 103. Second Civil War, causes of: 147. Second Coming: see Eschatology. "Second Creation": 113

Seconde Semaine, La: 65*

Secord, Arthur W.: 44

Secret will (God's): 114

Secret Garden (Burnett): 118

Secret History of the Calves-Head Clubb: 116

Secreta Secretorum: 40, 128

Secretaryship (for the Foreign Tongues): 30*, 44*, 55. M's account, Phillips' account: 55

Sects: 51, 83*. M's idea of perfection like that of: 83. Sectarianism: 9*, 114; M's earliest sectarianism: 114

Secular: offices: 51. Music: 121. M's rising secular tones: 147. Secularism: 47, 69*

Secundus, Johannes: 4, 64

Security: 51

Sedan, France: 44

Seder Olam: 123

Sedgwick: H. D.: 58. Joseph: 114. Obadiah: 44, 91. William: 98, 144, 147, 38; works: A 2nd View of the Army Remonstrance: 147; The Spirituall Madman (eulogizes the king): 147

Sedley, C.: 58. Sir Charles: 44

Sedulius, Caelius: 44, 57, 65, 74, 3, 64. Works: "Epistola ad Macedonium": 74; Opus Paschale: 74; Carmen Paschale: 57, 74

Seebohm: 3. Frederic: 18, 110, 129

Seed of the Woman: 93

Seekers: 7, 38. Seekerism: 114*

"Seemliness": 70

Seeley: Sir John: 16, 34, 79. John Robert: 87; on varied talents of M: 87

Segar, Sir William: 40, 44

Segni, A.: 6

Segrais, Jean-Regnault de: 122

Segregation, principle of: 9*

Segusianus, Eusebius: 10

Seile, Henry (pr., bks., 1619-61): 44, 91

Seinam (Zeinam): 49

Seine River, France: 44

Seissel, Claude de, De Monarchia Franciae Sive De Republica Galliae: 82. See also: Seyssel, Claude de

Sejanus (Ben Jonson): 88, 131

Sejanus: 19

Selandica Castra: 49

Selby, William: 40

Selden Society, Publications of the: 45

Selden: 3, 88. Gilbert: 45. John: 9, 7, 10, 10, 4, 24, 30, 40, 41, 42, 44*, 45, 51, 60, 73, 77, 113, 114, 128, 142*, 144, 22, 82, 101, 137, 94; works: De Jure Naturali et Gentium: 74; History of Tithes: 147; Uxor Hebraica: 91; Law of Nature and of Nations: 82; The Hebrew Wife: 30, 82; De Diis Syriis: 77, 142, 55

Select Essays, With Some Few Miscellaneous Copies of Verses Drawn By Ingenious Hands: 115

Select Reviews: 44

Select Specimens of Ancient Eng. Poetry (Headley): 88

Selene. See Moon

Seletune: 49

Seleucia (the great): 19, 49, 73, 144. See also: Telassar

Seleucus: 144

Self: 96. Self-assertion (improper): 47. Self-assurance (M's): 40. Self-confidence: 51. Self annihilation: 25*. Selfhood: 25; see also: Satan. Self- contempt: 47. Self-deification: 47*; see also: Demonic; Fall of man; Pride; Sin. Self-denying Ordinance: 44. Self-esteem (proper): 47.

Self (continued): Self examination in M: 30*. Self-government: 51; benefits of: 51; kings not better than: 51; limited in civil affairs: 51; manliness of: 51. Self-knowledge: 114*, 122*, 124*; see also: Magnanimity; Wisdom Self-interest: 51. Self-love: 124*. Self-representation, M's supposed, the Richardsons on: 88. Self- respect: 51; see also: self- esteem. Self-righteousness: 47; see also: Legalism; Pride. Self- vindication (in M): 30*. Selfish interests: 51. Selfishness: 51; of the Bps.: 51; of the Presbyterians: 51

Sellar, William Y.: 56, 137

Seller, Abednego: 116

Sellers: Henry: 40, 44. R. V.: 125

Sellin, P. R.: 6, 101

Selling: 3

Selneccerus, Nicolaus: 65

Selous, H. C.: 97

Seltzer, Leon E.: 122

Selvaggi: 28, 44

Selwood: 49

Semaine...contre celle du Sieur du Bartas: 65

Semele: 56, 73, 90

Semenzi, Giuseppe Girolamo: 65

Semi-chorus: 92

Semi-Pelagian: 71

Semicolon: 88

Semiramis (Semyramus): 73, 111

Semitic: study: 40. Semitics: 40; at St. John's College, Cambridge: 40; M's beginnings in before 1625: 40.

Semmelroth, Otto: 93

Sena. See Siena

Senaar: 49

Senas: 73

Senate: House, Cambridge: 40. Of Rome: 51. Perpetual: 9, 147

Senault, Jean-François: 93. Pattern of Patience: 74

Sendivogius (Sendigovius), Michael: 7, 93

Seneca, the Younger: 133

Seneca, Lucius Annaeus (the Elder): 1, 2, 4, 20, 23, 33, 40*, 18, 44, 56, 57, 60, 68, 70, 73, 74, 77, 90*, 112, 114, 123, 125, 128*, 132, 142, 144, 145*, 3, 26, 71, 82, 88, 91, 92, 93, 64, 115, 130, 149, 148, 117. Works: De Providentia: 57, 74; Natural Questions: 77; To Marcia, on Consolation: 50; Epistulae: 60; "Ad Helviam...de Consolatione": 74; De Beneficiis: 74; "De Constantia Sapientis": 74; "De Ira": 74; "Epistle LXXIII," "Epistle CX," "Epistle CXVI," "Epistle CXX," "Epistle CXXIII": 74

"Seneschal of England": 44

Sengelius: 10

Senior year: M's: 40. Studies: 40

Seniores sophistae: 40

Senir: 73

Sennaar: 73

Sennacherib: 73

Senocke. See Sevenoaks

Sensabaugh, George F.: 44*, 128, 143, 115. Works: "Milton on Learning": 74, 83; M in Early America: 82; That Grand Whig Milton: 82

Sense: good: 51. Substitution of impressions of one, for those of another, Warton on: 88. And sound, Todd on: 88

Senses: 25

Sensibility: Hume's artistic, as shown by his paraphrases: 88. Developed, of the Richardsons: 88. Periods of great physical: 88. Warton's highly developed: 88. Wide range of Warton's: 88. Todd's limited: 88

Sensory impressions, Warton on character of M's: 88

Sensual idolatry: 51

Sensuality: 47, 113*, 141. And the Fall: 141. In M: 141. In music: 121. As the Fall: 113. In the Fall of Satan and the rebel angels: 113. In M's nature: 113. Legitimate when under the control of intelligence: 113

Sensuous effects of style valued by Warton: 88

A Sentence in Mercurius Politicus (attr. to M): 44

Sentence structure: 98. Psychologically analyzed by the Richardsons: 88

Sententia (exercise in theme writing): 20, 40

Sententiae Pueriles: 20

Sentimentalism: 71

Seon: 144. Seon's Realme (Amorrean Coast): 49, 73; see also: Arnon

Seotterall, Joseph: 44

Separation of Church and State, M on: 51*

Separation: 124*

Separatists(ism): 7, 9*, 60, 114*, 147. Exodus to Holland: 147. See also: Brownism; Pilgrims

Sepher ha-Zohar: 123. See also: Zohar

Sepher Yetsirah: 123

Sepher, Raziel: 142

Sephiroth, the: 113

Sepin, Gervais: 64

Sepmaine, ou Création, La: 65*

Sepmaines, Les Divines (Du Bartas): 118. (La Primiere): 70, 118

Septuagint: 40, 41, 42, 44, 68, 73, 74, 22

Septuaginta: 40

Sequara, Rozaling Lucy: 44

Sequel to an Antidote to the Miseries of Human Life, A: 115

Sequestration, Committee for: 44. Sequestration of Delinquent's Books: 44

Serafino della Salandra: 77, 120

Seraphim: 142*. Rabbinical Hayyoth: 142

Serapis: 73, 144

Serarius, Nicolai: 79

Serarius: 68

Serbonian bog: 19, 49, 73, 144

Serenate: 121

Serenity (M's, though blind): 44

Sergeant at Arms: 44

Sergestus: 2

Serica: 144

Sericana: 19, 49, 73. See also: Cathay; Imaus

Series: 98

Serious and meditative poetry, superiority of: 88

<u>Serious and Faithful Represenation of the Judgments of Ministers of the Gospel Within the Province of London</u>: 9, 60, 147

Seriphia(n): 73

Serjeants' Inn, London: 44

Serjeantson, M. S.: 128

Serlio, Sebastiano: 39

Sermo: 40

Sermon(s): On the Martyrdom of King Charles I: 116. Preach'd before King Charles II: 116. Preach'd before the Honourable House of Commons: 116; at St. Margaret's: 116. Preach'd at St. Andrew's Plymouth: 116. Preached at the Magnficent Coronation: 116. Preached at Whitehal Upon The 29th of May: 116. Preached before the King: 116; at White-Hall: 116; on the 30/31 of January, 1680/81: 116; on the 30th of January, 1684/85: 116. Preached before the Lord Mayor: 116. Preached before the Right Honourable the Lord Mayor: 116; and Alderman, etc.: 116. Preached in the Parish Church of St. James: 116. Preached on the Anniversary: 116. Preached upon September the 9th, 1683: 116

Sermons: 40, 51. In M: 15*

<u>Serpent Salve</u>. See Bramhall, J.

Serpent(s): 17*, 41, 42, 50*, 54, 142, 144, 36*, 72*. Of Genesis: 142. Associated with hero: 123. Its upright posture: 93. Identity of: 36. Equals pleasure: 36. Ability to speak: 36*; language of Scripture used ironically by: 119. Semi- human form of: 36. Motives for tempting Man, Eve: 36. Interrogation of: 36. Condemnation of: 36. Satan's instrument: 93. See also: Satan

Serpentarius: 89

Serraliona: 49, 73, 144

Serranus: 44. C. Atilius Regulus: 73

Serrell, George: 16

Servant(s): 44*, 122. M's and family's: 44*. Of God: 123. Christ's form of: 123. Angel as, king as: 123

Servetus, Michael: 16, 60, 114, 93, 63, 71, 148, 32, 55

Service of Burial of the Dead: 126

Service: 47, 121

Servitude: 51

Servius: 90*, 121, 123, 21. H. M.: 1, 4, 57, 81. Tullius: 73

<u>Sesame and Lilies</u> (Ruskin): 111

Sesotris: 73

Sessions House, London: 44

Sestiada: 73

Sestius, Publius: 73

Set: 1, 90

Seth: 128, 142, 4, 32, 36. As recipient of Messianic prophecy: 123. See also: Protevangelium

Setia: 49, 73

Seton, John (1498?-1567): 40*, 91

<u>Sette Giornate del mondo creato, Le</u> (Tasso): 65, 70

Setting of M's poetry: Peck, Warton on: 88. Todd on contemporary: 88

Settlement on Anne at marriage: 40

Seven degrees: 93

Seven eyes of God: 25

<u>Seven Deadly Sins, The</u>: 45

Seven Deadly Sins: 44

Sevenoaks (Sevenocke, Senocke), co. Kent: 44, 45

Seventeenth-Century News (and News-Letter): 44

Seventeenth Century Background, The (Basil Willey): 139, 131

Seventeenth Century Studies presented to Sir Herbert Grierson (C. S. Lewis): 131

Seventh Age: 93

Several Proceedings in Parliament: 44

Severia: 49

Severien of Gabala: 65

Severn River: 29, 49, 73, 72. See also: Sabrina

Severn, Charles. See Ward, John

Severus: Alexander: 73. Cornelius: 44. Sulpicius: 73, 74, 123, 82; Sacred History: 82

Sevil(le): 73, 49

Seward: Anna: 44, 58*, 88; admires M's minor poems: 58; on M's sonnets: 58. W.: 97

Sewell: Arthur: 9, 15, 23, 34, 44, 60, 63*, 84, 86, 102, 110, 123, 138, 141, 93. G.: 58. J. M.: 115; Miscellaneous Poems with Several Specimens from the Author's Manuscripts Version of the Poems of Ossian: 115. M.: 58. W.: 58

Sex: 47, 67. In PL: 137. Sexual: imagery: 118; shame, as a consequence of the Fall: 113; relations: 93; demonic antagonism to: 47. Sexuality: 17*, 25. See also: Love; Copulation

Sexagesima Sunday: 40

Sexby, Edward (d. 1658) (and Silas Titus): 44, 116, 91

Sexton, Barbara. See Ayloffe, Barbara

Sextus: Empiricus: 114. Sextus IV, Pope: 29

Seybolt, R. F.: 41

Seymour, Sir Edward: 44, 116

Seyssel (Sesell), Claude de: 73, 82

Sezincote: 45. House: 97

Seznec, Jean: 123, 93, 97

SeBoyar, G. E.: 123

Sforze, Francesco: 40

Sgurolulus: 40

Sguropulus (Sgouropolos), Sylvester: 44, 91

Shaaber, Matthias A.: 44

Shabbington: 45

Shad: Sir John: 45. Maud: see Ayloffe, Maud

Shadow: 79

Shadows Flying Away (John Saltmarsh): 147*

Shadowy Female. See Female will

Shadwell, Thomas: 117

Shafer, R.: 68

Shafte, J.: 128

Shaftesbury Place, London: 44

Shaftesbury: Earl of: 60, 97. Anthony Ashley Cooper, 3rd Earl of: 12, 15, 58, 145, 88, 117; praises PL: 58, 116

Shaftsbury (Paladur, Septonia, Skepton): 49

Shah Abbas: 19

Shakespeare: John: 45. Thomas: 45

Shakespeare, William: 1*, 2, 4, 5, 6, 7, 8*, 12, 15*, 17, 18, 19, 20, 23, 27, 31, 40*, 41, 44*, 45, 52, 35, 73, 56, 58*, 59*, 60, 68, 69, 70*, 77, 76, 79, 84, 86*, 87*, 89, 90, 95, 98*, 102, 103, 105, 108, 111*, 113, 114, 118, 120, 122, 123, 124, 126, 127, 128*, 129, 132*, 133*, 134, 135*, 136*, 139, 141, 142, 145, 3, 14*, 26, 32, 39*, 46, 53, 62, 71, 72, 82, 88*, 91, 92*, 93*, 97*, 64, 101, 109, 115*, 130*, 131, 137*, 146*, 149, 148, 150*, 117*, 21, 13, 25, 94. Power of compression: 136. Genius of humanism: 136. Blake's illustrations to: 25. His characters: Dogberry, Lady Macbeth, Falstaff, Iago, Ulysses, MacDuff: 124. On decorum: 66. Imagery of: 8*. Influence on M: 104. Influence on PL: 55. Contrasted with M: 87. Compared with M: 87, 146. Similes and metaphors in: 87. An objective poet: 87. 18th c. view of: 87. As an example of Schiller's "naive" poet: 87. And Goethe: 87. Sonnets of: 58*, 87, 146; autobiographical reading of: 87; impersonality of: 87; 19th c.

attitude toward: 87; compared with M's: 87; Hazlitt's objections to: 87; Pattison on: 87. M preferred to: 87. Tennyson's debt to: 87. Works: All's Well that Ends Well: 69*; Antony and Cleopatra: 141, 46, 146; Coriolanus: 141, 46; Cymbeline: 35, 52; Hamlet: 35, 52, 60, 142, 92, 115, 146, 149*, 148; Julius Caesar: 141; King John: 77; King Lear: 35, 52, 46, 92, 146, 149*, 148, 25; Macbeth: 60, 124, 46, 82, 146, 149*, 148, 25; Measure for Measure: 82; Merchant of Venice: 60; Midsummer Night's Dream: 146; Much Ado About Nothing: 69; Othello: 52, 109, 145, 149*, 148; Richard III: 82, 109; Romeo and Juliet: 52, 59, 92, 146; Sonnets: 141; The Tempest: 74, 145; Timon of Athens: 52; Troilus and Cressida: 35, 124, 11; Twelfth Night: 11; The Winter's Tale: 35, 69, 87, 82; As You Like It: 35; Henry IV, V, VI: 35; Phoenix and the Turtle: 35. See also: "On Shakespeare"; Shakespeare's Family: 45

Shakespeare's Fight with the Pirates (Pollard): 135

Shakespeare's Last Plays (Tillyard): 134

Shakespearean scholarship and M criticism: 88

Shakespearian Punctuation (P. Simpson): 135*

Shalmaneser: 19

Shame: 47, 51*. As topic of deliberative rhetoric: 123. Result of Fall: 46

Shapcot, Col. Robert: 44

Shape (character dressed for masque): 50

Shapiro, Karl: 128

Shares, Mr.: 45

Sharp: J.: 58. John: 44. Nicholas: 44

Sharpe, J.: 97

Sharrock, Roger: 37

Shastid, Thomas Hall: 16

Shattuck, Roger: 14

Shaunburg, See William VI

Shaw: 15, 35. Mr.: 40. Dr.: 44, 73, 88; Physical Observations on Arabic Petraea: 88. B.: 36. C.: 58. George Bernard: 65, 76, 111, 138, 71, 72, 91, 92, 137. John M.: 40, 54, 93, 115; Poems by the Late Dr. John Shaw: 115. Lemuel: 98. Dr. Ralph (d. 1484): 91

Shawcross, John (T.): 29, 44, 59, 75*, 100, 123, 135*, 11, 39, 106, 148, 150, 21

She weepeth continually: 121

Shearman's Hall, Shrewsbury: 44

Sheba, Queen of: 143, 32

Shechem. See Sechem

Sheed, F. J.: 79, 81

Sheep: 143. Neglected, and the fold, feed them, hungry, cherish them, silly simple: 143

Sheerness: 103

Sheffield: Capt.: 45. Elizabeth: see Cope, Eliz. John, Earl of Mulgrave: 15

Sheiras (Sheirs, Sheres). See Shiers

Shekinah (Shekhina): 60, 113

Sheldon: Gilbert, Abp. (1598-1677): 44, 45, 93; Dignity of Kingship: 91. Richard: 93

Shelford, Robert: 93

Shelley Memorials: 98

Shelley: Mr.: 45. H. C.: 58. Percy Bysshe: see separate entry. Richard: 44. Thomas: 44. Sir Timothy: 131

Shelley, Percy Bysshe: 1, 4, 15, 27, 31, 34*, 35, 50, 58*, 60, 70, 73, 79, 52, 84, 86*, 87, 95, 98, 112, 111, 113, 118, 128, 132, 133, 94, 141, 14, 38, 46, 53, 71, 88, 97, 64, 109, 130*, 131, 137, 146*, 149, 148, 150, 55, 140, 21; admires M: 58; influenced by l'Allegro, Nativity, PL: 58; Satan's Fall the result of injured merit: 107; Zastrozzi: 146; on M's Satan: 87; blank verse of: 87; letters: 146; prefaces: 146; his reading of M: 146; works: A Defence of Poetry: 60, 146; Hellas: 60; A Philosophical View of Reform: 60, 146; Address to the People: 146; Adonais: 146; Cenci: 146; Laurels: 146; M's Spirit: 146; Ode to Liberty: 145; On the Devil and Devils: 146; Queen Mab: 146; Speculation on Morals: 146; Vindication of Natural Diet: 146.

Shelton, Thomas: 64

Shem: 32

Shenstone, William: 58, 105, 117

Shepheardes Calender, The: 12, 20, 29, 70, 83*, 139, 88. E. K.'s notes to: 88

Shepherd: R.: 58. T. R.: 58

"Shepherd of Hermas": adoptionism: 107. Subordinationism: 107

Shepherd's Hunting (Wither): 29

Shepherds at birth of Christ: 44

Sheppard: Sir Fleetwood: 44. J. T.: 56, 92*, 148. Sir John: 134. Samuel: 145

Sheppey: 49

Sherastan (Scorastan, Sharston): 49

Sheratt (Shurratt), Richard: 44, 45

Sherborne: 45

Sherburn (Shirburn): 49, 89. Edward: 44. George: 12, 44, 58, 113

Sherburne, Sir Edward: 145

Sheres: Mr.: 44, 45. Thomas: 45. See also: Shiers

Sherfield: (Cherfield), Mr.: 44, 45. Henry: 143; proceeding against, defense of, and punishment: 143

Sheridan: E.: 58. R. B.: 35, 58, 105; The Critic: 35. T., quotes PL: 58. Sheridan's Lectures on the Art of Reading: 88

Sheriff of London; of Middlesex co.: 44

Sheriffhales Academy: 78

Sherive, C. H.: 58

Sherley: 45. Thomas: 128

Sherlock: Bp. Thomas: 32. William: 116, 32

Sherman: 130. John: 93. Stuart: 115

Sherpherd's Garland (Drayton): 29

Sherrat. See Sheratt

Sherrington, Sir Charles: 93

Sherry, Richard: 20, 56

Sherwin: P. F.: 113. Richard: 44

Sherwood: Francis: 44

Sherwyn, Richard: 44

Sheshet, Rabbi: 16

Shetland: 49

Shiel, James, "Boethius' Commentaries on Aristotle": 82

Shiells, R.: 58

Shiers: Edward: 45. (Sheires), George: 44, 45. (Sheirs), Robert: 44, 45. Thomas: 44

Shilleto (Shillito): A. R.: 44. C.: 58

Shilo (Silo): 49

Shimei: 44, 73

Shinar: 144

Ship of Fools, The (Brant) (warns against the dangers of knowledge): 83

Shipley, co. Derby: 44

Shipley: 45. Arthur E.: 44 J.: 58

Shipman, T., on PL: 58

Shippen, W.: 58

Shipton under Wychwood, co. Oxon.: 44, 45

Shirburn Ballads: 68

Shire Hall, Cambridge: 40

Shirley: 70, 120, 133. Elizabeth: see Cotton, Eliz. Frederick J.: 93. James: 29*, 84, 39, 55; The Triumph of Peace: 94. John: 128

Shirokalga: 49

Shirooan: 49

Shirte, Roger: 45

Shoberie: 49

Shoel, T.: 58

Shooting stars: 89

Shoreditch Church, London: 44

Shorer, M.: 23

Shorey, Paul: 68, 79

Shorr, Philip: 128

Short Answer to the Tedious Vindication of Smectymnuus: 26

Short Answer: 103

Short Declaration of the Mistery of Iniquity (in which Thomas Helwys braves the wrath of James): 147

Short Discourse Between Monarchial and Aristocratical Government (Henry Robinson): 147

Short History of the Anabaptists: 9

Short History of the Eng. People (Green): 70

Short Title Cataolgue: 40*. See also: Pollard, A. W.; Wing

Short View of the Late Troubles in England: 116

Short View of the Prelatical Church (attr. to M): 44

Short-sightedness: 51

Short, But Just Account of the Tryal of Benjamin Harris: 116

Short, John: 45

Shorte Introduction of Grammar, A (Lily): 20

Shorter Catechism: 60

Shorter Oxford English Dictionary: 44

Shorthampton: 45

Shorthouse, Joseph Henry: 7, 87. _John Inglesant_: 87

Shortyard: 45

Shotbolt, John: 54

Shotover, co. Oxon.: 44, 28, 45*, 94

Shower (Bartholomew): 115

Shower, John: 37. Serious Reflections on Time and Eternity: 45

Shrewsbury, co. Salop: 40, 44. M's journey to: 40

Shrewsbury: 40, 45. Duke of: 44. Charles Talbot, Earl of: 44

Shropshire: 44, 45, 49

Shumaker, Wayne: 4, 37, 60, 79, 110, 118, 128, 14, 36, 61, 93, 106, 137

Shurratt. See Sheratt

Shusky: 19

Shuster, George N.: 143

Shute: Mr.: 44. Christopher: 40

Shuter: Mr.: 45. Mrs. (Powell): 44, 45. Hopton (Hope): 44, 45

Shutford: 45

Shylock: 45

Sibbes, Richard: 40, 79, 142, 32, 93*. _Light from Heaven_: 142

Siber: 49

Siberia: 19, 49

Sibley, Agnes Marie: 115

Sibma(h): 19, 49, 73, 144

Sibthorp, H.: 58

Sibyl: 2, 60, 90

Sibyllae: 73

Sicanian: 73

Sichardus: 73

Siciliensis, infamis ille reus: 73

Sicily (Sicania, Sicilia, Trinacria): 19, 44, 49, 103, 144, 94, 3. Sicilian: muse: 73; cave: 3. Sicilians: 51, 3. See also: AEtna; Enna; Scylla

Sickness, M and: 44

Siddall, William: 40

Siddons: Mrs.: 97. S., abridges PL: 58

Sidenham: 45

Sideris River: 19

Sides, Henry J.: 44

Sidgwick, Henry: 87

Sidney family, Spenser's relation to: 83. See also: Sidney, Lady; Sidney, Sir Henry; Sidney, Philip

Sidney Redivivus: 116

Sidney-Sussex College, Cambridge: 40, 44, 45

Sidney, Sir Philip: 1, 4, 12, 15, 17, 20, 23, 27, 28, 18, 73, 29, 30, 31, 34, 71, 82, 88, 37, 40, 44, 45, 52, 56, 58, 59, 60, 69, 70*, 79, 92, 64*, 101, 131, 137, 83*, 87, 100, 103, 108, 110, 114, 116, 120, 122, 123, 124, 128, 129, 132, 26, 32, 38, 39, 46, 53, 146, 21, 13. And M compared: 146. Works: _Arcadia_: 35, 69, 11, 46, 82,

94; Defense of Poesy: 11; An Apology for Poetry: 69, 82

Sidney: 112, 133, 3, 106. Lady, reason for her being called "widowed": 83. (Sidneium), Algernon (1622-83): 44, 73, 116*, 38, 91, 115, 146, 117, 13. Sir Henry: 19, 83. Humphrey: 44. Sir Philip: see separate entry. Phillip, Lord Lisle: 38

Sidon: 49. Sidonian: 73; virgins: 144

Sidonius, Apollonaris: 21

Siduri: 32

Siebeck, Hermann: 93

Siebert: Frederick S.: 44. Th.: 141

Sieciethovia: 49

Siege tradition, in epic: 123

Siegel, Paul N.: 93

Siegfried: 149

Siena (Sena): 44, 103, 94

Sierksma, F.: 141

Sierra Leone: 19

Sieveking, A. F.: 70

Sievers, Edward: 40

Sigebert of Gembloux: 93

Sigebert the Small: 3

Sigeferth: 40

Sigeius: 49, 73. See also: Ganymede

Sigelm: 3

Siger: 3. Siger of Brabant: 32. Leonard, "Image of Job in the Renaissance": 74

Sigerson, G.: 57. The Easter Song of Sedulius: 57

Sight: 128

Sign(s): 51, 123, 11, 96. Fallible: 51. Of likes and equals: 123. Of the Bible: 103. The Pied bull, London: 103. The Spread Eagle: 103

Signatures: on Anne's indenture: 40. M's: 40. In 1623 (M's): 40

Significance of music: 121

Significant form, speechers: 100*

Sigonus (Sigonius), Carlo (Carlus): 57, 73, 82, 94. Works: De Occidentali Imperio: 57, 82; De Regno Italiae: 82

Sikes: George: 44, 59, 91. J. G.: 40

Silence: 2, 90. Sacred: 96. Rhetoric of: 96

Silenus: 73, 90

Silesia: 49. See also: Frederick William

Silesianus (Selesius), Angelus: 60, 27

Silius Italicus: 20, 44, 90, 122, 88, 64. Punica: 74

Sills, Kenneth C. M.: 111, 93

Silo (A. V. Shiloh): 73

Siloa: 49, 73, 72. Siloa's Brook: 143, 106. See also: Solomon, Garden of

Silton: 45

Silvagni, D.: 6

Silvan(us): 73

Silver Age: 36

Silvercon. See Spiering

Silverstein, Theodore: 69

Silvestri, Feliciano: 44

Silvestris, Bernardus: 32

Silvette, Herbert: 128

Simancas (Simancos), Spain: 44

Simcha (joy): 125

Simeon: Biblical: 44, 73. Simeon of Durham: 73, 3. Sir George: 44. Rabbi: 123. ben Yohai, Rabbi: 38

Similarity, argument from: 123*. See also: Likes

Simile(s): 8. Pearce and Addison on Homeric: 88. Exact correspondence to their subjects of, emphasized by Callander: 88. PL, simile in: 53; see also: PL. See also: Allusion and simile

Similitude, M's discussion of: 20

Simita, Gabriel: 40

Simmes, William (composer): 44

Simmias: 64

Simmons: Mary: 91. Matthew: 40, 44*, 45. (Symmons, Symonds, Simmonds), pr., bks.: 103, 135, 91, 55; see also: Parker, W. R., "Milton, Rothwell and Simmons." Robert: 25. (Symmons) Samuel (pr., publisher): 1, 40, 44*, 50, 103, 135, 28, 91, 130, 117, 55, 13; called Simons by Phillips: 55

Simoentis: 73

Simois River: 44, 49

Simon: 72. Simon, Abraham (sculptor, M portraits, bust): 44. Simon bar Cochba: 38. Father: 6. Simon ha-Darshan: 41. Simon Magus: 73, 36, 114, 38. Richard: 22. Peter: 73. Thomas (artist, engraver): 44. Ulrich: 93

Simonds, Walter: 44, 45

Simonides: 40. Of Ceos: 93

Simons (Simmons), Samuel: 28

<u>Simple Cobbler, The</u>: 71

"Simple" plot: 92

Simplicity: and grandeur: Bentley, Newton, Warton on: 88. Classical simplicity, majesty and grace, the Richardsons on: 88. Richardsons attracted by, and homeliness: 88. Praised by Monboddo: 88. Beautiful, valued by Todd: 88

Simplicius: 5, 40, 73, 32

Simplification of M's syntax, Bentley's: 88

Simplon Pass: 44

Simpson: Mr.: 117. Cuthbert A.: 32, 64. David: 115; <u>A Plea for Religion and the Sacred Writings</u>: 115. E. (author and editor): 135*. Evelyn M.: 79, 128, 39, 93. Lewis P.: 115. Nathaniel: 40. P. (author and editor): 135*; see also: Jonson, Ben, individual titles. Percy: 39. Sidrach: 59, 120. T. M.: 97

Sims: Mr: 44. James H.: 17, 37, 60, 110, 123, 32, 64, 101

Simson: Andrew: 40. John: 40. Otto von: 106

Sin: 1, 2*, 17, 19, 31*, 41, 47*, 51, 54, 56, 63, 67*, 98, 102, 111, 113, 118, 124, 127*, 139, 144, 143, 46, 71, 101, 109, 130, 55. Transition to from innocence: 118. In Heaven: 50. Pact with Satan: 46. Dominance of appetite over soul: 46. Traditional view: 93. And celestial and infernal trinity, and Death, and degree: 101. As discord: 121. Deformity and misery of: 122. Causes of: 123. Original: 47, 124, 139, 48. Human and Demonic: 47. God's attitude towards: 47. Forms of: 47. Results of: 47. And Venus: 143. Lavish act of: 143. And Death build causeway: 143. Man dead in: 143. All born servants of: 143. Definition of: 71. Allegorical figure in PL: 70, 73, 113. The daugher of Satan: 113. As character: 72*, 140*, 55; sources as character: 55. See also: Demonic; Fall; Guilt; Self-deification; Death; Evil; Pride; Satan; Sin and Death; Eve

Sin and Death: 50*, 76, 128*, 106. As "creators": 75. Birth of: 128. Foreknowledge of: 128. As agents of Satan: 75. Allegory of: 63. Biblical basis of allegory: 119. Language of Scripture used ironically by: 119

Sinaean: 73

Sinai (Horeb, Oreb): 19, 49, 73, 3, 72

Sinarum Regio: 144

Since she whom I lov'd (John Donne): 131*

Sincerity: 51

Sinclair: George: 142. Upton: 118

Single-handed exploit: 122

Singleton: Charles: 5, 76, 79, 39. H.: 97. J.: 58. Mary (i.e., Frances Brooke): 117. R. C.: 58. Ralph H.: 64

Sinibaldus, Johann: 82. <u>Geneanthropeia</u>: 82

Siniories: 51

Sinistrari, Ludovico Maria: 142. <u>Demoniality</u>: 142

Sinlessness, as the source of perfection: 83*

Sinnamus (Cinnamus), Johannes: 73

Sinon: 2, 44, 56

Sins of the bishops: 51

Sion (Zion): 49, 73, 3

Sion: Sion College, London: 40, 44. Sion Hill: 143, 106; and sacred Muse: 143. Sion House: 103. Sion's Plea: 73

Siope: 73

Sippell, Theodor: 7

Sir Gawain and the Green Knight: 76

Sir Orfeo: 150

Sirach: 2

Siradia, Albertus Alasco, Count Palatine of: 44

Siren(s): 2, 40, 44, 70, 73, 90, 111, 121, 3, 72

Sirenus: 123. See also: Tasso

Sirius: 89

Sirluck, Ernest: 1, 6, 54, 59, 79, 123, 53, 93, 137, 148, 21. "M's Critical Use of Historical Sources": 82

Sirocco: 144

Sisson: Charles J.: 9, 44, 108. Thomas: 44

Sistine ceiling: 139

Sisyphus: 60, 73

Sittim: 49, 73

Situation, poetic: 53*

Sitwell, Edith: 1, 15, 60, 138, 64. Sacheverell: 27

Six clerk: 45

Six Ages: 93. Sixth Age: 143

Six, J.: 58

Sixesmith, Thomas: 40

Sixtus: V: 6, 40. VI: 29. Of Siena: 32

Sizar: 40

Skazanie o Adami i Evi: 65

Skeat, Walter W. (ed. Epitaphium Damonis): 45, 83, 112, 136. See also: Milton, John, Works

Skeleton Key to Finnegans Wake (J. Campbell and H. M. Robinson): 139

Skelton: A.: 58. John: 111, 114, 128, 133. Sir John: 40. Richard: 143

Skelton's Engraved Illustrations of ...Oxfordshire: 45

Skemp, A. R.: 36

Skene, G.: 58

Skeptics and skepticism: 40, 114*, 71

Skilled music: 121

Skinner: 3, 149. Mr.: 40, 44. Anabella: 120. Mrs. Bridget (mother of Cyriack): 44, 120. Cyriak (Cyriack, Cyriac): 9, 16, 28*, 30, 44*, 51, 59, 63, 84, 87, 103, 120, 62, 91, 137, 117, 55, 94; anonymous biographer: 55; see also: MS. Sonnets XXI, XXII. Daniel: 28, 44*, 63*, 102, 103, 116, 135, 82, 150, 55; his father, Daniel: 44, 150; see also: De Doctrina Christiana. Edward: 44. John: 123, 11, 32, 36, 93. William: 44, 120

Skinners Company: 40

Skinnerz, N.: 44

Skippon: Gen.: 45. Philip: 44

Skurray, F.: 58

Skynner, Robert: 44

Slakey, R. L.: 59

Slany, Sir Stephen: 40

Slapp (Stap), Mr.: 44

Slare, Frederick: 10

Slatford: Anthony: 45. Job: 45. John: 44, 45

Slatter, Anthony: 44, 45

Slatyer, William: 44

Slaughter's Coffee House: 97

Slaughtersford, co. Wilts.: 44

Slavery: 47, 51. See also: Freedom

Sleep: 2, 90. Of the soul: 107. Sleep wish: 118

Sleiden (Sleidanus), John (Johannes) Philippson: 40, 44, 41, 60, 70, 73, 114, 82, 91, 22, 93. Commentarii de Statu Religionis Reipublicae: 82*

Sleswich (Slesvicus): 49

Sligo, Viscount: 103. See also: Scudamore, John

Sloane Ayscough MS. 1446 (British

Museum): 7*, 40

Sloane, William: 44

Slobotca: 49

Sloss, D. J.: 25

Slough, co. Bucks.: 44

Slovo Adama ko Lazariu: 65

Sluperius, Jakob de Sluyper: 64

Sluterus, M. Serverinus: 40

Smalcaldia: 49, 73. League: 38

Smalcius, Valentin: 22

Small: Mr.: 44. William: 44, 97

"Small poets" (Greek): 40

Smalle, Peter: 93

Smalley, Beryl: 110, 93. Study of the Bible in the Middle Ages: 74

Smart: Christopher: 15, 58, 35, 117; praises L'Allegro and Il Penseroso: 58. J. A.: 148. John Semple: 16, 40, 44*, 56, 59*, 86, 102, 112, 113, 132, 144, 26, 150; on M's sonnets: 58; see also: Milton, John, Sonnets. Peter: 33

Smeaton, Oliphant: 44

Smectymnuo-Mastix: 44, 103

Smectymnuus Redivivus: 44, 91

Smectymnuus: 8, 9*, 30, 44*, 45, 51, 113, 114, 144, 26, 62, 91*, 94; works: Vindication: 91; Answer to a Book: 91; see also: Of Reformation.

"Smectymnuus," pseudonym of 5 ministers: 103, 60, 93. "Smectymnuus" the compounded signature to the Puritan Manifesto: 136. Smectymnuans, on language: 66

Smedley, E.: 58

Smeducci, B.: 6

Smert Kayina: 65

Smethwick, Francis: 10

Smetius, Henricus: 40

Smiglecki, Marcin: 40

Smirke, R.: 97

Smit, W. A. P.: 6, 95

Smith: (Smythe), Mr.: 44, 45; see also: Hatton, Lord. A.: 58. A. J.: 23, 79, 53. Adam, Wealth of Nations: 82. C.: 58*. Charles (publisher): 44. D. Nichol: 44. E.: 58. E. F.: 58. Edward: 44.

Smith: G. G.: 79. G. Gregory: 66, 122, 128. George: 44, 144. Gregory: 70. G. C. Moore: 40. H.: 105. H. F. Russel: 9, 15, 116, 115. H. W.: 86. Hallett: 110, 39. Henry: 44, 54, 143. Henry Preserved: 110. J.: 58. James: 35, 44, 125, 145, 131. Joaquim: 97. John (Cambridge Platonist): 79, 114, 93, 132, 15, 23, 44, 45, 102, 108, 142, 14; works: "Discourse...of Prophesie": 74; Discourses: 81; The Mysterie of Rhetorique Unvail'd: 79. John Christopher: 102, 117. Logan Pearsall: 1, 44, 86, 105, 141, 137; M and His Modern Critics: 83.

Smith: M.: 58. Mary (Morrison): 45. Matthew: 44. Bp. Miles: 40, 93. "Obituary": see Smith, Richard. Paul E.: 40. Peter: 44. Philip: 45. Preserved: 60, 93. Ralph: (bks., 1642-84): 91. (Smyth), Bp. Richard: 40, 44, 45, 93. Dr. Richard (1500-63): 91; The Obituary of Richard Smyth: 45. Robert M.: 44, 59; Varient Issues of Shakespeare's Second Folio and M's First Published Poem: 44. Robertson: 41. Samuel: 40, 64. Sir (Dr.) Thomas: 18, 9, 10, 19, 40, 44, 45, 58, 73, 82, 55; The Commonwealth of England: 82*. W.: 23, 58, 59. Sir W. C.: 58. William: 115; The Works of Wm. Smith: 115. (Smyth), William: 44*, 45. William (the Quaker): 93. William Robertson: 100. W. Taylor, "Job": 74. Mrs. Wheeler: 44

Smithfield: 45, 49, 103, 3

Smock Alley, London: 44

Smoke in the Temple (John Saltmarsh): 147

Smoking a Segar in the Manner of Milton: 115

Smolensko: 49

Smollett, T.: 58, 86

Smoothness: sublimity as opposed to, in Comus, stressed by Warton: 88. Vigour preferred by Dunster to: 88

Smyrna (Smirna): 44, 49, 73

Smyrnaeus, Quintus: 73

Smyth: H. W.: 92. Henry: 40. John: 79, 114; one of the founders of the Baptists, writes The Last Book of John Smith: 147. P.: 58. W.: 58.

Zephaniah: 114

Smythe: Mr.: 44; see also: Smith. Oliver: 20, 40. Richard: 44; The Obituary of Richard Smyth: 45

Snart, C.: 58

Snawsel, Robert: 93

Sneeze, compared to storm: 128

Snell: Bruno: 125. P.: 58

Snelling: Bathsheba: see Huet. John: 44

Sneyd, Rev. Walter: 44

Snobbery: 51

Snorri Sturlason: 19

Snow-White and the Seven Dwarfs: 130

Snow, Edward: 39

Snow: 128*. Causes: 128

Snowden, Richard: 115. The Columbiad: Or a Poem on the American War: 115

Snyder: D. J.: 56. E. D.: 58

Soames, W.: 58

Soane, Sir J.: 97

Soarez, Cyrien: 40

Sobieski, John (Jan), King John III of Poland (1624-96): 60, 116, 91, 55

Sobriety: 51

Social background of M's works, studied by Peck, Warton, Todd: 88

Social contract: 9*. Social order: 8. Social thought: 31. Social well-being: 51

Sociality, M and: 137

Societies, fraternal: 7*

Societies, political: 51

Society for Diffusion of Useful Knowledge: 44

Society of Antiquaries: 44

Society of British Artists: 97

Society of Jesus, Records of English Province of (ed. Foley): 44

Society of Jesus: 27

Society: 51

Socinian(s): 44, 51, 73, 103, 3, 22*, 32, 71. Socinianism: 7, 34, 114*, 22*, 38, 71, 78*

Socinus (Lelio Sozzini): 55

Socinus, Faustus (Socino, Fausto): 44, 74, 22, 32, 71, 55

Socrates (Scolasticus): 30, 44, 57, 73, 114, 116, 123, 3, 93. Church History: 82*

Socrates: 4, 5, 7, 18, 19, 29, 37, 40, 51, 52, 57, 60*, 67, 68, 70, 73, 81, 112, 114*, 122, 125, 136, 141, 142, 145, 3, 53, 62, 71, 72, 88, 64, 109, 146, 25. On immortality of the soul: 80. "Poor Socrates" mentioned: 80. M's references to: 112. "Myth of Er" quoted: 80. Socratic discourses: 73, 125

Soden, Godfrey, I.: 93

Sodom (projected work): 136

Sodom and Gomorrah: 139

Sodom: 19, 49, 73, 144. See also: Asphaltic Pool

"Sodom Burning" (M's): 44

Sofala: 19, 49, 73, 144. See also: Ophir

Sofia: 44

Softened forms in M, Peck, Newton, Lofft on: 88

Sogdiana: 19, 49, 73, 144

Sohn, Georg: 40, 93

Soissons: 49

Solar system: 89

Soldiers Casting Lots for Christ's Garments: 25

Soledade, Felix Joseph da: 65

Solemn League and Covenant: 9, 51, 113

Solerti, Angelo: 6, 122

Soli: 44, 3

Soliciter: 45

Soliloquies (St. Augustine): 131

Soliloquy: 31

Solinus: 19, 128, 3. Caius Julius:

73

Solitude, delights and fruits of: 30

Solitude: 54

Solofky: 49

Solomon ben Isaac: 26

Solomon: H. C.: 16. J. W.: 97. M. H.: see Solomon, H. C.

Solomon: 2, 19, 30, 51, 54, 57, 60, 68, 70, 73, 74, 103, 112, 114, 122, 125, 127, 139, 142, 144, 143, 3, 32, 71, 72, 91, 106. Song of: 54, 3, 62, 106. At court: 143. Temple destroyed: 143. Wisdom of: 106. Garden of: 49. See also: Bible; Hinnom; Temple of Solomon

Solon: 40, 60, 73, 112, 114, 3

Solstices, the: 89

Solway: 49

Solyhull: 45

Somatic imagery: 118*. Definition of: 118. Introductory examples: 118. In the Iliad: 118. Inclusiveness of: 118. Modernity of M's use of: 118

Somatic states: 118. Appropriateness of describing in poetry: 118

Some Discourses Upon Dr. Burnet and Dr. Tillotson: 116

Some Observations Upon The Keeping The Thirtieth of January: 116

"Some Particulars...Concerning the Office of Requests": 44

Some Remarques Upon a Late Popular Piece of Nonsence: 116

Some Succinct Remarks on the Speech of the Late Lord Russell: 116

Some Thoughts Concerning Education: 78

Some Versions of Pastoral (Empson): 134, 139

Some, Robert: 114

Somers Tracts: 44

Somers, John, Lord Baron: 44, 117

Somerset House: 44, 103

Somerset: Edward Seymour, Duke of: 38. Lord J.: 6

Somerset: 45, 49. Somersetshire: 44, 45; Archaelogical and Natural History Society, Proceedings of the: 45; Record Society, Publications of the: 45

Somerset's Masque (Campion): 29

Somerton: 49

Somerville (Somervile), W.: 58*

Sommer, H. O.: 128

Sommers, Lord: 28, 94

Somnium Scipionis: 121

Somnus. See Sleep

Son (of God): 17*, 31*, 50*, 70*, 63*, 107*, 111*, 113*, 118, 47*, 127*, 72*, 71, 106*.

Son (of God, associated with, compared to). Abraham: 119. Biblical Rock: 119. Christ of New Testament: 119. Creator: 113. David: 119. Demiurge: 60, 113. Moses: 119. Orlando Furioso, XIV: 60. Orpheus: 106. Paul: 119. Reason: 113. Satan: 119. Saul: 119. Solomon (contrasted with by Satan): 119. Spenser's Sapience: 60.

Son (of God, character). Character: 119. Characterized by Satan: 119. A 2nd God: 107. Substance but not essence of God in pseudo-Clementine Homilies: 107. As defined by synecdoche and metonymy: 118. As Title: 123*. As sacrificer for Man: 107, 72. In judgment of man: 47*, 50, 72. In creation: 72. In Battle of Heaven: 72. Chariot of during battle: 119. Advocate of man: 72. Christian heroism: 106. As Light: 106. Creative agent: 106*. Creative speeches of analyzed for audience appropriateness: 118. Exaltation of: 118. Inspires men: 107. Head of angels: 107. The Creator (in ante-Nicene Fathers): 107. Christ among men: 107. Attributes derived: 107. Ante-dates creation (in Lactantius): 107. As judge, atonement, incarnation: 47*, 54, 107*. M's title for: 107. Priest and prophet: 107, 106*. Power over fallen angels: 107. Rules demons through fear: 107. Mediator before Fall: 107. Patience in temptation shown by: 119.

Son (of God, origin of). Only begotten of Father: 119. 1st begotten: 72. Creation of: 113. Sole manifestation of Father: 113. Begets himself: 107. Begotten within time: 107. Metaphorical begetting: 107. Metaphorical generation: 107. Literal begetting: 107. Relation to

God and man: 47. Generation a mystery in Irenaeus of Lyons: 107. Visible at time of metaphorical begetting: 107. Visible in De Doctrina Christiana: 107. Self-originated in pseudo-Clementine Homilies and Recognitions: 107. Unknown to angels prior to metaphorical begetting: 107. Creator external to his creation: 107.

Son (of God, various). Annointing, the 2nd stage in his development (according to M and Origen): 107. Victory over temptations foreshadowed: 119. Triumph over Satan foreshadowed: 119. Ultimate victory prophesized: 119. Prophesies own death and resurrection: 119. Praised by angels: 119. Temptation to seek fame rebuffed by: 119. Converses with Adam in Paradise: 119. Fallen pair and Serpent judged by: 119. Birth of (as Jesus) foreshadowed: 119. Echoes New Testament language of Paul: 119.

Son (of God). See also: Christ; God; Reconciliation; Redemption; Salvation; Satan; Trinity; PL; PR

Sonata: 121

Soncinae, Paulus Barbus. See Barbo

Sondheim, Moriz: 93

Sondheimer, Janet: 122

Sonds, Mr.: 44

Song for St. Cecila's Day (Dryden): 70

Song of Roland, The: 70, 122

Song of Solomon: 35, 44, 70, 132, 72. See also: Solomon; Bible

Song of Songs. See Song of Solomon

Song of Victory, A (Gill the Younger): 20

Song: 121*, 92. In PL: marriage song of triumph: 50; entire epic as: 118; transitions from speech to: 118. Songs and music in masques: 29*. Songbooks: 40

Songs and Sonnets (John Donne): 131

Songs of Innocence and Experience: 25

Songs the drunkards made, libelling the Gills: 20

Sonnet(s): 26*, 58*. The 18th c.: 58*, 87; vogue of, due to M's minor poems: 58. 19th c.: 87. The Elizabethan: 58*, 87. Shakespeare's, Richardson's quote from: 88. The Italian: 58*; Newton on: 88. See also: Sonnets (M's)

Sonnets (M's). In general: 15, 70*, 87*, 103, 112, 111, 73*, 146, 113, 129, 132*, 55*. Warton on the austerity of M's: 88. Italian: 132, 87. Pearce's references to: 88. Newton on the grandeur of M's: 88. Their prototypes: 129. Sonnet by M senior: 40. Wordsworth, Dr. Johnson on: 87. Compared with Shakespeare's: 87. Victorian attitude toward: 87. Quality of: 87. As model for Victorian sonnet: 87. Departed from Petrarchan form: 87. Compared with Elizabethan: 87. Popularity of: 87. Pattison on: 87. Personal quality in: 87. Themes of: 87. Imitations of: 87. Image of M the man in: 87. References to blindness in: 16. Sonnets to Chimentelli, lost: 44. Function, origins of rites and ceremonies in poems: 126. Relationship of religious ritual and ceremony to style and strcture of poems: 126. Types of rites and ceremonies in poems: 126. Values of religious rites and cermonies in poems: 126. Sonnets: I: 55. IV: 112. II-VI (Italian), mentioned: 55, 112; VII: 55, 118; VIII, IX, X, XI: 55; XII: 55, 112, 87; XIII- XVIII: 55; XIX: 55, 126*; XX, XXII, XXIII: 55. Sonnets in imitation of M's: 58

Sonnets (Shakespeare): 1609: 135*. Sonnets of Shakespeare: 139

Sonning: 45

Sons of Belial. See Belial

Sons of God: 113, 144

Sontag, Susan: 14

Sophia (daughter of James I): 40

Sophie, Princess: 44

Sophism: 40

Sophisma: 40

Sophist (Plato): 5, 112

Sophist(s): 123, 71. Satan, Belial as: 123*. Maker of idols: 123. Character of: 123. Hero as: 123

Sophisters: 40

Sophistry: 40, 47, 51

Sophocles: 2, 4, 6, 15, 30, 40, 44, 51, 52, 56, 58, 60, 68, 70, 73, 74, 76, 90, 103, 125, 132, 3, 26, 53, 71, 72, 82, 91, 92*, 93, 64, 101, 130, 146, 149, 148, 117, 21, 13. Works: Ajax: 92*; Antigone: 82, 92*;

Electra: 92*; Oedipus at Colonus: 92*; Oedipus the King: 92*; Oedipus Tyrannus: 82; Philoctetes: 92*; Trachiniae: 82, 92*

Sophomore: 40

Sophron: 70, 112. Sophron Mimus: 73

Sophronia: 58

Sophrosyne: 5

Sora: 49

Sorani, Aldo: 44

Soranzo, Giovanni: 65, 77

Sorbières, M. (French traveler): 103

Sorbonists: 73, 3

Sorcery: 114*

Sordello: 111

Sorec: 49, 73

Sorek: 144

Sorel, Georges: 60

Sorell, Thomas: 44

Sorenzo, Giovanni, Adamo: 74

Sorokin, Pitirim Alexandrovich: 60

Sorrells, Mr.: 44

Sorsby, Arnold: 16, 44, 128

Sospetto d'Herode: 65

Soterichus: 60

Soteriology. See Atonement; Grace

Sotheby: Samuel Leigh: 16, 40, 44*, 63, 120; Ramblings in Elucidation of the Autograph of Milton: 44, 82, 43. W.: 58

Sotheby's auction rooms: 44*

Sotheran, Henry, Ltd. (book dealer): 44

"Sothis" (Sirius): 89

Sotona: 36

Soucy, François du: 65

Soul: 113, 144*, 142, 46. Origin of: 114. Creation: 93. Tripartite: 93. Analogous to Godhead: 93. Distension and objectification of: 96. Biblical view: 48. Greek theory of: 48. M's doctrine of the: 113, 22, 48. Nature, kinds, faculties of: 128. Pre-existence of: 142. As spirits: 142. Hierarchy of reason, will and appetite: 46. Hierarchy reversed by Fall: 46. In isolation after Fall: 46

"Soul-sleepers": 44

Soul's Mortality. See Mans Mortallite

Soumet, Alexandre: 65

Sound, William, Surmaster of St. Paul's: 20, 40

Sound: 121. The Richardsons' appreciation of, in poetry: 88. The Richardsons on meaning of sounds: 88. Sound-board: 121. Sound and sense, Todd on: 88

Sources: 92. Of M: 88*. Of M's theory: 121*. M's, of Hume's, Richardsons' notes: 88. And influences upon (including alleged plagiarism): 117*. M's, Peck's: 88*. Of "St. Maur": 88. And Paterson: 88. Newton's treatment of M's verse: 88. Marchant's, James Buchanan's, T. Warton's, Loffts, Bowle's, Stillingfleet's: 88. Of Newton's, Callander's, Dunster's editions: 88. Of Todd's edition of "Comus": 88. Of Todd's large edition: 88

Soury, J.: 41

South Cadbury, co. Somerset: 44

South Carolina Gazette, The: 115

South Gate of Old Exchange: 44

South Kensington Museum, London: 44

South Pole: 150

South Sea: 144

South, Robert: 23, 40, 44, 116, 145

Southamptonshire: 45. Southampton: 49; Earl of: 45

Southern cross: 89

Southern hemisphere: 150

Southern California, Univ. of: 44

Southern Passion (13th c. Eng. poem): 74

Southey, Robert: 1, 6, 68, 87, 115, 146*, 21, 58*, 13, 97. Interest in subject of Deluge: 87. On Burnet's Sacred Theory: 87. And M compared: 146. Indifferent to M: 58. Influenced by L'Allegro and Il

Penseroso: 58. Works: Joan of Arc: 115; Thalaba compared to SA: 87

Southwark, London: 44, 45, 49

Southwell, Edward: 123. Robert: 4, 81, 108; Saint Peters Complaynt: 74

Southworth: Henry: 45. Margaret: see Duck, Margaret

Sovereign Right of the People over Tyrants (attr. to M): 44

Sovereign Salve to Cure the Blind (attr. to M): 44

Sovereignty: 122*

Soviet Russia, divorce laws in: 71

Sowernam, Ester: 128

Sozomen (Sozomenus): 73, 90, 116, 93. Church History: 82

Spa (Spada), Belgium: 44

Space: 25. Vast in PL: 50. Entropy of: 96. Automorphistic concept of: 96. Musical and Ramistic: 96

Spada, Governor: 6

Spaeth: Duncan: 60. Sigmund G. (M's Knowledge of Music): 8, 16, 40, 44, 60, 70, 100, 112, 110, 118, 128, 14, 93, 106

Spagna, A.: 6

Spagnoli, G. B.: 32

Spain (and Spanish): 49, 19, 44, 103, 3, 150, 94. See also: Philip IV, King of Spain; Cardenas; Spanish

Spalatto: 49, 73

Spalding(e), Robert: 40, 42

Spang, William: 44

Spangenberg: H.: 93. Wolfert: 68

Spanheim: 44, 73, 117. (Spanhemius), Ezekiel (Ezechiel): 7, 10, 28, 30, 44*, 73, 117. Frederich, Jr. and Sr.: 10. Wigandus: 10

Spaniard(s): 19, 103, 3. See also: Spain

Spanish Friar, The (Dryden): 2, 130. See also: Dryden

Spanish: 40, 150. Language: 103. Lit.: Peck, Bowle, Todd on: 88. Poets: 70. Spanish Armada, The: 103

Spanmuller, Jakob. See Pontanus, Jacobus

Spanuoli, Baptista. See Mantuan

Spargo, Sister Emma Jane Marie: 79

Sparke: Edward: 93. Michael Sr. (bks., 1620-53): 91. Nicholas: 40

Sparks: 40

Sparrow: John: 7, 114; "Latin Verse of the Renaissance": 74. Richard: 40, 44

Sparta (Lacedaemon, Spartan Land): 49, 51, 3. Their prelatical: 73. Spartan: 44. Spartans: 51

Spartacus: 73

Spartan twins (constellation): 73

Spasmodic school of poetry: 87

Speaight, Robert: 93

Speake: George: 45. Mary (Pye): 45

Speaker: the: 51. Speakers, persuasive: 51. Speaker's power, the: 51. Speaking: 51

Special types of reasonings: 51

Special Spirit: 71

Specific: the: 51. Arguments, instance, measures, policy, problems, statements: 51

Spectacle Makers Guild: 16

Spectacle: 92

Spectator, The: 12, 40, 70, 88, 130, 94. See also: Addison, Joseph

Spectre: 25

Speculation: 47

Speculum mundi: 65

Speculum Humanae Salvationis: 74, 36, 99

Spedding, James: 87

Spee, Friedrich: 64

Speech for the Liberty of Unlicenc'd Printing. See Areopagitica

Speech of Mr. John Milton: 51

Speech Day at St. Paul's School: 40

Speech: 51. Habits: 51. Freedom of: 31

Speeches and Prayers of Some of the Late King's Judges, The: 116

Speeches. See Signficant form

Speed, John: 19, 40, 44, 82, 93. Historie of Great Britaine: 82*

Speedwell (ship): 44

Speght, Thomas: 88

Speiser, E. A.: 64

Spelling: 19, 28, 40, 117

Spellings: of the Richardsons: 88; Richardonsons on phonetic value of M's: 88. Peck, Lofft, Todd on: 88. M's original, and Hawkey: 88. Newton's treatment of: 88. Lofft derives them from M's pronunciation: 88. And vocabulary, Todd's systematic study of M's: 88. Todd on, and pronunciation, rhyming: 88

Spelman, Sir Henry: 40, 73, 114, 147, 88, 93. History of Sacrilege (research on tithe collecting): 147

Spence, Joseph: 12, 58, 88, 117

Spencer, De legibus Hebraeorum: 41

Spencer: 149. Mr.: 44. Lady: 44, 117. Grand-child of M: 28. Lady Alice, Countess Dowager of Derby: 29, 55. Benjamin: 9, 54. Sir Edward: 38, 91. Francis: 44. Herbert: 35. Jane: see Cope, Jane. John: 1, 40, 45, 100, 38, 93. Sir John: 45, 55. Martha: 44. Margaret: 44. T.: 23. Theodore: 44, 69, 86, 102, 93. T. J. B.: 86, 39

Spender, Stephen: 108

Spengler, Oswald: 27, 87

Spenser, Edmund: 1*, 2, 4, 5, 6, 7, 8, 9, 12, 15*, 17, 18, 19, 20, 23, 27*, 29, 31, 33*, 34, 37, 40, 77, 35, 44*, 50, 51, 52*, 107, 111, 114, 120, 56, 54, 58*, 59, 60*, 63, 65*, 69*, 70*, 73, 75, 76*, 79, 81, 83*, 84, 86, 87, 90*, 98, 100*, 102, 103, 107, 108*, 112*, 110, 113, 121, 122*, 123*, 125, 126, 127, 128*, 129, 133*, 134, 135, 136, 139*, 142, 141, 144, 145*, 11, 14, 26*, 32*, 38, 39*, 132*, 3, 46, 53, 71, 72*, 82, 88*, 91, 92, 93*, 97, 64*, 94, 101, 106, 109, 115, 130*, 131, 137, 146*, 149, 148*, 117*, 21, 55, 13, 25*. Influence on M: 55*. And Lycidas, Comus, PL: 129. And M compared: 146. His pastoral poetry: 129. His Puritanism: 129. Has less influence in 18th c. than M: 58. Bower of Acrasia: 141. Works: Amoretti: 69, 87. Epithalamion: 69. The Faerie Queene: 35, 58*, 60*, 68, 69*, 74, 79, 77*, 142, 11, 46*, 109, 146, 148*, 150, 25; as visionary poem: 25; as narrative: 25; Books I and II: 126; Sapience: 126; examples of medieval tradition of the Christ-Knight in: 61; Belphoebe: 109; Britomart: 109; Hymne in Honour of Beautie, An: 69; Hymne in Honour of Love: 35, 69, 77; Hymne of Heavenly Beautie: 60; "Letter to Raleigh": 74; Prothalamion: 69; Shepheardes Calender: 35, 69, 79; View of the Present State of Ireland: 82

Spenser Handbook, A (Jones): 83

Spenser-Harvey correspondence, the: 83

Spenser: John: 64. Peregrine: 44. Sylvanus (son of poet): 44; his wife: 44. William (grandson of poet): 44, 137, 150

Spenser's Influence on PL: 112

Sperter, Julius: 7

Speroni, Sperone: 40, 70

Spheres (study of): 40, 121*, 128. Configuration of: 89. Sphere- metal: 121. Inhabited by spirits: 128. Music of: 128, 93. Spherical shell: 89. See also: Copernicus; Ptolemy

Sphinx Philosophica: 40

Sphinx Theologica: 40

Sphinx: 8, 90

Spice Islands: 150

Spicer, John: 45

"Spicie Drugs": 150

Spicq, Ceslaus: 93

Spiering, Peter, Lord of Silvercrone (Swedish ambassador): 44

Spiller, Robert E.: 115

Spina, Allesandro di (invention of spectacles by): 16

Spinckes, Ann. See Cope, Anne

Spingarn, Joel Elias: 18, 15, 66, 70, 100, 122, 123, 101. Critical Essays of the 17th c.: 74

Spinn House, Cambridge: 40

Spinoza, Baruch de (Benedict): 15, 34, 41, 71, 93, 148, 83, 38, 87, 113, 13, 142, 146. The influence of the Greek idea of perfection on: 83. The Chief Works: 142

Spire: 49

<u>Spirit of the Fhanatiques Dissected</u>, The: 103, 116

Spirit World of M and More, the: 112

Spirit(s): 143, 9*, 144. Use of word: 107. The problem of: 92. Animal, vital, natural: 128. Cordial: 128. The Spirit: 9*; definition of: 113; no distinction between matter and: 113; the fruits of, conceals not sin, source of truth, indispensable, law of and life, life of: 143; and Samson: 143; insight into the author's, demanded by Marchant: 88; Logos produces: 107; in M: 107; M's use of the word: 107; nature of: 107; not to be invoked: 107; in Origen: 107; probably does not enter PL as an entity: 107; Mask: 104. Spirits, two present at Creation: 41. See also: Holy Spirit

<u>Spiritual Journey of A Young Man, A</u>: 54

Spiritual: 51,60, 122*, 143*. vs. natural: 60. Structure of the universe, paralysis, nakedness, regeneration, in individual conscience, and virtues of, renaissance imperative: 143. Hero: 122*. Franciscans: 38. Tendency of the Richardsons: 88. Guidance, unintelligence: 51. Liberty, necessity of commonwealth to guarantee: 51. Power, nature of: 51

Spirituality: in M's treatment of the Deity, the Richardsons on: 88. Peculiar, of the 17th c. appreciated by Dunster: 88

<u>Spirituall Madman</u> (William Sedgwick): 147

Spirituals: 114

Spitalfields (Spital Fields), London: 44*

Spitteler: 141

Spittle House End, Cambridge: 40

Spitzer, Leo: 4, 23, 59, 39, 72, 93

Spleen: 128

Spofford, Harriet: 16

Spoken language, Bentley treats Eng. not as a written but a: 88

Spon: Dr. Charles: 44. Isaac: 44

Spondanus, J.: 1

Sponde (Spondanus), Jean de: 123

Spondee (Spondanus), Henri de: 93

Spondees: after pyrrhics, Todd on: 88. Dr. Bridges on: 88

Spongano, R.: 6

Spontaneity: 70. M's imitation of, Peck on: 88. M's, Thyer of: 88. See also: Endowment, creative; Inspiration

Spontaneous generation: 128

Spoor, Friderici (Friedrich, pr.): 44, 91

<u>Sportive Wit</u>: 103, 94. See also: Phillips, John

Sports: 40

Spragg, John: 45

Sprague, Homer: 128

Sprat: 133. Bp.: 28. Dr. Thomas: 10, 15, 23, 37, 114, 116, 128, 145, 88, 91, 117

Spread Eagle: M's father's shop: 40. Bread Street, M's house: 44. See also: White Bear

Sprenger, James: 142

Sprigg(e): Mr.: 45. Joshua: 9, 45, 60, 93; <u>Ancient Bounds</u>: 74. William: 45; distributed <u>A Modest Plea For An Equal Common-Wealth</u>: 147

Spring Gardens (M's residence): 44, 103

Spring, E.: 92

Spring: 8. Eternal: 144

<u>Springer's Weekly Oracle</u>: 115

Springsguth, S.: 97

Sprott: Ernest: 40, 44. S. E.: 86

Sproughton, co. Suffolk: 44

Spry, Robert: 38

Spurgeon: C. F. E.: 128. Caroline: 108

Spuridion, Bp. of Cyprus: 82

Spurstow, William (1605-66): 44, 51, 91, 93. See also: Smectymnuus

Spurstowe, William: 142

Square, significance of: 75. See

also: Circle

Squires, V. P.: 16, 113

Stability under a grand council: 51

Stacey, W. David: 93

Stacy, Frances: 44, 45

Stadius, Iohannes: 40

Stafford Close: 44

Stafford House: 97

Stafford: Marquis of: 91. Mr.: 91. Anthony: 77, 93

Stafford: 102. City or co.: 44, 45, 49. Staffordshire: 49

Stage: 92. Technique, Peck's interest in: 88. Pronunciation, Sympson on: 88. Production of Comus, Warton on: 88. Elizabethan, studied by Warton: 88. M's love of the: 113. Craft: 92. Directions: 92. Lyric: 92. Possibilities (for PL): 50. Adaptations: 117

Stagirite: 73. See also: Aristotle

Staines: 40

Stainton (sic) St. John: 40

Stairs: 143*. As way to salvation: 143*. Appearance of: 143. And causeway to Hell: 143. To Heaven, Biblical basis for: 119. See also: Ladder

Stalbridge, Henry: 33

Stalin: 34, 60

Stamford: 49. Bridge (Battle Bridge): 49

Stampa, Gaspara: 120

Stanbridge, John: 40

Stance: 72. See also subentries under titles of poems

Standard: Anne: 45. Elizabeth (Ashworth): 45. Thomas: 45

Standards (Angelic Order): 142

Standen, J.: 58

Standing Committee of Oxford: 103

Standon: 45

Stanes: 49

Stanfield, C.: 97

Stanford: California: 44. Univ. Publications: 44

Stanford: Donald E.: 115. W. B.: 79

Stange, G. Robert: 87

Stanhope: Dr.: 44. Charles, 2nd Lord: 44. Elizabeth: 45. Sir John: 45

Staniford, Daniel: 115. The Art of Reading: 115

Stanley: Mr.: 44. Sir Edward: 62, 91. Ferdinando, Lord Strange, 5th Earl of Derby: 55. George: 44. Grange: 45. Sir Thomas: 5, 44, 145, 92

Stanningston: 45

Stanstead Abbey: 45. Stanstead Park, co. Sussex: 44

Stanton Harcourt: 45

Stanton St. John, co. Oxon.: 28, 40, 44*, 45

Stanton: 45

Stanyhurst, Richard: 40, 66

Stanzaic form: 40

Stanzaic Life of Christ: 36, 99

Stap (Slapp), Mr.: 44

Stapeley, co. Cheshire: 44

Staphorstius: 94, 117

Staple Inn, Admission Books of: 45

Staple Inn: 40, 45

Staple: Sarah: 44. William: 44

Stapleton: Lady Barbara: 45. Lawrence (Laurence): 14, 93, 101. Margaret: see Wildgoose, Lady Margaret. Sir Philip: 44, 45. Thomas: 93

Star Chamber: 44, 45, 51, 73, 103, 94

Star Inn: 40

Starbuck: 98

Stark, Miriam Lutcher, collection: 44

Starke, John: 44

Starkey: George: 9, 44*, 60, 103, 116; Royal Blood: 91. John (bks., publisher, 1658-89): 44*, 91, 55;

called Starky by Philips: 55

Starkman, M. K.: 23

Starnes: DeWitt T.: 102, 123, 32, 93, 39. And Ernest W. Talbert, Classical Myth and Legend in Renaissance Dictionaries: 60

Stars: 17, 89*, 128*, 144. Creation and function, derivation of light, falling stars a sign of wind, influence of, number, Pole star, substance, sustenance: 128. Grouping into constellations, in navigation, as inhabited worlds, belief as to; in the astronomy of M's time, structure of stellar universe, creation of in PL, ancient beliefs as to influence of, triple, variable: 89. Atlas of, the first, binary, catalogues of, clusters of, colours in, distance of, double, fluctuation of light in, galaxies, groups, insulated, light years of, multiple, nature of nebulae, number visible, periodical, quadruple, single, temporary: 89. Fixed: 89, 128. See also: Comets; Firmament; Meteors; Zodiac

Stasima: 92*

State church: 7, 51. Abolition of: 51. Argument against: 51. And M, M on the: 147

<u>State of Innocence</u>...<u>by a Gentleman of Oxford</u>: 88

<u>State of Innocence</u> (Dryden): 134, 88, 94. <u>State of Innocence</u> and <u>Fall of Man</u> (Dryden): 65, 118

State Paper Office, Whitehall: 94, 150

<u>State Papers, Domestic, Calendar of</u>: 40. <u>State Papers, Calendar of</u>: 45*

<u>State Papers</u>: 45

<u>State Trials</u>: 44

State, the: 70, 51*. And church government, differences between: 51. States: 25

Statement of Faith of the 3rd Council of Constantinople: 74

Statement: 51. Statements, pithy: 51

States General: 51

Statesman (Plato): 112

Statesman: 51. Orator, ideal of M and the ancients: 20

Statesmanship (M's): 129

Stationers' Company: 40, 44, 51, 136, 94. Petition for M's arrest: 136. See also: Company of Stationers

Stationers' Hall: 40, 51, 103

<u>Stationers' Register</u>: 40, 44*, 103

Stationery supplies: 40

Statius, Publius Papinius: 2, 4, 33, 40, 50, 57, 90*, 111, 122, 123, 133, 134, 32, 36, 53, 88, 64, 130, 117, 21. Works: <u>Achilleid</u>: 74; <u>Thebaid</u>: 57, 36

"Statuary in Rome": 98

"Statutes and Antiquities, Of": 44

Statute Staple (11 June 1627): 40, 44

<u>Statutes at Large</u> (ed. Keble): 44

Statutes of Cambridge Univ.: 40

Statutes of Christ's College, Cambridge: 40

Statutes of Colet. See Colet, John

Statutes of Queen's College, Cambridge: 40

Stauffer: Donald A.: 143. Ethelbert: 93

Staunton, Mr.: 44, 45

Staupitz, John: 114

Steadman, John M.: 23, 29, 60, 110, 111, 14, 39, 93, 106, 21, 101. On Haemony: 104. <u>M's Epic Characters</u>: 48

Stearne, John: 142

Stearns: J. B.: 56. Samuel: 115; <u>Thomas's Massachusetts, Connecticut, Rhode Island, Newhampshire and Vermont Almanack</u>: 115

Stebbing: Rev. Henry: 87; on M's character: 111. William: 144

Stebbins, Eunice B.: 128

Stechow, W.: 27

Stedman: Mr.: 44. Rev. Thomas: 44

Steel, David: 88

<u>Steele Glas, The</u> (Gascoigne): 83

Steele: 130. A.: 58. R., on M: 58. Sir R.: 97. Sir Richard: 145, 115, 55, 60; <u>The Tatler</u>: 82, 109. Robert: 40, 128. William, Attorney-

General: 44

Steen: 27. Cornelius van den (a Lapide): 93

Steeplehill Copse: 44, 45

Steere, Richard: 58, 115. Works: The Daniel Catcher: 115; Earth's Felicities, Heaven's Allowances: 115; A Monumental Memorial of Marine Mercy; Upon the Coelestial Embassy Perform'd by Angels: 115

Steevens, George: 44, 58, 87, 88, 97. Definition of sonnet: 87

Stefan(us), St.: 73

Stegmann: Joachin: 22. Josua: 22

Stein: Alfred: 150. Arnold: 1, 4, 15, 17, 23*, 37*, 52*, 66, 75, 76, 79, 81, 86, 105, 110, 111, 118, 122, 123, 127, 128, 139, 11, 14, 32, 36, 53, 85, 93, 101, 106, 109, 140*; Heroic Knowledge: 74; dual nature of Paradise: 61; on poetic success of PR: 61; reconciles M's attitude towards learning and wisdom: 61; on return of Samson to God and his people: 61; works: Answerable Style: 60*, 95, 48; "Milton's War in Heaven": 60; "Satan and the Dramatic Role of Evil": 60. G.: 23. Gertrude: 35

Steinbeck, John: 95

Steiner: George: 14. M.: 93

Steinweg, Carl Albert: 100

Stemmata Dudleiana (Spenser): 83

Stendahl: 1, 39. Krister: 93

Stent, Peter (bks.): 44

Stentor: 73

Stephanoff, F. P.: 97

Stephanus: 28, 40, 63. (Stephen), Charles or Robert (lexicographers): 44, 123, 32. Henricius: 40, 123; see also: Estienne. Robertus (Estienne, Robert): 123

Stephanus' Thesaurus: 20

Stephen: 130. St. Stephen: 111. Sir Leslie: 16, 44, 58, 86, 87, 137. P.: 92

Stephens, St., Church, Walbrook: 40

Stephens: Mr.: 44. E.: 58. G.: 65. James: 65. R.: 94. S. B.: 97. William: 116

Stepney: 45. William: 40

Stereoscopic technqiue (Bunyan's): 47

Sterlinbridge (Sterling, Sterlinium): 49

Sterling Library: 44

Sterling: G.: 58. Joseph: 58, 117

Sterling: 73, 149

Stermont, Jacobus: 44

Stern: 7. Alfred: 40, 44*, 45, 63, 113, 144, 91, 21; Milton und zeine Zeit: 44. Sterne: Catharine: see Ayloffe, Catharine. John: 40. Laurence: 59, 86, 64. Thomas: 45

Sternhold and Hopkins (Psalter): 42, 126. Sternhold, versions of Pslams: 20

Sternhold, Thomas: 40

Sterry: Mr.: 44. Nathaniel: 44. Peter (d. 1672): 23, 44, 59, 67, 79, 114, 142, 91, 93*; surnames by: 38; works: "Catechism": 81; Discourse: 81, 38

Stesichorus: 40, 90

Stetinum: 49

Stettin. See Charles X; Frederick William

Steuart, Adam: 9

Steuchius, Augustinus: 74, 64. Enarrationes in...Job: 74

Stevens and Brown (bks.s): 44

Stevens: B. F. (bks.): 44. David H.: 28, 40, 41, 44*, 45, 59, 86, 102, 113, 132; Reference Guide to M: 44; M Papers: 44. Richard: 45. W. B.: 58. Wallace: 81, 14*, 25; 105, 36; "necessary fiction" in poetry: 61

Stevenson: Rev. Mr.: 44. John: 45. M.: 58. Robert Lewis: 136, 137. W. B., Poem of Job: 74. William: 44

Stevenstone: 44

Stevin, Sinon: 10

Steward: Mr.: 44. John: 44. William: 45

Stewart: Francis: 40. Helen A.: 44. J. A., works: "Cambridge Platonists": 83, 110; The Myths of Plato: 48. James T.: 93. John: 40. Stanley: 32

Stichoi eis ton Adam: 65

Stichomythia: 92

Stiefel, Jesaias: 7

Stier, Hans: 40*

Stigel, Johann: 83*

Stigliano, Prince of: 103

Stilicho: 57

Still And Soft Voice (William Walwyn, in which he explains his creed): 147*

Stillingfleet: Benjamin: 58, 88, 117; oratorio from PL: 58. Bp. Edward: 114, 142, 32, 93, 148; works: Origenes Sacrae: 74; A Discourse Concerning the Idolatry Practiced in the Church of Rome: 142

Stillman, D. G.: 135

Stillwell, Margaret Bingham: 40

Stilpo: 44

Stimulation: the Richardsons' demand of, in poetry: 88. Of the mind, effect of poetry dependent on, Thyer, Warton on: 88

Stimulus and response, as nonsequential: 118

Stintzing, Roderich: 93

Stirling, Brents: 148

Stoa: 44, 49, 3. Painted: 73

Stobaeus: 90

Stock responses: 118

Stock Circle, the: 40

Stock Talmadge co., Oxon.: 44

Stock(e), Rev. Richard: 40*, 44

Stockarus, J. J.: 44

Stockdale, M. R.: 58

Stockenham: 45

Stocker (ambassador for Schaffhausen in Piedmont): 10

Stocker, Gertrude. See Ewens, Gertrude

Stockholm, Sweden: 44*, 103, 49

Stockwood, John: 20, 40, 56

Stodder, Clement K.: 44

Stoehr, T.: 59

Stoic(s): 27, 40, 73, 79, 125, 144, 145, 3, 71*. Philosophy: 5, 70. Influence upon "Cosmopolitanism": 107

Stoicism: 15, 17, 60, 113, 114, 123, 141, 32, 36, 71, 72, 146. Temperance and self-control: 60. Message of: 71. Christ and: 60. M's: 60, 132; M and: 88. See also: Milton, John

Stoke Lyne: 45

Stoke Newington, London (Public Library): 44

Stoke, co. Suffolk: 44

Stokenchurch: 45

Stokes: Adrian: 5. H. P.: 40. John H.: 16. Whitley: 64

Stolberg, F. L.: 58

Stoll, Elmer Edgar: 18, 1, 15, 23, 24, 52, 56, 86, 102, 110, 60, 76, 87, 113, 141, 133, 138, 144, 143, 92, 109, 130*, 137, 146. "Certain Fallacies and Irrelevancies in the Literary Scholarship of the Day": 83

Stonar (Lapis Tituli): 49

Stone: Mr.: 45. Anne: 44. Barton W.: 115. C. F.: 14. Darwell: 93. E. M.: 36. F.: 58. Lawrence: 39

Stonetows: 40

Stonehouse, Mary G. T.: 44

Stoner family: 45

Stonestreet: Katherine: 120. William: 120

Stonte, Edward: 45

S'too him Bayes: 116, 91

Stop: 121

Stopes, C. C.: 45

Storace, Miss: 97

Storm and Stress. See Sturm und Drang

Storm(s): 128. Storm scenes: 99

Stormaria: 49. See also: Frederick III

Stormont, D.: 58

Storrs, Sir Ronald: 18

Story of Genesis and Exodus (13th c. Eng. poem): 65, 74, 149

Story, as means of solving cognitive problems: 118

Stothard, Thomas: 97*, 146

Stoughton: family: 44. John: 93. Sir Nicholas: 44

Stoupe, Mr.: 30

Stouppe (Stuppius), Rev. Jean Baptiste: 44, 59, 73

Stour: 49

Stourmouth: 45

Stow Wood, co. Oxon.: 44

Stow: Joane: see Upton, Joane. John: 17, 20, 40*, 44, 128, 82*, 93; Annales: 82*

Stowe MS. Catalogue of, in British Museum: 44

Stowe, co. Bucks.: 44

Stowe: 97. Harriet Beecher: 118, 137

Stowford Close, co. Oxon.: 44

Stowmarket, co. Suffolk: 40, 44

Stowood: 44, 45

Stowre: 49

Stoye, J. W.: 6

Strabo, Walafrid: 68

Strabo: 5, 19, 31, 40, 70, 90*, 128, 144, 32, 88

Strachey: Lytton: 95, 137. William: 32

Strack-Billerbeck: 41

Strack, H. L.: 36

Strada, Famiano: 40, 149, 13

Straddale: 49

Stradling, Sir John: 65, 122, 123, 32, 93. Divine Poems: 74

Strafford, Earl of (Thomas Wentworth): 10, 44, 45, 70, 73, 103, 113, 116, 26, 94, 144

Strafford, Niobe: 149

Strage degli Innocenti, La: 65*

Strahan, A.: 58

Strand Bridge: 103

Strand, London: 44*, 45

Strang, W.: 97

Strange and Terrible News from Cambridge: 142

Strange Relation of a Young Woman Possest with a Devil, The: 142

Strange: Lord: 44, 45. Francis (scrivener): 44. T.: 58

Strangeness, Hume's sense of, and beauty: 88. See also: Eccentricity; Uncommon

Strangford, Viscount: 58

Strasburgus, Jacobus: 65, 64. Works: Oratio Prima: 74; Oratio Secunda: 74

Strassburg (Strasburgh), Germany: 44, 49, 73, 3

Strat-Cluid: 49

Stratford, co. Essex: 44

Stratford: Elizabeth: 44. Thomas: 117; influenced by PL: 58; on M: 58

Strathmann, Earnest A.: 44, 93

Stratman, Carl J.: 40

Stratton St. Margarets: 45

Straus, O. S.: 9

Strauss: Leo: 60. Richard: 39, 137

Stravinsky, Igor: 39

Strawberry Hill: 44, 97

Strawson, William: 93

Streater, Robert (painter, M portrait): 44

Streatham, co. Surrey: 44

Strebaeus: 40

Street: Sir John: 44. Olive: 44, 45. Thomas: 44. Sir Thomas (judge): 44

Streeter, Mrs.: 44

Strelley: 45. Francis: 45. George: 45

Strength: 2

Stress, Lofft on: 88. See also: Accent; Emphasis

Stretton-on-the-Fosse: 45

Strich, Fritz: 27

Stricken, Johann: 65

Strickland, Walter (Striclandium): 10, 44, 73, 91

Strife. See Eris

Strigelius, Victorinus: 74, 64. Liber Job: 20

Striggio, A.: 6, 64

Strindberg, August: 111

Stringed instruments: 121

Stringer, Thomas: 44

Strittmatter, Dom Anselm: 60

Stroganov, A. G.: 117

Strong: A. H.: 110. E. K.: 58. Nathaniel: 115; England's Perfect Schoolmaster: 115. William: 93

Stroud, William: 40

Stroup, T. B.: 59

Strozzi: Giovanni B.: 6. Guilio: 6

Structure(s): 51*, 11*. Educational: 51. Of sound: 124*. Masque: 29. In PL: 11*. Of PL: 106; Bentley on: 88; Pearce on, or large parts of PL: 88; Dunster on: 88. In SA: 11. Analysis of: 92. Pearce on, gradation in: 88. Principle of economy in, pedantically applied by Newton: 88. Syntactic, enhancing clarity: 88. Dunster's interest in literary: 88. Dunster's analysis of: 88. Dunster's study of connection between character of: 88. Addison and Dunster on: 88. Structure and structural principles: 67*. Structural patterns: in syntax, rhythm, 12-book version of PL: 104*. See also: Form

Struther, William: 93

Struthers, J.: 58

Strutt, J.: 58, 97

Struve: 89

Strya: 49

Strype, John: 20, 40, 114, 143

Stuart: A.: 59, 120. Sir Charles: see Richmond. Dorothy Margaret: 44. Mary: 103

Stuart: House of: 44, 45, 51*, 31, 44, 103*, 71. Regime: 51. Stuart kings: 60. Political theory: 83

Stubbe: Henry: 9*, 114, 91. Sir Henry: 44. Philip: 44

Stubbs: Philip, Anatomy of Abuses: 45, 82, 88. William, Select Charters: 82

Stubington, H.: 44

Stubler, Elizabeth: 128

Stuckius, J. R.: 10

Student(s): 40, 51*, 143. Regulations for: 40. Social rant of: 40. Immature: 51. Quandry of the: 143. And critics: 143. And truth: 143. And M's poetry: 143. Christian vision by: 143. Discipline of: 143

Students Admitted to the Inner Temple: 44. See also: Inner Temple

Studia leviora: 40

"Studies in the Epic Language of PL" (thesis, Black): 135

Studies in the M Tradition (Good): 70, 88

Studies in M (S. B. Liljegren): 88

Studies in Philology: 44*, 112, 88

Studies in Philosophy: 48

Studies in Shakespeare, M, and Donne (Fries, et al.): 112, 135

Studies in 17th-c. Poetic (Wallerstein): 111

Studies: 51, 144. M's in school: 20*. M's study habits: 40, 44. M's account of own: 30*, 44*. Order of at St. Paul's: 40

Studley: Marian: 16. Peter: 114

Study in M's Christian Doctrine, A (Sewell): 134

Study of the Prose Works of John Donne (E. Simpson): 135

Stunica, Didacus á, In Job: 74

Stupidity: 51

Sturbridge: 49, 73. See also: Barwellianus

Sture: 49

Sturm und Drang: 7, 87, 97

Sturm: Johannes (Hans): 40. Johannes C.: 10, 20, 40, 44, 73, 18

Sturm: 3

Sturminster Newton Castle: 45

Sturmius, Johannes. See Sturm, Joannes C.

Stuteville: John: 40. Sir Martin: 40, 44. (Stuttvyle), Thomas: 44

Stuttgart, Germany: 44

Stuttvyle, Thomas. See Stuteville

Styant, William: 45

Stygian: 73

Style, Thomas: 44

Style: 67, 117*. M's: 46. Dating of, in PL: 50. Strength of in PL: 118. Syntactical analysis of: 118. Literary: 70. M on: 30

Styles: family: 45. John: 40. (Style), Robert: 45

Styles: theory of: 66. The 3: 81

Styx River: 44, 49, 73, 90, 3

"Suarez," De Angelis: 95. See also: Guazzo

Suarez, Franciscus: 4, 40, 63, 116, 32, 93

Subconscious, the, appreciated by the Richardsons: 88

Subject: 51. Erudition and, of PL, valued as principal features of the poem: 88. Judged by Newton to be less important in poetry than manner: 88. Of poetry, professional and actual, Warton on: 88

Subjected Plain: 96

Subjection: 51

Subjective: character of the: 96. Elements in M's work: 129. Method of the Richardsons: 88. Subjectivity: 96

Sublime, the: 5*, 87*, 97*, 25. In M's epics: 87. Longinian Sublime, described: 87. Natural Sublime: described, Victorian interest in, in Miltonic religious epics, in Montgomery's <u>The Omnipresence of the Deity</u>: 87. See also: Allegory

Sublimity: 87, 146, 117*. Effect of on readers, characteristics of: 87. Of music: 121. And humanism: 136. Of style and subject, the Richardsons on: 88. Of PL, Newton on: 88. As opposed to smoothness in Comus, Warton on: 88. See also: Majesty; Grand; Grandeur

Sublunar vault: 128*

Subordinationism: ante-Nicene Fathers': 107. Athenagoras of Athens: 107. Clement of Alexandria: 107. Irenaus of Lyons: 107. Justin Martyr: 107. M: 107. Novatian: 107. Origen: 107. Tatian: 107. Tertullian: 107. In PL, De Doctrina Christiana: 93

Subpoena: 45

Subsidy Rolls: 40

Substance: 40, 96. A performer: 40. Evil, good: 51. Of Godhead: 93

Sucana: 49

Succoth: 49, 73

Suckling: 58, 120, 130. Sir John: 73, 84, 145, 91, 150, 55. Sir John (the Elder): 44, 86. Sir John (the Younger): 44, 45, 55

Sudbury: Elizabeth: 120. James: 120. John: 120. John, Jr.: 120. Joseph: 120. Katherine: 120. Parnell: 120

Sudley, Lord Thomas Seymour: 51, 73

Sudorius, Nicholas: 40

Suessanus, Augustinius Niphus (Nifo, Agostino de Sessa): 123

Suetonius: 20, 40, 73, 126, 128, 38, 82, 64

Suevi, the: 71

Suevia: 49

Suffenos: 73

Suffering: as a source of perfection: 83, 122. In SA: 125*. See also: Patience; Martyrdom; Fortitude; Endurance

<u>Suffolk in 1674</u>: 44

<u>Suffolk Green Books</u>: 44

Suffolk House: 44

Suffolk Institute of Archaeology, <u>Proceedings</u>: 44

<u>Suffolk Records</u>: 44

Suffolk, Earl of, Theophilus Howard,

Warden of the Cinque Ports: 40, 44

Suffolk: County: 44, 45, 49. East, County Council: 44

Suffrage: aristocratic plan of: 51. Limitation of: 51. M on: 51

Sugar Loaf (sign): 44

Sugden, E. H.: 19

Suger, Abbot: 27, 79

Suggestions: 51. Stimulating, the Richardsons on: 88. And mystery: 88. And vagueness, Warton on: 88

Suicide: 47, 92. Milton on: 80

Suidas: 4, 23, 40, 60, 64, 88, 90, 123, 128. Index Scriptorum: 74

Suliard: Eustice: 45. Jane: see Ayloffe, Jane. Margaret: see Ayloffe, Margaret (Foster)

Sulla (Sylla), Lucius Cornelius: 51, 60, 103

Sulmo: 49

Sulpicius (Sulpitius): 3. Johannes: 40. Severus: 68, 113

Sultan: 19

Sumatra: 19, 40, 144

Sumerians: 32

Summa contra Gentiles: 20

Summa Theologica: 27

Summanus: 73

Summary: 51

Summatra: 49, 57. See also: Chersonese

Summer home of the Miltons: 40

Summero-Akkadians, the: 89

Summers, Montague: 128, 142. The History of Witchcraft and Demonology: 142. See also: Dryden

Summers: J. E.: 39. Joseph H.: 15, 17, 23, 37*, 60, 66, 75, 79, 81, 86, 100, 110, 111, 118, 126, 14, 32, 53, 85, 93, 101, 106, 109, 115, 140, 21. The Muses' Method: 109

Summerson: Sir J.: 97. John: 39

Summons to House of Lords (M's): 44

Summum bonum: 123. See also: Good, highest

Sumner, Charles R., Bp. of Winchester: 23, 40, 41, 44, 63*, 70, 102, 107, 113, 114, 22, 43, 117, 55. Translator of De Doctrina Christiana: 63. See also: Milton, John, Works: De Doctrina Christiana

Sumpsimus: 40

Sun (bookshop): 44

Sun: figure in "Nativity Ode": 29. Sun worship (in PL): 15

Sun: 50, 89*, 90*, 128*, 144, 72*. As symbol for Christ: 100*. Creation and composition, creative power, effects of Fall on, functions, purity of, source of light, sustenance: 128. Created, effects of, ruler: 144. Central nucleus of, chemical constitution of, the chromosphere, distance of, eclipse of, gravity force of, heat of, light of, magnitude, nature of: 89. Nebular surroundings of, parallax, the photosphere, rotation, spots in, star as a: 89. Masculine: 144. Center of universe: 144. Suns, others: 89

Sündenfall, Der: by Ezzo: 65. By Immessen: 65

Sunderburg: 49

Superego, actions in PL which derive from: 118

Superiority, appeal to feeling of: 51

Superman: 47

Supernatural, the: 145

Supernumerary syllables: Bentley, Pearce, the Richardsons, Peck, Calton, Newton, Warton, Lofft, Dunster and Blair, Todd's treatment of: 88. See also: Elision; Contraction; Hypercatalectic

Superstition: 8, 19, 51, 114

Supplement to Burnet's History of My Own Time: 116

Suppliants, The: by Aeschylus: 70. By Euripides: 70

Supplicat: 40. Supplicats for degrees: 44

Supralapsarianism: 71

Supreme Court of Judicature: 45

Suratta: 49

"Surge, age, surge" (M's): 44

Surmaster at St. Paul's: 40

Surphlet, R.: 128

Surrey, Henry Howard, Earl of: 102, 132, 133, 117, 55, 58, 120, 130

Surrey: 45, 49

Surridge: Rev. H. A. D.: 44. Miss M. K.: 44

Surtz, Edward: 110

Survey of that Foolish, Seditious, Scandalous, Prophane, Libell, the Protestation Protested (Hall): 9, 73, 147

Survey of Cornwall (Carew): 88

Survey Gazateer of the British Isles, A: 45

Survey: historical: 51. Of Scriptural passages: 51. Of studies: 51

Surveys and Tokens: 45

Surville, Marguerite-Eleanore Clothilde de Vallon-Chalys, Madam de: 44

Sus: 19, 49, 73. See also: Almansor

Susa: 19, 44, 49, 73, 144. See also: Choaspes

Susannah (13th c. Eng. poem): 74

Susenbrotus, Johannes: 40

Susiana: 19, 49, 73, 144

Suso, Heinrich: 7

Suspense, use of: 51

Suspension: 98

Sussex: 44, 45, 49

Sutro Library, San Francisco: 44

Suttaby, Crosby and Corral (publishers): 97

Sutton Colefield (Coldfield), co. Warwick: 44, 45

Sutton, Thomas: 37, 102, 114, 93

Suzman, A.: 23

Svendsen, Kester: 1, 6, 15, 17, 23, 44, 54, 59, 60, 100, 66, 68, 75, 86, 87, 102, 105, 110, 123, 128*, 82, 93, 97, 101, 106, 115, 137. Works: Milton and Science: 48

Svengali: 34

Svoboda, Karl Maria: 5, 86, 142. La Demonologie de Michel Psellos: 142

Svogliati Academy, Florence: 44, 55

Svogliati: 103, 121

"Swain": 72

Swain, J.: 58

Swalbach: 44

Swalcliffe: 45

Swale, John (bks.): 44

Swan: C.: 58. John: 65, 77, 102, 128*, 32, 93. (Swann), Nicholas: 44

Swann, Arthur: 44

Swans: 40

Swanswich, (Gnavewic, Swanwine): 49

Swanton, John R.: 118

Swanwick, A.: 58

Swardson, H. R.: 37

Swart-star (Sirius): 89

Swearingen, Roger: 37

Sweden (Suecia), and Swedish: 44*, 49, 103, 3. King and Queen of: 20. Committee for Affairs of: 44. Treaty with, drawn up by M: 16. Swede: 3. See also: Charles Gustavus X; Christina

Swedenberg, H. T., Jr.: 122, 128

Swedenborg, Emmanuel: 142, 46, 97, 146, 25. Swedenborgianism: 78. See also: Marriage of Heaven and Hell

Swedish ambassador. See Bonde

Swedish Intelligencer: 20

Sweet Echo: 121

Sweet, Henry: 44

Sweeting, John (bks., 1639-61): 91

Swete, J.: 58

Swetnam, Joseph: 128, 64

Swettenham: family: 44. Elizabeth: 44

Swift: 133, 3. John: 93. Jonathan: 1, 15, 17, 54, 35, 58, 60, 63, 75, 86,

87, 102, 114, 136, 139, 72, 88, 91, 97, 115, 146, 150, 117, 13; admires PL: 58; Gulliver's Travels: 35; see also: Gulliver's Travels. T.: 58

Swifte, E. L.: 58

Swilland, co. Suffolk: 44

Swimming: 40

Swinburne, Algernon Charles: 35, 58, 86, 87, 15, 132, 71, 149, 148. A. C.: Uses Nativity meter: 58. Political sonnets of: 87. Devotion to classical authors: 87. On Dante worshippers: 87. Works: Dirae: 87; Erechtheus: 87; Before a Crucifix: 35

Swire: 49

Swiss: 103. Evangelical Cantons, including Appenzell, Basel, Bern, Bienne, Geneva, Glarus, Grisons, Mulhausen, St. Gall, Schaffhausen, Zurich: 44*, 103

Swithelm: 3

Switzerland (Helvetia), and Swiss: 44, 49, 103. See also: Stockarus

Sword: M's skill with: 40, 44. Small: 40

Sybil: 57

Sychaeus: 56

Sydenham: Col.: 103. Humphrey: 114, 93*. Thomas: 16. (Sidnamum), William: 73

Sydway, Mr.: 44

Syene: 19, 49, 73, 144. See also: Merope

Syford, Constance M.: 69

Syfret, R. H.: 60

Sykes Davies, H.: 86

Sykes, Norman: 93

Sylburgius, Friedericus: 40

Sylla: 73, 120

Syllables, terminal, uncolloquial length in: 118

Syllogism: 51. Rhetorical: 51

Sylphs: 142

Sylva de Medrano, La: 88

Sylva Synom.: 40

Sylvan, Sylvans: 90

Sylvester (Silvester), St.: 73

Sylvester, Joshua (translator of Du Bartas): 1, 15, 17, 37, 40, 58, 63, 65, 68, 79, 84, 102, 108, 114, 118, 121, 122, 123, 127, 129, 132, 133, 142, 26, 32*, 39, 88, 91, 93, 64, 137, 148, 150, 117, 55, 94. Works: Bethulians Rescue (trans. of Du Bartas' Judit): 74; Du Bartas His Divine Weekes and Workes (trans. of Du Bartas' Sepmaine and Seconde Sepmaine): 74; Fragments...of Bartas: 74; Job Triumphant: 74; translation of Fracastoro's Joseph: 74; Urania (trans. of Du Bartas' Uranie): 74. See also: Du Bartas

Sylvius, Aeneas: 60

Symbol: 47, 69*. Symbolic meaning in PL: 83. See also: Accommodation

Symbolism: 27*, 104*, 113, 125*, 143*, 25*. Christian imagery: in Mask: 104, 143; Lycidas: 104*. In M's poetry: 113. In PR: 125*. Satan's perplexity over: 125. Dalilah and the community: 125. Dalilah as injustice: 125. Samson's reflection of image of Dalilah: 125. In the stairs: 143*. Pervasive: 143. Purpose of: 143. Petrification of: 143. Coleridge's characterization of: 143. Intrinsic meaning: 143. Indispensable in religion: 143. Phallic, of apple, ark, dove, garment, golden flower, harrow, lark, loom, mill: 25. Of plow, polypus, sandals, serpent, thyme, weaving, web: 25. See also: Albion; Jesus

Symbolists, French, sensitive to physical impressions: 88

Symeon: family: 45. Sir George: 44, 45*. John: 45

Symes, Valentine: 44

Symmachus: 73, 93

Symmeren: 49

Symmes, Anne: 44

Symmetrical structure: in PL, temporal: 100*. Narrative: 100*. In Benlowes: 100. Bible, Lamentations: 100. Revelations: 100. Corneille, Dante, Spenser, Virgil, Racine, Ross, Sceve: 100. German middle age: 100

Symmetry: 92*. Concept of: 96. In word-order: 88

Symmons: 70. Charles: 16, 58, 87, 136, 93, 146, 117; Life of Milton: 87; see also: Milton, John, Prose Works. Edward: 144. J.: 58. Matthew (pr.): 44; see also: Simmons. (Symonds), Samuel: 3; see also: Simmons

Symond's Inn: 45

Symonds: Rev. Edward: 44. Mr. John Addington: 5, 18, 87, 111, 138, 64; on SA, on Dr. Johnson's concept of prosody, on prosody: 87. (Symons), Katherine: 45. R.: 6. Samuel: 45. William: 44

Symons: A.: 58. Arthur: 79, 136; on Coleridge: 136. S. (pr.): 94. (Symonds), Walter: 44, 45

Sympathy: 51. Sympathies: 51

Symphony: 40, 121*

Symplegades: 90

Symposium (Plato): 52, 112*, 121, 62

Sympson: Newton's collaborator: 88. David: 44. J.: 58

Symson: Andrew: 114. William: 40

Syncellos: 41

Syncellus, Georgius: 57, 65, 68, 113, 77. Chronographia, ab Adamo usque ad Diocletianum: 57

Syncopation: 121

Synecdoche: defined and illustrated: 118. Of objects and actions: 118

Synergist: 71

Synesius of Cyrene: 5, 93

Synod of Dort: 40

Synopsis Chroniche: 65

Synopsis Historion: 65

Syntax: 88*. In M: 15, 20, 40

Synthesis, lack of, in Peck's criticism: 88

Sypher, Wylie: 27, 52, 101, 115

Sypherd, W. O.: 62

Syphilis, alleged cause of M's blindness: 16*

Syracuse: 3. Syracusans: 112

Syria: 19, 49, 32, 92. Syrian: 3; shepherdess: 73; dialect: 51

Syriac: 40, 42, 44, 73, 103. Bible: 74. New Testament: 40, 41. See also: Bible

Syrinx: 73, 90

Syrtis: 19, 49, 73, 144

System in music: 121

Systema Grammaticum (Farnaby): 20

Systematic intelligence, Peck's lack of: 88

-T-

T., C.: 128

T., F.: 117

T., H.: 117

T., I. See Toland

T., J.: 117. See Tonson, Jacob

Tabb, John B.: 16

Table Talk (Coleridge): 70

Tablet of Cebes, The: 122

Tabula Hebr. Gramm.: 40

Tabulae Codicum Manu Scriptorum...in Bibliotheca Palatina Vindobonensi: 44

Tacitus, Cornelius: 19, 40, 44, 57, 73, 84, 114, 123, 144, 145*, 3, 32, 62, 82, 88, 93, 146, 117, 13

Tact: 51. Lack of: 51

Taenarian, Taenarum: 73

Taenarus: 49

Tagus River: 19, 49, 73

Taihohu Univ., Formosa: 40

Taillepied, Noël: 93

Taine: 132, 130. H. A.: 87, 110; on M's character: 87. Hippolyte: 76, 71

Tainton. See Taynton

Tajano: 44

Takells Mead, co. Surrey: 44

Talaeus, Audomari (Omer Talon): 20, 40

Talbert, E. W.: 29, 102, 123, 32

Talbot: family: 44. Lady: 44. C. H.: 36. G.: 58. Sir John: 44

Tale of the Two Swannes: 130

Talents, parable of: 72

Tallack, William, George Fox, the Friends, and the Early Baptists: 83

Talleyrand, Charles Maurice de: 60

Tallis, Thomas: 40, 121

Tallman, Warren: 125

Talmud: 15, 40, 41, 42, 73, 128, 136, 142, 32, 36*, 88. Babylonian: 74. Talmud, the Babylonian: 36; 'Abodah Zarah, Sanhedrin, Shabbath, Sotah: 36. Aboth of Rabbi Nathan, Baba Bathra, Berakoth, 'Erubin, Hagigah, Hullin, Niddah, Pesahim, Yebamoth: 36. Talmudic learning: 40. Talmudist: 3

Talthybius: 92

Talus: 45, 73

Tamar (man, not river): 73

Tamar (Tamara) River: 44, 49, 73, 3

Tamburlaine (Marlowe): 134

Tamburlaine: 19

Tamira: 49

Tammuz: 143

Tamworth: 45, 49. Dorothy: see Cotton, Dorothy

Tanais: 49. River: 144

Tancke, Joachim: 100

Tancred: 123. See also: Tasso

Tandridge, co. Surrey: 44

Tanet: 49

Tanevot, Alexandre: 65, 117

Tangley, co. Oxon.: 44*, 45*

Tangut: 49

Tangye, Sir Richard: 44

Tani, Gino: 29

Tanner: J. R.: 40. John S. (M portraits, medals): 44

Tannevot. See Tanevot

Tannhäuser: 149

Tansillo da Nola, Luigi: 120, 64. Lagrime di S. Pietro: 74

Tantalus: 60, 73, 90, 123, 72

Taperell, J.: 58

Tapestry: 70

Taplow, co. Bucks.: 44

Taprell, R.: 58

Taprobane(a): 19, 40, 49, 73, 144. See also: Summatra

Tarentum. See Henri Charles

Targ, William, and H. F. Marks, Ten Thousand Rare Books: 44

Targioni-Tozetti, G.: 6

Targum: 1, 40*, 41*, 42, 22; see also Onkelos. Jerusalem: 60, 123. Palestine: 123. Targumists: 73. Targum of Jonathan: 44, 36

Tarkington, Booth: 16, 44

Tarpeia Musa: 73

Tarpeian Rock: 44, 73

Tarquin: 44. Tarquins: 51

Tarquinius Priscus ("Old") Lucius: 73. Tarquin(ius) Superbus ("proud) Lucius: 73

Tarrant, W. G.: 116

Tarshish: 19

Tarsus: 19, 49, 73, 3, 72. Saul of: 51

Tartar(s): 73, 19*, 44. Tartar War: 44. Tartar King: 3

Tartaria: 19, 49, 144

Tartarus (Tartarean): 44, 56, 73, 90*, 98, 3, 72

Tartessian: 73

Tartessus: 49. See also: Tarsus

Tartu: 44

Tasburgh, Charles: 40

Tasker, R. V. G.: 31

Tasso, Bernardo: 120, 122

Tasso, Torquato: 1, 2, 4, 5, 6*, 10, 15*, 19, 23, 27, 28, 30, 37, 40, 44*,

50, 52, 56, 58, 59, 60, 65, 66, 68, 69, 38, 39, 77, 70*, 73, 74, 84, 86, 90, 102, 103, 108, 112, 111, 118, 120*, 122*, 123*, 127, 128, 129*, 132, 133, 135, 142, 144, 145, 3, 26, 32, 53, 88*, 92, 93, 94, 97, 64*, 101, 106, 109, 115, 130, 137, 146*, 149, 117*, 21, 55, 13, 25. His theory of epic poetry: 129. His influence on M: 129. And M compared: 146. Satan and force of evil (Jerusalem Delivered): 149.

Tasso, Works: Aminta: 122, 55; On Heroic Virtue: 74; Della Virtu Eroica e della Carita: 60, 122, 123; Del Poema Eroica: 60; Gerusalemme Liberata: 50, 60, 74, 122*, 46, 109, 146, 149, 77, 123*, 142, 82, 115; Il Mondo Creato: 60, 74, 122, 123; Prose Diverse: 60; Discorsi dell Poema Heroico: 74, 122, 123*; Discorsi dell'Arte Poetica: 74, 122, 123; Gerusalemme Conquistata: 74, 122, 142, 46; Goffredo: 74; Rinaldo: 122; Il Messagiero: 123; Il Calaneo o vero de gli idoli: 123; Sette Giornate del Mondo Creato: 149

Tassoni, Alessandro: 122, 82. Pensieri Diversi: 82

Taste: good: 51. Massey's differs from his theory: 88. Dunster's, different from Warton's: 88. Todd's more advanced than his theories: 88

Tat: 57

Tate: Allen: 23, 86, 124, 131; comments of, on PL: 83. John: 44. N.: 58; influenced by M: 58

Tatian: 24, 32. Disciple of Justin Martyr: 107. Logos is the 1st begotten of God: 107. Subordinationist: 107. Address to the Greeks: 36

Tatius: 64

Tatler, The (Steele): 58, 97

Tatlock, J. S. P.: 57, 63, 93

Taubmannus, Fredericus: 65, 64, 77, 15, 94, 117. Bellum Angelicum: 74, 77

Tauler, John: 7*, 114

Taunton: 44, 49

Taurica (Tauric Fields): 49; see also: Crim. Tauric pool: 73

Taurini: 49

Tauris: 19, 49, 73. See also: Bactrian; Casbeen; Ecbatan; Hispahan

Taurus Mountains: 19, 73

Taurus: 49, 73. See also: Niphates

Taus: 49

Tausig, Karl: 39

Tautologies, condemned by Bentley: 88. See also: Repetition

Tavard, George H.: 79, 81

Tavern life: 8

Taverner: John: 44. Richard: 40

Tavernier: 88

Tavistock (Tavestock, Tavistoc): 45, 49

Tawney, R. H.: 15, 59, 60, 86, 108, 147, 39. Writes of the Puritan reaction to the Statute of Monopoly: 147

Tawze: 49

Taxation: 83

Taxes: 44*

Tayler, Edward: 110, 39

Taylor: 130. Mr.: 44. Alfred E.: 37, 112, 93. Col.: 44. Dick, Jr.: 60, 110, 123, 23, 101, 140; "Storm Scene in PR": 74. Edmund: 7. Edward: 79, 110, 93, 115. Eva G. R.: 40.

Taylor: F.: 59. F. J.: 143; and cause of Reformation: 143. F. Sherwood: 75. George Coffin: 1, 23, 44, 60, 63, 75, 77, 102, 110, 122, 123, 128*, 144, 36, 14, 93; theological commonplaces: 107; M's Use of Du Bartas: 74. G. C. T.: 133. G. Rattray: 93. Henry O.: 128, 143; on spiritual death: 143; and Benedict's regula: 143; and Honorius of Autun: 143; on medieval religious art: 143; and Isidore: 143.

Taylor: Isaac: 19, 87. J.: 58, 97, 99*. James: 44. Bp. Jeremy: 9, 15, 23, 27, 44, 54, 69, 114*, 116, 120, 102, 39, 142, 147, 32, 88, 91, 93, 146*, 148, 150, 13, 94; and M compared: 146, 13; compiler of liturgies: 126; on church and kings: 147; works: Contemplation of the State of Man: 60; Great Exemplar of Sanctity: 74; The Whole Works of Jeremy Taylor: 60, 142.

Taylor: Jerome: 79. Joane Blackborow: 44. John: 40, 44, 115, 32; works: An Inquiry into the

Principles and Policy of the Government of the U. S.: 115; Traitors Perspective Glass: 91. John (another, "Water Poet"): 103, 116. Peter: 25. Rene: 39. Thomas: 7, 54, 108, 114, 128, 93, 99*; Christs Combate: 74. Vincent: 93. W.: 15, 58

Taynton (Tainton): 45

Tayth: 49

Tchekov: 92

Te Deum: 126

Teachers: 51. At Cambridge: 30. M's at St. Paul's: 20*, 30. See also: Chappell, William; Gill, Alexander; Young, Thomas

Teaching: 51, 84. M on teaching of language, politics: 51. M on teachers: 51. Teaching as a monopoly: 40

Tears of Lamentation, etc.: 103

Tears or Lamentations of a Sorrowful Soul: 121

Tears, Sighs, Complaints, and Prayers: 103

Technical: modes of persuasion: 51. Ingenuity of Bentley's method: 88. Terms, defended by Pearce: 88. Peck's observations on M's, borrowed: 88. Newton interested in intellectual and, rather than emotional problems: 88. Technical treatises: 58. Technical words in M: 70

Technique in music: 121

Tecla, manuscript of: 73

Tegg, T.: 97

Teia: 49. Teia(n) Musa: 73, 3

Teignmouth, Lord: 44

Teilhard de Chardin, Pierre: 52, 111

Teitelbaum, Eve: 25

Telamon: 44, 73, 3

Telassar: 49, 73, 144. See also: Eden; Seleucia

Telegonus: 73

Telemachus: 56

Teleology: 96

Telephus, King of Mysians: 44, 73, 3

Telescope: 17, 40, 89, 128

Telesio, Bernardino: 6, 114

Telesius: 142

Tell-me-why-story, use of by children: 118. PL as: 118

Telling vs. presentation: 118

Telling House, London: 44

Tellus: 56

Telta: 49

Temes. See Thames

Temesa: 49. Temesaean: 73

Temir: 1, 73

Tempe Restored (Townshend): 29*

Tempe, vale of: 144

Temperance: 9*, 24, 44, 51, 113, 122, 123, 125*, 139, 144, 93. M's praise of in Comus: 113. And righteousness toward ouselves: 125. And magnanimity, wisdom, justice, joy, learning: 125. And Samson: 125. In unfallen and fallen hero: 123. The theme of PL: 83. Background history: 125. As guardian of moral threshold: 125. As achieved effect: 125. And harmony, grace, decorum, passion: 125. And discipline: 125*. M's concept of: 125. And "integrity of life": 125

Tempest, in PR, as adversity symbol: 123*

Tempest, The (Shakespeare): 139, 88

Tempier, Stephen (Etienne): 77. Opiniones ducentae undeviginti: 77

Temple of Gnidus: 58

Temple: the: 72*; building of Pandaemonium associated with: 119. Temple Bar: 27, 44, 103. Temple Classics: 44. Temple Court: see Upleadon. Temple, London: 44, 45; see also: Inner and Middle Temples. Temple of Dagon: 72*. Temple of God: 107. Temple of Solomon: and Renaissance art, and PL: 106. Temple of Venus: 27

Temple: Sir Peter: 44. Sir Thomas: 44, 144; sermon by: 38. W.: 141. Abp. William: 15, 93. Sir William: 15, 47, 60, 35, 145, 143, 115; on reason and love, judgment, freedom, and redemption: 47

Temporal structure: 100*. See also:

Symmetrical structure

Temporality, and mutability: 48

Temporis Partus Masculus (Bacon): 112

Temptacion of Man in Paradyce: 65

Temptation: 47, 125*, 46. Ordeal: 123*. Motif: 122*. Temptation, time: 50. Evil: 123. Tradition of: 125. Belial and: 125. Of appetite: 125. Scale of: 125. Satan's breaking the rules: 125. On the tower: 125. Temptation of the angels, Parthia, Rome, Athens: 46. In the wilderness: 93. Of man: see Fall. Temptations, exposure to: 51. Temptations of Christ: 46, 99*, 119; by "fraud" or "violence": 99. Length of: 99. Temptation (of Eve and Adam): 31*, 46. See also: Trial; Adam; Eve; Satan; Serpent

Temsford: 49

Ten Brink, Bernhard, Early Eng. Lit.: 74

Ten Commandments, authority conferred by: 51

Ten Tribes: 19

Tenach (Tanach): 40

Tenant: by the courtesy: 45. For term of years: 45. In dower: 45. In tail: 45

Tender Conscience Religiously Affected (tithes as oppression of the poor): 147

Tenerife (Teneriff) Mt.: 19, 49, 73, 150

Tenison, Thomas, Abp. of Canterbury: 44

Tennant, Frederick R.: 15, 36, 93

Tenniel: 35

Tennis: 40

Tennyson, Alfred Lord: 4, 27, 34, 35, 58*, 59, 73, 86, 87*, 89, 95, 105, 111, 118, 120, 132, 139, 143, 26, 71, 64, 130, 137, 149, 150, 55. Library at Somersby, at Cambridge, religious attitude of, interest in classical authors, attitude toward the sonnet, Byronic moods of: 87. Pre-Cambridge poems on Byron, M's influence on early poems, poems of Cambridge period, early knowledge of M, interest in M's use of language, Miltonic influence on Cambridge poems: 87.

Tennyson (continued): Geographical descriptions in poetry, and the "Apostles," problem of fate and free will in poetry, passion vs. reason in his poetry, allegiance to conscious artistry, interest in theology, political sonnets of, perfected art of, youth of, poems of apprenticeship, M and Virgil favorite poets of: 87. And, on M: letter to aunt on SA, studies M's blank verse, interest in M's Eden, interest in M's Hesperian Gardens and idyllic scenes, echoes of M in later poetry, blank verse imitative of M's, on M's imagination, concept of M as artist, attitudes similar to M;s, relationship to M, admired M's artistry, attitude toward M, M's influence on, concept of poetry similar to M's, compared with M: 87. And PL: recitations by, passages of loved by, knowledge of, attitude toward, : 87. On Lycidas: 58, 87. 1st Reform Bill: 87. Influence of poetry on Victorian readers: 87.

Works: "Milton" (Alcaios): 87; "To Virgil": 87; "Merlin and the Glean": 87; "The Deity": 87; "On Sublimity": 87; "Ode to Memory": 87; "Persia": 87; "Milton's Mulberry": 87; "Recollection of the Arabaian Nights": 87; "The Lotos-Eaters": 87; "Oenone": 87; "Lucretius": 87; "Aramageddon": early version of: 87; M element in: 87; "The Hesperides," M's influence on: 87; sonnets: "Written on hearing of the Outbreak of Polish Insurrection": 87; "Montinegro": 87; "Salve Lux Renata": 87; Idylls of the King, reason vs. passion in: 87; In Memorium: 109; compared with Shakespeare's sonnets, faultless verse of, idea of fate and free will in, idea of fame in, blank verse of: 87; Poems, M's influence on: 87; Poems, Chiefly Lyrical, M's influence on: 87; The Love's Tale and Timbucktoo, blank verse of: 87. The Devil and the Lady: 87; Poems by Two Brothers: 87; Maud: 35

Tennyson: Charles (Alfred's brother): 87. Charles (Alfred's grandson): 87. Rev. George Clayton (library of): 87. Hallam: 87

Tenor: 121

Tenses (M's use of): 15

Tenterden: 45

Tenure for life: 45

Tenure of Kings and Magistrates: 52, 103, 89, 112, 111, 113, 116*, 129, 144*, 94*, 55. And the Golden Rule: 144*. Principles of: 144. Seneca quoted: 144. Obedience conditional: 144. King's power limited: 144. People's sovereignty: 144. King is accountable: 144. M's account: 55. Compared with Pro Populo Adversus Tyrannos: 116. Presentation copy of: 44. See also: Milton, John, Works

Terah's faithful son: 73

Teredon: 19, 49, 73, 144. See also: Balsara; Euphrates

Terence in English (Bernard): 20

Terence School, Cambridge: 40

Terence: 18, 20, 40*, 44, 56, 70, 73, 95, 82, 88, 64, 117. Eunuch: 82

Terentius Christian: 40

Terentius: 3

Teresa of Ávila, St.: 23, 27, 39

Term Catalogues: 44*. See also: E. Arber

Terms, college, at Cambridge: 40

Ternate: 19, 49, 73, 150. See also: Banda; Tidore

Terra Moriath: 144

Terrell, John. See Tyrrell

Terrestrial Paradise: 19. Terrestrial Universe: 71

Terror: 2. Of another Stuart regime: 51

Terry: John: 93. M.: 58. Milton S.: 22. Roderick: 44. Seth Sprague: 44

Terseness: Hume on M's: 88. The Richardsons on, causing obscurity: 88. Calton unable to do justice to M's: 88. M's valued by Dunster: 88. And regarded as derived from the Latin: 88. Monboddo on M's: 88

Tertullian, Quintus Septimius Florens: 18, 24, 34, 40, 44, 54, 57*, 59, 63, 65, 68, 73, 74, 113, 114, 125, 139, 141, 142, 144, 145, 3, 32, 36, 38, 71, 82*, 88, 93*, 101, 115. "Word" derived from wisdom: 107. Subordinationist: 107. Chiliasm: 107. Works: De Spectaculis: 57, 82; An Answer to the Jews: 36; Prescription against Heretics: 36; The Flesh of Christ: 36; Treatise of the Soul: 36; "Adversus Praxeas": 74; Against Praxeas: 60; Apology: 74; Apologeticum: 82; Contra Marcion: 60; "Of Patience": 74, 36; The Ante-Nicene Fathers: 142

Terza, Dante della: 39

Tesauro: 1, 39

Tesiphon: 144

Test and Corporation Acts: 78

Test Act(s): 103, 147

Testam Graecum: 40

Testament of the Protoplasts: 65

Testament of Adam: 65

Testament of Moses: 65

Testament of Solomon: 142

Testament: Old: 51, 143. New: 51, 143. Ladder in: 143. Angels and saints of: 143. Greek: 44. See also: Bible

Testamentum Patris Nostri Adam: 123

Testi, Fulvio: 121, 117

Testimonia: 62

Testimony of the President, Professors, Tutors, and Hebrew Instructor of Harvard College in Cambridge, against the Rev. Mr. George Whitefield, and his Conduct: 37

Testimony to the Truth of Jesus Christ: 44, 91

Testimony: 51*. Divine: 122. Divine and human: 123*. As artificial proof: 123

Tethys Festival (Daniel): 29

Tethys: 56, 73, 90, 104

Tetius, H.: 6

Tetnal: 49

Tetrachordon: 54*, 124, 94, 102, 103, 112*, 111, 113*. Imagery of: 8*. On the freedom of the will: 83. On the dignity of man: 83. Use of the term "Perfection" in: 83. See also: Milton, John, Works

Tetragrammaton: 41, 123

Tetuan (Tituan): 44

Teucrigenas: 73

Teumesius: 49, 73

Teutonic lands: 3

Tevenot, Melchisedech: 16, 30

Tew, Little: 45

Tewksbury, Gardner, co. Gloucester: 44

Texas, Univ. of: 44

Text: presuppositions and structure of: 96. M's: 117*. M's, treatment of, Hume's, Bentley's: 88. M's treatment of, Pearce's, the Richardsons on, Peck's, Hawkey's, Newton's, Calton's, Marchant on, Wesley's, Lofft's, Todd's: 88. Milton Restor'd and Bentley Depos'd, on Bentley's: 88. A Friendly Letter to Dr. Bentley on Bentley's: 88. Textbooks: 20, 40; advocated by Brinsley: 20*; use at St. Paul's: 20*

Textor, John Ravisius: 40

Textual problems, dealt with by F. Thynne: 88. Aims of Bentley's commentary: 88

Tha 'alibi (Abu Mansur 'Abd Al Malek): 123

Thacher: Samuel Cooper: 115; Catalogue of the Entire and Select Library of the Late Rev. Samuel Cooper Thacher: 115. Thomas: 115; A Discourse on the Errors of Popery: 115

Thackeray: 149. Annie: 37. H. St. J.: 36. W. M.: 35, 136, 97, 149

Thackham, Thomas: 44

Thalaba: 130

Thaler: A.: 58, 113. Alwin: 144

Thales: 73, 114, 123, 3, 92; astronomical work of: 89. Milesius: 128

Thalia: 73, 3

Thame: 45, 73. Co. Oxon.: 44

Thames: Thames River: 40, 49, 103, 44, 3; see also: Thame. Thames (Temes) Street: 44, 45

Thammuz: 2, 57, 73, 90, 127, 144, 72. Biblical authority for: 119.

Thamyris: 16, 60, 73, 90, 3

Thanatos. See Death

Thanet, Earl of: 103

Thanksgiving Sermon For the Deliverance of Our King: 116

Thanksgiving Sermon Preach'd, A: 116

Tharmas: 25

Tharsis: 142

Thatched House, Islington: 44

"That Nature is not Subject to Old Age": 72. See also: Milton, John, Works

Thaumantia proles: 73

The Trial. See Kafka

Theaetetus (Plato): 112

Theanthropos: 107

Theater of Voluptuous Worldings (Van der Noot): 83

Theatre of the World. See Ortelius, Abraham

Theatre: 8, 30, 40. The Eng.: 97. M's attitude toward: 137. Theatre Royal: 27. Theatricals, M (college): 121

Theatrum Ortelli Epit.: 40

Theatrum Poetarum (att. to M, and Phillips): 44, 70, 111, 116, 94

Thebaid (Statius): 111, 134

Theban monster: 73

Thebes (Echionius, Ogygius, Thebae): 49, 70, 73, 90, 144, 3, 92; see also: Ismenian. Thebes, Egyptian: 49, 73; see also: Arabia

Thebez (Thesbitis Terra): 49, 73

Thel: 25. The Book of Thel: 25

Thelwall, J.: 58*

Thelwel: 49

Theme: 40, 69. Ethical view: 140*. Felix culpa view: 140*. Problem of: 92. Latin composition: 40. Themes, prose: 20*

Themis: 1, 73, 90

Themistius: 40

Themistocles: 60, 73, 123

Themylthorp, Nicholas: 40

Theobald: John: 117. Lewis: 1, 88, 97, 130, 117; on M: 58

Theocrisis: 65

Theocritus: 1, 4, 12, 17, 27, 33, 40, 44, 73, 90*, 103, 121, 144, 3, 32, 39, 72, 93, 97, 64*, 146, 148, 117, 21,

13. Works: Idylls, "Idyll XVII": 74; Infant Herakles: 74

Theoctista (Theoctistus): 44, 73

Theodicy: 60

Theodolus: 36. Eclogue: 36

Theodore: 60, 3. Theodore bar Khoni: 36; Book of Scholia: 36. Theodore of Mopsuestia: 74

Theodoret (of Cyrrhus): 24, 57, 65, 68, 73, 74, 77, 114, 144, 83, 93. Works: In Exodum: 74; Church History: 82

Theodoretus: 123

Theodoric: 73

Theodorus: 101, 146. Canterbury Bp., a Grecian monk of Tarsus: 73. Theodorus Prodomus: 123

Theodosius I: 44, 73, 3. II, the Younger: 51, 73. Emperor: 82, 21

Theodote: 73

Theodotion (the heretical): 73, 93

Theodotus the Patriarch: 73

Theognis: 40, 73, 90

Theogony (masculine): 139

Theogony (Hesiod): 118, 3

Theologia Germanica: 7, 114

Theologian(s): 51. M as, influenced by early Fathers: 107

Theological Works of the Reverend Mr. Charles Leslie, The: 115

Theological: renewal: 47. Virtues: 122. Index: 82. Studies (M's): 44

Theology: 40*, 50*, 51, 113, 146. M's: 50, 43; how derived: 107; attitude towards: 113. Of PL, difficulty in classifying: 107. Negative: 93. Natural: 93. Affirmative: 93. 17th c.-Protestant: 8, 31

Theomachia (John Goodwin): 147

Theon: 82. Progymnasmata: 20

Theophanes, Isaac: 44, 89

Theophanes, St.: 73

Theophania, comoedia nova: 65

Theophile: 77

Theophilus: 32, 117*. Theophilus, "the worthy emperor": 73. Theophilus of Adana: 114. Theophilus of Antioch, St.: 24, 60, 36, 93; 1st to use the term "trinity": 107; God incomprehensible, immanent word and external logos, logos the 1st born of God, logos speaks to Adam in Eden: Three Books of Theopilus to Autolycus. Theophilus Loncardiensis: 40

Theophrastus von Hohenheim: 142. Four Treatises: 142

Theophrastus, The English: 58

Theophrastus: 6, 40, 73, 79, 128, 3, 82, 64

Theophylactus: 99*. Of Bulgaria: 68

Theorbo: 121

Theorists, modern: 51

Theory: 51. Of music: 121*. Theories: Massey's differ from his taste: 88; regarding poetry, Warton's: 88; Dunster's immature, critical, different from his practice: 88; Todd's less developed than his taste: 88

Theosophy: 7. Theosophists: 142, 71. Theosophical Brotherhood: 7

Theotormon: 25. Theotormon woven: 25

Theriaca (Nicander): 3

Theriotes: 72

Thermodoon: 49. Thermodoontea River: 73

Thersites: 2, 123, 71

Thesaurus linguae Latinae: 68, 55

Thesaurus Cicernonianus (Nizolius): 20

Thesaurus Poeticus: 40

"These Shapes of old transfigured by the charms" (attr. to M): 44

These Tradesmen are Preachers in and about the City of London: 44, 91

Theseus: 2, 44, 123, 11, 92

Thesis, or consultation in theme writing: 20

Thespian drama: 92

Thessala saga: 73

Thessalia (Haemonia): 1, 44, 49. Thessalian witch: 19

Thessalonians: 3. Epistle to the: 73. See also: Bible

Thessalonica: 49

Thessaly (Haemonia): 1. See also: Thessalia

Thestylis: 73, 90

Thetford, co. Norfolk: 44

Thetford, Isle of Ely, co. Cambs.: 44, 49

Thetis: 44, 73, 90, 3

Thevenaz, Pierre: 39

Thévenin (usually misspelled Thevenot), François, M. D.: 44, 73, 113

Thevenot, Dr. See Thévenin

Thiard, Gaspard Pontus de. See Tyard, de

Thibaut de Maisières, Maury: 77, 64

Thiodamantaeus. See Hylas

Third Age: 143

Third Collection against Propery and Tyranny; 44

Third Conference: 44

Thirlwall, C.: 92

Thirty Queries (John Goodwin): 147

Thirty Years' War: 8, 83, 71

Thirty-Nine Articles: 81, 103, 107, 134, 71, 78

Thomas à Becket: 71

Thomas Aquinas, St.: 24*, 31, 41, 60, 77, 79*, 93*, 130. Works: De Regimine Principum: 60; Summa Theolgica: 60, 77*. See also: Aquinas, Thomas

Thomas, St.: 3. Thomas, St., the Apostle: 111

Thomas: 72. A.: 58. B.: 58. Dylan: 15. Edmund: 58. Edward: 58, 150. Joseph: 25. L.: 58. Randall: 44. Roger: 44. Thomas: 40, 123. W.: 58. W. C.: 97. William: 9, 30, 40, 44, 91. William, Bp. of Worcester: 44. William, M. P.: 44

Thomas Cisterciensis: 68. Thomas of Cantimpré: 128. Thomas of Malmesbury: 93. Thomas the Rhymer: 40

Thomason: 3. Catharine: 59, 26; see also: M's Sonnet XIV. Elizabeth: 59, 120. George (bks., including his collection in the British Museum and catalogue of it by G. K. Fortescue): 44*, 59, 84, 103, 120, 38, 91*. Katherine (Mrs. George): 44, 120, 130. William: 120

Thomism: 81

Thompson: 3. Mr.: 44. Anthony: 10. C. J.: 16. Campbell: 64. Elbert N. S.: 1, 15, 19, 60, 68, 77, 86, 102, 108, 112, 110, 113, 128, 144, 43, 71, 92, 101, 109, 130; "The Theme of PL": 83. Edward: 144. Capt. Edward (ed. of Works of Andrew Marvell): see Marvell, Andrew.

Thompson: F.: 58. Francis, D. D.: 5, 44, 87, 145. G. (translator): 58. J.: see Tonson. James A. K.: 40, 86; The City of Dreadful Night: 46. Nathaniel (pr.): 44. Samuel (bks.): 44. Stith: see Grebanier. Thomas: 44. W. (of Queen's College, Oxford): 58. W. (of Trinity College, Dublin): 58. William: 117. See also: Thomson

Thomson: 130, 149. A.: 58. Mrs. Catherine: 94. G.: 141. Gladys S.: 44. J. A. K.: 92. James: 7, 15, 58*, 87, 105, 97, 109, 115, 146, 117, 55, 13, 94; influenced by M: 58*; on M: 58; preface to Areopagitica: 58; works: Seasons: 58*, 115; Winter: 115. John: 115; The Letters of Curtius: 109. See also: Thompson

Thonain, E.: 6

Thone: 144. The wife of: 73

Thoreau, Henry David: 37, 71, 72

Thorley: 40

Thorn, R. J.: 58

Thornbury: Ethel M.: 60. George Walter, and Edward Walford: 44; see also: Walford, Edward

Thorndike: A. H.: 16. Lynn: 16, 57, 75, 128, 93

Thorne, William: 40

Thornehill Copse: 44, 45

Thornhill: J.: 97. W. J.: 58

Thornthwaite, J.: 97

Thornton: John Wingate: 115. Thomas: 40

Thoroton, Robert: 45

Thoroughness: 51

Thorowgood, G.: 54

Thorp: Thomas (bks.): 44. Willard: 115

Thorpe: Mr.: 44. Francis: 44. James E., Jr.: 115. James: 44, 52, 56, 86*, 100, 123, 142, 146, 25; M Criticism: Selections from Four Centuries: 142

Thorton, Roger de: 40

Thory, John: 40

Thoth: 57

Thou God of Might: 121

Thou, Jacques Auguste de (Thaunus): 40, 58. See also: Thuanus, Jacobus

Thought(s): 47, 123. Originality of M's: 113. Figures of: 20. See also: Reason; Dianoia

Thrace (Odrysia; Thressa; Thracia; Thracian): 44, 49, 73. Thracian: lute: 3; Thracian bard: 3, 73

Thraldom: 51

Thrale: Mrs. H.: 58. Richard (bks.): 44

Thrascias: 144

Thrascias: 73, 90

Thrasea(s) Paetus: 73

Thraso, boasting: 73

Thrasybulus: 73

Thrasymachus: 112

Three: Classes of Men: 25; see also: Milton; Rintrah; Satan. Three Cranes Inn: 40. Three Cups Inn: 40. Three Bibles (bookshop): 44. Three degrees: 93. Three eras: 93. Three Pigeons (pr.'s shop): 44. Three Pigeons (sign): 44

Threthowan, Illtyd: 79, 81

Throckmorton: Mr.: 45. Job: 44. Nicholas: 44

Throgmorton: Frances: 108. Winifred: see Powell, Winifred

Thrones: 142. Rabbinical Aralim: 142

Thuanus: 65. Jacques (Jacobus) Auguste de Thou: 73, 82; Historia Sui Temporis: 82*

Thucydides: 5, 20, 34, 40, 44, 145, 92, 93, 146, 117

Thule: 49; see also: Utmost Isles. Frozen Thule: 73

Thunder: 50, 128*. Causes and kinds: 128. Thunderbolt: 128. See also: Chariot of paternal deity

Thurenne. See Turenne

Thurian, Max: 93

Thurland, Sir Edward: 44

Thurloe (Thurloium), John, Secretary of State: 10, 16, 30, 44*, 73, 103, 116, 38, 91, 94

Thurston: John (artist): 44, 97. Linda: 39. Thomas: 44

Thusca (Thuscia). See Tuscan

Thyatira: 49. The much-praised Bp. of: 73

Thyer, Robert: 1, 4, 56, 60, 102, 105, 118, 53, 88*, 92, 117*

Thyestes: 56, 90, 139, 92. Thyestean banquet: 73

Thyme. See Symbolism

Thymos: 122

Thynne: Fr.: 88. Sir James: 44. William: 88

Thyoneus: 73

Thyrsis: 1, 44, 70, 90, 128, 144, 143, 72. See also: Attendant Spirit

Thysius, A.: 54

Tiamat: 36

Tibaltiana: 73

Tiber River: 44, 49, 3

Tiberias (town): 49, 73

Tiberius, Emperor: 19, 49, 73, 3

Tibullus, Albius: 4, 20, 40, 44, 90, 88, 64, 130, 148, 117

"Tibullus." See "Ad Messallam"

Tibur: 49

Tichborne, Robert (regicide): 44, 93

Tichonius: 38

Tickell: R.: 58. T., edits PL: 58

Ticknor, George: 44

Ticktack (a game): 40

Tides: 128

Tidore: 19, 150

Tiebi: 49

Tiebout, C.: 97

Tieck: 7. Johann Ludwig: 136. Ludwig: 44

Tiepolo, Giovanni Battista: 1, 27

Tigerstedt, E. N.: 100

Tighe, M.: 58

Tigris River: 19, 49, 73, 144, 32*. See also: Euphrates

Tihany, L. C.: 19

Tikune Zohar: 113

Tilbury: 44

Tillage: 51

Tilley, William: 117

Tillich, Paul: 47, 101. On demonic: 47. On incarnation: 47

Tillier, François: 64

Tillingham, co. Essex: 44

Tillotson: Geoffrey: 1, 12, 150. John, apb. of Canterbury: 40, 44, 114, 116, 145, 115

Tilly, Johann Tserclaes, Count, Imperial General: 10

Tillyard: Arthur: 45. E. M. W.: see separate entry. E. V. M.: 141*. Phyllis B. (translator): 20, 112, 128, 92

Tillyard, E. M. W.: 1, 4, 5, 6, 8, 9, 12, 15, 16, 18, 20, 23, 24, 27, 29, 31, 33, 34*, 37, 40, 41, 44, 52*, 56, 59, 63*, 66, 68, 69, 73, 75, 76, 77, 79, 81, 84, 86*, 102, 104, 105, 108*, 110, 114, 122, 123, 124, 125, 127, 118, 128*, 132, 133, 135, 136, 142, 139, 138*, 144, 14, 143, 26, 36, 62, 85, 91, 92*, 93, 99, 54, 101, 106, 109, 130*, 137*, 148*, 150, 140*, 21, 48, 25. On the epic: 48. Drama in Comus: 143; epilogue of Comus: 143. On SA: 143. Fall attributed to levity and uxoriousness: 107. PL occasionally heretical: 107. Muse unidentifiable: 107. Tone of mortification in PR: 61. Works: The Elizabethan World Picture: 142; The Eng. Epic and Its Background: 60, 74, 48; The Eng. Epic Tradition: 88; Milton: 60, 74*, 95, 77, 48; comment of, on the theme of PL: 83; The Miltonic Setting Past and Present: 60, 74, 95, 142; Studies in M: 95, 48; and Phyllis B.: 75; edited M's Private Correspondence and Academic Exercises: 44, 83

Tilmannus, Godefridus: Allegoriae Simul et Tropologiae: 74

Tilney, Edmund: 54

Tilson, Edward: 44

Timaeus (Plato): 5, 29, 112, 121, 111, 130

Timaeus of Locri (man, not title): 3

Timarchus: 73

Timber (Ben Jonson): 70, 135

Timberlake: family: 45. (Tymberlacke), Mr.: 44, 45. Henry: 45. John: 45. Margaret: 45. Thomas: 45

Timbrel: 121

Time Vindicated (Jonson): 20, 29

Time: 44, 76*, 124*, 125*, 128, 11, 93, 25. As kairos: 25. In PL: 48; historical of: 125. Intrusions from: 124. Perspective of: 124. Moments of (detached and enclosed): 124. Midwife of Truth: 128. Problems of: 128. A physical phenomenon: 128. Adapted by M, inconsistently used in PL: 50. Narrative, closing off of, mythical, torture of, God's, the worry of, resignation to, and timing, M's imaginative sense of: 125. Perception and structure of: 96*

Times, London: 44. Times Literary Supplement: 45, 144, 150. See also: London Times

Timmer, B. J.: 36

Timmis, Randle: 44

Timna (city): 49, 73, 72

Timnath, the woman of: 92

Timocharis: 89

Timoleon: 16, 73. Timoleon: 98

Timolus: 49

Timon of Athens: 128

Timotheus of Miletus: 121

Timothy: St. Timothy: 73, 139, 3. Epistles of: 44; 1st Epistle of Paul to: 74

Timpler, Clemens: 40

Tinctoris, Johannes: 93

Tindal: Mathew: 32. W.: 58

Tindal's Ground, Bunhill: 44

Tindale: 3

Tindall, W. Y.: 9

Tine: 49

Tinqoesia: 49

Tinker, Chauncey B.: 137

Tinling, Marion: 115

Tinna: 49

"Tintern Abbey" (Wordsworth): 118, 130

Tinterne: 49

Tintoretto: 6, 27

Tipping: Edward: 45. Elizabeth: 45. "Eternity": 45. Sir George: 45. John: 45. Thomas: 45. William: 45

Tipton, Edmund: 44

Tir-nan-og: 118

Tiraboschi, Girolamo: 18

Tiresias (Tyresias): 16, 30, 44, 60, 73, 90, 3, 62, 72

Tirinus, Jacobus: 68

Tirvalore Tables: 89

Tirzah: 25

Tischbein, W.: 97

Tisiphone: 73, 111

Tissardus, Franciscus: 40

Titan(s): 1, 57, 60*, 73, 90*, 123, 144, 72. War of the: 118

Titanomachia, Greek myths of: 48

Titchfield: 45

Tite, Sir William: 44

Titelmann, Franciscus: 74. In Job: 74

Tithes: 9*, 44, 51, 114*, 147. Abolition of: 51. Defended by Harrington: 147. Denounced by Fox: 147. In hands of laymen: 147. Osborne effective opponent of: 147. Petitions concerning: 147. Undergoes searching scrutiny: 147. Controversy over: 38. Lilburne, Milton, Overton, Presbyterians, Quakers, Selden, Spelman, Winstanley, on the issue of tithes: 147

Tithonia: 73. Tithonia Arva: 49

Tithonus: 73, 90, 72

Titian: 6, 122, 39, 146

Title: 92. Titles: in marriage: 54; argument from: 123*

Tituan. See Tetuan

Titular: 73

Titus: 73, 3, 36, 38. Silas: 91. Silius: see Sexby

Tityos: 56, 111, 72

Tityrus: 44, 56, 73, 3

Tityus: 60

Tiverton: 45

Tixeront, L. J.: 93

Tixier: 40. See also: Textor

Tmolus: 44, 73

To the Honourable Convention: 116

To All that Love Peace and Truth: 59

To All that Professe Chritianity (George Fox): 147

To Aristus, in Imitation of Milton: 58

"To his Coy Mistress" (Andrew Marvell): 115, 131

"To our Queen": 98

"To the Virgins to make much of Time" (Robert Herrick): 131

Toad, Satan as: 50

Toase, Charles A.: 44

Tobacco-mens' Company: 44

Tobacco: 40

Tobias: 77, 142, 3

Tobit: 142. Book of: 66

Tobol: 49

Tobolsca: 49

<u>Tod des erstne Menschen, Der</u>: 65

<u>Tod Abels, Der</u>: 65

<u>Tod Adams, Der</u>: 65

Todd: 7, 128*, 43. Henry John: 1, 4, 5, 16, 19, 33*, 40, 41, 56, 57, 59, 60, 63, 68, 73, 77, 102, 104, 128*, 132, 144, 142, 62, 88*, 91*, 92, 93, 64, 146, 149, 117*, 55, 21, 94; works: editor of <u>Poetical Works</u>: 44*; the <u>Torah</u>: 142. J., study cited: 80

Toffanin, Giuseppe: 18

Tofte, R.: 59

<u>Toilers of the Sea</u> (Hugo): 1

Toinet, Raymond, <u>Poèmes Heroïques-Epiques</u>: 74

Tokefield, Thomas (clerk): 44

Toland, John: 7, 9, 28*, 40, 41, 44, 45, 58, 59, 63, 70, 73, 86, 102, 116*, 88, 91, 97, 94, 130, 146, 150, 117*, 55. See also: Milton, John, Works: <u>Complete Collection of the Works</u>, with prefatory life of M by John Toland

Toledo, Ohio: 44

Toledo, Spain: 49. 12th Council of: 73

Tolerance: 51. Appeal for: 51. Christian: 51. M on tolerance of opinion: 51

Tolerating a monarch, reproach for: 51

<u>Toleration Act and the Bill of Rights</u>: 147

<u>Toleration Discuss'd</u>: 116

Toleration: 7*, 9*, 51, 114*, 147*, 78*. M's advocacy of: 113. M's last appeal for: 147. Asked 1st by Baptist sect: 147. As Civil War issue: 147. Campaign of London ministers against: 147. Dangers of: 147. In the army: 147. Would nullify Covenant: 147. Zealots in the army: 147. Austin, Barebones Parliament, Bastwick, Burton, Cromwell, Goodwin, Knollys, Lilburne, Overton, Prynne, Saltmarsh, Vane, Vicars, Walwyn, Williams, on the issue of toleration: 147. M on the issue: 143, 147. Toleration of Jews: 93; of Catholics: 147, 93; see also: Catholics. Toleration Acts: 78. In <u>Agreement of the People</u>: 147

Toletus, Franciscus: 40

Toliver, Harold E.: 14, 106

Tolkein, J. R. R.: 64

Tollemache, Wilbraham: 44

Tollinton, Richard B.: 93

Tolomei, C.: 59, 120

Tolouse (Tolosa, Toulouse): 44*, 49, 103

Tolstoy, Leo: 111, 133. <u>Resurrection</u>: 46

<u>Tom Jones</u>: 136

<u>Tom Swift and His Submarine</u>: 1

<u>Tom Tyler and His Wife</u>: 44

Tomasen, Christian: 10

Tomasini, Jacob: 82. Petrarcha Redivivus: 82

Tombes, John: 114

Tome of Leo: 74

Tomis: 3, 21

Tomitano: 73

Tomitanus Ager: 49. See also: Corallaeis

Tomkins: J.: 121. John: 20, 44. Joseph: 44. P. W.: 97. (Tomkyns), Thomas (composer): 28, 44

Tomkis, Thomas: 40, 128

Tomkyns, Rev. Thomas: 28, 44, 103, 116, 94

Tomlins: E. S. and T. E.: 58. Henry: 44. Richard: 10. Richard (bks.): 91. Sir Thomas E.: 45

Tomlinson, Charles: 58, 87. <u>The Sonnet, Its Origin, Structure and Place in Poetry</u>: 87

Tommaseo and Bellini: 120

Tomson, Mr.: 44, 45

Tonal and tempo patterns in <u>Mask</u>, PL: 104

Tone: 121

Tonge, Eres: 44

Tonnage and poundage: 103

Tonson: Messrs. (bks.s): 44. Jacob (the Elder, publisher, bks.): 28, 40, 44*, 58, 86, 116, 88, 91, 94, 97, 149, 150, 117, 55; his nephew, Jacob, the Younger: 44*. Richard (bks.): 44

Tooke: Benjamin (pr.): 44. Christopher: 44

Tooma (Tooina): 49

Toothlesse Satirs (Hall): 20

Tophet: 144, 143

Topia y Rivera, Alejandro: 65

Topic of degree: 51

Topica (Cicero): 20

Topics (Aristotle): 20

Topliff, Nathaniel: 115. Poems, Moral, Descriptive, and Political: 115

Topographical poems: in blank verse: 58*. Not known to be Miltonic: 58

Topos, magna parvis conferre: 118

Topsell, Edward: 60, 105, 128*

Torah, The: 142, 36

Torah: 41

Torchester (Tovechester): 49

Toricelli: 89

Tories (attitude toward M): 87

Torksey: 49

Torments of Hell: 93

Torniellus, Augustinus: 68

Torquatus, Lucius, Manlius: 73

Torquemada, Antonio de: 128*

Torrance, Thomas F.: 93

Torriano, Giovanni: 40

Torricelli, E.: 6, 10, 44

Tortolletti, Bartolommeo: 64. Juditha: 74

Tortona, Italy: 29

Tortuga (Association): 49. See also: Providence

Tossanus: Daniel, Sr.: 10. Daniel, Jr.: 10. Elizabeth: 10. Johanna: 10. Maria: 10. Paul: 10*, 40. Renata: 10. Samuel: 10

Tostadus (Tostatos), Alfonsus (Alonso, Alphonso): 68, 77*

Totalitarian state: 31

Totila: 93

Totness: 49

Tottel, Miscellany: 129

Toucan, cluster in: 89

Touch: 121

Toulouse: 44*, 49, 103

Tournay: 49, 73

Tourneur: Cyril: 15, 33, 35, 86, 108, 21; Atheist's Tragedy: 35. Timothy: 44

Tourreil, Maistre de: 44

Tours, France: 44, 49

Touteville, Daniel: 93

Tovell (Tovey), Nathaniel: 28. See also: Tovey

Tovey: D. C.: 58. Nathaniel (M's tutor): 40*, 42, 44, 84, 137, 55. Richard: 103

Tower: the Tower: 45, 103. Tower House, London: 44. Tower of London: 40, 44, 49. Tower Ward: 44

Towerhill: 49

Towers, Joseph: 44

Towersey: (Dowersey), Elizabeth: see Jackson, Eliz. Jane: 45. Richard: 45. William: 45

Town and gown fighting: 40

Town Hall, London: 44

Town(e), Robert: 79, 114

Towneley Plays: 65, 123, 134, 36

Towneley, Creatio: 143

Townesend gate: 45

Townesend, Richard: 44, 45

Townley, James: 44, 89

Townlye, Zouch: 20

Townsend: 44. Richard H.: 115; Original Poems by a Citizen of Baltimore: 115. G.: 58. H.: 97. John: 44. William: 44

Townshend: Aurelian: 1, 29*, 39, 64, 21. George Ferrars, 3rd Marquis: 44. George John Patrick Dominic, 7th Marquess: 44

Toxophilus (Ascham): 3

Toynbee: Arnold J.: 48*; on the Genesis myths: 48; on myths and modern fiction: 48; Study of History: 74, 48*. Margaret: 44. P.: 58. Paget: 40, 111, 64

Tozer, H. F.: 64

Traces of God: 81

Trachinia(n): 73. Cliffs: 19

Trachiniae (Sophocles): 70, 73, 3

Tractarians: 87

Tractate on Education: 51, 121, 129, 94. On perfection: 83. On the purpose of learning: 60. M's use of the term "Perfection" in: 83. See also: Of Education; Milton, John, Works

Tractatio de Officio Regis (Wycliffe): 83

Tracts, printed: 40

Tracy, John: 40

Trade: 51, 150. Trade winds: 150. M's attitude towards: 8

Trading flood: 150

Tradition(s): 27*, 47, 67, 143, 25. Preserved in symbols: 143. In M's thought: 143. And Scripture: 143. Ancient, in Selden's notes to Polyolbion: 88. Peck on country and foreign: 88. Knowledge of local, Meadowcourt's, Warton's: 88. Country, Warton on: 88. Protestant view of: 93. Value of: 25. Corruption of: 25. Christian: 25

Traditional: 27*. Beliefs, education, methods, practices: 51. Traditional view (M's): 50. Traditionalism: 19, 27

Traducianism: 107, 93. Traducianist (M): 107

Traductions de la Bible (ed. Jean Bonnard): 74

Tragedia von schöpfung: 65

Tragedie Nouvelle de Samson le Fort: 68

Tragedy on Fall of Man: M's drafts for: 149. M's summary of: 149. Grounds for dissatisfaction: 149

Tragedy: 17*, 27*, 40, 50*, 70*, 125, 128, 132, 72*, 146, 117*, 21*, 25. Medieval interpreation of by Manso and Chorus: 125. And insight: 125. And the self: 125. Function of, structure of, subject matter of: 70*. Renaissance theory of: 46. M's ideas on: 132. In PL: 15. "Elegiac": 72. And epic: 149. Restriction of scope of: 149*. Tragedies, Attic: 51

Tragic flaw: 70. Flaw in Samson: 70. Hero: 70. Comedy: 70. Person: 122. Poet, function of: 123. Reversal: 70. Sense: 70. Experience in SA: 125. The final stages of: 125

Tragödie von Verordnung der Stände: 65

Traherne, Thomas: 23, 60, 76, 123, 93, 101, 132, 130. Works: Meditations: 60; Centuries, Poems and Thanksgiving: 60; Commonplace Book: 82

Training: humanitarian, medieval, military: 51

Traitor's Perspective Glass: 103, 116

Trajan, Emperor: 44, 51, 73

Trallis: 73

Transactions of the Royal Irish Academy: 115

Transcendence, experience and idea of: 96*

Transfer of land: 45

Transferred epithets: 118

Transfiguration: 47. See also: Accommodation

Transformations: 104

Transhistory: 47

Transit instrument: 89

Transitions: 51

Translations: 58*; see also: Blank verse; Hexameter; Prose; Rime.

Translation in school: 20*, 40*, 44. Translation, double system: 40. Translations, M's: of letters: 44*; projected, of Homer: 44. M's influence on, unfortunate: 58. Of M: 117*

Transproser Rehears'd, The: 103, 116

Transubstantiation: 93

Transverse: 121

Transversion (structural principle): 67

Transylvania: 49, 73. Transylvanian: 3

Trapaud, E.: 58

Trapnel, Hannah: 38

Trapp: J.: 105, 99*. John: 58, 74, 93; Annotations upon the Old and New Testament: 74*. Joseph: 86, 117

Trask: John: 114. Willard R.: 122

Travel: M on: 51. Travel literature: 128. See also: Bourne; Cowley; Hakluyt; Mandeville

Travelers' Book: 44

Traveller, The (Oliver Goldsmith): 131

Travels into Persia (Travernier): 88

Traver, H.: 36

Travers: Hope: 60, 93, 101. John: 45. Rebecca: 7. Walter: 38

Traversi, D.: 23

Travess, Philip: 44

Travesty: of disputatio: 40. Of epic: 123

Travis, G.: 58

Treason Act: 103

Treason Arraigned, etc. (L'Estrange): 103, 116, 147. See also: R. L'Estrange

Treason: 51

Treasury Books, Calendar of: 45

Treasury, Commissioners of: 44

Treatise of Christian Doctrine: 94. See also: Milton, John, Works

Treatise of Civil Power in Ecclesiastical Causes: 103, 102, 113, 116

Treatise of Execution of Justice: 44, 116

Treatise of Magistracy (attr. to M): 44

Treatise of Monarcy: attr. to M: 44. By Philip Hunton: 147

Treatise of Reformation Without Tarrying for Anie (Robert Browne): 147

Treatise of Schemes and Tropes, A (Sherry): 20

Treatise on the Passions of the Soul (Descartes): 118

Treatise upon Education: 88

Treatise Concerning the Trinity (Gill the Elder): 20

Treatise: 141. Treatises, educational: 51

Treatment of God: 117*

Treaty of Ripon: 103

Trebellius Pollio: 73

Trebisond: 49, 73

Tree of Knowledge: 17*, 24, 41, 47, 123, 128, 144, 32*, 36*, 72, 93. Vine, fig: 36. Allegorical meaning of, type of cross, tree of death, prohibition of, not prohibited: 36*. Effect of: 36*. As instrumental cause of sin: 123. In relation to covenants, to Church: 32. Location of, questions concerning, symbolic meaning of: 32. In PL: 32. See also: Information; Knowledge; Reason; Wisdom

Tree of Life: 17, 24*, 47, 123*, 32*, 36*, 72. As sacrament: 123. In relation to covenants, questions concerning, symbolic meaning of, as pledge: 32. In New Jerusalem: 32. In PL: 32. Analogous to, allegorical meaning of, equated with Tree of Knowledge: 36. Nature, size of, denial of: 36. Location of: 32; in Paradise: 119

Tree: Beerbohm: 39. Sir Herbert: 86

Tree: 96

Trees and plants: 128*. Amarant, apples of Asphaltus, arecca betula, balm, banyan (see Indian fig tree), cassia, Christ's thorn, cinnamon, crocus: 128. Cypress, elm and vine, fennel, haemony, Hellebore, hyacinth, Indian fig tree, lettuce, moly: 128. Mushroom, mulberry, myrrh, nard, nepenthes, pine, spices, sycamore, tree grafting: 128

Tregaskis (bks.): 44

Treip, Mindele: 21

Trelawny, E. J.: 113

Trelcatius, Lucas: 93

Tremellius, John Immanuel: 40, 41, 42, 68, 43, 93

Tremisen: 19, 49, 73. See also: Almansor

Trenchard, John: 44

Trent (Treanta): 49, 3, 43, 130; River: 44, 73. Trent (Tridentum): 49. Trent, Council of: 40, 44, 73, 123; Trentian Council: 71

Trent: W. P.: 63, 143. William: 16

Trevelyan, Sir G. M.: 9, 33*, 54, 144, 147, 143, 101. On Laud's purpose and method: 143. Cites the effect of Bible reading on the national character: 147

Trèves, Gallic School of: 40

Trevir: 49

Trevis, John: 44, 45

Trevisanus, Bernhardus: 7, 100

Trevor-Roper, H. R.: 44, 39

Trevor, Sir John: 44

<u>Trew Law of Free Monarchies</u>: 116

<u>Trial of Elizabeth Duchess Dowager of Kingston for Bigamy, The</u>: 117

Trial: M and the concept of: 52. Of patience and faith: 123*. See also: Temptation

Tribonian: 73. Tribonianus: 54

<u>Tribute to George Coffin Taylor</u>: 44

Trickett, Rachel: 39

Triclinius, Demetrius: 40

Triers, Committee of: 9

Trigge, Francis: 93

Trigonometry: 40, 89. Trigonometric terms: 40

Trilling, Lionel: 60, 86, 87

Trimeter iambic: 40

Trimley (Trymly), co. Suffolk: 44

Trinacrian: 73

Trinculo: 70. Trinculos(e): 73, 3

Trinity: 7, 27, 47, 60*, 63, 103, 113, 139, 144, 36*, 71*, 92. M on the: 113. Portrayal of: 110. Father, Son: 36*. Holy Ghost: 36. In Bible, in tradition, in M: 93. During creation: 93. Metaphors on: 93. Trinitarianism: 71. See also: Anti-Trinitarianism; God; Christ; Messiah

Trinity Act: 78

Trinity College, Cambridge: 40*, 44*, 45, 103, 94, 150. Trinity College, Gale manuscripts: 20. Trinity College Library, Cambridge: 40. Trinity College Manuscript: 17, 19, 28, 29*, 40, 133, 44*, 77, 104, 92, 132*, 94. M's "Outlines for Tragedies": 60. See also: Cambridge MS.

Trinity College, Dublin: 40, 44, 45

Trinity College, Oxford: 40, 44, 45

Triolo, Alfred: 21

Triones: 3

<u>Trionfa della Castita</u> (Petrarch): 70

<u>Trionfi</u> (Petrarch): 29

Tripart method of expounding a text: 40

Tripe, A.: 58

Triple equation: 99*

Triple Tyrant: 73

<u>Triplex vita</u>. See Active life; Contemplative life; Voluptuous life; Paris, Judgement of

Tripos at Cambridge: 40

Triptolemus: 73, 3

Trismegistus, Hermes: 60

Trissino, Giovanni Giorgio: 1, 4, 6, 50, 56, 66, 120, 122*, 123, 129, 64, 130*, 117. Works: <u>Italia Liberata</u>: 74; <u>Poetica</u>: 74; <u>Quinta et la Sesta Divisione della Poetica</u>: 74

Tristan: 139

Tristitiae Remedium: 103, 121

Tritheim, Johann (Trithemius, John: 114, 142. Octo Quaestionem Libellus: 142

Triton: 49, 126, 72. Ocean's trumpets: 73, 90, 104. River: 73, 144. See also: Irassa; Nyseian Isle

"Tritum est vetustate proverbium" (M's): 44

Triumph of Beauty (Shirley): 29

Triumph of Peace (Shirley): 29

Triumph: 103

Triumphs: 29

"Triumphs of Oriana": 44, 113, 121

"Triumphs: Spectacle vs. Sense" (Furniss): 29

Trivial arts: 40

"Trivial Education of John Milton, The (Clark): 20

Trivium: 40, 103, 3. Trivial-quadrivial curriculum: 45. Trivium, linguistic arts of the: 20

Trivulzeana Library: 40

Troas: 49

Trobridge, John: 44

Troeltsch, Ernst: 7, 60, 32, 93

Trogus, Pompeius: 40

Troilus and Creseide (Chaucer): 134, 88

Troilus and Cressida (Shakespeare): 88, 130

Trojan(s): 71. Dardanian: 44

Trojetes: 49

Trollope, A. W.: 35, 58

Tromp: 120. Admiral: 103

Tron Church, Edinburgh: 44

Tronchin, Theodore: 40

Tronsarelli, Ottavio: 29, 64

Tropes, meaning, parts: 20

Trophonii Antrum: 49

Trophonius: 73, 3

Tropology, as form of Biblical interpreation: 68

Trost, Martin, Hebrew Grammar: 42

Trot, Robert (bks., 1645-9): 91

Trotman, Mr.: 44

Trott, John: 44

Trotter, Elizabeth: 44

Troy (Ilium, Ilion, Pergamus, Troia): 19, 44, 49, 70, 90, 3, 72, 92. See also: Dardanius

Troy, W.: 23

Troyes: 49

True and Infernal Friendship, Or the Wisdom of Eve: 115

True and Perfect Narrative of the Inhumane Practices: 116

True and Perfect Picture of our Present Reformation: 44

True Account and Declaration of the Horrid Conspiracy: 116

True Account of the Author of a Book Entitled Eikon Basilike: 116

True Character of an Untrue Bishop (attr. to M): 44

True Description...Cardinal Wolsey ...and William Laud (attr. to M): 44

True Difference between Christian Subjection and Unnatural Rebellion: 116

True Narrative of the Horrid Plot and Conspiracy: 116

True Notion of Passive Obedience Stated, The: 116

True Patriot, The: 117

True Protestant Bridle: 116

True Protestant Mercury: 116

True Relation of the State of the Case (by a Rump apologist): 103, 147

True Religion, Heresy, Schism, Toleration: 113

True State of the Case (Army): 147

Truelove: family: 44. Anne (cousin): 44. Henry (cousin): 44. Katherine (cousin): 44. Margaret (great-aunt): 44. Margaret (cousin): 44. Margaret Jeffrey (aunt): 44.

Paul (cousin): 44. Richard (cousin): 44. Robert (cousin): 44. Sara (cousin): 44. William (uncle, great-uncle, cousin): 40, 44

Truisms: absurd, in Paterson's notes: 88. Massey's, The Monthly Review on: 88

Trumbull: Benjamin: 115; An Appeal to the Public, Especially to the Learned, with Respect to the Unlawfulness of Divorces: 115. John: 71, 115*; works: M'Fingal: 115*; Ode to Sleep: 115; The Progress of Dulness: 115. Sir William: 44

Trumpington Road: 40. Trumpington Street, Cambridge: 40

Trusler, John: 25

Trussel, John: 40

Trust: 51. In perpetual grand council: 51. In royalty, Presbyterian: 51. In God: 51; form and effect of saving faith: 123; opposite of carnal reliance, idolotry, presumption, and distrust: 123

Trustees for sale of King's Goods: 44

Truth and Innocence Vindicated: 116

Truth Brought to Light: 44, 116

Truth: 7, 47, 51*, 60, 122*, 128, 11, 96. New: 51. Present: 51. Birth of: 128. In poetry, Peck on: 88. Figure in "Nativity Ode": 29

Truthtellers, the need of, in Parliament: 83

Tryals of Thomas Walcot, William Hone, The: 116

Trymly. See Trimley

Tryon, Thomas: 7

Tryphiodorus: 40

Tsanoff, Radoslav A., "The Notion of Perfection": 83

Tschirch, Fritz: 100

Tsikal: 68

Tubal-Cain: 73, 127, 123

Tübingen, Germany: 44

Tucker, W. J.: 58

Tuckney, Anthony: 40, 114

Tuckwell, W.: 33

Tudman, Mr.: 44

Tudor School-boy Life (Watson): 3

Tudor(s): 103. Political theory: 83

Tudor, Mary: 128. False pregnancies: 128

Tuer, Andrew E.: 40

Tuition: 40

Tuke, Thomas: 93

Tullibardine, Lord: 44

Tullius: Tully: see Cicero. Tullius Marcus: see Cicero

Tulloch, John: 7, 15, 40, 63, 87, 112. On M's Puritan temperament: 87. On M's Puritanism: 87. On De Doctrina Christiana: 87. Eng. Puritanism and Its Leaders: 87

Tully: 2, 20. See also: Cicero

Tunbridge Grammar School: 40

Tune (Tine): 73

Tung, Mason, on PL: 104

Tuningus, Gerardus: 73

Tunis: 19, 44

Tunstall: 3

Tupper: F.: 92. J. W.: 68, 113, 92

Turberville, George: 40, 58, 64, 77. Eglogs: 77

Turchestan: 49, 73

Turell, Ebenezer: 115. The Life and Character of The Rev. Colman: 115

Turenne (Thurenne), Henri de la Tour d'Auvergne, Vicomte de, Marshal of France: 10. And his wife: 44

Turin: 70, 103

Turk's Head: the: 51. Bookshop: 44. Sign, London: 44. Tavern: 103

Turkestan: 19

Turkey (and Turks): 19, 31, 44, 103. Turkish: 49; tyrants: 60; see also: Bizance. Turks: 19, 44, 51, 103; as scourges of God: 93

Turkish Historie: 40

Turley, Edward: 44

Turmel, Joseph: 93

Turn-again Lane (satirical name): 44

Turnbull: Gavin: 58. George Henry: 40, 44*

Turner: Mr.: 44. A. T. and W. A.: 6. Albert M.: 89, 87. Amy Lee: 128. Christopher: 44. Dawson: 44. Rev. Everett S.: 44. Francis: 116. John: 44. Joseph: 118. J. M. W.: 87, 97. Paul: 37, 134. Robert: 40, 142; translations by: 142. Professor W. Arthur (and Mrs.): 44*; on M: 80

Turnham Green: 44, 103

Turning of verses: 20

Turns of Words and Thoughts: 145

Turnus: 1, 2, 17, 56*, 60, 73, 90, 123, 3. See also: Virgil

Turon de Beyrie, Marquis: 44

Turon: 49

Turpin: 73

Turquet, Lewis de Mayerne: 128

Turretin (Turrettini): family: 30, 73. Two brothers in Geneva: 44

Tursellinus, Horatius: 117

Turyn, Alexander: 40

Tuscan(y) (Hetrurian, Thuscan, Etruria, Hetrusca Ditio, Thuscus): 44, 73, 49. Grand Duke of: 6, 103. Tuscan: artist, the: 73, 89; see also: Galileo. Tuscan: air: 121, 3; mariners transformed: 73; verse: 40; tongue: 3. See also: Italian; Florence

Tusculan Disputations (Cicero): 112

Tusculan: 3. Tusculun... retirements: 73

Tusculum: 44, 49

Tusser, Thomas: 40

Tutbury: 73. Horse fair: 40

Tutor(s): function and role of: 40, 51. M's: 40, 44*. Royal: 40. Tutoring (M and): 19, 44*

Tuve, Rosemond: 12, 15, 17, 23*, 29, 34, 37, 52, 66, 69, 79, 86, 104, 123, 128, 145, 14, 143, 39, 53, 72, 93, 64, 101*, 21. Metaphors and images in _Lycidas_: 61. On M's imagery: 61. And orthodoxy: 61. On pagan and Christian elements in M: 61

Tuveson, Ernest L.: 23, 104, 93, 101, 148

Tuvil, Daniel: 114, 144, 93

Tweed River: 44, 49, 73, 3

Twelfth Century Homilies: 99

Twelfth Night: 134

Twells: 94

Twelve Tables, the Roman: 3

Twenty Thousand Leagues Under the Sea: 1

"Twicknam Garden" (John Donne): 131

Twining, T.: 58, 92

Twisden, Sir William: 40

Twiss: H.: 58. Sir Travers: 116

Twisse, William: 114, 38

Two cities: 93

Two Choice and Useful Treatises: 142

Two Cranes Court, London: 44

"Two handed engine": 73. As rod: 104. As sword: 104

Two Letters: 78*. See also: Historical Account

Two Speeches: 116

Two Temples, the: 98

Two Views of Education (Cooper): 3

Twyn, John (pr.): 44, 116

Twynne, Thomas: 40, 128

Tyard, Pontus de: 93

Tyburn, London: 44, 103

Tyche. See Chance

Tycho Brahe: 40, 89*, 114. "Urianenburg": 89. Astronomical work of: 89. The "Tychonic" hypothesis: 89. View as to the stars: 89. Death: 89. See also: Tychonic systems

Tychonic systems: 102

Tye, Thomas: 121

Tyers: J.: 97. Thomas: 44

Tyffe, Mr.: 44

Tyler, Moses C.: 44, 115

Tylston, Dr. Thomas (also his son): 44

Tymberlacke. See Timberlake

Tymme, Thomas: 77, 128, 32, 93. Dial. Phil., 1612: 77

Tympani: 40

Tyndale, William: 33, 40, 79, 116, 147, 143, 22, 93, 149. And Christian faith: 143. And ivy tree: 143. On Romish ceremonies: 143. Translates Bible and is burned: 147. His New Testament: 143

Tyndarus: 73

Tynley, Robert: 93

Type-typet: 73

Type characterization in epic and traditional drama: 118

Typee: 98, 136

Types and typology: theory of: 79*. In "Lycidas": 79. Rhetorical function of: 79. In PL:, SA: 79. See also: Allegory; Typology

Typhlos: 73

Typhon (Typhoean, Typhoeus): 56, 57, 60, 90, 144, 3, 72, 73

Typographical Antiquities (Ames): 135

Typology: 15, 67, 123, 93. Christian: 96*. See also: Types

Tyrannical Government Anatomized (trans. of Buchanan's Baptistes, attr. to M): 44

Tyrannicide: 9*

Tyrant(s): 122, 51*, 147. Definition of: 51. Just punishment of: 51. Arguments for deposing, church divines sanction death of, liberty dependent on death of, punishment of, treatment of, heathens' treatment: 51. And men of destiny: 147

Tyras (Tyral): 49

Tyre (Sarra): 49, 144

Tyro, Marcus Tullius: 73

Tyrrany: 9*, 17, 51*, 113, 123, 144*, 46, 93. Hatred of: 51. M's denunciation: 51. M's conception of: 113. Popularity as theme in exercises: 20. Symbolized by Babylon and Egypt: 46. Tyrannical: characters of monarchy: 51; methods: 51; policy: 51; interpretation: 109

Tyrrell: Mrs.: 44. Alice: 44. Anthony: 45. James (1642-1718): 45, 91. Sir James: 44, 45, 116. Johan: 44. John: 44. Sir John: 45. Richard: 44. Sir Thomas: 45. Sir Timothy: 45

Tyrrhen Sea (Southern Sea, Tyrrhenus Pontus): 49, 73. See also: Circe's Island

Tyrrhenia: 144

Tyrtaeus: 40

Tyrwhitt, Thomas: 88

Tyson, M.: 58

Tythe-Takers Cart Overthrown (Lupton): 147

Tythes no Maintenance for Gospel Ministers: 147

Tythes No Property to, nor Lawful Maintenance for a Powerful Gospel-preaching Ministry (John Crook): 147

Tytler: A. F.: 58. H. W.: 58

Tyton, Francis (pr.): 44

Tzetzes, Johannes: 73, 90, 123

Tzidkiel: 41

-U-

Uberti, F. degli: 6

Ubertinus (Hubertinus, Clericus Crescentinas): 123

Ucalegonium: 49, 73

Uccello: 15

Udall: John: 40, 42, 93, 99*; Combate betwixt Christ and the Devill: 74. Nicholas: 20, 40; see Erasmus, Paraphrase

Ueber den Ursprung des Uebels: 65

Uffenbach, Zacharias Conrad von: 117

Ugolino: 111, 97

Ugolinus, Blasius: 22

Ulac, A. See Vlaccus, A.; Vlac(q)

Uladislau: 49

Ulfeldt, Corfitz: 10

Ullmann, Walter: 93

Ulloa, Alfonso d': 40

Ulpian: 116

Ulrich: Rev. Mr.: 44. Hans Jacob: 10. Heinrich: 10

Ulro: 25

Ulster (Ultonia): 49, 73, 103

Ultima Thule: 19

Ultimate reality, as expressed in music: 121

Ulugh-beg: 89

Ulysses: 1, 2, 12, 19, 29, 44, 51, 70, 90*, 103, 73, 111, 3, 11, 32, 97, 130. See also: Homer; Odyssey

"Ulysses Errores": 144

Unamuno y Jugo, Miguel de: 60

Uncle Tom's Cabin (H. B. Stowe): 118

Uncommon: expressions, Pearce's liberal attitude towards: 88. Newton's objections to, unless classical: 88. See also: Eccentricity; Strangeness

Uncritical: method, Peck's: 88. Acceptance of other peoples' opinions, Peck's analysis of: 88

Under-Woods (Jonson): 45, 135

Undergraduate work: 40

Underhill: Edmund: 45. Evelyn: 7, 75, 110. Thomas (pr.-bks., 1641- 59): 7, 44, 91, 55

Understanding: 51

Underwood, John (scrivener): 44

Undines: 142

Unemotional method, Newton's: 88

Unequals: argument from: 123*. Negation of: 123

Ungeleichen Kinder Eve, Die: 65

Unger: Dominick J.: 93. Emma, and William A. Jackson: 44*

Unhappy endings: 92

Union List of Serials: 44

Union Theological Seminary: 44

Union: 96. And fellowship with Christ: 63. Between a commonwealth and Christianity: 51

Unison: 121

Unitarian(s): 71, 78*. Unitarianism: 63. Unitarian Tracts: 78*

United Netherlands: 51

United Provinces (Batavia, Foederatae Provinciae): 49, 51. See also: Low Countries; Netherlands

United States: 45. Cumulative Book Auction Records: 44. Literary Gazette: 63. United States Magazine, The: 115

Units of attention: 51

Unity(ies): 50, 51, 113. Among all Protestant sects: 51. Of body and soul in M's thought: 113. Of God, of man and God: 113. Of time and action: 123. The 3 unities: 70, 92

Universal Asylum and Columbian Magazine, The: 115

Universal Magazine, The: 115

Universal Spectator: 88

Universal: histories: 93. Insight: 51. Universality: of appeal: 51; of music: 121

Universe as Pictured in Milton's PL, The: 112

Universe: 50, 128. Man less than: 73. Infinite: 128. Theological: 128. Cyclic: 107. M's views of: 128. See also: Copernicus; Milton; Ptolemy; Creation; Nature; Providence

Universiteits-Bibliotheek, Amsterdam: 44

Universities of Europe in the Middle Ages (Rashdall): 3

Universities: criticism of: 114*. M's idea about: 20, 113. Changes by 1600: 40

University microfilms: 44

University of Michigan Press: 112

University of Toronto Quarterly: 44

University wits: 133

University Carrier: 121. See also: Milton, John, Works

University College, Oxford (windows): 81

Unlimited Prerogative of Kings Subverted: 60

Unorthodoxy, M and: 44, 51, 107

Unrhymed lines compared by Peck to discords: 88

Unrighteous Judge (John Goodwin): 147

Untaught Bard: An Original Work, The: 115

Unwin, William: 117

Upcott, William: 25

Upis: 73, 3

Upleadon (Temple Court), co. Hereford: 44

"Upon a Fly" (attr. to M): 44

Upon the Circumcision: 112. See also: Milton, John, Works

Upper Bench, Court of: 44

Upright posture of man: 93. Of serpent: 93

Upsala, Sweden: 44

Upton: Elizabeth (Bence): 45. Joane (Stow): 45. John: 44, 45, 56, 88, 117; Critical Observations on Shakespeare: 95. Mary: see Knightley, Mary. W.: 53

Ur: 19, 49, 73

Urania (muse): 1, 41, 42, 44, 60, 70, 73, 89, 90, 103, 111, 113, 144, 3, 71, 72, 109. See also: Muse

Urania, or the Heavenly Muse: 65

Urania, sive De Stellis: 65

Uranie, ou Muse Celèste, L': 65

Uranologie: 65

Uranus: 34, 57, 73, 89, 90. See also: Heaven

Urban VIII, Pope: 6*, 44

Urbana, Illinois: 44

Urbanus Sylvan: 117

Ure, Peter: 60

Urfé, Anne D': works: Hymne de Saincte Susanne: 74; Julic: 74

Uriah: 73

Uriel: 1, 2, 17, 31, 41, 50, 57, 63, 70, 73, 76, 89, 98, 102, 112, 111, 123, 127, 128, 142*, 144, 71, 130, 55, 140, 72

Urim: 100. Urim and Thummim: 41, 73, 98. See also: Chariot of Paternal Deity; Enthronement of Christ

Urizen (character): 146*, 25. As tyrant: 25. And Satan: 25. As destroyer: 25. See also: Jehovah; Satan

Urizen, The Book of: 25. Its epic impulse: 25. And Genesis: 25

Urn-Burial (Thomas Browne): 34, 131

Urquhart, Sir Thomas: 44, 59

Urreta, Friar Luis di: 32

Ursinus, Zacharias (real name Bar): 40, 41, 47, 63, 73, 123, 142, 32, 93; Summe of Christian Religion (trans. Dr. Henry Parry): 74, 142. Ursinus Cathechism: 40. On freedom: 47

Urstisius: 44, 3

Urstitius (Wurstisen), Christian: 40

Urthona: 25. See also: Los

Uruk: 36

Usa. See Ouse River

Use of Daily Publick Prayers: 9

Useful art: 70

Uselessness of kingship: 51

Usher. See Ussher

Ushers and submasters: 40

Usk, co. Monmouth: 44. Usk (Osca) River: 49

Usnea: 16

Ussher: G. Neville: 115; The Elements of Eng. Grammar: 115. Abp. James of Armagh: 10, 30, 40, 42, 44, 45, 51, 54, 60, 63, 84, 102, 118, 113, 134, 136, 142, 143, 22, 26, 32, 91, 101, 148, 117, 55, 94, 137; on Christ the Mediator: 143; a better paradise: 143; and baptism: 143; and creation: 143; and age of world: 143; works: Judgment of Dr. Rainolds Touching the Originall of Episcopacy: 57; A Body of Divinity: 142; The Whole Works: 142. John: 9, 115

Ustiug: 49

Usurpation: 47. See also: Self-deification

Usury: 45. Usurer: 45

Uther: 44, 73.

Utilitarianism, Meadowcourt's literary, and classicism: 88

Utley, Francis L.: 44, 92

Utmost Isles: 49. See also: Thule

<u>Utopia</u> (Sir Thomas More): 52, 112. Utopian plan: 51

Utopia: 73, 136, 143. Born of crisis: 147. Politics: 3. Utopian schemes, M on: 80. Utopianism: 60, 38*

Utrecht (Ultrajectum), Netherlands: 44. Compact of: 51

<u>Utter Routing of the whole Army of all the Independents and Sectaries</u> (John Bastwick): 147

Uwins, T.: 97

Uxbridge: 40, 49, 73

Uzzah: 114

Uzzean: 49, 73

Uzziah: 73

Uzziel: 41, 73, 142, 72

-V-

V., J.: 44. See also: Upton, John

<u>Vacation Exercise</u>: 112, 129, 132. See also: Milton, John, Works

Vacation(s) in the country (M's): 44

Vaccus: 30

Vadianus (Joachim Von Watt): 32

Vagueness: and dreaminess appeal to Hume: 88. Or subtlety of mood, Bentley's inability to appreciate or analyze: 88. And irrational suggestiveness, Pearce's valuation of: 88. Pearce on M's technique of handling vague mental states: 88. Of effect appreciated by the Richardsons: 88. Stimulating, Warburton on: 88. Suggestive, Massey on: 88. Stimulating effect of: 88

Vahlen: 132

Vaiguts: 49. See also: Pechora

Vala: 25. See also: <u>The Four Zoas</u>

Valdarno: 49, 73. See also: Arno; Florence

Valderama, R. P. P.: 142. <u>Histoire General du Monde</u>: 142

Valdes: Juan: 114. Pierre: 59, 120

"Valediction Forbidding Mourning" (John Donne): 63, 131. "Valediction of Weeping" (John Donne): 131

Valencia: 3

Valency: M. J.: 122. Maurice: 93

Valens (Emperor): 73

Valentine: 120. Henry: 93. T.: 59

Valentinia(n): 49, 3; see also: Wall of Severus. The Gnostic: 79. The Great, Roman Emperor: 44. Valentinian II: 73; Valentinian III: 73

Valentinus: Basilius: 7. Gregorius: 60

Valerianus, Joannes Pierius: 123

Valerius Flaccus: 90. See also: Flaccus

Valerius Maximus: 20, 40, 128, 88

Valerius Publicola ("friend of the people"): 73

Valéry, Paul: 12, 65, 14, 39

Valiant-for-Truth, Mr.: 143

Valier, Bertucci, Doge (Duke) of Venice: 44

Valla, Lorenzo della: 18, 4, 20, 40, 74, 114, 142, 22, 92, 93

Valle, Jerome: 74, 64. <u>Jhesuida</u>: 74

Vallombrosa: 19, 44, 49, 73, 72

Vallongnes, Pierre de: 64

Valmarana, Odoricus (Odorico): 1, 60, 65, 77*, 122, 123, 88. <u>Daemonomachie</u>: 74

Valori: Mr.: 44. Baccio: 44

Valour: 122*

Valpy: R.: 58. T. R.: 97

Values: 51. Scale of: 31. Aesthetic: 51. Traditional nature of in PL: 118

Valvasone, Erasmo di: 1, 15, 65, 77, 122, 123, 141, 142, 64. Works:

Angeleida: 74, 142, 77; LaGrime di Santa Maria Maddelena: 74

Van de Perre, Paulus: 44. See also: Dutch agents

Van der Gucht, Benjamin (painter): 28, 44. J.: 97. Michael (engraver): 44

Van der Noot (identified as Diggon Davie): 83

Van der Plas, Pieter (painter, M portrait): 44

Van Aizema, Leo: 30. See also: Aizema

Van Buren, Paul: 93

Van Cleve, Edward M.: 16

Van Dale, Anthony: 142

Van Den Vondel, Joost. See Vondel

Van Doren: Carl: 98. Mark, comments of, on PL: 83, 110; and M's faults: 143

Van Dyke: (Dyck), Sir Anthony (painter): 44, 103. Henry: 16

Van Eyck: 90

Van Helmont, Jean Baptiste: 142. Two Hundred Queries: 142

Van Noppen, L.: 149

Van Sinderen, Mr. and Mrs. Adrian: 44

Van Tieghem, Paul, Littérature Latine de la Renaissance: 74

Van Trompe, Admiral: 59

Van Unik, W. C.: 36

Van Vechten, Carl: 60

van Zanten, Jacob: 117

Vandals: 71. See also: Christina, Queen; Charles X; Frederick III; Frederick William

Vandelli, G.: 5

Vanderbank, J.: 97

Vane: 51. Charles: 44, 59, 103. Sir Henry: 7, 9*, 10, 28, 44*, 59, 60, 79, 103, 113, 114, 116, 84, 40, 120, 142, 147, 26, 32, 82, 91, 94, 146, 117; leader of Parliamentary Independents: 147; on state church: 147; on toleration: 147; and state church issue: 147; influence on Parliament: 147; trial and execution of: 147; works: A Healing Question Propounded and Resolved...with a Desire to apply Balsome to the Wound before it becomes incurable: 147; The Retired Man's Meditations: (inveighs against magistrates in): 142, 147; see also: M's sonnet XVII. Sir Henry (the Younger): 44, 59, 38*. Lady Frances: 44, 91

Vanhomrigh, Miss: 58

Vanière, J.: 58

Vanini, Lucilio: 114

Vanists: 7

Vanities, Limbo of: 123

Vanity of the Present Churches: 9, 147. Of and in learning: 114

Vanity: 51, 122*. See also: Merit

Vanlore: Lady Mary: see Powell, Lady Mary. Sir Peter: 45

Vann, Gerald: 93

Vapors: 128

Varchi, Benedetto: 5, 6, 40, 44, 60, 120, 122, 123, 64. Works: Della Poesia: 74; Hercolano: 74

Vardanes: 19

Variana: 49, 73

Varier: 40

Variety: 51. M's, in PL: 50

Varinus: 128

Variorum edition of Spenser's Minor Poems: 83

Variorum edition of Milton: Newton's: 88. Todd's: 88

Varius: 123, 21

Varley: F. J.: 45. Mrs. J.: 44

Varro, Marcus Terentius: 18, 40, 44, 57, 70, 73, 74, 100, 114, 123, 128, 3

Varthema: 19

"Varying the Phrase": 20

Vasari, Giorgio: 5, 27

Vasco da Gama: 150

Vashti: 73

Vasilowich, Ivan: 19

Vasletus, Ludovicus: 40

Vatablus, Francis(cus): 41, 42, 73, 22, 32

Vates, M as: 87

<u>Vathek</u>: 15

Vatican: 44, 49, 103, 3. Visit to: 30

Vatinius, Publius: 73

Vaudemont, Mlle. de: 29

Vaudois: 103, 94. See also: Piedmont

Vaudoyer, L.: 97

Vaudray, Mr.: 44, 45

Vaughan: Edward: 68. Henry: 12, 15, 16, 18, 23, 44*, 59, 60, 76, 79, 81*, 84, 86, 114, 123, 128, 145*, 38, 85, 91, 93, 101, 109, 131, 55; compared with M: 80; Biblical allusions, use of; childhood, concept of; digressive movement, "early days," concept of; eucharistic poems; Herbert's influence; illumination, experience of; nature-imagery, use of; pre-existence, concept of; secular poems: 81*. Lord: see Carbery. Richard: see Carbery. Robert: 44. Thomas: 7, 81, 114, 123, 128*, 142, 93; works: <u>The Works</u>: 142; <u>Anima Magica Abscondita</u>: 142. Sir William (W. W.): 40, 44, 114, 93

Vauquelin de la Fresnaye, Jean: works: <u>Art Poetique Francois</u>: 74; <u>Israelide</u>: 74

Vautrollier, Thomas (pr.): 44

Vauts, Moses à: 54

Vauvenarques, Marquis de: 60

Vaux: Edward: 103. George: 44

Vauxhall: 58. Pleasure Gardens of: 97

Vavasour, Sir William: 44

Vavassor, Francis: 44

Veale: Mr.: 44, 45. Abraham: 40

Veblin, Thorsten: 114

Vecchi: Horatio: 6. Orazio: 44, 121

Vedelin: 94

Veer, Gerrit de: 19

Vega Carpio, Lope de: 58, 65

Vega, Garcilaso de la: 64

Vegetius: 128

Vegius: 40. Maphaeus, "13th Book" of <u>Aeneid</u>: 74. See also: Virgil, <u>Aeneid</u>

Vehemence: 53. And rhetoric: 53. In PL: 53. Vehement language: 51; vehemence in M's language: 66*

Velasquez, Diego: 35, 39

Veldkamp, J.: 113

Velle, Pietro Della: 121

Vellutello: 111

Venables, G. S.: 58

Vendler, Helen Hennessy: 14, 101

Vengeance: 122

Venice (Veneta Respublica, Venetiae): 19, 29, 44*, 49, 103, 94, 3. M's visit to: 6. Great Council of: 51. Venetians: 44. See also: Contarini; Valier

<u>Venite</u>: 126

Venn: 120. J. A.: 45. Dr. J.: 134. John (and J. A.): 40*, 44*, 45*. Col. John: 91

Venner, Thomas: 114, 38

Venning, Ralph: 114, 93, 109

Venosa, Italy: 44. Prince of: 121

Vent, the: 45

Ventris: Mr.: 44. Michael: 118

Venus (Amathusia, Cytherea, Heavenly Beauty): 2, 17, 29, 44, 56, 60, 69*, 89, 90*, 128, 144, 3, 32, 72, 25. Genetrix: 72

Venus (Hesperus): 89*. Atmosphere, axis, brilliancy of, density of, diameter of, distance from the sun: 89. Evening star as, light and heat received by, morning stars as, orbit of, phases: 89. Revolution, rotation, no satellite, surface of, vegetation on: 89. Organisms on, M. E. Perrier's hypothesis: 89. Accurate definition of, impossible: 89. Transit of: 89

<u>Venus and Adonis</u>: 70, 139, 71, 88

Venus de Milo: 5

Venusian poet. See Horace

Verallo, Giacinto: 65, 77

<u>Verax Prodromum in Delirium</u>: 44, 91

Verax, Theodorus: 103. "Verax, T.": 59. See also: Walker, Clement

Verbal curiosities in poetry: 30

<u>Verbal Index to Milton's PL</u>: 117

Verbeke, Gerard: 5

Verdant Isles: 49. See also: Azores; Green Cape

Verden. See Charles X

Verdeyn, René: 40

Verdi: 6

Verdier, Anthony du: 60

Verdune, John: 73

Verdüssen, Jerome (Hieronymus) (Dutch pr.): 44, 91

Verepaeus, textbook by: 20

Vergateria: 49

Vergerius, P. P.: 40, 60

Vergil. See Virgil

Vergil, Polydore: 40, 128, 93, 32

Vergilii evangelisantis Christiados libri XIII: 65

Vergivian. See Irish Sea

Vergivium...salum: 73

Verheiden, Jacobus: 73

Verisimilitude: 70, 122. In poetic characters: 123*

Veritas: 90

Verity, A. W.: 1, 15, 16, 19*, 23, 33*, 40, 44, 57, 59, 60, 63, 68, 73, 86, 87, 89, 110, 123, 128*, 132, 142, 144, 88, 92*, 148, 150. On M: 80. Editor of <u>Comus</u> and <u>Lycidas</u>: 44. See also: Milton, John, Works: PL:

Verity: 41*, 3, 43

Vermandois (Vermanduiorum Agrum): 49

Vermeer, Johannes: 27

Vermigli, Pietro Martire (Peter Martyr): 68, 122, 123, 93

<u>Vermont Baptist Missionary Magazine</u>: 115

Vernacular: 5, 30*, 40

Verne, Jules: 1, 135

<u>Verney Papers, The</u>: 45. Verney case, the: 38

Verney: Sir Edmund: 44. Frances P.: 44. Sir Ralph: 44

Vernon MS.: 36

Vernon: Judith: 44. George: 44. Ralph: 40. William Warren: 111

Vernulaeus, Nicolaus: 40

Verona, Italy: 44, 49, 103, 3. Veronese: 139

Verrall: A. W.: 44. John: 125

Verrall: 35

Verres, Caius (Gaius): 51, 73, 3

Verrio, A.: 97

Versatility: in music: 121. Peck's, advantages of: 88

Verschaeve, Cyriel, <u>Vondel's Trilogie</u>: 95

Verse: 121. And Voice, as sirens: 72. Rhymed, discussed: 55. Verse form(s): Latin: 40; of Middle Ages and Renaissance: 40. Writing exercises in: 20*, 40. Technique of, Thynne on: 88. Hume's appreciation of valuable irregularities in M's: 88. Bentley on, Newton and Dunster on M's: 88. Classical theory of, misapplied by Bentley: 88. Little attention paid by Pearce to M's: 88. Irregularities in M's, recognized as deliberate by Pearce: 88. Studied by the Richardsons according to their personal acoustic impressions: 88. Richardsons on adaptation of, to subject: 88. Richardsons on classical models of M's: 88. Richardsons on analysis of, superior to that of later critics: 88. Peck on verse, on music and, on deliberateness of M's handling of: 88. Calton's liberality in matters of (admits hypercatalectic verse, opposed to Newton's conservatism in metrical problems): 88. Sympson appreciates the variety of M's, contrasting it with classicist monotony: 88. Warton does not understand the technique of M's: 88. Lofft on, of PL: 88. Dunster on technique of, and classical allusions as mere decorations of poetry: 88. Dunster shows Newton's misapplication of classical principles in dealing with M's: 88. Of Comus, Todd on: 88. Stillingfleet on: 88. Todd's erudtion in matters of: 88. Todd's treatment of M's: 88

Versification, individual titles of: On the Death of a Fair Infant; Vacation Exercise; On the Morning of Christ's Nativity; On Shakespeare; On the Univ. Carrier; An Epitaph on the Marchioness of Winchester; L'Allegro; Il Penseroso; On Time; At a Solemn Music; On the Circumcision; Lycidas: 55. See also: Milton, John, Works

Versification: 40, 70, 55*. And rhyme: 117*. M's: 129. SA: 55. 18th c. criticism: 55. See also: Style; Verse forms

Verstigan. See Rowlands

Versündigte und begnadigte Aelteren: 65

Vertue: George (artist, engraver, M portrait): 28, 44*, 70, 97, 55. Henry: 54; Christ and the Church: Or, Parallels: 74

Vertumnus: 1, 73, 90

Verulam (St. Albans): 49

Verunas: 44

Verus: 73

Verwey, H. de la Fontaine: 44

Very Copy of a Paper Delivered to the Sheriff's, The: 116

Very, Jones: 115

Vesalius, Andreas: 16

Vesey. See Veysey

Vesing, Mr.: 44

Vespasian, Emperor: 73, 38

Vespucci, Amerigo: 6, 128

Vessey (Vessy), Capt. Robert: 44

Vesta: 60, 73, 90*, 144, 72

Vestiary symbolism: 122

Vesuvius: 19

Vetch, Major, Milton at Rome: 87

Vettori, Mr.: 44, 70

Vetus Comoedia: 73, 3

Vetus Interpretes (Vulgate): 40

Veysey (Vesey): Richard (innkeeper): 44, 45. Robert: 45. Walter: 45

Via media, in polity: 114

Via Jacobaea, Paris: 44

Viarre, Simone: 39

Vibration: 121

Vicar of Hell (Sir Francis Brian or Bryan): 73

"Vicarius": 58

Vicarious atonement: 113

Vicars: John: 144, 93; expresses his fears of toleration in The Schismatick Sifted: 147. Thomas: 20, 40

Vicary, Thomas: 123

Vice-chancellor: 72. Of Cambridge Univ.: 40

Vice: 51. Figured by bestial shapes: 123

Vicente, Gil: 65

Vicious and profane persons: 44

Vickars, Samuel: 40

Vico Mercurio: 40

Vico, Giambattista: 139

Vicomercato, Francesco: 18

Vicqfort, D.: 44

Victor I, "Bp. of Rome": 73, 91. B.: 58. Claudius Marius: 65, 74, 32, 36*, 64; Alethia(s): 74, 36*

Victoria and Albert Museum, London: 44

Victoria Art Gallery, Melbourne: 44

Victoria County History of Buckingham: 44

Victoria County History, Suffolk: 40

Victoria, Queen: 40, 142

Victoria: 144

Victorians and M: 87*, 136. M's effect on: 87. Reaction to PL: 87. Varied responses to M: 87. M's kinship with: 87. Interest in biography: 87. Double personality of: 87. Concept of the sonnet: 87. Attitude toward the sonnet: 87. Taste for Sublime in art: 87. Taste for religious lit.: 87. Attitude toward Satan of PR: 87. Less of belief in supernatural: 87. Decline in religious imagination: 87. Regarded M as Puritan: 87*. Reaction to Dr. Johnson: 87. Interest in M's form, style, metrical skill: 87. Attitude toward M's theology after 1850: 87*. Change in attitude toward Bible: 87. Effect of scientific developments on: 87. Lack of interest in M's religious ideas: 87. Effect of Bible criticism on: 87. Interest in conscious artistry as opposed to interest in unpremeditated art: 87. Concept of term "artist": 87. Demand for poetry on modern subjects: 87. Veneration for M: 136. Late-Victorian view of M: 87

Victorinus of Pettau: Chiliasm: 107. One third of angels fell: 107

Victorinus Petavionensis: 65

Victorius, Petrus (Vettori, Pietro): 123

Victory: 2, 143. In court masque: 143. Christ's: 143

Vida, Marco Girolamo: 15, 50, 70*, 121, 133, 117, 65, 74, 56, 58, 60, 122, 123, 142, 88, 64, 99, 148, 55, 21. Works: Christiad: 74, 149, 142; Christias: 149; De Arte Poetica: 74

Vidier, A., and P. Perrier: 44. See also: Perrier, P.

Vidler, Alexander R.: 93

Vienna (Vienne): 49, 3. Council of: 3

Viereck, Peter: 52

View of the Present State of Ireland, A (Spenser): 70

Vigenere, Blaise de: 5

Viger, Francois: 40

Vigilius: 68

Vignier, Nicolas (the Younger): 93

Vigny, A. de: 6

Vigor: Hume on M's passionate, restrained: 33. Bentley sides with, as opposed to sweet smoothness: 88. Austere, passionate, admired by Bentley: 88. Of M's manner emphasized by the Richardsons: 88. In poetry valued by Richardsons: 88. Peck prefers false elegance to: 88. M's grim, Newton demands the conventional grand manner instead of: 88. Preferred by Dunster to smoothness: 88

Villa (Italy): 44

Villa, Marquis of: 28, 94. See also: Manso

Villafranca: 49

Village Book. See Miller, Edna

Villani, Giovanni: 44, 93. Croniche: 82

Villanovanus, Arnoldus: 122

Villars, Montfaucon de: 142. Comte de Gabalis: 142. See also: Gabalis

Ville, A. de: 6

Villehardouin, Geoffroy de: 93

Villenave, Mathieu Guillaume Thérèse de: 115. La Jacobiniade: 115

Villeré. See Philaras:

Villey, Pierre: 16

Villiers: Mr.: 44. George, Duke of Buckingham: 40, 45, 115; see also: Buckingham; Daubray

Villon: 1. Annette: 150

Vinaver, Eugene: 25

Vincennae: 49

Vincent of Beauvais: 40, 128, 36, 93. Works: Speculum Historiale: 74, 36; Speculum Naturale: 36

Vincent: J.: 58. Nathaniel: 93. Thomas: 44

Vinci, Leonarado da: 100

Vindication...against Edwards: 78

Vindication of the Answer, A: 59, 103

Vindication of the Ministers: 9

Vindication of the Primitive Christian: 116

Vindication of the Ways of God to man, as the theme of PL: 83

Vindication of Churches Commonly Called Independent (Henry Burton): 147

Vindication of King Charles I: 116

Vindication of Lord Russell's Speech and Paper: 116

Vindication of Royal Commission: 91

Vindication of Some Among Our Selves: 116

Vindiciae veritatis (Henry Burton): 147

Vindiciae Carolinae: 44, 116

Vindiciae Contra Tyrannos: 103, 116. See also: Languet

Vindicius Liberius: 116

Vine: 54*

Viner, Sir Robert: 10

Vinetus, Elius: 40

Vinogradoff, Paul: 93

Vinta, Francesco: 64

Vio, Thomas de. See Cajetan

Viol: 40, 121. Books: 40. Viol de gamba: 40

Violence: 47, 51, 11*, 92. In Comus, Lycidas: 11. In M's prose: 50. Of language: 11. Of "War in Heaven": 11. Of Samson: 11

Violet, Thomas: 44

Viraginia(n): 49, 73

Viret, Pierre (Viretus, Petrus): 73, 123, 93

Virgil, Publius Vergilius Maro: 1*, 2*, 4, 5, 6, 12, 15*, 16, 17, 18, 19, 20*, 27, 30, 33*, 34, 35, 37, 40*, 44*, 50, 52, 56*, 57, 58*, 59, 60, 68, 70*, 73, 74*, 76, 84, 86, 87, 89, 90*, 98, 95, 100, 102, 103, 104, 105, 108, 112, 111, 113, 114, 118*, 120, 121, 122*, 123, 124, 125, 126, 127, 128, 129*, 132*, 133*, 136, 141, 142, 144, 145, 3*, 26, 32*, 36*, 39, 46, 53, 72, 82, 88*, 93, 97, 21, 101, 64*, 106, 94, 109, 115*, 130*, 137, 146*, 148*, 150*, 117*, 13, 25, 21. Thought no greater than M: 58*. Admired by Tennyson: 87. Consummate artist: 87. As poeta doctus: 123. And M compare: 2*, 35, 146, 87. Dido: 109. Aeneas: 109. First eclogue, relation of, to Spenser's September Eclogue: 83. Works: Aeneid: 2*, 35, 81, 95, 21*; 57, 74*, 77, 36, 46, 109, 146, 149*, 143*, 25; Eclogues: 81, 36, 21*; Georgics: 74, 81, 36, 21; Eclogue IV, IX: 74; Fourth Georgic: 109. See also: Aeneid

Virgil (Character in the Commedia): 111*

Virgilio, Johannes de: 64

Virgin Mary: life of Jesus reviewed by: 119. As "second Eve": 119

Virginal(s): 40, 121

Virginia Almanack, The: 115. Virginia Almanack for the Year of Our Lord God 1770, The: 115

Virginia: 44, 49

Virginity: 27, 54, 69, 93, 25. Images of: 8. See also: Chastity

Virgins: 89. Virgin birth: 113

Virtue: 24*, 27, 31*, 40, 47, 51*, 54, 104, 103, 125*, 143*, 142. M on: 51. Cloistered, M: 107. Indefatigable: 51. Cardinal: 143. Classified: 143. Christian: 143, 73, 40. Aristotelian: 40. Heroic: 123. Unity of: 125. Problem of interrelationship of: 125. Splintering of in Christian Doctrine: 125. M's travesty of in Pandemonium: 125. Truce within and free: 143. Victorious: 143. 15 steps to: 143. See also: Wisdom; Legalism; Moralism; Fortitude; Humanity; Justice; Piety; Temperance; Milton, John, Works

Virunnius: 3

Vischer, Peter: 117

Visiak, E. H.: 1, 16, 44, 45, 86, 112, 128, 132, 85, 92, 93, 137, 146. With H. J. Foss, ed. of Comus: 44. See also: Comus; Lament for Damon (ed. E. H. Visiak)

Vision of the Twelve Goddesses (Daniel): 29

Vision of Delight (Jonson): 29, 88

Vision of Heaven in heroic literature: 123

Vision(e) of Purgatory: 116

Vision, A: 58

Vision: 51, 67, 96*, 25. And rhetoric: 25. Types of: 25. Organization: 25. And action: 25. See also: Divine Wisdom

Visions (apocalyptic): 67

Visions of Government: 116

Visitation of London 1633, 1634, 1635: 40

Visitations of the Almighty: 58

Visitors: 30

Visscher: 10

Visser, Martinus: 63

Visteni, Nicholas: 44

Visual: effects, observed by Callander, David Steel on: 88. Images: 118*. Difficulty of discussing objectively: 118. An example of precise: 118. Cinematographic technique in: 118. Borderline instance: 118. Example of sharp: 118. Developed but generic: 118. Clear but inappropriate: 118. Examples of general: 118. Imagination: 60

Visualization: excessive and irresponsible: 118. Of M's scenes by Pearce: 88. Pearce on need of, as opposed to vague generalization: 88. Pearce on gradation of: 88. Pearce's, of nature more acute than Bentley's: 88. The Richardsons', of M's scenes: 88. Careful, helps explain M's language: 88

Vita contemplativa: 143

Vita di Dante: 111

Vita Adae et Evae: 65, 123

Vita Nuova: 111

Vitalian: 3

Vitalism in 17th c. thought: 118

Vitalist-mechanist controversy: 128

Vitorelli, Andre: 21

Vitruvius Polio, Marcus: 44, 73, 100, 128, 3, 39, 93, 97

Vittel, Christopher: 7

Vittone: 27

Vittori, L.: 6

Vittorino da Feltre and Other Humanist Educators (Woodward): 3

Vittorino da Feltre: 5, 3

Vituperation, in theme writing: 20

Vivante, Leone: 14

Vivarius, Jacobus: 65

Vivers, Richard: 44, 45

Vives on Education (Watson): 3

Vives, Juan Luis: 19, 20, 40, 54, 56, 60, 114, 144*, 145, 3, 93, 55. _Introduction to Wisedome_: 74

Vivian, T. (translations): 58

Viviani: Mr.: 44. V.: 6

Vlaccus, Adrian: 30, 59, 91

Vlacq, Adrian (Adriaan) (Dutch pr.): 44*, 55, 94

Vlitius, James: 44

Vocabulary: influence of literary associations on value of M's: 88. Shifting value of elements of, felt by Pearce: 88. Discussions of M's by: Hume, the Richardsons, Peck, Paterson, Newton, Dodd, Warton, Letter to Warton, Dunster, Todd: 88. Vocabularies, printed: 40. See also: Classical; Italian; Hebrew; Rabbinical; Anglo-Saxon; Technical; Archaic; Neologisms; Dialect; Word-formation

Vocal: chords: 121. Music: 121

Voegelin, Eric: 125

Vogelius, Janus Augustus: 40

Vogelweide, Walther von der: 100

Vogler, Thomas: 25

Voice: 121

Voigt, Georg: 18

Voith, Valten: 65

Voiture: Mr.: 44. Vincent: 44

Volateran: 128

Volcano: 128

Volga (Edel, Tolga): 49. See also: Astracan; Nagay

Volhinnia: 49

Volhusky: 49

Volkel, Johannes: 22

Volkelius: 148

Volney, C.-F., Comte de: 97

Vologda: 19

Volpone (Jonson): 70, 135

Volscia: 73

Voltaire, Francois Marie Arouet de: 6, 12, 15, 27, 34, 37, 18, 44*, 58, 73, 105, 111, 113, 123, 141, 142, 11, 88, 93, 115, 137, 149, 117*, 55, 13, 94, 97, 146*

Volubility, Warton condemns mere moralizing: 83

Voluntarism in M's Paradise, example of in imagery: 118. Voluntaryism: 114

Voluptas: 90

Voluptuous life: 123

Volusius, Annals of: 73

Volz, P.: 141

Von Berge, Ernest Gottlieb: 117

Von Hügel: 130

Von Schwind, Moritz: 70

Von Watt, Joachim: 32

Von Zezen: 44

Vondel, Joost van den: 6, 15, 17, 42, 50, 60, 65*, 68, 70, 77, 123, 129, 141, 32, 142, 36, 92, 94, 64, 137, 149*, 130. Works: Adam in Ballingschap: 95, 36, 149, 55, 77, 149; summary: 149*; characterization of Eve, of Satan, called Lucifer: 149*; temptation scene: 149; Lucifer: 77, 95, 36, 149*, 55; need of epic form: 149; quoted: 149; motive for rebellion: 149; campaign: 149; opposition: 149; expulsion: 149; revenge on Adam: 149; Samson of Heilige Wraeck: 55; Het Pascha: 95; Argument: 77, 95

Voragine, Jacobus de: 64

Vorst, Conrad: 114

Vorstius, Johann: 32

Vortiger(n): 73, 94

Vossius (Voss): Isaac: 10, 44*, 103, 32, 88, 117; Gerhard Jan: 6, 10, 20, 40*, 142, 22, 93, 94, 137; works: De Origine et Progressu Idolatriae: 142; De Theologia Gentili: 74

Vowell, Peter: 44

Vowels, Todd on retention and omission of, in M's spellings: 83

Voyage of St. Brendan: 128

Voyeurism: 139

Voyon, Simon de: 93

Voysin, Joseph: 113

Vriendt, Floris de: 123

Vuillier, Gaston: 29

Vuinmannus, Nicolas (Wynman, Nicolaus): 123

Vuinthauserus, Vuolfgangus: 123

Vulcan: 2, 56, 73, 90*, 144, 130

Vulgate: 40, 42, 63, 22, 36, 71, 78, 99. Bible: 74. See also: Bible

Vulteius: Hermann: 10. Johann: 10

Vulture: 144

Vultzes: 73

Vyecocke, Mr.: 44

Vyner: Honor: 120. Sir Thomas: 120. Thomas, Jr.: 120

Vyse, W.: 58

-W-

W., B.: 116

W., E.: 44

W., G.: 44

W., J. See Wyeth

W., N.: 44

W., P.: 116

W., R.: 44. See also: Waring, R.

W., T.: 117

Waad: Mr.: 44, 45. Armagil: 45. James: 45. Sir William: 45

Waddell, Helen: 33, 64, 148

Waddington: Mr.: 44. Raymond B.: 93. Samuel: 136

Wade: Gladys I.: 81. S. G.: 36

Wades-Mill: 45

Wadham College, Oxford: 40

Wadley Coppice: 45

Wadstein, Ernst: 93

Wadsworth, J.: 40

Wager-motif: 48

Wagger, John: 44

Waggon to London, charge for: 40

Waggoner: G. R.: 101. H.: 23

Wagner: Antiony R.: 44. Richard: 113, 114, 139, 14, 39, 137; Gotterdammerung: 46

Wagstaffe: John: 114, 142. Thomas: 44, 116

Wain, travel by: 40

Wain, John: 52, 86, 105

Wainwright: Mr.: 45. Arthur W.: 93. Rebecca (Downer): 45

Waite, A. E.: 7, 142

Waites, Alfred: 115

Waith, Eugene M.: 123, 39

Wake, William: 116

Wakefield: Sir Charles: 44. Gilbert: 58, 115. Roger: 40. Thomas: 40, 42

Wakering, co. Essex: 44, 45

Wakerley. See Weckherlin, G.

Walaeus, A.: 54

Walafridus, Strabus: 99

Walbancke, Matthew (pr.): 44

Walch, Johann Georg: 68

Waldenses, History of the (Giles): 3

Waldenses: 7, 44, 3, 73. Waldensians: 60, 128, 38, 82

Waldere: 36

Waldock, A. J. A.: 1, 15, 17, 23, 34, 37*, 56, 52, 60, 66*, 81, 95, 86*, 105, 123*, 128, 136, 139, 141*, 142, 36*, 84, 110*, 122, 53, 93, 146, 150*, 140*, 48. PL ocassionally heretical: 107. Ambiguity in PL: 61. Poetic satisfaction in PL: 61. On Adam and Eve's sin: 80. Criticism of Waldock's theory: 48. PL and Its Critics: 74, 142, 83, 95*, 109*, 48*

Waldron: Mr.: 44. Henry: 44

Wales (Cambria, Demetia, Deomed, Genounia, Guinethia, North Wales, South Wales): 44, 45, 49. North: 44. Prince of: 97

Walford, Edward: 16, 44, 45. And Walter Thornbury: 44. See also: Thornbury, G. W.

Walker-Ames Lecture (Tillyard): 131

Walker: Mr. (relative of M): 44. A.: 135. Dr. Anthony: 23, 40, 116. Alice: 79. Clement (d. 1651): 9, 44, 103, 147; History of Independency (scoffs at M): 147, 91. Daniel P.: 39, 93. Sir Edward: 44. Ferdinando: 128. George: 32. Grace: see Duck, Grace.

Walker: Henry: 103. J.: 58; author of Rhetorical Grammar: 88. John: 44, 142, 93; works: A Diallogicall Discourse of Spirits and Devils: 142; A Summary Answer to all the Material Points in any of Master Darel, His Books: 142. Joseph: 40. Joseph Cooper: 88. Matthias (pr.): 44. Richard J. B.: 44. Robert (painter, M portrait): 44. Thomas: 45. W. S. (translator): 58. William: 44

Walking as recreation: 40, 44

Walkington, Thomas: 64

Wall of Antonius: 49

Wall of Severus (Adrian): 49

Wall: Adam: 40. Heyling: 44. John: 44, 93. Moses: 44, 147, 38; letter to M: 147. Richard: 44. W. E.: 58

Wallace: G.: 58. J. M.: 23, 39. John: 44. Karl R.: 115. Malcolm W., The Life of Sir Philip Sidney: 83. Robert (on M's prose): 87. Ronald S.: 79

Wallen, John (bks.): 44

Waller: A. R.: 23, 44, 122; see also: Hazlitt, William, Works. Anne: 44. Dorothy: see Cope, Dorothy. E.: 84. Edmond of (Kaesgrave): 44. Edmund: 15, 16, 44*, 59, 105, 121, 116, 120, 124, 32, 145, 91, 115, 94, 131, 146, 117. Sir Hardress: 9. Walter: 44. Sir William: 44, 120, 94, 64, 137; contrasted with M: 58

Wallerstein, Ruth: 29, 76

Walley: Alice: 44. (Whalley), William: 44

Wallin, Elizabeth: 45. See also: Wallwin, Elizabeth

Wallingford: 49. House: 103; Wallingford-House Cromwellians: 51

Wallington, co. Surrey: 44

Wallis: Elisha?: 91. John: 10*, 40, 44, 114

Walloons: 103

Wallop, Robert: 44

Wallope, Sir Henry: 40

Wallwin: (Walwyn), Elizabeth: 45; see also: Wallin, Eliz. Judith: see Harris, Judith. Walter: 45

Walmesley: (Wallmisley), George: 44. Roger: 44

Walne, Peter: 44

Walpole Society: 44

Walpole: Horace: 12, 35, 40, 58, 70, 97; on M: 58; see also: Orford, Earl of. Michael: 93

Walsall: Dr.: 44. Samuel: 64

Walsh: C. M.: 93. Dorothy: dramatic tension in PL: 61; experience and poetry: 61. Thomas: 16. William: 17, 58; ignores Lycidas: 58. Pope's letter to: 88

Walsingham: Sir Edward: 45. Elizabeth: see Ayloffe, Elizabeth. Sir Francis: 64. Thomas: 93

Walsted Delves: 45

Walsted: (Walstead, Wheelsted), Francis: 44, 45. Thomas: 45

Walter von Chatillon (of Chatillon): 133

Walter: family: 45. Miss: see Cope, Mrs. Sir John: 45. Mary: see Cope, Mary. Sir William: 45

Walters: D.: 58. J.: 58. Lucy: 44

Waltham (town): 49

Waltham: Geoffrey: 45. Katherine (Duck): 45

Walthar, Balthazar: 7

Walther (Waltherus), Rudolph: 89, 122, 123, 143, 64. Monomachia Davidis et Goliae: 74. See also: Gualter

Walthew (Walthewe): Mr.: 45. Robert: 44, 45

Walton-on-Thames: 45

Walton: 15. Col.: 44. Bp. Brian: 40, 41, 42, 44, 22, 93, 94. Eda Lou: 108. Geoffrey: 86. Izaak: 40, 44, 59, 86, 91, 94, 55

Walton's Bible: 113. Walton's polyglot, Biblia Polyglotta: 43; see also: London Polyglot

Walwins Wiles: 147

Walworth, Leonard: 44

Walwyn, William: 9, 44, 60, 147*, 32, 38, 91. Characterization of Goodwin's people: 147. Denounced as dangerous communist and anarchist: 147. Emphasizes social compulsion of the gospel: 147. Intellectual creed: 147. Intellectual leaders of the Levellers: 147. Leveller and extreme tolerationist: 147. Liberal Puritan: 147. Strife with the Independents: 147. Works: A Still and Soft Voice (explains his creed): 147*; Word in Season (defends the Independents): 147; The Compassionate Samaratane (for free press): 147; The Fountain of Slaunder Discovered (his apology): 147; hue and cry after: 147; The Second Part of Englands New-Chaines Discovered (imprisoned for writing): 147; Parable of Physitians (plea for toleration): 147; A Whisper in the Eare (respected for writing, believes in the triumph of truth): 147; Parable, or Consulatation of Physitians upon Master Edward: 147; Walwyns Just Defence: 147. See also: Wallwin; Wallin

Wanading: 49, 3

Wandalbertus Prumiensis: 65

Wanderer, The: 15, 36, 109

Wandering, as metaphor: 106

Wanderings of Cain: 65

Wanley, Nathaniel: 128, 93

Wapping: 45

War in Heaven: 17, 41, 50*, 67*, 76, 100*, 113, 118*, 75, 123*, 11*, 72*, 93, 106*. And Chaos: 75. And the poet's role: 75. And narrative technique: 75. "Accommodated" truth in: 118. Unsuitability in: 118. Inconsistencies and contradications in: 118. As ironic: 118. Poetic success in: 118. Failures in: 118. Most brilliant passages of: 118. Between church and its foes: 123. As epic theme: 123. And peace as subject for deliberative rhetoric: 123*. Choric song, two accounts, length of, when inserted in PL, position changed in PL: 50

War(s): 47, 51, 58, 25. M on: 137. Religious: 71. Condemned: 144. Not best epic subject: 50. Bps.' (Episcopal): 44, 51. Second Bps.': 51. English Civil: 44. Wars of Roses: 44. See also: Battle

Warbeck, Perkin: 73

Warble: 121

Warburton: 132. George: 93. J.: 68. Sarah: see Powell, Sarah. Bp. William: 12, 15, 58*, 59, 144, 88*, 92, 109, 130, 146, 117*, 55, 13, 25; on M: 58

Warcupp: Robert: 44. Rodolph: 44

Warcutt (Warrutt), Thomas: 44

Ward: 7. Mr.: 40. E. M.: 97. Edward: 44, 116. Mrs. Humphry, Robert Elsmere: 87. J.: 58, 59, 97. John (composer): 44*. Nathaniel: 38, 71; sermon by: 38. Richard: 101. Robert (Stafford): 82, 99, 137; Animadversions of Warre: 82. Samuel: 10, 40, 114, 93. Seth: 10, 37, 114

Ward's English Poets: 86

Wardall, Thomas: 44

Wardhouse: 49

Wardle, W. L.: 36

Wards and Liveries, Court of: 45

Ware Park: 45

Warewell: 49

Warham (Werham): 49

Waring: Mr.: 44, 45. Luther Hess: 60. Richard: 44; see also: W., R. Thomas: 44

Warkworth: 45

Warly, John: 115

Warner: 133. Sir George G. (ed. Nicholas Papers): 44; and J. P. Gilson, British Museum Catalogue of Western Manuscripts in the Old Royal and King's Collections: 44; see also: Nicholas Papers; Nicholas, Sir Edward. John: 147; sermon, The Devilish Conspiracy, Hellish Treason: 147. Rex: 141, 101. Walter: 40, 114. William: 19, 93

Warning: 50*, 51. To Adam: 50. Shifted in PL: 50. To and by Uriel: 50

Warnke, Frank J.: 110, 39, 101

Warping the argument: 51

Warr: Joseph: 147; Privliedges of the People: 147. T.: 45

Warrant to search Prynn's house: 44

Warren: Mr.: 45. A.: 97. Alice (pr., 1660-62): 91. Austin: 101, 115. Charles: 115. Edward: 93. James: 115, 117. John: 44, 45; The Devilish Conspiracy, Hellish Treason: 147. Robert Penn: 12, 125, 53. Thomas: 45. William (Fairfield): 32, 112, 128

Warrington Academy: 78

Warrington, 1st Earl of (Henry Booth): 116

Warrior: 122*

Warrutt. See Warcutt

Warsaw: 49

Warsley: 45

Warters, A.: 64

Warton: John: 58. Rev. John: 88. Joseph: 12, 33, 58*, 86, 97, 146, 117*, 55; imitates M's trans. from Horace: 58; on M: 58; says L'Allegro and Il Penseroso are neglected: 58; uses Nativity meter: 58.

Warton, Thomas: 4, 15, 19, 28, 29, 33*, 40*, 44, 58*, 59*, 70, 73, 120, 128, 132, 134, 143, 39, 43, 53, 88*, 91, 92, 64, 109, 130, 146*, 149, 150, 117*, 55, 13. Thomas Sr., influenced by M: 58*. Thomas Jr.: 58*. Borrowings from M: 58. Editor of M's minor poems: 58. Influenced by L'Allegro and Il Penseroso: 58. On M: 58. The Wartons: 94, 130. Works: History of Eng. Poetry: 74; Poems Upon Several Occasions (ed.): 44*; M's Minor Poems (ed.): 109. See also: Milton, John, Works: Poems

Warwick(shire): 44, 45*, 49. City or co.: 44, 45. Visitation of: 45. Castle: 45

Warwick, Black Book of: 45

Warwick: Christopher: 44. T.: 58. Sir Philip: 116

Wase, Christopher. See Wasse, Christopher

Wase, W.: 45

Washbourne, Thomas: 44

Washbrooke, co. Suffolk: 44

Washburn, Azel: 115. Two Discourses Delivered in the College Chapel: 115

Washington: Mr.: 44. George: 60, 115*. Joseph: 44, 116

Washington, D. C.: 44

Wassailing: 51

Wasse, Christopher, trans. Sophocles'

Electra: 44, 91

Waste Land, The (Eliot): 72, 130

Wasteland: 72

Wastell, Simon: 68

Watch (M's): 44

Watch-Word to the City of London (Winstanley's socialist manifesto): 147*

Watcher angels: 36. Fall of: 36. See also: Angels

Water nymphs: 90

Water Colour Society: 97

Waterford, Ireland: 44

Waterhouse: Benjamin: 115; A Journal of a Young Man of Massachusetts Late a Surgeon on Board an American Privateer: 115. E. K.: 97. Edward: 114. G.: 44

Waterland, Daniel: 32

Waterloo, A.: 97

Waterperry, co. Oxon.: 44

Waters (above and under the firmament), the: 89

Waters: Henry F.: 44. Robert: 142; John Selden and his Table Talk: 142

Waterstock: 45

Waterworth, Stephen: 44

Waties, Edward: 29

Watkins: Mr.: 44. D.: 44. Oscar D.: 93. W. B. C.: 23, 29, 37, 60, 75, 81, 125, 128, 14, 93, 101; Anatomy of Milton's Verse: 74

Watling Street: 44, 49

Watlington, co. Oxon.: 44

Watney: Oliver: 44. Vernon: 44

Watson: 90, 3*. Mr.: 117. Caroline: 44. Edward W.: 93. Foster: 20, 40, 56, 60, 77, 112, 128. G.: 23, 86*. J. R.: 59. Philip S.: 93. Rev. R. L.: 44. Richard: 44. Sara: 128. Sarah Ruth: 29. Thomas: 37, 64. Dr. Thomas (suggested as a possible "wolf"): 83. Sir William (sonnets in Miltonic tradition): 87

Watt: F. W.: 122. Ian: 54. Robert: 44. William: see Grebanier

Watteau, A.: 97

Watts-Dunton, W. T.: 59, 120

Watts: A. W.: 15. G. F.: 97. Isaac: 58*, 70, 86, 32, 115*; borrows from Lycidas: 58; inflUeced by PL: 58; on M: 58; works: Divine Songs for Children: 115; The Improvement of the Mind: 115; Few Happy Matches: 115. James: 44. William: 81

Waugh, Arthur: 44

Way of Virtue: 31*

Way to the Peace and Settlement of these Nations (Peter Corneliszoon Plockhoy): 147

Way: A. S.: 58, 92. Albert: 44

Waybridge: 45

Ways: 143. To Heaven and Hell: 143

Weaknesses, national: 51

Wealth: 51. Wealthy, the: 51

Weathers, Winston: 128

Weaver, Thomas: 44

Weaver's Discourse of Funeral Monuments: 88

Weavers Hall, London: 44

Weavers, Company of: 44

Weaving. See Symbolism

Web. See Symbolism

Webb: Alice: 44. C. C. J.: 93. Daniel: 58, 97, 117. Edward (Edmund): 45. Elizabeth: 44. F.: 58. John: 37, 44, 45. Margaret: 45. R. K.: 87. (Web), Richard: 93. William: 44, 45*

Webb's Observations on Poetry and Musick: 88

Webbe: Bp. George: 93. Joseph: 7, 40. William: 1, 4, 56, 66, 46, 150

Webber: Mr.: 45. Mrs.: 44. Anne (sister-in-law of M's brother, Christopher): 44. Isabel (mother-in-law of M's brother, Christopher): 44. Isabel (sister-in-law of M's brother Christopher): 44. John (father-in-law of M's brother, Christopher): 44. Katherine (sister-in-law of M's brother, Christopher): 44. Margaret: 44. Thomazine (M's sister-in-law): 28. Tomasine: see Milton, Tomasine. W.: 44. William (brother-in-law of M's brother,

Christopher): 44

Weber, Die (Hauptmann): 118

Weber: K.: 6. Max: 60; The Protestant Ethic and the Spirit of Capitalism: 83. Walter: 98

Webster: Daniel: 16. Elizabeth (Mrs. Elijah): 44. John: 9, 15, 35, 37*, 44, 66, 114, 118, 134, 142*, 39, 131, 146, 148; army preacher, mineralist: 114; works: Academiarum Examen: 37, 142; The Displaying of Supposed Witchcraft: 142. Noah: 115; works: Dictionary: 70; A Grammatical Institute of the Eng. Language, Part Second: 115; A Philosophical and Practical Grammar of the Eng. Language: 115. T. B. L.: 92*, 64

Weckherlin (Weckherlyn), Georg Rodolf: 7, 10*, 16, 30, 40, 44*, 94

Wedgwood, J. (T.) (engraver): 44, 97

Wedmore: 49

Weedon, Venus. See Newman, Venus (Weedon)

Week of creation: 100*. Week of uncreation (Satan's): 100*

Weekes, N.: 58

Weekly Intelligencer: 44

Weekly Magazine, The: 115

Weekly Monitor, The: 115

Weekly Monitor: A Series of Essays on Moral and Religious Subjects, The: 115

Weekly Museum, The: 115

Weekly Post: 59

Weekly Visitor, Or Ladies' Miscellany, The: 115

Weeks, John E.: 16

Weelkes (Weelks), Thomas (composer): 44

Weelsted. See Walsted

Weems: (Wemes, Weyms), James: 44. Mason Locke: 115; A History of the Life and Death, Virtues and Exploits, of General George Washington: 115

Weemse (Weemes, Wemyss), John: 1, 24*, 40, 41, 79, 102, 22, 32, 93. Christian Synagogue: 74

Wegleiter, Christoph: 10

Wehnert, E. M.: 97

Weidhorn, Manfred: 60, 75

Weigel: 7. John A.: 115

Weigelius, Valentine: 79. Weigelians: 7

Weikherlyn, Geo. R.: 103

Weil: H.: 92. Simone: 125. Bernard: 6; Literary Criticism in the Italian Renaissance: 74

Weinberg, B.: 6, 39

Weingarten: 7

Weir, H.: 97

Weisinger, Herbert: 39, 93

Weissenbach, Mr.: 44

Weitz, Morris: 110

Weland: 141

Welbeck Abbey, co. Notts.: 44

Welby: Mr.: 45. John: 40. T. E.: 133. William: 44, 45

Welch, Claude: 93

Welcome (Bonavento) (ship): 44

Weld, Mr.: 40

Welde, Thomas: 114

Welfare: national: 51. Of England: 51. Of humanity: 51

Well of Life: 128, 72

Well-being: 51

Welldon: 3. J. E. C.: 112, 71

Wellek, René: 12, 27, 86

Weller, Catharine: 115. Works: The Medley: 115; The Sabbath: 115

Wellington, Duke of: 97, 150

Wells-Dymoke, Edmund Lionel: 44

Wells, co. Somerset: 44

Wells: 44, 45. Mrs. Elizabeth (née Dymoke): 44. H. G.: 34, 141, 137. J. E.: 58. John: 44, 128. Stanley: 39

Welsford, Enid: 15, 27, 29, 143, 39, 101, 148, 21. And M's lack of judgment: 143. Comus and Pleasure

Reconciled to Vertue: 143

Welsh: dialect in Tudor times: 83. Mountains: 40. Poets: 44

Welsted, L. (praises M): 58

Weltchronik: 65

Welwood, Elizabeth: 44

Wemys(s). See Weemes, John

Wendel, Francois: 93

Wendelin, Marcus Friderik: 40

Wendell Smith, H.: 15

Wendey, Rev. Thomas: 44

Wendland, Anna: 44

Wenman: Elizabeth: see Ashworth, Eliz. Richard: 45. Sir Thomas: 44

Wense, Wilhelm von der: 7

Wentworth Hebrew Lecturer: 40

Wentworth: 94. John: 40. Sir Peter: 44, 116. Thomas: see Strafford. See also: Strafford, Earl of

Weolud: 49

Werblowsky, R. J. Zwi: 1*, 27, 34, 37, 52, 60, 34, 110, 128, 142, 93. Lucifer and Prometheus: A Study of Milton's Satan: 142

Werder, Diederich von dem: 10

Werdmüller, Otto: 93

Werge, J.: 58

Werner, Heinz: 118

Wertermore: 49

Wesembechius: 44. Mathew Wesenbeck: 73

Weser River: 44

Wesley Museum, London: 44

Wesley: Charles: 137. John: 7, 142, 88, 97, 115, 130, 146, 117; edits PL, praises M: 58; the importance of Perfection to: 83; A Plain Account of Christian Perfection: 83. S., Jr.: 58; parodies Miltonic descriptive poetry: 58. S., Sr.: 58; praises PL: 58. Samuel: 16, 44

West: Agnes: see Ayloff, Agnes. B.: 97. Benjamin: 115; works: The New England Almanack: 115; The North-American Calendar: Or the Rhode-Island Almanack: 115. Capt.: 44. G.: 58. J.: 58. R.: 58*. R. L.: 97. Rebecca: 60. Robert H.: 1, 15, 17, 34, 66, 110, 123, 128, 142, 93, 106, 137, 146; influenced by L'Allegro: 58; works: The Invisible World: 142; "Literal-Minded Defense of Milton's Battle in Heaven": 60; M and the Angels: 60, 95. Thomas: 45

West Cheap: 40

West Frieseland: 44

West Indies: 150

West Ord, co. Durham: 44

West-Saxons: 49, 3

West Wycombe, co. Bucks.: 44

Westall, R.: 97*

Westbury, co. Wilts.: 44

Westby, S.: 58

Westchester: 73

Westcomb, Richard: 44

Westcott: Brooke F.: 143. Cassius D.: 16

Westcourt: 45

Westermann, Claus: 25

Westermarck, Edward: 75, 93

Western Empire: 49

Westmacott, R.: 97

Westmaria: 49

Westminster Abbey: 40, 44, 45, 94, 97. Muniments: 44

Westminster Assembly: 9*, 40, 113, 103, 141, 32, 38*, 78, 94. Meets to determine status of state church: 147. See also: National synod

Westminster Cathedral: 103

Westminster Confession: 63, 32, 78, 22, 71

Westminster Hall: 3, 44, 49, 103

Westminster School: 20, 40, 42

Westminster, Palace of: 97

Westminster: 40, 44*, 45*, 49, 51, 73, 103*, 3

Westmoreland: family: see Fane

family. Mary Fane, Countess of: 44*; see also: Fane, Mary (Mildmay). Earl of: see Fane, Francis; Fane, Mildmay

Weston, co. Salop.: 44

Weston: Edward: 93. J.: 58, 86. Jessie L.: 69. S.: 58

Westphal, Rudolph: 100

Westrawe, Ann: 44, 45

Westwellowe: 45

Wey (Wye) River: 49

Weyms. See Weems

Weynman: Elizabeth: see Brome, Eliz. Sir Thomas: 45

Whale and His Captors, The: 98

Whale, J. S.: 79, 93

Whaler, James: 37, 40, 56, 76, 81, 86, 100, 102, 105, 111, 128, 53, 101. Works: "Grammatical Nexus of the Miltonic Simile": 74; "Similes in PL": 74

Whales: 144

Whaley: 49

Whalley: Col. Edward: 44, 73, 38; see also: W., E. George: 146. Henry: 44. John: 117. T. S.: 58. See also: Walley

Whalter, James: 118

Wharey, J. B.: 37

Wharfs and Quays (Keys), London: 44. See also: Custom House

Wharton: Mr.: 44. Edith: 149. Philip: 40

Whateley: M.: 58. William: 54*, 123, 93. See also: Wheatley; Whately

Whately: E.: 58. William: 148. See also: Whateley

Whatman, Edward: 54

Whear, Degory: 10

Wheatfield: 45

Wheatley (Whateley), co. Oxon.: 44*, 45*, 103, 94. MS.: 36

Wheatley Copse (Coppice): 44, 45

Wheatley: F.: 97. Seizure of, and M: 44*

Wheeler: James: 150. T.: 59. Trundle (satiric name): 44

Wheelock (Whelocke), Abraham: 40, 42

Wheels (as an angelic order): 142

Wheelsted. See Walsted

Wheelwright, Philip: 23, 76

Wheldrake, co. York: 44

Whelocke, Abraham. See: Wheelock

Whelpley, Samuel: 115. A Sermon on the Immortality of the Soul: 115

When David Heard: 121

"When in your language I unskilled address": 44

"When the assault was Intended": 103. See also: Milton, John, Works: Sonnet VIII

Whetcombe, William: 45

Whetstone of Wit (1557): 40

Whetstone, George: 66, 70

Whibley: 3. Charles: 93. Leonard: 40; Companion to Greek Studies: 74

Whichcot(e): 112, 132. Benjamin: 1, 9, 15, 23, 40, 60, 102, 114, 93, 137

Whiffen, E. T.: 58

Whigs: 60, 87, 94. M admired by: 58

Whilton, John: 45

Whip for the House of Lords (John Lilburne): 147

Whipping at St. Paul's: 40. M whipped by Chappell (?): 44

Whish, M.: 44

Whisper in the Eare (William Walwyn): 147

Whistler: 15, 35

Whiston: John (bks.): 44. William: 32, 25

Whitaker: Mr.: 44. Jeremiah: 93. Nathaniel: 115; works: An Antidote Against, and the Reward of, Toryism: 115; The Reward of Toryism: 115. Richard (pr.): 44. Richard (bks., 1619-48): 91. Virgil K.: 116. William: 40, 79, 93

Whitby, Daniel: 32

Whitcomb, Benjamin: 44

White Jacket: 98*

White: J. (chaplain): 94. Jeremiah: White: Mr.: 44. A. T.: 44. Andrew D.: 142, 143. Andrew W.: 44. Anthony: 93. Antonia, Frost in May: 95. Daniel (bks., 1619-48): 91. Edward: 40. H.: 58. Harim: 93. Helen C.: 93, 106. H. Kirke: 58.

44. John: 10, 44, 79, 32, 39, 93, 115; The Country Man's Conductor: 115. Robert (engraver, M portraits): 44. Thomas Holt: 58, 117. Thomas: 40, 44, 116; Pantheologia: 74. W. A.: 44. William: 44

White: White Bear, London (Bread Street): 44, 44*. White Hart (sign), London: 44. White Horse (bookshop): 44. White Lion (sign): 44. White Rose: see Rose

Whitefield, George: 71, 146

Whitehall, London (Alba Aula): 27, 29, 40, 44*, 45, 49, 73, 103*. Debates: 9, 115

Whitehead: 112. Alfred North: 1, 37, 47, 76, 133, 143, 93; Reformation symbols: 143; on development of religion: 47. C.: 32. George: 114, 93. T. M.: 44. Thomas: 40. W.: 58

Whitehorne, Capt. William: 44

Whitehouse: J. (trans. Stolberg): 58. Walter A.: 93

Whitelaw, R.: 58

Whiteley, D. E. H.: 93

Whitelock(e): 51, 94. (Withlock, Witeloch, Whitboch), member and President of Council of State, Keeper of the Greal Seal: 16, 30, 44*, 45, 59, 73, 103, 120, 121, 38, 39, 117; Bulstrode, Memoirs...of: 45, 121. D.: 36. Sir James: 20, 40, 45, 59. R. H.: 45

Whites, co. Suffolk: 44

Whitfield (Whitfelde): Mr.: 44, 45. H.: 58. Henry: 45.

Whitford, B.: 122

Whitgift, Abp. John: 40, 41, 42, 38, 71, 64

Whiting: George Wesley: 1, 9, 19*, 24, 44, 68, 69, 75, 77, 36, 100, 102, 108, 110, 116, 123, 128*, 142, 32, 91, 93, 64, 101, 21; works: "The Politics of M's Apostate Angels": 60; "Tormenting Tophet": 60. John: 44. Thomas: 44

Whitley: W.: 97. William Thomas: 79; A History of British Baptists: 83

Whitlock, Bulstrode. See Whitelock, Bulstrode

Whitlock, Richard: 114, 145, 93

Whitman: C. H.: 64. Walt: 35, 58, 98, 112, 113, 133, 46, 71, 72, 115, 131, 149, 25

Whitney: 15, 45. Elizabeth: see Greere, Eliz. (Cope). Geoffrey: 29, 123. J. P.: 20. Lois: 69. Thomas: 45

Whittier, John Greenleaf: 44, 115

Whittier's Unknown Romance: 44

Whittingham: C.: 97. William: 73

Whittington series: 45

Whittington: George (bks.): 44. Robert: 40

Whittler, John: 115

Whole Booke of Psalmes (Ravenscroft): 20

Whole Duty of Man: 103. See also: Allestree

Whore of Babylon: 25

Whorwood: family: 45. Brome: 45. Diana: see Master, Diana. Elizabeth: 45. Field: 45. Jane (Ryther): 45. John: 45. Thomas: 45*. Sir Thomas: 45*. Urusla (Brome): 45. William: 45. Sir William: 45

Whyte: Lancelot L.: 93. Samuel: 115, 117; Modern Education, Respecting Young Ladies as Well as Gentlemen: 115

Wibbandun: 49

Wichita Falls, Texas: 44

Wickedness: 51

Wickham: 45. E. C.: 59

Wickstead, Richard: 44

Wicksteed: 111. Joseph H.: 93. Philip H.: 5, 93

Widda. See William VI

Widdowes, Daniel: 128

"Widdowes daughter of the glenne": 83

Widdrington: Ralph: 64. Sir Thomas: 44. Baron William: 45. See also: Witherington·

Widmanstadius, Johannes Albertus: 40

Widmer: Kingsley: 37, 110, 93, 101. Richard: 44. Thomas: 44. William: 44

Wiegel, Valentin: 114

Wiener, Peter F.: 60

Wier, Jean (Wierus, Joannes): 123, 128, 142. Works: <u>Histoires Disputes et Discours des Illusions et Impostures des Diables</u>: 142: <u>Pseuo-Monarchia Daemonum</u>: 142

Wife (husband/wife relationship): 31, 54*

Wife of Bath: 54

Wife-beating: 54

Wiffen, J. H.: 40

Wigan: 45

Wigandus: writer on divorce: 44. Johann: 44

Wigganbeorch: 49

Wiggintoa: 45

Wigglesworth, Michael: 58, 71

Wight (Vectis), Isle of: 44, 45, 49, 73

Wightman, Elizabeth: 44

Wigingmere: 49

Wigmore, Michael: 93

Wikandus (Vigand), Johannes: 73

Wike Copse (Coppice): 44, 45

Wilberforce, Bp.: 35

Wilbraham: Mr.: 44. Sir Thomas: 44

Wilbur, Richard: 110

Wilby(e), John (composer): 40, 44, 121

Wilcock, John: 45. See also: Wilcox

Wilcocke, S.: 58

Wilcocks, Thomas: 123

Wilcox: Mr.: 44, 45. John: 45; see also: Wilcock. Rowland: 45. S. C.: 14. Thomas: 114

Wild, John: 44, 45, 99

Wild: 10. Wild beasts: 99

Wilde, Oscar: 35, 54, 58, 87, 39, 137. "On the Massacre of the Christians in Bulgaria": 87

Wilder: Amos: 79. Thornton: 137. William H.: 16

Wilderness (Desert): 49, 99

Wildgoose, Lady Margaret (Stapleton): 45

Wildman: Sir John: 9, 91; works: <u>Putney Projects</u> (attacks the Independents): 147; <u>A Cal To All The Souldiers of The Armie</u>: 147. William: 40

Wile, Udo J.: 16

Wiles, Roy M.: 64

Wiley, Margaret: 128

Wilford, John: 44. See also: Wilsford

Wilhelm II, Margrave of Hesse: 64

Wilhelm V, Landgraf von Hessen-Kassel: 10

Wilkenfield, Roger B.: 39. On Mask: 104

Wilkes: G. A.: 86, 122, 123, 101, 146. John: 44

Wilkie: D.: 97. Robert: 40. William: 58, 110, 117

Wilkin, Simon: 128

Wilkinfeld, Roger B.: 101

Wilkins: David: 44. George (composer): 44. Dr. John, Bp. of Chester: 1, 10*, 23, 35, 37*, 44, 77*, 79, 102, 114*, 144, 128, 32, 91, 55; An Essay Towards a Real Character and a Philosophical Language: 37; On the Principles and Duties of Natural Religion: 37. William: 44

Wilkinson: Mr.: 40. Christopher (pr.): 44. David: 29, 21. John: 64. L. P.: 59. Robert: 40, 54

Wilks, Rev. Mr.: 58

Will: 7, 9*, 31, 51, 144. Freedom of: 51; see also: Free will. Of God: 51. Of the people, responsiveness of a commonwealth to: 51. The nature of: 48

Will (M's last will): 44*, 55. Testimony of Christopher Milton, quoted: 55. Testimony of Elizabeth Fisher, quoted: 55. See MS., followed by identifying name and number

Willcock: G. D.: 135. Gladys: 79. J.: 9, 23, 59

Willems, Alphonse, Les Elzevier (1880): 91

Willemsz, Marcus (Dutch pr.): 44

Willet, Andrew: 24*, 40, 44, 67, 77*, 102, 142*, 36, 93. Works: Hexapla in Genesin: 142, 36; Synopsis Papismi: 142

Willetts, W.: 34

Willey, Basil: 1, 12, 15, 23, 31, 35, 52*, 56, 63, 68, 84, 86*, 102, 108, 110, 128, 139, 138, 141, 144, 133, 36, 109, 131. The 17th-c. Background: 109

William: I, the Conqueror: 29, 60. Of Orange (William III): 51, 16, 40, 44, 83; William and Mary: 116*

William VI, Landgrave of Hesse and ruler of Hersfeld (Herefeldt), Katzenelnbogen (Cutzenhellebogen), Ziegenhain (Decia Ligenhain), Nidda (Widda), and Schaumburg (Schaunburg): 44

William, Sir Peter: 10

William: of Malmesbury: 44, 82*, 93; De Gestis Regum Anglorum: 82. Of Ockham (Occam): 83, 82. Of Saint-Thierry: 114. Of Shoreham: 36; On the Trinity, Creation, Existence of Evil, etc.: 36. Of Tyre: 93. Of Worcester: 88. The Silent (1533-84): 149

Williams: Mr.: 44, 45. Arnold: 1, 15, 17, 23, 24, 37, 54, 60, 68, 75, 77, 95, 102, 105, 108, 110, 123, 128, 142*, 144, 32, 36, 93, 101, 148; aspect of M's theology from Renaissance Commentaries on Genesis: 107; works: The Common Expositor: 60, 142, 48; "The Eng. Moral Play before 1500": 60; "Wisdom of the Chaldeans": 142. C. M.: 44. Charles: 1, 40, 86*, 102, 105, 110, 123, 127, 133, 138*, 139, 141, 93, 101, 130*, 137, 150; attributes Fall to injured merit: 107. E.: 58. Edward: 115; The Christian Preacher: 115. George Walton: 50, 93. Bp. Griffith: 93.

Williams: H. M.: 58. J.: 58. J. (pr.): 44. J. B.: 16, 44; see also: Muddiman, J. B. J. L.: 97. John: 45, 146. John (1582-1650): 91. John (bks., 1635-83): 91. John, Bp. of Lincoln, Abp. of York: 10, 40, 44, 45, 51, 94. Kathleen: 25. Norman Powell: 15, 17, 123, 36*, 93; The Ideas of the Fall and of Original Sin: 83. Nicholas: 44. R.: 129. R. C., "Epic as Discussed by 16th-c. Critics": 74. R. D.: 21. Ralph C.: 122. Raymond: 53.

Williams, Roger: 7, 9*, 16, 44*, 51, 60, 102, 103, 108, 114*, 120, 147*, 26, 38, 115, 137, 148. Against any state church: 147. Disapproves of the Covenant: 147. Extreme tolerationist: 147. Intellectual transitions: 147. In the Massachusetts colony: 147. Puritan idealist: 147. Toleration principles: 147. With the Plymouth colony: 147. Toleration for Papists and Arminians: 147. Throws off the code of Calvin: 147. Writes of the difference between Puritans and Separitists: 147. Works: The Bloody Tenet Yet More Bloody (asserts his principles in): 147; An Appendex to the Cleargie of the Four Great Parties: 147; Queries of Highest Consideration: 147, 115; The Boudy Tenet: 147*, 115; The Fourth Paper Presented by Major Butler: 147

Williams: T. C.: 58. Thomas (minister): 115; The Age of Infidelity: 115. Thomas: 44, 64, 115. W. (of Gray's Inn): 58. W. (of Halifax): 58. W. R.: 45. Walter: 116

Williams's Library, London: 44

Williamson: Francis: 44. George C.: 23, 37, 44*, 86, 102, 93, 131; M's mortalism results from 17th-c. beliefs: 107; works: "Milton and the Mortalist Heresy": 60; "M the anti-Romantic": 60. Sir Joseph: 10, 44, 116, 94, 150. William: 44

Willibrode (Willibrord, Wilbrod): 73, 3

Willier, William: 44

Willingham, Mr.: 44

Willis: and Clark: 40. Nathaniel Parker: 98. Robert: 40. Thomas: 10, 16, 44. William: 116

Willmot, Richard: 44

Willmott, Rev. Robert: 87. "Life of Milton": 87

Willoughby: family: 15, 45*. (Willughby), Miss: see Peckham, Mrs. Bridget: 45. Edward: 44, 45*.

Edwin: 44. Elizabeth (Atkinson): 45. Elizabeth (Littleton): 45. Frances: see Ewens, Frances (Rogers). Francis: 40, 45. Sir Francis: 45. George: 45. H. R.: 92. Henry: 45. Hugh: 45, 103. Sir Hugh: 19, 150. John: 45. Percival: 45. Sir Percival: 45. Richard: 45. Robert: 44*, 45*. Rogert, Lord Brooke: 45. Thomas: 44, 45*. Sir Thomas: 45. William: 45. Winifred: 45

Wills, J.: 58

Willughby. See Willoughby

Wilmer, William H.: 16, 44, 128

Wilmerding, Lucius A.: 44

Wilmington Almanac, or Ephemeris For the Year of Our Lord 1794: 115

Wilmot, John. See Rochester

Wilsford, Mr.: 44. See also: Wilford

Wilson: Anthony: 44. Dudley B.: 93. E. F.: 128, 64. Elkins: 108. H. S.: 69. James: 115; works: _The Works of the Hon. James Wilson, L.L.D._: 115; _Considerations on the Nature and Extent of the Legislative Authority of the British Parliament_: 82. J. of Lanarkshire: 58. J., _Art of Painting_: 58. John (several): 40, 44, 59, 87, 39, 130; on PL: 87; hostile toward writers of religious epics: 87; attitude toward religious epics: 87; on natural Sublime: 87; on degeneration of Satan: 87; on M the Puritan: 87; on M's treatment of Satan in PL: 87. J. Dover: 58, 102. L. A.: 6. R.: 97. R. McL.: 36. Richard (tax collector): 44. Thomas: 9, 18, 20, 23, 40, 66, 114, 116, 122, 123, 93, 64; works: _Art of Rhetorique_: 79, 82; _A Christian Dictionary_: 79. Sir Thomas: 93. William (pr., 1640-65): 91

Wilstach, Paul: 115

Wilton (Ellandune): 49

Wilton: Nicholas: 44. Thomasine: 44

Wiltshire, The Natural History of: 45

Wiltshire, The Topographical Collections: 45

Wiltshire: 45*, 49

Wimpina, Konrad (Koch): 114

Wimsatt, William K., Jr.: 12, 23, 34, 56, 79, 100, 123, 128, 39, 53. And Cleanth Brooks: 66

Winandermere (Wonwaldermere): 49

Winburne: 49

Wincanton: 45

Winch, Humphrey: 44

Winchester (Caerguent, Wintonia): 44, 45, 49, 3. College: 44. School: 40

Winchester: Bp. of: 103, 21; see also: Andrewes. Marchioness of (Jane Savage): 40, 26; see also: Paulet. (Paulet), John Paulet, Marquis of: 40

Winchilsea, Countess of: 58. Parodies M: 58

Winckelmann: 88. J. J.: 97. Johann: 87; Apollonian view of Greek culture: 87

Wind(s): 90, 128*, 144. Causes and kinds: 128. Creative power: 128. Wind-egg: 128. Wind-chest: 121. Wind instruments: 121

Wind, Edgar: 23, 79, 123, 39, 64, 106

Windelband, Wilhelm: 113, 71

Windham: Mr.: 44. Thomas: 44

Winding Sheet for the Good Old Cause: 51

Windmill (satirical sign): 44

Window: 143. Ancient and fair in St. Edmonds: 143

Windsor Castle: 29. The Waterloo Chamber: 97

Windsor: Arthur Lloyd: 87, 116. Eleanor: see Brome, Eleanor. P. L.: 41. William Lord: 45

Windsor: 45, 49, 73, 103

Wine: 144

Wing: Donald: 40, 44*, 116, 128. John: 54

Wingate, Edmund: 40

Wingfield, R.: 58

Wingren, Gustaf: 93

Winifrid(e) of Devon: 73, 3

Winkelmann, J. J.: 44

Winklhofer, Alois: 93

Winny, James: 79

Winshemius, Vitus: 40

Winslow, E.: 44

Winsor, Justin: 40

Winstanley, Gerrard: 7, 9, 60, 79, 108, 114, 147*, 32. Against divination of theologians: 147. And the Diggers: 147. Appeals to Cromwell for help for the Digger movement: 147. Appeals to London and the army: 147. Criticizes Agreement of the People: 147. denounces tything priests: 147. Derives his fundamental economic principle from the Scriptures: 147. Early Puritan: 147. For laborers: 147. Looks on tithes as kingly thievery: 147. On economic change: 147. Opposes the established church: 147. Proposes communistic state: 147. Rationalism of: 147. Works: An Appeal to all Englishmen: 147; A New-Years Gift for the Parliament and Armie: 147; The Saints Paradise (records his discouragement): 147; A Watch-Word to the City of London (a socialist manifest): 147*; Light Shining in Buckingham-shire: 147

Winstanley: J.: 58. William: 28, 86, 116, 91, 93, 130, 145, 150

Winter solstice, position of determined by the Chinese: 89

Winter's Tale, The (Shakespeare): 134

Winteringham (Wintheringham), co. York: 44, 45

Winters, Yvor: 34, 105, 110, 124, 142. Faults in PL: 143

Winterton, Ralph: 40

Winthernsey (Winthornsey). See Withernsea

Winthrop, John (two different): 10, 44, 38

Winton: 44

Winwed: 49

Winyett, Guy: 44

Wippedsfleot: 49

Wirheal: 49

Wirl, J.: 4

Wirtemberg (Wurtemburg): 49

Wisdom of the Ancients, The (Bacon): 134

Wisdom: 24, 47, 51*, 54, 60*, 63, 122*, 125*, 139, 144, 143, 53*, 93, 96, 107. Feminine in M: 107. Feminine, in Origen: 107. Foreknowledge equals wisdom in M: 107. As idea in M: 107. As idea in Origen: 107. Personified by Origen: 107. Precedes word according to Tertullian: 107. As heroic virtue: 123*. Of Samson: 114. In PR: 123*. Of the heart: 125. Religious and civil: 51. Created by virtue: 40. Of Solomon: 113. Undaunted: 51. Lit. in the Bible: 40. Attends Son of God; 143. The sum of: 143. And poetry: 53*. See also: Reason; Tree of Knowledge

Wisdom: 58

Wise, Thomas: 20

Wise: administration: 51. Men: 51

Wiseman, Richard: 16

Wismar. See Charles X

Wissenburgus, Wolfgang: 32

Wistatston (Wisterson), co. Cheshire: 44

Wit Restored: 44, 91

Wit: 40, 51. Defense of: 30. In PL: 40

Witbock. See Whitelocke

Witch-burning in New England: 136

Witchcraft: 7, 114*, 128, 142. Belief in: 89. Tracts against: 142. Investigation of by Dr. Harvey: 142. Writers against: 142. Wier's attempt to defend: 142

Witgeornesbrug: 49

Witham: 49

Withdrawal: 125. As theme in SA: 125*. Final gesture that sums up the play: 125. As man's great temptation: 125. See also: Knowledge

Wither, George: 15, 20, 29, 40, 44, 45, 58, 60, 114, 128, 129, 135*, 26, 38, 39, 71, 91, 130, 93. Psalter: 74

Witherington, William: 44, 45. See also: Widdrington

Withernsea (Winthernsey, Winthornsey), co. York: 44, 45

Witherspoon: Alexander M.: 44, 63, 110. John: 117

Withgarburgh: 49

Withlock. See Whitelocke

Witness: 45, 51. To sister's marriage settlemen: 44

Witney: 45

Witt, E. E.: 58

Witte, Petrus de: 93

Wittenberg: 49

Wittkower, Rudolph: 27*, 100, 39, 106

Wittreich, Joseph A.: 14, 25. Rhyme scheme in _Lycidas_: 61

Wives (M's). See Powell, Mary; Woodcock, Katherine; Minshull, Elizabeth; Milton, John, Life

Wixel: 49

Wodderborn, John: 16

Wodderspoon, John: 44

Wodenote, Theophilus: 93

Wodensbeorth (Wodens Mt., Wodensburg): 49

Wodensfield: 49

Wodhull, M.: 58

Wodley, J.: 45

Wogan, C.: 58

Wolcot, J.: 58

Wolf: pr.: 40. Jerome: 20. Lucien: 7

Wolf: Church of Rome: 143. Roman and ravening wolves: 142. The great Wolf: 142. Grevious Wolves: 143. In England: 83. Wolves: 144

Wolfe: General: 97. Don M.: 6, 9, 23, 31, 44, 52, 59, 60, 75, 79, 86, 102, 108, 116, 122, 128, 85, 93; and William Alfred: 66; works: editor of Works: 44*; _Milton in the Puritan Revolution_: 83, 82, 48; see also: Milton, John, _Complete Prose Works_. Edward: 44. Humbert: 65. Reginald: 93. Reyner: 40

Wolff, H. F.: 16

Wolffhart, Conrad: 20. See also: Lycosthenes

Wölfflin, H.: 23, 27

Wolfson, Harry A.: 5, 40, 57, 60, 110, 125, 93. _Philosophy of the Church Fathers_: 74

Wolgast, Elizabeth H.: 125

Wolgemut, Michael: 93

Wollaston: 45. W.: 58

Wollaton: 45

Wolleb, John (Wollebius, Johannes): 1, 24, 44, 63, 79, 77, 142, 93, 102, 123, 22, 130, 148, 55. Theological writer: 44. Works: _Abridgement of Christian Divinity_ (trans. Alexander Ross): 74, 142; _Compendium Theologiae Christianae_: 74

Wolodimira: 49

Wologda (Vologda): 49

Wolseley: Sir Charles: 116, 32, 91

Wolsey: Thomas, Cardinal and Abp. of York: 44. Cavendish's Memoirs: 88

Wolsey's curriculum for school at Ipswich: 20

Wolverhampton: 45. _Chronicle and Staffordshire Advertiser_: 44

Wolzogen, Mr.: 44

Woman: 8, 31, 41, 54*, 141*, 144. Warrior: 122. Intellect: 50. Inferiority of: 141. Ambivalence of symbol: 141. As image for unconscious: 141. As mother-image: 141. Created inferior to man: 93. Fall of: 93. Subjection to man symbolized: 119. Barred from college: 40. Language books for: 40 See also: Mariology

Women: M and: 40. M's conception of: 113*. Meredith on: 113. M's attitude toward: 87, 71, 80. M's susceptibility to: 113. M's attitude toward sex and relations with women before marriage: 137.

Wonder: 122*. Effect of heroic poem: 123. See also: Effect of epic poem; Miracle; Marvellous; Admiration

Wonderfull Deliverance, A: 59

Wonderfull Workmanship of the World: 65

Wonders of the Invisible World: 71

Wood Street: 44, 45, 103

Wood: A. Skevington: 93. Anthony à: 7, 10, 16, 20, 28*, 40*, 44*, 45*, 63, 73, 87, 103, 114, 116, 91, 64, 94, 130, 137, 146, 150, 117, 55. Christopher: 45. E. J.: 44. George

A.: 144. J.: 97. James Playsted: 115. Louise A.: 63; Milton's Antitrinitarian Conception: 74. Dr. Robert: 91. Thomas: 93

Wood: 143. Drear wood in Comus: 143. Meaning of: 143. Ladder of 2 woods: 143. Gods: 90. Enchanted: 123. Nymphs: 90. See also: Tasso

Woodberry, George E.: 71, 137

Woodbine, George E.: 116

Woodbridge: Mr.: 44. William: 115; A Sermon on the Care of the Soul: 115

Woodcock: family: 44. Elizabeth: 44, 120*; see also: Goddard; M's mother-in-law. Elizabeth, Jr.: 120. Honor: 120. Katherine: see separate entry. Mary: 120. Richard: 120. Capt. William (M's father-in- law): 28, 44, 103, 120

Woodcock, Katherine (Catharine), M's 2nd wife: 8, 16, 28*, 30, 59, 103, 120, 132, 136, 26, 62, 91, 92, 109, 131, 146, 148. Sonnet to: 131. See also: Milton, John, Life; Milton, Katherine Woodcock

Woodcocke, Thomas (bks.): 40

Woodfill, W. L.: 40

Woodford, S.: 58

Woodhead, A.: 99*

Woodhouse, A. S. P.: 1, 4, 6, 9*, 18, 23, 27, 29, 44, 52, 59, 63, 66, 69, 75, 76, 79, 81, 84, 86, 102, 104, 108, 110, 116, 123, 125, 128, 134, 142, 139, 143, 39, 72, 85, 93, 101, 101*, 106, 109, 130, 146, 148*, 21*. Interprets Comus: 143. Rule of reason in M: 143. Biographical critical of M: 61. Christ as hero: 61. Christ's divinity and humanity contrasted: 61. Works: "The Argument of Milton's Comus": 60; "Pattern in PL: 60; "Theme and Pattern in PR": 74; Puritanism and Liberty: 60, 83; "The Approach to Milton": 83

Woodhouse: Elizabeth: 45. J.: 58. Lucy (Cotton): 45. Philip: 45. Thomas: 45

Woodhull, Marianna: 63, 77, 102

Woodington, Mr.: 44. See also: Woodrington

Woodley, G.: 58

Woodman: Allen (mercer): 44. John (yeoman): 44

Woodmere, New York: 44

Woodperry: 45

Woodress, James: 115

Woodrington, John: 44. See also: Woodington

Woodroff, Jane. See Coxeter, Jane

Woods, Leonard: 115. Works: Envy Wishes, then Believes: 115; A Sermon Delivered Before the Massachusetts Missionary Society: 115

Woodstock, co. Oxon.: 40, 44. Woodstock Park: 45

Woodward: 3. Rev. Charles: 44. Hezekiah: 44, 103. John: 44, 32. W. H. (trans.): 20; Desiderius Erasmus concerning the Aim and Method of Education: 82

Woodworth, John: 115. The Spunkiad: Or Heroism Improved: 115

Woody, Thomas: 115

Woold Keys (Quays), London: 44*, 45*

Woolf: R.: 36. Virginia: 35, 76, 133, 39, 137

Woollcombe, K. J.: 79, 93

Woolley, C. Leonard: 64

Woolnoth, T. (engraver): 44

Woolstilstan (Woolaston), co. Staffs.: 44

Woolton, Bp. John: 93

Woolvercot (Woln'cote), co. Oxon.: 44

Worcester (Worcestershire): 40, 44, 45, 49, 103

Worcester College, Oxford: 44

Worcester: Marquis of: 44. Samuel: 115; An Address, on Sacred Music: 115

Word in Season (William Walwyn): 147

Word of God: 60*, 107, 3, 143*, 144, 71*, 72*. And Puritans: 143. And ministers: 143. The key to the kingdom: 143. Christ: 143. A sword: 143. And church reform: 143. Sole judge: 143. True wisdom in: 143. In baptism: 143. M's debt to: 143. Power of: 143. Foundation of religion: 143. Knowledge of: 143. See also: Christ; Logos; Son; PR

Word to the Wavering, A: 116

Word to Purpose: Or a Parthian Dart: 147

Word: and image: 79. Formation, M's, Todd on: 88. Order: Pearce on logical value of: 88; and meaning, the Richardsons on: 88; inverted, Peck on, Newton on: 88; symmetry in: 88. Words: 96*; of song: 121

Worde, Wynkyn de: 40, 32

Wordsworth: Christopher: 40, 44, 112, 146. Dorothy: 44, 146

Wordsworth, William: 7, 8, 12*, 15, 16, 27, 28, 34, 35, 40, 44, 45, 58*, 59, 39, 53, 71, 97, 64, 106, 68, 70, 73, 76, 79, 86*, 87*, 98, 105, 110, 118, 120, 124, 132, 133, 136, 139, 144, 3, 14*, 26, 94, 115, 130*, 137, 146*, 149*, 150, 55, 48, 13, 25. Borrowings from M: 58*. On M: 58. On M's sonnets: 58. Wherein like M: 58. On Shakespeare's sonnets: 87. Sonnets of: 87. Sonnets in Miltonic tradition: 87. Interpretation of PL: 83. Imagery of: 8. Definition of poetry: 87. Tennyson on blank verse: 87. Annotations to Knight's Taste: 146. Annotations to PL: 146. Letters: 146*. And M compared: 146*. Others' reminiscences: 146*. Quoted: 149. Works: Advertisement: 146; Artegal and Elidure: 146; Celebrated Epitaphs Considered: 146; Convention of Centra: 146; Country Church-Yard: 146; Excursion: 146; Friend: 146; Intimations Ode: 35; Italian Itinerant: 146; Laodamia: 146; Laying the Foundation-Stone: 146; Legislation for the Poor: 146; Lines on the Expected Invasion: 146; Lines Written in Macpherson's Ossian: 146; Lycoris: 146; on M: 146; Preface (1800): 146; Preface (1815): 146; The Prelude: 109, 146; Resolution and Independence: 35; "Scorn not the Sonnet": 87; Sonnets: 146*; Tintern Abbey: 8; Upon Epitaphs: 146; Vallombrosa: 146; We are Seven: 35

Worffeild, Mr.: 44

Working with hands, M on: 80

Works and Days (Hesiad): 3

Works of the Late Revered Mr. Samuel Johnson: 116

Works of John Milton, The, Columbia edition: 112, 116

Works of Milton (ed. Frank A. Patterson): 74

Works of Ralph Cudworth, The: 112

Works: 47. Certain projected works of M: 136. And faith: 93. Good: 122. See also: Legalism

World of Wonders: 40

World, The: 58

World: 40, 50, 144, 96*. Training school for virtue: 107. Infinite: 144. Finite: 144. Creation ex nihilo: 144. Lures and Threats: 123*. Disputed origin of: 144. In Origen and M: 107. Tree in world mythology: 118. Use of the word: 107. Signficance of the world in M's time: 89. See also: Providence; Fortune; Creation; Nature

World's Classics: 44

Worldly Hero: 122*

Wormay, John: 44

Worminghall: 45

Worminghurst, co. Sussex: 44

Wormius: Olaus: 44. Wilhelmus: 44

Wornall: 45

Worndall: 45

Worringer, W.: 23

Worseley, Philip Stanhope: 64

Worship, freedom of: 31

Worshipful Company of Mercers: 103

Worsley: Mr.: 44. Benjamin: 44

Worster (Vigornium): 49

Worthies of England, History of the: 45

Worthington, John: 7, 10, 40, 44, 81, 142*, 93. The Diary and Correspondence of Dr. John Worthington: 142

Wortman, Tunis: 115. Works: An Oration on the Influence of Social Institutions upon Human Morals and Happiness: 115; A Treatise, Concerning Political Enquiry and the Liberty of the Press: 115

Wostenholme, John: 40

Wotton, Sir Henry: 1, 6, 15, 16, 28, 30, 40, 44*, 56, 59, 84, 100, 103, 133, 113, 132, 136, 145, 39, 88, 91, 93, 94, 106, 109, 130, 117, 55. Letter quoted: 55

Woty, W.: 58*

Wrangham, F.: 58

Wrath: 122, 25. Theme of in PL: 104. Of God: 93. Of Jesus: 93

Wraughton, William: 33

Wray, D.: 58

Wraysbury, co. Bucks.: 44

Wreay, Eduard: 10

Wren: Sir Christopher: 10, 27, 44, 86, 88. Bp. Matthew: 40, 64

Wrenn, C. L.: 33, 105, 128

Wrestling: 40, 51. "Wrastling": 40

Wright: Dr. (an aged clergyman in Dorsetshire): 150, 94. Rev. Mr.: 44. Andrew: 45. Bernard A.: 6, 9, 44, 59, 60, 76, 84, 86*, 100, 110, 116, 128, 135*, 141, 85, 93, 101. Edward: 40, 44, 77. Elizabeth: see Croke, Eliz. F. A.: 92. I. C.: 58. J., of Derby: 97. Jane: see Lowe, Jane. John (pr.): 44. John (another?): 44.

Wright: Leonard: 93. Louis B.: 15, 54, 102, 108, 128, 93, 115. Martin: 45. Natalie: 40. Nathalia: 20, 98. Nathaniel: 44. R. A.: 28. Robert: 45. Sir Robert (judge): 44. Thomas: 44, 128. Thomas Goddard: 115. William Aldis (ed. <u>Facsimile of the Manuscript of Milton's Minor Poems</u>): 44, 59, 63, 79, 135. W. S.: 44

Wrighter, Clement: 44, 113

Writ: 45. Writ of Error: 73

Writers: Christian: 51. Classical: 51. Early: 51. Of the text letter (scribes): 40

Writing: 51. In Petty School: 40

<u>Written in the Inimitable PL</u>: 115

Wroth, Lady Mary: 120

Wulfer: 3

Wullenius, Mr.: 44

Wunstius, Andreas: 68

Wyatt: 132, 133. A. J.: 92. Sir Thomas: 23, 40, 45, 58, 59, 120, 128, 131

Wycherley, William: 87, 146

Wychwood: 45

Wyclif (Wycliffe, Wycliff, Wicklef, Wickleffe, Wickliffe), John: 1, 7, 23, 40, 44, 51, 68, 73, 83, 114, 3, 38, 71, 93, 99, 150

Wycombe, co. Bucks.: 44. See also: West Wycombe

Wyer, Richard: 40

Wyeth, Joseph (and Mrs.): 44. See also: Ellwood, Thomas

Wykes, Dr.: 44

Wylshman, Walter: 93

Wyndham, John: 44

Wyngaerden, Adrian: 91

Wythe, George: 115

-X-

Xanthippe: 112

Xanthus: 2, 49

Xavier, P. H.: 99

Xenocrates: 123

Xenophanes: 68, 71, 92

Xenophon: 8, 12, 17, 18, 19, 30, 40, 44, 58, 73, 74, 112, 114, 122, 123, 132, 133, 145, 3, 32, 39, 71, 72, 82, 64, 146. Works: <u>Cyropaedia</u>: 46; <u>Memorabilia</u>: 74

Xerxes: 19, 60, 73, 46. Bridging Hellespont: 19

Ximenes, Cardinal: 40

Xiphilinus: 73

-Y-

Yahwe: 11. And Satan: 48. Encounter between Yahwe and the Serpent: 48. Yahwism: 32

Yalden, Thomas: 116

Yale: Univ.: 44*. Univ. Library: 44. Press: see Milton, John, Complete Prose Works. <u>Yale Literary Magazine, The</u>: 115. <u>Yale Milton</u>: 73. Yale Studies in English: 44

<u>Yalkut Shimeoni</u> (Yalkut Shime 'oni): 41, 57

Yanning, William: 44, 45

Yapp: Ann: 44. William: 44

Yara: 49

Yardley, Edward (archdeacon): 44

Yate, Peter: 45

Yates: Frances A.: 29, 40, 79, 123, 39, 93. Jane: 44. John: 93

Year Books of Probate: 45

Year: divisions of the: 89. Of creation: 93

Yearsley, A.: 58*. Admires PL: 58

Yeatman, H. F.: 58

Yeats, W. B.: 1, 5, 12, 15, 63, 86, 95, 110, 124, 127, 134, 136, 139, 14, 36, 46, 53, 61, 72, 101*, 130, 131, 25

Yelverton: Charles (alias Kempe): 40. Christopher: 40. Sir Henry: 40, 44. Thomas: 40

Yeo, Richard (medallist): 44

Yeomans, Charles: 44

Yeraslave: 49

Yewelme. See Ewelme

Yezer-ha-ra: 36

Yiddish: 40

Yin and Yang: 48

"Ynkhorne termes": 20

Yoder, Audrey: 128

Yonge, Charles D.: 16

York (Caerebranc, Eboracum), city and co.: 40, 44, 45, 49, 73, 103, 3. Abp. of: 103. York Academy: 78. York Library: 36. York School: 42

York tune: 40, 121

York Plays: 65, 36*. York mystery plays: 123

York Street (Petty France), London: 44

York: House of: 44. Duchess of: see Mary of Modena; Hyde, Anne. Duke of: 44. Duke of (Charles I): 40. Duke of (later James II): 103; see also: James II. Robert: 44

Yorke: Mr.: 44. C. (sonnets of): 58. P., 2nd Earl of Hardwicke (sonnet of): 58. P., Viscount Royston: 58. Philip: see Hardwicke. William: 44

Yorkshire Diaries: 40

Yosippon: 1, 63, 86

Youde, J.: 58

Youga: 49

Young: 7, 3, 97, 130, 149. Mr. (pr.): 44. Bartholemew: 40. Sir Charles: 44. Edward: 44, 86, 87, 58*, 113, 88, 115, 146, 55; borrowings from M: 58; works: Night Thoughts: 58*, 95; Conjectures on Original Compositions: 87. Hugh W.: 40. John, Bp. of Rochester: 83, 114.

Young: Karl: 93. Katherine: see Powell, Katherine. M. J.: 58. (Junius), Patrick (1584-1652): 30, 40, 42, 44, 91, 94. Peter: 40. Robert (pr.): 44. Roger: 40. Stark: 5. Thomas: see separate entry. Thomas, "Student of Staple Inn": 40. W.: 58. William: 40

Young, Rev. Thomas, 1587-1655 (M's tutor): 9*, 15, 19, 20*, 28, 30*, 40*, 41, 42*, 62, 71, 72, 26, 32, 38, 91, 44*, 51, 57, 68, 70, 73, 34, 103, 112, 113, 132, 93, 94, 64, 109, 137, 146, 148, 55, 136. His father (William): 44. His son: 44. His wife: 44. Calvinist: 147. See also: Smectymnuus

Younger Brother: 1, 29, 40, 143

Younger, John: 44

Youth: 51, 90; see also: Hebe. "Youth of M, the": 112

Youth's Instructor in the Eng. Tongue, The: 115

Youths Behaviour (Hawkins): 20

Yoxford, co. Suffolk: 44

Ypsilanti, Prince: 31

Yvelin, Nicholas: 64

Yvronia: 73

-Z-

Z., A.: 117

Zabkiel: 142

Zabrella, Giacomo: 40

Zachariä, Friedrich Wilhelm: 65, 117

Zachariae: 10

Zacharius: 77

Zachary: 73. Pope: 116, 142

Zack, Baron von: 40

Zadkiel: 142

Zagorin, Perez: 44, 93

Zaleucus: 73, 3

Zamzummin: 123. See also: Giants, Biblical

Zanardus, Michael: 40

Zanchi, Basilio: 64

Zanchius (Zanchi), Jerome: 4, 16, 63, 65, 73, 74, 77, 114, 128, 142*, 3, 22, 32, 36, 93, 64, 109. Works: <u>De Operibus Dei</u>: 142, 36; <u>Operum Theologicorum</u>: 142

Zanon: 6

Zarlino, Gioseffo: 100

<u>Zeal Examinel</u> (anonymous tolerationist tract): 147

Zeal: 51, 63, 122. In language, attitudes toward: 66. "Zeal": 136; M's word for his diatribes: 136

Zebede(e): 73

Zechariah: 64

Zedler, J.: 128

Zeidler, Jakob: 6

Zeigler: 6. Hieronymus: 117

Zeitlin, Jacob: 41

Zelandia: 49

Zellius, Matthäus: 44, 73

Zeno: 5, 23, 44, 114, 123, 125, 3, 71. See also: Stoa; Stoics; Icenorum

Zeno: 74. "De Job": 74. St.: 143

Zenobia: 54

Zenophon. See Xenophon

Zephon: 2, 50*, 56, 60, 70, 73, 102, 111, 123, 128, 142, 144, 71, 72, 140

Zephyr(us): 44, 73, 90, 144, 72

Zephyritis: 73

Zergolta (Surgoot): 49

Zero, use of with place value: 40

Zesen, Filip (Philip) von, <u>Charles II</u>: 44, 91

Zeus: 1*, 2, 17, 34, 60, 90, 141*, 144, 71, 72, 92. And God: 141. Static world order of: 141. See also: Jupiter; Jove

Zeuxis: 73

Ziegler: Caspar: 44, 91. (Zieglerus), Hieronymus: 65, 68, 77

Zigabenus, Euthymius: 99*

Zilboorg, G.: 128

Zillman, Lawrence J.: 87. <u>John Keats and the Sonnet Tradition</u>: 87

Zimansky, Curt A.: 110

Zimmer, Heinrich: 76

Zimmerman, Lester Fred: 115

Zimmermann, Johann Jakob: 7

Zinsser, Hans: 63

Zinzendorf, Count: 10

Zion: 44

Ziphon: 42

Zippora(h): 73

Zirkle, C.: 128

Ziska, Ján (Zisca, Zizca, John): 16, 73

Zitt, Hersch L.: 93

Zoas: 25

Zodiac: 73*, 89, 123*, 142. Aries, Cancer, Scorpio: 128. Zodiacal watch: 100; see also: Poetic universe

Zodiacus Vitae: 65. <u>Zodiake of Life</u>: 65

<u>Zohar</u>: 1, 24*, 34, 40, 41, 63, 86, 113*, 123, 132, 136, 141, 144, 32, 36, 71

Zoilus: 2, 44, 130

Zollicoffer: David: 10. Hermann: 10. Johannes: 10, 44. Tobias: 10

Zollikofer, Johannes. See Zollicoffer

Zonaras, John (Johannes): 65, 68

Zones of earth: 128. Zone, the Frozen (Antarctic): 49

Zonta, Leontine: 60

Zophiel: 73, 142. Relation to Iophiel, Zophiel, or Zaphkiel: 142

Zora: 49, 73, 92

Zorn, Mark: 39

Zoroaster: 113, 88. Zoroastrianism: 15, 71. Zoroastrians: 60

Zorobabel: 30, 70, 112, 3

Zosimus (Zozimus): 73

Zouch: Edward: 40. T.: 58

Zouche, Richard: 64

Zuccari, Federico: 39

Zuckermann, B.: 35, 44

Zuinglius. See Zwingli

Zunder, Theodore A.: 115

Zuntz, G.: 143

Zurich (Zuric, Tygurus): 27, 44, 49. See also: Swiss Evangelical Cantons

Zwicky, Laurie Bowman: 128

Zwingli, Ulrich (Zwinglius, Huldrych): 7, 51, 60, 73, 114, 123, 3, 32, 71, 82, 93. Works: Annotationes in Evangelium Matthai: 74; Short Pathwaye to the...Understanding of ...Scriptures (trans. John Veron): 74. Zwinglianism: 40. Zwinglians: 143